India Studies in Business and Economics

The Indian economy is considered to be one of the fastest growing economies of the world with India amongst the most important G-20 economies. Ever since the Indian economy made its presence felt on the global platform, the research community is now even more interested in studying and analyzing what India has to offer. This series aims to bring forth the latest studies and research about India from the areas of economics, business, and management science. The titles featured in this series will present rigorous empirical research, often accompanied by policy recommendations, evoke and evaluate various aspects of the economy and the business and management landscape in India, with a special focus on India's relationship with the world in terms of business and trade.

More information about this series at http://www.springer.com/series/11234

Nripendra Kishore Mishra
Editor

Development Challenges of India After Twenty Five Years of Economic Reforms

Inequality, Labour, Employment and Migration

Springer

Editor
Nripendra Kishore Mishra
Department of Economics
Banaras Hindu University
Varanasi, Uttar Pradesh, India

A line related to Foreword was mistakenly published in the Preface of this book and has now been removed.

ISSN 2198-0012 ISSN 2198-0020 (electronic)
India Studies in Business and Economics
ISBN 978-981-15-8264-6 ISBN 978-981-15-8265-3 (eBook)
https://doi.org/10.1007/978-981-15-8265-3

This Springer imprint is published by the registered company Springer Nature Singapore Pte Ltd.
The registered company address is: 152 Beach Road, #21-01/04 Gateway East, Singapore 189721, Singapore

Preface

India embarked on the path of economic liberalization since 1991 and witnessed fast economic growth by the turn of the millennium. In fact, feeble attempts toward economic reforms had already started since the mid-1980s, and most economists agree that structural break in the growth of GDP started from the early 1980s. The need for change in economic policy was being felt from the early 1980s, and there were some attempts to do so in the late 1980s, which is famously known in policy circle as 'M Document.' In 1980, the size of the Indian GDP was larger than that of China, which fared poorly in all indicators of development as compared to India. During the same period, countries of South East Asia were doing better than India not only in terms of GDP growth but also in the indicators of human development. Political crisis post-1989 under coalition governments halted any attempt to address the simmering economic crisis, and it ultimately fell upon a minority government to carry out full-fledged economic reforms from 1991 onward. These economic reforms paid large dividends in later periods as India traced a trajectory of high economic growth. This 'golden run' continued for nearly 20 years. It is now more than a quarter of a century since the initiation of economic reforms. Slowly and steadily, all pretensions of the mixed economy have been shed, and there is hardly any hesitation either on the part of the state or public in accepting that India has absolutely adopted the capitalistic path of development. Ironically, the word 'socialist' continues to define the state in the preamble of the constitution. The 25 years of market reforms have also seen changes in other spheres such as coalition power politics largely based on communal and caste equations, the rise of the middle class, and the emergence of service sector, especially IT-enabled services, as the driver of growth and pro-business rather pro-market economic policy. By 2020, the embrace of the market is complete, and planning as an instrument of economic policy is a thing of the past.

These years of liberalization have been years of 'celebration of growth,' and euphoria overgrowth has been the principal driving force of policy. In a very subtle shift, the concept of development stands replaced by the idea of growth in popular discourse with the latter being touted as a panacea for all ills. A growth in GDP is supposed to usher in development along all social indicators as well. This view has been advocated globally by neo-liberal economists and multilateral agencies. In India, this shift in the perception of 'development' was effectuated very forcefully in 2014 when the Hindi word for development *vikas* was pushed into the growth narrative without spelling out its content. It only became evident later that it was actually the growth that was sought to be pursued. The idea of 'development' itself has become a topic of debate with a definite tilt toward pushing through growth in the name of development. Sadly, this has been done without any theoretical or empirical evidence as it is suited to neo-liberalism (global capital), to the 'new' Indian state, to newer coalitions of interest groups, and also to the new 'aspirational India.'

It is now time to evaluate these past 25 years under the liberalized economic regime which has achieved substantial gains but also lost ground on several counts; probably the latter is greater than the former. No doubt, the size of the economy and per capita income has gone up. After some letup in the 1990s, there has been sustained reduction in poverty, while the rate of unemployment remained fairly stable till 2011–12. However, the rate of unemployment shot up sharply from 2011–12 to 2017–18. Indicators of health and education have improved. The private sector has come of age. There had been some acceleration in the growth rate of wage rate and earnings of labor, but it collapsed later. At the same time, inequality or disparities in income/consumption and wealth have gone up considerably. There are newer forms of inequality. Economic growth has not been poverty reducing. The content and the process of growth have been unequalizing. Unemployment remains a challenge as it was two decades ago. The period after 2014 has been even more challenging according to the Centre for Monitoring Indian Economy (CMIE) and Periodic Labor Force Surveys (PLFS). One does not have any information about poverty after 2011–12, but there are indications that it might have gone up. The share of labor in value added is declining. The labor class is in distress, especially unskilled workers. Migration has become an important coping up strategy with continued agrarian distress. The neglect of these issues over the last 25 years came to the fore as the economy came to a grinding halt in the Covid-19 pandemic. The pandemic exposed several fault lines in society, polity, and economy. The class character of the state, role of public institutions, and 'othering' of the working class, especially migrant workers, have become clearly visible. The pandemic has proved right our presumption that the economic reforms have worked wonders on many fronts, but they have been equally punishing on more counts.

Contributions in this volume address these questions from multiple perspectives. Problems in conceptualization of development and Indian development model are compared with other countries. Newer forms of vulnerability and sources of inequality are highlighted, and distress in labor market is examined from multiple lenses. Connections between agrarian economy and rural distress are established. Migration is addressed in a wider conception of labor mobility. A common conclusion is that many vital issues of development have been neglected in the last 25 years of economic reforms in pursuit of growth.

This volume emanates from a seminar organized by the Department of Economics, Banaras Hindu University, Varanasi, on the theme of 'Twenty Five Years of Economic Reforms in India' in March 2018 in honor of Prof. Ravi Srivastava. The sub-themes in the seminar, which constitute the sections of the book too, were essentially areas of his work. Prof. Ravi Srivastava, who superannuated in 2018 from Jawaharlal Nehru University (JNU), has had a very close academic interaction with the Department of Economics, BHU, Varanasi. I am full of gratitude to Prof. Srivastava as he has been a great source of inspiration to me throughout my academic journey. I express my sincere thanks to all contributors who are known experts in their respective areas of research. I am also thankful to Prof. R. P. Pathak, former Dean, Faculty of Social Sciences, Prof. A. K. Gaur, the Head of the Department, and all my colleagues and students. I am also thankful to the Indian Council of Social Science Research, New Delhi, Department of Planning, Government of Uttar Pradesh, and the Tata Trust, Mumbai, for their financial support for the seminar. Ms. Sudha Passi has very diligently done copy editing of this volume. I am thankful to Ms. Nupoor Singh and Ms. Jayaraniprem Kumar from Springer for their cooperation and valuable support.

I dedicate this volume to my parents who raised me in challenging circumstances and encouraged my pursuit of knowledge to satiate my spirit of enquiry.

Varanasi, India

Prof. Nripendra Kishore Mishra

Contents

About the Editor

Nripendra Kishore Mishra is a Professor in the Department of Economics at Banaras Hindu University (BHU) Varanasi. He has 22 years of teaching and research experience, specializing in development economics, and was a Visiting Researcher at the Rural Development Institute, Chinese Academy of Social Sciences (CASS), Beijing. He started his career at DAV College, Gorakhpur and moved on to become a Reader and Professor at BHU, Varanasi. Prof. Mishra has published more than 15 research papers in respected journals and has completed 9 research projects funded by national and international agencies. His work with NCEUS and the Ministry of Minority Affairs has had a significant impact on government policymaking. Recently, Prof. Mishra has successfully created a panel of poor households with a gap of twenty years in backward regions of Uttar Pradesh and Bihar. Prof. Mishra's primary area of research of is poverty, employment, labour, informal economy, women's empowerment and rural non-farm sector, particularly in Uttar Pradesh. Prof. Mishra is associated with many professional organization and journals in various capacities.

Introduction

Nripendra Kishore Mishra

Abstract India has achieved high growth in the last twenty-five years of economic reforms and is now counted as one of emerging economies in the world. There has been a reduction in poverty, but inequality has gone up. Broad health indicators have improved, yet it cannot be called a healthy country. Many development deficits have been bridged in the last twenty-five years. Still, some development challenges are persisting, and newer challenges have come up. Some of these are taken up for further investigation.

1 Background

In the last 25 years since economic reforms were ushered in India, the country has emerged as the world's fifth largest economy with one of the fastest growth rates on the globe. News that India's GDP has surpassed that of developed countries such as the UK and France have been greeted with jubilation.[1] There is now talk of becoming a USD five trillion economy given India's enormous growth potential. However, lost in this din is the discussion about the per capita income, unemployment rate, incidence of poverty, health and education outcomes, and other social indicators. Growth in itself is neither good nor bad. It does bring in more goods and services but that is only a beginning of the complex process of development (Rao 1964; Ramirez et al. 1997; Mulok et al. 2012). What really matters is the general effect of growth on development. But somehow growth is being passed off as development, as if it automatically and proportionally results in development. This usage has been trending of late as the generic Hindi term for development *Vikas* is being used to highlight growth as if the two are synonyms. As a result, the connotation of development has

[1] IMF's October 2019 World Economic Outlook data puts India's nominal GDP at USD 2.94 trillion ahead of UK (USD 2.83 trillion and France (USD 2.71 trillion).

N. K. Mishra (✉)
Department of Economics, Banaras Hindu University, Varanasi, India
e-mail: nripendra.mishra@gmail.com

N. K. Mishra (ed.), *Development Challenges of India After Twenty Five Years of Economic Reforms*, India Studies in Business and Economics,
https://doi.org/10.1007/978-981-15-8265-3_1

shrunk to expansion of the commodity sector ignoring many other dimensions of the term. On the contrary, it is growth that has been pushed into the narrative of '*Vikas*'. While growth has caught the imagination of the nation, its content and nature, and even equitability, have yet to capture popular attention and space in public debate.

No doubt, 25 years of economic reforms or neoliberal economic policies have transformed Indian economy and society in many ways: The size of GDP and per capita income has gone up, absolute poverty has declined, access to health and education has improved immensely, life expectancy at birth has gone up, and infant mortality rate has gone down. In fact, this list can be extended by adding many other achievements, some of that have definitely come about in the new economic regime. Also, the state has withdrawn from many sectors allowing the market forces to decide their course. It has become the predominant ideology with subscription not only of the ruling class but also of backing from the common man too. A new middle class has emerged as the epitome of a 'New India' or 'Aspirational India'. Indeed! India has changed dramatically in the liberalization years.

Nevertheless, it has remained the same in more ways than some. Even as some stubborn old issues continue to bog down growth, new challenges have emerged putting a big question mark on the efficacy of neoliberal policies that have been in place for a quarter of a century. Among the new challenges pointed out by economists are jobless growth (Kannan and Raveendran 2019; Tejani 2015; Mukherjee 2014; Alessandrini 2009; Bhalotra 1998), social protection (Jha 2013; Mehrotra et al. 2014; Kapur and Nangia 2015), rising economic inequality (Himanshu 2019; Dev 2016; Pal and Ghosh 2007), rising cost of health and education (Gumber et al. 2017; UGC 2008; NCEE 2005), unequal access to resources (Kumar and Saleth 2018; Barik and Thorat 2015; Beck 1995), growing non-standard forms of employment (Landau, Mahy, and Mitchell 2015; Srivastava 2016), and declining share of labour in value added (Jayadev and Narayan 2018; Maiti 2018, 2019; Abraham and Sasikumar 2017). Women are withdrawing from the labour force (Bhalla and Kaur 2011; Chaudhary and Verick 2014; Sanghi et al. 2015) and gender differentials in wages are widening (ILO 2018; Bhattacharjee et al. 2015; Khanna 2012). Investment in human capital has taken a back seat. It has also brought in dispossession and displacement (Mehdi and Chaudhry 2015; Tilak and Jandhyala 2006). Therefore, the content and nature of growth are very important. But, realization of high growth rather than addressing the real issues of development has gained popular attention aptly promoted by the corporate-controlled media and political class. This suits the political class as well as it is not compelled to grapple with the complex process of development, and a singular focus on GDP growth rate suffices. Thus, it becomes pertinent to review these 25 years from the perspective of development by taking stock of progress on old issues and emerging challenges. It is also important as there has been a complete change in the nature of the state in these years as a whole set of neoliberal policies have replaced the earlier policy of state-mediated development (Kohli 2007). A classic case is the decline of state role in public health and higher education sectors.

It is against this backdrop that this book seeks to revisit some old issues of development along with the new challenges. The volume emanates from a seminar on the same theme organized by the Department of Economics, Banaras Hindu University,

Varanasi in March 2018 in honour of Professor Ravi Srivastava, Director, Centre of Employment Study, Institute of Human Development, New Delhi, and formerly Professor of Economics, Centre for the Study of Regional Development, Jawaharlal Nehru University, New Delhi. The issues covered are essentially ones that have been the area of work of Prof Srivastava. The present volume is divided into five interlinked sections viz.

I. The challenge of development
II. Poverty and inequality
III. Labour, work, and employment
IV. The agrarian question
V. Labour mobility.

A brief overview of the structure of the volume and papers contained in each section is discussed in the following sections.

2 The Challenge of Development

Of late, the word 'development' has been used in many contexts, often quite unrelated to the received understanding of the term. A chasm in this received understanding is used to push through the 'convenient' meaning of development. Therefore, there is a need to redefine what one means by development in times of emergence of 'aspirational India'. The perception of development is different for different classes and regions. This has been evident in public discourse during the last 5 years. Does the conventional conception of development in terms of material availability properly explain the observed 'development deficit' in India of present time? One needs to revisit the idea of development, where the latter is defined in a much broader sense including institutions. It also requires an exploration to know who is paying the cost and who is reaping the benefits of development (or growth). The past 20 five years have witnessed growing inequality between various groups, suggesting the non-inclusiveness of development (or growth). While Arvind Subramanian and Ashok Lahiri flag many present challenges of development, B V Singh et al. take an altogether different view of development in India.

Arvind Subramanian[2] compares the Indian development experience with several countries and concludes that the Indian model is distinctly different from any other available development model. A striking point made here is about the sequencing of economic development and political development. Europe had slow growth and economic development along with political development. But East Asia and many other countries first had economic development followed by political development. The case of India is altogether different. It had political development in the form of

[2]This paper by Dr Arvind Subramanian is an edited version of his valedictory speech delivered at the said seminar.

democracy and universal suffrage right after independence, when economic development was in a nascent stage. In a way, it belongs to neither camp and yet has witnessed dramatic development in the period under study. This proposition of Subramanian brings into discussion an important issue of relationship between political and economic development and, by extension, between politics and economy. Sen (1999) argues that democracy is an essential condition for sustained economic development over a long period of time. The case of East Asia shows that investment in human capital and welfare state are preconditions for sustained development. But, China presents a puzzle. In the early 1980s, all indicators of development in China were worse than India (Basu 2009; Desai 2003). The situation was reversed by the late 1990s in spite of the fact that political development in China has not taken off at all. So far, evidences point that sustained economic development is best executed in a pluralist democracy. This inference has far-reaching effects on many of the current debates in India. A section of media has linked the slowing down of economy with political issues of the time (BBC 2019; Subramanian 2019). Kohli (2006) states that economic policies are influenced by the political interests of ruling parties. However, Subramanian restricts himself to comparing the Indian model with other available models.

Ashok Lahiri in his paper on 'Development challenges of India after twenty-five years of economic reform' takes the discussion further and argues that the answer to the question of how have we done after the 1991 reforms depends on 'relative to which period of our own past' and 'relative to which other country'. While comparison between the pre-reform and post-reform period of India shows that the last 25 years have been 'gratifying', the comparison with East Asian countries (including China) is 'sobering'. India has not done as well as East Asian countries have done in this period. Of course, there are issues of political development in these countries as pointed out by Subramanian. An interesting observation is that fiscal laxity in India has been greater than many of these countries raising doubts on the role of public spending in boosting growth. Lahiri lists eight issues as development challenge in the near future, namely, fiscal rectitude, market versus state, agricultural reforms, farm loan waivers, minimum support price, the role of cooperatives, physical infrastructure, and social infrastructure. The economic policy needs to have a definite response to these issues. So far, there has been considerable back and forth response on these issues. However, it appears that Lahiri places greater importance on physical infrastructure as compared with social infrastructure despite the fact that there has been a major change in the understanding of economic theory in recent times and investment in social infrastructure is supposed to have higher social rate of return (Bathla, Kumar, and Joshi 2018). The emphasis on physical capital as the driver of development is quite consistent with the new definition of development being forwarded in India in recent times. One is still not sure whether underdevelopment of India is caused by the lack of roads, ports, railway lines, and power or it is the absence of quality healthcare and education. Available research is quite inconclusive (Mohanan and Hay 2016; Sahoo 2011; ADB 2007).

A mechanical meaning of development is being propounded and there are reasons to believe that it may not be complete. Sen (2005) raises some important questions about the process and consequences of development. Development of what, development of whom, and who defines what development is—these are the questions that need to be answered. There is a yearning to find an alternative meaning of development, which is best reflected in experiments like the happiness index (Royal Government of Bhutan 2012). Is it that the idea of development is too West-centric or obsessed with commodities and objectivity? Is it correct to have a universal meaning of development or a one size fits all definition of development? The 'capability approach' does provide a window to peep into this question. But here again, this issue stands unresolved.[3] Alkire (2002) argues that valuable freedoms are to be obtained from the context itself, which means that there cannot be a universal definition of development. B V Singh, Siddharth Singh, Ravish K. Shukla, and Lav Jee attempt to understand development through an alternative method by using an experiment in their paper on 'Secrets of the Heart: Adding Subjectivity to the Policy Prescriptions for a Pleasant Economic Development'. It is argued that the quest for objectivity (which is based on pre-conceived meaning of certain terms including development) and reliance on scientific methods has not yielded a complete understanding of development and consequently policy fails to address the 'felt needs' of intended beneficiaries. These methods rely on *ex-post facto* information and thus fail to predict the future. Most of the time, the policies derived from theoretical conclusions overlook the whole construct of human being; which includes social relationships, impulses, political affiliation, likes–dislikes, and spiritual setting and belief systems. Therefore, development planning needs to be supplemented by other methods capable of deconstructing established meanings. Individual behaviour is non-linear and often non-rational if the latter is defined in the conventional sense of the term. This can be addressed only by including subjective elements that factor the needs and desires of targeted people in policy and decision-making, the paper argues citing a case study from Varanasi city on the labour force engaged in spiritual tourism.

3 Poverty and Inequality

The concepts of equity and justice have undergone a remarkable change over time. As intolerance over stratification and differentiation has grown, the very concept of inequality has undergone a radical transformation with the discussion now focused on 'inequality of what' and 'inequality among whom'. The need of the hour now is to extend the idea of the transformed notion of inequality to development, so as to reflect its implications for 'growth with justice' in the Indian context. While the earlier belief in an inverted U-shape curve describing the relationship between economic growth and economic inequality has been questioned in light of extensive cross-country data for longer periods, there is a very little analytical exploration into what might happen to inequality between different social groups, or across spatial units, in terms

[3]For details, see debate between Sen (1993) and (Nussbaum 2003, 2011).

of income and non-income dimensions in the course of rapid economic development. In spite of renewed interest in the issue of inequality across the world, discussions on inequalities based on ethnic, racial, or caste groups have been less visible than general or interpersonal inequality. Rising disparities has become a defining feature of the last 25 years of the Indian economy. The conventional way of looking at inequality only in terms of income is no longer considered appropriate. It is also not clear how growth has impacted inequality and what has been the functional impact of inequality on issues like labour force participation. This issue needs investigation by bringing in a wider conception of inequality. Declining share of labour in value added is directly linked with rising functional inequality.

The idea of inequality has undergone many changes; believed to be a non-issue by classical economists and considered as the most important issue by Marxists. Somehow, there was either neglect or tolerance of inequality in mainstream economics, at times considered as the only natural in human society. Interestingly, Kaldor (1955) and Kuznet (1955) are celebrated while Kalecki is ignored by mainstream economics. D N Reddy, in his paper 'Toward understanding the nature of inequality in India in terms of changing perceptions on its sources and solutions', traces the evolution of this concept right from Mill, Marshall, and Clark to Piketty. He shows how conceptualization of inequality has changed with time and how multilateral institutions like IMF, which did not accord much importance to the inequality question till the late 1990s, have changed their position and now regard it as the central question of modern times. The Oxfam Annual Report (2017/2018) is a telling example of newfound concern of mainstream economics with respect to inequality. Of course, Piketty (2014) has been the pioneer in bringing the inequality discourse on the agenda. For a long time, inequality research has been obsessed with Kuznet (1955) without actually understanding it. Reddy points out these fallacies in the conceptualization of inequality and argues that broadening the scope of research on the multidimensional nature of inequality has also resulted in questioning the conventional wisdom that disparity is the result of differences in skills and talents. Piketty (2014) and (Stiglitz 2015) have highlighted the role of policy and politics in inequality. Reddy argues that one of the main dimensions of contemporary political economy is the emergence of finance capital and the complex role of finance, property (real estate), and avoidance of taxation as drivers of inequality. It is shown that growing inequality is a challenge to sustainable growth and reduction in poverty is only possible through reduction in inequality. Inequality, as measured by consumption Gini declined till 1970s. But, it has steadily risen after 1991. Income Gini, as measured from IHDS data, is much higher (0.55) than consumption Gini (0.37), and wealth Gini is even higher (0.74). Often, inequality is associated with skill premiums. Reddy argues against this and shows that the majority of billionaires in India has 'rent thick' sectors as their primary source of earnings. Post reform period has witnessed a rise in the share of the top decile in national income and there is a clear phenomenon of the 'hollowing out' of the middle class. It is suggested that income from labour and income from capital should be differentiated and taxed differently and there is a need to change the international tax system.

Arup Mitra's paper 'Growth, inequality and labor force participation' agrees with Reddy's findings on the rising disparity in earnings in post-reform period. Mitra points out that inequality is being perpetuated by unequal access to health and education between the poor and the rich. Inequality in access to education is so glaring, that in HDR 2013, India's education index loses more than 40% of its value once adjusted for inequality. In other words, education and health inequality are much sharper than expenditure inequality. However, the association between growth and inequality presents a mixed picture at the disaggregated level. Many states registered a rapid growth and witnessed a decline in inequality in either rural or urban areas. On the other hand, there are states that rapid growth has experienced a rise in inequality over time. The cross-sectional picture suggests that along with economic growth inequality tends to rise only in rural areas, while in urban areas, which show higher levels of growth than rural areas, inequality does not necessarily rise. He argues that inequality and poverty are mostly unrelated. In the equation for poverty being a function of both growth and inequality, inequality shows no effect except in the urban context for the year 2004–05 when it takes a positive coefficient as one would expect, i.e., with an increase in inequality, poverty tends to rise. Existence of large informal employment in the form of working poor, rise in capital intensity even in the so-called labour-intensive organized manufacturing sector, and services led-growth are important factors that led to a rise in inequality. The binary nature of service sector and relative stagnancy of manufacturing sector have also contributed to rising inequality.

There has been a revival of the 'trickle-down' hypothesis in policy circles—quite contradictory to the received understanding in theory—and a narrative is being built suggesting that growth is the panacea that would take care of poverty and inequality. The relationship between growth and poverty is mediated by inequality. This issue is examined by Nripendra Kishore Mishra and Manish Kumar Singh in their paper on 'Inclusiveness of economic growth in Uttar Pradesh' where the state is the focus of attention. The current focus on inequality largely originates from an observation that recent economic growth in many countries has disproportionately benefitted the upper income groups. India has experienced an unprecedented high rate of growth in recent times but that has been accompanied by rising inequality in spite of poverty reduction. But, it is yet not clear how far this growth is inclusive and what the extents of income gain are for the poor. Mishra and Singh examine the pro-poorness of growth in Uttar Pradesh in reference to India. The state witnessed a loss in its growth momentum after 1970s, which has been one of the major reasons for its not so impressive decline in poverty ratio, unlike other Indian states. Many other states took advantage of liberalization and succeeded in accelerating their growth rate and consequently in drastically reducing their poverty ratio. Uttar Pradesh failed to do so, which is why it is continuously lagging the national growth rate. While consumption Gini has gone up in rural India from 1993–94 to 2004–05 and has remained constant from 2004–05 to 2011–12, it is almost the same in rural Uttar Pradesh right from 1993–94 to 2011–12. And it is consistently lower than national Gini. This suggests that even if rural MPCE in Uttar Pradesh is lower than national rural MPCE, and the difference has widened further, inequality has not risen in rural

Uttar Pradesh. This is in stark contrast with urban areas. Inequality is much higher in urban Uttar Pradesh than India and very high as compared with rural Uttar Pradesh in 2011–12. Growth should have reduced poverty in rural India by 12.17%. But the actual reduction turns out to be only 8.47% because of adverse redistribution, which has taken off 3.69% of potential decline in poverty. Redistribution effect is able to do so only marginally (0.75%) between 2004–05 and 2011–12 in rural India, where total change in poverty (16.10%) is very close to growth effect (16.85%). But, actual change in poverty (12.31%) is higher than growth effect (11.55%) in case of rural Uttar Pradesh from 2004–05 to 2011–12. Here, redistribution effect (0.75%) is working in the same direction and helps in reduction of poverty. Redistribution effect has played a much stronger role in urban India. Growth effect (13%) is highly moderated by redistribution effect (6.95%) and actual change in poverty turns out to be only 6% during 1993–94 and 2004–05. However, redistribution effect is moderated from 2004–05 to 2011–12. Although change in total urban poverty in U.P is lower than that of India, yet redistribution effect is stronger in Uttar Pradesh and ironically, it is stronger during 2004–05 and 2011–12. It means that urban poverty reduction in Uttar Pradesh has been drastically pulled down by redistribution against poor right from 1993–94 to 2011–12. Also, it is only rural Uttar Pradesh that has demonstrated a clear tendency towards pro-poor growth during 2004–05 and 2011–12. During the first time period, the gap between actual growth rate (AGR) and Poverty Equivalent Growth Rate (PEGR) had been wider in rural India but it considerably narrowed down in the second period. While AGR of rural Uttar Pradesh was very close to PEGR in the first time period, the former exceeded the latter in the second time period suggesting pro-poorness of growth. There is some narrowing down of gap between AGR and PEGR in urban India. There is only marginal narrowing down in urban Uttar Pradesh However, it must be noted that this analysis is limited up to 2011–12 only and one has reason to believe that these inferences would stand altered once data are available for a later period.[4]

4 Labour, Work, and Employment

There have been major changes in the world of work and employment during the 25 years of economic reforms. This process, in fact, had started in the 1970s itself but gained primacy in 1990s, especially after the 'Washington Consensus', and has been accelerated further in the wake of digitalization, platform economy, and artificial intelligence (AI). The deepening of transnational production and accumulation has essentially led to accelerated fragmentation of tasks and a significant 'de-centring' of production from the North (developed world) to select destinations in the South (developing countries) with significant impacts on labour regimes. This 'de-centring' is characterized by a shift of production from advanced capitalist countries to a handful of developing countries, where metropolitan capital has strengthened its

[4]This inference is based on a report of Business Standard (Roychoudhury 2019).

presence to take advantage of, inter alia, relatively inexpensive labour and raw materials as well as to tap the markets. Both these important features of contemporary capitalism, organically embedded in the overall neoliberal architecture, have changed the dynamics of labour utilization, labour reserves, conditions of work, etc. Furthermore, the world of work is changing with greater automation and digitalization. The link between output and employment is no longer as strong as it used to be. Declining employment elasticity is a new normal. This has important implications for labour and employment, which is reflecting in diversification of activities of rural households. Rural labour is responding to labour market signals within its own boundaries. This is further compounded by declining absorption of labour in agriculture and manufacturing, resulting in out migration from rural economy and growing urban informal employment. Thus, changes in global capitalism, agrarian crisis, migration, unemployment, and growing urban informal economy together provide a complete picture of the state of labour in India. This distress of labour is also reflected in the declining quality of employment, quite contrary to ILO's focus on decent employment. The quality of employment is also associated with skills and it is often argued that low-quality employment is a consequence of low skills and the latter is unevenly distributed. Lower caste[5] groups are found to be working in low earning activities in informal manufacturing. If that be the case, then how do we explain the observed pattern of concentration of low caste groups in low skills and low earning activities? Is it the caste or skill that determines this outcome? Public wage employment programmes like Mahatma Gandhi National Rural Employment Generated Scheme (MGNREGS) are supposed to be one option of providing employment. Therefore, one needs to look at the labour question in light of these newer developments and linking it up with growing distress in rural economy.

The most striking feature of recent times in the world of work is growing informalization and precarity of work. ILO detail definitions of these concepts. Ravi Srivastava, Balakrishuna Padhi, and Rahul Ranjan in their paper on 'Structural Change and Increasing Precarity of Employment in India' argue that observed precarity of employment is a combination of three interrelated processes, namely, changes in employment structure, negligible growth in total employment and slow growth in non-agricultural employment, and growing informalization of the formal sector. A very powerful and highly relevant argument is made by authors that informal employment in India should be determined on the basis of job security and not the availability of social security and therefore authors use written contract as designating formal employees as those employees who have a written contract. This becomes all the more important in present times when adhoc, incomplete and inadequate social security measures have been provided for workers.[6] It is shown that there is shift in employment from agriculture to industry and services, increase in regular/salaried employment, and increase in formal sector employment. The economy has failed to create adequate employment and a major reason for this is declining LFPR. Most of this decline is for rural areas and for women. Rising youth unemployment is a

[5]Traditional categorization of Hindu society explained later.

[6]This has been further highlighted by Pushpendra and Dipak Kumar Singh in this volume.

very distinguishing feature. It is concluded that there has been a significant degree of informalization of employment in the formal sector of the economy, and among regular/salaried workers who form the predominant section of the formal sector workforce. This has counteracted the potentially positive effect of the economy-wide shift towards regular/salaried work and towards formal sector growth.

Labour distress in the period of economic reforms is manifested as declining share of labour in value added, growing unemployment, decreasing employment elasticity, and slow growth in wages. It is intricately related with global political economy and internal dynamics of global capitalism. Therefore, only internal explanation of distress of labour is not sufficient. Praveen Jha and Satadru Sikdar in their paper 'Contemporary capitalism and employment challenges: some reflections on India' attempt to take up the issue of labour distress in the country in the larger context of functioning of global capitalism. They have spelt out some important markers of contemporary capitalism such as doing away with controls on capital, reconstitution of class power within 'capital in general' in favour of 'finance capital', capitalism of generalized monopolies, and profound technological changes. These markers appear to generate several adverse tendencies for workers across the globe and India is no exception. Growing financialization of accumulation, structural changes in contemporary capitalism, and hegemony of finance capital have serious adverse consequences for the world of work and workers. Jha and Sikdar, in support of their observation, cite the recent Periodic Labor Force Survey PLFS (2017–18), wherein the rate of unemployment has gone up and Labour Force Participation Rate—LFPR for women has reduced drastically.[7] Remarkably, wage growth has been almost close to zero during 2011–12 and 2017–18 (Srivastava and Padhi 2020). This is organically connected with the neoliberal economic policies that have increased the divergence between growth rates and labour absorption. Since the mid-1990s, persistent and deepening agrarian distress has been accompanied by the lack of gainful employment in non-agricultural sectors. In spite of increasing GDP growth rates, labour absorption rates were stagnant till 2004–05 and have been falling subsequently. Apart from lower absorption of labour, rise in bad quality of employment or non-standard forms of employment (ILO 2015) has become a defining feature of the Indian labour market and informality is one of the main reasons for it.

Vinoj Abraham in 'Structural change and rural households in India: An analysis of the nature of transformation in their economic activities' explores labour distress at the level of households. Movement of households from agriculture to non-agricultural sector after 1993–94 entailed manifold changes in the economic activities of households. The conventional division of labour in terms of gender, skills, and age was replaced by new arrangements. Abraham examines this shift in employment for the period from 1993–94 to 2011–12 and finds that entry into non-agricultural employment in rural areas is gender specific, with the employment in the sector limited to

[7] PLFS data, held back by the government for a long period of time, were officially released only after 2019 general elections. The predominant view on PLFS is that the period 2011–12 to 2017–18 has been devastating for labour (Kannan and Raveendran 2019; Mehrotra and Parida 2019). However a divergent view is taken by (Bhandari and Dubey 2019).

males while females move away from the labour market to enter either education or domestic activities. Further, the rise in non-agricultural employment has been mainly construction-driven. Households were found shifting completely to non-agricultural activities rather than adopting a more risk-averse strategy of activities. Possibly, the number of members from each household in the labour market is declining as a household shift from agriculture to non-agriculture sector. This is especially true for households who find agriculture unviable. The shift has necessitated increasing division of labour both within the household and at the production site; caregiving and social reproduction become exclusive and increasing activity of women while the male head of household moves to non-agriculture and sons move to acquire better education. Abraham draws a very interesting inference that propensity of the head of a household to be in agriculture is independent of his age. According to him, a key feature of the transformation in rural areas is that it is not dependent on individual features such as age or factors associated with age, such as education, health, or the age composition of population. Rather, social and economic conditions encourage the rural population towards non-agricultural activities. The question of inter-generational mobility is examined within limitations of available data. A large share of sons of older parents engaged in non-agriculture preferred to remain in non-agriculture and this tendency has accentuated with time. But preference of sons of older parents in agriculture to remain there has also been declining with time. Among the younger parents too, the sons tend to shift away from agriculture, but the shift is mostly towards education. Land ownership is an important determinant of diversification in rural households, lack of which drives sons to follow their fathers in the non-agriculture sector. Rise in the size of landholding increases the probability of sons of agricultural households staying put in the occupation. Yet, between 1993–94 and 2011–12, more sons, whose fathers were in agriculture and owned land of some size, shifted away from agriculture. Moreover, smaller the land size larger was the propensity among sons to leave agriculture, despite their fathers being in agriculture. This is in contrast to landless agricultural workers; when one was landless, there was greater propensity to be in agriculture, but when one owns land, then land size matters inversely for sons to remain in agriculture. But, if households owned land and even then fathers worked in non-agriculture sector, there was an increasing tendency for sons to shift to agricultural activity as the size of the land increased. This implies that the shift from agriculture to non-agriculture sector for sons whose fathers were in non-agricultural employment, is governed largely by land ownership, especially the size of landholding. In fact, a larger part of non-agriculture sector is itself in the informal sector and this diversification of households from agriculture to non-agriculture has significant implications for labour market. The shift to non-agriculture is mostly in the form of casual wage labour in the informal sector. There has been a sizable improvement in regular salaried employment also but that has been mostly contractual and in the informal sector devoid of any social security.

Even if the regular salaried workers have better working conditions than casual wage workers, one has little information about their method of job search. It is generally accepted that job search in informal sector is through social networking, but, it must have changed with IT revolution, especially with mobile telephony. Rajendra

P. Mamgain, in his paper on 'Wage employment, informality, and social networks in Indian labor market', examines the composition of regular salaried workers and the method of their job search. Mamgain finds almost half of regular salaried employment being in informal sector that naturally means absence of social security. It is expected that all regular employees working in public as well as private organized sector should have at least written job contracts and social security. Surprisingly, a significant 38% of regular workers working in public sector do not have any written job contract and social security indicating the precarious nature of their employment. Based on primary data of urban labour market from four cities, viz, Lucknow, Pune, Delhi/NCR, and Coimbatore, Mamgain concludes that contractual employment has emerged as the new form of recruitment, wherein workers are not directly employed by a principal employer but through a contractor for specific jobs. This form of recruitment is increasingly being used by employers to not only reduce labour costs but also control labour. The share of such workers both in public and private sector has increased substantially over the years, particularly after the economic reforms of early 1990s. Mamgain's findings are supported by many other studies also (Jahn 2015; ILO 2015). He also finds caste[8] considerations playing a significant role in employment in the deeply stratified Indian society, as a result of which the Scheduled castes (SC) or former untouchables and Scheduled Tribes (ST) have lower incidence of regular salaried work than other (higher) caste groups. The most prominent source of job information is informal social networks, which include friends, relatives, family members, caste networks, etc. The probability of using social networks for job search tends to reduce with every increase in the number of years of education. Similarly, as the income levels of workers increase, the odds in favour of using social networks decline significantly.

The labour issue has been taken up mostly as that of wage employment in policy and academic circles; ignoring the fact that more than half of workers are self-employed. Often earnings of the self-employed workers are below the market wage rate, which is a classic case of self-exploitation of labour. The shift from wage employment to self-employment is considered a sign of maturing of economies, provided the latter is voluntary, and brings in earnings higher than the market wage rate. Thus, self-employment becomes a stepping stone for entrepreneurship as observed in developed economies. Eventually, the size of self-employed workers becomes low with the rise in per capita income of an economy. However, labour markets in low- and middle-income countries differ fundamentally from those in advanced economies/countries. In labour-abundant economies like India which are characterized with high degree of unemployment, the reported large percentage of

[8]Ancient Hindu tradition structures society on a hierarchical multi-tier caste system comprising the *Brahmins* (priests and educators), *Kshatriyas* (warriors), *Vaisyas* (traders), and *Shudras* (artisans and farmers). There were also the *ati-shudras* (outcastes engaged in lowly jobs as scavenging, cleaning, tanning, etc.) The castes placed at the top of the hierarchy enjoy most privileges and rights that decrease in a graded manner from the top to bottom. The purity of caste was maintained by proscribing inter-caste dining and inter-caste marriages. The *ati-shudras* were regarded as 'untouchables' with no right to education and property. Although untouchability and any kind of caste discrimination are banned in India, caste prejudices continue to run deep in the society.

self-employed workers is primarily own account workers (OAWs) working in own account enterprises (OAEs). Therefore, the rate of wage employment is low and self-employment is high. The employment structure in poor countries contrasts drastically with that of rich countries. In the USA, for example, own-account workers account for only about 5% of employment, whereas about half of all employment is in firms with more than 500 employees (Hipple 2010). Self-employment could also be an indication of distress in the labour market. The choice between self-employment and wage employment essentially rests on relative differentials in earnings and the probability of getting decent wage employment. One also needs to factor in implicit costs involved in self-employment, including the use of family labour and own inputs. Banerjee and Duflo point out that 'while there are many petty entrepreneurs among the Indian middle class, most of them do not seem to be capitalists in waiting. They run businesses, but, for the most part, only because they are still relatively poor, and every little bit helps. If they could only find the right salaried job, they might be quite content to shut their business down' (2007: p 21). Yet raising productivity of self-employed workers or small businesses can contribute significantly to reducing the vulnerability of workers at the bottom of the pyramid, provided there is no discrimination. Caste-based discrimination in ownership and performance of enterprises is prevalent in India and it is shown that SC/ST owned, and operated enterprises fail to become a viable livelihood alternative to wage employment, which could be one of the reasons for preponderance of SC/ST in wage employment, more so in casual wage labour.

It thus makes sense to examine the caste profile of ownership and performance of enterprises in India, which is carried out by P. P. Sahu and Manik Kumar in their paper 'Entrepreneurial avenues for Scheduled Tribes communities in non-farm-enterprise sector: prospects and challenges'. The share of enterprises (unincorporated enterprises as covered by National Sample Survey Organization (NSSO)) owned by SCs and STs is lower in urban areas as compared with rural areas. The proportion of enterprises owned by STs remained more or less stable while those owned by SCs declined during 2011–16. In rural OAEs segment, the ST-owned enterprises declined in manufacturing, while their share increased in trading and service sector activities. There is a noticeable shift from manufacturing to trading and service sector enterprises both in OAEs and establishments in rural areas. In urban areas, the share of ST-owned enterprises is lower as compared with their rural counterparts even in same activity. The ST-owned enterprises were limited to a very few selected activities in manufacturing sector and were largely in traditional industry groups with highly labour-intensive production process. Not only is the share of ST-owned enterprises low but economic returns to their enterprises are also lower than those owned by other social groups. Per enterprise (and per worker) gross value added for ST-owned enterprises are lower as compared with those owned by higher castes (other social groups). This pattern holds true both in OAEs and establishments and also in rural and urban areas. The same trend is seen for fixed capital and gross value added as well. The ownership of enterprises by different social groups (along with a host of other factors) is associated with the performance indicators of an enterprise. Thus, ST-owned OAEs do not perform better than those owned and managed by SCs,

Other Backward Castes (OBCs), and other castes in terms of relative efficiency. If earnings of enterprises owned by SC or for that matter by any lower economic group are low, wage employment is a better source than self-employment, especially when options like Mahatma Gandhi National Rural Employment Guarantee Scheme (MGNREGS) are available. There have been major changes in the labour market with the introduction of MGNREGS; important among them are tightening of rural labour market and rise in rural wage rate. This is supported by many studies (Himanshu and Kundu 2017; Deb et al 2014; Himanshu et al 2013).

Examining the impact of MGNREGS with latest data, Ashok Pankaj and Mondira Bhattacharya in their paper titled 'MGNREGS and rural labor market in India', finds that the scheme has not only led to a rise in wages of rural labour, reduction in male–female, and rural–urban wage disparities, but also there is empowerment of labour through their increased bargaining position. The idea of minimum wages had been there on paper for long, but the enactment of MGNREGA (Mahatma Gandhi National Rural Employment Guarantee Act) is seen as a landmark legislation making it obligatory for the State to provide work to rural populace on demand and save them from slipping into dire poverty. An upward push of wages due to MGNREGS is explained by additional employment effects, increased bargaining position, and reduced vulnerability of the rural poor through assured employment.

Aggregative analysis suffers from a serious limitation especially in geography like India, where the national average does not always reflect regional realities. India is one country that can be best understood only when research is disaggregated, at least at the level of states. At times, the contrast is so startling that it is difficult to accept this average value of India. One does not know whether states are converging or diverging (Goli et al. 2013; Li et al. 2018), but one does know that there are extremely opposite states within the country. Uttar Pradesh is one state that poses a serious challenge to the national development effort, and therefore, its challenge needs to be explicitly recognized (NITI Aayog 2018; Parker and Kozel 2005; Rasul and Sharma 2014). Out of the many questions pertinent for Uttar Pradesh, this volume has taken up two issues, namely, subcontracting linkages in informal enterprises and skill mismatch. In his paper, 'Subcontracting linkages in the informal manufacturing sector in Uttar Pradesh', Udai Bhan Singh observes that NSSO data in unincorporated enterprises generally report a decline in subcontracting over time (Basole et al. 2014). He, however, finds that this decline has been sharper in rural areas of the state. What is not mentioned is that the nature of subcontracting has changed in last 10–15 years and the NSSO data on enterprise round have been unable to incorporate this change. With this caveat in order, it is shown that the extent of subcontracting significantly varies among the sub-industry categories and sub-contracted works are prevalent in both labour-intensive and capital-intensive enterprises. The extent of subcontracting has increased more than two times among the relatively capital-intensive enterprises. However, it has declined significantly among labour-intensive enterprises. Also, the manufacturing sector in Uttar Pradesh appears to be supporting both views—stagnation and development—with respect to subcontracting. Furthermore, subcontracting linkages between formal and informal enterprises have developed mainly in the Western region, which is also the most industrialized part of the state, lending credence to the development view. GVA per worker is below the notional income in almost 90% of enterprises in 2015–16. This percentage is relatively higher in labour-intensive enterprises, i.e., mostly OAEs, and in sub-industry categories like food products, beverages, tobacco products, cotton ginning, cleaning and baling textiles, wearing apparel, leather products, etc., which implies that large firms exploit informal manufacturing firms and use them for cost-cutting. Uttar Pradesh is also marked for unemployment and its 'not so good' quality of education, which is also reflected at national level in programmes like 'Skill India'. The central government's argument is that there is shortage of employable workforce despite rising Gross Enrolment Ratio (GER) in primary, secondary, and university level education, casting doubts on the usefulness of education system of India, which is exemplified in case of Uttar Pradesh (Goldman, Kumar, and Liu 2008; Biswal 2011). I.C. Awasthi and Puneet Kumar Shrivastava, in their paper on 'Skill inequality among social groups in India: regional analysis in Uttar Pradesh', point to the skill gap in different regions of the state during 2003–04 and 2011–12. Decomposition of skill inequality across regions shows a clear regional imbalance. Out of total caste inequalities, more than 90% is due to within-group inequalities while the remaining are due to between-group inequalities in all the four regions of the state. Also, inequality has increased at a faster rate in the western and central regions. It is found that inequality in general education within the disadvantaged groups is higher as compared with the 'general' category or higher castes for all regions during both time periods. While in the case of Technical and Vocational Education and Training (TVET), the situation is just reverse—lower inequality prevailed within the weaker sections (SC, ST, and OBCs) and higher inequality was found within the upper caste groups (general) in all the regions.

A common thread that runs throughout this section on labour, wages, and employment is that labour distress is more pronounced in rural economy and the discussion is mainly centred on workers in the non-agricultural sector. Yet, one has to factor in the role of agriculture in rural distress and declining labour absorption in agriculture as the latter still happens to be one of the largest employment providers in India. A complete picture of the world of work and workers can be had only by including state of agrarian economy, which is dealt within the following section.

5 The Agrarian Question

The Indian debate on agrarian transition has indeed provided great clarity on the role of agriculture in economic and social transformation. From the perspective of capital, agriculture assumes importance in terms of its ability to supply cheap labour for accumulation in non-agricultural activities along with the supply of food and acts as a market for industrial goods and services. The state looks at agriculture in a similar way but in the context of development it has to do with generating agrarian surplus for financing industrialization, supply of wage goods, and speeding up structural transformation of the economy to a higher level of income and development.

For labour, agrarian transition assumes importance in terms of the evolving agrarian relations that determine the share of wages or earnings in output. Simply put, it means how much structural transformation of the economy can be enabled by agriculture, so that alternative means of livelihood are available outside of agriculture and ultimately secure a higher standard of living. While there are commonalities in these perspectives, the impact of agrarian change can be different for different groups. However, it is a fact that agriculture itself is going through a crisis of unprecedented scale. Although agrarian crisis has been discussed in quite detail in the literature, yet there is need to place it in the context of labour and employment, especially with regards to its implications on rural to urban migration and changes in the pattern of labour mobility.

K P Kannan, in his paper on 'Structural transformation and the agrarian question in the Indian Economy: some disturbing concerns from a laborist perspective', examines the structural change in Indian economy linking it with the agrarian question. The observed structural transformation away from agriculture has not been accompanied by a structural transformation away from rural employment and the rural nature of urban employment. There is a fourfold pattern where only a few states qualify for a meaningful structural transformation even in the limited sense of moving away from the agricultural sector for majority employment. Also, this structural transformation is partial and limited to three out of five broad social groups. Rural economy is characterized by the phenomenal growth of the non-agricultural sector in terms of output as well as employment. The incremental workforce of 91.6 million during 1993–94 and 2011–12 has wholly been absorbed by the non-agricultural sector along with 10.9 million of those already engaged in agriculture. This has meant that a 4.6% decline in employment in agriculture. However, it is mostly casual wage labour, which has left agriculture. But, peasants have registered an increase during this period. Kannan argues that this is not a sign of increasing proletarianization but increasing peasantization of Indian agriculture that is not in tune with the spread of capitalist market relations and transactions in the Indian rural economy. If employment is measured in terms of 'rurality of employment', it is found that while much of the movement of labour has been away from agriculture to non-agriculture, it was less so from rural to the urban economy. Therefore, the agrarian transition question may be replaced by a rural transition question. States with no structural transformation so far and continuing to be in the group of low per capita income represent the most difficult part of the structural transformation story because there it is a combination of no structural transformation, and low per capita income accompanied by low product per worker in both agricultural and non-agricultural sectors. These states, including Uttar Pradesh and Bihar, account for close to 38% of the total population. The overall picture, therefore, is one of the partial structural transformations covering 15 states accounting for half the total population of the country.

Rakesh Raman and Khursheed Ahmad Khan, in their paper on 'Failing agriculture and frazzled farmers: the inside story of India's most populous states-U.P. and Maharashtra', take a different view of rural distress. They argue that agricultural crisis and agrarian crisis are two distinct phenomena and prefer to call it 'crisis in agriculture'. They have also computed a Crisis index for major states in India. Tamil Nadu, Kerala,

Karnataka, Andhra Pradesh, and Maharashtra have highest index while Punjab and Haryana have the lowest index. Crisis of agriculture is an all India phenomenon, only its intensity varies across states, and it is more intense in southern India than the northern states. Maharashtra and Uttar Pradesh are subjected to further investigation. The analysis is limited to the trienniums ending 2004 and 2015. While Vidharbha and Western regions suffer the most in Maharashtra, Marathwada is relatively better off. In Uttar Pradesh, Bundelkhand region is the worst performer while the situation is far better in its Western and Eastern regions. District wise analysis shows that within the crisis-infested states/regions, there could be some 'comfortable zones' while within the so-called less troubled states/regions, there could be some 'difficult zones'. Further, marginal and small farmers have higher crisis index as compared with the semi-medium and medium farmers. It has been found that the cropping intensity and productivity per hectare in rupees for marginal and small farmers in both the states are higher than that of medium and large farmers. But, very high cost of production, adherence to old technology, high dependency of population, greater reliance on non-institutional credit, and inability to get remunerative prices for their produce—all combine together to turn the tide against marginal and small farmers. Furthermore, social group is the main determining factor of the crisis followed by total factor productivity, irrigation facilities, alternative livelihood opportunities, and land holdings.

If there is crisis in the rural economy, its labour has two options, either to diversify into non-agricultural sector, or to move out as a coping strategy. Limitations of the first option have already been highlighted in earlier papers. The second option of moving out or out-migration is often cited as the most preferred option that has been taken up in the next section.

6 Labour Mobility

The distress in rural economy has resulted in massive out migration. As surplus labour from agriculture is being withdrawn very rapidly, it has often been 'erroneously' pointed out that India too is reaching the 'Lewisian turning point'. There is a distinct difference between India and other countries having experienced the Lewisian turning point. In case of India, the out migration is largely from rural economy to the urban informal economy and not to the urban industrial sector. Thus, unlike the Harris-Todaro framework, it is a push force that has generated migration in India. Yet, migration has drastically changed the rural economy. The impact of remittances on rural economy is a typical example. In fact, labour shortage during peak agriculture season has been reported from even labour-abundant regions. Out migration of males from villages has also brought about a change in gender norms in the hinterland. There has been a change in the strategy and duration of migration too. Long-term migration is being replaced by short-term migration and daily commuting has become an important type of labour mobility from satellite towns and rural areas to emerging commercial hubs or centres across India. There are ample migration literatures dealing with the macro-dimension of migration based on NSSO and Census data. Of late, the frequency or spells of migration have gone up while duration of migration has come down, especially that of workers. However, secondary data sources are either outdated or inadequate to capture this change in the nature of labour mobility. It needs to be reiterated that once migration is defined in terms of activity space instead of the conventional wisdom of defining, it in terms of change in the usual place of residence, much of the received understanding on migration stands challenged. Four papers in this section on labour mobility are based on primary data to unearth the hitherto neglected dimensions of labour mobility. These papers examine labour movement in a much more nuanced way, including short-term migrants and daily commuters; a category that has yet to receive adequate attention in migration research.

Tulika Tripathi examines labour mobility in eastern Uttar Pradesh, southern Uttar Pradesh, and north Bihar, based on a panel of primary data for the period from 1996–97 to 2017–18. This is a repeat survey of Living Standard Measurement Survey LSMS—1997 (World Bank 1998) for the selected region. This region is one of most backward regions of India and the largest source of out migration of unskilled and semi-skilled workers. Rural employment generation schemes such as MGNREGA and improvement in Information Communications Technology or ICT and transport have significantly impacted the nature of labour mobility in this region. Movement to far off places, i.e., inter-state mobility, has increased substantially during 1997 and 2017. In fact, individuals from well-off communities, i.e., upper caste, higher MPCE class, and land-owning class are migrating for long durations. The gender pattern of migration remains the same; a one-off flow for men and fixity for women. While long-term migration has increased for higher caste individuals, short duration migration has increased for OBC and SC/ST. Over the two decades mapped for the study, the class-caste pattern of migration has remained the same. However, there has been a tremendous increase in migration within the same district and a sharp decline in migration to other states. It is hypothesized that the rising service and construction sector in small towns and cities such as Allahabad, Gorakhpur, and Patna have generated many job opportunities making them more employable and popular destinations of daily commuters and seasonal migrants hailing from poor and relatively lower caste groups. Tripathi attributes the rise in seasonal migration and daily commuting to the availability of transport, especially motorcycles in villages, and rural penetration of ICT in the banking sector. The large presence of motorcycles in villages has dramatically affected labour mobility in this Eastern Uttar Pradesh and North Bihar region.

Daily commuters from rural areas to cities in search of work, mostly as casual workers in the construction sector or in urban informal economy, have become an important stream of migrants, which is not covered in many studies on migration. Bhaskar Majumder and V Narayan in their paper, 'Migrating to the roads in the cities in Uttar Pradesh: some reflections', capture these migrants (street labourers) from six major cities of Uttar Pradesh in a field study. The major reasons for migration to city are either landlessness or inadequate landholding that failed to fulfil the subsistence needs of households in the migration zone. The average wages per month at the destination for such migrant labourers, both intra-state and inter-state, are around four times what they earn in their native lands. Interestingly, neither the positive rural–urban wage-differential nor agricultural wage rate, which has no impact on the urban wage rate, is the determinant of migration for these labourers. Rather it is their joblessness for more than 6 months in rural areas along with their landlessness that forces them to migrate to cities. An interesting observation is made by Majumder and Narayan about the conflict of interest between local urban labour and migrant labour that the latter did not crowd out existing local labour has not risen as their work profiles are different. Albeit this point as has come up in discussion about international migration and about immigrants from Bangladesh to India (Banerjee 2020).

The question of labour mobility or migration has caught popular imagination recently when huge mass of migrant workers started their march to their respective source destinations after lockdown of economy. The whole question of safety nets and social security for workers, especially migrant workers, has become a matter of public debate. Pushpendra and Dipak Kumar Singh are motivated by this and examine the social security architecture in their paper on 'Mobility and Threshold Social Security' by assessing the policy and legal framework of social security in India and argue for reconceptualising social security as a redistribution strategy that creates comprehensive entitlements for migrants and other workers. It is argued that a multidimensional, inclusive, and equity-oriented conceptualization of social security sets a social policy agenda for the state, markets, industry associations, trade unions, civil society organizations, and other actors and would require them to reorient their goals accordingly. A strong case is built by authors in favour of a threshold level of social security instead of a minimalist social security.

Another paper in this section based on extensive primary data of sugarcane-cutters in Maharashtra examines the migration pattern of a particular class of workers. Anurag Asawa in his paper, 'Mapping of migrants based on caste, origin and destination: an insight into the sugarcane cutter migrants in Maharashtra', uses a very large field data from 2004–05 to 2012–13 to claim that most of these migrants are below the age of 35 years and with very poor education levels. Every second migrant belongs to the Other Backward Caste (OBC) category and out of them almost every third migrant belongs to the Vanjari sub-caste. Beed, Ahmednagar, Jalgaon, Aurangabad, and Nashik are districts of origin for almost 80% migrants. Ahmednagar, Pune, Nashik, Kolhapur, and Satara are the top five districts of destination for almost 77% migrants. The flow of migrants is from less developed areas to more developed areas, and the caste of migrants also indicates that they belong to the poor strata of the population. Marathas, from the general or upper-caste category, are a 'surprise' inclusion, as they are seen as a very influential community in some parts of the state.

Processes and results of short-term and long-term migrations are different for households at micro-level. So far, migration literature has not paid adequate attention to this. Ray, Naaz, Khasnobis, and Majumder in their paper titled 'Internal migration and inclusive development: insights from the field', attempt to address this research gap by using case studies from three districts of the West Bengal state in eastern India. Temporary seasonal migration is mostly a distress phenomenon. People without adequate (farm) land in rural areas, mostly married males with little formal education, and belonging to the socially disadvantaged groups (STs and Muslims) are more likely to migrate. The predicted probability of migration of an unmarried 35-year-old male with 4 years of schooling and hailing from a Hindu upper caste household of five members with 35 *kathas*[9] of land is 19%. In contrast, for a 30-year-old married male from an ST or Muslim landless family of four persons, without any formal schooling, the predicted probability multiplies three times at 62%. There is no conclusive proof of the success of migration as a coping and poverty alleviation strategy. The nature of employment and earnings of migrants is questionable. Most of them are in unskilled casual wage employment outside the state. Seasonal or temporary migration is facilitated mostly by labour contractors followed by family/relatives, while long-term settled migration is facilitated more by family members or relatives.

7 Summing Up

The last 25 years of economic reforms have had a significant impact on the country's development. While there have been improvements in many areas, there remain areas that have witnessed either stagnation or deterioration. This period has also been characterized by a complete change in the nature of state. Neoliberal policies are an accepted doctrine now; the debate is only about its degree. Papers in this volume have highlighted some issues that continue to pose a challenge to development. The challenge of poverty and inequality is examined and it is suggested that there has to be a change in the nature of the growth process to make it more inclusive and equitable. Neither the observed 'growth euphoria' seems to be seized of this issue nor does the existing growth curve seems to be directed towards the desired direction of equitability. This inability of growth accompanied by changes in global capitalism and technology has posed a serious challenge to working class and rural economy in India even as newer strategies, including diversification away from agriculture, are being devised to cope with growing disparities. The present volume seeks to fill this gap in received understanding on these issues. The researchers in this book strongly recommend an interventionist role for the state in the current scenario. Uttar Pradesh has been a major challenge to national development efforts. It continues to remain the most laggard state in many development outcomes. Any national initiative is bound to become a failure, if this most populous state in the country does not come out of development deficit. Therefore, a special attention is given to it in this volume.

[9] *katha* is a traditional unit area of land measurement. It varies for different states in India. In West Bengal and Uttar Pradesh, one katha is equivalent to 720 sq feet.

References

Abraham, V., & Sasikumar, S. K. (2017). *Declining wage share in india's organized manufacturing sector: trends, patterns and determinants*. I.L.O. Asia -Pacific Working Paper Series.

Asian Development Bank. (2007). *Transport sector in India – Focusing on results*. Operations Evaluation Department, Asian Development Bank, no. June.

Alessandrini, M. (2009). Jobless growth in Indian manufacturing : A Kaldorian approach. *Centre for Financial & Management Studies, 1*, no. November: 1–32.

Alkire, S. (2002). Dimensions of human development. *World Development, 30*(2), 181–205.

Banerjee, A. (2020). *No evidence that low skill immigrants are bad for economy*. Retrieved from, January 8, https://www.youtube.com/watch?v=3-CG4kIXC64.

Banerjee, A. V., & Duflo, E. (2007). The economic lives of the poor. *Journal of Economic Perspectives, 21*(1), 141–67. https://doi.org/10.1257/jep.21.1.141.

Barik, D., & Thorat, A. (2015). Issues of Unequal Access to Public Health in India. *Frontiers in Public Health (October)*. https://doi.org/10.3389/fpubh.2015.00245.

Basole, A., Deepankar, B., & Rajesh, B. (2014). Determinants and Impact of Subcontracting: Evidence from India's informal manufacturing sector, Economics Department Working Paper Series, 169, Retrieved from https://scholarworks.umass.edu/econ_workingpaper/169

Basu, K. (2009). China and India: Idiosyncratic paths to high growth. *Economic and Political Weekly, 44*(38), 43–56.

Bathla, S., Kumar, A., & Joshi, P. K. (2018). Regional income inequalities and public investments in rural India. *Agricultural Economics Research Review, 31*(1), 13. https://doi.org/10.5958/0974-0279.2018.00002.2.

BBC. (2019). Viewpoint: How Serious Is India's Economic Slowdown? *BBC News*. Retrieved from, August 27, https://www.bbc.com/news/world-asia-india-49470466.

Beck, T. (1995). How the poor fight for respect and resources in village India. *Human Organization, 54*(2): 169–81. https://doi.org/10.17730/humo.54.2.208v3n31088272g7.

Bhalla, S. S., & Kaur, R. (2011). *Labor force participation of women in India: some facts, some queries*. Asia Research Centre, Working Paper 40, London School of Economics.

Bhalotra, S. R. (1998). The puzzle of jobless growth in Indian manufacturing. *Oxford Bulletin of Economics and Statistics, 60*(1), 5–32. https://doi.org/10.1111/1468-0084.00084.

Bhandari, L., & Dubey, A. (2019). *Emerging Employment Patterns of 21st Century India*. Indicus Foundation White Paper, 1–48.

Bhattacharjee, S., Hnatkovska, V., Lahiri, A. (2015). The evolution of gender gaps in India. *India Policy Forum, 11*(1).

Biswal, K. (2011). Secondary education in India: development policies, programmes and challenges. Create pathways to access, Research Monograph No. 63. Resource document. Retrieved from, April 13, https://eric.ed.gov/?id=ED522057.

Chaudhary, R., and Verick, S. (2014). *Female labor force participation in India and beyond*. ILO Asia-Pasific Working Paper Series.

Deb, U., Nagaraj, N., Kumar, R., Bhattarai, M., Padmaja, R., Parthasarathy Rao, P., et al. (2014). Dynamics of rural labor markets in India: implications for inclusive development strategy. *Policy Brief, 27*, 1–12.

Desai, M. (2003). *India and China: An essay in comparative political economy*. In IMF Conference on India/China.

Dev, S. M. (2016). *The problem of inequality*. Indira Gandhi Institute of Development Research, Mumbai. Retrieved from, April 13, 2020 https://doi.org/10.1057/9780230524491_4.

Goldman, C. A., Kumar, K B., & Liu, Y. (2008). *Education and the Asian surge: A comparison of the education systems in India and China*. Center for Asia Pacific Policy.

Goli, S., Perianayagam, A., and Reddy, B. (2013). Socioeconomic progress across the major Indian states : Converging or diverging. Resource document. *Munich Personal RePEc Archive*. Retrieved from, April 13, 2020, https://mpra.ub.uni-muenchen.de/59668/.

Gumber, A., Narayanan, L., & Dhak, B. (2017). Rising healthcare costs and universal health coverage in India: An analysis of national sample surveys, 1986–2014. Gujarat Institute of Development Research, Working paper series no. 246 July 2017 Ahmedabad. http://gidr.ac.in/pdf/wp-246-2579.pdf

Himanshu. (2019). Inequality in India: A review of levels and trends. Resource document. United Nations University World Institute for Development Economics Research. https://doi.org/10.35188/UNU-WIDER/2019/676-0.

Himanshu, & Kundu, S. (2017). Rural wages in India: Recent trends and determinants. *Indian Journal of Labor Economics* (vol. 59(2)). Springer.

Himanshu, Lanjouw, P., Murgai, R., & Stern, N. (2013). Non-farm diversification, poverty, economic mobility, and income inequality: A Case Study in Village India. Resource document. Policy Research Working Paper 6451. https://doi.org/10.1111/agec.12029.

Hipple, S. F. (2010, September 2010). Self-Employment in the United States. *Monthly Labor Review*

ILO. (2015). Non-standard forms of employment. *International Labor Organization*. https://doi.org/10.1164/rccm.201209-1671OC.

ILO. (2018). India Wage Report, Wage policies for decent work and inclusive growth. Retrieved from, July 03, 2010 https://www.ilo.org/wcmsp5/groups/public/—asia/—ro-bangkok/—sro-new_delhi/documents/publication/wcms_638305.pdf.

Jahn, E. J. (2015). Don't worry, be flexible! Job satisfaction among flexible workers. *Australian Journal of Labor Economics, 18*(2), 147–68.

Jayadev, A., & Narayan, A. (2018, March). The evolution of India's industrial labor share and its correlates. Centre for Sustainable Employment Working Paper 2018-4 4.

Jha, R. (2013). Welfare Schemes and Social Protection in India. ASARC Working Paper 2013/10. Retrieved from, July 04, 2020, https://papers.ssrn.com/sol3/papers.cfm?abstract_id=2303988.

Kaldor, N. (1955). Alternative theories of distribution. *The Review of Economic Studies, 23*(2)(1955–1956), 83–100

Kannan, K. P., & Raveendran, G. (2019). From jobless to job-loss growth: gainers and losers during 2012–18. *Economic and Political Weekly, 54*(44), 38–44.

Kapur, D., & Nangia, P. (2015). Social protection in India: A welfare state sans public goods? *India Review, 14*(1), 73–90. https://doi.org/10.1080/14736489.2015.1001275.

Khanna, S. (2012). Gender wage discrimination in India: glass ceiling or sticky floor Delhi School of Economics, Centre for Development Economics (CDE) Working Paper No. 214. Available at http://dx.doi.org/10.2139/ssrn.2115074

Kohli, A. (2006). Politics of economic growth in India, 1980–2005, Part II: The 1990s and beyond. *Economic and Political Weekly, 41*(14), 1251–59.

Kohli, A. (2007). State and redistributive development in India. *UNRISD Seminar Held at IGIDR, 3*(1), 149–57. https://doi.org/10.1174/113564009787531226.

Kumar, M. D., & Saleth, R. Maria. (2018). Inequality in the Indian water sector: challenges and policy options. *Indian Journal of Human Development, 12*(2), 265–81. https://doi.org/10.1177/0973703018793727.

Kuznet, S. (1955). Economic growth and income inequality. *American Economic Review, 45*(1), 1–28.

Landau, I., Mahy, P., & Mitchell, R. (2015). *The regulation of non-standard forms of employment in India, Indonesia and Viet Nam, Conditions of Work and Employment Series, No 63*. Geneva: International Labor Office.

Li, Y., Rama, M., and Zhao, Q. (2018, December). States diverge, cities converge: Drivers of local growth catch-up in India. World Bank Policy Research Working Paper 8660.

Maiti, D. (2018). Trade, Market Imperfections and Labor Share, Working papers 292, Centre for Development Economics, Delhi School of Economics.

Maiti, D. (2019). Trade, Labor Share, and Productivity in India's Industries, ADBI Working Paper Series, No. 926, Tokyo, Asian Development Bank Institute.

Mehdi, A., & Chaudhry, D. (2015). *Human capital potential of India's Future Workforce*. New Delhi: Indian Council For Research On International Economic Relations.

Mehrotra, S., Kumra, N., & Gandhi, A. (2014). India's Fragmented Social Protection System: Three Rights Are in Place; Two Are Still Missing, United Nations Research Institute for Social Development, Working Paper 2014–18, Geneva.

Mehrotra, S., & Parida, J. K. (2019). India's Employment Crisis : Rising Education Levels and Falling Non-agricultural Job Growth, CSE Working Paper, 2019-04, Azim Premji University, October.

Mohanan, M., Hay, K., & Mor, Nachiket. (2016). Quality of Healthcare in India : Challenges, Priorities, And The Road Ahead, *Health Affairs*, *35*, 10.

Mukherjee, S. (2014). Liberalisation and jobless growth in a developing economy. *Journal of Economic Integration, 29*(3): 450–69. Available at https://doi.org/10.11130/jei.2014.29.3.450.

Mulok, D., Kogid, M., Asid, R., and Lily, J. (2012). Is economic growth suficient for poverty alleviation? empirical evidence from Malaysia. *Cuadernos de Economía*, 26–32.

NCEE. (2005). India education profile. *National Center on Education and the Economy*.

NITIAayog. (2018). *Strategy for New India @ 75*. Resource document. Niti Aayog. https://niti.gov.in/sites/default/files/2019-01/Strategy_for_New_India_0.pdf

Nussbaum, M. C. (2003). Capabilities as Fundamental Entitlements: Sen and Social Justice. *Feminist Economics* 9(2–3): 33–59. Retrieved from, July 02, 2020 https://doi.org/10.1080/135457002200 0077926.

Nussbaum, M. C. (2011). Creating Capabitities: The Human Development Approach. Retrieved from July 01, 2020, https://apps.ufs.ac.za/media/dl/userfiles/documents/News/2012_12/2012_12_10_Martha_Nussbaum_UFS_December_2012.pdf.

Oxfam Annual Report. (2017/2018). Retrieved from, July 03, 2020, https://www-cdn.oxfam.org/s3fs-public/file_attachments/story/oxfam_annual_report_2017-2018_final_2.pdf.

Pal, P., & Ghosh, J. (2007). Inequality in India: A survey of recent trends. DESA Working Paper No. 45, ST/ESA/2007/DWP/45, Economics and Social Affairs, United Nations.

Parker, B., & Kozel, V. (2007). Understanding poverty and vulnerability in India's Uttar Pradesh and Bihar: A Q-squared approach, World Development 35(2)

Piketty, T. (2014). *Capitalism in the twenty-first century*. The Belknap Press of Harvard University Press.

Ramirez, A., Ranis, G., & Stewart, F. (1997, December). Economic growth and human development. Yale Economic Growth Center, Discussion Papers, no. 787.

Rao, V. K. R. V. (1964). Price policy and economic development with special reference to India. *Economic and Political Weekly, 16*(41), 1649–52.

Rasul, G., & Sharma, E. (2014). Understanding the poor economic performance of Bihar and Uttar Pradesh, India: a macro-perspective. *Regional Studies, Regional Science 1*(1): 221–39. Available at https://doi.org/10.1080/21681376.2014.943804.

Royal Government of Bhutan. (2012). *Defining a new economic paradigm*. Bhutan Report. Retrieved from, June 29, 2020, https://sustainabledevelopment.un.org/content/documents/617BhutanReport_WEB_F.pdf.

Roychoudhury, A. (2019, March 15). 108 economists, social scientists raise doubts on credibility of govt data. *Business Standard News*. Retrieved from, Accessed on June 29, 2020, https://www.business-standard.com/article/economy-policy/108-economists-social-scientists-raise-doubts-on-credibility-of-govt-data-119031500054_1.html.

Sahoo, P. (2011). *Transport infrastructure in india: developments, challenges and lessons from Japan*. Japan External Trade Organization: Institute of Development Economics.

Sanghi, S., Srija, A., & Shrinivas, V. S. (2015). Decline in rural female labor force participation in India: a relook into the causes. *The Journal for Decision Makers, 40*(3), 255–68. https://doi.org/10.1177/0256090915598264.

Sen, A. (1993). *Capability and well-being, resource document*. Oxford Scholarship online. November 2003: Retrieved from, June 30, 2020 https://doi.org/10.1093/0198287976.001.0001.

Sen, A. (1999). Democracy as a Universal Value. *Journal of Democracy*. Retrieved from, June 28, 2020, https://doi.org/10.2478/v10193-011-0020-1.

Sen, A. (2005). *The argumentative Indian.* History and Identity, Allen Lane: Writings on Indian Culture.

Srivastava, R. (2016). Structural Change and Non-Standard Forms of Employment in India. International Labor Organization, Working paper no. 68.

Srivastava, R., & Padhi, B. (2020). Collapse in wage/salary income growth in India, 2011–12 to 2017–18. Centre for Employment Studies Working Paper Series WP 01/2020. Retrieved from, June 27, 2020, https://doi.org/10.1017/CBO9781107415324.004.

Stiglitz, J. E. (2015). The origins of inequality and the policy to contain it. *National Tax Journal, 68*(2): 425–48. http://10.0.67.158/ntj.2015.2.09.

Subramanian, A. (2019). India Facing 'Great Slowdown', Economy Headed to ICU: Ex-CEA. *The Economic Times*, December 18. Retrieved from, December 19, 2019https://economictimes.indiatimes.com/news/economy/policy/economy-trapped-in-four-balance-sheet-problem-ex-cea/articleshow/72867290.cms?from=mdr.

Tejani, S. (2015). Jobless growth in India: an investigation. *Cambridge Journal of Economics, 40*(3), 843–70. https://doi.org/10.1093/cje/bev025.

Tilak, Jandhyala. B.G. (1985). Analysis of Costs of Education in India. The National Institute of Educational Planning and Administration (NIEPA), Occasional Paper, no. January 1985.

Tilak, Jandhyala B.G. (2006). Economics of human capital in India. *The Indian Economic Association.* Retrieved from, July 03, 2020, https://doi.org/10.1007/978-981-13-0250-3_1.

UGC. (2008). *Higher Education in India: Issues related to expansion, inclusiveness, quality and finance.* P. Duriasamy: University Grants Commission, New Delhi.

World Bank. (1998). Uttar Pradesh and Bihar Survey of Living Conditions, 1997–98, LSMS

The Challenge of Development in India

Some Reflections on Development Challenges of India

Arvind Subramanian

Abstract Indian economy started growing much before reforms of 1991. In fact, last 25–30 years have been golden age for many other developing countries. There are mainly two models of sequencing of economic development and political development. But, Indian model is distinctly different from other models. One model is Western Europe and North America that are now very rich and advanced countries with high standards of living and fantastic social indicators. The second model of development is of the East Asian countries that have been very successful. India belongs to neither camp in the sense that first we neither grew as slowly as those countries over long period of time nor have we grown very rapidly. This paper compares Indian model with other models and shows its uniqueness. However, this model brings up many challenges also that are discussed in this paper.

To begin with something that is actually true, not just for India but for almost the entire developing world is that the last 25–30 years have been the best of times for the developing world including India, China and other countries as well. So, whenever we think about issues like poverty, inequality and many other social indicators not doing well, one should look at all these indicators for India and for others countries as well. Per capita GDP, the level of poverty, life expectancy, infant mortality, adult mortality—all these indicators today are far better than they were 25 or 30 years ago. So in some way, this is the golden age for India, not in terms of responsibility of any one government but the cumulative effect of whats happened in the last 25–30 years. That has been true around the developing world like China and East Asia. There are

This is an edited version of the valedictory addressed delivered by Dr Arvind Subramanian at an international seminar on "Development Challenges of India after Twenty Five Years of Economic Reforms" on 18 March, 2018 at Department of Economics, Banaras Hindu University, Varanasi.

A. Subramanian (✉)
Former Chief Economic Advisor, Ministry of Finance, Government of India, Non-Resident Senior Fellow, PIIE, New Delhi, India
e-mail: arvindsubramanian2011@gmail.com

Professor, Ashoka University, New Delhi, India

N. K. Mishra (ed.), *Development Challenges of India After Twenty Five Years of Economic Reforms*, India Studies in Business and Economics,
https://doi.org/10.1007/978-981-15-8265-3_2

countries in Africa, eastern Europe and Latin America which have done very well. So we call this the age of economic convergence which means that poorer countries are catching up or converging to the standard of living in the advanced economy. So in that sense, this is the best of times.

Here, a small note about 25 years of economic reform is in order. One piece of fact about India which is important to remember is that why serious reforms began in India in 1991 only, in the aftermath of the crisis that we had. In fact, India's growth took on around 1980s. We had about almost 40 years of rapid economic growth of about 6% and 6.5%. So, while the reforms may have begun in 1991, India's economic growth took on 10 years before reforms and in fact, in one of the papers that I have written on the Indian Economy with Dani Rodrick, poses this as a puzzle. How come the Indian economy started growing rapidly 10 years before the economic reforms began? So, that is an interesting thing that one should keep in mind that the reforms began in 1991 but India's growth and India's prosperity took a turn for the better around 1979–1980. One may go into why is the case but that is something that is useful to keep in mind.

One may ask whether the Indian economic model has been successful or not. I would say, it is not been obviously as spectacularly successful as China or South Korea or Japan, but on the other hand, its been much better than many other countries in Africa, in Southern Asia and so on. Now there is something very special about the Indian development model because it is very useful to always think about India's performance relative to other countries. So, if we look at the last 200 years of economic development, there have been two very successful models of economic and political development.

One model is Western Europe and North America that are now very rich and advanced countries with high standards of living and fantastic social indicators. Of course, now they are also facing challenges of rising inequality, but broadly it is a very successful economic model and political model as well. But what is distinctive about these countries? They grew or developed over about 200 and 250 years. So their success was gradual, they grew at about 2% to 2.5% for 150–200 years, from about 1820 till today. Over a long period of time, they grew slowly and became successful. The other distinctive thing about them is their political development went hand in hand with economic development. In contrast to India, not everyone got the right to vote immediately in USA or Western Europe. It happened slowly over time. So economic and political developments were both slow and went hand in hand. Today of course all these countries are democracies and have very good accountable political institutions. So, economic and political developments were slow and simultaneous, that is the first model.

The second model of development is of the East Asian countries that have been very successful and there the broad pattern is economic development happened much more rapidly and in about 50–70 years in different countries in different periods. But beginning 1950, It was Japan, Singapore, Taiwan, Korea, China, Malaysia to some extent and Thailand. These countries grew very rapidly over a much shorter space of time.

So the first contrast is that while former model is of development that is slow and over very long period of time and the latter is of was very rapid development which had happened relatively quickly. Second, in most of latter category of countries, political development came after the economic development. So China, for example, is still not a democracy. Korea became democracy much later. Indonesia became democracy 20 and 30 years after it got started growing very rapidly. So these are the two successful models of development one, with slow growth, slow and simultaneously economic and political development and second, rapid growth and sequential development, first economic development and then political development.

India belongs to neither camp in the sense that first we neither grew as slowly as those countries over long period of time nor have we grown very rapidly. Many of these latter category of countries have grown at about 8% or 9% or 10% for 20, 30 or 40 years. India has grown at about 5% or 6% for about 40 years. And the second big difference is that India's economic development happened along with political development. So India had to embark on this journey of economic development being a country with universal franchise where everybody could vote. That is why the Indian economic and political development model is actually very different from these two models and that has created its own opportunities and own challenges. So, I call this model of India as the precocious development model because India became a democracy much earlier than it should have, given the experience about other countries and also because in our economic development model we are very different from the Asians, in a sense that we have done much more services and much less manufacturing than those other countries did. So I call this the precocious development model, doing things well in advance of what most countries did at a comparable point in time. This is a very useful way of thinking about the Indian economy.

However, this model has brought in many challenges. While some of them were settled in the planned development process of India, many of them are still continuing. The idea of federalism is one of that which has been brought into debate in recent times with the introduction of Goods and Service Tax (GST). It is a major reform that the government has undertaken. It is going to have a lot of positive effects, creating one market in India, eliminating barriers to the movements of goods between states of India. Also, GST has been exceptional in creating a new model of cooperative federalism. What do we mean by cooperative federalism, essentially we think about GST, the States have to give up the right to tax and the Centre had to also give up right to tax but both of them have to come together and take these tax decisions together. So now, any tax or any good or any services apart from few things that kept out had to be decided jointly by the Centre and the 29 States in the GST Council. This is a really fantastic model for how India needs to evolve in tackling all the challenge in implementation of GST, which have been mentioned in last 3 months and I would argue that those challenges can no longer be done either by the centre or by the states acting on their own. They have to come together to do so. There are many important issues involved like what is done for taxes, what is going about the revenue, what is going to do for compliances, what is going to do for formalizing the economy, bringing more people in tax slab. But above all, I think about GST as the future of

India in terms of creating a truly federal India where states both compete with each other in a number of dimensions but also the state and centre come together to jointly resolve a number of problems.

Now, let me first, then go to a most specific challenge that we all are facing which is agriculture and let me tell you why I think the cooperative federalism model is actually going to be very critical even in solving the problems of agriculture. Now we all know what the problems of agriculture are. Fundamentally, we need to raise farm incomes and agricultural productivity, that is one and also we need to protect farmers against all the risks that they face whether in terms of prices, weather, or some other shocks. Farmers face more variability of income than the other sectors do. So, we need to increase their income but we also need to increase their resilience to these weather and price shocks that are always going to affect agriculture, that is the fundamental problem.

In the Economic Survey (2017–18), we tried and analyze what is going to be impact of climate change on agriculture and it turns out that climate change, increases in temperature, reduction in rainfall which we have seen largely in India, are going to have a big effect on agricultural productivity. So, this challenge that we face in agriculture is going to be compounded by the effect that going forward the weather and climate are going to be much more unfavourable for agriculture. Farmers in Maharashtra are agitating. But if you think about Maharashtra, only about 20% of the land there is irrigated. So you see immediately water and the public using water, irrigation and agricultural technology and research are big challenges. We are neglecting this a lot and need to do much more on that. But my own view more and more is that if we want to fundamentally raise, or at least protect farmers and build some resilience, we should think seriously about giving farmers something like a universal basic income for all farmers.

I am very excited by the fact that two states in India have started this. Telangana and Karnataka have started the scheme, wherein Telangana, for example, from beginning of year 2018 for every season of Kharif and Rabi, all farmers are going to get Rs 4000 per hectare as income which means Rs 8000 for every farmer based on landholding. It is a very promising thing. Of course, there are going to be a lot of problems in implementing this but in some ways I want to bring back cooperative federalism, because the puzzle is this. Agriculture is a state subject. So, whenever people say agriculture is in distress, I immediately ask the question—why have not the state governments for the last 30–40 years responded to the problem of farmers. Why is it always seen as something that the centre has to solve and not the centre and the states coming together. Therefore going forward, the centre and the states should come together and try to solve this. So, for example, if you take something like a universal basic income for all farmers. One possibility is, for example, that the centre provides a lot of subsidies to farmers—the fertilizer subsidy, minimum support prices and so on. So the question is can the centre and states come together and say, look some of these subsidies that have very harmful effects like fertilizers subsidy, for example, have very negative consequences for soil quality, for health, for productivity in the long run. Why cannot we change the manner in which we support farmers by instead of giving them support in the form of wasteful subsidy and why not give them and why cannot centre and the states come together in solving this problem.

Another big challenge in India, in the long run, is about human capital. There is one area in the last 50–60 years, where India has not done very well it would be health and education.

In the Budget, 2018–19, the Government announced big scheme for health. Let's see how it play out. But if you take education for example and if you look at the studies done by 'Pratham' over the last 10 years, what they find is that, if you look at the primary education in India our enrolment rates are almost close to 100. Almost every child goes to school in India but if you look at what they actually learn in school it's not very encouraging. Going by ASER reports of last 10 years, learning outcomes (the ability to read, the ability to some basic arithmetic) are at a very low level and flat. In fact in the Economic Survey, we calculated something like a poverty count or a poverty ratio that reflects into learning and it is found that it is actually very high. So education or human capital is something that we are lagging behind tremendously. There are a couple of reasons for this.

One, there is no doubt that when we became independent, there was a general neglect of basic and primary education. There was much more of an emphasis on higher education and we set up all these impressive institutes of higher education. But for some reason, the early founding fathers did not emphasize the basic education. In terms of our economic development policies that was perhaps one of the biggest failures of early policymakers. Now, let me give second more controversial thought, of looking around the world historically. One finds that education spread very rapidly in many of countries, like, China, Western Europe and Scandinavia. Universal education was something that society really valued either because the church in Europe and Scandinnavia said we must (everyone, every child must be educated) or in Japan or China (the Chinese communist party thought that was very important). Therefore education spread in these countries. The controversial thought that I want to put forward is that there is something about Indian society, namely, Indian hierarchy that makes or that made at least universal education not so valuable. If you have a very hierarchical society then you do not value equality as an ethic or equality as a fundamental value. Somewhere caste system and all these other things come into the play. And there may be historical or cultural origins for not having education. A stratified society like caste system does not have ethics of equality. Primary education has been a state subject forever. The thought that is always crossed my mind is why is that in the history of India, we not had more politicians who had said that vote for me I will educate your child or vote for me I will create a good health system or universal education system. Why has that never happened in India? Why do the politicians say vote for me I will give free power, vote for me I will give my community some benefits or vote for me I will provide reservation. Fundamentally, the advancement of human capital, health and education has never been on political agenda for some reason and has never resonated in the political process.

I remember in the last U.P. election, there were hundreds of advertisements counting highway between Lucknow and Delhi have been built. That was meant to show how successful a politician was and therefore the implicit message was—I build infrastructure, I build this road, therefore vote for me. Why is that no politician had said there are 30, 40 or 50 million uneducated children and I will create good schools. For me, this is a kind of critical political economy question that needs more reflection and more research including why Uttar Pradesh lags behind on social and human capital indicators. It is worth thinking about that can we create a dynamic U.P. Why do not we make it a politically advantageous proposition for human capital, for the government to invest in human capital?

Development Challenges of India After 25 Years of Economic Reform

Ashok K. Lahiri

Abstract Performance of Indian economy in post-reform period may be considered to be gratifying if compared with pre-reform period. But, if compared with other comparable countries, it is sobering only. After 25 years of economic reforms, there are some critical challenges to be faced in near future. Fiscal rectitude is the most important challenge. The policy also needs to settle the question of 'market failure' versus 'state failure'. Agricultural reforms, availability/waiver of farm loans, role of minimum support price and creation of physical and social infrastructure are going to be key questions in future.

1 Crisis of 1991

The country has completed a quarter century since the economic reforms were launched after crisis of 1991. A crisis was brewing because Indian industry was shackled by unnecessary and harmful cobwebs of bureaucratic control in the form of industrial licensing. In industry, Government decided who to produce, what to produce, how to produce, for whom to produce and at what price to sell. Imports were restricted under quotas and high tariffs. Protected from international competition, industrial efficiency suffered. Importing machinery, intermediate goods, and industrial inputs meant navigating several bureaucratic layers to obtain the necessary permit or license. Then, there was the emphasis on the public sector; it was supposed to be at the commanding heights of the economy. The shortcomings of the market, the so-called market failures, were well known. Government failure or the limitations of the government were not. By the second 5-year plan, the famous statistician Prasanta Chandra Mahalanobis, the doyen of statistics and the founder of the Indian Statistical Institute, was firmly in the saddle at the Planning Commission. Mahalanobis was a firm believer in the public sector and anticipated that in 15 years' time surpluses of

---

A. K. Lahiri (✉)
Member 15th Finance Commission, Government of India, Gurgaon, India
e-mail: ashoklahiriin@yahoo.com

N. K. Mishra (ed.), *Development Challenges of India After Twenty Five Years of Economic Reforms*, India Studies in Business and Economics,
https://doi.org/10.1007/978-981-15-8265-3_3

the public sector would render the need for extra taxation superfluous in the Indian economy (Dhar 2003). Alas, the experience was to be quite to the contrary.

As the government borrowed and spent well above what it earned from taxes, public debt mounted with burgeoning fiscal deficits. There were spill-over of such deficits into frequent balance of payments crises. After the Suez crisis in 1956, the country had been in the midst of a balance of payments crunch and had to go to the International Monetary Fund (IMF) for a stand-by arrangement.[1] Then, rapidly, in quick succession, for balance of payments problems, India had to go to the IMF in 1962, 1963, 1965, 1981, and 1991.

Only a few had anticipated the limited capacity of the government to administer an industrial licensing regime. One of these exceptions was Chakravarti Rajagopalachari or Rajaji, also known as Kautilya of Indian politics of his time. In 1961, he coined the memorable term 'permit-quota-license raj'. Overall, it would be unfair to blame our predecessors and policymakers of those times for their touching faith in socialist planning and the abilities of the public sector. India was also not alone in voting in favour of socialism; even two noted economists—Joseph Schumpeter in 1942 and Nobel laureate Paul Samuelson in 1967—had predicted the victory of socialism over capitalism (Schumpeter 1942; Samuelson 1967). In the 1967 edition of his famous textbook 'Economics: An Introductory Analysis', Samuelson had extrapolated the Soviet Union catching up with the USA in terms of gross national product between 1977 and 1995. In the 1973 edition, Samuelson had predicted that the Soviet Union's per capita income would continue to grow and probably match that of the USA by 1990 and overtake it by 2010. In the event, the Soviet Union, under Gorbachev, disappeared by the end of 1991.

What the government under Prime Minister Narasimha Rao, with Dr Manmohan Singh as his Finance Minister, did in 1991 was to start an end of the era of socialist planning with industrial licensing, quantitative restrictions on imports and high-custom tariffs. The hallmark of the 1991 reforms was external and internal liberalisation and the dismantling of the 'permit-quota license raj' and reining in the fiscal excesses.

2 Post-reform Performance[2]

So, how have we done after the 1991 reforms? The answer depends on 'relative to which period of our own past' and 'relative to which other country'. If we compare the country's performance since the launch of the reforms in 1991 with that in the past, the answer is gratifying. We have grown faster than in the past; poverty has

---

[1] Indeed, India had balance of payments problems right after independence and approached the IMF for a loan right in 1948 because of UK's difficulties in releasing the sterling balances that it owed to India.

[2] This section is from the 5th Raja Chelliah Memorial Lecture delivered at the Madras School of Economics, Chennai on February 9, 2018.

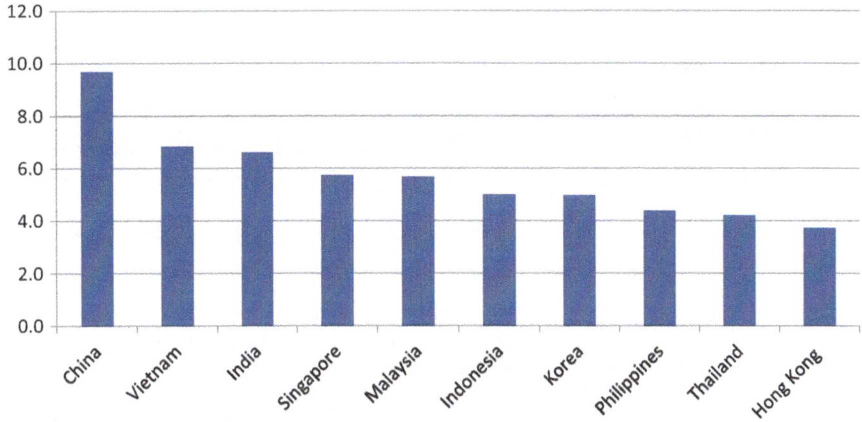

Fig. 1 East Asia and India—Real GDP growth 1991–2017 (Annual, in per cent). *Source* IMF Data Mapper. http://www.imf.org/external/datamapper/NGDPDPC@WEO/OEMDC/ADVEC/WEOWORLD/CHN/HKG/IND/IDN/KOR/MYS/SGP

gone down more rapidly though not enough; we have had no periods of sustained high inflation like after the two oil price shocks in the 1970s; and we have had no balance of payments crisis compelling us to seek exceptional balance of payments support from multilateral bodies such as the IMF.

Comparing how we have done relative to our not-too-distant neighbours in the east is a more sobering experience. We take People's Republic of China, Hong Kong, Indonesia, Republic of Korea, Malaysia, the Philippines, Singapore, Thailand and Vietnam for comparison. For little more than a quarter century, China has grown at about one and a half times the speed of India (Fig. 1).[3] Even Vietnam has grown slightly faster than India. We may have done better than the other seven in terms of growth, but not fast enough for a rapid catch up. These seven started in 1991 with per capita incomes between two and a half to 48 times that of India.[4]

What about macroeconomic stability? India stands out as the country with the highest rate of inflation, next only to Vietnam and Indonesia (Fig. 2). Our performance on the balance of payments front has been the worst (Fig. 3).[5] Among the 10 countries under consideration, apart from Vietnam, India is the only one which had a current account deficit.

If we look at the fiscal position of the general government, that is centre, states and local governments combined, we find that India has had the largest general

[3]By China we mean People's Republic of China. Similarly, Korea refers to Republic of Korea.

[4]In 1991, compared to India's per capita income of \$318 (=100), per capita income of China was \$359 (=113), Hong Kong \$15,190 (=4,775), Indonesia \$848 (=266), Korea \$7,523 (=2,365), Malaysia \$2,845 (=894), the Philippines \$807 (=254), Singapore \$14,504 (=4,560), Thailand \$5,902 (=1,855) and Vietnam \$2,172 (=683).

[5]We consider 1997–2017, the period after the East Asian Crisis partly because current account data are not available for China prior to 1997.

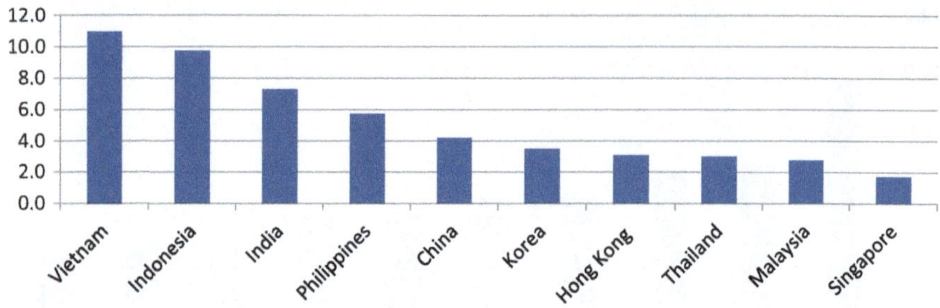

Fig. 2 East Asia and India—Average Annual CPI Inflation 1991–2017 (In per cent). *Source* IMF Data Mapper. http://www.imf.org/external/datamapper/NGDPDPC@WEO/OEMDC/ADVEC/WEOWORLD/CHN/HKG/IND/IDN/KOR/MYS/SGP

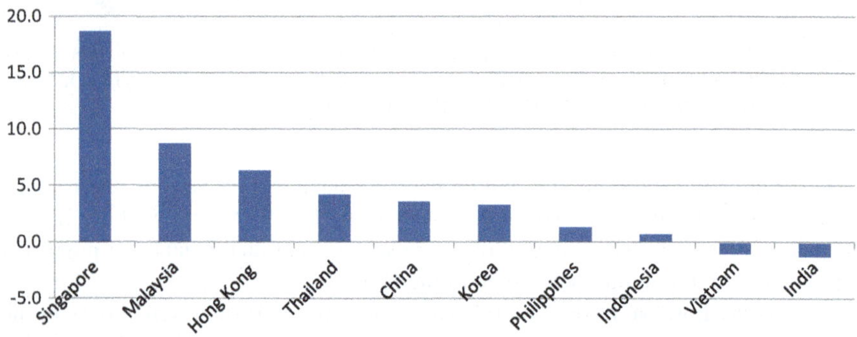

Fig. 3 East Asia and India—Current Account Balance, Average, 1997–2017 (as a proportion of GDP, in per cent). *Source* IMF Data Mapper. http://www.imf.org/external/datamapper/NGDPDPC@WEO/OEMDC/ADVEC/WEOWORLD/CHN/HKG/IND/IDN/KOR/MYS/SGP

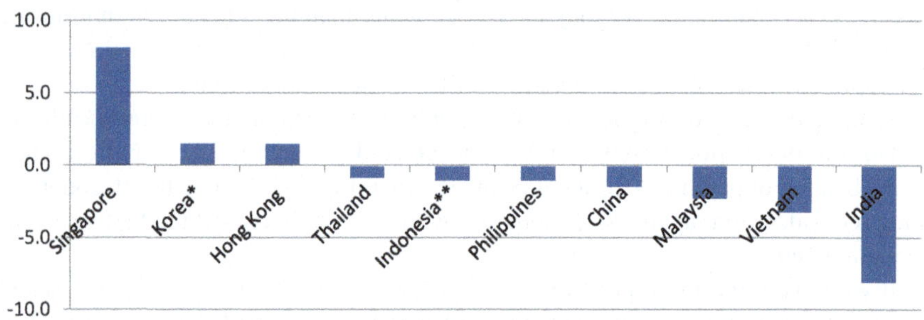

Fig. 4 East Asia and India—General government net lending, 1991–2017 (Per cent of GDP). *Source* IMF Data Mapper. http://www.imf.org/external/datamapper/NGDPDPC@WEO/OEMDC/ADVEC/WEOWORLD/CHN/HKG/IND/IDN/KOR/MYS/SGP

government net borrowing as a proportion of GDP (Fig. 4).[6] It is true that not all countries in East Asia generate fiscal surpluses, but all the countries under consideration were fiscally far more conservative than India. They incurred fiscal deficits, but none, on the average, as large and persistent as that of India. None had as large debts or as adverse primary balance as India.[7]

3 Development Challenges and Way Forward

3.1 Fiscal Rectitude

Now, in comparison with other neighbours in East Asia, the question that we can ask is: why has India not grown faster? The answer surely does not lie in insufficient fiscal stimulus. If government borrowing and spending more held the key to higher growth, India should have grown faster than Vietnam and even China. It is more than likely that structural factors, such as lack of physical infrastructure, inability to transform money spent on public education and health into appropriate outcomes, slow agricultural reforms and facilitation of business, and insufficient progress in liberalising land and labour markets, inhibited growth. Over-expansionary fiscal policy resulted only in higher inflation and weaker balance of payments outcomes. Higher inflation and balance of payments problems may have actually hurt our growth and development performance.

Going forward, the fiscal laxity needs to be corrected. There is no need to generate fiscal surpluses, or even balanced budgets, but there is a need to restrict fiscal deficits to reasonable levels. Some deficit for creating assets should be welcome as long as productivity rises in response. But, not an excessive fiscal deficit that is inconsistent with macroeconomic stability. Exigencies will arise and the government will need to respond to downturns and demand recessions with fiscal stimulus. But there needs to be restraint in normal times. Exhausting the fiscal space by expansionary stance even in relatively normal years leaves a government with little elbow room to respond by a stimulus package without jeopardising macroeconomic stability, when a demand shortfall actually arises. The Fiscal Responsibility and Budget Management Acts that the Centre and the States have need to be observed, and the story cannot continue to be one of the missed timelines and shifting goalposts.[8]

---

[6]General government net lending reported by the IMF does not correspond to general government fiscal surplus reported by Indian official statistics primarily because of the differential treatment of disinvestment receipts.

[7]We disregard Singapore's high public debt (110.6% of GDP in 2017 as Singapore's public debt consists largely of Singapore Government Securities (SGS) issued to assist the Central Provident Fund (CPF), which administers Singapore's defined contribution pension fund.

[8]The NDA government that got the FRBMA passed did not last to promulgate the Rules. United Progressive Alliance (UPA) came to power after the general election of 2004, and continued in office for a second term. Under the first UPA government, the FRBM Rules came into force from July 5, 2004. While notifying the Rules on July 2, 2004, an amendment to the Act was passed for a 1-year postponement of the target year for eliminating the revenue deficit to 2008–09. Before the ink on

3.2 Principle

With the reforms, the state has moved away from socialist planning and intervening in general in what should be produced where, how and when, or at what price a product has to be sold. This has been described pejoratively as a 'neo-liberal' move with the state in retreat. The challenge, I believe, now is to be clear about the underlying principle that should guide the reforms going forward. The principle that should guide the reform is the state doing neither too little nor too much in the economic sphere. India has suffered from the consequences of both the extremes for a considerable period of time.

India under British rule for nearly two centuries had a government that did too little not only for promoting industry but even in physical infrastructures such as roads and power supply or social infrastructures such as health and education. The colonial government's main aim was collecting taxes, maintaining peace and order, getting raw materials, such as tea and jute, to the home country and selling manufactured products to India. A professed laissez-faire attitude in the colony—sometimes in sharp contrast to what the government was doing in its own country, for example, with

---

the FRBM Act was dry, the Finance Minister, in his Budget Speech for 2005–06, pressed the pause button vis-à-vis the FRBM Act because of the drastically changed pattern of devolution and funding recommended by the 12th Finance Commission. In March 2005, Shankar Acharya published an article in Business Standard entitled 'Farewell fiscal responsibility?' What followed indeed looks like a farewell to fiscal responsibility. The FRBM path of fiscal correction was halted from 2008 to 2009 because of unanticipated changes in the prices of fuel and fertiliser. Outlays on major subsidies shot up from Rs 67,498 crore in 2007–08 to Rs 1,23,581 crore in 2008–09. Off-budget bonds issued to the petroleum and fertiliser companies amounted to a further Rs 95,942 crore or 1.8% of GDP in 2008–09. On August 28, 2008, the central government asked the 13th Finance Commission to lay down a revised road map for fiscal consolidation. With elections for the 15th Lok Sabha scheduled for April–May, 2009, an Interim Budget for 2009–10 followed on February 16, 2009. A new Finance Minister, in office for only 3 weeks, called the economic circumstances extraordinary and announced extraordinary measures. The FRBM targets were relaxed to boost demand and counter the impact of the global financial meltdown. Post-election, the Budget for 2009–10 presented on July 6, 2009, included a fiscal stimulus package. Between 2008–09 and 2009–10, as a proportion of GDP, the fiscal deficit shot up from 6.0% to 6.5%, with an even bigger increase in revenue deficit from 4.5% to 5.2%. Of course, the medium-term commitment to fiscal consolidation and a return to the FRBM targets at the earliest were reiterated. In the context of FRBM, the 13th Finance Commission, in its report submitted on December 29, 2009, argued against disturbing the existing classification of revenue and capital expenditure in an ad hoc manner. Yet, in what was described as the 'Godzilla of all fudges played out in this country in the guise of fiscal consolidation', Budget 2011–12 quietly introduced the concept of 'effective revenue deficit'. It is the revenue deficit adjusted for grants to states for asset creation. The Budget of 2012–13 went farther. Through the Finance Act, known for its missile-like efficiency for getting passed without elaborate discussion or amendments, it changed the FRBM Act itself. The Centre's commitment to eliminate its revenue deficit was dumped for the elimination of the tenuous concept of 'effective revenue deficit'. The amended FRBM Rules of May 7, 2013, stretched the time for its elimination by 6 years to March 31, 2015, and for bringing the fiscal deficit down to 3% of GDP by 8 years to March 31, 2017. In 2018–19, as a proportion of GDP, the budget estimate of revenue deficit of the central government continues to be far above zero at 2.2%! The Finance Bill currently in Parliament removes the elimination of revenue deficit as a target and stipulates the target date for containment of fiscal deficit below 3% of GDP to March 31, 2021.

instruments such as protective tariffs—suited them well.[9] There was an unwillingness to accept anything that could even closely resemble 'market failure'.

In the first four decades after independence, under socialist planning, what followed is the other extreme of the state trying to do too much. If the colonial rulers did not recognise 'market failure', governments in India in the first four decades after independence refused to consider the possibility of 'government failure'.

The right principle guiding the reforms forward should recognise the limitations of both markets and government. Quite a few goods and services—for example, financial markets, natural monopolies such as public utilities, markets dominated by a few big players, or pharmaceutical products—cannot be left entirely to the mercy of the markets. They need rules and regulations and a regulatory body such as the Reserve Bank of India or Securities and Exchange Board of India (SEBI), Electricity Regulatory Commission, Competition Commission, or Central Drugs Standard Control Organization to avoid systemic risks, exploitative pricing, and health and safety risks. Neither can markets solve the problems of illiteracy, poor health, poor roads or water supply.

Similarly, the government cannot solve all problems, particularly the problem of resource allocation at the micro level, that is what and how much to produce, where, and with what technology. Undoubtedly, there has been progress in this area, but rather haltingly. The last rites of the erstwhile Planning Commission provide a good example of this halting progress.

After independence, in conformity with socialist practice, a formal model of planning was adopted in India, and a Planning Commission, with the Prime Minister as chairman and also reporting directly to the Prime Minister, was established on March 15, 1950. There was no mention of a Planning Commission in the Constitution, nor was it set up by law; it was simply an arm of the central Government of India set up through a Cabinet resolution. The Planning Commission provided the institutional structure for planning under the permit-license-quota raj. It, along with its detailed Five Year Plans, had outlived its utility for channelling private investment after the introduction of market-based reforms in 1991. In his first Independence Day speech in 2014, Prime Minister Narendra Modi announced the scrapping of the Planning Commission. By a press release on January 1, 2015, after a life of 65 years, the erstwhile Planning Commission died to be replaced by the National Institution for Transforming India (NITI) Ayog.[10]

---

[9]For example, the British market, when the textile industry first started coming up in the island state, was protected by duties of 70–80%. The Indian textile industry, on the other hand, during its formative years between 1896 and 1925, had the benefit of import tariff protection of 3.5% neutralised by an equivalent excise duty on domestic textiles.

[10]http://pib.nic.in/newsite/pmreleases.aspx?mincode=61.

3.3 Agricultural Reforms

The third challenge is agricultural reforms. A sector that produces only 16–17% or less than a sixth of the gross value added, but provides half the employment in the economy cannot but be in distress. There is an urgent need for accelerated agricultural reforms. The recent farm loan waivers across states totalling around 1.0–1.5% of 2017–18 gross domestic product has brought the issue of agricultural reforms to the centre stage. The enduring solution of course lies in providing employment in alternative sectors, particularly in industry. But, this is a task that can be achieved only over time. Questions can be raised about the course that reform is following in agriculture.

3.4 Cheap Farm Loans and Farm Loan Waivers

Emphasis on cheap credit had started under Indira Gandhi in 1972 with the Differential Rate of Interest (DRI) scheme. Banks, mostly government-owned, had to allocate at least 1% of loans to weaker sections, including small and marginal farmers, at highly subsidised 4% annual interest, a rate adopted against the advice of an expert group appointed for this purpose. DRI continues, but with very limited success. Targeted borrowers are apathetic about its small amounts, and the banks lukewarm with the high administrative costs.

Loan waiver is an extreme form of cheap credit—zero interest and no repayment date. In July 1975, the 20-point programme during the emergency included planned liquidation of rural indebtedness through moratorium on debt recovery from landless labourers, small farmers and artisans. Cheap credit for the rural poor to procure income-generating assets started with a bang with the Integrated Rural Development Program (IRDP) launched on a pilot basis in 1978. Extended rapidly to four million households by 1987, it was adjudged the 'worst-ever development programme' by some studies of effectiveness. Loans were either highjacked by the rich and well-connected, or wasted with inadequate attention to forward (e.g. marketing of milk) and backward (e.g. fodder for cattle) linkages.

Through *loan melas* in the 1980s, Sri Janardhan Poojary, Minister of State for Finance, first under Indira Gandhi and then Rajiv Gandhi, made revolutionary contribution in popularising cheap credit. Initially, the ruling Janata Party in Karnataka, Poojary's home state, protested. Soon realising that the senior Congress leader had emerged as a friend of the poor by misusing banks, it declared itself not against loan melas, but the partisan manner of allowing only Congress functionaries to mediate loans. Imitation is the best form of flattery, and over time, by promising and granting farm loan waivers, all parties started paying their tribute to the iconic Poojary. Janata Party, with Devi Lal as Deputy Prime Minister, did so in 1989. After farmers' suicides in Vidarbha, an expert group on agricultural indebtedness, in mid-2007, recommended a few steps, but not a debt waiver. Yet, United Progressive

Alliance's Finance Minister Chidambaram's Union Budget, 2008–09, went ahead with a waiver.

Andhra Pradesh, under Telegu Desam's Chandrababu Naidu, and Telangana under Telangana Rashtra Samithi's K. Chandrasekhar Rao gave such waivers in 2014. Tamil Nadu, under AIADMK's Puratchi Thalaivi did so in 2016. In 2017, in Uttar Pradesh, the government announced the Kisan Karz Mafi Yojana, or Peasant Loan Waiver Scheme to redeem the Bharatiya Janata Party's (BJP) election promise. Rahul Gandhi had announced 'Karz maaf, bijli bill half' in his election campaign, and the waiver would have come even with a Samajwadi-Congress victory in UP.

Promise of farm loan waivers in election campaigns has become standard fare for almost all political parties. Lack of access to institutional credit and low agricultural productivity, and reliance on unscrupulous moneylenders are at the root of rural indebtedness. Yet, politicians prefer cheap institutional credit to more institutional credit. Loan waivers can be given by the stroke of a pen, and before elections, their concerns are more immediate and practical than strategic and long term.

Waivers are problematic at best. They send a wrong message on servicing of loans. Those who repaid, regret why they did so. One waiver triggers expectation of more to follow. The less you repay, the more you gain in the future. Incentive to repay on time weakens. Credit culture deteriorates. Once bitten twice shy, banks avoid lending in jurisdictions where waivers are granted. Waiver's temporary relief comes at the cost of lower credit inflows. Furthermore, even when the governments repay the loans on farmers' behalf, such repayments often come with a delay because of their stressed fiscal situation. They also raise the question about whether paying for loan waivers is the best use of scarce government resources in helping the agricultural sector.

Loan waivers are clearly not in conformity with the spirit of the reforms. Yet, intense competition among parties to distribute freebies, including loan waivers, continues. Stopping the culture of political parties promising farm loan waivers will continue to be a challenge going forward.[11]

3.5 Minimum Support Price

The Indian State's involvement in agriculture has been primarily by interventions in the input markets, such as for fertiliser, through subsidies, and in output markets through minimum support price (MSP), public procurement through the government-owned Food Corporation of India (FCI) and public distribution system.

---

[11]The freebies provoked even the judiciary to step into stop the practice. Noting the discriminatory nature of drought-related loan waiver only to small and marginal farmers, the Hon'ble Madras High Court has directed Tamil Nadu to extend the benefit to all farmers. The Hon'ble Supreme Court has observed that promises of freebies to lure voters shake the roots of free and fair polls, and directed the Election Commission (EC) to frame guidelines for regulating contents of manifestos. In response, the guidelines issued by the Election Commission on April 24, 2015, in the form of 'Model Code of conduct for the Guidance of the political parties and candidates', does not hold out much hope for success. http://eci.nic.in/eci_main1/current/manifestos_27052015.pdf.

MSP has a long history going back well before the reforms. The Government had appointed a Foodgrains Prices Committee under the Chairmanship of L. K. Jha in August 1964. The Committee in its report had recommended a minimum price which would be assured to farmers through support operations as well as a procurement price for wholesalers and retailers such that producers are able to secure 'a rupee or two' more than the minimum price. The procurement price was also the 'maximum price'. As far as consumers were concerned, the Committee had also fixed the ex-mill price—that is the price after the paddy has been milled, bagged and sewn—of rice as well as the maximum retail price.[12] The Committee had recommended the producer price for three varieties of wheat—red, common white and superior—as well as for four types of coarse grains—jowar, bajra, maize and gram and left the job of fixing the maximum producer price for these for the Agricultural Prices Commission to be appointed.[13] From 1968 to 69, the Government announced only the MSP and the MSP became the MSP-cum-procurement price. The MSPs were announced around the time of sowing and applied to the period when the crop was harvested and sold.[14]

Politically, given the enormous farm lobby, procurement price became a very sensitive issue. Dharm Narain (1975), Chairman of Agricultural Prices Commission during 1970–1975, described it well by saying 'the procurement price is more politics than economics'. The S. R. Sen Committee was appointed in 1979 to go into the cost of cultivation to decide the procurement price. But the procurement price often was more than what was recommended by the Commission. Furthermore, given that farmers often had to sell their foodgrains to traders at prices lower than the MSP, even the decision as to where the FCI would carry out its procurement was politically determined.

Food policy of the Government suffered from conflicting objectives, which included promoting production and self-reliance, reducing undue fluctuations in foodgrains prices, and protecting the vulnerable sections of the people. The Central Government made foodgrains available to the states at the central depots at a uniform central issue price. The Central Government also reimbursed the difference between the economic cost of the FCI—the price paid to farmers together with other incidental operating and storage costs including handling, transportation and wastage—and the central issue price in the form of subsidies. Procurement incidentals, such as mandi fees and cesses, and distribution cost could be as much as a third of the economic

[12]The Committee was aware of the innumerable varieties of rice, and fixed only the minimum and maximum prices of only one 'coarse variety of paddy in each state' and left the job of fixing the prices of different varieties to the state governments.

[13]http://cacp.dacnet.nic.in/ViewQuestionare.aspx?Input = 2&DocId = 1&PageId = 66&KeyId = 511 The Agricultural Prices Commission became the Commission for Agricultural Costs and Prices in 1985.

[14]'The agricultural crop year in India is from July to June. The Indian cropping season is classified into two main seasons-(i) Kharif and (ii) Rabi based on the monsoon. The Kharif cropping season is from July–October during the south-west monsoon and the Rabi cropping season is from October to March (winter)'. http://www.arthapedia.in/index.php?title = Cropping_seasons_of_India-_Kharif_%26_Rabi Rabi marketing season is April–June, and Kharif marketing season is October–December.

cost. Beyond the central depots, the state governments shared the responsibility of reaching the foodgrains to the fair price shops and running the PDS. The only way the consumers could be provided with foodgrains at a reasonable price while farmers could be paid a 'remunerative price' was through subsidies. Food subsidies for the Central Government mounted as the over-all cost of procuring the grains—known as economic cost—went up much faster than the price collected from the states for distribution to the consumers through PDS with or without further subsidies from such governments. A solution to the problem did not lie in increasing the central issue price collected from the consumers because offtake was already falling short of allocation of foodgrains.

The S. R. Sen Committee had clearly pointed out that a mechanical fixation of price on the basis of cost of cultivation will freeze the price relationships to the demand–supply situation prevailing in the past and thereby obstruct allocation of resources as per changing economic situation. By the early 1970s, economists had pointed out how the artificially high price for foodgrains and the availability of new high-yielding varieties of seeds, particularly wheat, was leading to a shift of acreage from other food and cash crops, and was likely to result 'either in a progressively increasing stockpile of wheat or will seek for it an export outlet'. Furthermore, Dharm Narain (1972: A-6) had pointed out 'Since, given the ruling international prices for this cereal, domestic wheat cannot be exported without a sizeable subsidy, the feasibility as well as the desirability of this course of action will have to be properly assessed. The building and carrying of a progressively rising stock of wheat is, likewise, a costly operation and it would be neither desirable nor possible to undertake it on a continuing basis'. But, that is what precisely happened over time, stocks piled up and grains were exported with large subsidies to cover the difference between the world price and economic cost of procuring grains. And, now again there is demand for mechanical fixation of MSP at levels 'at least 50% more than the weighted average cost of production'! This surely is not in line with the spirit of the reforms. How to reform the agricultural output markets and the MSP regime is going to continue to be a challenge. In this context, there are lessons to be learnt from the success story of milk.

3.6 Lessons from Milk

Production of milk had gone up in two decades from 17 million tonnes in 1951–52 to only 22 million tonnes in 1971–72. Milk was 'cheap, but not available' through the government outlets in urban centres in the late 1960s and early 1970s. With the White Revolution, output more than doubled in each of the next two decades to 56 million tonnes in 1991–92 and 128 million tonnes in 2011–12.

The National Dairy Development Board (NDDB), founded in 1965, launched Operation Flood with the sale of skimmed milk powder and butter oil gifted by the European Union through the World Food Programme. The triple objectives of 'a flood of milk', augmenting rural incomes, and ensuring reasonable prices for consumers were not only attained but also in a sustainable way. The backbone of the programme was the 'Anand Pattern' of cooperatives of milk producers in different parts of the country. 'Amul', the brand name of the Gujarat Co-operative Milk Marketing Federation Ltd., owned by more than 3.5 million milk producers in Gujarat, became a household name. Over time, government undertakings, such as the Delhi Milk Scheme (DMS) or Bihar State Dairy Corporation, were handed over to the NDDB.

Generally, success in agriculture has been limited in areas other than milk. Indeed, relative to many other agri-products, milk has got some unique characteristics. For example, milk is more homogenous than rice, making it easier to procure, transport and store. Rice comes in many varieties such as Basmati, Gobindabhog, and Sona Masuri. Furthermore, milk is produced every day through the year unlike many seasonal agricultural commodities, such as mangoes. Yet, despite these unique characteristics, three important lessons from milk, particularly the 'soft touch' nature of government intervention, are noteworthy.

First, not government undertakings, but cooperatives, successful in many countries such as New Zealand, the Netherlands and Denmark since the 19th century, were promoted for milk. In milk, without the shadow of a gigantic public sector undertaking, very little entry barriers promoted competition in procurement, transportation, storage, and distribution. Milk was delicensed in 1991 and subjected to the Milk and Milk Product Order (MMPO) of 1992 under the provisions of Essential Commodities Act, 1955. But, MMPO, even before its repeal in 2011, was more for maintaining the quality of milk supply by large dairies.

The nature of government intervention in wheat and rice was starkly different. The FCI was set up in 1964, a year before NDDB. FCI's mandate was to carry out price support operations for safeguarding the interests of the farmers, to distribute foodgrains throughout the country for the public distribution system, and to maintain adequate levels of operational and buffer stocks of foodgrains to ensure National Food Security. There was even a 10-month long abortive move to nationalise the wholesale trade in wheat in April 1973 under Indira Gandhi!

A monolithic and gigantic central government undertaking to deal with vital foodgrains along with the system of MSP and procurement at MSP made the economics of wheat and rice, including where to procure and at what price, and also the wage bill of the FCI, vulnerable to political pressures. Before the Punjab polls in February 2014, Prime Minister Modi had suggested unbundling FCI into three parts for procurement, storage and distribution.

In January 2015, the High Level Committee (HLC) under the chairmanship of Shanta Kumar gave its report on restructuring the FCI. The HLC recommended handing over all procurement operations of wheat and rice in Andhra Pradesh, Chhattisgarh, Haryana, Madhya Pradesh, Odisha and Punjab to state governments, as they have sufficient experience in and reasonable infrastructure for procurement. It recommended that FCI should 'move on' to help the states in the east—like Eastern Uttar Pradesh, Bihar, West Bengal, and Assam—which still awaited the green revolution and where small farmers dominate and sell much below MSP. It is time to act on either the Prime Minister's suggestion or the HLC's recommendation.

Second, there has been no MSP for milk. MSPs, as the HLC has pointed out, continue to distort the market for 23 agricultural goods. Furthermore, FCI procurement is restricted to wheat and rice with MSPs doubling up as procurement prices. As recommended by the HLC, the government should revisit its MSP policy.

Third, the country has made considerable progress in horticulture with its output of 269 million tonnes surpassing that of foodgrains for the first time in 2012–13. But there is scope for much more progress in horticulture. Its demand is going up rapidly with increasing income. Because of the labour-intensive nature of fruits and vegetables and higher value realisation, their promotion can also generate prosperity for the small farmers. For this, a major requirement is cold chain or logistics support for storage and distribution to maintain the inventory within predetermined ambient parameters. Particularly glaring is the acute shortage of pack-houses with conveyer belt systems for sorting, grading, washing, drying, weighing, packaging, pre-cooling and staging, and of reefer vehicles with active refrigeration designed for environment-controlled carriage of products.

Much of the white revolution is due to the rapid development of milk processing and distribution infrastructure, e.g. developing and installing automatic milk collection units for quality verification and bulk coolers at the village level, processing and packaging plants, tankers to transport the milk at 4°c, and bulk vending machines. A lesson from milk for horticulture is the need to facilitate the development of the requisite infrastructure through private sector initiatives. How to make it come about will continue to be a challenge.

3.7 *Physical Infrastructure*

The fourth challenge is building up our physical infrastructure. With the benefit of hindsight, it is clear that, relative to China, we invested too little in the post-independence period. While China invested between 31 and 39% of its GDP during 1971 and 2000, we invested only 18 to 24%. And also, we invested too little in physical infrastructure. We realised this inadequacy late only when there were perennial power outages, roadways choked up with traffic, urban centres starting to look more like shanty towns and long waiting periods for getting freight moved by railways.

In infrastructure, while fast-growing emerging economies invested around 7–10% of their GDP, India invested only about 3% of GDP in the first 50 years of independence (Chatterjee 2017). By the late-1980s, researchers were talking about infrastructural bottlenecks. But, even with this awareness, enhanced outlays on infrastructure were delayed further because of limited fiscal space. There were obvious difficulties in the form of burgeoning fiscal deficits, and political challenge in shifting expenditure from revenue items such as subsidies.

The publication of the India Infrastructure Report in 1996 played a major role in attracting attention to this important sector. We have made progress since then. As a proportion of GDP, infrastructural investment climbed from 4.8% in 2002 to a high of 8.4% in 2011. According to the World Bank's Logistic Performance Index, India ranked 35 with a score of 3.42 in 2016, up from rank 54 and score 3.08 in 2014, rank 46 and score 3.08 in 2012, rank 47 and score 3.12 in 2010, and rank 39 and score 3.07 in 2007.[15] The corresponding improvement in terms of infrastructure, according to the World Bank, is to rank 38 and score 3.34 in 2016, up from rank 65 and score 2.88 in 2014, rank 52 and score 2.87 in 2012, rank 52 and score 2.91 in 2010, and rank 42 and score 2.90 in 2007. But, there are miles to go before our physical infrastructure is adequate to support accelerated economic growth and development.

First, we need to start compiling the data on infrastructural investment with how well or how badly we are doing. There is a lot to be learnt from Peter Drucker's quote 'If you can't measure it, you can't improve it'. No data on infrastructural investments are available from official sources except for the past, to the best of my knowledge, from the erstwhile Planning Commission. The numbers about how much we need in terms of infrastructural investment are quite intimidating. Under the 12th Plan (2012–17), the target for infrastructure investment was Rs. 56 trillion. Estimates suggest that actual achievement may have been only around Rs. 39 trillion (Chatterjee 2016). Instead of 7–10% of GDP, India invested only 5.% of GDP in infrastructure in 2015.[16]

Second, we need to clarify the definition of infrastructure. For a long time, we have focused on six infrastructure or core industries, namely crude oil, petroleum refining, coal, electricity, cement, and finished steel. Indeed, these are very important segments of the economy, we need to monitor them closely as we have in the past, but all of these are not what we normally mean by infrastructure. Infrastructure is the basic physical structure and facilities which are essential for the operation of the economy and cannot be substituted by imports.[17] You can import finished steel or refined petroleum products, but you cannot substitute facilities such as roads, ports and power supply lines by imports. The inclusion of the six core industries in infrastructure often leads to quite a bit of confusion. For example, when you read about 926 infrastructure projects, worth Rs.13 trillion and accounting for 7.2% of all outstanding projects, stalled at end-September 2017, they include a large number of steel and cement projects (Vyas 2017, Mampatta 2017). This number does not provide what we are looking for in terms of stalled infrastructure projects.[18]

---

[15] LPI consists of six components, namely customs, infrastructure, international shipments, logistics quality and competence, tracking and tracing and timeliness. https://lpi.worldbank.org/international/global.

[16] See ADB report 'Meeting Asia's Infrastructure Needs,' February, 2017. https://www.adb.org/publications/asia-infrastructure-needs.

[17] Perhaps, infrastructure should include only electricity, roads and bridges, telecom, railways, irrigation, water supply and sanitation, ports, airports, storage and gas supply network. There is merit in deliberations to decide on a rigorous definition.

[18] DBOD Circular of November 25, 2013. https://rbi.org.in/Scripts/NotificationUser.aspx?Id = 8591&Mode = 0 The definition of subsectors identified by the RBI in its circular for classifying credit as 'infrastructral lending' is more satisfactory. It divides the sectors into the following categories—transport, energy, water and sanitation, communication, and market and social infrastructure. But even here, I find fertiliser (capital investment) included under 'market and social infrastructure'. Fertiliser is indeed very important for the economy, but I doubt if it qualifies to be included under 'infrastructure'.

Third, we need to fully recognise that the public sector alone cannot fill the gap in infrastructure, and the private sector has to come in. Let us look at the numbers. If we take Rs. 165 trillion as the ballpark figure for GDP, we need to invest Rs.12–16 trillion per year in infrastructure.[19] According to the Union Government's 2017–18 budget, the entire capital expenditure budgeted by the Central Government was Rs. 3 trillion in 2017–18. If you look at the composition of the Centre's capital outlay, except for the capital outlay on defence of Rs. 916 billion, for Ministry of Finance of Rs. 411 billion, and for Ministry of Home of Rs. 132 billion, almost the entire capital outlay is on infrastructure. For 2017–18, a back of the envelope calculation yields a figure of Rs. 1.35 trillion capital outlays budgeted for infrastructure by the Central Government, notably with Rs. 552 billion for railways and Rs. 542 billion for roads.[20] If we make the heroic assumption of an equivalent sum spent by State Governments, the total infrastructure investment by the general government is unlikely to have been more than Rs. 3 trillion, or a fifth or at best a quarter of what was needed.

Given the need for fiscal consolidation, the unlikely prospect of a major jump in revenues of the government and the limited scope for any radical expenditure restructuring in the short run, reliance on private investment appears to be unavoidable.[21] Private investment in infrastructure is not so much a matter of choice but a necessity.[22] Given the fiscal reality and the country's needs, the debate about private investment in infrastructure should be focused not on its desirability but about 'how'

---

[19]The Asian Development Bank, in its report titled 'Meeting Asia's Infrastructure Needs', has estimated that $4.36 trillion is needed to fix India's infrastructure deficit by 2030. That entails more than $300 billion of spending every year for the next 13 years.

[20]Included under infrastructure investment are capital account allocations under Ministries of Civil Aviation, Communications, Railways, Road Transport and Highways, Urban Development, Water Resources, River Development and Ganga Rejuvenation.

[21]Prior to the mid-1990 s, barring for some historic exceptions, such as Kolkata Electric Supply or BEST in Mumbai, the public sector fully financed, owned and managed infrastructure projects and took all the associated risks. The role of the private sector was restricted to the traditional procurement model. The state engaged the private sector only to build (and often design) the asset. The asset was ultimately owned and operated by the state. Experience with the state taking all the risks was not particularly happy. With the state taking all the traffic risks in railways, money went for connecting VIP constituencies by rail rather than expanding congested rail corridors with maximum freight and passenger needs. Inefficiencies, delays and failures took years to come to public notice. Recently, regulatory reasons accounting for the bulk of stalled infrastructure projects in the public sector came to public notice expeditiously. Perhaps, without similar private sector projects stalled by regulations, the problems would have surfaced only after a number of years.

[22]India has made substantial progress in promoting private investment in infrastructure since one of the first toll roads in India—a 12-km long toll road linking Indore to the industrial township of Pithampur in Madhya Pradesh—was opened in November 1993. Some landmarks in the promotion of PPP in infrastructure were the delicensing of electricity generation in 1991, amendment of National Highways Act 1956 in 1995, granting licences to eight cellular mobile telephone service operators in four metro cities and 14 operators in 18 state circles in 1994, and setting up of Infrastructure Development Finance Company (IDFC) in 1997. India has come a long way in promoting public–private partnerships (PPP) in infrastructure. Some point out that India has become the world leader in PPP. Vinayak Chatterjee: 'PPP in India: The story so far'. Business Standard, January 21, 2013. http://www.business-standard.com/article/opinion/vinayak-chatterjee-ppp-in-india-the-story-so-far-112051400022_1.html Government of India's database

to bring it in in the most efficient and welfare-enhancing way. For this what we need is to solve the four main problems of: implementation, regulatory capture, financing, and incomplete contracts.

The ambition behind the vision for the Three Gorges Dam in China has been compared with that of the pyramid-building Pharaohs. The 607 feet tall and 3,319 yards wide dam has created a lake stretching over 640 kms! The National People's Congress approved the dam in 1992 and construction started on December 14, 1994 and was completed in 2006. The dam was expected to be fully operational in 2009, but the last of the 32 turbines was connected to the grid only on July 4, 2012. Now, compare this with the Bangalore-Mysore Infrastructure Corridor (BMIC) in the southern state of Karnataka in India. It is a 4–6 lane 111 km tolled expressway project connecting the state capital of Bengaluru (old name for Bangalore) and important city of Mysuru (old name Mysore). A tender for developing the BMIC was invited by the state government of Karnataka on September 28, 1988, before the People's Congress in China approved the Three Gorges Dam in 1992! The BMIC is still not complete. Much of the implementation problems related to land acquisition and obtaining the regulatory and environmental clearances. Solving these will continue to be major challenges.

3.8 Social Infrastructure

The last, but not the least, is the challenge of improving social infrastructure, namely education and health. We lag behind our East Asian neighbours in terms of education and health indicators. Here, the main challenge is to shift the focus from only building more schools, primary health centres and hospitals to making sure that there are no problems of absentee teachers, or teachers who do not teach, health centres with no doctor or medical staff and medical supplies. Improving the quality of service will require active involvement of the user community. Encouraging this involvement

on infrastructure projects in the public domain lists 1,555 projects in the PPP mode. InfrastructureIndia.Gov.in, https://infrastructureindia.gov.in/project-list?id = 1&searchType = Government%20Infrastructure%20Projects%20(PPP) By grants of Rs. 287 billion, the government has entered into agreements to get these projects, costing Rs. 9.7 trillion, implemented through the private sector. The modalities tried include build-operate-transfer (BOT), build-own-operate-transfer (BOOT), design-build-finance-operate-transfer (DBFOT), and operation and management contract (O&M). Duration of the concession period can be as varied as 24 months to 9,999 months, and the bidding parameter used for the award of contract varied from highest premium or minimum grant to tariff or user charge, annuity, revenue share, concession duration, lease rent and cost of construction. Since January 2016, a hybrid annuity model is also being tried. Under the BOT model though, private players build, operate and maintain the road for a specified number of years before transferring the asset back to the government. Under the BOT-annuity model, the toll revenue risk is taken by the government and the private party is paid a pre-fixed annuity for the construction and maintenance of the road. Under EPC (engineering, procurement and construction) model, the private player is paid to lay the roads with no further role for the private player in the road's ownership, toll collection or maintenance. The hybrid-annuity model combines EPC (40%, released in five tranches linked to milestones) and BOT-Annuity (60%).

will be a major challenge going forward. In this context, what we may also consider is the delegation of teacher recruitment and monitoring to local bodies and the levy of a minimal user fee to generate a sense of entitlement among the users. The user fee need not even go to the consolidated fund of the government, it can remain with the parent–teacher society in a school or the Rogi Kalyan Samitis in health centres or hospitals and used for purposes such as purchasing books or sports equipment in schools, and beds and bed linen in hospitals.

4 Conclusion

Though the challenges may look formidable, pessimism is unwarranted. Other countries have met them in the recent past and India can also do it. Japan had grown at spectacular rates during the 1950s, more than doubling its per capita GDP. Apart from Japan, quite a few other countries to the east of India—the so-called East Asian Tigers, namely Hong Kong, South Korea, Singapore and Taiwan—started growing fast as well during the 1960s and 1970s. All the countries increased their per capita GDP at constant 2010 US dollar terms by a factor of over six times between 1960 and 1990. With high single-digit rates, their per capita income doubled every decade over much of the second half of the last century. Such historically unprecedented growth rates of per capita income over three decades totally transformed the very nature of living for most of the population. Korea, for example, even joined the rich country club of OECD in 1996.

Electorate in India has matured and become enlightened, they exercise their ballot judiciously, and are hungry for development. Their emphasis now is on 'bijli, sadak, pani' and not 'roti, kapda, makan'. Political parties' stress on 'vikas' shows they are adjusting to the new demands of the electorate and reinforces my optimism.[23] 'People have a tendency to blame politicians when things don't work, but one 'get the politicians one deserve', former US President Barak Obama told Italians in May

[23]In a CNN IBN Centre for the Study of Developing Societies (CSDS) all-India post-poll survey of 22,301 respondents, after the 2014 Lok Sabha election, when asked what the single most important issue was while voting in the recent Lok Sabha election, 19.0% mentioned inflation in general and hike in the price of LPG, petrol and diesel in particular, 11.6% corruption, 10.9% lack of development, and 7.5% unemployment and jobs. Issues such as MNREGA, and poverty were mentioned as the topmost issue only by 0.3% and 1.9% of the respondents. Question 5. http://www.lokniti.org/pdf/All-India-Postpoll-2014-Survey-Findings.pdf. The survey is conducted by Lokniti—Programme for Comparative Democracy—established in 1997 as a CSDS research programme. The National Election Studies series attempts to understand the larger forces and the long-term changes taking place in democratic politics and society. The most recent in the National Election series has been the National Election Study 2009 and 2014. Question 23 d. http://www.lokniti.org/pdf/All-India-Postpoll-2014-Survey-Findings.pdf asks: Should the government spend more on infrastructure than on subsidising the poor? Almost half (48.3%) of the respondents strongly or somewhat agreed with the proposition, with less than a quarter (21.3%) strongly or somewhat disagreeing and the rest expressing no opinion.

2017. If the wisdom of the Indian electorate is not misplaced, the development challenges after 25 years of reform will be successfully met.

References

Dhar, P. N. (2003). *The Evolution of Economic Policy in India–Selected Essays*. New Delhi: Oxford University Press.

Schumpeter, Joseph. (1942). *Capitalism, Socialism and Democracy*. New York: Harper & Row.

Samuelson P (1967) Economics: An Introductory Analysis, McGraw Hill.

Dharm, N. (2004). Combating the wheat lobby, Cross Section, March 1975, quoted in M. Raghavan: "Politics of Procurement and Price Support", Economic and Political Weekly, Vol. 39, No. 5 (Jan. 31–Feb. 6, 2004), pp. 506–508.

Dharm Narain: "Growth and Imbalances in Indian Agriculture," Economic and Political Weekly, Review of Agriculture March 1972. P. A-6

Vinayak Chatterjee: "Is India investing enough in infrastructure?" Business Standard, April 17, 2017. http://www.rediff.com/business/special/special-is-india-investing-enough-in-infrastructure/20170417.htm

Vinayak Chatterjee: "A NIIF-ty solution for the times," Business Standard, February 14, 2016

Mahesh Vyas: "Implementation-Stalled Projects inch up", CMIE, October 4, 2017, https://www.cmie.com/kommon/bin/sr.php?kall=warticle&dt=2017-10-03%2016:23:01&msec=266.

Sachin Mampatta: "Value of stalled projects rises to a record Rs13.22 trillion in September quarter," Mint, October 3, 2017. http://www.livemint.com/Politics/eJsGqshJCG4VPGvthnDUVN/Value-of-stalled-projects-reaches-yet-another-high.html

Secrets of the Heart: Adding Subjectivity to Policy Prescriptions for a Pleasant Economic Development

B. V. Singh, Siddharth Singh, Ravish Kumar Shukla, and Lav Jee

Abstract Growth and development efforts worldwide and their guiding economic principles have been well rooted in one theory or the other. They apply scientific rational approaches as per their beliefs in positivist and postpositivist designs; they are objective and materialistic; they believe in independence of the mind and body. As a result, they address more to history than offer solutions to the futuristic desires of the masses. They lack predictive ability. Therefore, most of the time development drives produce dissatisfaction and dejection for those who were intended to benefit from them. Also, many a time, policies derived from theoretical conclusions overlook the whole construct of the human being. They tend to ignore subjectivity. If life is for stability, tranquility, and felicity, development policies must recognize masses as both angelic and corporal. For the approval of 'heart—the seat of happiness, aspects of subjectivity—intuitions, faiths, whims, and aspirations that one dreams about must find their place in policies meant for people. The aspects of subjectivity not only provide pictorial information about the real individual, but also address the question of freedom of masses and enable them to penetrate into the future. Subjectivity provides space to the "synthetic a priory" part of the construct for a pleasant development. This paper deals with the spectrum of personal construct for secrets of the heart by dividing the shades of spectrum into "rational" and "extra rational" colors. It shows how shades of rationality—absolute, relative, environmental, or emotive—are necessarily a priory analytic and posteriori synthetic; they dissect and explain. Therefore, optimization—constrained or unconstrained—deals with partial

B. V. Singh (✉) · L. Jee
Department of Economics, Banaras Hindu University, Varanasi, India
e-mail: bhupendravsingh@gmail.com

L. Jee
e-mail: cmishra792@gmail.com

S. Singh
Department of Economics, DAV PG College, Varanasi, Uttar Pradesh, India
e-mail: siddharthvns19@gmail.com

R. Kumar Shukla
Department of Economics, Government College, Chinor, Gwalior, India
e-mail: ravishshuklashukla21@gmail.com

N. K. Mishra (ed.), *Development Challenges of India After Twenty Five Years of Economic Reforms*, India Studies in Business and Economics,
https://doi.org/10.1007/978-981-15-8265-3_4

and loses the holistic. The "extra rational" parts—emotions and beliefs—extend the agenda of personal construct. They are found to be better predictors. One feels, therefore one believes, and the belief enables a judgment that is pleasant. The scientific neglects stages of development in which the "Principle of Pleasure" plays an important role. It ignores the role of "identity," "memory," and "conscience." It ignores the role of the "will" and it ignores "heart" as the ruling organ. It rejects "felicity" and as such the role of fantasies and fictions. The three parallels—Freudian, Indian Yogic Psychology, and Arabic—approaches add holistic to the construct resulting in chaotic and contradictory/complementary forces producing indeterminacy and nonlinearity. It is captured by "poetic logic" as an individual's words are vivid, livid, and mutes. For them "time" is not linear and not equally spaced but is an intuitive comprehension. Therefore, future can be penetrated through experiments that enable intuitive judgments stimulated by carefully chosen "tools." The paper concludes by making propositions such as the individual is holistic—both physical and beyond; the decision frontier is in a state of flux—nonlinear and chaotic; it is easier to deduce from the whole than to add up to get the whole; it is the "Principle of Pleasure" that governs; time and space are intuitive judgments; a futuristic data set is experimental—spurred by stimulants. How one may actually do it is given as a "postscript" to the argument. A simple case study of development of spiritual tourism in Varanasi city is explored. The study uses experimental data and its propositions to consolidate the subjective whims to find alternative strategies to make development a pleasant experience for local populace. It has successfully shown the difference between optimized and loved strategies. It suggests that pleasant betterment of the labor force in spiritual tourism can be achieved by shifting them elsewhere rather than creating more tourism options.

1 Introduction

Growth seen as an increase in aggregate physical output found its course in change of labor, capital, and technology, where only technology had unlimited expansion while that of labor and capital were limited.[1] The question of capital accumulation, use of the accumulated capital, capital–labor ratio, and other such considerations guided developmental policies worldwide. Many governments invested in research and development and in innovations; given this belief. Some others who believed this but doubted its success due to weak and untrue assumptions found refuge in bringing forth institutional reforms and ensuring conducive social environment.[2] Growth was pursued through a knowledge-based economy—wherein consumption and production were based on intellectual capital. Thus, intellectual property rights became an important addition to institutions. The Endogenous Growth Theory argued that

[1]Neoclassical arguments.

[2]Institutional arguments.

economic growth was mainly an endogenous contribution caused by faster innovation and investment in human capital.[3] When growth took the form of development it incorporated very difficult and nay saying political and economic issues. Alternative developmental paradigms endeavored to construe the debate through cultural and moral considerations.[4] They argued for modernization through agriculture, industry, and service sectors.[5] They believed in import substitution and industrialization and supported investment in infrastructure development.[6]

In addition, the question of regional development incorporated another dimension consideration of "the space" in the discourse. Pace could be defined as a nation, part of nation, region as socio-cultural-politico-economic divides. The spatial divides as complete and integrated units might develop to have interrelationship as endorsed by "Labor Division" arguments. Therefore, there could be diversified relational space as per the specifics[7] It seemed like arguing for an economic system that attracted and caused conditions for long lasting, interdependent, and uniform development.

The "space" has wedged upon economic thinking in explaining the way an economic system functions. It is understood as endowments generating geographic advantages such as availability of raw materials, human and social capital, as also economies that reduce production and transaction costs. The regional approaches may be categorized into two main groups: locational theories and regional development theories. The first provides a methodologically scientific disciplinary identity using microeconomic foundations and macroeconomic methods. They use techniques such as system theory that aims at extension of demand and production areas. The second group, which is more macroeconomic in nature, talks of locational specifics. They are abstract and intend to identify regional growth determinants that increase employment and individual well-being. References can be given to regional Keynesian and neoclassical growth theories. There have been attempts to wed the two approaches. The Growth Pole Theory of Perroux (Campbel 1974), the role of multinationals (Lipietz 1980; Blomstrom and Kokko 1999), endogenous determinants, learning regions deserve references.

Since 1990, there have been some efforts to incorporate the indeterminate behavior of individuals who found a match in the concept of nonlinear dynamics in social

[3]There have been efforts to understand the role of culture, trust, respect, self-determination (Khan et al. 2010).

[4]For example, Bourdieu (1985a, 1998) and Putnam (1993, 1995) seem to propose two social traditions and explain the role of "civil society" in attaining sustained development. They represent opposite forces of social dimension. The discussion leads to conclude the divides of "social integration" and "social conflicts" to ensure consensus and economic development.

[5]The context of Dependency Theory. The arguments of imperialism and neo-imperialism can also be added.

[6]However, few others found no support for a relationship between infrastructure and economic development.

[7]A comprehensive account of Local Developmental Strategies has been given by the ILO implementation of economic and social interventions to create an environment where social activities support economic objective and vice versa (ILO 2013, p. 2).

sciences. Researchers used more advanced mathematical tools to understand the qualitative aspects (Nijkamp and Reggiani 1992a, b; Nijkamp and Reggiani 1993a, b) of individual behavior. These approaches relaxed assumptions of constant returns and perfect competition. They analyzed a dynamic growth mechanism with increasing returns and transportation costs. The system had many equilibria and it used optimization techniques.[8] However, these efforts also seemed to overlook the question of disaggregate specifics as did the other traditional models.

The question of poverty found an important place in the development discourse in the mid-70s of the last century since the emphasis shifted from relative to absolute poverty. The failure of trickle-down theory was considered as one of the seven sins of planning (Haq 1976). The emergence of the human development index (HDI) shifted the debate on development to discussion on poverty. The three-dimension HDI has now been extended to include multidimensional poverty index (MDI) (UNDP 2018). The capability approach was seen as deprivation to lead a life one believed worth living. Development was viewed as development vis-a-vis capability. Means without capabilities were useless (Sen 1989a, 1999, 2004a, b).[9] Sen's critics argued that his approach is against liberalism, more individualistic, and very difficult to theorize. Martha Nussbaum (2011a, b) gave an extended version by annexing the theory of justice deriving from the concept of human dignity and suggested to "guarantee the same to all up to a defined level."

What to do with "capabilities" has been argued by many economists. To mention a few—Robeyns (2003a) suggested a procedural approach for experimenting capabilities; emphases were given to list priorities explicitly, methodological justification, and sensitivity to the situation. Alkire (2005a) suggested valuation in two steps; first, theorizing and then participatory evaluation by the group.

By and large worldwide, growth and developmental efforts, guiding economic policies, and other policies have been well rooted in one theory or the other. The intentions have been justifiable, so have been the theories and policies given certain beliefs in Scientifics—positivist and postpositivist designs and well-considered rational approaches; admissible to reason. They are objective, materialistic, and believe in independence of the mind and body. They use *ex post facto* information and rely upon a form of world comprehendible by *analytic* a priori and *synthetic posteriori*. In this way, these theories are more a history than ways to look into the future. These efforts at growth seem to believe that only aggregates matter, and specifics at some disaggregate level do not matter. For example, who owned the capital, labor, or technology seldom matter. It ignores, for that matter, the characteristics of leadership—a good leader can make a win possible with an insufficient army.

---

[8] See also, Pike et al. (2007).

[9] Although Sen admits the importance of "consequence" and how people feel about their lives and the overall question of distribution, he also emphasized that resources should not be treated exclusively for fair distributional justice. His contribution may be listed as individual characteristics, local environment and variation in social conditions, conventions and customs and distribution within family.

2 Transcendental to the Silver Lining

But somewhere some aspects have been missing as almost all parts of the world are facing dissatisfaction with the local masses resulting in different forms of dejection prone to insurgencies or immediate insurgencies. For example, despite, let us say, honest efforts by the federal and several state (provincial) governments, farmers' suicides in India remain unanswered. Displacement of natives for development projects caused huge demonstrations and nay saying. Mob lynching and other emotional outbursts do have a cause of concern as extreme cases.[10] The development projects have been a failure in providing satisfaction to the local people. Everywhere, the aspirations of local people are seen as restraints rather than guiding principles for development drives. Such drives are considered as threats to their routine lifestyles and places from where they are detached and displaced.[11] The loss of livelihoods (crises of water, grazing fields, and livestock); threat to culture; and crisis of identity, traditions, social relations; and nature on the whole of which their life could have been a part were identified as reasons of local dismay and dejection. The projects also caused pollution threatening the existing ecosystems. All such cases of protests portray the fact that the development drives created contrary to what they actually aimed at and made life of the people worse than before. They were not as per people's needs, wishes, and imaginations.

A development project must have social approval at the grassroots level given the diversities of the population. Most of the time, policies derived from theoretical conclusions overlook the whole construct of human being, which include a social relationship, impulses, political affiliation, likes–dislikes, and spiritual settings and beliefs. Furthermore, it is an unacceptable proposition that they (the object of study) do not understand but the intellectual elites can understand.[12] There have been tendencies to cut the size of existence of those for whom the exercise of development is undertaken. As the intellectual elites have the authority they can author. Knowledge derived from *a priory analytic* and *posteriori synthetic* has added more to scholarly arrogance than making the life of stakeholders more vivid and expedient.

In the uproar of excess of objectivity and scientism, people's whims have been ignored as darkened phenomena, especially in economics. If life is also for stability, tranquility, and felicity, then developmental policies must recognize people both as angelic and corporal. As the question of happiness finds a place in academic discussions, aspects of subjectivity—intuitions, faiths, whims, and aspirations that one dreams about—must find their place in the toolbox to respond to the dissatisfactions and dejections resulting in mass protests and insurgencies. The aspects of subjectivity not only provide pictorial information about the real individual but also address

---

[10]See Notes to Chap. 3, in Taleb (2007), referring wisdom (madness of the crowd: collectively we can both get wiser or far more foolish. But my conjecture is that we fail in more complicated predictions—economic variables for which crowds incur pathologies—two heads are worse than one.).

[11]See also Anthony (2001).

[12]Who will judge the judges?

the question of freedom of masses and the use of their intuitions, faiths, whims, and aspirations as guiding principles to penetrate into future. Avoiding them as "irrational" and in turn dealing them with force is in no way prudent for a democratic and enlightened society. And even when approved, the challenge remains on how to incorporate the subjective aspects into objective policies.

Should we include *synthetic* a priori[13] knowledge and regard religion, myths, and metaphysics (and other issues of faith) as useful? Development theories and beliefs, implicit therein, possess very weak predictive ability in the sense that they are not able to predict outliers.[14] However, not addressing outliers and catastrophes is quite injurious to future planning. On the methodological note, they (*a priory analytic* and *posteriori synthetic*) seem to begin with simple static models and then transform the structure to the dynamic world by adding more complications. There are limits to such added complications as they become insolvable gradually. It can be maintained that deriving simple from complicated,[15] static from dynamic, and partial from total could be more useful and handy.

The present endeavor does not reject the existing conventional knowledge that is objective, materialist, universal, quantitative, easily transformable to simple linear mathematics and provides facilities to test them on *ex post facto* data with axiomatic techniques and artificial assumptions that offer useful explanations in meaningful ways. Rather, it claims to construe upon the individual construct to capture the subjective whole in order to predict future aspirations. Also, it boasts of providing alternatives to incorporate such aspirations in developmental policies to enable a pleasant solution that is loved by people.

On the methodological side, the effort extends the agenda to find a pleasing solution and deductive arguments to add to the inductions. It intends to devise techniques to incorporate "subjective whims" in policymaking and proposes to find solutions to gaps between whims and authoritative developmental paradigm. It may be considered more democratic and may entail a political freedom of masses. It refers to the freedom of the ethnic groups to choose a particular quality of development in terms of their geographical, cultural, personal, and social value structure and relationship. It speaks of design and to live a life they love to and have cherished for generations. It attempts to preserve their identity that has stood the test of time vis-a-vis some time even forsaking fruits of modern amenities. It pertains to incorporating special problems of different socio-cultural-ethnic groups and stakeholders.

It proposes to extend the discussion of personal construct to dimensions not yet considered to derive prescriptions. It also proposes to take the whole existence of the individual into account—scientific, physical, or beyond. The expression of

---

[13]"*A priory synthetic* judgments are possible" constitutes the central idea of Kant's "Critique of the Pure Reason." (Russell Reprint 2007, p. 642).

[14]The question of prediction is one important aspect where techniques in economics (may be true for whole social sciences) have been measurably insufficient. Because it deals with phenomena of highly nonrepetitive nature, economics is considered to be no more than at the edge of the science (and equally on the edge of the history). (Hicks 1984; Baranzini and Scazzieri 1986).

[15]Bourke (1991).

such totality finds outlets in words that are no objective representations[16] of the imagery inside. There are gestures and postures and also the mutes. Sometime silence expresses the words. Therefore, efforts to capture such imagery by codified words are superimposition of ideas of the observer. However, the image can find different expressions in different individuals—seemingly illogical. They are interacted, coordinated, contradicted, or concluded realities—realities that govern behavior. Given this understanding, there are inconsistencies amid social and economic theories and inconsistencies at the level of methodology.[17]

It is obvious that economists themselves may sympathize with the poor and put forth numerous suggestions to address their pitiable conditions, assuming their authority (over the subject) but will not permit the real economic actor—the poor—to possess the same construct. The world (authors) has belittled the individual who has been a victim of artificial assumptions or, to say, "ignorance."

3 Spectrum of Personal Construct: The Rational

The pure reason that is output of intelligence belittles the world and produces ignorance[18]; ignorance produces sorrow that finds joy in lamentation offering explanation. Many such theories are lamentations as they explain but do not understand[19]; they are specially acceptance of failure to predict the future.[20] The rational expectation in purity may predict only those events that have already taken place, as assumptions of rationality use "reason." Reason can dissect and analyze. It can artificially generalize[21] (fooled by randomness). It does not foresee the "nonhappened" that perhaps can be solved "intuitively"[22] and by "faith."

Rationality: Rationality means having reasons that are pure and perfect. They produce what is reasonable. A rational individual attempts to optimize the uses

[16]It can be seen as failure of "Picture theory of Meaning" and use the language game in expressing. Language makes expression possible and also limits the possibility of expression.

[17]"There is incongruity between the official and actual stances on methodology. Such accepted methods presuppose, for their validity and widespread use, the ubiquity of spontaneous events regularities, while the significant social regularities of the sought-after kind have yet to be discovered" (Lawson 1997).

[18]Lock says "Since the mind, in all its thoughts and reasoning, hath no other immediate object buts its own idea, which it alone does or can contemplate, it is evident that our knowledge is only conversant about them" and "knowledge is the perception of agreement and disagreement of two ideas" (quoted by Russell 2017, p. 637).

[19]*Sorrowful person finds joy in lamentation* (Gibran, Secret of Hearts).

[20]See also, "Historical fractures" (Taleb 2007); "This long history*** lasted a dozen centuries, longer than the entire history of France, encountering the first Arab sword, the Greek language and thought, all the heritage went up in smoke, as if it never happened."

[21]Artificiality of a bell-shaped probability curve (Taleb 2007).

[22]See Table 11.1 "Trader and Scientific Approach" (pp. 192, Taleb 2007). See also Thaler and Sunstein, (2009, Soft Copy) for other such cases of judgment.

of scarce resources. This is a simplistic and artificial definition, wherein decisions are taken by axioms. This rationality is absolute and devoid of ethics and other considerations that are natural to human society.

In the late nineteenth century ample literature cropped up on this weakest hangover of the Rationalist Movement in Europe. It added considerations like relative rationality and, most importantly, bounded rationality. While relative rationality trusts good or bad reasons, admissible or not admissible reasons, useful or not so useful reasons, bounded rationality seems to put bounds on reasons by given information.

Bounded rationality argues and tries to explain by putting limits to unlimited information, incorporating importance of time and space. It addresses complexities of the situation. The method finds solution to problems of decision-making by "simple" arguments rather than complex mathematical structures (Simon 1957). It offers a simple connect between the rational and so-called psychological aspects, as it claims. It is maintained that bounded rationality is not a departure from economic reasoning but an extension of actual rational behavior. It helps in taking a judgment by a process identified as heuristic or proximal. It rejects untrue optimization that relies upon unreal and constructed assumptions about knowledge, motto, gains and losses, and beliefs about life as a whole. Bounded rationality points out the human limitation to resort to rational behavior rather than declaring them to be much more than rational. However, proponents of bounded rationality lament that humans prefer rational behavior but can practice it only in a limited sense.

On a positive note, the concept of bounded rationality incorporates the idea of an "adaptive toolbox" and heuristic that includes collection of rules[23] that are simple to implement and are adjusted as per time and space. It focuses on context-based solutions that are "satisficing." It is obvious that individuals respond to different "space and time" differently. One can argue that bounded rationality is pure rationality with some reservations posed by time and space that are reflected as "environment." It incorporates psychological plausibility by continuing cognitions that are emotional as well as paying heed to social laws.

The two other competing as well as overlapping ideas are ecological and social rationality, the outside worlds and social considerations, respectively. Therefore, the theoretical individual, according to Gibran (2009), is the "martyr in this belittling world, and a victim of ignorance."

4 Spectrum of Personal Construct: The Extra Rational

The heart has its own reasons which reason knows not. It is a journey in multidimensional sky that is the reflection of being—beyond linear time and space. Therefore, what rationality cannot solve is solved by emotions—especially love. It corresponds to the "Throbbing heart which is like a bird flying in a spacious sky of love" (Gibran 2009).

[23]For examples of such other rules, see Thaler and Sunstein (2008).

Emotions: Seeing from a view of sapiens (humans) that ignores the power of emotions is, sadly, short-sighted. The very name *Homo sapiens*, or the thinking species, is misleading in light of the new appreciations and vision of the significance of emotion in our lives that science now offers. Our personal values are expressed in terms of emotions. They are representatives of cultural essence. Emotions are not necessarily postcognitive. People can experience emotions without conscious awareness and without cognitive mediation (Goleman 1996, 2006, 1996).

They are an enabling force that fills failures of intelligence. "It is like a book—in whose pages one reads the chapter of happiness and misery, joy and pain, laughter and sorrow" (Gibran 2009). There could be many more. We do not know the seat of emotions in the physical body of humans but are sure that they give shape and realization to different cognitive resources. They energize such resources. They are the extrarational part of the rational, as nonlinearity is to linearity and as chaos and catastrophe are to order. They are subjective to the objective. They influence decision-making to the extent that the motto of taking decisions is governed by emotions. Effective decision-making stems from emotional process. We all know from experience, when it comes to shaping our decisions and actions, the "gut feeling" counts every bit as much—and more than thought. We have gone too far in emphasizing the value and importance of pure rationality. It is a surge of relief. "When the heart becomes congested with secret, the eyes begin to burn from searing tears, and the ribs are about to burst with the growing of the heart's confinement, one cannot find expression of such a labyrinth except by surge of relief' (Ibid). Proposition that 'our deepest feelings, our passions and longings, are essential guides that our species owes much of its existence to their power in human affairs, that power is extraordinary: only a potent love urgency of saving a charioted child could lead a parent to override the impulse for personal survival.' Seen from their self-sacrifice was arguably irrational (Goleman 1996, 2013). Human satisfaction comes in the form of emotional experience. Psychology considers that emotions and reasons are contiguous. Rationality does not produce solution; finally, it is found by emotions that are supported by other sources of belief. Therefore, emotional intelligence is the sum total of rationality, emotions, and sets of belief systems.

Emotions and beliefs are contiguous. Emotions are guided by belief systems that are formed by past experiences—derived by history or fiction, cultural, social, or personal values[24] pertaining to the society one lives in. On the other hand, emotions also guide belief system. Rational actors depend upon emotional belief, so to say. Feeling is believing that as the evidence is given by emotion. The "influence of emotions upon beliefs can be viewed as the port through which emotions exert their influence upon human life" (Mercer 2010). Therefore, beliefs rely on internally generated inference most of the time alien to the scientific judgment process. It diminishes the risk that it may be wrong (Fiedler and Bless 2000).

---

[24]Singh (2018).

Beliefs: Belief systems[25] are like information stock. It may not be real but is representative of human construct. It enables one to take judgments. Beliefs, as they are formed, are also representative of group behavior in that each member acts in accordance with the collective belief, although they may act individually.

A belief system may be formed by contradictory possibilities, absence of coherence, and compartmentalization. It is a broken sequence and denial of linear logic. Therefore, group of literature (true or false), vague and scientific history, religious practices (atonements, rituals, ceremonies, penances, etc.), and commands of priests and pundits all contribute to formation of beliefs. They also emanate from habits, illogical, and intuitive practices. It may be argued that people think that they are acting rationally but ultimately it comes to their belief system to take a judgment. Reasons enable arguments but beliefs enable judgment. Beliefs are updated and refined on the basis of new information.[26] It is also argued that beliefs distort rationality. They are found better predictors. One feels, therefore one believes; even if he says, "I think, I believe."

5 Spectrum of Personal Construct: The Holistic

The individual thinks like a poet and claims:

> As a most enlightened person regarding the need of heart which is like a bird flying in the spacious sky of love… It is like a vase replenished with the wine of ages that has been pressed for shipping souls… It is like a book in whose pages one reads the chapters of happiness and misery, joy and pain, laughter and sorrow (Gibran 2009).

A complete human being has emotions, reasons, and information. They have social relations and considerations, perceptions, experiences, history, and literature. They have a physical body and capacities and a location in geography and time. Some momentary psychic experience is not denied. There are moments of mysticism or cosmic consciousness—intuitive glimpses into higher realities for an immortal soul, or aesthetic apprehensions of the evolutionary in human. He has the ultimate value—cosmic love; in one aspect cosmic love is found all aspects of existence. There is imagery to the symbolism of subliminal consciousness. There is symbolism and simile. The list goes on. Therefore, it is both angelic and corporal.

The development of human being can be seen to have stages in which love plays an important role. According to Freud's psychoanalysis, there are stages of *id*, *ego*, and *super ego,* which follow the principle of pleasure, reality principle, and the principle of morality. "Id" contains drives and memories; it is impulsive. It may not be logical or rational; actually it is fantasy oriented. It remains with the individual forever. Ego

---

[25]"Do you recall his dreams and beliefs"; Gibran, Secrets of the Heart.

[26]Theory of Partial Belief, Laplace's Law of Succession and Bayesian Forecasting. "Hume's account of partial belief is an extension in a quite natural way of his account of non-partial belief. Partial belief, according to him, is a consequence of the mind's capacity to divide its force equally among distinct alternatives" (Hume et al. pp 39–60).

is that part of human construct that is influenced by worldly knowledge, or it depicts pragmatic approach. The id is chaotic while ego is reasonable. Superego includes values and morals of the society. It also includes conscience. But it can be argued that it is the "Pleasure Principle" that can be fundamental while the other two can put some restraints (bounds).

There are, however, alternative systems of the construct of the individual that have gone unattended in the tempest of occidental reasoning. We present only a very brief account of the oriental systems—Indian and Islamic; and then we can decide if they are apt to extend the agenda of personal construct to further detail. Indian Vedanta System relies on the four important constituents of human construct [Sankritayan, R, 1944 (2017)]. They are *buddhi* (intellect), *ahankara* (identity), *manas* (memory), and *chitta* (conscience).[27] The *buddhi* mentioned as intellect slashes the object apart and tries to analyze. It subdivides deeper and deeper.[28] It knows only the material world.[29] There has been tremendous development of knowledge derived upon capabilities of the reason. But as it derives from and refers only to past, it can only analyze that which has occurred in the past. It artificially uses the art of "Theories of Random Numbers."[30] It looks at the past that is present (Gibran 2009).

Ahankara (identity[31]) is fundamental to existence as it is given by a particular body capability, color, features, family one belongs to, power position, etc. It is also governed by geographical location, religion, and the quest to be recognized.

Manas (memory[32]) only receives and does not create. It is a faculty of mind that coordinates sensory impressions before they are presented to the conscience. *Manas* is atomic, an instrument, a sense organ, always active, nonmorphological. It is based on *sanskara* (cultural essence). Perceptive materials are conversed and analyzed with the help of *manas*, hence it is a super-sense (Sharma and Vyas 2015). "It is like a vase replenished with the wine of ages …looks at life as the spring looks at the winter" (Gibran 2009). The *chitta* (conscience) has different meanings. It is pure intelligence without memory. It is the source of all creation that we know by true and divine love.

[27] These four divides can be extended to 16 and with further detail they can be extended to many more. The discussion of "evolutes" refers to 25 (Sankhya); *Yoga Sutra,* referred *to as* Yogic Psychology classified them under *five* heads, (Chatterji and Dutta 2018, p. 275).The Sanskrit terms used for constituents do not have exact equivalents in English. The translations offered in parentheses are the closest meanings).

[28] Such divisions lose properties of undivided parts. Social Intelligence and intelligence of the mass are different (See, Goleman 2006).

[29] The theories in economics are dissection and explanations; therefore, this could be one reason why they lack predictive ability.

[30] Probability is principally a branch of applied skepticism, not as engineering discipline (Taleb 2007). Rhetoric can be constructed randomly, but not genuine knowledge (Ibid, p. 72).

[31] However, the term 'Identity' means differently; the powerful moral idea that has come down to us; the universal human psychology of thymus. The natural demand for dignity that gives us a language for expressing resentments if such recognition is not forthcoming (Fukayama 2018, p. 163).

[32] It is also translated as mind in Sankhya System. It is made up of parts and so can come into contact with different senses simultaneously; however, the *vaisheshika* differs. They argue that the organs cannot function simultaneously (Sharma 2003; p. 161).

The Arabic and Islamic psychology and philosophy of mind give details of the body, mind, and soul.[33] Beginning with Al-Kindi and Al-Razi, they consider that mind is part of soul (Admonson and Porman 2015; Sharif 1963). The separation of soul and body provides the ability to know things not perceptible with empirical means and leads to common sense, imagination, and memory. Therefore, memory goes beyond the body. Al-Kindi describes four types of intellect: one that is universal; two, that gives the abstract idea of the world; three, that enables part of abstract ideas to part of acquired but passive knowledge; and four, when it becomes active after encountering worldly objects. Al-Razi talks of three souls—the rational or the divine one, the animal that has placed in the heart, and the vegetative that has placed in the liver. Obviously, in the view of the two, the soul and the intellect have varying meanings; but they go beyond worldly reasons.

Al-Farabi, another known philosopher, talks of the soul that has triple functions—being formal, efficient, and final cause (Davidson 1992) the potential intellect that has capabilities to possess the basic axiom of thoughts and to receive all other intelligible notions. The individual intellect when perfected can come closer to the agent intellect. Individual intellect leads to the form of practical intellect that perceives the senses—likes or dislikes, attractive or repulsive—which combined with imagination lead to action.

Avicenna argues that common sense coordinates information with already possessed impressions (past memory) in order to produce a unified picture (He calls it a cognitive faculty) to help take decisions.[34] He proposes a function of "estimative faculty—*waham*" that enables all animals including humans to sense "nonsensible" intentions that are intrinsic to the object. They are the extrasensible property. He also acknowledges the existence of the faculty of intuition in addition to estimation. He observes that there are people who excel without much prior experience empirically or rationally. The third innate power of estimative faculty is recollection—memory.

For Avicenna, the cognitive faculties deal with practical and empirical issues, the tradition—a credible source of practical decisions—comes into play a deterministic role only through the approval of the soul (Davidson 1992; Inati 1996). The estimation with cognitive facilities is responsible for fantasies and fiction in our dreams and thoughts. Similar to the concept of "tendencies" (*vasana*),[35] he speaks of the unused ineligibles accumulated to agent intellect and exhibited as habits.

As a concluding remark to the excerpts mentioned in preceding arguments, it is clear that simple assumptions of rationality, be it absolute, relative, or bounded, are only axiomatic and produce only one benefit: they are simple and understandable by syllogisms. No single source can enable decision-making.

---

[33]These terms connote different sets of organizations, definitions and functions with reference to different philosophers although, many a time, there are overlaps.

[34]Avicenna has divided the inner self into five parts- *Hiss-i-mustalaq, Hifz-i-majmuyi, Indrak-ila shayri, Indrak-i-shaura and Hifz-i-maani.* See Sankritayan (2017) p. 120.

[35]The Bhagwat Gita.

6 Spectrum of Personal Construct: The Decision-Making

The literature on decision-making begins with the definition that a decision is an oriented and a definite choice out of at least two options. It involves mental functions such as memory, reasoning, problem solving, emotions, and other motivational functions. Although it has acknowledged the influence of conscious and unconscious factors limited to psychoanalytic sources, it does not incorporate the direct role of beliefs, for they are not substantiated by scientific exercises. They deal with components in terms of decision situation, decision-maker,[36] and decision process. The literature believes in the two basic premises–humans have limited information and limited processing capabilities. The models usually describe the process in words and avoid mathematical treatments.[37]

The naturalistic models are adaptive in nature and include situational awareness. Analytical models are concerned with how decision-makers select a course of action. They assume that people use combinations of simple decision rules to find an option that meets the minimum requirements. Kahneman and Frederick (2002) propose two alternative systems of processing the information—reflective system logical and analytical, based on new information with substantial efforts deductively, slowly, sequentially, and consciously; and intuitive system, wherein information is processed automatically, effortlessly, associatively, unconsciously, and, often, emotionally. However, Evans (1984) proposed the same in different terms; heuristic and analytical systems. The former is not directly governed by consciousness, rapid information processing; the latter refers to the opposite. Heuristics in decision-making have certain strategies, as it is referred. They include elimination by aspect strategy and satisficing strategies, Relevant Que Strategy and strategy of past experience (Tversky 1972; Ginerenzer et al. 1999).

Beresford and Sloper (2008) have given an account of descriptive approaches. The information processing approach focuses mainly on adaptive decision-maker framework when none of the alternatives is declared the best. This pertains to conscious process. The prospect theory relies on making decisions involving risk or uncertainty. The Theory of Reasoned Action and Planned Behavior link attitude and behavior while making choices. Heuristics strategies are adopted to solve choice problems. The role argued for a prospect theory of emotions in decision-making has mainly two meta goals to meet: first, minimizing the experience of negative emotions and second, maximizing the ease of justification to oneself and to the others (Bettman et al 1998).

[36]The ethical conduct, personal integrity, willingness to assume responsibility, courage, intellectual skills, etc. deserve a mention..

[37]The descriptive theories describe how people actually think, however, normative descriptions aim at how one ought to reason. The first has the empirical validity and the second has suggestive mode.

The essence of Prospect theory[38] is the mathematical model that tries to predict. Kahnemann and Tversky (2013) presented decision-making under risk, since then it has been developed and modified by economists who have been striving to refine the mathematics of the model and by psychologists who have been interested in understanding the psychological process.

The brief account of literature on decision-making clearly outlines that it is partial, ad hoc, and artificially defines the human being assuming that they are given with the understanding to work to optimize. The literature mainly deals with industrial setups and not the day to day individual perception of development strategies. Again it is objective, materialist, attempted universal, quantitative, easily transformable to simple linear mathematics, and provides facilities to test them on *ex post facto* data with axiomatic techniques and artificial assumptions. It does not "read the chapter of happiness and misery, joy and pain, laughter and sorrow." It is not a "surge of relief." It does not take into account the whole of the human construct that can produce a piece of knowledge useful to predict the future. It does not incorporate the role of belief systems in taking decisions. The belief system may be formed by contradictory possibilities, absence of coherence, and compartmentalization. It is broken sequence and linear logic. It ignores the stages of development in which the principle of pleasure plays an important role (Freud). It ignores the role of "identity," "memory," and "conscience" (Indian Vedanta system), as also of the "will" that is responsible for desires and dislikes and the heart as the "ruling organ." It also ignores intelligible imprints that originate as sensible forms and are conveyed to the "imaginations." It rejects "felicity" (Al-Farabi) and ignores the role of estimation that can influence and be responsible for fantasies and fictions in our dreams and thoughts (Avicenna).

7 Spectrum of Personal Construct: The Labyrinth

The world outside is dynamic and chaotic. It shows an aperiodic behavior that makes long-term prediction impossible (Strogatz 1994). The system is inseparable. "Whenever parts of system interfere, or cooperate, or compete, there are nonlinear interactions. Most of everyday life is nonlinear and the principle of superposition fails spectacularly" (ibid p. 2). So is the world inside. The policies derived from theoretical conclusions overlook the whole construct of human being; which include a social combination of complementary, contradictory, and parallel impulses; and produce a chaotic and catastrophic surface where upon a deterministic point of optimal decision becomes impossible. The solution to the complex, chaotic, and aperiodic behavioral labyrinth is found in qualitative expression that reflects representativeness of the

[38]The prospect theories use canonical and axiomatic approaches including Bayesian Probability and other standard probability models. They assume unlimited capacity of cognitive power, rationality, and unlimited supply of information. The beliefs, intensions, knowledge, and desires are often artificially constructed. Sometimes influences like fatigue, stress, experience, and complexity of task are also incorporated.

individual (ibid; p. 2). Therefore, it is easier to take the intuitive[39] narration from the individual and drawing aspects of concern. Such a futuristic data set is experimental and is generated as immediate[40] and intuitive judgments spurred by stimulants. This leads to the question of "poetic logic" and finding solutions.

The individual's narrations do not reflect the pictorial and simple meaning of the expression, as they are metaphorical,[41] figurative, and mythopoetic. It has tropes and euphemism. Thus, poetic logic transcends primal and primal models of experience and takes into account the human sensorium, imaginations, and the innermost construct that include vivid, livid, and hidden parts. It is a realization of the whole. As a result, it proposes limitations to complete reliance on mathematical formulation to understand.[42] In this way, all knowledge could be one and is an interacted, coordinated, contradicted, or concluded reality. Poetic logic has a far greater role in creating, understanding, or analyzing quantitative data. It reflects limitations to the representativeness of data.[43] Therefore, for policy prediction to comply with future aspirations, two different riddles have to be solved: first, to get a representative of the whole, and second, to find quantities to represent qualities—the data question.

8 Finding Sweeter and More Gentle Dreams

It is maintained that the rationalist—positivist and postpositivist—designs of developmental paradigms have caused dissatisfaction of the masses for whom they were created. The scientific paradigm not only failed to incorporate stakeholders, but also lacked predictability and usefulness in the terms of the desired developmental course that leaves the world as it was ever—the permanence of development. The reason why this kind of knowledge could not solve social problems in futuristic mode lies in ontological and epistemological beliefs and, in turn, on the methodological reliance on objectivity of quantities and other optimization techniques. This is due to the reliance only on *a priory analytic* and *posteriori synthetic* canons of inquiry.

---

[39] 'Space and time, Kant Says, are not concepts; they are forms of "intuitions"—looking at (Russell 2017, p. 642).

[40] An emotive and whimsical judgment is immediate while well-considered and delayed judgments are cognitive (Goleman 2013).

[41] No theory formulated in language can ever penetrate the world of realty. It can, however, reveal it serendipitously, through metaphor. Metaphor is a trace to poetic thinking, which constantly creates connections among things. This is why metaphors and "metaforms" have such emotional power; they tie people together, allowing them to express a common sense of purpose in an interconnected fashion. Danesi (2004).

[42] A rejection of Descartes mind and body and Leibniz arguments (Thilly 2005, pp. 281,376).

[43] "I defend the relevance of fiction for social science investigation. Novels can be useful for making some economic approaches—such as behavioural economics or signalling theory—more plausible. Novels are more like models than is commonly believed. Some novels present verbal models of reality. I interpret other novels as a kind of simulation, akin to how simulations are used in economics. Economics can, and has, profited from the insights contained in novels." Cowen (2005).

With the understanding of Scientifics, a complicated model of simulation can be constructed and the *ex post facto* data[44] can be raised using regular sampling designs and analytics. Given the form of the world and axioms, they produce many results and doubts continue despite the belief of existence of universal truth—a fantasy. It is the denial of poetic logic. Pure reason that is output of only intelligence belittles the world and produces ignorance by offering explanations—a lamentation.

The whole construct of human being includes wills, value systems, social relationships, impulses,[45] political affiliations, likes–dislikes, spiritual setting, and beliefs. There are "momentary psychic experiences, moments of cosmic consciousness, and intuitive glimpses into higher realities of an immortal soul or only aesthetic apprehensions." In one aspect of cosmic love, we find all aspects. The basic guiding force of human behavior is love that seeks pleasure, worldly knowledge, and moral considerations come later (Freud). The "intellect" dissects, "identity" transports one's own definition of oneself, "memory" carts special characteristics cherished by generations, and "conscience" is the ideal—transcendental to time and space-universal memory (Indian Yogic philosophy). The construct has a role of "will," "desires and dislikes," "imaginations," and "attainment of felicity." There is a role of "fantasies and fictions" and "dreams and beliefs" (Persian and Arabic contribution). In all, pleasure principle—angelic or corporal—plays a central role. Looking through heart is a journey into the multidimensional sky that is the reflection of being beyond linear time and space. The being is like "a vase replenished with the wine of ages that has been pressed for shipping soul***** It is like a book in whose pages one reads the chapter of happiness and misery, joy and pain, laughter and sorrow." Taking judgment by heart is "a surge of relief" that has no trivial solutions. Let the sweeter and more gentle dreams than those one encounters in awareness rule as "lovers encounter comfort and condolences in dreams" (Gibran 2009).

We conclude by way of making the following propositions:

P1 Axiomatic and ad hoc (a priori *analytic and posteriori synthetic*) discussions on development add to explanations and not to understanding. The affected party (individual) is kept out of the decision process by making artificial assumptions.

P2 The individual is rational and emotional. He has beliefs and identity. He has cultural essence that is "filled with the wine of ages." He has conscience that is transcendent. It is worldly, cosmic, and mystic. The existence is holistic—both physical and beyond.

P3 The decision frontier of the individual comprises interacted, coordinated, contradicted, and concluded realities. It is in a state of flux, nonlinear, and chaotic.

P4 It is easier and useful to deduce from the qualitative whole (pictorial whole) that is a mythopoetic expression. A simple can be derived from the complicated, static from dynamic, and partial from total.

[44]The customary data raising, it may be argued, is imposed meaning by the researcher's perception, as the measure is artificially found by assuming the pictorial meaning.

[45]For a complete review of such impulses, see Singh (2018).

P5 The individual seldom optimizes (satisficing or heuristic) and he cannot optimize; it is the *Principle of Pleasure* (ecstasy) that governs his thinking and actions in chase of happiness. It is fantasy oriented.

P6 It is through love that one can penetrate the other and the future. As "time and space" are only intuitively known, therefore, future can be known intuitively or as a loved one.

P7 A priori *synthetic* solution—the intuitive one—is possible and that can add the subjective aspect if dealt carefully.

P8 A futuristic data set is experimental—generated as immediate and intuitive judgment spurred by stimulants.

P9 A genuine strategy can be the solution point (possibly modal point) of deductive and inductive judgments

9 A Postscript

Theories of development neglect the subtle concerns of common man who has beliefs and dreams regarding pleasant and happy living. Such futuristic and loved concerns (fantasies) need to be incorporated into the development discourse to combat developmental dissonance and, in turn, individual dissonance. But individual concerns produce a complicated decision surface such that a realistic and unique solution is not possible. Therefore, a deductive proposition for such concerns can be derived from a whole that enables a solution to the chaotic and complex decision surface. It is possible through intuitive and immediate judgments.

We present development of "Spiritual Tourism" in Varanasi Region; a simple aspect of "Creative Economy"[46] as a case study for the incorporation of subjectivity to enable a pleasant development strategy. Although it deals with many aspects, only one dimension—Development of Labor Force for religious tourism, is taken up here.

Methodology[47]: It is maintained that a complex construct produces action tendencies guided by dissonance as the difference or gap between aspirations/dreams and realized (due to government endeavor) ones—read as development dissonance. Solution to so arrived development dissonance leads to context-specific subjective perception of development.

---

[46] Singh (2019).

[47] For the detail and other alternative exercises, see Singh (2019).

The Variables: We started with 17 aspects (defined as variables). Some found no place in the discussion and a few new ones were added leaving us with 14 in all (Refer Box 1) for carrying over.

Box 1: List of Variables

Adventure Sports (ASR)	Cleaning and Waste Disposal (CGW)
Improvement in Connectivity (ITC)	State of Sewage Water (SWG)
Online Booking Revenue (OBR)	Balance between Activities (BCW)
Labor Force for Religious Offerings (LRO)	Expansion of New Town (ENN)
Darshan Hassel Reduction (DHR)	Source of Information (SIC)
Crowd Management (CUS)	Safety of Tourists (STC)
Tourist Visit Purpose (WRP)	Opinion about Varanasi Items (OBI)

The Data: The experiment was conducted on groups of stakeholders (emic and etic) using images[48] of developed sights as stimulants to trigger the whims. Time (τ)[49] is defined as intuitive judgments. For the quantification of qualitative data, five coders were asked to make entry for each variable using the content in the transcript and video recordings from five groups for each stage of development. Variables were given entries for measures. Tables contained columns on directly mentioned, metaphoric, and euphemism, respectively. A weight of 3, 2, and 1 was assigned to each of them, respectively. Recurrence was also marked to assign additional weights to each of the columns. A point on scale of 1–5 was marked for the remaining columns of Intentionality, "Situationality," Coherence, Informative, and Acceptability to assign additional weightage to the variables.

Deciphering Dissonance: Difference equations derived from various alternative econometric models[50]—universal characteristics, pleasing to many, and pleasing to all—have been used to trace development dissonance. The graphs are plotted for three cases of imagery, realized, and dissonance. The analysis of the graphs helps us to arrive at policy prescriptions.

Results: Regression Results for Realization and Imageries are given in Tables 1 and 2 (Appendix). The Expansion Path[51] for Dissonance is given in Table 3 and graphs pertaining to Table 3 in the figures that follow (Appendix) (Figs. 1, 2, 3, 4, 5 and 6).

For Table 1—The Realization—it is apparent from the perusal of OLS estimate of the three models that coefficients of LRO remain same and only levels of confidence

[48]They are—1. Pertaining to a miserable condition (at time $\tau - 1$); 2. As the developed scenario (Govt. efforts)—the realizations (at time τ); 3. The future imagery (the Fantasies, at time τ;).

[49]τ—it is pronounced as Tau.

[50]Three models—Simple Linear, deflated by Square of Errors, Step wise Correction by relevant variables are estimated using Two Estimating Functions—OLS and Best fit(Min. χ^2)—for the data sets. Standardized $y_i = [Y_i - \text{Mean } Yi]/SEY_i$, weighted by Distance $Y_i * [1 - (yi - \text{mode})/\text{range}]$, $Yi * [1 - (yi - \text{max of } yi)/\text{range}]$ are estimated.

[51]$AB^{\tau} + C$;A, B, C are the estimated parameters of expansion path derived from the Difference Equation y_{τ} = extracted from the estimated models.

Table 1 Labor Force for Religious Offerings (LRO): The Realization

Universal/Mean Standardized as per t-distribution			Kernel Index as per deviation from Mode Value			Kernel Index as per deviation from Maximum Value		
Individual Variable	OLS Estimate (Min. $\sum e^2$)	Best Fit Estimate (Min. χ^2 *)	Individual Variable	OLS Estimate (Min. $\sum e^2$)	Best Fit Estimate (Min. χ^2 **)	Individual Variable	OLS Estimate (Min. $\sum e^2$)	Best Fit Estimate (Min. χ^2 ***)
	Coefficient (t-stat)			Coefficient(t-stat)			Coefficient (t-stat)	
LRO C	0.99 (1394.59) 3.55E-16(1.01E-13)	0.50 0.97	LRO C	3.00(463.19) −1.35(−0.99)	2.99 0	LRO C	3.00(58825.41) −0.02(−1.02)	1980261−2E + 09
LRO Error^2 C	0.99(1124525)−12.73(-3878.245) 0.003(813.85)		–	–		–		–
LRO ENH BCD WRP C	0.99 (977.51) -0.0001(-0.09) 0.002 (0.19) 0.004 (0.49) 3.55E-16(9.50E-14)		LRO ENH WRP CGD C	2.99(333.93) 0.0006(0.22) 0.003(0.46) 0.001(1.29) −4.62(−1.84)		LRO BCD ENH WRP C	3.00(52027.82) 1.10E-05(0.15) −3.05E-06(−0.07) 1.44E-06(0.26) −0.03(−1.01)	

Source: Singh (2019). Culture and economic development: An experiment for deciphering dissonance. Unpublished thesis, BHU
*Initial Value for Min.χ^2 is coefficient from Robust Equation, **Initial Value for Min.$\chi^2$is coefficient from Deflated Equation***Initial Value for Min.χ^2 is coefficient from Deflated Equation

Table 2 Labor Force for Religious Offerings (LRO) The Image

Universal/Mean Standardized as per t-distribution			Kernel Index as per deviation from Mode Value			Kernel Index as per deviation from Maximum Value		
Individual Variable	OLS Estimate (Min. $\sum e^2$)	Best Fit Estimate (Min. χ^2 *)	Individual Variable	OLS Estimate (Min. $\sum e^2$)	Best Fit Estimate (Min. χ^2 **)	Individual Variable	OLS Estimate (Min. $\sum e^2$)	Best Fit Estimate (Min. χ^2 ***)
	Coefficient (t-stat)			Coefficient(t-stat)			Coefficient (t-stat)	
LRO C	0.99 (1859.34) 3.55E-16 (1.35E-13)	0.16 −1.38	LRO C	0.003 (5.59) 0.13(0.98)	0.003 0.4	LRO C	5.95E-07(43574.46) −7.74E-09(−1.02)	5.4E + 07 −19256116
LRO Error^2 C	0.99 (1499371) −16.98 (−3878.24) 0.002 (813.85)		–	–		–		–
LRO ENH BCD WRP C	0.99 (1303.35) −0.0001 (−0.09) 0.0002 (0.19) 0.0003 (0.49) 3.55E-16(1.27E-13)		LRO ENH WRP CGD C	0.003(4.73) 0.0001(0.60) -3.84E-05 (-0.52) -0.0001(-1.18) 0.40(1.66)		LRO BCD ENH WRP C	5.95E-07(38539.17) 2.94E-12(0.15) -8-18E-13(-0.07) 3.87E-13(0.26) -8.72E.09(-1.01)	

Source Singh (2019). Culture and economic development: An experiment for deciphering dissonance. Unpublished thesis, BHU
*Initial Value for Min. χ^2 is coefficient from Robust Equation, **Initial Value for Min. χ^2 is coefficient from Deflated Equation
***Initial Value for Min. χ^2 is coefficient from Deflated Equation

Table 3 Labor Force for Religious Offerings (LRO): The Dissonance (Dissonance = Imagery − Realized) Expansion Path: $AB^{\gamma} + C$

		Universal/Mean Standardized as per t-distribution		Kernel Index as per deviation from Mode		Kernel Index as per deviation from Maximum	
		Min. $\sum e^2$	Min. χ^2	Min. $\sum e^2$	Min. χ^2	Min. $\sum e^2$	Min. χ^2
Imagery	A	0.2	−1.64	0.40	0.40	2592	2591.96
	B	0.99	0.16	0.003	0.003	5.95E-07	−5.4E + 07
	C	0.2	−1.64	0.40	0.40	8.7E-09	−0.03
Realized	A	0.3	1.98	2.32	0	2592.01	2593.98
	B	0.99	0.50	2.99	2.99	3	0.50
	C	0.3	1.98	2.32	0	0.01	1.98

Source Singh (2019). Culture and economic development: An experiment for deciphering dissonance. Unpublished thesis, BHU

Fig. 1 LRO_Universal (Min. $\sum e^2$)

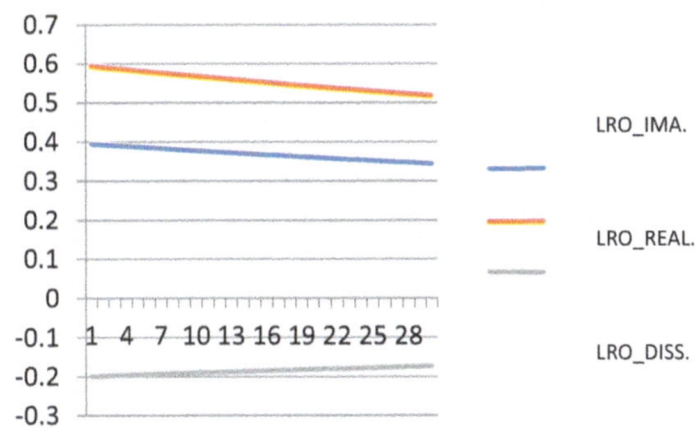

Fig. 2 LRO_Satisficing_Many (Min. $\sum e^2$)

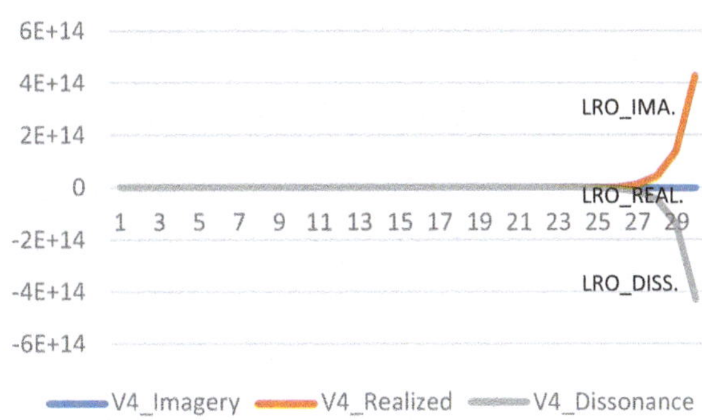

Fig. 3 LRO_Satisficing_All (Min. $\sum e^2$)

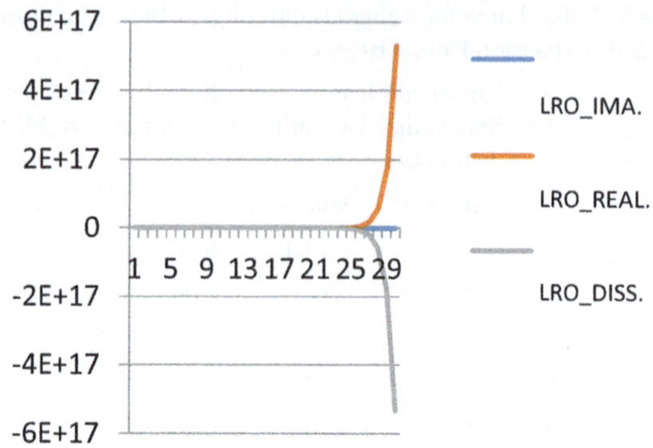

Fig. 4 LRO_Universal (Min. χ^2)

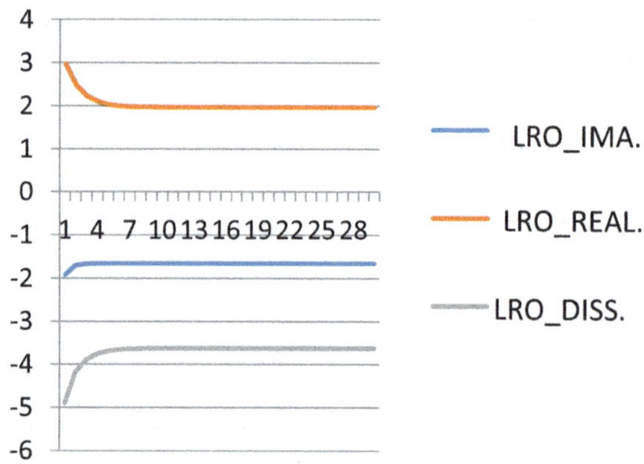

Fig. 5 LRO_Satisficing_Many (Min. χ^2)

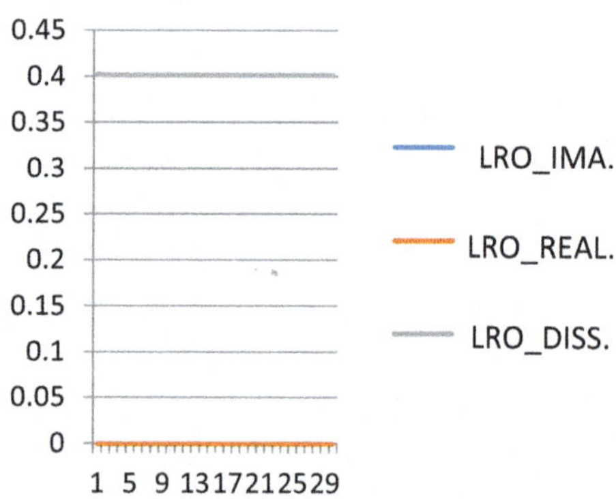

Fig. 6 LRO_Satisficing_All (Min. χ^2)

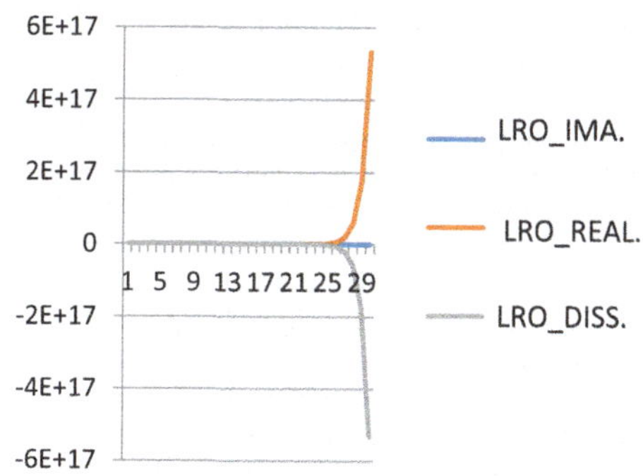

change that are seldom paid heed to in policy prescriptions.[52] The negative intercept term (as universal belief) maybe because of perceived initial negative perception[53] of past happiness by the labor force. However, the intercept and the coefficient change giving a different perception by the masses regarding the realized minimum (positive—0.97 increased from zero) and desired rate (0.50 decreased from 0.99) of efforts. When loved/pleasing strategies were tried, "pleasing to many" increased stupendously to 3.00 and an unaffordable high when resorted to "pleasing to all." The alternative models (rows) do not make any substantial changes.[54]

The future image (dreams) depicts not quite different picture for the universal beliefs (coefficients being 0.99 and intercept being zero), but it reduces to zero when the two alternative strategies are attempted. Can we examine the proposition that to work as religious labor force is not a dreamed occupation? A policy of shifting such laborers to other activities is required for a pleasant solution. A clearer picture emerges when difference equations for realization, imagery, and dissonance are plotted. It declines continuously for universal values and declines sharply for pleasing strategies. Can we have a combination of the two strategies as a justified solution?

References

Adamson, P., & Porman, P. E. (2015). The philosophical work of Al- Kindi. Oxford University Press, Published in Karachi, Pakistan.

Alkire, S. (2005a). Needs and capabilities. *Royal Institute of Philosophy Supplements, 57,* 229–252.

Alkire, S. (2005b). Why the capability approach? *Journal of Human Development, 6*(1), 115–135.

Amin, H., Sharma, R., Vyas, H. A., & Vyas, M. K. (2015). Concept of Manas in Sa–m. khya Darsfana. *Indian Journal of History of Science, 50,* 125–130.

[52] A possible exhibit of "Fooled by Randomness".

[53] "as spring looks at the winter" Gibran, Secret of Heart.

[54] It raises doubts against additions to apprehension in terms of precessions—a possible exaggeration.

Anthony, O. S. (2001). Displacement, resistance and critique of development: from the grassroots to the global. Desk Study Four, Refugee Studies Centre of the University of Oxford, revisited: https://www.rsc.ox.ac.uk/files/files-1/wp9-displacement-resistance-critique-development-2002.pdf, date 20th April, 2020, time 02:08 PM

Baranzini M, Scazzieri R (1986) Foundations of economics: structures of inquiry and economic theory. Oxford, UK; New York, NY, USA: Blackwell.

Beresford, B., & Sloper, T. (2008). *Understanding the dynamics of decision-making and choice: A scoping study of key psychological theories to inform the design and analysis of the panel study.* York: Social Policy Research Unit, University of York.UK.

Bettman, J. R., Luce, M. F., & Payne, J. W. (1998). Constructive consumer choice processes. *Journal of consumer research, 25*(3), 187–217.

Blomström M, Kokko A (1999) Regional integration and foreign direct investment: A conceptual framework and three cases. The World Bank.

Bourdieu, P. (1985a). a) The genesis of the concepts of habitus and field. *Sociocriticism, 2*(2), 11–24.

Bourdieu, P. (1985b). b) The social space and the genesis of groups. *Theory and Society, 14,* 723–744.

Bourdieu P (1998) Acts of resistance: Against the new myths of our time. Polity Press. Soft copy: http://digamo.free.fr/bourdieu98.pdf, date 22th April, 2020 at 11:42 AM.

Bourke, P. (1991). *An introduction to fractals* (p. 5). Noongard: The University of Western of Australia, Consulta.

Campbell, J. (1974). A note on growth poles. *Growth and Change, 5*(2), 43–45.

Cowen T (2005). Is a novel a model?. The Street Porter and the Philosopher: Conversations on Analytical Egalitarianism, 319–37. http://www.sscnet.ucla.edu/polisci/faculty/chwe/austen/cowen2005.pdf, date: 22th April, 2020 at 11: 58 AM

Danesi, M. (2004). *Poetic Logic the Role of Metaphor in Thought, Language, and Culture.* Madison, WI: Atwood Publishing.

Davidson, H. A. (1992). *Alfarabi.* Avicenna and Averrose on Intellect: Oxford University Press, New York.

Evans G W (Ed.) (1984) Environmental stress. CUP Archive.

Fiedler, K., & Bless, H. (2000). *The formation of beliefs at the interface of affective and cognitive processes* (pp. 144–170). Emotions and beliefs: How feelings influence thoughts.

Fukuyama, F. (2018). *Identity: Contemporary identity politics and the struggle for recognition.* MTL Manipal: Profile books.

Gibran K (2009). The collected works of Kahlil Gibran. Maple Press 493–496.

Gigerenzer G, Todd PM, ABC Research Group. (1999). *Simple heuristics that make us smart.* New York: Oxford University Press.

Goleman D (1996 (2013)) Emotional intelligence. Why it can matter more than IQ, Bloomsbury, Publishing India Ltd. New Delhi

Goleman, D. (2006). *(2007)) Social intelligence.* The new Science of Human Relationships: Penguin Random House, UK, Pub.by Arrow Books.

Haq, M. (1976). *The poverty curtain: Choices for the third world.* New York: Columbia University Press.

Hicks, J. (1984). Is economics a science? *Interdisciplinary Science Reviews, 9*(3), 213–219.

Inati, S. C. (1996). *Ibn Sina and mysticism: remarks and admonitions: part four.* London and New York: Kegan Paul International.

International Labour Organization. (2013). Local development strategies In: The informal economy and decent work: A policy resource guide supporting transitions to formality. Geneva: International Labour Organization

Jaakko H et Al (1976) Belief and Probability, Part of Synthesis Library for Springer Link (SLYI, Vol104).

Kahneman, D., & Frederick, S. (2002). Representativeness revisited: Attribute substitution in intuitive judgment. *Heuristics and biases: The psychology of intuitive judgment, 49,* 81.

Kahneman D, Tversky A (2013) Prospect theory: An analysis of decision under risk. In Handbook of the fundamentals of financial decision making: Part I (pp. 99–127). Singapore.

Khan MM, Zhang J, Hashmi MS (2010) Cultural values and economic growth in Asia: An empirical analysis. International Journal of Business and Social Science, 1(2).

Lawson, T. (1997). *Economics and reality*. London: Routledge.

Lipietz, A. (1980). Inter-regional polarisation and the tertiarisation of society. *Papers in Regional Science, 44*(1), 3–17.

Mercer, J. (2010). Emotional beliefs. *International Organization, 64*(1), 1–31.

Nijkamp P, Reggiani A (1992 a) Interaction, Evolution and Chaos in Space. Springer-Verlag Berlin Heidelberg

Nijkamp, P., & Reggiani, A. (1992b). *Static and dynamic spatial interaction models: an integrating perspective*. Amsterdam: Serie Research Memoranda.

Nijkamp P, Reggiani A (1993) Complex Behaviour in Spatial Networks. In Nonlinear Evolution of Spatial Economic Systems (pp. 248–271). Springer, Berlin, Heidelberg.

Nijkamp, P., & Reggiani, A. (Eds.). (1993b). *Nonlinear evolution of spatial economic systems*. Berlin: Springer.

Nussbaum, M. C. (2011a). *a) Creating capabilities*. USA: Harvard University Press.

Nussbaum, M. C. (2011b). b) Perfectionist liberalism and political liberalism. *Philosophy & Public Affairs, 39*(1), 3–45.

OPHI. (2018). *Global multidimensional Poverty Index 2018: The most detailed picture to date of the world's poorest people*. UK: University of Oxford.

Pike, A., Rodríguez-Pose, A., & Tomaney, J. (2007). What kind of local and regional development and for whom? *Regional Studies, 41*(9), 1253–1269.

Putnam, R. D. (1993). *Making Democracy Work: Civic Traditions in Modern Italy*. Princeton: Princeton University Press. Princeton, New Jersey.

Putnam, R. D. (1995). Bowling alone, revisited. The Responsive Community (Spring): 18–33. Forthcoming in a collective volume edited by Axel Hadenius. Cambridge University Press. New York.

Robeyns, I. (2003a). a) Sen's capability approach and gender inequality: selecting relevant capabilities. *Feminist economics, 9*(2–3), 61–92.

Robeyns, I. (2003b). The capability approach: an interdisciplinary introduction. In Training course preceding the Third International Conference on the Capability Approach, Pavia, Italy.

Russell B (2017(1946)) History of western philosophy: Collector's edition. Routledge. Printed in Saurabh India pvt ltd. New Delhi.

Sharif, M. M. (1963). *A history of muslim philosophy*. Wiesbaden: Harrassowitz. Published by Pakistan Philosophical Congress.

Sen A (1989 a) Indian development: Lessons and non-lessons. Daedalus, 369–392.

Sen, A. (1989b). b)Women's survival as a development problem. *Bulletin of the American Academy of Arts and Sciences, 43*(2), 14–29.

Sen, A. (1999). *Development as Freedom*. New Delhi: Oxford University Press.

Sen, A. (2004a). *Chapter 1 Cultural Liberty and Human Development*. United Nations Development Programme: UN Human Development Reports.

Sen, A. (2004b). Capabilities, lists, and public reason: continuing the conversation. *Feminist economics, 10*(3), 77–80.

Simon, H. A. (1957). *Models of man; social and rational*. USA: Wiley.

Singh, S. (2018). Different Aspects of Economic Decision Making for a Culturally Charged Economic Actor: A Review of Literature. Available at SSRN 3385589.

Singh, S. (2019). Culture and economic development: An experiment for deciphering dissonance. Unpublished thesis, BHU.

Strogatz, S. H. (1994). *Nonlinear dynamics and chaos: with applications to physics, biology, chemistry, and engineering (studies in nonlinearity)* (1st ed.). USA: Perseus Books.

Taleb, N. N. (2005). Fooled by randomness: The hidden role of chance in life and in the markets. 2nd ed. Texere, New York.

Taleb, N. N. (2007). *The black swan: The impact of the highly improbable.* India: Penguin.
Thaler RH, & Sunstein C R (2008) Nudge: Improving decisions about health, wealth, and happiness. Yale University Press, New Haven & London
Thilly, F. (2005). *A history of Philosophy.* New Delhi: SBW Publication.
Tversky, A. (1972). Eliminpation by aspects: A theory of choice. *Psychological Review, 79*(4), 28.

Poverty and Inequality

Toward Understanding the Nature of Inequality in India in Terms of Changing Perceptions on Its Sources and Solutions

D. Narasimha Reddy

Abstract This paper enquires about changing perceptions of inequality in terms of its sources, consequences, and the solutions that have been thrown up by the emerging research findings on the issue. The conception of inequality is a dynamic one and has seen many transitions. This paper surveys this transition starting from Aristotle to Piketty and shows that the shift to multidimensionality of inequality, besides locating the issue in historical context in terms of social, political, and economic dimensions also calls for differentiation of types of inequality. The conventional wisdom that inequality is the result of the differences in skills and talents is questioned and other sources of inequality, mainly policies and politics, are brought into debate. The relationship of inequality with growth, poverty, and labor market outcomes is analyzed and it is shown that inequality is a constraint on growth and poverty reduction. If one were to simplify the problem of inequality into two dimensions, viz., inequality of opportunities and inequality of outcomes, perhaps there is no other country in the world other than India which faces the inequality of opportunities as deep, because of its centuries of history, and as wide because of its universal nature across all regions of the country. India is one of the very few countries which do not collect information on income through household surveys. This paper uses many alternative data sources for India and shows that there is a clear phenomenon of 'hollowing out' of the middle class. Fiscal policy, especially taxation, has an important role in reducing inequality. But, reliance on fiscal policy only may not be sufficient and there is a need for radical policy and political mobilization.

1 Introduction

In recent times, there has been growing evidence that ever since the unfolding of the process of economic globalization in countries under neoliberal economic regimes that witnessed retreat of the state and the entrenchment of privatization, there has

D. Narasimha Reddy (✉)
University of Hyderabad, Hyderabad, India
e-mail: duvvurunarasimha@gmail.com

N. K. Mishra (ed.), *Development Challenges of India After Twenty Five Years of Economic Reforms*, India Studies in Business and Economics,
https://doi.org/10.1007/978-981-15-8265-3_5

been unbridled increase in inequality of income and wealth, even as large sections of people remained poor and deprived. This has drawn widespread mobilization and protests in many countries, especially in Latin America, correctives did bring about positive changes in favor of better life for the marginalized and the working class in general (Roberts 2012). In India, even as it is revealed that there has been growing inequality of income and wealth, and even as it is increasingly clear that the accelerated growth of the last few decades, instead of "trickling down" in an inclusive way to the lower rungs of the society, it has actually been adding wealth to the top rungs of the rich. There is a continued obsession with "growth", and hardly any larger debate on the ramifications of growing inequality on the prospects of progress of the democratic polity that would ensure equitable and fair access to the fruits of growth to people. The limited objective of this paper is to help inform the debate on the changing perceptions on inequality in terms of its sources, consequences, and the solutions that have been thrown up by the emerging research findings on the issue. Based mostly on the review of recent literature and secondary sources of data, the presentation of this paper is divided into five sections. The brief introduction is followed by the second section that deals briefly with the changes in the conceptualization of inequality. The third section refers to the changes in the perceptions about the sources or drivers of inequality, which apparently are much against the conventional wisdom. It also brings together the findings on the adverse effects of inequality. Based on these emerging findings on the various ramifications of inequality, the fourth section presents the trends in inequality in India. The last section is about the emerging policy perspectives on containing inequality within reasonable bounds that would make growth fair, inclusive, and sustainable.

2 Inequality: A Concept in Transition

The concept of inequality has changed over time. Amartya Sen asserts: "concepts of equity and justice have changed remarkably over history, and as the intolerance of stratification and differentiation has grown, the very concept of inequality has gone through radical transformation …I should argue that the historical nature of the notion of inequality is worth bearing in mind before going into an analysis of economic inequality as it is viewed by economists today"[1] (Sen 1973). In a comprehensive account of inequality from Aristotle to White (2003) brings out as to how Aristotle conceptualized inequality in ethical framework, and how ethical considerations continued to dominate the Classical school particularly J. S. Mill's egalitarian framework, only to be challenged by the framework of subjective methodological individualism of the Neoclassical school. And again, it was the turn of Sen to revive the normative ethical framework in discussing inequality in the context of well-being.

[1] The reference "today" should be seen as 1960s and early 1970s around which it was written and at which point the Pareto dictum that inequality changes but "stable in the long run" was still dominant mainstream conception.

Mill differentiated between "earned" income, and property obtained from free use of mind and body, and "unearned" income from rent. He was for equal distribution of income by taxing land. Mill insisted on equality of opportunity and the role of education in achieving it. By the latter half of nineteenth century, there emerged a shift from the classical economics to neoclassical rational value-free approach, and all ethical and egalitarian considerations were sought to be purged out. For Marshall and J.B. Clark income distribution was to be seen solely in terms of marginal productive theory. "No matter how unequal the income distribution is, as long as it follows the marginal productivity rule, it is a good and just income distribution. …with the rise of Pareto and the ordinalist approach to welfare economics, this non-egalitarian criterion comes to dominate mainstream economics" (White 2003). For Pareto, the only basis for preferring a more equal income distribution over a less equal one was "sentiment." Interestingly, Pareto who was known for his theoretical contributions, was also, perhaps, one of the earliest empirical researchers. In 1895, he conducted an empirical study of the distribution of income in different European countries and cities at different times in the nineteenth century and concluded distribution of income was roughly constant across these times and places. His interpretation was that "the income distribution may change over time, but it is remarkably stable," and become the Pareto Law. His proposition was that attempts to decrease inequality by redistribution of income were futile in the long term (White 2003). Pigou, based on better empirical evidence questioned Pareto's findings and theory. But Pigou's arguments, since it was based on utilitarian approach, were vehemently dismissed as unscientific by Lionnel Robbins (White 2003). And Pareto's proposition that, changes notwithstanding, income distribution would be stable in the long run, continued to rule as the law for the neoclassical mainstream and to inequality and income distribution were relegated as issues of not much importance in economics. But yet the growing evidence of increasing inequality and deliberate efforts to ignore the same, remained an embarrassment.

It is at this historical context in the career of inequality analysis, in the 1950s Kuznet's undertook a systematic analysis of interpersonal income inequality with a particular focus on the behavior of the share of the upper income groups on the basis of innovative sources of data.[2] Kuznets used for the first time a combination of the income tax returns (USA introduced income tax in 1913) and national income tables for the USA, in the construction of which he played a pioneering role. He presented his results in his famous presidential address, 'Economic Growth and Income Inequality' (Kuznets 1955) to the American Economic Association. According to his findings, income inequality evolved along an inverted "U," increasing in the initial stages of development and narrowing later on, which has become the famous "Kuznets Curve" or "inverted U" hypothesis of income inequality and economic growth relationship. But in the existing cold war context of the 1950s, Piketty (2014) points out, some of Kuznets observations that his finding would help to "keep the underdeveloped countries within the orbit of the free world" acted as a political weapon, and he was seen as a bearer of good news in the face of the spectre of Marx's proposition that dynamics

[2]Part of this paragraph draws from Haque (2019).

of private capital accumulation inevitably lead to the concentration of wealth in ever fewer hands, resulting in a kind of apocalypse of capitalism. Though there was hardly any work on inequality in the mainstream economics at that time, Kuznets' hypothesis which in a way resonates with "Pareto Law" that changes notwithstanding, inequality will be stable in the long run—came to be treated as an empirical anchor for the neoclassical *a priori* proposition. Thus, "Kuznets Curve" came as an ideological boost to the mainstream economics profession which hastened to convert it as a "natural law" of development and distribution (Lee and Gerecke 2012).

The irony is that Kuznets' more circumspect and cautious remarks were totally ignored. Kuznets in his lecture did caution that his proposition was of speculative nature based on "5% empirical information and 95% speculation, some of it tainted by wishful thinking." He went on to emphasize that inequality was much larger issue and closed his lecture with the following words: "Effective work in this field necessarily calls for a shift from market economics to political and social economy" (Kuznets 1955, p. 28). Mainstream economics, instead of initiating new research with a broader framework suggested by Kuznets, used his findings as settled conclusions and propagated the notion that with the turnaround from underdevelopment to development, growth would bring about decline in inequality and hence "growth should take the driving seat and distribution the back seat" in economic development (Lee and Gerecke 2012). In the mainstream neoclassical economics, the place accorded to research on inequality has since been virtually closed. Though die-hard mainstream may hold on to it, the impact of over three decades of globalization with growing market orientation through deregulation and privatization, there has been relatively high growth in most of the developed and in the large emerging economies, but there was no sign of inequality wearing off in the latter stages of development. On the contrary, there has been growing evidence that income disparities within countries have been on the increase, and in many cases, to the levels inconscionable. The paradox is that multilateral agencies such as the International Monetary Fund, which promoted the neoliberal agenda across countries, are the very agencies that are sponsoring extensive research on the impact of inequality and policy interventions to overcome the same (IMF 2007; Oxfam 2017a). Beginning with 2000, there has been a great spurt in research on various dimensions of inequality. But the real breakthrough in terms of methodology in the true Kuznetsian spirit came with Piketty: "…no one has ever systematically pursued Kuznet's work, no doubt in part because the historical and statistical study of tax records falls into a sort of academic no-man's-land, too historical for economists and too economistic for historians. That is a pity, because the dynamics of income inequality can only be studied in a long-run perspective, which is possible only if one makes use of tax records" (Piketty 2014, p. 17). By emphasizing that inequality is complex and multidimensional, Piketty's work liberates inequality research from narrow economic confines and orients toward understanding capital and power relations by drawing from wide range of information sources including income and wealth accounts, household income and wealth surveys, fiscal data coming from tax sources, inheritance, wealth data including wealth rankings, and of course, national income data. In broadening the scope of inequality research "…it makes one think about the overwhelming cultural-ideological-economic-political complex that power of wealth creates which conditions the public to emulate values that make people band together any threats to possession of wealth, however unequal it might be." (Piketty 2017, p. 545).

The shift to multidimensionality of inequality, besides locating the issue in historical context in terms of social, political, and economic dimensions also calls for differentiation of types of inequality. Conventionally, the focus has been on the functional and interpersonal distribution of income. In the classical political economy, including Marx, the emphasis was on income and its functional distribution among social classes based on their role in the production system as workers, capitalists, or owners of land receiving incomes in the form of wages, profits, and rents. While functional classification still assumes continued importance, there was a shift in emphasis in the neoclassical period toward interpersonal distribution of income, which overtime has come to assume significant importance in public policy both for the purposes of measurement of inequality (UNCTAD 2011), and for public intervention for taxation or public fiscal transfers. While both in the functional and the personal distribution, the focus has been on the outcomes, viz., income and wealth, which are also seen in vertical distribution at different levels. The growing inequalities, and along with it certain social classes or groups suffering persistent low income or wealth in spite of overall growth, have brought the dimension of inequality of opportunities or the horizontal inequality to the fore in recent times. Horizontal inequalities refer to inequalities between groups with specific characteristics that their members and the others recognize as important aspects of their identity. These groups could be defined by culture, gender, ethnicity, religion, race, caste, geographic location, and age, among other characteristics. These are the results of systematic discrimination and exclusion, and they can prevent individuals within marginalized groups from achieving their full potential, and in contributing to society's prosperity. Horizontal inequalities manifest themselves in unequal opportunities and outcomes across socioeconomic, political, and cultural dimensions (UNDP 2013, p. 27).

3 Changing Perception on Sources of Inequality

The broadening of the scope of research on the multidimensional nature of inequality has also resulted in questioning the conventional wisdom that inequality is the result of the differences in skills and talents. For over three decades, it was argued that income inequality in the USA centered on the dispersion of wages and the increased premium for skilled or educated workers, due to varying skill-based technological change and globalization. But research in recent years has brought out that much of the inequality is due to shift of income and wealth to the very top 1 to 10%. "Stories based on the supply and demand for skills are not enough to explain the extreme top tail of the earnings distribution; nor is it earned incomes" (Alvaredo et al. 2013). Piketty did emphasize the role of politics and policy: "One should be vary of any economic determinism in regard to inequality of wealth and income. The history of the distribution of wealth has always been deeply political, and it cannot be reduced to purely economic mechanisms" (Piketty 2017, p. 545). The Economist (2014), supposed to be largely on the mainstream path, also endorses by pointing out that "skill-based technological change" or "superstar economics" are incomplete explanations of rising inequality, and they may actually leave out the more interesting half of the story.

Stiglitz (2015) discussing the origins of inequality points out that during the eighteenth and nineteenth centuries, there were two views on inequality, one was the Marxist view that attributed it to exploitation and market power and the other was neoclassical view based on their marginal productivity theory of distribution attributing to the differences in productivity linked earnings. In the late nineteenth and the twentieth centuries, the concern about inequality was linked to monopoly capital. He points out that today's capitalism is different, and that USA "inequality is not, for the most part, the result of economic forces. It is not, in this sense, the result of inexorable economic laws" (Stiglitz 2015, p. 427). But it is because of policies and politics, and much of the rents are derived by using political influence in land grants, modification of zoning of urban land, preferential provision of tax laws, giving away of country's natural resources and in the financial sector, insider trading and sophisticated front running, fees for credit/debit card monopolies (Stiglitz 2015, p. 432). Stiglitz feels that the "real issue is not capitalism in the twenty-first century, but politics in the twenty-first century." Under the neoliberal regimes, state acts as the agency to shift incomes from citizens to the capital (Baker 2014). A study of inequality in India blames squarely the policy flaws as the source (Shetty 2018).

The World Inequality Report 2018 (Alvaredo et al. 2018) brings out that in recent decades, especially since 1980s, income inequality increased in almost all regions of the world with different speed, ranging from the lowest in Europe to the highest in the Middle East. Role of national policies and institutions significantly influenced income inequality. By 1980s, the postwar egalitarian era came to an end in most of the countries. Globalization and the ensuing neoliberal regimes witnessed extensive shift toward deregulation and privatization. Tax systems grew less progressive and declining share of public investment brought about massive educational inequalities. Between 1980 and 2016, top 1% captured almost 50% of the growth in income. Increasing economic inequality has been largely due to unequal ownership of capital. Increasing privatization and income inequalities fuelled rise in wealth inequality. Since 1980s, there have been large transfers of wealth from public to private ownership. Between 1970 and 2016, the ratio of private capital to national income increased from about 2 to 3.5 to 4 to 7 across countries. In developed countries, increase in public wealth was negative or zero, and the ratio of net public wealth to net national income turned negative in the USA and UK (Alvaredo et al. 2018).

Arrow et al. (2000) suggest that growing inequality is due to the demise of egalitarian concerns in public policy and refer to three sources of the demoralization of the egalitarian project in the USA. First is the moral dimension, i.e., the concept of fairness, which no longer enjoys consensus on what it entails and therefore does not provide much guidance in egalitarian support. Second is the shift in public knowledge of causes of inequality. Poverty and inequality, once considered systematic impediments such as discrimination and class bias in schooling and employment, are now sought to be explained by either cultural or genetic factors. The third reason for the demise of egalitarian consensus is the shift in public understanding of the underlying causes of inequality, seen simply as immune to public policy to improve employment, training and expanded education. A study on rising inequalities in Asia points to the inequality of opportunities in the form of discrimination and social exclusion as the main source of inequality (ADB 2012). Corak (2013) draws attention to the phenomenon of the "The Great Gatsby Curve"—more inequalities arising due to less mobility across generations. In a more polarized labor market like that of the USA, the substantial rise in the income shares of the top 1% will result in access to high quality of human capital investment in their children. The intergenerational transmission of employment and wealth would mean higher rate of transmission of economic advantage to the top and more deeper inequality.

One of the main dimensions of contemporary political economy is the emergence of finance capital and the complex role of finance, property (especially, real estate) and the avoidance of taxation as the drivers of inequality. According to the Organisation for Economic Cooperation and Development (OECD), the off-shore registration of companies in low-tax jurisdictions is estimated to cost $240 billion annually, equivalent to 4–10% of global corporate tax revenue, to the treasuries of G-20 nations (Jones 2017). There is growing evidence that current levels of extreme inequality exceed what can be justified by merit in terms of talent, effort, and risk taking. Jacobs (2015), in a very significant paper that challenges the merit as the source of inequality, reviews several sources of extreme wealth through an analytical framework known as "the ladder of demerit." The six rungs of the ladder from higher to lower—consists of crime, cronyism, inheritance, monopoly, globalization, and technology. The higher rungs are clearly not meritocratic. The lower ones, it is pointed out, reward talented people multiple times what can be justified based on merit. By drawing empirical evidence largely from *Forbe's* list of billionaires, he provides a tentative indication of the relative importance of each rung: "Fifty percent of the world's billionaire wealth is found to be non-meritocratic owing to either inheritance or a high presumption of cronyism. Another 15 percent is not meritocratic owing to presumption of monopoly. All of it is non-meritocratic owing to globalisation. By contrast, crime and technology are found to be negligible sources of extreme wealth" (Jacobs 2015). Monopoly rents from sectors such as telecommunications, air travel, and broadcast frequencies fuel excess returns to owners and shareholders at the expense of the rest of the economy (Jacobs 2015; Oxfam 2017; Oxfam 2018). A study on the sources of wealth in India finds a similar pattern: "Out of India's forty-six billionaires in 2012, twenty had drawn their primary wealth (at least originally) from sectors that can be classified as 'rent thick' (real estate, construction, infrastructure or ports, media, cement, and mining). The remaining twenty six billionaires had drawn their primary wealth from 'other' sectors (IT/software, pharmaceuticals and biotech, finance, liquor and automotives, and so on). Overall, 43% of the total number of billionaires, accounting for 60% billionaires' wealth in India, had their primary sources of wealth from rent-thick sectors" (Gandhi and Walton 2012).

3.1 Adverse Impact of Inequality

There is growing evidence on the adverse consequences of rising inequality. Some of the early studies like that of Berg and Ostry (2011) provide evidence as to how inequality could undermine growth process and its sustainability. Their findings show that "growth spells" are likely to be shorter in countries with higher inequality, and reduced inequality and sustained growth may thus be two sides of the same coin. Stiglitz (2012) supports these claims by showing that income inequality is associated with unstable economies and unsustainable economic growth. Rajan (2010) argued that the 2008 financial crisis was a consequence of high-economic inequality. His proposition was that as the inequalities increased the U.S. consumers in the lower rungs of income reacted to a decrease in their permanent incomes since the early 1980s by reducing saving and increasing borrowing. The debt-driven consumption demand could not be sustained after a while, resulting in a financial bubble creating the crisis. An extensive review paper of the IMF is devoted to the studies sparked off by these findings (Treeck and Sturn 2012). There have been a number of studies on the impact of inequality on labor markets. For instance in a major collection of studies on labor markets, institutions, and inequality, Berg (2015) shows that between the early 1990s to the early 2010s, except in Latin America and some African countries, inequalities increased in most of the regions, including China and India. Jaumotte and Buitron (2015) report a rise in inequality in labor markets in advanced economies, with particular concentration of incomes at the top of the distribution. During the same period, there was erosion of labor market institutions, decline of unionization, and decline of minimum wages. Interestingly, it is also shown that there exists a strong negative relationship between unionization and top earners' income shares.

Lanker et al. (2019) using data from 164 countries comprising of 97% of the world's population presents a scenario of global poverty from 1981 to 2030. The findings show that declining income inequality is likely to be more effective in reducing poverty than rise in growth rate per se. It also finds that it would be difficult to achieve the Sustainable Development Goal-10 of reducing global poverty to 3% of the population by 2030 without addressing reduction in inequality. UNDP (2013) examining inequality from the perspective of well-being brings out the adverse consequences of growing inequality. It finds inequality undermines development by hindering economic progress, weakening democratic life, and threatening social cohesion. Inequality, it is argued, is not only intrinsically unfair, but it makes achievement of widespread well-being difficult, if we include not only material but also relational and subjective well-being. "Increases in income inequality over the last 20 years have been largely driven by broad globalisation, but domestic policy choices have played an important role too" (UNDP 2013).

4 The Indian Context[3]

If one were to simplify the problem of inequality into two dimensions, viz., inequality of opportunities and inequality of outcomes, perhaps there is no other country in the world other than India which faces the inequality of opportunities as deep, because of its centuries of history of discrimination, and as wide because of its universal spread across all regions of the country. The inequality of opportunities was the primary challenge with which the new Republic of India came into existence in 1950 and the Constitution did engage with the issue and addressed it with the world's first comprehensive provisions of affirmative action. While the progress on the desired lines has been acceptably limited, there exists a system of Directive Principles of State Policy (DPSP) by effective implementation of which could be faced upto a certain extent, if there is political will. The inequality of outcomes was expected to be taken care by the strategy of growth with distributive justice in tandem with DPSP. The available evidence does show that the strategy which was to a large extent the framework for policies and programs, though was not up to the expectations, in spite of relatively low levels of growth did bring down inequality for the first three decades (Reddy 2019). However, with the early winds of liberalization in the 1980s and a complete regime change toward neoliberalism and globalization since early 1990s, there has been unbridled surge in inequalities in income and wealth with exasperating impact on inequality of opportunities as well.

India is one of the very few countries which do not collect information on income through household surveys. And hence it has rightly earned the snide remark that India has entered the digital age without any surveys for collecting income data from households (Chancel and Piketty 2017). For quite some time, consumer expenditure data based on all-India consumer household expenditure by the NSSO served as the proxy for income inequality estimates. But it is well known that consumption expenditure as a proxy for income would be gross underestimation of income especially of the higher income groups. Notwithstanding these limitations, the consumption Gini as a proxy for income did bring about one thing, that is, a tendency for inequality to decline in the pre-liberalization era from mid-1950s (0.35) to mid-1970s (0.30) but started rising later to 0.33 in 1993–94, and further to 0.37 in 2011–12 (Mahendra Dev 2017, Barbosa et al. 2016). In the later period, the consumption expenditure gap between different consumption classes also showed an increase. For instance, the share of top 10% in the total consumption expenditure increased from 27% in 1983 to 33% in 2011–12.

The only other source of household income data is the India Human Development Survey (IHDS)[4] available since 2005. Though IHDS data do not cover the entire country, the sample size is considered fairly large enough to provide indicative measures of distribution of income. The IHDS results showed income inequality of 0.54 Gini in 2004–05, and it further increased to 0.55 by 2011–12. The IHDS data

[3]This section draws partly from the author's joint paper on a larger theme (Haque and Reddy 2019).

[4]IHDS has been jointly organized by researchers from the University of Maryland and the National Council of Applied Economic Research (NCAER), New Delhi.

act as a shock to the comfort with which the consumption expenditure based Gini was used as a proxy to show that inequality in India was very low. Now it is clear that India is in the highest income inequality zone, and the current estimates show that income inequality is the second highest in the world next only to South Africa and some Middle East countries (Milanovic 2016; Alvaredo et al. 2018).

For the estimation of household wealth in India, the only source available as of now is the NSSO decennial All India Debt and Investment Survey (AIDIS). However, there are some measurement issues, comparability problems, under-reporting of wealth, under-sampling of the super-rich, etc., which point to the limitation of the data (Jayaraj and Subramanian 2006; Anand and Thampi 2016). Yet the data do help in capturing the broad trends, and the datasets are put to extensive analysis of inequalities of not only of wealth but also income over a period across different social groups and urban–rural areas (Anand and Thampi 2016; Vamsi 2010). The AIDIS data on wealth reveal that the level of inequality which was already at a very high level (Gini 0.65) by mid-1990s, has steeply increased since the middle of the first decade of 2000s to reach the extreme level of 0.74. The wealth shifts have been increasingly toward upper deciles: "Considering wealth inequality by deciles revealed that only the topmost decile increased its share in asset ownership after 2002… this trend of wealth consolidation has worsened since then, and narrowed to the top 10% and perhaps even lower; by 2012, the top 5% alone owned half of the wealth" (Anand and Thampi 2016). This is corroborated by the other sources, such as Forbes' Indian Rich lists, according to which the wealth of the richest Indians that it reported amounted to "less than 2% of national income in the 1990s, but increased substantially throughout the 2000s, reaching 10% in 2015, and with a peak of 27% before the 2008–09 financial crisis" (Chancel and Piketty 2017). A more interesting and revealing aspect is the demystification of the notion of talent and risks that are widely propagated as the sources of high income and wealth. As pointed out earlier, out of India's 46 billionaires in 2012, 20 had drawn their primary source of wealth (at least originally) from sectors that can be classified as "rent-thick" (real estate, construction, infrastructure or ports sectors, media, cement, and mining) (Gandhi and Walton 2012).

The major breakthrough in the analysis of inequality comes from Piketty's pioneering efforts along the path set by Kuznets in utilizing innovative sources of data and simplified methods of presentation of the results. In the case of India, income tax data since 1922,[5] the NSSO consumption expenditure survey data, the National Accounts data, the IHDS income, and consumption data and the UN statistics population data are utilized to estimate the levels and trends in income inequality (Chancel and Piketty 2017; Alvaredo et al. 2018). The data enable long-term analysis right from 1922 to 2013–14, and bring as to what difference that a regulatory regime of growth with distributive justice in the prereform period could make compared with the neoliberal regime with the market forces and private profit seeking as the main driving forces of growth. Table 1 shows that there was actually an increase in the share of bottom 50% of the adult population in the national income from 19% to 24% in the first three decades from mid-1950s to mid-1980s. And the middle-income group

[5]In India, income tax was introduced in 1922.

Table 1 Changes in income of different classes as a share of GDP (%) in India

Income Group	Mid-1980s	1982–83	2000	2013–14
Top 10%	40	30	40	55
Middle 40%	40	46	40	29.6
Bottom 50%	19	23.6	20.6	14.9

Table 2 Share of different groups in the total national income generated in India: before and after liberalization (in percentages)

Income group	Before Liberalization 1951–1980	After Liberalization 1980–2014
All	100	100
Top 10%	24	66
Middle 40%	49	23
Bottom 50%	28	11

Source Chancel and Piketty 2017

too experienced an increase in the share while the share of the top 10% declined from 40% to 30%. But the trend was completely reversed since mid-1980s with all the increase in the income moving up to the rich top 10% while rest of the population experienced sharp decline in the share especially since the early 2000s.

Table 2 captures the growing inequality of incomes during the three decades under the neoliberal regime compared with the three decades of the prereform period. What is striking is that not only that all the rise in income was shifting to the top 10% or the steep decline in the share of the middle class from about one-half of the national income in the first 30 years to less than one-fourth in the later period. The classification of 'middle 40%' includes a substantial proportion of 'lower middle class' and a thin section of a relatively a rich urban middle class that enjoyed the benefits of the globalization. Thus, it is a clear phenomenon of "hollowing out" of the substantial section of the middle class as well. It is widely believed that it is the middle income group that helps to boost the demand and sustain economic growth. It would be interesting to see how the middle-income group is faring in China in comparison with India. Table 3 shows the pace of growth of the adult per capita income of different income groups and their respective shares in the total income generated during the period between 1980 and 2014 in India and China. China's overall per capita income during the period was three to four times higher is not surprising. But the cause for concern is that top 10% India has been appropriating two-thirds of the total income, leaving only one-third to the rest of the 90% comprising middle- and bottom-income groups, which certainly a case of extreme inequality in income distribution, while the China's story seems to the reserve with the top 10% getting less than one-third of the total income generated during the period. What is significant is that in China the middle 40% could get a share of 43% which is a substantial support for sustained demand and growth, while India's middle group ends with 23% which poses a serious question on the possibility of future sustained growth.

Table 3 Adult Per Capita Income Growth and the Share Captured from the Growth of Income: 1980–2014 in India and China (in percentages)

Income Group	Growth of Income		Share Captured From Growth of Income	
	India	China	India	China
Entire adult population (100%)	187	659	100	100
Top 10%	394	1074	66	29
Middle 40%	93	615	23	43
Bottom 50%	89	312	11	13

Source Chancel and Piketty (2017) and Alvaredo et al. (2018)

In spite of the methodological improvements by way of accessing innovative sources of data and novel ways of analysis, the unraveling of the social dimensions of inequality of outcomes and opportunities in India still remains relatively little explored. Though the AIDIS data provide certain broad trends on the social dimensions of inequality of consumption expenditure and to an extent wealth, the income dimension remains a dark area. Neither income tax data nor National Accounts could help in this regard. Collection of the comprehensive income data either as a part of the present NSSO surveys or through separate explicitly designed surveys becomes an urgent imperative for deeper understanding of the nature of inequality in India.

In recent years, there has been increasing number of studies on inequality in India. There are special issues of journals, and focused thematic reports with a comprehensive collection of studies, like, for example, *India Social Development Report 2018* with a theme "Rising Inequalities in India," (Haque and Reddy 2019). The complexity and the spread of deep rootedness of the nature of inequalities in India could be seen from the evidences brought as attempted to bring together in this report, in terms of differences by gender, interstate and intrastate, rural–urban, agricultural—nonagricultural, intra-agricultural and in access to employment, education and health facilities. And yet there is no resonance of the concern among the people and politics. There appears to be persistence of a false hope that adding a prefix "inclusive" to each program and depicting every decimal increase in growth rates as development could carry the day. There is still obstinate resistance to recognize the deep damage the growing inequality does to the social fabric of the country, and hence hardly any effort to face it head-on. The Government of India's performance in terms of efforts at reducing inequality could best be summed up in the following observation: "In 2015, the leaders of 193 governments promised to reduce inequality as part of the Sustainable Development Goals (SDGs). Without reducing inequality, meeting the SDG to eliminate poverty will be impossible. Now Development Finance International and Oxfam have produced the first index to measure the commitment of governments to reducing the gap between the rich and the poor. The index is based on a new database of indicators, covering 152 countries, which measures government action on social spending, tax and labour rights—three areas found to be critical to reducing the gap. This preliminary version of the Commitment to Reducing Inequality (CRI) Index finds that 112 of the 152 countries surveyed are doing less than half of what they could to tackle inequality. *Countries such as India and Nigeria do very badly overall*, and among rich countries, the USA does very badly. At the same time, countries such as Sweden, Chile, Namibia and Uruguay have taken strong steps to reduce inequality" (Oxfam 2017, emphasis added).

The dualistic nature of Indian society, perpetuated by the neglect of Dalits, Adivasis, and ethnic minorities, inequality in the distribution of education and health care and lack of these facilities in rural areas where the poor are concentrated, disguised unemployment, and low-labor productivity in agriculture, high incidence of open unemployment in urban areas, slow pace of growth of rural infrastructure and nonfarm activities, and above all inappropriate choices of investment, technology and policies come in the way of balanced and egalitarian social and economic development. Besides, the major challenge is the income and wealth inequalities that have been surging at an unprecedented pace. Unless India's policymakers come to grips with these problems, there will continue to be large pockets of poverty, high degree of economic inequality as well as continued marginalization of some social and ethnic groups. Political inequality among various social groups may further accentuate the problem, because unequal distribution of control over resources and of political influence would perpetuate institutions that protect the interests of the most powerful, to the detriment of the have-nots.

5 Policy Perspectives

Ever since the notion that inequality is only a transitory phenomenon and that it would wither away with growth and development is challenged, there has been a range of measures that have been commended as a part of the policy interventions, including policy shift that would envisage more space for state in the affairs of the economy. Fiscal policy assumes highest priority, followed by strengthening of labor market institutions. And of course, a kind of precondition for their effectiveness is social and political mobilization and a broad consensus against inequality. The fiscal measures suggested to reverse the growing inequality range from steeply progressive income taxation, taxes on wealth and estate duties, increased public expenditure on social goods such as education and health, fiscal transfers such as universal social security, basic income transfers, and so on (Piketty 2014; Baker 2014; IMF 2017a; Milanovic 2017; Oxfam 2018).

A study of the impact of tax and expenditure policies with a sample of 150 countries for the period between 1970 and 2009 (Martinez-Vazquez et al. 2012) shows that progressive personal income taxes and corporate taxes reduce income inequality. But it also found that the impact of corporate taxes eroded in open globalized economies. Interestingly, with the entrenchment of neoliberalism between 1990 and 2009, the net effect of tax policies was to increase inequality by 1.53 points of Gini, but it was moderated by political compulsions of welfare expenditure policies that brought a decrease of inequality by 0.97 of the Gini. However, with the background of decades of fiscal policies that prioritized fiscal consolidation at the expense of social expenditure and progressive taxation, the shift to progressive fiscal policy becomes challenging (UNDP 2013). There have been steep cuts in corporate taxation in the name of making domestic economies attractive for capital. Globally, average corporate tax rates were reduced by almost half from 49% in 1985 to 24% in 2019. For instance, in recent years, corporate tax in India has been reduced from 35 to 25%. Further, there has been a steep decline in income tax rates and tax burden (Shetty 2018). Since 1960s, countries that witnessed largest reductions in marginal income tax rates are also (like USA, UK) countries that have experienced the largest increase in top incomes, but there is no evidence that reduced tax rates increased growth rates. Interestingly, it shows that high-income earners respond to lower top tax rates, not by increasing productive work effort as pointed by the standard supply-side story but instead by finding ways to extract a larger share of economic pie at the expense of others in the economy (Saez 2017). In India, the marginal rates of income tax which reached a peak of over 75% in the early 1970s declined to about 60% by 1990, and since then it has been reduced down to 33% which is much lower than that of most of the developed countries.

There are two major challenges to the shift toward more progressive taxation measures to reverse the process of growing inequality. One is the need for political commitment to overcome the resistances to bringing back progressive income taxation from the present comfort of the rich which is used to the neoliberal low tax regimes. The second is an innovative restructuring of the entire income tax system that internalizes the emerging knowledge on the sources of inequality, which means a progressive tax system that differentiates "earned income" from "unearned income" or "rents," that which recognizes the role of inheritances in aggravating inequality, that which responds to the need for plugging the loopholes in the international tax system in which MNEs operate, and that which is designed with appropriate institutional mechanisms, both at the national and international levels to negotiate and implement the shift.

As pointed out earlier, the present research on sources of inequality has also thrown up new thinking on the concept of "income" and "wealth" and to differentiate "income" and "wealth" by their source for treatment of regulation as well as taxation. There is growing consensus that income from labor and income from capital should be differentiated and taxed differently. With the exception of the salaries and bonuses of employees like investment managers, most of the income from wages and salaries should be treated as "earned income" and subjected to relatively less steep rates of income tax. Most of the earnings from capital, with some exceptions, should be treated as "unearned" income and subjected to steeply progressive taxation. It is argued that major unearned income in the form of rents stem from government interventions in the economy that have the effect of redistributing income upward. The sources of such rental income would include financial sector, monopolies in pharmaceuticals, telecommunications, etc. Taxing these sources (rents) would act to an extent in reversing upward redistribution of income (Baker 2014). Stiglitz (2015) differentiates returns to capital into four types, viz., pure rate of interest, returns to risks like capital market speculation, excessive remuneration to the positions like investment managers, and rents arising from monopoly power and suggests steeply progressive taxation on such capital incomes. He also suggests that high levels of taxes on land (real estate) and capital gains on land would also reduce inequality by encouraging more investment into real economy and enhance growth. Atkinson (2015), based on his life-long experience in the study of inequality, made 15 comprehensive proposals toward public policy that would contain inequality. One that is of far-reaching significance is in terms of differential treatment of earned and unearned income. He suggested "Earned Income Discount," once the income is differentiated into "earned income," "capital gains," "interest," and "profit" for tax purposes. In effect, it would mean progressively steeper taxes with the increasing element of "unearned" nature in income.

One of the major proposals that is gaining wider support relates to inheritance and wealth taxes (Stiglitz 2015; Saez 2017; Atkinson 2015; The Economist 2017). Globally, there is a kind of paradox relating to inheritance tax policy. Even as the role of inheritances is seen as the increasing source of inequality of wealth, and consequently earning the epithete for the present capitalism as "patrimonial capitalism," there has been growing resistance to inheritance taxes in most of the countries. Except in Japan, there is decline in inheritance taxes, even as inheritances are increasing. For instance, flow of inheritances has tripled in France since 1950s, and among Europe's billionaires' half have inherited their wealth. And this proportion is rising. In OECD countries, share of inheritance taxes in public revenue declined from about 1% in 1960s to less than 0.5% presently. Many countries including India, Norway, Australia, Canada and Russia abolished inheritance tax, and (it is scheduled to go in USA by 2015) in the US (The Economist 2017). After a survey of the state of inheritance taxes across countries, The Economist (2017) concludes: "A fair and efficient tax system would seek to include inheritance taxes, not eliminate them." Atkinson (2015) suggested broader tax on wealth differentiated by source, namely, inheritance, gifts, and property with differential tax rates.

6 Inequality and Reforms in International Tax System

One of the major sources of tax revenue loss to both developed and developing countries is the international tax system, which enables the multinational enterprises to shift their profits from the countries where they earn to locations widely known as off-shore "tax havens" with low tax or hardly any tax. The evolution of tax havens has been made possible by the "arm's length" principles of international corporate tax system laid down under League of Nations almost a century ago. This system treats multinational enterprises as loosely connected "separate entities." This, it is by now, well known is a fiction. Multinationals with a wide network of their affiliates that are tightly connected by the present hyper technology of communications draw great strength by their "unitary" nature. But use this so-called "arms length" separate entity fiction to shift profits from their affiliates operating in high-tax locations to their affiliates in low-tax locations, causing enormous corporate tax losses to countries where the economic activity is actually carried out. There are varying estimates of tax losses caused to countries by the multinational enterprises under the facility of tax havens. These range from $500 billion to $600 billion a year, of which the share of the low-income countries could be as high as $200 billion (Shaxson 2019). Besides corporates, rich individuals also take advantage of tax havens where they could stash their illicit fortunes.

Though there have been growing reports of the corporate tax losses through the system of multinational enterprises being treated as "separate entities" not much concerted action was taken against it for a long time. But since 2008, financial crisis the world has woken up to the fact that tax losses though tax havens have been huge and required global action. The result has been several initiatives. One is the Common Reporting Standard (CRS), initiated by the OECD. This is a regime to exchange financial information automatically across the countries so as to help tax authorities track offshore holdings of their taxpayers. Though there are limitations, it is reported that by July 2019, the CRS enabled sharing of tax information by 90 countries on 47 million accounts with about 20–25% of tax haven deposits which also resulted in voluntary disclosures that yielded $95 billion additional tax revenues to OECD and the Group of 20, which includes India. The second initiative of OECD was the "base erosion and profit sharing" (BEPS) project, to realign taxation with economic substance. But it failed because it was within the old principle of "arm's length" that treats multinational enterprise affiliates as separate entities. The Independent Commission for the Reform of International Corporate Taxation (ICRICT), which includes scholars and tax experts, including Piketty and Stiglitz, has proposed an alternative to the failing BEPS system. The proposal is based on the fact that multinationals (MNCs) are groups of entities that are under a single management control and have a single set of owners and should therefore be taxed as "unitary firms." A unitary approach would mean apportioning MNC's global profits to different countries on the economic basis of their share in the combined global production and sales. The ICRICT proposed "unitary tax with formulary apportionment" (ICRICT 2019; Ocampo 2019), and it is considered as simpler, fairer, and more rational than the current system (Shaxson 2019). There has been wider support for change in the existing system. In March 2019, the then IMF Chief, Christine Lagarde called the "arms' length" principle "outdated" and "especially harmful to low-income countries." She urged "fundamental rethink" and move toward formula-based approach to allocate income for corporate taxation (Lagarde 2019). Hope is that change would come and help countries for better action against growing inequality through growing international pressure. The other dimension is the regular intervention of financial flows much of which hunts speculative profits from stock markets. There has been a revival of the demand for "Tobin Tax" or financial transactions tax like the one in force in countries like Japan (Piketty 2014; Baker 2014).

The other side of fiscal policy in addressing inequality relates to the public expenditure policy. The extent of fiscal redistribution as a corrective to inequality, besides progressive direct taxes, would depend on the "in-kind transfer spending (such as education and health), which can reduce the inequality of "full income" (that is disposable income adjusted for in-kind transfers). "In-kind transfers such as those for education and health also affect market income inequality over time by changing the distribution of human capital, including across generations by promoting social mobility" (IMF 2017a, p. 6). There is growing evidence on the relationship between expenditure on education and health and reduced inequality. A study of 13 developing countries shows that "spending on education and health lowers inequality and its marginal contribution to the overall decline in inequality is, on average, 69 percent" (Lustig 2015). There are other studies on the relationship between income inequality and education expansion. Educational expansion would reduce educational inequalities which in turn put strong downward pressure on income inequality (IMF 2017a, p. 9). Public expenditure toward achieving nationally appropriate social protection systems for all (ILO 2017) would also be a critical part of mitigating inequality.

7 Beyond Fiscal Policy

Atkinson, while strongly supporting the role of fiscal policy believes that reduced inequality cannot be achieved solely through fiscal measures (Atkinson 2015). Emphasizing the need for moving beyond tax and transfer instruments, Atkinson pleads for a radical policy to reduce inequality that engages the whole of government, would include, besides taxation, technology, employment, wages, and social security that would have an impact in reducing inequality. Though these proposals are made with specific reference to UK, these have wider policy relevance to most of the developed as well as developing countries. Atkinson argues that the direction of technological change need not be assumed as being entirely exogenous but could be subjected to policy control. Hence it should be the explicit concern of policymakers to invest in publicly funded research toward innovations in technology that would lead to employability of workers and take into consideration the human dimension of service provision. Since in a market economy, the balance of power is weighed against consumers and workers, the role of trade unions should be reinforced by founding a Social and Economic Council involving all the social partners. There should be a national pay policy consisting of two elements: a statutory minimum wage set at a living wage and a code of practice for pay above minimum wage, agreed as a part of "national conversation" involving the Social and Economic Council. The employment policy should aim at reduced unemployment and guarantee public employment at minimum wages for those who seek it. Social security measures should be strengthened and child benefit should be paid to all children. Atkinson was optimistic that these proposals are eminently doable within the capitalist system.

While the emerging fiscal and other policy measures provide a concrete basis to move toward mitigating inequalities, and achieving fair and inclusive growth, in countries like India the equally challenging task is to engage with deep-rooted inequality of opportunities because of centuries of history of widely prevalent social discrimination. Reducing horizontal inequalities, tackling social inclusion and ensuring equity in access to opportunities will further require strengthening the agency, voice and political participation of groups that experience disadvantage on account of their identity (UNDP 2013). Finally, the discussion of the policy strategies would be incomplete and end up as mere aspirational without any promise of its practical prospects, if we do not find any answers to the following questions: Is the social and political mobilization against inequality, and in favor of the shift in policy agenda possible in the face of present entrenched neoliberalism? Are there any recent instances of public intervention reversing the rising trend in inequality and moving toward more inclusive development?

For these questions, we do get fairly clear answers from the economic and political developments of one region in the world, i.e., Latin America. Roberts (2012) in his very illuminating study of politics of inequality and redistribution in Latin America provides a graphic picture of the developments with the neoliberal entrenchment in the last two decades of the twentieth century (1980s and 1990s) and the developments in the "post-adjustment" period (2002–2010). He calls the earlier period, 1980s and 1990s, as a period of "dual transitions" to political democracy and to market liberalization, and the latter period, 2000–2010, as the period of "repoliticisation of inequality" and redistribution. In the first period, there was an electoral turn in most of the political groups including left, and toward democratic governments but with political hegemonies. On the economic front, there was almost obsessive liberalization of trade, investment, and financial markets. The process of international integration was near complete (Maia 2014). There was privatization of public enterprises, shift in employment from formal to informal (UNCTAD 2011). By 1990s, 85% of job growth was informal in nature. There was increasing labor market segmentation, weakening of unions with sharp decline in trade union density. Labor market reforms were more towards flexibility, and health care increasingly shifted from state to private. There was welfare interventions first in the form of poverty relief and later in the form of conditional cash transfer to keep children in school. Marketization had demobilizing effect on collective activity despite democracy (Bellinger et al. 2011).

Economic downturn at the end of the twentieth century paved the way for political mobilization and leftist electoral victories since 1998. Between 1998 and 2011, there were leftist presidents in 11 different countries accounting for two-thirds of Latin American population. The "left" turn appears to be with a kind of Latin American characteristics: "…Latin America did not turn left politically because more people came to identify as leftist; it turned left because many citizens who did not identify themselves as leftist nevertheless began to vote for leftist candidates and parties" (Roberts 2012, p. 10). Another characteristic that was typical of Latin America was, in spite of neoliberal policies, citizens' emphasis was on state, and LA remained statist and there was strong support for state in enterprise ownership, job creation, health care, and citizen welfare. In the later period, social mobilization resulted in building up support for social democratic parties. Indigenous groups developed collective strength to militate for change, celebrating indigenity, developing horizontal identities, and foreign alliances across desperate ethnic groups. Evans (2017) observes that "inequalities increased if poor people internalize stigmatized identities, but through association and exposure to egalitarian discourses, people may revise their self perception and believe they deserved dignity." The revival of social mobilization from below and mass protest helped "repoliticize" inequality, "politicize" social deficits and bring redistributive policies to central place on the political agenda (Roberts 2012). The result was equity gains both under conservative governments as well as leftist ones. The positive trend toward reduced inequalities, and secure and better conditions of living for workers were witness across the region. LA that had high levels of inequality of per capita incomes experienced a declining trend from a Gini of 0.55 in 2000 to 0.496 in 2012, largely due to longer years of schooling, larger and more progressive transfer payments ranging from 17 to 21% of GDP, lower dependency ratio, and higher work participation rates especially of women (Lustig et al. 2015). Latin American experience of inequality reduction through progressive policy turn brings to the fore the role of social movements and ideational shifts. As Alice Evans (2017) hopes, publicizing Latin American collective success (during 2000–2010) in reducing inequality might embolden campaigns elsewhere for a movement against growing inequalities. Hopefully, these could be lessons for countries like India as well.

References

ADB. (2012). *Asian Development Outlook: Confronting Rising Inequality in Asia*. Manila: Asian Development Bank.

Alvaredo, Facundo., Lucas Chancel, Thomas Piketty, Emmanuel Saez and Gabriel Zucman (2018), World Inequality Report, World Inequality Lab.

Alvaredo, Facundo., Anthony B. Attkinson, Thomas Piketty, and Emmanuel Saez (2013) "The Top 1 percent in International and Historical Perspective", *Journal of Economic Perspectives*, Vol. 27, No. 3, Summer 2013, 3–20.

Anand, I and A. Thampi (2016) "Recent Trends in Wealth Inequality in India" *Economic and Political Weekly*, Vol. 51, No. 50.

Arrow, K., Bowles, Samuel, & Durlaf, Steven. (2000). *Introduction*. Meritocracy and Economic Inequality: Princeton University Press, Princeton, IX–XV.

Atkinson, B. A. (2015). *Inequality: What is to be done?*. London: Harvard University Press.

Baker, Dean (2014) "Economic Policy in a Post-Piketty World". Truthout, April 21.

Barbosa, Alexandre, de Fuilas., Maria Cristina Cacciamali, et al. (2016). *Growth, Labour and Inequality in Brazil and India: A Comparative Study*. Delhi: Oxford University Press.

Berg, Andrew G., & Ostry, Jonathan D. (2011). *Inequality and Understanding Unstable Growth: The Sides of the same coin?* (p. 8). International Monetary Fund, Washington, April: IMF Staff Discussion Note.

Berg, Jamine (Ed.). (2015). *Labour Markets, Institutions and Inequality: Building Just Societies in the 21st Century*. Geneva: Intenational Labour Organization.

Billinger, Paul, Jr, B., & Moises ARce, (2011). Protest and Democracy in Latin America's Market Era. *Political Research Quarterly, 64*(3), 688–704.

Chancel, Lucas. And Thomas Piketty (2017) "Indian Income Inequality, 1922–2014: From British Raj to Billionnaire Raj?" WID. World Working Paper Series N2017/11, Wealth and Income Database.

Corak, Miles (2013) "Income Inequality, Equality of Opportunity, and Intergenerational Mobility", *Journal of Economic Perspectives*, Vol. 27, No. 3, Summer 2013, 79–102.

Evans, A. (2017). "Politicising Inequalities: The Power of Ideas", Working Paper, Kings College, London, June 2017.

Gandhi, Aditi, & Walton, Michael. (2012). Where do India's Billionaires Get their Wealth? *Economic and Political Weekly, XLVII, 40,* 10–14.

Haque, T. and D.N. Reddy Eds. (2019) India Social Development Report 2018: Rising Inequalities in India, Council for Social Development, and Oxford University Press, New Delhi.

ICRICT (2019) A Roadmap to improve Rules for Taxing Multinationals, Independent Commission for the Reform of International Corporate Taxation.

ILO. (2017). *Global Wage Report 2016-17: Wage Inequality in the Workplace.* Geneva: International Labour Organisation.

IMF. (2007). *World Economic Outlook: Globalisation and Inequality.* Washington, October: International Monetary Fund.

IMF. (2017a). *Tracking Inequality.* International Monetary Fund, Washington DC, October: Fiscal Monitor.

IMF. (2017b). *IMF Fiscal Monitor: Tackling Inequality, October 2017.* Washington DC: International Monetary Fund.

Jacobs, D. (2015) "Extreme wealth is not merited", Oxfam Discussion Papers, www.oxfam.org, November.

Jaumotte, Florence, & Buitron, Carolina Osorio. (2015). Inequality and Labor Market Institutions. International Monetary Fund, Washington: IMF Staff Discussion Note.

Jayaraj, D., & Subramaniam, S. (2018). The Distribution of Household Assets in India: 1991–1992 to 2012–2013. *Indian Journal of Human Development, 12*(2), 181–203.

Jones, Gareth A. (2017) "The Geographies of Capital in the Twenty-First Century: Inequality, Political Economy, and Space", in Heather Boushey, et.al. edited, After Piketty: The Agenda for Economics and Inequality, Harvard University Press, Cambridge, Mass, 280–303.

Kuznets, Simon. (1955). Economic Growth and Income Inequality. *American Economic Review, 45*(1), 1–28.

Lagarde, Christina (2019) "An Overhaul of the International Tax System can wait no longer" *The Financial Times,* March 11.

Lanker, C., Daniel Gersyon Mawer, Maria Negre and Espen Beer Prydy (2019) "How Much Does Reducing Inequality Matter for Global Poverty?" Policy Research Working Paper, 8869, World Bank Group, Washington.

Lee, Sangheon. And Megan Gerecke (2012) "Inequality and Economic Growth Revisiting Kuznetsian Political Economy of Inequality", Keynote Paper on the theme "Wages and Wage Share" at the 54th Annual Conference of the Indian Society of Labour Economics, Varanasi, 20–22 December.

Lustig, Nora (2015) "The Redistributive Impact of Government Spending on Education and Health: Evidence from Thirteen Developing Countries in the Commitment to Equity Project", Commitment to Equity (CEQ) Working Paper No. 30, Tulana University.

Lustig, N., L. F. Lpez-Calva, E. Ortiz-Juarez (2015) "Deconstructing the Decline in Inequality in Latin America", in Basu, Kaushik and Joseph Stiglitz, (eds) Proceedings of IEA Round Table on Shared Prosperity and Growth, Palgrave-Macmillan.

Mahendra Dev, S (2017) "Inequality, Employment and Public Policy", Presidential Address, 59th Annual Conference, The Indian Society of Labour Economics, Thiruvananthapuram, 16–18 December.

Maia, Alexandre Gori & Esther Menezes (2014) "Economic Growth, Labour and Productivity in Brazil and the United States: A Comparative Analysis" *Revista de Economia Politica,* (Review of Economics and Politics), Vol. 34, No. 2, Sao Paulo, April/June.

Martinez-Vazquez, Jorge., Violata Vulovic and Blanca Moreno Dodson (2012) "The Impact of Tax and Expenditure Policies on Income Distribution: Evidence from Large Panel of Countries", (Hacienda Publica Espaniola) *Review of Public Economics,* 200(2012), 95–130.

Milanovic, B. (2016) "The Question of India's Inequality", http://glineq.blogspot.in/2016/05/the-question-of-india's-inequality.html.

Milanovic, B. (2017) "Increasing Capital Income Share and Its Effects on Personal Income Inequality", in Heather Boushey et.al. edited After Piketty: The Agenda for Economics and Inequality, Harvard University Press, Cambridge, Mass. 235–258.

Ocampo, J. (2019). "Arresting Tax Avoidance by MNCs" *The Hindu Business Line*, November 13.

Oxfam (2017) "Great Expectations: Is the IMF turning words into action on inequality?", Oxfam Briefing Paper, www.Oxfam.org.

Oxfam (2018) Reward Work, Not Wealth, www.Oxfam.org.

Piketty, T (2014) Capital in Twenty First Century, Harvard University Press

Piketty, T. (2017) "Toward a Reconciliation between Economics and Social Sciences" in Boushey, H. et.al. ed. op.cit., pp. 543–566.

Rajan, R. G. (2010). *Fault Lines: How Hidden Fractures Still Threaten the World Economy*. Princeton University Press: Princeton.

Reddy, D. Narasimha (2019) "Persistent Inequalities in India: Challenges in Overcoming Inequalities of Opportunities" in Haque and Reddy eds., Op.Cit.

Roberts, K. M. (2012). The Politics of Inequality and Redistribution in Latin America's Post-Adjustment Era", United Nations University and World Institute for Development Economics Research, Working Paper No. 2012/08.

Saez, E. (2017). Research Agenda after Capital in Twenty-First Century. in Heather Bourshey et.al. edited After Piketty: The Agenda for Economics and Inequality, Harvard University Press, Cambridge Mass, 304–321.

Sen, A. (1973). *On Economic Inequality*. Oxford: Clarenden Press.

Shaxson, N. (2019). "The billions attracted by tax havens do harm to sending and receiving nations alike", Finance and Development, September 2019.

Shetty, S. L. (2018)."Neglect of Growing Income and Asset Inequalities: A Flaw in Public Policy Discourses in India", *Indian Journal of Human Development*, (12(2), 149–180.

Stiglitz, Joseph, & E., (2015). The Origins of Inequality, and Policies to Contain It. *National Tax Journal, 68*(2), 425–448.

The Economist (2014). Our Crony-Capitalism Index: Planet Plutocrat: The Countries where Politically connected businessmen are most likely to prosper. *The Economist*, March 15.

The Economist (2017). Briefing Taxing Inheritances, *The Economist*, 25th November 2017.

Van, T. K., & Simun, S. (2012). Income Inequality as a cause for the Great Recession? A Survey of Current Debates, Conditions of Work and Employment Series No. 39, International Labour Office, Geneva.

UNCTAD. (2011). *Evolution of Income Inequality: Different Time Perspectives and Dimensions*. Trade and Development Report, UNCTAD: Chapter III.

UNDP. (2013). *Humanity Divided: Confronting Inequality in Developing Countries*. New York, November: United Nations Development Programme.

Vakulabharanam, V. (2010). Does Class Matter? Class Structure and Worsening Inequality in India. *Economic and Political Weekly, 45*(29), 67–76.

White, K. (2003). Inequality and the Case for Redistribution: Aristotle to Sen. In: Paper at History of Economics Society Annual meeting, June 4–7, 2003, Duke University, http://history-of-economics.org/wp-content/uploads/2016/12/2003/pdf.

Growth, Inequality and Labour Force Participation

Arup Mitra

Abstract The Indian economy has experienced high growth in recent times which has been accompanied by a reduction in poverty with rising inequality. Rising inequality is rooted in the nature of growth itself which is highly skewed towards the service sector. The nature of service sector in itself is of a type which contributes to rising inequality. This is routed through little expansion in employment opportunities and declining labour force participation. It is argued that employment is central to the inequality question.

1 Economic Growth

During the reform period, particularly in the 2000s, economic growth shot up to an unprecedented high level until at least the global financial crisis occurred. Rodrik and Subramanian (2005) further argued that growth was triggered in the reform period by an attitudinal shift on the part of the national government towards a pro-business (as opposed to pro-liberalization) approach. However, the composition of growth has been primarily dominated by the services sector. Contrasting the historical experience of many developed countries, the share of service sector in total value added increased much before the industry could rise to a reasonable high level. Rapid productivity growth in the services sector contributed to an accelerated economic growth in India (Goldar and Mitra 2010).

However, the dominance of the services/tertiary sector before the secondary sector's relative size could outweigh that of other sectors did invite concerns at least in the past (Rao 1954, 1986). Bhattacharya and Mitra (1989) urged that higher is the discrepancy between the industry and agriculture growth, the higher is the growth of services across Indian states, implying that higher levels of per capita income originating from industrialization leads to higher demand for services. In a later work, Bhattacharya and Mitra (1990) argued that a wide disparity arising

A. Mitra (✉)
Faculty of Economics, Institute of Economic Growth, Delhi 110007, India
e-mail: arup@iegindia.org

N. K. Mishra (ed.), *Development Challenges of India After Twenty Five Years of Economic Reforms*, India Studies in Business and Economics,
https://doi.org/10.1007/978-981-15-8265-3_6

between the growth of income from services and commodity-producing sector tends to result in inflation and/or higher imports leading to the adverse balance of trade. This is particularly so if the tertiary sector value added expands because of rising income of those who are already employed and not due to income accruing to the new additions to the tertiary sector workforce. In other words, if expansion in value-added and employment generation both take place simultaneously within the tertiary sector, there will be a commensurate increase in demand for food and other essential goods produced in the manufacturing sector. However, if the expansion of the tertiary sector results only from the rise in income of those who are already employed in this sector, the additional income, as per Angel's law, would largely generate demand for luxury goods and other imported goods since the demand for food and other essential items has already been met (Bhattacharya and Mitra 1989, 1990).

A variety of other reasons have also been put forth to rationalize the growth of the services sector. Factors like increasing role of the government in implementing the objectives of growth, employment generation and poverty reduction, expansion of defence and public administration, the historical role of the urban middle class in wholesale trade and distribution and demonstration effects in developing countries creating demand patterns similar to those of high-income countries have been highlighted to offer a rationale for the expansion of the tertiary sector (Panchamukhi et al. 1986). As the elasticity of service consumption with respect to total consumption expenditure is higher than unity even in countries with very low per capita consumption (Sabolo 1975), the rapid growth of the tertiary sector has been further rationalized in terms of a strong demand base existing in the economy. Besides, sub-sectors like transport, communication and banking do contribute significantly to the overall economic growth as they constitute the basic physical and financial infrastructure. Especially the role of information technology (IT) and business process outsourcing services (BPOS) in enhancing the economic growth is said to be significant (World Bank 2004). In addition, the new growth theorists indicate that skill-intensive activities exert positive externalities on the rest of the economy, and thus the concentration of new activities in the tertiary sector with the initiation of IT industry can raise productivity and growth (Romer 1990). All this tends to suggest that services too hold the possibility of playing the role of engine of growth.

It may be important to identify certain other factors like urbanization, trade and investment and, more importantly, increasing inequality, which possibly contributed to the rapid growth of the tertiary sector and led to the divergence between the relative size of the tertiary and the secondary sectors. In India, for example, public consumption of services and consequently the pay hikes of the government and the semi-government employees would explain the high growth of services during the second half of the nineties. However, other than that among the demand-side factors it is the export of services which recorded the most spectacular growth over 1997–2005 (Rakshit 2007). Mitra (2011) further noted that the employment effects of such rapid growth in services exports are rather limited both in the formal and the informal sectors.

Besides, the ratio of household purchase of services to private consumption of services has gone up speedily during this period. Household purchase of services amounting to almost 40 per cent of services GDP has played an important role in accelerating the growth of the tertiary sector. The household income elasticity of services (estimated at 1.5 over the 10-year period) is indeed too high for a poor country like India and this has resulted primarily from an increasing inequality of income and introduction of a whole spectrum of new services which households have started consuming (Rakshit 2007). Hence, factors affecting income distribution and household preferences other than the government consumption and exports need to be considered in explaining the dominance of the tertiary sector over the industry.

From policy angle, trade and financial sector reforms and lifting of barriers to entry of private enterprises in certain services which were earlier reserved for the public sector have also played a major role in providing an impetus to the tertiary sector growth in India. In her analysis of developing countries, Joshi (2004) noted that urbanization raised the share of the tertiary sector in total employment.

One important aspect, which needs to be highlighted in this context, is a positive relationship between the level of per capita income and the intensity of use of services in manufacturing industries (Francois and Reinert 1996). Banga and Goldar (2007) in the Indian context noted that the importance of services as an input to production in the manufacturing sector increased considerably in the nineties compared to the eighties. As the authors pointed out, the real value of services used in manufacturing grew at the rate of 0.4 per cent per annum in the 1980s and the growth rate increased sharply to around 16 per cent per annum in the nineties. Economic policy changes in the nineties, particularly the trade reforms, created a condition favourable for increased use of services in manufacturing.

The positive spillover effects of the services-led growth on the rest of the economy cannot be ignored either. It contributed to the growth in other sectors too (Mitra and Schmidt 2008). For example, the growth in ICT led to a rise in TFPG in the manufacturing sector as well. But, the time series analysis (Goldar and Mitra 2010) pursued on sectoral shares of the GDP indicates that industry's capacity to impact on the services sector is much more than the services' impact on the industry. Hence, the key to stabilization in economic growth is the growth in the industrial sector through liberalization of economic policy affected the nature of India's growth pattern, providing a boost to the services sector. Besides, the welfare implications of the services-led growth are quite serious. There is not much scope for the productive absorption of the unskilled and semi-skilled workers since the high productivity segment within this sector is highly skill-intensive. The secondary effects on unskilled labour market are actually very low.

2 Inequality Issues

Economic growth in India has been associated with rising inequality as suggested by several indirect indicators. Unfortunately, in the Indian context, we do not have information on income distribution and therefore it is difficult to measure income inequality over time. However, the National Sample Survey Organization gives us data on consumption expenditure and the distribution of households based on expenditure size classes. From this, the expenditure inequality has been estimated though it is believed to be much less than the income inequality. Since the upper income households tend to save more and spend less, the expenditure inequality is usually a gross underestimate. Nevertheless, there is evidence in favour of rising inequality over time across several states.

According to the World Bank, between 1994 and 2005, the income share held by the highest 10 per cent of the population increased from 26 per cent to 28.3 per cent, while that of the bottom 20 per cent decreased from 9.09 per cent to 8.64 per cent. According to the OECD, between 1993 and 2008, India'sGini coefficient increased from 0.32 to 0.38. As per the Human Development Report (HDR) 2013, India ranked 136th (134th in 2011) in the Human Development Index (HDI). Strikingly, when the HDI is adjusted for inequality, the index loses its value by as much as 29.3 per cent.[1] Inequality in earnings has doubled in India over the last two decades, making it the worst performer on this count of all emerging economies. The top 10 per cent of wage earners now make 12 times more than the bottom 10 per cent up from a ratio of six in the 1990s. Moreover, wages are not smoothly spread out even through the middle of the distribution. The top 10 per cent of earners make almost five times more than the median 10 per cent, but this median 10 per cent makes just 0.4 times more than the bottom 10 per cent.[2] India's reform process resulted in opportunities that could be taken advantage of by a limited few or those who had access to resources. The inequality is being perpetuated by unequal access to health and education between the poor and the rich. Inequality in access to education is so glaring, that in HDR 2013, India's education index loses more than 40 per cent of its value once adjusted for inequality. In other words, education and health inequality are much sharper than expenditure inequality. Among many other indicators India's inequality in education and India's poorest people who don't have access to basic needs like food and clean water, and in huge numbers die from starvation, malnutrition, and treatable diseases, are glaring distortions of development.[3] Many states reported a rise in inequality over 2004–05 and 2010–11. At the all India level growth during this period turns out to around 7 per cent per annum but this growth has been associated with a rise in inequality both in the rural and urban areas. India's Gini coefficient has gone up from 0.26 to 0.28 and from 0.35 to 0.37 in the rural and urban areas respectively. There is evidence of the growing concentration of wealth among the elite. The consumption of the top 20 per cent of households grew at almost 3 per cent per year in the 2000s as compared to 2 per cent in the 1990s, while the growth in consumption of the

[1] K. K. Kundu (2013) "India has a problem with inequality, and it won't be solved easily", May 25, *Business standard.* https://www.business-standard.com/article/opinion/india-has-a-problem-with-inequality-and-it-won-t-be-solved-easily-113052500705_1.html.

[2] Times of India, December 7, 2011.

[3] Ground Truth by Charles M. Sennott. https://www.globalpost.com/dispatches/globalpost-blogs/groundtruth/india-education-increasing-inequality.

bottom 20 per cent of households remained unchanged at 1 per cent per year as per the consumption expenditure surveys of the National Sample Survey Organisation.[4]

In fact, at the state level, we get to see a very mixed picture. Many states registered a rapid growth and witnessed a decline in inequality in either rural or urban areas. On the other hand, there are states which with rapid growth experienced a rise in inequality over time. The relationship between the change in inequality between 2004–05 and 2011–12 and per capita economic growth rate over the same period across the Indian states indicates that higher is the growth, the lower is the extent of rise in inequality.[5] However, expenditure inequality, as mentioned above, is usually underestimated and therefore, the expected positive relationship between growth and income inequality may have existed.

As regards the relationship between growth and inequality we see a positive association in the rural context while its impact is insignificant in the urban areas. Possibly because rural areas are at lower levels of growth, inequality tends to rise conforming to Kuznet's observation. On the whole, the cross-sectional picture suggests that with economic growth inequality tends to rise only in the rural areas, while in the urban areas which shows higher levels of growth than the rural areas, inequality does not necessarily rise.

Based on the cross-sectional data economic growth is seen to reduce poverty, though the role of other factors is also important. Inequality and poverty are mostly unrelated. In the equation for poverty being a function of growth and inequality both (Table 1), inequality again shows no effect except in the urban context for the year 2004–05 where it takes a positive coefficient as one would expect, i.e. with an increase in inequality poverty tends to rise. Theses results are seen, as mentioned above, from the cross-sectional data. Otherwise, in the process of growth inequality seems to have gone up over time.

One important indicator of gross inequality is an overwhelming proportion of workers engaged in the informal sector. 'Employment problem' in the Indian context cannot be conceptualized merely in terms of open unemployment rate because many cannot afford to remain unemployed for long. On the other hand, the set of working poor is prevalent, implying residual absorption of workforce in low productivity informal sector activities. Even in the non-agricultural activities, the incidence of the informal sector employment is over and above 70 per cent (NSS 2009–10). The set of informal workers is extremely large which includes the self-employed in the informal sector (ranging from street vendors to those who operate micro enterprises with less than ten workers), regular hired workers in the petty enterprises in the informal sector and casual and contractual workers both in the informal and formal sectors without any employment or social security.

The services led-growth is an important factor which led to a rise in inequality in the process of growth and the rise in inequality further led to a growth in services' consumption by the middle- and higher income groups. The focus of government

---

[4]Times of India, December 7, 2011.

[5]Change in inequality = 0.054 – 0.0055 growth rate in per capita Net State Domestic Product.
(2.97)* (−2.03)* Adj R 2 = 0.093.

Table 1 Poverty, growth and inequality

Indep Var	Dep Var RPOV04-05	Dep VarUPOV04-05	Dep Var RPOV11-12	Dep VarUPOV11-12	Dep Var RPOV04-05	Dep VarUPOV04-05	Dep Var RPOV11-12	Dep VarUPOV11-12
PCNETSDP04-05	−0.0005 (−2.96)**	−0.0004 (−3.85)**			−0.0006 (−2.60)**	−0.0004 (−2.27)**		
PCNETSDP10-11			−0.0003 (−3.71)**	−0.0002 (−3.81)**			−0.0004 (−2.62)**	−0.0003 (−2.17)**
RLR04-05	83.43 (1.34)				88.19 (1.41)			
URL04-05		57.35 (2.01)*				57.71 (1.96)**		
RLR11-12			19.50 (0.37)				15.95 (0.30)	
ULR11-12				5.78 (0.25)				3.72 (0.16)
URBAN2001					0.17 (0.93)	−0.0103 (−0.08)		
URBAN2011							0.16 (0.82)	0.06 (0.43)
Constant	28.42 (2.17)**	15.31 (1.76)*	30.30 (2.49)***	20.12 (2.63)**	27.21 (2.06)**	15.22 (1.70)	30.71 (2.50)**	20.62 (2.62)**
Adj R2	0.18	0.32	0.31	0.29	0.18	0.30	0.30	0.27

Note R for rural and U for urban, POV for poverty and LR for Lorenz Ratio (inequality). PCNETSD is per capita net state domestic product. URBAN is the percentage of population in urban areas

Source Author's calculation

policy has been on the services sector. In the policy circle, there is a strong view that China may specialize in the production and export of manufacturing products while India would pursue on the lines of services activities. However, the services-led growth has serious implications in terms of employment generation and inequality. In the high-productivity services sector, the labour demand exists mainly for those who are highly skilled. Hence, the unskilled and semi-skilled labour remained mostly outside the purview of growth except for some nominal secondary effects of the high-productivity services sector.

The role of industry in generating employment opportunities particularly for the unskilled variety of the workforce is much stronger than that of the high-productivity services sector which is geared to absorbing the educated and skilled workers. Though this sector through secondary effects could generate employment opportunities for the unskilled and semi-skilled workers to some extent (Mitra and Schmid 2008), the manufacturing sector holds a much greater potential to employment generation and consequently in reducing inequality, as we have learnt from the historical experience of the developed nations. However, in the Indian context, the spread of the industrial sector has been highly limited being confined to a few states only. Other than this spatial aspect, the adoption of capital-intensive technology also restricted the employment growth in the organized/registered (a synonym for the formal) manufacturing sector. Import of technology from the developed countries, which has become cheaper in the wake of import liberalization, holds the possibility of adding to economic growth undoubtedly. However, the technology which is imported from abroad is mostly capital intensive in nature because it was invented to suit the economies characterized by labour scarcity. Import of such technology while contributing to growth does not necessarily generate employment opportunities, rather it reduces the labour content per unit of output (Kato and Mitra 2008).

On the whole, though economic growth has been quite fast and, at the same time, the incidence of poverty has declined considerably notwithstanding a rise in inequality the missing link between growth and poverty reduction in terms of fast employment growth is definitely a major concern. The overall employment growth scenario is so disheartening that it is difficult to believe that the percolation effect of growth occurred to benefit the poor (Table 2).[6] Not enough attention has been paid to improving the quality of the labour-intensive manufacturing goods. The most surprising part is the rise in capital intensity even in the so-called labour-intensive organized manufacturing sector. Import of capital-intensive technology even in labour-intensive industries has led to such sluggish growth in employment. Though labour market reforms have not been carried out in India on a significant scale, yet several indirect routes were followed to allow the firms to introduce labour market flexibility without providing labour with any safety net. This seems to have aggravated overall inequality and wage inequality especially.

[6]The overall disheartening employment generation has been further exacerbated between 2009–10 and 2017–18 as reported by PLFS, 2018. Since, the argument does not change even with results of PLFS, the latter is not used in analysis.

Table 2 Long-run growth rate in employment (1983–2009–2010) % p.a

Categories	Usual Status (ps + ss)	Weekly Status	Daily Status
Rural Male	1.6	1.7	1.7
Rural Female	0.8	1.8	1.4
Urban Male	3.0	3.1	3.2
Urban Female	2.6	3.3	3.3
Total	1.7	2.1	2.0

Note Based on NSS per thousand distribution applied to population figures derived from census estimates
Source Key Indicators of Employment and Unemployment in India, 2009–10, NSS (66/10), Ministry of Statistics and Programme Implementation, Government of India, June 2011 and Employment and Unemployment Situation in India, 2004–05, (Part-I), NSS 61st Round, Report No. 515(61/10/1), National Sample Survey Office, Ministry of Statistics and Programme Implementation, Government of India, September 2006.

The other issue relates to enrolment and skill formation. While the jobs are increasingly becoming skilled, the supply of labour is much in excess of demand in the unskilled category. In spite of a rise in the enrolment ratio, the skill gap has risen considerably. The efforts of the government to raise literacy and enrolment cannot be discredited. However, when it comes to the quality of education there is a sharp discrepancy between what is available for the low-income households and what can be accessed by the middle and high-income households. Education inequality is a major cause of income inequality. The quality of education available for the low-income households is extremely poor which does not enable the labour to get absorbed in high-productivity jobs.

Though in the rural areas the employment guarantee programmes were initiated there are severe leakages. On the positive side, these programmes raised the rural wage rate and provided consumption support to several households below the poverty line. However, these programmes were carried out in a haphazard manner and hence did not help asset creation either at the household or community level. Moreover, these programmes are confined to rural areas only. In the urban context, there is no major employment programme though there is the need for such programmes given the vast size of the urban informal sector, having considerable overlaps with urban poverty.

3 Labour Market Participation

Turning to labour market participation the male workforce participation rates for all ages are seen to be relatively high and are nearly 50 per cent both in the rural and in the urban areas if we consider the main or usual principal status workers (Table 3).

Table 3 Workforce Participation Rate (WFPR) and Labour Force Participation Rate (LFPR)

Category	WFPR (%) Population Census-2011	LFPR (%) Labour Bureau-2011–12
Rural Male	41.6 (17.5)	79.4 (6.4)
Rural Female	16.7 (53.2)	33.9 (48.0)
Urban Male	48.7 (15.5)	73.7 (7.6)
Urban Female	11.9 (36.0)	19.1 (46.9)
Persons Rural	29.5	57.9
Persons Urban	30.9	48.0
All Males	43.8	77.9
All Females	15.2	30.0
All Persons All Areas	29.9	55.4

Note (1) Though the Labour Bureau (LB) estimates refer to the year 2011–12—close to the population census year, 2011—they are not comparable with each other because the population census estimates are work participation rates for all age groups covering only the main (equivalent to the usual principal status) workers whereas the LB estimates are for age groups 15 and above and they cover all workers (usual principal and subsidiary status) and those who are unemployed
(2) Figures in parentheses are the coefficient of variation based on the state-level data.
Source Population Census, 2011 and Labour Bureau, 2011–12.

Secondly, the inter-state variations measured in terms of coefficient of variation are limited (17.5 and 15.5 per cent in the rural and urban areas, respectively). On the other hand, the female participation rates are significantly lower than their male counterparts (Table 3) and more so in the urban areas, implying that the rural–urban differentials in the case of women are more pronounced than in the case of males. Besides, the inter-state variations are sizable in the case of females, reflecting the influence of economic, social and cultural factors (coefficient of variation being 53.2 and 36.0 per cent in the rural and urban areas, respectively). The participation rates in the north-eastern and the southern regions, for example, are considerably higher than the northern states. A relatively lower magnitude of variation in the urban areas may be taken to signify the possibility of convergence (to a limited extent though), while the dominance of the social factors in the rural areas can be said to be more prominent. But the interpretation can be quite erroneous: the female work participation rates being by and large lower in the urban areas than in the rural areas indicate the limited impact of education on participation in the face of social factors. In fact, why the participation rate of Indian urban women is still so low, given that the per capita income and the educational attainment levels are higher than their rural counterparts, is an important research question. Participation rates and per capita income do not suggest any significant positive relationship in the case of females though among males such a pattern can be somewhat deciphered. In relation to females, only a subset of the cross-sectional observations (at the state level) at the most may conform to this pattern.

In terms of determinants, the study by Mitra and Okada (2018) clearly brings out the importance of infrastructure, education and health and urbanization on labour force participation of both the gender. This, in turn, points to three types of factors which are instrumental in resulting enhanced participation rate. The first set refers to the creation of greater volume of jobs motivating participation, the second enhances the ability of the individuals to participate and the third, the most important one, facilitates the accessibility of the capable ones to the locations where jobs are available. Hence, strategies for creating clusters with greater employment potentials (which in turn is cost-effective in making pro-poor growth happen), concerted efforts for human capital formation and investments to remove barriers between jobs and their seekers need to be pursued aggressively.

The negative impact of fertility and household size on rural female work participation comes out sharply: greater domestic burdens in large households do not allow women to participate explicitly in the labour market. Though the urbanization level does not show a positive effect on rural women participation at the state level, the beneficial effects are evident at the district level for both the gender. On the other hand, in the urban context, the participation rates of both females and males vary positively with the level of urbanization. In other words, the urban areas in states and districts with higher levels of urbanization unravel higher levels of participation both for females and males in comparison to the states or districts with lower levels of urbanization, revealing the agglomeration effects. With a greater concentration of infrastructure and activities, labour demand tends to increase.

While industrialization and growth in services both show a positive effect on participation, though very mildly, especially in the case of urban women, growth shows a rising impact only in the case of urban males. Also, there is evidence of poverty induced participation in agricultural activities, suggesting clearly the importance of rural diversification for participation to pick up in the rural context. Hence, from the policy point of view, a great deal will have to be done in terms of building infrastructure, initiating employment-oriented industrialization and encouraging rural diversification.

References

Banga, R., & Goldar, B. (2007, June 30). Contribution of services to output growth and productivity in Indian manufacturing: Pre and post reforms. *Economic and Political Weekly, 42*, 2769–2777.

Bhattacharya, B. B., & Mitra, A. (1989). Agriculture–industry growth rates: Widening disparity: An explanation. *Economic and Political Weekly, 24*(34), 1963–1970.

Bhattacharya, B. B., & Mitra, A. (1990). Excess growth of tertiary sector in Indian economy: Issues and implications. *Economic and Political Weekly, 25*(44), 2445–2450.

Francois, J., & Reinert, K. A. (1996). The role of services in the structure of production and trade: Stylized facts from a cross-country analysis. *Asia-Pacific Economic Review, 2*(I), 35–43.

Goldar, B. N., and Mitra, A. (2010). Productivity increase and changing sectoral composition: Contribution to economic growth in India. In P. B. Nayak, B. N. Goldar, & P. Agarwal (Eds.), *India's economy and growth: Essays in honour of V.K.R.V. Rao* (pp. 35–68). New Delhi: Sage.

Joshi, S. (2004, September 11). Tertiary sector-driven growth in India: Impact on employment and poverty. *Economic and Political Weekly,* pp. 4175–4178.

Kato, A., & Mitra, A. (2008). Imported technology and employment: Evidence from panel data on Indian manufacturing firms. In S. R. Hashim & N. S. Siddharthan (Eds.), *High-tech industries, employment and global competitiveness* (pp. 180–194). New Delhi: Routledge.

Mitra, A. (2011). Trade in services: Impact on employment in India. *The Social Science Journal, 48*(1), 72–93.

Mitra, A., & Okada, A. (2018). *Labour market participation in India: A region-and gender-specific study*. Springer.

Mitra, A., & Schmid, J. (2008). Growth and poverty in India: Emerging dimensions of the tertiary sector. *Service Industries Journal, 28* (8), 1–22 (Routledge).

Panchamukhi, V. R., Nambiar, R. G., & Metha, R. (1986, December). *Structural change and economic growth in developing countries*. Paper presented at the VIII World Economic Congress of the International Economic Association Theme 4, New Delhi.

Rakshit, M. (2007, February). Services-led growth: The Indian experience. *Money and Finance, 3,* 91–126.

Rao, V. K. R. V. (1954). Changes in India's national income – A static economy in progress, cited in S. Sivasubramonian's PhD thesis on National income of India 1900–01 to 1946–47, Doctoral dissertation, Delhi University, New Delhi.

Rao, V. K. R. V. (1986). *Balance between agriculture and industry in economic development*. New Delhi: Sage Publications.

Rodrik, D., & Subramanian, A. (2005). From Hindu growth to productivity surge: The mystery of the Indian growth transition. *IMF Staff Papers, 52*(2), 193–228.

Romer, P. M. (1990). Endogenous technological change. *Journal of Political Economy, 98*(3), 71–102.

Sabolo, Y. (1975). *Indian service industries*. Geneva: ILO.

World Bank. (2004). *Sustaining India's services revolution: Access to foreign markets, domestic reform and international negotiations*. Bangalore: South Asia Region.

Inclusiveness of Economic Growth in Uttar Pradesh

Nripendra Kishore Mishra and Manish Kumar Singh

Abstract The introduction of neo-liberalism in most of the developing countries raged the growth–inequality debate. It is evident from various available literatures that economic growth has been used as a major instrument to reduce poverty but, this expansion has been also accompanied by rising inequality in many developing countries including India. In order to deal with growing inequality, the major aim of India's Eleventh Five-year Plan was inclusive growth. In India, the picture at sub-national level is completely different because many states, especially the BIMARU (Bihar, Madhya Pradesh, Rajasthan and Uttar Pradesh) states, are lagging behind in both traditional and economical terms hence, a disaggregated analysis at sub-national level becomes necessary. This paper examined the impact of growth and inequality on poverty reduction by decomposing the change in poverty into growth effect and redistribution effect and estimating the pro-poor growth index and poverty equivalent growth rate for the rural and urban Uttar Pradesh using the CES 1993–94 (50th round), CES 2004–05 (61st round) and CES 2011–12 (68th round) data sets. The result indicates that poverty rate has highly declined in 2004–05 to 2011–12 as compared to 1993–94 to 2004–05 for both rural and urban area and effect of growth has dominant on poverty reduction in each time period. Interestingly, the growth of rural Uttar Pradesh has been inclusive during the period of 2004–05 to 2011–12, whereas in the urban area, increasing inequality hinders this inclusiveness.

1 Introduction

The growth–inequality debate has gained centre stage following the publication of Thomas Piketty's book *Capital in the Twenty-first Century* in 2013. This debate has been raging for almost three decades since the introduction of neo-liberalism in

N. K. Mishra (✉) · M. K. Singh
Department of Economics, Banaras Hindu University, Varanasi, India
e-mail: nripendra.mishra@gmail.com

M. K. Singh
e-mail: rathourmani92@gmail.com

N. K. Mishra (ed.), *Development Challenges of India After Twenty Five Years of Economic Reforms*, India Studies in Business and Economics,
https://doi.org/10.1007/978-981-15-8265-3_7

most developing countries as a means to bring them out of poverty. Expansion in the world output (or growth) has no doubt witnessed a decline in absolute poverty, as measured by Head Count Ratio (HCR), in many developing countries. However, the period of high growth has also been accompanied by growing inequality, or simply speaking, accumulation of wealth in the hands of a chosen few. This has also been the experience of India, which has experienced high economic growth with growing inequality (Chancel and Piketty 2017; Himanshu 2018). While there has been a reduction in poverty in the last two decades, the situation has become worse for the group at the bottom of income distribution. The current focus on inequality largely emanates from an observation that the recent economic growth in many countries has disproportionately benefitted the upper income groups, while the lower income groups have received a lesser share of Gross Domestic Product (GDP). The expansion of GDP has resulted in some income growth in lower income groups by default and resulted in the reduction of poverty as measured by the standard poverty line and HCR. The consequence of this has been high growth accompanied by a rise in inequality and some decline in poverty. Had it been just the opposite, where growth disproportionately benefitted the lower income groups, the outcome would have been high growth accompanied by a reduction in inequality and drastic decline (or complete removal) in poverty. This brings into question the nature of high growth experienced by many developing countries and its relationship with poverty, which is often discussed in the framework of 'inclusive growth'. While economic growth means only a high level of output or income irrespective of its distribution, inclusive growth aims at providing benefits of growth to every section of the society. There are two possible routes to achieve inclusive growth; either focus on the process that actual growth includes many people who participated in that growth or focus on the outcomes of the growth process (Klasen 2010). Inclusive growth has an indirect relationship with pro-poor growth because the ultimate aim of both these concepts is to reduce poverty and inequality. The debate on pro-poor growth originated from the celebrated work of Chenery et al. (1979), where the focus was on redistribution with growth. This model criticized the trickle-down hypothesis, which claimed that growth itself would reduce poverty. While the term inclusive growth was never defined at that time, it came to be known as 'pro-poor' during the 1990s. Pro-poor growth can be defined as the growth which provides better opportunities to the poor in order to uplift their economic conditions (IMF et al. 2000; OECD 2001). Kakwani et al. (2004) defined pro-poor growth as one which benefits the poor proportionately more than the non-poor. Thus, it shifted attention to the extent of income gains of the poor from growth.

India has experienced an unprecedented high rate of growth in recent times that has been accompanied by poverty reduction but rising inequality. But, it is yet not clear how far the growth has been inclusive and what are the extents of income gains of the poor. That is why the major aim of the country's Eleventh Plan (2007–12) was inclusive growth to deal with these inequalities and to promote the overall well-being (GOI 2011b). The proposed inclusiveness is difficult to assess because of the three reasons which may be summarized as follows.

(a) Growth is multidimensional in nature,
(b) the data on inclusiveness can be found only after a time lag and
(c) its impact may not be visible immediately (Oommen 2011).

In comparison, growth performance is more logical to assess despite being a complicated process. Inclusive growth is hard to define or capture (Ranieri and Ramos 2013), but the identification of more features will help in the specification of the meaning and concept of inclusive growth. Thorat and Dubey (2012) argue that growth was more poverty-reducing during 2004–05 and 2009–10.[1] Although poverty reduction is beneficial for some groups as compared to others, yet the adverse effects of inequality, specifically on the urban sector, have also been evident. Bhanumurthy and Mitra (2004) argued that the growth/mean effect dominates in both periods (1983–93 and 1993–2000) over the inequality effect and the population shift effect. Growth effect, which is beneficial for poverty reduction, seems to have gone up in the reform period. Mishra (2015) shows that reduction in poverty, more so in rural areas, has occurred due to the growth in total income. It has led to a reduction in poverty in rural areas but an increase in the urban areas.

However, these studies are very aggregative and the picture may be different at the sub-national level. There are huge variations across states. Inter-state inequalities in terms of per capita income and consumption have increased after the economic reforms and states like Uttar Pradesh (U.P.) are lagging far behind (GOI 2011a).[2] U.P. is also a part of BIMARU (Bihar, Madhya Pradesh, Rajasthan and U.P.) group of states that are traditionally and economically lagging behind other states in India. In 2012, just Bihar, Madhya Pradesh and U.P. were home to 44% of the poor in the country (Narayan and Murgai 2016). U.P. has the largest share in India's population and poverty, making it the highest shareholder of poverty among BIMARU states (Pathak 2011). U.P. was once positioned as the pacesetter for India's economic and social development. But now it shows far less promise (World Bank 2002). Thus, it is quite necessary to undertake a disaggregated analysis of economic growth and its impact on poverty and inequality in the state and ask if the state's economic policies have promoted inclusive growth. It is even important to revisit the growth poverty relationship in the framework of pro-poor growth, especially at the sub-national level. Also, there is a need to examine the distribution of growth benefits among the poor and non-poor, and how much growth is required to make it pro-poor.

This paper attempts decomposition of poverty into growth effect and inequality effect. Further, it estimates the pro-poor growth index (PPGI) and poverty equivalent growth rate (PEGR) to find the answer to the aforementioned questions. Although the focus is the state of Uttar Pradesh, yet it is referred to in the context of India as a whole.

[1] National Statistical Commission (NSC) in its 32nd Meeting held on 23–24 April, 2010, considered the use of the 2009–10 NSSO quinquennial survey as the base year for both the price indices as well as revision of the national income estimates and felt that, being a non-normal year, may pose problems; hence, it was desirable to repeat the survey once again in respect of consumer expenditure issues.

[2] This is also mentioned in a study of World Bank (Uttar Pradesh: growth, poverty and inequality 2016).

The paper is organized into four sections. Section 2 provides us with the technical framework, wherein the methodology of decomposition of change in poverty into growth and inequality effect, PPGI and poverty equivalent growth rate are discussed. While Sect. 3 examines the relationship between poverty and inequality, Sect. 4 examines the growth and poverty relationship in the state. Section 5 comprises conclusion and policy suggestions.

2 Technical Framework

2.1 Decomposition of Change in Poverty

Datt and Ravallion (1992), Kakwani (1993) have shown that change in poverty can be decomposed into a component due to change in mean income (constant inequality) and a component due to change in inequality (mean income constant). However, they argue that the change in poverty due to the change in mean income is known, but the change in mean income due to the change in inequality is residual. The rise in Monthly Per Capita Consumption Expenditure (MPCE) always helps in reducing poverty but the rise in inequality can occur both ways. It can either help in reducing poverty or may harm the poor people (Chen and Ravallion 2001; Kakwani and Pernia 2000). Mazumdar and Son (2001), Son (2003), Mishra (2015) have introduced a new poverty decomposition method by including what they term as 'population shift' effect without any residual term. But the population shift effect is still a contested idea and does not provide significant insight; therefore, we do not attempt it. We followed Kakwani and Pernia (2000) method due to several reasons. First, it is an exact decomposition analysis, having no residual term. Second, this decomposition analysis is extended for the measure of pro-poor growth by an index which is called PPGI. Therefore, this paper attempts to decompose the poverty change into growth effect and inequality effect, which means understanding the contribution of growth in poverty reduction when inequality is constant and contribution of inequality in poverty reduction when growth is constant. If the inequality effect is negative, growth would lead to a change in the distribution of income in favour of the poor, and if inequality effect is positive it means change in the distribution of income in favour of the rich.

Let the change in poverty between two periods j and k be ΔP_{jk} and the incidence of poverty be

$$P = P(z, \mu, L(p))$$

where P is a poverty measure that is fully characterized by the poverty line income (z), the mean income or expenditure (μ) and the Lorenz ratio ($L(p)$).

The change in poverty can be defined as

$$\Delta P_{jk} = f(G_{jk}, I_{jk})$$

where G_{jk} (growth effect) denotes the change in poverty due to the change in the mean income when inequality does not change and I_{jk} (inequality effect) denotes the change in poverty due to the change in inequality when income does not change.

Kakwani and Pernia (2000) propose a method that takes care of the weaknesses that are found in the previous ones where the inequality effect is a residual. They propose a method and define the mean and inequality effect as

$$\begin{aligned} G_{jk} =& 1/2[Ln[P(z, \mu_k, L_j(p))] - Ln[P(z, \mu_j, L_j(p))] + Ln[P(z, \mu_k, L_k(p))] \\ & - Ln[P(z, \mu_j, L_k(p))]] \end{aligned} \quad (1)$$

and

$$\begin{aligned} I_{jk} =& 1/2[Ln[\theta(z, \mu_j, L_k(p))] - Ln[\theta(z, \mu_j, L_j(p))] + Ln[\theta(z, \mu_k, L_k(p))] \\ & - Ln[\theta(z, \mu_k, L_j(p))]] \end{aligned} \quad (2)$$

It is noted that the poverty line (z) will be the same in both periods. Hence, the decomposition of poverty can be written as

$$P_{jk} = G_{jk} + I_{jk} \quad (3)$$

The sum of growth effect and redistribution effect is defined as the total change in poverty during periods j and k in Eq. 3.

2.2 *Pro-Poor Growth Index (PPGI)*

The decomposition of poverty change, however, explains only the contribution of growth and redistribution in poverty change; it is not able to explain which group (whether poor or rich) is enjoying more of this growth benefit. Is that growth process pro-poor or pro-rich? Before answering this question, one needs to estimate the PPGI, which measures the degree of pro-poorness of growth (Kakwani and Pernia 2000). The PPGI shows the relationship between total poverty reduction and poverty reduction which results from the distribution of natural growth.

Suppose there is a positive growth rate of g_{jk} percent between periods j and k, then poverty elasticity can be defined as

$$\eta = P_{jk}/g_{jk}$$

This is the proportional change in total poverty when there is a positive growth rate. Likewise, we may define

$$\eta_g = G_{jk}/g_{jk}$$

$$\eta_I = I_{jk}/g_{jk}$$

where η_g is the proportional change in poverty when the growth rate is positive and relative inequality does not change. Similarly, η_I is the proportional change in poverty when inequality changes without change in mean income. Thus, we can write,

$$\eta = \eta_g + \eta_I \quad (4)$$

The above Eq. (4) shows that the proportional change in poverty is summation of the two factors, namely, η_g which is income effect of growth on poverty and η_I, which is inequality effect on poverty.

Then, we can write the index of pro-poor growth (φ) as,

$$\varphi = \eta/\eta_g$$

where φ will be greater than 1 if $\eta_I < 0$, which means that growth is strictly pro-poor. If $0 < \varphi < 1$, it means that $\eta_I > 0$ but poverty still declines due to growth. This situation may be generally characterized as trickle-down. If, $\varphi < 0$, economic growth in fact badly hurts the poor and it leads to an increase in poverty.

2.3 Poverty Equivalent Growth Rate (PEGR)

PPGI only indicates that growth is pro-poor or pro-rich, but if growth is pro-rich, then it will be necessary to know how much more growth is required to make it pro-poor. Thus, one estimates the poverty equivalent growth rate (PEGR) proposed by Kakwani et al. (2004), which not only includes the magnitude of growth but also the amount of benefits received by the poor from the growth. They argue that proportional poverty reduction is monotonically increasing function of the PEGR which implies that greater PEGR leads to a larger proportional reduction in poverty. Thus, the maximization of PEGR means maximum poverty reduction.

$$\text{PEGR} = \frac{\eta}{\eta g} \times g_{\text{jk}}$$

where $\eta = Proportional\ change\ in\ total\ poverty$

$\eta g = growth\ elasticity\ of\ poverty$

$g_{\text{jk}} = growth\ rate\ of\ mean\ income$

or

$$\text{PEGR} = \frac{\textit{Proportional change in total poverty}}{\textit{growth elasticity of poverty}} \times \textit{growth rate of mean income}$$

The PEGR is derived by multiplying PPGI by the growth rate of mean income. Growth is pro-poor (anti-poor) if the PEGR is greater (less) than the mean income growth rate. If the PEGR lies between 0 and the mean income growth rate, then growth is accompanied by an increasing inequality wherein poverty still declines. This situation may be characterized as a trickle-down process when the poor receive proportionally lesser benefits of growth than the non-poor.

2.4 Data

The basic data used in this study is consumption expenditure survey (CES) of National Sample Survey (NSS) unit record data for the years 1993–94 (50th round),[3] 2004–05 (61st round) and 2011–12 (68th round) on mixed recall period.[4] NSSO CES data report consumption expenditure of households in nominal terms. For this study, the nominal expenditure has been converted into real expenditure at constant (2011–12) prices. The price deflator used to convert the household expenditure at constant prices is the implicit price deflator derived from the poverty line of India for rural and urban areas separately. Poverty lines are Rs 816 (rural), Rs 1000 (urban), Rs 768 (rural U.P.) and Rs 941(urban U.P.) (GoI 2011a, b). This is estimated by the methodology of the Tendulkar Committee through MPCE mix recall period. MPCE is calculated by using the deflated MPCE data.

3 Poverty and Inequality in Uttar Pradesh

Uttar Pradesh was one of the better-performing states in terms of aggregate growth until the 1970s. Thereafter, it has experienced a continuous decline in aggregate growth. The state's per capita income was 97% of the national per capita income in 1951. It gradually fell to 68% of this average in 1971–72 and hovered close to this level till 1991–92 (67.5%). Thereafter, it again started falling gradually to 50.5% in 2001–02 and then to 40.5% in 2014–15 (Srivastava and Ranjan 2016). This loss in growth momentum and failure to build on the foundations laid in the early years has cost U.P. very dearly. It has continuously slipped down with its growth rate always lagging the national growth rate (Refer Fig. 1). This loss in growth momentum has been one of the major reasons behind the 'not so impressive' decline in poverty ratio in U.P. unlike other states of India. It could be argued that many states took advantage

[3]In this period, the geographical boundary of U.P. included Uttarakhand but for the comparability of data, NSS region 'Himalayan' has been excluded from 50th round.

[4]CES 1993–93 (50th round) reported every estimation on URP so verification of the MRP estimation see; Himanshu (2007), Recent Trends in Poverty and Inequality: Some Preliminary Results.

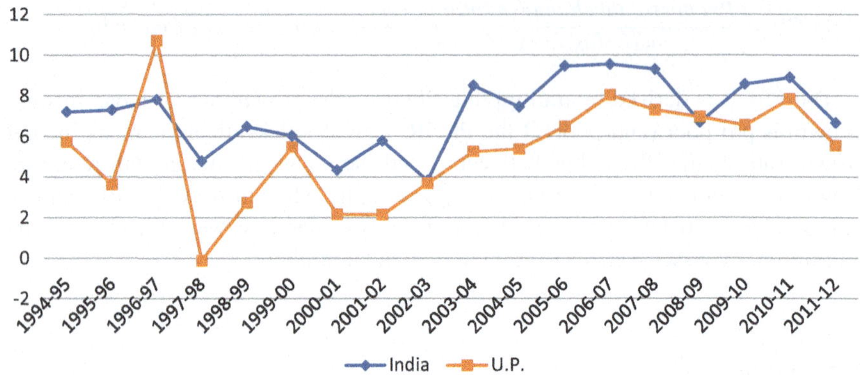

Fig. 1 Growth rate of Gross Domestic Product (India) and Gross State Domestic Product (U.P.) (1993–94 to 2011–12) at a constant price (2004–05 base years). *Source* Directorate of Economics & Statistics of, Uttar Pradesh and Central Statistics Office

of liberalization and succeeded in accelerating their growth rates and consequently reducing their poverty ratio drastically. Uttar Pradesh failed to do so and that is why it's growth is continuously falling short of the national growth rate. This divergence from the national average is also reflected in the MPCE, HCR and Gini Index.

It is evident from Fig. 2a and Table 2 (Appendix) that MPCE in rural U.P. has always been lower than the national average and this difference is widening over time. Rural MPCE of U.P. is only 83% of national rural MPCE in 2011–12. The same story is repeated more glaringly in case of urban U.P. Here, it is only 78% of national urban MPCE in 2011–12. This indicates that while growth in rural income is slower than urban income in U.P., in either case, it is significantly lower than the national level. According to Deaton and Drenze (2002), states with more poor people reported slower growth in MPCE. It has to be so as the growth rate of U.P. GSDP was 5.5% as compared to 6.5% growth of GDP for India in 2011–12 (Table 1).

HCR in rural India and rural U.P. is almost equal in 1993–94 and 2004–05. However, the decline is much sharper at the national level after 2004–05 and raises several questions. HCR of rural U.P. is significantly higher than rural India in 2011–12. But, urban HCR in U.P. has been always higher than national urban HCR, right from 1993–94 to 2011–12. During 1993–94 to 2011–12, this difference has further widened; to the extent that poverty level in urban U.P. is twice that of urban India (Fig. 2b). The period 2004–05 to 2011–12 appears to be significant as difference in MPCE and HCR of U.P. (rural and urban) and India has further widened (Refer Fig. 2a, b).

One may ask whether the change in inequality explains the observed changes in MPCE and HCR? Gini index (consumption) is computed for the referred time periods to understand the implication of change in inequality. While Gini has gone up in rural India from 1993–94 to 2004–05 and has remained constant from 2004–05 to 2011–12, it has been almost same in rural U.P. right from 1993–94 to 2011–12 (Refer Fig. 2c and Table 2 in Appendix) and it is consistently lower than national Gini.

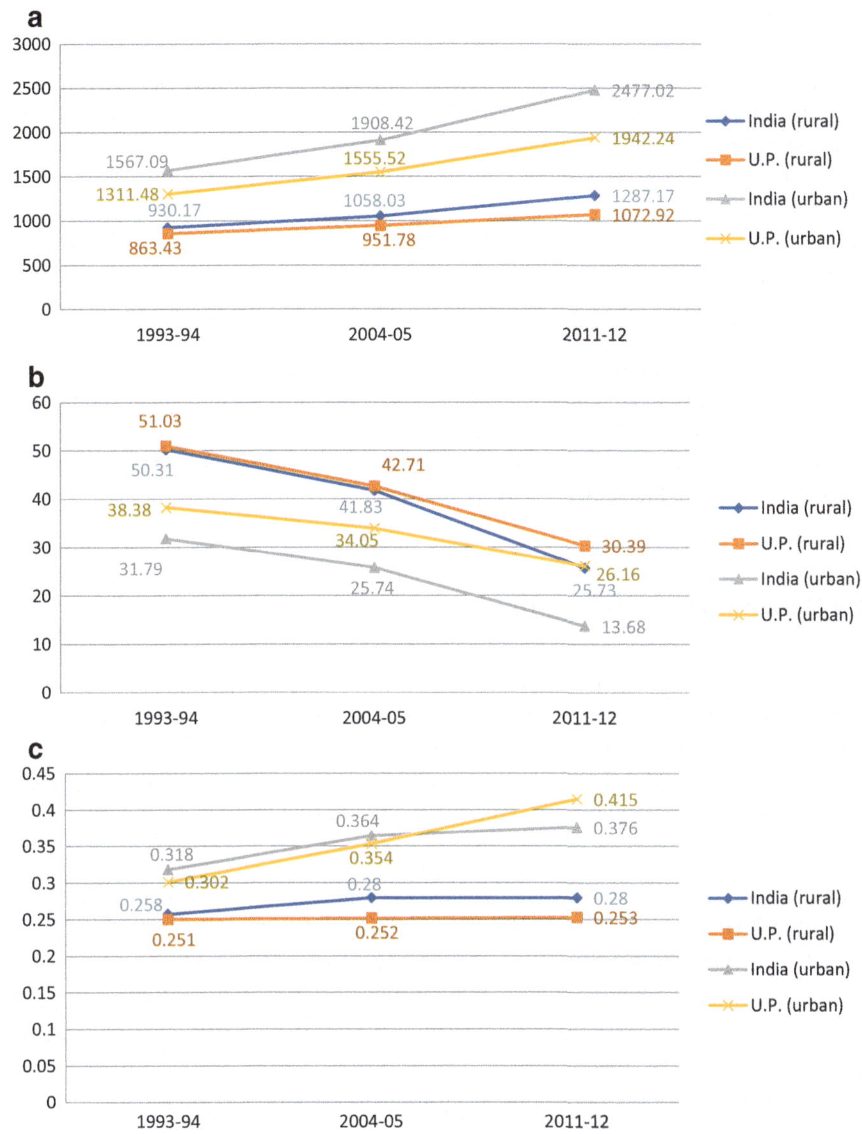

Fig. 2 **a** MPCE of India and U.P. **b** HCR of India and U.P. **c** GINI index of India and U.P. *Source* Author's own computation based on unit record data of NSSO 50th, 61st and 68th rounds

This is a bit puzzling and suggestive that even if rural MPCE in U.P. is lower than the national rural MPCE and the difference has widened over the years, inequality has not risen in rural U.P. This is in stark contrast with urban U.P. While Gini had been lower in urban U.P. as compared to the national Gini during 1993–94 to 2004–05, the trend reversed during 2004–05 to 2011–12. This is suggestive that inequality is much higher in urban U.P. than India and very high as compared to rural U.P. in 2011–12.

The overall picture depicts an acceleration in growth followed by a decline in poverty and rise in inequality and in MPCE. Growth in MPCE (mean income) always contributes to reducing poverty. But the latter may have been brought about by the decline in inequality (Chen and Ravallion 2001; Kakwani and Pernia 2000). Thus, the decline in poverty may have been caused by either positive growth or decline in inequality. This has been a widely contested issue in literature which involves questioning of methodology as well as empirical estimates. Economic growth began to slow down sharply in South Korea during 1996–97 but the incidence of poverty continued to fall significantly because the distribution of consumption became more equal (Kakwani and Pernia 2000). Kapoor (2013) finds that states with a higher level of initial inequality have a lower growth elasticity of poverty and suggests that the more equal the initial income distribution, the more responsive to growth is poverty. In spite of the observed methodological and empirical issues involved, it still makes sense to investigate the growth–poverty relationship.

4 Growth–Poverty Relationship

Change in poverty can be decomposed into growth effect and inequality effect. Table 1 shows the total change in poverty and decomposition of poverty into growth effect and inequality effect for India and Uttar Pradesh from 1993–94 to 2004–05 and 2004–05 to 2011–12. The decomposition analysis is done to assess the impact of growth and inequality on poverty reduction. The negative sign of growth effect explains the

Table 1 Decomposition of Poverty change (in %) of India and U.P. (1993–94 to 2004–05 and 2004–05 to 2011–12)

Period	Total change in poverty		Explained by			
			Growth		Redistribution	
	India	U.P.	India	U.P.	India	U.P.
Rural						
1993–94 to 2004–05	−8.47	−8.32	−12.17	−9.63	3.69	1.31
2004–05 to 2011–12	−16.10	−12.31	−16.85	−11.55	0.75	−0.75
Urban						
1993–94 to 2004–05	−6.05	−4.32	−13.00	−12.30	6.95	7.97
2004–05 to 2011–12	−12.24	−7.88	−13.40	−16.75	1.15	8.87

Source Author's own computation based on unit record data of NSSO 50th, 61st and 68th rounds

negative relationship between growth and poverty reduction, whereas the positive sign of redistribution effect signifies the rise in poverty with an increase in inequality.

Table 1 presents the decomposition of change in poverty into growth effect and redistribution effect. It is seen that during 1993–94 to 2004–05 total change in rural poverty has been similar for U.P. and India. But, a potential reduction in rural poverty through growth effect is moderated by the redistribution effect. Growth would have reduced poverty in rural India by 12.17%. But actual reduction turns out to be only 8.47% because of adverse redistribution, which has taken off 3.69% of potential decline in poverty. This rise in inequality during 1993–94 to 2004–05 in rural India is also shown by a rise in the Gini index during this period. Thus, the redistribution effect has produced a counterforce in poverty reduction. Interestingly, redistribution effect is able to do so only marginally (0.75%) in 2004–05 to 2011–12 in rural India, where the total change in poverty (16.10%) is very close to growth effect (16.85%). It is to be noted that Gini for rural India during this period has almost remained constant. What happens in the case of rural U.P.? Potential impact on poverty reduction through growth effect (9.63%) is lessened by the redistribution effect (1.31%) and actual change (8.32%) is slightly lower. But, a remarkable feature in case of rural U.P. for 2004–05 to 2011–12 is the change in the role of redistribution effect. The actual change in poverty (12.31%) is higher than the growth effect (11.55%). Here, the redistribution effect (0.75%) is working in the same direction and helps in the reduction of poverty. Again, it is to be noted that the Gini index for rural U.P. has remained constant during this period. Also, it is not necessary that the redistribution effect always works in the opposite direction of growth effect. Generally, redistribution is in favour of rich and against poor, but there can be a situation wherein redistribution is in favour of poor as obtained in case of rural U.P. during 2004–05 to 2011–12.[5] This is a bit puzzling also as a change in MPCE in rural U.P. has been almost equal during 1993–45 to 2004–05 and 2004–05 to 2011–12. Possibly, households are clustered around poverty line and interventions like Mahatma Gandhi National Rural Employment Guarantee Act (MGNREGA), National Rural Health Mission (NRHM), rise in rural wages and revamping of the Public Distribution System (PDS) during 2004–05 to 2011–12 might have resulted in redistribution in favour of the poor in rural U.P. during this period. It might have been due to the large size of rural poverty in U.P.

The redistribution effect has played a much stronger role in the urban area (Table 1). Growth effect (13%) is highly moderated by redistribution effect (6.95%) and actual change in poverty turns out to be only 6% in urban India during 1993–94 to 2004–05. However, the redistribution effect is moderated in 2004–05 to 2011–12. The corresponding Gini index for this period shows a dramatic rise in the first period and only a marginal rise in the second period in urban India. Although the change in total urban poverty in U.P. is lower than India, yet the redistribution effect is stronger in U.P. Ironically, it is stronger during 2004–05 to 2011–12 than the previous period. It means that urban poverty reduction in U.P. has been drastically pulled down by redistribution against poor right from 1993–94 to 2011–12. It is

[5]Kakwani and Pernia (2000) find negative impact of inequality on poverty for South Korea during 1990–98.

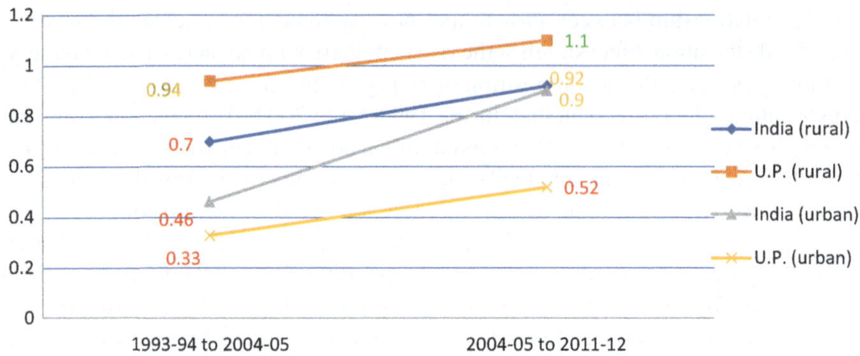

Fig. 3 Pro-poor Growth Index, India & U.P. (1993–94 to 2004–05 & 2004–05 to 2011–12). *Source* Author's own computation based on unit record data of NSSO 50th, 61st and 68th rounds

observed that urban Gini index has consistently gone up in U.P. during this period indicating that recent growth has benefitted only a few people and led to increasing disparities and inequalities (Dev and Ravi 2007).

So far, a mixed picture has emerged and it is not clear how much of the recent high growth has been pro- or anti-poor. One possible tool to answer this question is to estimate the pro-poor growth index. Figure 3 and Table 3 (Appendix) presents the PPGI for the periods 1993–94 to 2004–05 and 2004–05 to 2011–12. Growth is called pro-poor if PPGI is greater than one as discussed in the methodology section.

Figure 3 is quite revealing and partly supports the earlier contentions of researchers. In general, there is a tendency towards having a pro-poor growth in India beginning from 1993 to 1994. Of course, the degree varies across sectors. PPGI in 2004–05 to 2011–12 is better than in 1993–94 to 2004–05 in all sectors. However, it is not pro-poor in any sector except rural U.P., where it is greater than one. It is only rural U.P. which has demonstrated a clear tendency during 2004–05 to 2011–12 towards pro-poor growth. Does it mean that recent growth has not benefitted the poor at all and one needs to have a different growth than what one has had? Poverty equivalent growth rate (PEGR) is estimated to answer this.

Figures 4 and 5 and Table 4 (Appendix) present the mean income growth rate along with PEGR from 1993–94 to 2004–05 and 2004–05 to 2011–12. Growth is pro-poor if PEGR is greater than the mean income growth rate or actual growth rate (AGR). During the first period under study, the gap between AGR and PEGR is wider in rural India but it has considerably narrowed down during the second period (Fig. 4). While AGR of rural U.P. was very close to its PEGR in the first time period, PEGR exceeded AGR in the second time period suggesting pro-poorness of growth. Thus, during 1993–2004 AGR in the state was 10.23 while PEGR was 9.66; during the second period, PEGR steadily kept rising and surpassed AGR which at final count stood at 12.72 compared to 14.05 PEGR. Thus, rural U.P. has achieved the pro-poor growth which is better than the corresponding trend for the country as rural India is still approaching pro-poorness during 2004–05 to 2011–12. If the trend

Fig. 4 AGR & PEGR, rural India & U.P. *Source* Author's own, computation based on unit record data of NSSO 50th, 61st and 68th rounds

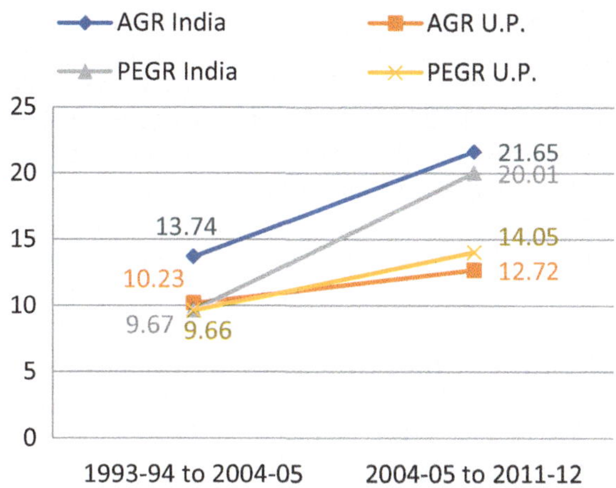

Fig. 5 AGR & PEGR, urban India & U.P. *Source* Author's own computation based on unit record data of NSSO 50th, 61st and 68th rounds

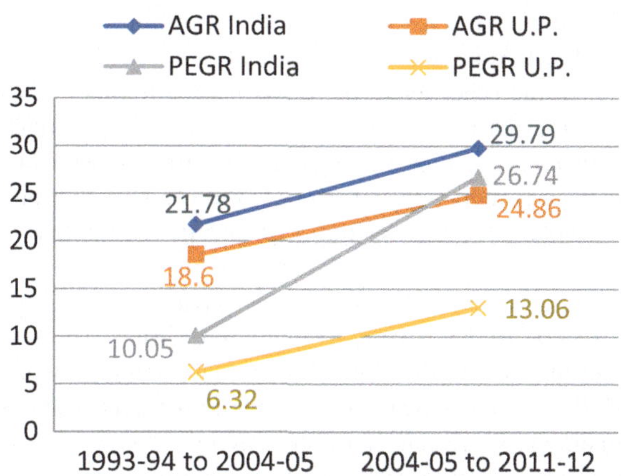

continues, rural India may achieve pro-poor growth, provided inequality does not alter the situation. The urban scenario presents the opposite trends (Fig. 5). While AGR for U.P. as well as India during both periods is more than PEGR, the gap between the two is narrowing down. While PEGR is catching up with AGR sharply in urban India lagging behind the latter by a few points (26.74 PEGR and 29.79 AGR), there has been only marginal narrowing down between the two in urban U.P. wherein the gap is of nine points (PEGR 13.06; AGR 24.86).

Based on the above discussion and empirical evidence, it may be argued that the distribution of MPCE is much better in the rural economy. In the case of rural U.P., growth has been pro-poor whereas rural India is lagging in pro-poor growth during the second period (2004–05 to 2011–12). It indicates that the distribution of MPCE has become more equal in rural U.P. as the Gini index is observed to be stagnant in both time periods. Schemes like MGNREGA, which introduced at the beginning of the second period, have resulted in pro-poor growth and an equitable and fair distribution of MPCE in the rural areas. These type of schemes help in the reduction of poverty in rural areas at a faster pace (Nayyar 2005). Impressive growth in real wages of casual labourers may also have been a major factor behind pro-poor growth and equitable distribution of income in rural U.P. According to Mamgain and Verick (2017) annual growth rate of real wages of casual labourers has been 4.46% for rural U.P. between 2004–05 and 2011–12, which is higher than urban U.P. (3.47%) for the corresponding period. The rapid growth of economy and agricultural productivity and a rise in the share of the non-agricultural sector in income and employment have contributed to the rise in rural wage rates (Chand and Srivastava 2014; Gulati et al. 2013), while others see it as a correction after a long stagnation (Drèze and Sen 2013).

Yet, rural poverty is high in Uttar Pradesh. Part of the reason is that as the level of MPCE is low despite being fairly distributed; suggesting that higher levels of MPCE may be required to make a significant impact on the reduction of rural poverty. In a state where 80% of the population lives in rural areas and 60% of it depends on agriculture, levels of earnings in agriculture and rural non-agricultural sector hold the key to reduction in rural poverty.

On the other hand, there has been a higher growth in MPCE and reduction in poverty in urban U.P. but it is accompanied by increasing inequality.[6] In urban U.P., MPCE is very high as compared to the rural area but higher inequality acts as a barrier to poverty reduction and pro-poor growth. Distribution of MPCE being more unequal, it is not able to make an impact as pro-poor or inclusive growth. One plausible reason for unequal distribution of MPCE is the slower growth rate of real wages of causal labourers in urban U.P. (3.47%) compared to 4.48% growth rate for rural U.P. during 2004–05 to 2011–12 (Mamgain and Verick 2017). Capital–skill complementarity and increase in the skill bias of agglomeration economies in the context of rapid skill-biased technical change have also played a major role in increasing inequality in urban area (Baum-Snow et al. 2018). Besides the one-off effect on poverty from a pure redistribution effect, the long-run impact of the improvements in the distribution of income will reflect on the growth elasticity of poverty (Kapoor 2013). Moreover, if attempts to reduce inequality fail, then it would become more difficult to address the problem of poverty and inclusive growth and the poor will not be benefitted via growth alone (Dang and Lanjouw 2018). Dealing with these inequalities would not only raise social justice but it could also promote inequality-deadening inclusive growth.

[6]Many studies for other regions have shown that high growth rate is accompanied by increasing inequality (see Weisskopf 2011; Chancel and Piketty 2017; Dang and Lanjouw 2018).

5 Conclusion

This paper has assessed the inclusiveness of economic growth between 1993–94 to 2004–05 and 2004–05 to 2011–12 in Uttar Pradesh. Change in poverty is decomposed into growth and redistribution effect, explaining the contribution of growth and redistribution in poverty change. Further, PPGI for the measurement of inclusiveness of economic growth is constructed and poverty equivalent growth rate is estimated. It is found that the contribution of growth is dominant in poverty reduction in both, rural and urban areas. Evidence shows that rural U.P. is lagging in pro-poor growth during the first period whereas in the second-period growth has been pro-poor. It has been possible because of the higher growth rate of real wages of causal labourers, equal distribution of income and successful implementation of anti-poverty schemes like MGNREGA. However, a whopping eighty percent of the state's population is still living in rural areas so promoting agriculture and non-agriculture sector and higher expenditure on anti-poverty schemes are required to pull people out of poverty. On the other hand, urban U.P. is lagging in pro-poor growth because of unequal distribution of income and steadily increasing inequality. Capital–skill complementarity, rapid skill-biased technical change and slower growth rate of real wages of causal labourers are major reasons behind growing inequality and pro-rich growth in urban U.P. Therefore, increasing the real wage of casual labourers, and equal distribution of growth benefits eventually become imperative to achieve pro-poor growth and reduce inequality.

This study highlights inadequacy of HCR-based poverty estimation and calls for further research on these lines, especially in the case of Uttar Pradesh. Though some explanations are offered, yet these are highly tentative and a more nuanced investigation is required to understand the challenge of U.P. The researchers do not have a complete explanation of the diametrically opposed picture of rural and urban U.P. This study indicates possible threads of future research on U.P.

Appendix

See Tables 2, 3 and 4.

Table 2 Indicators of living standard of India and U.P. (1993–94, 2004–05 and 2011–12)

	1993–94		2004–05		2011–12	
	India	U.P.	India	U.P.	India	U.P.
Rural						
MPCE	930.17	863.43	1058.03	951.78	1287.17	1072.92
HCR	50.31	51.03	41.83	42.71	25.73	30.39
Poverty gap	12.83	13.03	9.63	9.16	5.04	5.67
Severity of poverty	4.57	4.55	3.15	2.77	1.49	1.61
GINI	0.258	0.251	0.280	0.252	0.280	0.253
Urban						
MPCE	1567.09	1311.48	1908.42	1555.52	2477.02	1942.24
HCR	31.79	38.38	25.74	34.05	13.68	26.16
Poverty gap	7.64	969	6.07	7.80	2.70	5.29
Severity of poverty	2.67	3.48	2.04	2.53	0.79	1.51
GINI	0.318	0.302	0.364	0.354	0.376	0.415

Source Author's own computation based on unit record data of NSSO 50th, 61st and 68th rounds

Table 3 Pro-poor growth index for India and U.P. (1993–94 to 2004–05 and 2004–05 to 2011–12)

Period	Pro-Poor Growth Index (PPGI)			
	Rural		Urban	
	India	U.P.	India	U.P.
1993–94 to 2004–05	0.70	0.94	0.46	0.33
2004–05 to 2011–12	0.92	1.10	0.90	0.52

Source Author's own computation based on unit record data of NSSO 50th, 61st and 68th rounds

Table 4 Poverty equivalent growth rates for India and U.P. (1993–94 to 2004–05 and 2004–05 to 2011–12)

Period	Actual Growth Rate				Poverty Equivalent Growth Rate (PEGR)			
	Rural		Urban		Rural		Urban	
	India	U.P	India	U.P	India	U.P	India	U.P
1993–94 to 2004–05	13.74	10.23	21.78	18.60	9.67	9.66	10.05	6.32
2004–05 to 2011–12	21.65	12.72	29.79	24.86	20.01	14.05	26.74	13.06

Source Author's own computation based on unit record data of NSSO 50th, 61st and 68th rounds

References

Baum-Snow, N., Freedman, M., & Pavan, R. (2018). Why has urban inequality increased? *American Economic Journal: Applied Economics, 10*(4), 1–42.

Bhanumurthy, N. R., & Mitra, A. (2004). Economic growth, poverty, and inequality in indian states in the pre-reform and reform periods. *Asian Development Review, 21*(2), 79–99.

Chancel, L., & Piketty, T. (2017). *Indian income inequality, 1922–2015: From British Raj to Billionaire Raj?* WID.World Working Paper Series No 2017/11.

Chand, R., & Srivastava, S. K. (2014). Changes in the rural labour market and their implications for agriculture. *Economic and Political Weekly, xlIX*(10), 47–54.

Chen, S., & Ravallion, M. (2001). How did the worlds poorest fare in the 190s? *Review of Income and Wealth, 3,* 283–300.

Chenery, H., Ahluwalia, M. S., Jolly, R., Bell, C. L. G., & Duloy, J. H. (1979). Redistribution with growth. *Economist (United Kingdom).*

Dang, H.-A., & Lanjouw, P. (2018, December). *Inequality trends and dynamics in India—The bird's-eye and the granular perspectives.* WIDER Working Paper 2018/189.

Datt, G., & Ravallion, M. (1992). *Growth and redistribution components of changes in poverty measures a decomposition with applications to Brazil and India in the 1980s.* Living Standards Measurement Study: Working Paper No. 83, no. 83.

Deaton, A., & Drenze, J. (2002). Poverty and inequality in India a re-examination. *Economic and Political Weekly* 3729–3748.

Dev, S. M., & Ravi, C. (2007). Poverty and inequality: All-India and States, 1983–2005. *Economic and Political Weekly, 5*(3), 509–521.

Drèze, J., & Sen, A. (2013). *An uncertain glory: India and its contradictions.* Princeton University Press.

GOI. (2011a). *Indian economic policies towards inclusive growth: An approach to the twelfth five year plan (2012–17).* Government of India Planning Commission.

GOI. (2011b). *Mid-Term Appraisal Eleventh Five Year Plan 2007–2012* (pp. 1–475). Planning Commission Government of India, Oxford University Press.

Gulati, A., Jain, S., & Satija, N. (2013). *Rising farm wages in India: the 'pull' and 'push' factors* (pp. 1–30). Discussion Paper No. 5: COMMISSION FOR AGRICULTURAL COSTS AND PRICES Department of Agriculture & Cooperation Ministry of Agriculture Government of India, no. 5.

Himanshu. (2018). *Widening gaps: India ineqaulity report 2018.* Oxfam India.

IMF, UN, OECD, WBG. (2000). *A better world for all: Progress towards the International Development Goals.* Report: World Bank Group, International Monetary Fund, Orgnization for Economic Co-Operation and Development, United Nations.

Kakwani, N. (1993). Poverty and economic growth with application to C~Te D'ivoire. *Review of Income and Wealth, 2.*

Kakwani, N., & Pernia, E. M. (2000). What is pro-poor growth? *Asian Development Review, 18*(1), 1–16.

Kakwani, N., Khandker, S., Son, H. H. (2004). *Pro-poor growth: concepts and measurement with country case studies.* Working Paper 1 : United Nations Development Programme, International International Poverty Centre, no. 1.

Kapoor, R. (2013). Inequality matters. *Economic & Political Weekly, xlviII*(2).

Klasen, S. (2010). *ADB sustainable development working paper series measuring and monitoring inclusive growth: Multiple definitions, open questions, and some constructive proposals measuring and monitoring inclusive growth,* no. 12.

Mamgain, R. P., & Verick, S. (2017). *The State of Employment in Uttar Pradesh: Unleashing the Potential for Inclusive Growth. Ilo.*

Mazumdar, D., & Son, H. H. (2001, October). *Vulnerable groups and the labor market in Thailand: Impact of the Asian financial crisis in the light of Thailand's growth process.* University of Toronto.

Mishra, S. (2015). Decomposing poverty change: deciphering change in total population and beyond. *Review Income Wealth, 4,* 799–811.

Narayan, A., & Murgai, R. (2016). *Looking Back on Two Decades of Poverty and Well-Being in India.* The World Bank: Poverty and Equity Global Practice Group.

Nayyar, G. (2005). Growth and poverty in rural India: an analysis of inter-state differences. *Economic Political Weekly, 40*(16), 1631–1639.

OECD. (2001). *The DAC guidelines poverty reduction* (pp. 1–127). Organisation For Economic Co-Operation and Development.

Oommen, M. A. (2011). On the issue of 'inclusive growth.' *Economic Political Weekly, xlvi*(29), 158–159.

Pathak, D. (2011). *Poverty and Inequality in Uttar Pradesh: A Decomposition Analysis.* LAMBERT Academic Publishing.

Ranieri, R., & Ramos, R. A. (2013). *Inclusive growth: building up a concept.* Working Paper No. 104 International Policy Centre for Inclusive Growth (IPC-IG) Inter, no. 104.

Son, H. H. (2003). A new poverty decomposition. *Journal of Economic Inequality, 1,* 181–187.

Srivastava, R., & Ranjan, R. (2016). Deciphering Growth and Development. *Economic Political Weekly, II*(53), 32–43.

Thorat, S., & Dubey, A. (2012). Has growth been socially inclusive during 1993–94 – 2009–10? *Economic Political Weekly, xlvii*(10), 43–54.

Weisskopf, T. E. (2011). Why worry about inequality in the booming Indian economy? *Economic Political Weekly, XLVI*(47), 41–51.

World Bank. (2002). India poverty in India the challenge of Uttar Pradesh. Report No. 22323-IN, no. 22323.

Labor, Work, and Employment

Structural Change and Increasing Precarity of Employment in India

Ravi Srivastava, Balakrushna Padhi, and Rahul Ranjan

Abstract This paper analyses the nature and increasing precarity of India's employment in the last decade and a half. It examines the trends in informal employment in India in 2004–05, 2011–12 and 2017–18. The analysis reveals that there has been a significant degree of informalisation of employment in the formal sector of the economy, and among regular/salaried workers, who form the predominant section of the formal sector workforce. This has counteracted the potentially positive effect of the economy-wide shift from agricultural to non-agricultural employment, towards regular/salaried work and towards formal sector growth. This result reflects on the long-standing debate in India on the impact of formal labour relations on the formal sector employment. Formal employment is considered to be associated with very rigid labour laws restricting hiring and firing of workers. However, the paper shows that formal sector employment has expanded but with much greater informality of employment. This situation demands urgent attention in order to reverse the increasing precariousness of employment and engage policy levers in reducing the growing labour market inequalities in India.

1 Introduction

This paper analyses the nature and increasing precarity of India's employment in the last decade and a half. It examines how three interrelated processes have impacted on the trends in employment precarity in a contradictory fashion. The first of these

R. Srivastava (✉)
Centre of Employment Studies, Institute for Human Development, Delhi, India
e-mail: ravi.sriv@gmail.com

B. Padhi
Centre of Excellence in Fiscal Policy and Taxation, Bhubaneshwar, Odisha, India
e-mail: padhi.balakrushna5@gmail.com

R. Ranjan
Institute for Human Development, Delhi, India
e-mail: rkrahul555@gmail.com

N. K. Mishra (ed.), *Development Challenges of India After Twenty Five Years of Economic Reforms*, India Studies in Business and Economics,
https://doi.org/10.1007/978-981-15-8265-3_8

is a series of changes that appear to have occurred in India's employment structure. These are the shift in employment from agriculture to industry and services, growth of regular/salaried workers and the growth of formal sector employment. In principle, these changes allow for improvement in employment quality. They have to be understood, however, in the context of by the broader second set of changes demonstrating negligible growth in total employment, drop in labour force employment and in precarious agricultural employment, undertaken by women workers, combined with slow growth in employment outside agriculture, which has sent unemployment rates, particularly among the youth, surging to unprecedented levels. The final set of changes relates to growing informalisation of the formal sector of the economy.

Precarious employment, which is broadly understood as temporary and insecure employment,[1] is interpreted in this paper as informal employment, defined in the following section. Informality also comprises greater flexibility of employment achieved by capital in relation to labour. We show how informality has increased in the Indian economy and how it is driven by changes at the core of the economy, which have undone the potential beneficial impact of the structural changes in employment which we had referred to above.

2 Interpreting Informality

The debate on the informal sector took a different turn in the 1980s when it was realised that the informal sector was not a transitional phenomenon, but indeed the direction of global changes has increased the magnitude of informal sector employment. The International Labour Organization (ILO) took upon itself the task of defining the parameters for characterising informal sector enterprises and for estimating the size of informal sector employment across countries. The 15th ICLS (1993) Conference of the International Conference of Labour Statisticians (ICLS) outlined the characteristics of the informal sector. But it fell upon subsequent work by the committee of statisticians under what came to be known as the "Delhi Group" to fine-tune the definition of the informal sector and to give yardsticks by which comparable estimates could be obtained across countries.

While it was more or less understood that informal sector employment would be precarious, given the characteristics of this sector, it also was known that informal sector employment did not subsume the entire universe of precarious employment. In fact, there were forms of employment outside the informal sector, within the fold of the formal sector which shared the same characteristics. The categorisation of

[1]Kalleberg and Vallas (2018) define precarious work as "work that is uncertain, unstable, and insecure and in which employees bear the risks of work (as opposed to businesses or the government) and receive limited social benefits and statutory protections" (p. 1). ILO (2011) further adds that precarious work is "usually defined by uncertainty as to the duration of employment, multiple possible employers or a disguised or ambiguous employment relationship, a lack of access to social protection and benefits usually associated with employment, low pay, and substantial legal and practical obstacles to joining a trade union and bargaining collectively".

informal employment, whether within the informal sector or within the formal sector, was taken up by the 17th ICLS in 1997. Broadly speaking, informal employment has been defined as precarious employment, spanning all three sectors of the economy, viz. formal sector, informal sector and private households. The ILO provides a matrix which categorises informal/formal employment in these three sectors for different types of employment/activity types (Hussmans 2004, ILO 2013, pp. 32–38).

However, the definition of informal employment was broad and somewhat inconclusive. The ILO defines precariousness across two major dimensions, viz. job security, which includes protection against arbitrary dismissal (without due notice, etc.), and paid leave, and social security and leaves the precise definition of "precariousness" to individual countries.[2]

The definition of the informal sector and informal employment was taken up the National Commission for Enterprises in the Unorganised Sector (NCEUS), Government of India. The Commission produced a definitive report estimating the informal sector and informal economy and assessing the contribution of the informal sector to the Indian economy (NCEUS 2007).

This is how the NCEUS defined the informal sector and informal employment (NCEUS 2007, p. 3):

> The **unorganised sector** consists of all unincorporated private enterprises owned by individuals or households engaged in the sale and production of goods and services operated on a proprietary or partnership basis and with less than ten total workers.
>
> **Unorganised workers** consist of those working in the **unorganised sector** or households, excluding regular workers with social security benefits, and the workers in the formal sector without any employment and social security benefits provided by the employers.

These concepts have also been accepted by the National Statistical Commission's Working Group on Unorganised Sector Statistics (NSC 2012). The detailed methodology of estimation of the informal sector and informal employment was elaborated by the NCEUS in its Statistical Report (NCEUS 2008, Chap. 2). The report also provides details of data adjustments which were required in order for estimations to be made (ibid., Appendix 8). It may be mentioned that the NCEUS methodology, as well as the methodology followed in this paper, is distinct from the concept and methodology used by the NSO in its categorisation of unincorporated enterprises, regardless of the size of the workforce, as informal sector enterprises.

---

[2]See ILO (2013). According to paragraph 3(5) of the 17th ICLS guidelines, employees are considered to have informal jobs if their employment relationship is, in law or in practice, not subject to national labour legislation, income taxation, social protection or entitlement to certain employment benefits (advance notice of dismissal, severance pay, paid annual or sick leave, etc.) for reasons such as: the jobs or the employees are not declared to the relevant authorities; the jobs are casual or of a limited duration (e.g. through on-call arrangements); the hours of work or wages are below a specified threshold (e.g. below that qualifying for social security contributions); the workers are employed by unincorporated enterprises or by persons in households; the employee's place of work is outside the premises of the employer's enterprise (e.g. outworkers without an employment contract); or regulations are not applied, not enforced or not complied with for any reason (ibid. p. 39).

As can be seen from the NCEUS definition, unorganised/informal work in the formal sector was to be characterised both by employment security and social security benefits. But in the empirical estimation, given that the 55th Round of the NSS 'Employment & Unemployment Survey' (EUS) had only provided limited data on social security benefits to workers, the NCEUS used the only provision of social security benefits to characterise informal workers in the formal sector. Using its methodology and comparing the growth of formal/informal employment in the formal/informal sector between 1999–00 and 2004–05, the NCEUS came to the startling conclusion that the entire increase in the workforce in the interim period consisted of informal workers (NCEUS, Chap. 1). It also concluded that the share of informal workers had increased both in the formal sector and in the economy as a whole (ibid.). It may be mentioned that since 2004–05, however, the NSS Rounds on EUS, as well as the Periodic Labour Force Survey (PLFS) carried out since 2017–18, collect additional information on the nature of job contracts. This allows us to measure "job precariousness" along both axes (job security and social security).

The report of the ILO mentioned earlier (ILO 2013), went into these dimensions of informality and examined how different countries have operationalised the concept of informal employment. Table 2.8 in ILO (2013) has compiled country-specific definitions of informal employment. This shows that countries have used a combination of criteria (absence of job contracts, availability of paid leave or social security) to define informal employment but several (most) countries cited have adopted the absence of contracts as the intrinsic feature of informality.

Srivastava and Naik (2015) reviewed the ILO definitions and concepts along with the NCEUS recommendations. They argued that in India social security benefits in the organised sector had been extended to workers who were otherwise holding very precarious jobs, as temporary, casual or contract workers. Both the two major social security packages provided by the EPFO and the ESIC had made such provisions. Although temporary and contract workers may not be able to access organised sector social security in practice, the statutory framework provided for a disjuncture between employment security and social security benefits. Srivastava and Naik (ibid) therefore argued that employment security was a much more central feature of formal employment, given also that the provision of social security was contingent on employment. They also pointed out that ILO (2013) had shown that a number of countries had taken employment security as a key feature of formal employment. The paper also argued that capitalists/employers value labour flexibility even more than workers availing of some social security. It, therefore, argued that informal employment in India should be determined on the basis of job security, and not the availability of social security.

Job security is also not easy to define. At the very minimum, the following criteria could be used to define employment security: minimum tenure, notice procedure and severance pay/benefits. Data on these criteria is currently not being collected. But as pointed out earlier, the National Sample Survey (now the National Survey Office) has, since 2004–05, been collecting information on whether employees in designated industry groups have a written contract and the minimum period of such contracts. Srivastava and Naik (2015) used the availability of a written contract to designate an employee as a formal worker. Clearly, this is a very minimal criterion for employment security. As Mezaddri and Srivastava (2015) have shown, we can also consider degrees of formality and develop more stringent criteria to test the same.

This paper follows Srivastava and Naik (2015) in designating formal employees as those employees who have a written contract. In addition, self-employed and own account workers in the formal sector are also considered to be formal workers.

The operational criteria used to assign workers as belonging to the formal sector/informal sector follows Appendix VIII of NCEUS (2008) with two differences with respect to cooperatives and workers in households which are detailed in the explanatory note appended to Srivastava and Naik (2015).

This paper also makes new adjustments to the multipliers in the EUS and PLFS, based on the population projections made by the Registrar General of India.[3] These estimates also affect the size of the labour force and the workforce and hence diverge from earlier estimates made by the authors of this paper.

3 Structural Transformation of India's Employment Structure

3.1 The Shift from Agriculture to Industry and Services

The structural transformation of the economy and its implications for the employment structure is perhaps the most significant aspect of the set of changes which could have portended a beneficial impact for workers given the productivity differential between different sectors.

Between 1983 and 2017–18, the share of agriculture in total employment declined from over two-thirds (68.5%) to just over two-fifth (42%). Both industry and services gained in the share of total employment each of these nearly doubling. The share of industry in total employment increased from 13.7% in 1983 to 25.3% in 2017–18. The share of the services sector in total employment increased from 17.8% in 1983 to 32.7% in 2017–18 (see Table 1).

Within industries, the transformation was led by the construction industry. Employment in the construction industry increased from 6.8 million in 1983 (2.3% of total employment) to 52.8 million (11.6% of total employment) in 2017–18. Although manufacturing employment increased from 40 million to 58.2 million, its share in total employment did not change much and has remained static in the last few decades. Its share in total employment was 10.3% in 1983 and 10.8% in 1999–00. It increased to 12.9% in 2011–12 and remained at 12.8% in 2017–18.

[3]For the computation of census adjusted population figures, we have used the recent Census India (2019) projected population estimates for the year 2011–12 and 2017–18. See for details, Census of India 2011 Population Projections for India and States 2011–2036 Report of The Technical Group on Population Projections November, 2019.

Table 1 Changing share of industry groups in total employment

	1983	1993–94	1999–00	2004–05	2011–12	2017–18
Agriculture	**68.5**	**63.7**	**60.5**	**56.3**	**47.8**	**42.0**
Mining and quarrying	0.6	0.7	0.6	0.6	0.5	0.4
Manufacturing	10.6	11.5	10.8	12.3	12.9	12.8
Electricity, gas and water supply	0.3	0.4	0.3	0.3	0.3	0.5
Construction	2.3	3.2	4.4	5.7	10.6	11.6
Wholesale and retail trade	6.3	7.7	9.1	9.5	10.2	11.1
Hotels and restaurants	0.9	0.9	1.2	1.3	1.7	1.9
Transport, storage and communications	2.5	2.8	3.7	4.1	4.5	5.4
Financial intermediation	0.4	0.6	0.6	0.7	0.9	1.1
Real estate, renting and business activities	0.2	0.4	0.7	1.0	1.8	3.0
Public administration and defence	2.6	2.7	2.6	1.9	1.8	1.7
Education	1.5	1.7	2.1	2.5	3.1	3.9
Health and social work	0.6	0.6	0.7	0.8	1.0	1.3
Others services (90–99)	2.8	3.1	2.9	2.9	2.9	3.2
Total industry	**13.7**	**15.8**	**16.1**	**18.8**	**24.4**	**25.3**
Total services	**17.8**	**20.5**	**23.4**	**24.8**	**27.8**	**32.7**
Non-agriculture	**31.5**	**36.3**	**39.5**	**43.7**	**52.2**	**58.0**
Total	**100.0**	**100.0**	**100.0**	**100.0**	**100.0**	**100.0**

Source Authors own computation from NSS-EUS (1983 (38th), 1993–94 (50th), 1999–00 (55th), 2004–05 (61st), 2011–12 (68th)) and PLFS-I (2017–18)
Note Industry includes, the Mining, Manufacturing, Electricity and Construction, while the Service sector includes, Wholesale and retail trade, Hotels and restaurants, Transport, storage and communications, Financial intermediation, Real estate, renting and business activities, Public administration and defence, Education, Health and social work and Others Services (90–99). Industry Codes are concorded with National Industrial Classification (NIC) 2004

Within Services, the share of wholesale and retail trade in total employment increased from 6.3% in 1983 to 11.1% in 2017–18, and that of hotels and restaurants increased from 0.9 to 1.9% in the same period. The shares of Transport, storage and communication; Financial intermediation; and Real Estate, renting and business activities grew from 2.5% to 5.4%, 0.4% to 1.1%, 0.2% to 3%, respectively, between 1983 and 2017–18. The share of Education, and Health and Social Work grew from 1.5% to 3.9% and from 0.6% to 1.3%, respectively, between 1983 and 2017–18. However, the share of public defence and defence went down from 2.6% to 1.7% over the period and the share of Other Services has virtually stagnated.

Table 2 Increase in regular/salaried employment

Activity status	1983	1993–94	1999–2000	2004–05	2011–12	2017–18
Employment in million						
Self-employed	172.7	203.9	208.2	257.7	245.5	235.0
Regular/salaried worker	41.0	51.1	58.5	69.8	86.7	109.7
Casual worker	87.8	118.9	131.1	128.1	137.6	110.3
Workforce	301.4	374.0	397.8	455.5	469.9	455.0
Percent to total						
Self-employed	57	55	52	56	52	52
Regular/salaried worker	14	14	15	15	18	24
Casual worker	29	32	33	28	29	24
Workforce	100	100	100	100	100	100

Source Same as Table 1

3.2 *Increase in Regular/Salaried Employment*

A second change, linked to the first, is the significant shift in the activity status of employed persons in India in favour of regular/salaried workers which have taken place in recent decades. The activity-wise composition of the workforce shows small changes between 1983 and 2004–05 but faster change thereafter. Between 1983 and 2004–05, the share of self-employed workers among total employed changed marginally from 57% to 56% (see Table 2). The share of the casual workforce also dropped marginally from 29 to 28% and the share of the regular/salaried workers increased from 15 to 15%. These changes occurred at a more increased pace between 2004–05 and 2017–18. The share of self-employed workers in total employment declined from 56% to 52%, while the share of casual workers declined from 28 to 24% over this period. On the other hand, the share of regular/salaried workers in the total workforce increased from 15% in 2004–05 to 24% in 2017–18. Given the stagnation in the size of the total workforce after 2004–05, the numbers of both self-employed and casual workers were lower in 2017–18 than in 2004–05, whereas over this period, the numbers of regular/salaried workers increased from 69.8 million to 109.7 million.

3.3 *Increasing Formal Sector Share in Total Employment and Shift from Informal to Formal Sector*

Direct reliable estimates of the formal sector can be obtained from the EUS and the PLFS. As discussed in Sect. 2, the definition and the empirical categorisation of the formal sector here is drawn from the NCEUS with some modifications.

Table 3 Employment in the formal and informal sector

	2004–05	2011–12	2017–18
Percentage to total employment in formal sector and informal sector			
Formal sector	11.6	16.3	18.2
Informal sector	88.4	83.7	81.8
Total	100.0	100.0	100.0
Percentage change over 2004–05		2011–12	2017–18
Formal sector		44.8	56.5
Informal sector		−2.4	−7.6

Source Authors own computation from NSS-EUS (2004–05 (61st), 2011–12 (68th)) and PLFS-I (2017–18)
Note Formal and Informal Sectors are defined as in NCEUS (2008), with some empirical modifications introduced in Srivastava and Naik (2015)

Estimates have been prepared for 2004–05, 2011–12 and 2017–18. These show that the size of the formal sector increased from 52.9 million workers in 2004–05 to 76.7 million in 2011–12 and further to 82.8 million in 2017–18. Over the corresponding period, total employment in the informal sector declined from 402.8 million in 2004–05 to 393.3 million in 2011–12 and 372.2 million in 2017–18. Compared to 2004–05, employment in the formal sector increased although on a small base—by a significant 56.5%, while informal sector employment declined by 7.6%.

The result of these changes, presented in Table 3 shows that the share of the formal sector in total employment increased from 11.6% in 2004–05 to 16.3% in 2011–12 and further to 18.2% in 2017–18, with a corresponding decline in the share of formal sector employment. In absolute terms, formal sector employment increased 44.8% during 2004–05 to 2011–12 and by another 56.5% during 2004–05 and 2017–18. During the same period, absolute informal sector employment actually dipped by 2.4% during 2004–05 to 2011–12 and by 7.6% during 2004–05 to 2017–18.

The industry-wise details are given in Table 4. In the industries sector as a whole, the share of formal sector employment increased from 27.17% in 2004–05 to 32.65% in 2011–12 but dipped to 29.89% in 2017–18 still higher than the formal sector share in 2004–05. The share of formal sector employment in services increased steadily from 25.72% in 2004–05 to 29.48% in 2011–12 and further to 31.87% in 2017–18. Outside agriculture, the share of formal sector employment increased from 26.35% in 2004–05 to 31.01% in 2011–12.

Industry-wise, most industry groups show, and an increase in the share of the formal sector in total employment. In manufacturing, the share of the formal sector rose from 27.94% in 2004–05 to 35.47% in 2017–18. In wholesale and retail trade, the share of the formal sector increased from a low 3.78% to 7.55% over this period. The share of the formal sector in total employment increased between 2004–05 and 2017–18 in both Education and Health and Social work. The share of formal sector employment increased from 28.61% to 52.15% in Financial intermediation,

Table 4 Percentage of total employment in the formal sector by industry groups

	2004–05	2011–12	2017–18
Agriculture, hunting and forestry	**0.25**	**0.33**	**0.53**
Mining and quarrying	63.99	61.47	64.73
Manufacturing	27.94	33.32	35.47
Electricity, gas and water supply	92.03	90.85	81.16
Construction	18.49	28.47	20.47
Wholesale and retail trade	3.78	5.95	7.55
Hotels and restaurants	12.28	13.90	13.91
Transport, storage and communications	23.17	23.48	21.04
Financial intermediation	67.62	64.78	71.80
Real estate, renting and business activities	28.62	46.88	52.15
Public administration and defence	96.84	100.00	100.00
Education	67.72	74.04	75.52
Health-social work	52.65	59.13	63.80
Other services	4.19	8.11	9.17
Industry	**27.17**	**32.65**	**29.89**
Services	**25.72**	**29.48**	**31.87**
Non-agriculture	**26.35**	**30.96**	**31.01**
Total	**11.62**	**16.31**	**18.20**

Source Same as Table 3

from 28.61% to 52.15% in Real Estate and Business Activities. The industry groups where the share of the formal sector in total employment did not increase have been Transport, Storage and Communications; and Electricity, Gas and Water Supply. Other things remaining the same, this increase should have laid the basis for higher levels of formal employment in the economy.

4 Implications of the Stunted Growth in Employment and Declining Labour Force Participation

The total employment and the annual growth rate in employment are given in Table 5. Annual growth in total employment has been low throughout but has stagnated since 2004–05, turning negative between 2011–12 and 2017–18. Agricultural employment growth has been negative in the two successive periods after 2004–05. While the rate of non-agricultural employment has been higher than agricultural employment in all periods, it has not been high enough to push aggregate employment growth to reasonable levels, which as pointed out, declined between 2011–12 and 2017–18.

Table 5 Employment and annual growth rate

	Year/Round					
	1983	1993–94	1999–00	2004–05	2011–12	2017–18
Employment (million)						
Total	301.4	374.0	397.8	455.7	469.9	455.0
Agriculture	205.3	236.5	239.2	257.2	224.7	191.2
Non-agriculture	96.1	137.5	158.6	198.5	245.2	263.8
Annual growth rate in the preceding period						
Total		2.18	1.03	2.76	0.44	−0.54
Agriculture		1.42	0.19	1.46	−1.91	−2.65
Non-agriculture		3.65	2.41	4.59	3.07	1.23

Source Same as Table 1

A major reason for reflection of the economy's inability to create employment at a rapid rate is its inability to increase the labour force participation rate (LFPR) which has declined after 2004–05. As Table 6 shows, the total LFPR in the economy hovered around 43% between 1983 and 2004–05. But between 2004–05 and 2011–12, the LFPR dipped from 42.86% to 39.27% and then declined further to 36.84% in 2017–18. A sex-wise disaggregation shows that male LFPR remained almost unchanged but there was a significant decline in female LFPR by over 11% points between 2004–05 and 2017–18 from 28.85% in 2004–05 to 22.06% in 2011–12 and further to 17.14% in 2017–18.

Table 6 Labour force participation rate (all ages)

	Year/Round					
	1983	1999–2000	1999–2000	2004–05	2011–12	2017–18
Rural + Urban						
Male	55.13	55.61	54.13	55.96	55.50	55.48
Female	29.82	28.76	25.89	28.85	22.06	17.14
Total	42.92	42.70	40.47	42.86	39.27	36.84
Rural						
Male	55.49	56.08	54.05	55.51	55.14	54.79
Female	34.08	33.04	30.03	33.30	25.04	17.87
Person	45.07	44.95	42.36	44.72	40.48	36.76
Urban						
Male	54.01	54.29	54.34	57.03	56.28	56.84
Female	15.77	16.50	14.73	17.82	15.48	15.68
Person	36.08	36.42	35.51	38.32	36.63	37.01

Source Same as Table 1

Table 7 Unemployment rate—all ages

	1983	1999–2000	1999–2000	2004–05	2011–12	2017–18
Rural + Urban						
Male	2.30	2.11	2.56	2.26	2.15	6.26
Female	1.21	1.60	1.77	2.69	2.46	5.91
Total	1.93	1.94	2.32	2.40	2.23	6.18
Rural						
Male	1.40	1.43	1.77	1.60	1.73	5.84
Female	0.67	0.79	1.06	1.79	1.56	3.64
Person	1.13	1.20	1.52	1.67	1.68	5.32
Urban						
Male	5.14	4.05	4.59	3.81	3.04	7.07
Female	5.03	6.23	5.69	6.88	5.64	11.14
Person	5.12	4.52	4.81	4.49	3.57	7.90

Source Same as Table 1

A sector-wise disaggregation shows that most of this decline took place in rural areas and for women. This has been widely commented upon in the literature.[4] Female LFPR almost halved between 2004–05 and 2017–18 from 33.3% in 2004–05 to 17.87% in 2017–18. Although urban female LFPR was slightly lower in 2011–12 and 2017–18 compared to 2004–05, no long-term trend pattern is discernible from the results. Although in earlier years, rural female LFPR was almost twice the urban level, these two were almost convergent by 2017–18. Further analysis carried out showed that this decline was mainly because precarious female employment in agriculture (both paid and unpaid) went down in recent years. Thus, it needs to be noted that at one end of the employment spectrum, precarious jobs held by women in agriculture declined significantly, and this accounted for some of the shifts that we analyse later in this paper.

4.1 Rising Unemployment Rate

However, results further show other significant changes. Although the LFPR declined overall and for women, the availability of employment declined at an even faster rate in recent years after 2011–12 resulting in an increase in unemployment rates.

Table 7 shows the unemployment rate (all ages), disaggregated by sex, across sectors. The long-term trend in usual status unemployment rates which also happens to measure the lowest unemployment rate among the four measures of unemployment that the NSS data can generate (this is now down to three, with the PLFS), has been

[4] See for details Srivastava and Srivastava (2010), Srivastava (2016c, 2019), Kannan and Raveendran (2019), Rodgers (2020), Verick (2014).

Table 8 Unemployment rate among youth (15–29 years)

	1983	1999–2000	1999–2000	2004–05	2011–12	2017–18
Rural + Urban						
Male	5.09	5.11	6.19	5.41	6.01	17.85
Female	2.78	3.81	4.43	6.16	6.84	18.41
Total	4.32	4.69	5.66	5.65	6.23	17.96
Rural						
Male	3.13	3.51	4.36	3.94	4.94	17.36
Female	1.52	1.90	2.73	4.19	4.45	13.16
Person	2.53	2.94	3.81	4.03	4.80	16.52
Urban						
Male	10.80	9.64	10.93	8.77	8.25	18.79
Female	11.54	14.95	14.09	14.92	14.06	27.74
Person	10.94	10.76	11.52	10.09	9.49	20.70

Source Same as Table 1

remarkably stable over a quarter of a century between 2004–05 and 2004–05. But between 2004–05 and 2017–18, unemployment rates increased for all groups—urban or rural, male or female. Overall, male unemployment rates increased from 2.15% to 6.26% and female unemployment rates went up from 2.46% to 5.91%. While in rural areas, male unemployment rates exceeded those of women in 2017–18, it was the other way around in urban areas where female unemployment rates were as high as 11.14%, compared to an unemployment rate of 7.07% for men in 2017–18.

Further, the fragility of employment growth seems to have affected the young more than other groups. Unlike the aggregate unemployment rate, youth unemployment rates have shown a tendency to rise over the years—from 4.32% in 1983 to 5.65% n 2004–05 and 6.23% in 2011–12. But this rate almost trebled between 2011–12 and 2017–18, rising to 17.96%. As Table 8 shows, this rise occurred both among young men and among young women. Youth unemployment rates were higher in urban areas than in rural areas, higher among rural males than rural females, but in urban rates, unemployment rates were higher among young women than young men. Further analysis, not shown here, that although unemployment rates among the youth rise with increasing levels of education, the increase is significant across all education levels, from the lowest to the highest.

Thus, the results discussed in the preceding section have to understand in the context of the loss of precarious agricultural jobs, particularly for women; and the inability of the economy to increase jobs at a fast enough rate to absorb the young in recent years, among whom unemployment rates have increased at a phenomenal rate in recent years.

5 Precarity and Informality of the Workforce

For the purposes of this paper, we abstract from the several other challenges on the employment front briefly discussed in Sect. 4 and focus on the precarity of those who are in employment. As pointed out in Sect. 3, the structural transformation that the Indian economy has experienced in recent decades, with a shift of the employment structure towards regular salaried jobs in larger formal non-agricultural enterprises provides the preconditions for the creation of more stable and better quality employment. On the other hand, the push towards more flexible labour and non-standard jobs is increasingly precarious jobs (temporary, part-time, non-standard, and informal) the world over.

Between 2004–05 and 2017–18, the economy gained a paltry 4.6 million formal jobs. Most of this gain occurred between 2004–05 and 2011–12 (4.1 million). While informal jobs in the economy increased by 10.1 million between 2004–05 and 2011–12, there was a loss of 15.4 million informal jobs between 2011–12 and 2017–18, with the economy losing 5.3 million jobs in the aggregate in the entire period 2004–05 and 2017–18. As already pointed out, women in the rural sector of the economy have been moving out of the labour force and there is a significant decline in precarious agricultural work for women in the years since 2004–05 which has contributed to the overall decline in jobs (see Table 9).

The slow growth in formal jobs combined with either a slower growth (in percentage terms) in informal jobs has brought about a small increase in the share of formal employment in the country from 6% in 2004–05 to 6.7% in 2011–12 and 7% in 2017–18.

Table 10 shows that the industry-wise share of formal employment. This share has not improved between 2004–05 and 2017–18. Indeed, the reverse has happened. In other words, the results in Table 9 above are principally a result of employment moving away from agriculture but to sectors where informality has simultaneously increased.

Taking the broad sectors first, in the aggregate industries sector, the share of informal employment increased from 92.12% to 93.21% between 2004–05 and 2017–18. In the service sector as a whole, the percentage share of the informal employment increased from 81.87% to 83.86%.

Table 9 Formal and Informal Workers in the Indian Economy

	2004–05	2011–12	2017–18
Formal workers (million)	27.4	31.5	32.0
Informal workers (million)	428.3	438.4	423.0
Percent to total workers			
Formal worker	6.0	6.7	7.0
Informal workers	94.0	93.3	93.0

Source Same as Table 3

Table 10 Industry-wise percentage share of formal and informal employment

	Formal worker			Informal worker		
	2004–05	2011–12	2017–18	2004–05	2011–12	2017–18
Agriculture, hunting and forestry	**0.06**	**0.09**	**0.10**	**99.94**	**99.91**	**99.90**
Mining and quarrying	29.05	27.85	23.69	70.95	72.15	76.31
Manufacturing	8.30	7.89	8.24	91.70	92.11	91.76
Electricity, gas and water supply	69.58	59.15	46.74	30.42	40.85	53.26
Construction	1.71	2.87	3.00	98.29	97.13	97.00
Wholesale and retail trade	1.80	1.98	2.03	98.20	98.02	97.97
Hotels and restaurants	4.22	3.75	3.29	95.78	96.25	96.71
Transport, storage and communications	14.45	13.44	9.44	85.55	86.56	90.56
Financial intermediation	52.04	42.33	39.38	47.96	57.67	60.62
Real estate, renting and business activities	17.39	26.49	19.44	82.61	73.51	80.56
Public administration and defence	72.21	69.16	62.87	27.79	30.84	37.13
Education	52.41	50.18	44.73	47.59	49.82	55.27
Health-social work	37.62	36.62	32.78	62.38	63.38	67.22
Other services	3.46	4.55	6.09	96.54	95.45	93.91
Industry	**7.88**	**6.87**	**6.79**	**92.12**	**93.13**	**93.21**
Service	**18.13**	**17.95**	**16.14**	**81.87**	**82.05**	**83.86**
Total non-agriculture	**13.72**	**12.77**	**12.06**	**86.28**	**87.23**	**87.94**
Total	**6.01**	**6.71**	**7.03**	**93.99**	**93.29**	**92.97**

Source Same as Table 3

The more detailed industry-wise results show that informality increased in Manufacturing; Hotels and Restaurants; Transport, Storage and Communication; Financial Intermediation; Public administration and defence, Real Estate, Renting and Business Activities, Education, Health and Social Work. But informality declined marginally

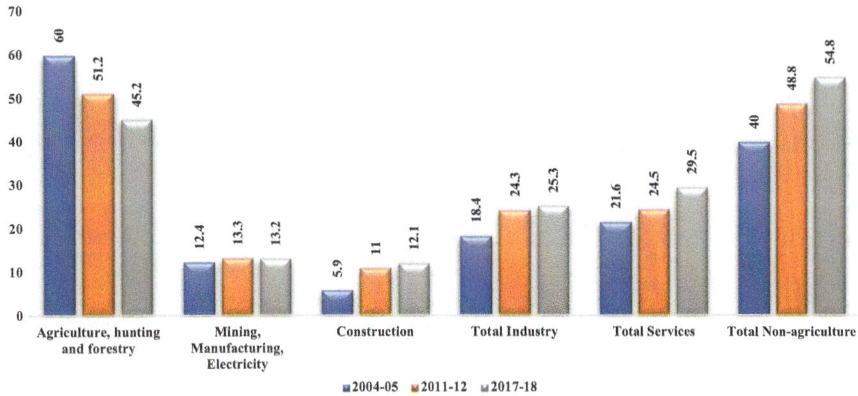

Fig. 1 Percentage contribution to total informal employment. *Source* Same as Table 3

from very high levels in the construction industry, and Wholesale and Retail Trade; and in Other Miscellaneous Services.

The shift in the employment structure away from agriculture almost entirely informal to industry and services, led to very marginal changes in the formalisation of employment, as these industries although less informal than agriculture, got more informalised in the recent decades. The share of agriculture in total informal employment declined from 60% in 2004–05 to 45.2% in 2017–18, but the corresponding contribution of the non-agricultural sector to informal employment increased from 40% to 54.8%. Both the industries and services sector contributed almost equally to this increase. The share of the services sector in total informal employment increased by 7.9%, from 21.6% in 2004–05 to 29.5% in 2017–18. Over the corresponding period, the share of industries by 6.9%—from 18.4% to 25.3% largely the contribution of the construction industry which grew rapidly at a high level of informalisation (see Fig. 1).

Since formalisation can principally occur through the category of regular/salaried work, whose significance, as noted in Fig. 2 has increased between 2004–05 and 2017–18, Fig. 2 summarises the share of formal and informal workers among all regular/salaried workers. Agriculture has a low share of regular/salaried workers, but among them, the share of formal workers increased from 5.1% in 2004–05 to 8.1% in 2011–12 but declined to 6.5% in 2017–18. The share of formal workers in manufacturing declined steadily from 26% in 2004–05 to 19.1% in 2017–18. Thus, in manufacturing, every four out of five regular/salaried worker was an informal worker in 2017–18. In industries as a whole, the share of formal workers among regular salaried workers declined from 31.3% to 22% in 2017–18. The share of formal workers declined across the board in services except for Other Services (NIC Div. 90–99). Overall, 43.5% if regular/salaried workers were formal workers with written contracts in 2004–05, but this percentage declined to only 31.2 in 2017–18. Thus, the shift in the activity status of the Indian workforce towards regular/salaried

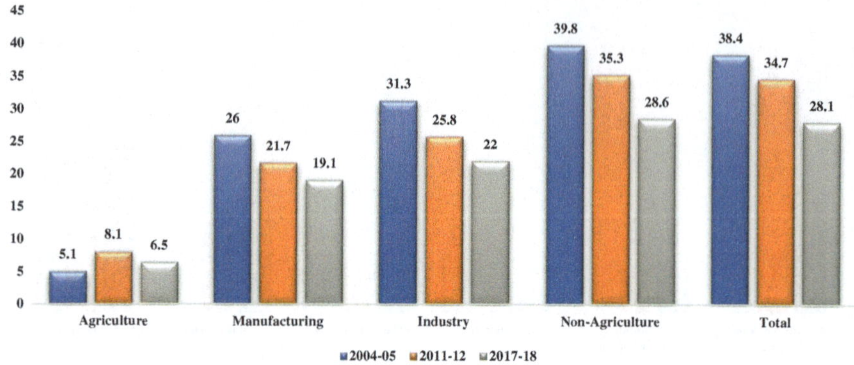

Fig. 2 Percentage of formal workers among regular/salaried workers across industry groups. *Source* Same as Table 3

work did not result in higher formalisation of the workforce due to the hiring of regular/salaried workers in informal settings and with formal contracts.

6 Formal and Informal Employment in the Formal Sector

As shown in Sect. 3, the formal sector of the economy has grown rapidly in recent years. Although its direct share in total employment is still small, it is still the leading sector of the economy, dominated by large capital and capital–labour relations shaped by such capital, unlike the informal sector where the role of capital is either fragmented or diffused and indirect. It is also in relation to the formal sector that there have been intense debates on labour market rigidities leading to slow growth of employment. On growth of formal sector employment, facts have already been discussed in Sect. 3. Here, we discuss the evolution of formal capital–labour relations in this sector since 2004–05.

The shares of formal and formal employment in the three periods/rounds and across different industry groups are discussed in Table 11.

In the formal sector as a whole, the share of formal employment was less than half (46.2%) in 2004–05. This fell to 37.4% in 2011–12 and further to 35.2% in 2017–18. The share of formal work in the minuscule formal agricultural sector was understandably the lowest—19.4% in 2004–05 and 17.8% in 2017–18. In the industries sector, only a quarter of workers (25/2%) were formal workers in 2004–05 and in 2017–18, this fell further, and only a fifth of the workers (20.5%) were formal workers. While in this segment, the construction industry was the least formal, the level of formalisation was low in manufacturing and declined further. The share of formal employment in manufacturing was 25.3% in 2004–05 and declined steadily to 21.6% in 2017–18. The level of formalisation was higher in services but declined by a significant level from 63.5% in 2004–05 to 46.5% in 2017–18. As would be

Table 11 Industry-wise percentage of formal workers in the formal sector

	2004–05	2011–12	2017–18
Agriculture, hunting and forestry	**19.4**	**21.6**	**17.8**
Mining and quarrying	44.0	43.0	36.0
Manufacturing	25.3	21.1	21.6
Electricity, gas and water supply	74.6	63.6	54.8
Construction	5.7	8.2	11.4
Wholesale and retail trade	23.1	23.4	19.4
Hotels and restaurants	26.2	19.8	18.7
Transport, storage and communications	56.5	50.0	39.6
Financial intermediation	68.7	61.4	50.7
Real estate, renting and business activities	51.2	50.3	33.0
Public administration and defence	73.2	69.2	62.9
Education	70.4	61.9	55.1
Health-social work	66.9	58.1	48.1
Other services	39.1	42.8	42.1
Industry	**25.1**	**18.8**	**20.5**
Service	**63.5**	**55.8**	**46.3**
Total non-agriculture	**46.5**	**37.6**	**35.5**
Total	**46.2**	**37.4**	**35.2**

Source Same as Table 3

expected the share of formal employment was high in public administration. Education, health and financial intermediation but declined in each of these sectors over time. Formalisation within the formal sector was low in wholesale and retail trade, and hotels and restaurants to begin with and declined over the years. By 2017–18, less than one-fifth of the employment in each of these sectors was formal. Given that these figures are for the formal sector and over a relatively short period of time of 13 years, the pace of informalisation is indeed remarkable.

Table 12 shows the share of formal workers across the government/public sector and the private formal sector. The government/public sector is considered to be a model employer, but the results in Table 12 show that due to outsourcing and contract-based employment, the share of formal workers has declined quite rapidly. In 2004–05, 72.1% of all workers in the government sector were formal workers but by 2017–18, this had declined to 55.1%. In the private formal sector, the share of formal workers was already low at 24.6% in 2004–05 and further declined to 20.8% in 2017–18. The aggregate industry sector, which was already highly informalised in 2004–05, with formal workers at 18.5%, showed an even lower percentage of formal workers—16.7% in 2017–18. The Services sector less informalised in 2004–05 with about two-fifth workers as formal. This declined to nearly one quarter (27%) in 2017–18. In the formal non-agricultural sector, the percentage of formal workers declined from about

Table 12 Industry-wise percentage of informal workers in government/public sector

	Government/Public sector			Formal private sector		
	2004–05	2011–12	2017–18	2004–05	2011–12	2017–18
Agriculture, hunting and forestry	**52.4**	**29.0**	**37.9**	**5.1**	**10.6**	**3.8**
Mining and quarrying	81.3	82.5	70.2	20.9	19.1	18.6
Manufacturing	73.8	75.2	40.6	21.9	18.9	20.3
Electricity, gas and water supply	76.8	70.6	61.5	62.2	41.3	36.6
Construction	16.3	13.6	22.4	3.1	3.4	4.4
Wholesale and retail trade	49.4	50.3	28.1	20.4	21.4	18.2
Hotels and restaurants	63.3	49.8	31.2	23.5	16.3	15.0
Transport, storage and communications	73.5	75.1	55.9	24.9	23.6	21.6
Financial intermediation	70.2	70.2	58.1	66.3	53.0	45.6
Real estate, renting and business activities	51.3	74.8	51.6	51.2	46.0	26.5
Public administration and defence	73.3	69.2	62.9	60.1		
Education	77.6	70.8	64.5	49.3	37.5	29.9
Health-social work	78.6	74.2	61.1	45.1	36.2	27.4
Other services	64.9	58.3	54.7	29.8	31.3	31.6
Industry	**61.1**	**30.2**	**35.3**	**18.5**	**15.1**	**16.7**
Service	**74.3**	**70.4**	**60.5**	**39.1**	**34.2**	**27.0**
Total non-agriculture	**72.3**	**58.9**	**55.3**	**24.9**	**21.9**	**21.0**
Total	**72.1**	**58.5**	**55.1**	**24.6**	**21.8**	**20.8**

Source Same as Table 3

*Only includes workers in the workers in the AGEGC sector (industry groups/divisions 012, 014, 015, 02 and 99) as per NIC 2004

a quarter (24.9%) in 2004–05, to about a fifth (21%) in 2017–18. Among industry groups which showed a significant increase in informalisation between 2004–05 and 2017–18 in the formal private sector were Hotels and Restaurants; Financial Intermediation; Real Estate and Business Activities; Education; Health and Social Work.

The formal sector of the economy is largely dominated by a regular/salaried workforce. The activity-wise composition of the formal sector workforce across industries needs to be comprehended in order to further understand the drivers of informality in the formal sector that has been observed above. Only two industry groups predominantly comprise of casual workers. The ACGEC subgroup in agriculture comprises just around a third of regular/salaried workers, with the rest being casual or self-employed workers. The formal sector in the construction industry mainly comprises casual workers—about four-fifth of all workers. The share of casual workers was quite high in mining and in manufacturing in 2004–05 but has declined since then. In manufacturing, the share of casual workers has declined from 25.3% in 2004–05 to only 13.9% in 2017–18. Self-employed and casual workers are also relatively more significant in wholesale and retail trade, and in hotels and communication. On the other hand, the share of regular employment has been very high in public administration and defence, education, real estate, financial intermediation, electricity, water and gas supply and health and social work. In each of these industries, the share of regular workers exceeded 90% in 2017–18.

The industries sector has a lower share of regular workers. This share was 57.6% in 2004–05. It declined to 51.1% in 2011–12 due to the increased share of construction industry employment and then increased to 60.5% in 2017–18. In the services sector, the share of regular employment was already high at 92.5% in 2004–05 and increased steadily to 96.5% in 2017–18. In the non-agricultural sector as a whole, the share of regular workers was 77% in 2004–05. It declined to 73.2% in 2011–12, due to the rapid growth in the casualised construction industry in this period, and then increased to 81.4% in 2017–18. These percentages remain more or less the same with the inclusion of the AGEGC sub-group (Table 13).

Since regular/salaried work comprises about four-fifth of workers in the formal sector, it holds the key to trends in informality/precarity in the formal sector. Results of the percentage of regular wage/salaried workers who were informally employed are given in Table 14. Formal employment relations declined significantly in all industry groups between 2004–05 and 2017–18. Among manufacturing workers, only 35.8% regular/salaried workers were formal in 2004–05. This went down by more than 8% points to 27.4 in 2011–12 and declined further to 26.3% in 2017–18. There was a systematic decline in formal employment across the tertiary sector. This decline could be seen even in public administration and defence (from 74.5% formal workers in 2004–05 to 63.4% formal workers in 2017–18), education (from 71.6% formal workers in 2004–05 to 55.4% in 2017–18) and health (from 69.9% formal workers in 2004–05 to 38.8% in 2017–18). Regular/salaried workers remained the most formalised in public administration and defence (63.4%), electricity, water and gas supply (56.8%), education (55.4%) and financial intermediation (52.9%).

Table 13 Activity status of formal sector workers (industry-wise, percent to total)

	2004–05			2011–12			2017–18		
	SE	REG	CAS	SE	REG	CAS	SE	REG	CAS
Agriculture, hunting and forestry*	**19.1**	**34.2**	**46.7**	**7.0**	**30.4**	**62.6**	**16.0**	**35.9**	**48.1**
Mining and quarrying	5.3	56.0	38.7	1.7	57.2	41.1	1.5	68.4	30.1
Manufacturing	6.1	68.6	25.3	4.1	75.9	20.0	4.9	81.2	13.9
Electricity, gas and water supply	0.9	94.6	4.5	0.1	95.3	4.6	0.7	96.6	2.7
Construction	8.5	12.9	78.6	4.6	10.6	84.8	6.3	14.4	79.2
Wholesale and retail trade	14.3	69.2	16.6	8.7	79.9	11.4	5.5	89.8	4.7
Hotels and restaurants	12.4	76.9	10.7	9.1	84.8	6.2	7.4	83.1	9.6
Transport, storage and communications	3.0	86.5	10.4	3.2	88.0	8.8	1.1	93.3	5.6
Financial intermediation	7.0	91.6	1.3	1.5	97.4	1.1	3.9	95.7	0.4
Real estate, renting and business activities	9.2	87.9	2.9	3.3	93.7	2.9	1.6	97.0	1.3
Public administration and defence	0.5	97.8	1.7	0.0	99.2	0.8	0.0	98.8	1.2
Education	1.1	98.1	0.8	0.6	99.1	0.3	0.5	99.4	0.1
Health-social work	1.8	95.0	3.2	1.4	96.0	2.6	0.7	98.7	0.7
Other services	17.3	73.2	9.4	6.6	85.9	7.5	3.4	90.9	5.7
Industry	**6.3**	**57.6**	**36.2**	**4.0**	**51.1**	**44.9**	**5.0**	**60.5**	**34.5**
Service	**3.4**	**92.5**	**4.1**	**2.2**	**94.6**	**3.2**	**1.6**	**96.5**	**1.9**
Total non-agriculture	**4.7**	**77.0**	**18.3**	**3.1**	**73.2**	**23.7**	**3.0**	**81.4**	**15.6**
Total	**4.8**	**76.5**	**18.7**	**3.1**	**72.8**	**24.1**	**3.2**	**80.8**	**16.0**

Source Same as Table 3

Refers only to the AGEGC subgroup within agriculture which excludes crop growing and includes industry groups/divisions 012, 014, 015, 02 and 99 as per NIC 2004

Note SE, REG and CAS mean Self-employed, Regular/Salaried Workers and Casual Workers, respectively

Table 14 Formal employment (percent) among regular salaried work in the formal sector

	2004–05	2011–12	2017–18
Agriculture, hunting and forestry*	**54.8**	**61.2**	**42.5**
Mining and quarrying	77.7	75.1	52.7
Manufacturing	35.8	27.4	26.3
Electricity, gas and water supply	77.9	66.5	56.8
Construction	37.3	25.9	34.1
Wholesale and retail trade	33.0	29.0	21.5
Hotels and restaurants	34.1	23.4	22.5
Transport, storage and communications	64.7	56.3	42.4
Financial intermediation	74.5	63.0	52.9
Real estate, renting and business activities	58.2	53.5	34.0
Public administration and defence	74.5	69.4	63.4
Education	71.6	62.5	55.4
Health-Social work	69.9	60.1	48.8
Other Services	50.5	48.9	45.6
Industry	**42.5**	**32.4**	**30.4**
Service	**68.3**	**58.8**	**47.8**
Total non-agriculture	**59.7**	**49.7**	**42.4**
Total	**59.7**	**49.8**	**42.4**

Source Same as Table 3
*Only includes workers in the workers in the AGEGC sector (industry groups/divisions 012, 014, 015, 02 and 99 as per NIC 2004
Note Total Formal–informal workers/sector has been computed based on NCEUS and Srivastava and Naik (2015) study

In sectors as a whole, the share of formal workers among regular/salaried workers declined from 54.8% in 2004–05 to 42.5% in 2017–18. In industries, this share declined from 42.5% to 30.4% over the corresponding period. In the service sector as a whole, the share of formal employment among regular/salaried workers remained higher than in services but declined from 68.3% in 2004–05 to 47.8% in 2017–18.

This informalisation of regular/salaried workers has proceeded with a rapid pace. While in 2004–05, two-fifth of regular workers were informal, by 2011–12, more than half were informal. By 2017–18, just under three-fifth (57.6%) had reported informal employment relations. It is the growing informality among the regular workers that has driven the growing informalisation of formal sector employment in India between 2004–05 and 2017–18.

There is evidence that the rapid informalisation of regular workers, even among those with relatively high levels of formal education, is a major determinant of the gap between formal and informal workers. Srivastava (2016b) examined the wage differences between these two groups of regular workers: regular workers without any written contract (informal regular employees), and regular workers with a written contract (formal employees). The mean log wage rate of the former is 0.886 higher than mean log wage rate of the latter. Using Blinder–Oaxaca decomposition, the difference was divided between differences in characteristics and differences in rewards to informal and formal labour markets (wage penalty). Approximately 54% of the wage differential was accounted for by differences in characteristics, whereas differences in rewards (wage penalty) accounted for approximately 46% of the wage gap. Srivastava and Manchanda (2015) analysed the pattern of wage inequality in India. They found increasing levels of inequality among regular workers in the formal sector, reflecting rising differences between very highly skilled regular workers and the rest, on the one hand, and the other regular workers. In a recent paper, Srivastava and Padhi (2020) examined the trends in wage pattern between 2004–05 and 2017–18. The relative wage gap between regular/salaried wage workers and casual workers declined between 2004–05 and 2011–12, and further between 2011–12 and 2017–18. In fact, real wages of regular workers declined between 2011–12 and 2017–18 and the decline was at a faster rate among formal sector workers, which as we have shown has informalised at a rapid pace. Thus, informalisation of regular workers has no doubt influenced wages and labour market dynamics in the formal sector of the economy.

7 Conclusion

There is clear evidence that despite changes in the employment structure of the Indian economy towards an increasing share of industry and services in total employment, growth in regular/salaried employment, higher growth and higher share of the formal sector in total employment, and a faster rate of decline of precarious agricultural work, the share of formal employment in total employment has remained virtually unchanged. This paper analyses the trends in informal employment in India in 2004–05, 2011–12 and 2017–18. It corroborates the findings of Srivastava (2012, 2016a, b, 2019), Srivastava and Naik (2015) which have shown that there has been a significant degree of informalisation of employment in the formal sector of the economy, and among regular/salaried workers who form the predominant section of the formal sector workforce. This has counteracted the potentially positive effect of the economy-wide shift towards regular/salaried work, and towards formal sector growth.

This result reflects on the long-standing debate in India on the impact of formal labour relations on the formal sector employment. Formal employment is considered to be associated with very rigid labour laws restricting hiring and firing of workers. Results examined by Srivastava (2016a, b), Srivastava (2019) have clearly shown that formal employment has grown in India at a fairly rapid rate. These results are again corroborated in this paper which shows that formal sector employment grew by 44.8% between 2004–05 and 2011–12 and again by 56.5% between 2004–05 and 2017–18. Although formal employment grew in the formal sector, the growth of informal employment within it was much faster, leading to an informalisation of the formal sector, and arresting the formalisation of employment in the economy. These trends reflect the push towards achieving higher labour market flexibility in the formal sector, a trend which gets amplified if we also consider the predominance of informal employment in the lower rungs of the value chain which has links with the formal sector. It has resulted in a higher wage premium for highly skilled formal workers and has steadily lowered the gap between regular/salaried workers and casual workers. The increasing precariousness of employment in the non-agricultural and formal sectors of the economy has created a large, vulnerable workforce, among whom, as argued by Srivastava (2019), the circular labour migrants are a growing chunk of workers.

This situation demands urgent attention in order to arrest increasing precariousness of employment and engage policy levers in reducing the growing labour market inequalities in India.

References

Hussmans, R. (2004). *Measuring the informal economy: From employment in the informal sector to informal employment*. Working Paper No. 53. Policy Integration department, Bureau of Statistics, ILO. Geneva.

ILO (International Labour Organisation). (2011). *From precarious work to decent work*. Policies and regulations to combat precarious Employment. Geneva: ACTRAV.

ILO (International Labour Organization). (2013). *Measuring informality: A statistical manual on the informal sector and informal employment*. Geneva: International Labour Office.

Kalleberg, A. L., & Vallas, S. P. (2018) *Precarious work. Research in the sociology of work* (Vol. 31, pp. 1–30). Emerald Publishing.

Kannan, K. P., & Raveendran, G. (2019). From jobless to job-loss growth. *Economic & Political Weekly, 54*(44), 39.

Mezaddri, A., & Srivastava, R. (2015). Capital-labour relationships in formal sector garment manufacturing in the Delhi National Capital Region of India. Labour Conditions and the Working Poor in India and China, First Report of the ESRC Project. https://www.soas.ac.uk/cdpr/publications/reports/file106927.pdf.

NCEUS (National Commission for Enterprises in the Unorganised Sector). (2007). Conditions of Work and Promotion of Livelihood in the Unorganised Sector, National Commission for Enterprises in the Unorganised Sector. New Delhi: Government of India.

NCEUS (National Commission for Enterprises in the Unorganised Sector). (2008, October). *Report on definitional and statistical issues relating to the informal economy*. New Delhi: Government of India.

NSC (National Statistical Commission, Government of India). (2012, February). *Report of the Committee on Unorganised Sector Statistics*.

Rodgers, G. (2020). Labour and employment in India: A 50-year perspective. *The Indian Journal of Labour Economics* 1–19.

Srivastava, R. (2012). Changing employment conditions of the Indian workforce and implications for decent work. *Global Labour Journal, 3*(1), 63–90.

Srivastava, R. S. (2016a). Myth and reality of labour flexibility in India and what is to be done? *The Indian Journal of Labour Economics, 59*(1), 1–38 (Springer).

Srivastava, R. S. (2016b). Structural change and non-standard forms of employment in India. International Labour Office, Inclusive Labour Markets, Labour Relations and Working Conditions Branch. Geneva: ILO (Conditions of Work and Employment Series; No. 68).

Srivastava, R. (2016). *Structural change and non-standard forms of employment in India.* Geneva: ILO.

Srivastava. (2019). Inequality and social security In India: Proposed changes in labour code explosive or a whimper? Oxfarm. Retrieved, from https://www.indiaenvironmentportal.org.in/files/file/state%20of%20employment%20in%20India.pdf.

Srivastava, N., & Srivastava, R. (2010). Women, work, and employment outcomes in rural India.*Economic and Political Weekly* 49–63

Srivastava, R. S., & Naik, A. K. (2015). Growth and informality in the Indian economy. In K. P. Kannan, R. P. Mamgain & Preet Rustagi (Eds.), *Development from the perspective of labour: Essays in honour of Prof. T. S. Papola.* New Delhi: Academic Foundation.

Srivastava, R. S., & Manchanda, N. (2015). Labour market inequality in India and its dynamics. *Indian Journal of Economics, Special Centennial Issue, XCVII*(384), 25–43.

Srivastava, R. S., & Padhi, B. (2020). *Collapse in wage/salary income growth in India, 2011–12 to 2017–18.* Working Paper 01/2020, Institute for Human Development, New Delhi, India.

Verick, S. (2014). *Women's labour force participation in India: Why is it so low.* International Labor Organization

Contemporary Capitalism and Employment Challenges: Some Reflections on India

Praveen Jha and Satadru Sikdar

Abstract The fact that India confronts massive challenges of employment and livelihoods is clearly evident from the relevant literature on the subject. The progress on these was hardly impressive during the first four decades after Independence from the British colonial rule, but the overall situation appears to have gone from bad to worse during approximately the last three decades of so-called economic reforms. And indeed, the last quinquennium appears to be a disastrous phase as per all the available data sources. The focus of this paper is on some of the critical issues, with respect to the above-noted themes in contemporary India, while locating these, very briefly, in the architecture of some of the major features of contemporary global capitalism, and India's own context of neo-liberalism.

1 Introduction

It is generally well acknowledged that both, the quantity and quality of employment, have been among the most serious challenges confronting the Indian economy; in fact, by most accounts, the gravity of the problem has increased during the period of so-called economic reforms since the early 1990s. As per the report of the International Labour Organization, *World Employment and Social Outlook: Trends 2019*, region-wise distribution of unemployed persons, in 2018, was the highest in Eastern Asia (39.3 million), followed by sub-Saharan Africa (25.3 million), Latin America (24.2 million) and Southern Asia (22.2 million). This report also suggests that South Asia and sub-Saharan Africa are among the most challenged regions with respect to the quality of work, with well over 70% of workers trapped in fragile and vulnerable employment conditions. India's count of the unemployed is likely to increase from 18.3 to 18.9 million between 2017 and 2019 (ILO 2019); furthermore, the share, as

P. Jha (✉)
CESP. School of Social Sciences, Jawaharlal Nehru University, New Delhi, India
e-mail: praveenjha2005@gmail.com

S. Sikdar
National Institute of Public Finance and Policy, New Delhi, India

N. K. Mishra (ed.), *Development Challenges of India After Twenty Five Years of Economic Reforms*, India Studies in Business and Economics,
https://doi.org/10.1007/978-981-15-8265-3_9

well as the absolute numbers of those in vulnerable employment, are also likely to increase. The portion of informal jobs, for all sectors and non-agricultural sectors, is put at approximately 90% and 80%, respectively.

A recent World Bank report titled "Jobless Growth?" paints a similarly bleak picture: "the demographic transition is swelling the ranks of the working-age population across most of South Asia. In this context, keeping employment rates constant would require massive job creation. But there is a widespread perception that increases in the working-age population have been offset by declining employment rates, and that women accounted for most of the decline" (World Bank 2018, p. 29). Based on its estimate of the number of people aged 15 and above, the Report projects that India will need to create at least 8 million jobs per year to even maintain current employment rates till 2025. We may also note that India's own official estimates of the net new entrants in the job market at the current juncture have been put between 10 and 12 million every year. In other words, even if we focus only on the quantity of jobs required, there is a huge challenge at hand. Further, given that India's GDP growth rate, for almost four decades now, has been quite respectable at more than 6% per annum, but employment elasticity has shown a secular decline for more than three decades now, it is obviously pertinent to ask whether rapid growth of GDP alone can address the challenges of livelihoods and additional employment generation.

Before we examine some of these issues in detail for India, it would be useful to flag a couple of major features of contemporary capitalism which appear to have impacted the world of work everywhere, in very profound ways; this is discussed in Sect. 2. Section 3 provides a brief overview, of the trends and patterns associated with some of the major indicators, with a focus on recent years, relating to work and well-being of workers. Section4 concludes the paper highlighting its core argument.

2 Neoliberalism's Challenges to the World of Work: Some Pointers

Of course, to construct a sketch of contemporary global capitalism is a herculean endeavour, if not an impossible one. Complexity and diversity of the underlying features, processes, etc., across different regions of the world make any such task hugely challenging. There is a large literature on the subject with which we cannot engage here. Nonetheless, at a high level of abstraction, it is possible to flag a couple of its most prominent markers, which have indeed shaped its dynamics in the recent times and have huge implications for workers everywhere.

The first point worth highlighting here is that since the 1970s, the era of what most observers in political economy tradition characterise as neo-liberalism, has been ascendant, and by 1990s, this regime clearly succeeded in establishing its hegemony in the global economy. Sure enough, neo-liberalism does not come in any one size or shape, temporally or across different countries, but its core philosophy has been: 'leave the economy to the market; market knows and does the best', which was captured quite well in the phrase 'Washington Consensus', coined and made famous by John Williamson. Harvey (2005) offers a good working definition of neo-liberalism as: "*Neoliberalism is in the first instance a theory of political economic practices that proposes that human well-being can best be advanced by liberating individual entrepreneurial freedoms and skills within an institutional framework characterized by strong private property rights, free markets, and free trade. The role of the state is to create and preserve an institutional framework appropriate to such practices.*" As already hinted, here we do not intend to analyse varieties of neo-liberalism across time and space, but essentially focus on a couple of key features at the core of neo-liberal capitalism, which is what capitalism has been for close to half a century.

Among the most important features which need to be underscored as being absolutely central to the working of neo-liberalism is doing away with controls on Capital. Gradually but surely, this has had profound implications for the reconstitution of class power in the global economy and society in multiple ways, two of which are worth highlighting: (a) enormous increase in the economic and political power of capital, *vis-a-vis* other constituents such as labour, citizens, etc., everywhere; and (b) within capital in general, phenomenal increase in power of finance capital. As is well-documented, multinational and transnational corporations (MNCs/TNCs) had already become very influential entities in the global economic system by the first half of the twentieth century, (for early and very illuminating discussions of this phenomenon, see Baran and Sweezy 1966; Galbraith 1967; Stephen Hymer 1969), and during the era of neo-liberalism their power has witnessed astronomical increases. A simple indicator of this phenomenon is the fact that, as per the recent estimates by the Transnational Institute (TNI), *of the top hundred economic entities, in terms of revenue,69 were corporations and only 31 were countries.* (Babic, Fichtner and Heemskerk 2017). In this list, Walmart comes at the top among corporations, after countries of G-7, along with China and Brazil, and occupies the tenth position. It is this dramatic increase in the economic heft of these corporations, and their increasing stranglehold on the global economic system, which justifies late Amin's (2019) claim that "contemporary capitalism is a capitalism of generalised monopolies". Amin suggests that the global economic system has reached a new stage in the centralisation of capital where leading corporations, mostly headquartered in the North, are in the drivers' seat and have established firm networks of control through "monopolies upstream and downstream" across the economies of the world (Amin 2019). One of its major implications has been strengthening of the processes of primitive accumulation, (which in any case is a permanent feature of capitalism), resulting in large-scale destruction of petty production and livelihoods of the masses in the Global South.

Another significant development during the era of neo-liberalism, and organically connected with doing away with regulations on capital, has been the reconstitution of class power within 'capital in general' in favour of 'finance capital', which relies primarily on accumulation through circulation and speculation; in its extreme and vulgar form, it is nothing but unbridled 'casino capitalism'. Paul Sweezy had pointed to this 'new finance' in his *The Triumph of Financial Capital,* almost a quarter-century ago: "the development in the last twenty years or so of a relatively independent—financial superstructure sitting on top of the world economy and most of its national units. It is made up of banks—central, regional and local—and a host of dealers in a bewildering variety of financial assets and services, all inter connected by a network of markets, some of which are structured and regulated, others informal and unregulated", (Sweezy 1994). As it happens, the growing power of this new finance has dramatically altered the processes and dynamics of accumulation in the global economy, and these have been analysed very carefully by several Marxist political economists. To quote Sweezy again: "Traditionally financial expansion has gone hand in hand with prosperity in the real economy. Is it really possible that this is no longer true, that now in the late twentieth century the opposite is more nearly the case; in other words, that financial expansion feeds not on a healthy real economy but a stagnant one? The answer to this question, I think, is yes, it is possible, and it has been happening. And I will add that I am quite convinced that the *inverted relation between the financial and the real is the key to understanding new trends in the world economy* (italics added)" (Sweezy 1994).

Another major marker of contemporary capitalism, which partly resembles, analytically speaking, above-noted characterisation advanced by Samir Amin, that "contemporary capitalism is a capitalism of generalised monopolies", is trans-nationalisation of capital from North to the South, both through direct investments in economic activities (FDI) as well as through the incorporation of domestic economic actors without making any direct investments locally, *e.g.* by making them 'suppliers'. These have resulted, as Patnaik (2005) puts it, in the loosening of "the traditionally enforced pattern of international division of labour". In other words, the traditional segmentation of economic activities and associated division of labour have been considerably diluted and a handful of countries in the Global South have become major hubs in a whole range of 'modern economic activities'. The case of East Asia, led by China, as the 'manufacturing workshop', and that of India as the 'office' of the world, have received considerable attention in the recent decades. These developments, relating to accelerated trans-nationalisation of economic activities have been analysed under the broad rubric of global commodity chains/supply chains/value chains/production networks (GCCs/GSCs/GVCs/GPNs), etc. We need not get into a discussion of these analytical frameworks here and their respective merits and disadvantages, and would only like to stress that such developments have had profound implications for contemporary capitalism and its various actors; further, in large measure, above-noted dramatic restructuring of global accumulation dynamics is organically connected with de-regulation of capital or, in other words, the ascendency of neo-liberalism.

From the point of view of workers, the above-noted 'de-centreing/de-segmentation', etc. have several important implications, the most obvious one being that employment and wages in the Global North cannot be insulated anymore from the exposure of huge labour reserves in the Global South, even though it may not lead to any significant expansion in labour absorption in the latter, due to adoption of relatively capital-intensive technology, destruction of petty production, etc., which are also organically connected with the restructuring in the overall global accumulation dynamics. Thus, trans-nationalisation of economic activities from the North to the select destinations in the South, as has been experienced during the last few decades, may lead to increases in the labour productivity in the latter without concomitant increases in the wages, while putting considerable pressure on wages and working conditions in the former. A major implication of such connected tendencies would be an increase in the share of surplus, along with a decline in the share of wages, in total output. All available evidences point exactly to such tendencies and outcomes in the global economy during the era of neo-liberalism, (Basu 2016). In fact, even in the most powerful economy in the World, viz. the USA, as noted by Stiglitz apart from a decline in the wage share, even the real wages have been almost stagnant since the late 1960s (Stiglitz 2018).

The third important feature associated with contemporary accumulation regimes, with significant implications for the world of work, worth flagging here, is connected with the profound technological changes often described as the fourth industrial revolution, which constitutes a large and complex canvas. Although it is indeed difficult to predict work and labour-related outcomes connected with the so-called 'Industry Four', due to several uncertainties including the economical–political–social ones, it appears that the global economy has witnessed a major acceleration in labour-saving technological changes in the recent decades, thus creating substantial pressure on the world of work.

In sum: important markers which have profoundly structured contemporary global capitalist dynamics and are organically connected with neo-liberalism, appear to generate several adverse tendencies for workers across the globe; further, there are no good news around the corner. Although, based on the major features of contemporary capitalism, which we have very briefly mentioned in the foregoing, one cannot jump to unequivocal conclusions regarding the prospect for employment, livelihoods, working conditions, etc., either for India or elsewhere, certain tendencies need to be taken seriously. First, growing financialisation of accumulation under the tutelage of neo-liberalism tends to put tremendous pressure on the real economy everywhere, privileging 'casino capitalism', which leads to increases in 'labour reserves'. Second, the other structural changes in contemporary capitalism, flagged in the foregoing, have contributed to significant increases in the share of surplus and downward pressures on the share of wages; these obviously exacerbate the problems of underconsumption and labour demand. Third, given the hegemony of finance capital, nation states are trapped into deflationary macroeconomic policies, resulting in compression of public investments and expenditure; these again have serious adverse consequences for the world of work and workers. With these brief remarks on the larger overall context of global capitalism, we now turn to the India story.

3 Persistent and Deepening Employment Deficits in India

Before highlighting some important characteristics of the contemporary world of work in India, it would be useful to say a few words about the existing relevant data sources. Though multiple official entities and institutions are involved in collection, compilation and dissemination of labour statistics,[1] most discussions on employment in India generally rely on the surveys of the Employment and Unemployment Situation (EUS) which have been conducted since the early 1950s by the National Sample Survey Organisation (NSSO), an organisation under the jurisdiction of Ministry of Statistics and Programme Implementation (MoSPI). Of course, covering the entire population, baseline statistics capturing quite a few important variables, are also generated by the Registrar of Census and the Census Commissioner, every 10 years, the last census being conducted in 2011. Apart from these major institutions, organisations like the Labour Bureau and Directorate General of Employment and Training (DGET), which are linked to the Ministry of Labour and Employment (MoLE), carry out sporadic and targeted surveys. A recent internationally comparable database constructed through a collaboration between the International Labour Organisation and the Reserve Bank of India known as the Capital (K), Labour (L), Energy (E), Material (M), Services (S) database or RBI-KLEMS database, maybe used to track year-wise log changes in GDP, sectoral growth rates and growth rates of employment between 1981–82 and 2016–17.

Apart from these sources, we also get useful labour statistics about the organised/formal sector from administrative sources such as Employees' Provident Fund Organisation (EPFO), the Employees State Insurance Scheme (ESIC) and National Pension System (NPS). Government database monitoring implementation of employment generation schemes like Mahatma Gandhi National Rural Employment Guarantee Act (MGNREGA), 'Support to Training and Employment Programme (STEP)' and others also provide limited real-time data on particular segments and target groups. Recent studies have also used data from private agencies like Centre for Monitoring Indian Economy (CMIE) which does Consumer Pyramid Surveys (CMIE-CPDX) in collaboration with Bombay Stock Exchange (BSE).

As mentioned earlier, the NSSO surveys have been considered most valuable sources for the world of work in India. The first NSS-EUS was undertaken in the Round 9 (May–September 1955); thereafter, there were experiments with survey designs of EUS up to the early 1970s. Based on the Dantwala Committee's recommendations, a more ambitious and relatively more comprehensive survey, covering several variables, including employment and unemployment was carried out in 1972–73 (i.e. the 27th Round of NSS). As suggested by the Committee, it was decided to carry these Surveys quinquennially; thus far, six such comprehensive surveys have been conducted, and the last one was 68th Round (2011–12).[2] With respect to the labour domain, these surveys provide data on the labour force participation rates (LFPR, i.e. the number of employed+the number of unemployed in the labour force) and the worker population ratio (WPR, i.e. the proportion of actually working or employed people with particular population segments) and unemployment rates (UR). The significance of this data is that it provides important information on, both organised/formal and unorganised/informal sector workers, through the collection of

[1] We have provided a brief review of these elsewhere (Jha 2009), and here we limit our readers to a bare minimum.

[2] The details about the available information have been discussed in other paper by Jha (2015).

data on regular, self-employed and casual workers. However, a major limitation of the quinquennial NSSO data was that it provided information with a gap of 5 years, which had obvious constraints from the point of view of policy interventions. Hence, it was decided, based on the Panagariya Committee recommendations, that annual periodic labour force survey (PLFS) should replace the hitherto quinquennial EUS, to collect important information on work related variables. It was proposed that data on LFPR, WPR and UR for the usual status (UPSS) and current weekly status (CWS),[3] for men and women in the rural and urban areas. It also recommended that rotational sampling be done for urban areas over four quarters of the year. In line with the recommendation of the said Committee, the first Annual PLFS was conducted between June 2017 and July 2018, and its report was published in May 2019. Most of the observations in this paper on the long term trends in the world of work are based on estimates which are calculated on the basis of different rounds of the NSSO (EUS) and PLFS data. Some references are also made to other data sources.

It comes out very powerfully from multiple data sources that the employment situation has been under huge stress in recent years. The recent annual PLFS, 2017–18 has shown that the unemployment rate has risen 2.77 times since the last EUS of 2011–12 and is at a 45 years high of 6.1% as per UPSS measure. Similarly, the decline in the growth rate of employment growth is also reported by the RBI-KLEMS database which shows that 7.7 lakh people became jobless between 2014 and 2016; though some recovery was made in 2016–17 with an addition of 2.89 lakh jobs, there was a net loss of approximately 4.89 lakh jobs between 2014–15 and 2016–17. According to the RBI-KLEMS database, there have been negative log changes in the rate of growth of employment in 12 sectors (out of a total of 27 sectors) in 3 years between 2014–15 and 2016–17. From a long-term perspective, the exponential growth rate in employment was 1.92, 1.72 and 1.47% in the periods between 1981–82 to 1989–90, 1990–91 to 1999–2000 and 2000–01 to 2009–10, respectively. But these came down sharply to 0.58% between 2010–11 and 2016–17.[4]

The secular upward trend in unemployment is evident for all regions and segments of the population through both the UPSS and CWS approaches as illustrated in the data presented by the PLFS 2017–18. Through the CWS, we can see that the unemployment rate in 2017–18 reached a high of 8.8% for rural and urban male workers; it was 7.7% rural women and 12.8% for urban women workers (Table 1 in Appendix). The same trend is also illustrated through the UPSS approach, which shows that unemployment rates for 2017–18 were 5.8 and 3.8 for rural males and rural females, respectively; for urban male and urban female workers, they were 7.1 and 10.8%, respectively.[5] The current PLFS shows that the LFPR for women in rural India is at the lowest level since 1993–94; it is 18.2% if estimated by UPSS approach and 16.1% by the CWS approach, the. Though there has been a miniscule increase in

[3]For different measures of employment/unemployment see Jha (2009).

[4]We have also calculated the average log change during these periods, as these were, 1.65, 1.48, 1.25% in between 1981–82 and 1989–90, 1990–91 and 1999–2000 and 2000–01 and 2009–10, respectively, and it has reduced to 0.47% in between 2010–11 and 2016–17.

[5]Based on Appendix Tables 18 and 36, Annual Report PLFS 2017–18.

urban LFPR for women (Table 2 of Appendix), this has not been enough to offset the steep fall in rural LFPR. The result has been a historical low in participation rates.

The scenario described above is organically connected with neo-liberal economic policies which have increased the divergence between growth rates and labour absorption; rural India has borne the brunt of the growing employment crisis. Since the mid-1990s, persisting and deepening agrarian distress has been accompanied by the lack of gainful employment in the non-agricultural sectors. Even today, about half the total population is dependent on agriculture and allied sectors for their livelihood, even though the sector only contributes a sixth to the GDP. Further, state-led efforts to induce the much talked about the process of diversification of employment from the mid-1970s to the late 1980s have received a massive setback with cutbacks in public spending, especially since the mid-1990s. Apart from this, there are also many other reasons, among which one important cause is accelerating displacement and dispossession, resulting in a huge expansion of labour reserves in rural India without adequate creation of gainful employment in the non-agricultural sector. The share of the manufacturing sector in the overall national income has been stagnant around 15–16% since the early 1990s and most of the growth has taken place in the service sector, a great deal of which is of a very vulnerable quality.

The growing dissonance between overall GDP growth rates and WPR is illustrated in Fig. 1, which shows the moving average of GDP and WPR shares for both rural and urban in different NSS and PLFS years. It clearly demonstrates that in spite of

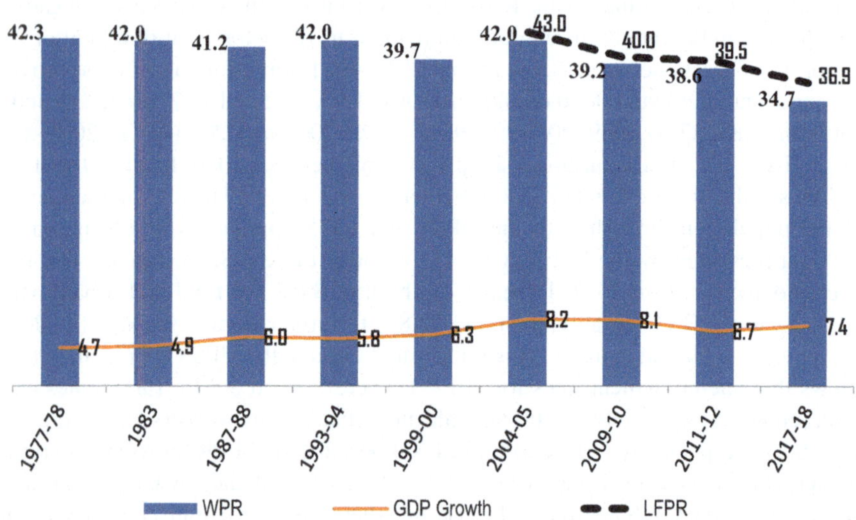

Fig. 1 GDP growth rate (3 Years MA) and workforce & labour participation rate. *Note* GDP figures from 1976–77 to 2012–13 are in 2004–05 constant prices, whereas GDP figures for 2016–17 to 2018–19 are in 2011–12 constant prices. *Sources* WPR compiled from Statement 10& LFPR from Statement 8, PLFS Annual Report 2017–18 and GDP from CSO

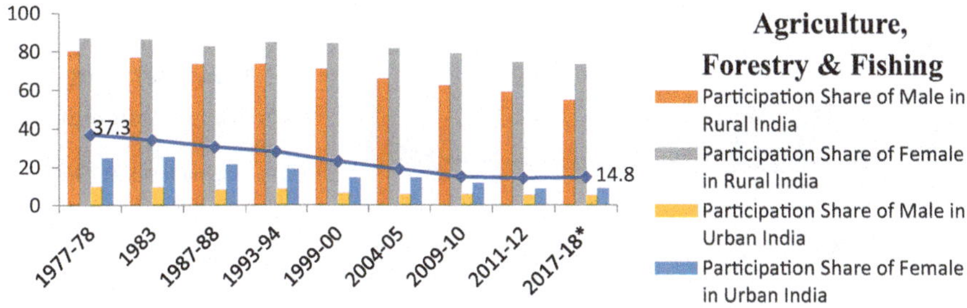

Fig. 2 Comparison of GDP and WPR shares in agriculture, forestry & fishing. *Note* GDP shares are 3 years moving average and figures from 1976–77 to 2012–13 are in 2004–05 constant prices, whereas figures for 2016–17 to 2018–19 are in 2011–12 constant prices and the share of GVA. *Source* WPR are based on NSS Report No. 554: Employment and Unemployment Situation in India, 2011–12, Statement 5.11 and Annual Report PLFS, 2017–18, Appendix Table 26 and GDP shares are calculated from data available from CSO

increasing GDP growth rates, labour absorption rates were stagnant till 2004–05, and have been falling subsequently.

The broad picture presented above can be nuanced through an analysis of the WPR across the major sectors and industry groups during the last four decades as shown in Table 3 of the Appendix. The results of Table 3 have been presented in Figs. 2, 3, 4, 5, 6, 7, and 8, which illustrate how the labour absorption of different sectors is either stagnant or declining from the late 1970s onwards. Figure two shows that in contrast to the overall trend, and most other major sectors, GDP share in agriculture and its allied sectors have sharply fallen although it continues to be the single largest employer in the economy. The WPR rates for rural men declined from 80.4 to 54.95% and, for rural women, they have fallen from 86.8 to 73.19% between 1977–78 and 2017–18.

The results for agriculture and allied sectors (from Table 3 and Fig. 2) presented above clearly point towards the significant fall in labour absorption. Ideally, such a fall should have resulted in a transition from labour absorption in agriculture to other non-agricultural sectors. However, the trends in the non-agricultural sectors (Table

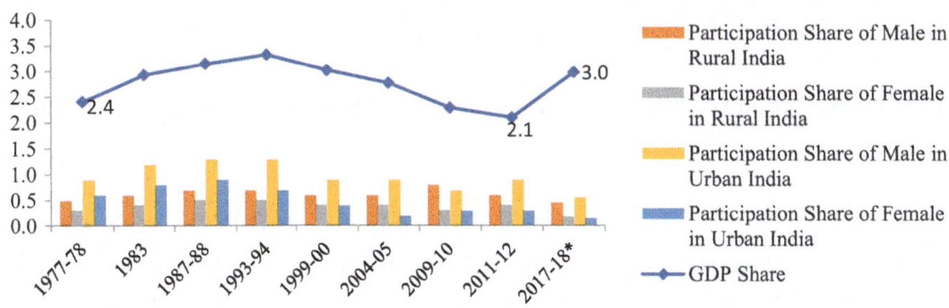

Fig. 3 Comparison of GDP share and WPR share in mining & quarrying. *Note* and *Source* Same as Fig. 2

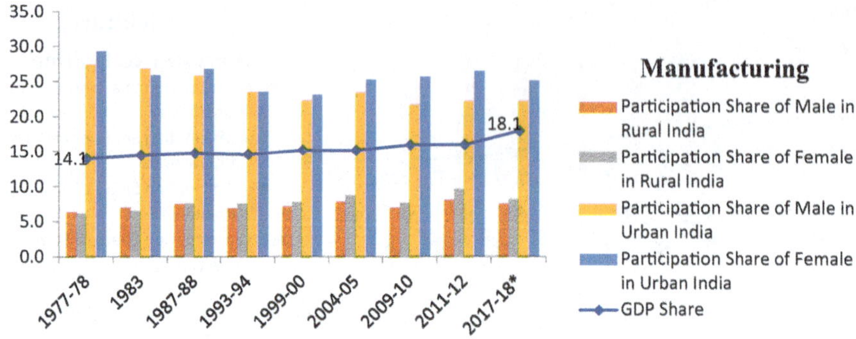

Fig. 4 Comparison of GDP share and WPR share in manufacturing. *Note & Source* Same as Fig. 2

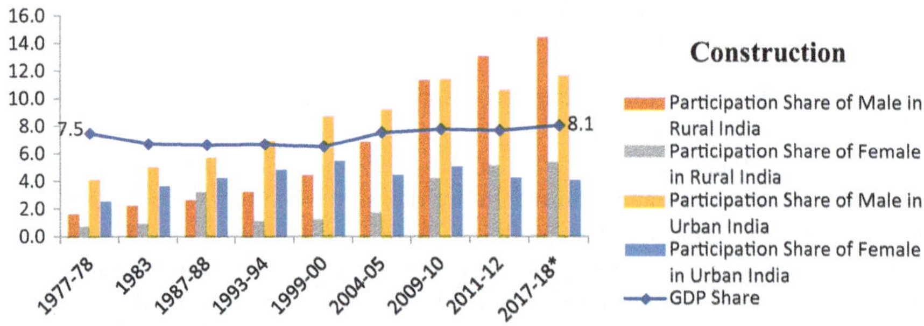

Fig. 5 Comparison of GDP share and WPR share in construction. *Note & Source* Same as Fig. 2

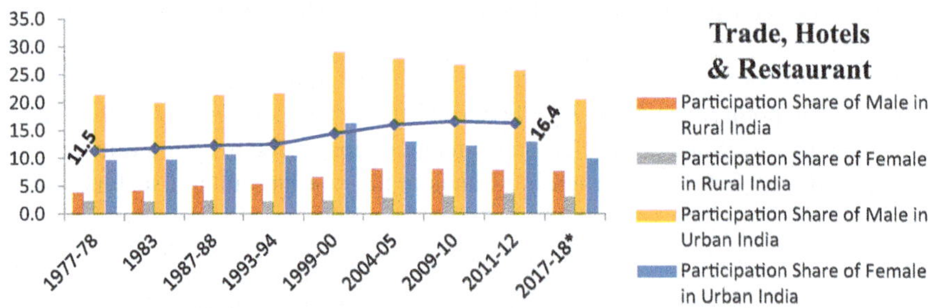

Fig. 6 Comparison of GDP share and WPR share in trade, hotels & restaurant. *Note & Source* Same as Fig. 2

3 and Figs. 3, 4, 5, 6, 7, 8) show that these sectors have largely followed the path of jobless growth. For example, the GDP share in Mining and Quarrying (Fig. 3) has experienced an upward turn between 2012 and 2018 (after it declined between 1993–94 and 2012), but the WPR has seen a continuous decline since 1994. Among

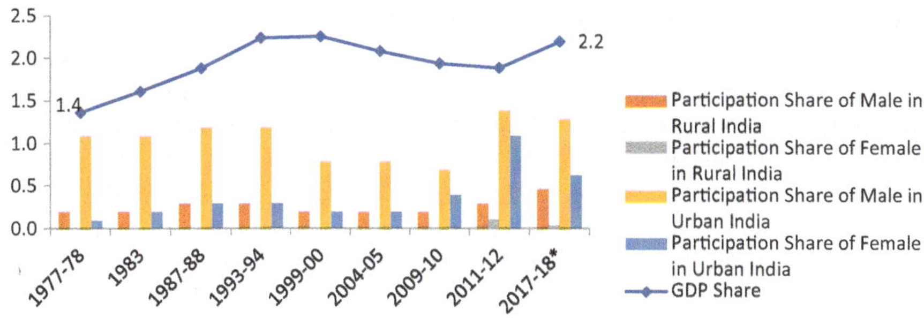

Fig. 7 Comparison of GDP share and WPR share in electricity, gas & water supply. *Note & Source* Same as Fig. 2

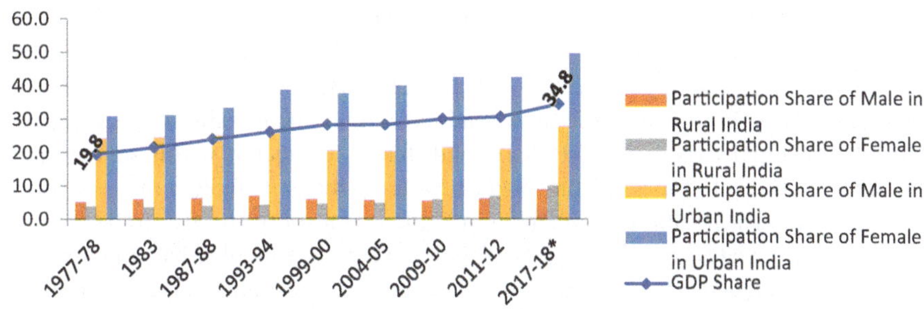

Fig. 8 Comparison of GDP and WPR Share in Other Services. *Note & Source* Same as Fig. 2

other factors, the privatisation of mines and incentives to reduce human intervention may be the source of its reduced capacity to absorb labour.

In contrast to this, the Manufacturing Sector has seen a relatively more stable trend where its GDP share has increased from 14% in 1977–78 to 18.1% in 2017–18 (Table 3 and Fig. 4); even during the 1990s, the sector seems to have shown stable growth, but without any expansion in its share in GDP. The WPR in this sector has remained between 22 and 25% for all segments of the population, thus showing no new creation of promising jobs for those who are actually losing employment in other sectors. As per the All India Manufacturers' Organisation (AIMO) survey, across 3 lakh industries, about 35 lakhs jobs were lost across different segments of manufacturing from 2014 to 2018. Also, the recent turmoil in the automobile sector has resulted in job losses to the tune of approximately 3.5 lakh. This slowdown is also having a negative impact on ancillary industries like combing automakers, spare part manufacturers and franchised dealers and garages (Reuters 2019).

Construction is another sector which has been seen as having good prospects for the creation of new jobs, in large measure, due to government incentives to private construction businesses in the last few decades. This sector has seen a slight growth since the middle of the 1990s (Table 3 and Fig. 5). Long-term trends in Fig. 5 also show that WPR of both male and female workers have been to the tune of 21–25%

in overall terms. It is significant that female WPR showed a marginally rising trend till 2012, but in the recent period, there has been a slight downturn, highlighting the contraction of employment between 2012 and 2018. Even schemes like MGNREGS and other government projects like PMGSY have failed to have a significant impact on employment generation.

Further, it is to be noted that most of the opportunities generated in this sector are largely in the nature of casual and irregular wage labour without any modicum of social protection. Hence, expanding opportunities in the construction sector only reflect the expansion of low-wage informal work, which, as the PLFS shows, has also contracted in the last 6 years.

The lack of labour absorption in these four producing sectors, which account for approximately 44% of the current GDP and about two-thirds of WPR in rural areas, is apparent from the data presented above. These trends of jobless/job-loss growth have been structured by uneven development where the emphasis has been on the service sectors. Data from RBI-KLEMS further illustrates that the overall GDP growth rate has largely been driven by the service sector, in which there is a preponderance of both vulnerable casual and self-employment (Table 4 of Appendix). The relationship between the GDP shares of different sub-sectors within services and the WPR is shown in Figs. 6, 7 and 8 (data for the same is in Table 3 of Appendix). There was an incremental improvement in WPR in transport, storage, trade (Fig. 6) and electricity, water sectors (Fig. 7). This is especially true of urban India which has seen an increasing WPR, especially in the category of ‘other services’ (Fig. 8). As PLFS report shows, 49.9% of female workers in urban India are engaged in ‘other services’, and of which, almost 15.1% engaged in the education sector, and 9.56% are engaged in ‘activities of households as employers’ as domestic workers and almost 6% are working in ‘human health and social work activities’. Relatively high presence of these workers in these segments represents persistence of informal sector as they largely work without any job security and social protection.

The lack of labour absorption across different sectors is accompanied by the high presence of low-wage and insecure employment. Though there has been an increasing trend of ‘real’ wages since the 1980s, it is also accompanied by wage inequality, especially in the urban/organised sector, and also between regular and casual workers during the same period (Jha 2015). Recent data presented by the PLFS 2017–18 shows the average daily wage rates for regular wage/salaried employees, self-employed persons (with 30 days recall periods), and for casual labour (with each day of the reference week) as illustrated in Fig. 9.

Table 3 of the Appendix and Fig. 9 clearly show that the average wages are higher for regular salaried employees in comparison with self-employed and casual workers. The PLFS 2017–18 also shows that the self-employed and casual workers in rural India are earning less than half of regular waged workers, which is already much less, i.e. about two-thirds of the accepted minimum standard (Varma 2019). The average earnings of self-employed workers are better than those of casual workers but lower than that of regular salaried workers. Gender and sectoral differences in wages are clearly visible from Fig. 9. There are substantial disparities in average

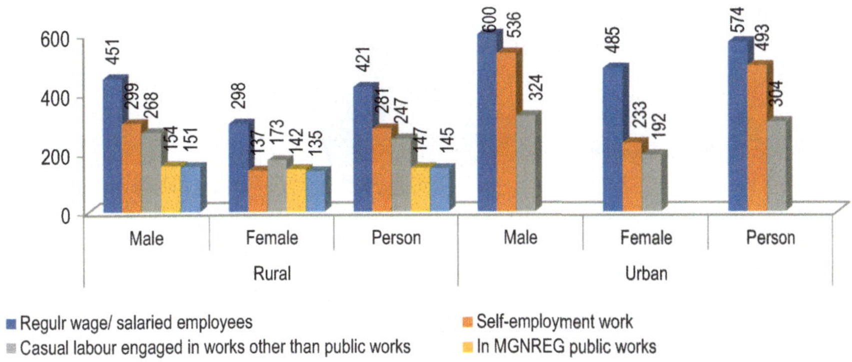

Fig. 9 Comparison of average daily wages among broad status of employment. *Source* Calculation based on Annual Report PLFS, 2017–18

wages[6] calculated for self-employed workers; for average, monthly wages for male workers are Rs. 16,067 and Rs. 8955 in urban and rural India, respectively whereas, for urban and rural women, they are Rs. 6993.75 and Rs. 4122, respectively. Further, for self-employed women workers in rural India, the average daily wage (i.e. average monthly wage divided by 30 days) is significantly less than the average daily wage for casual workers in non-public work and MGNREGS. The inequalities of wages across different types of jobs in diverse sectors show that a large share of workers are working for wages which are much lower than the declared minimum wages (Jha 2015; Papola and Kannan 2017) (Table 5).[7]

The unregulated low-wage employment scenario described above is reflective of the persistence and deepening of informality. Casual workers and own-account enterprises, 85% of whom work with only one or two hired workers, form the bulk of the working population and structure low-wage and insecure work. Even though the world of work has been characterised by a high ratio of informal workers in the pre-reform period, this has been exacerbated by a relentless informalisation of work in the formal sector. In 1999–2000, the share of informal workers in the so-called organised sector was 37.8% and it had increased to 54.4% in 2011–12, according to the 68th round of NSSO. As per the same round of the NSSO, 97% of the self-employed in the rural and 98% in the urban areas are in the informal sector; 78% of the rural casual labourers and 81% of the urban casual labourers are in the informal sector.

---

[6]The PLFS report has presented quarterly average wage for these broad categories, and we have calculated the average wage of these quarterly figures.

[7]According to the NCEUS report (2009), 85% of all casual workers in rural areas and 57% of them in urban areas get wages below the minimum wages in 2004–05. The difference in the proportion of workers below the minimum wage norm in rural areas and urban areas is more marked for the non-agricultural workers, with urban workers being considerably worse-off. Among industry groups, the proportion of men below the minimum wage is higher in trade, whereas among women it is highest in manufacturing in rural and urban areas. Thus, an overwhelming majority of workers both in the rural as well as urban areas get wages which are well below the stipulated minimum wage in the country.

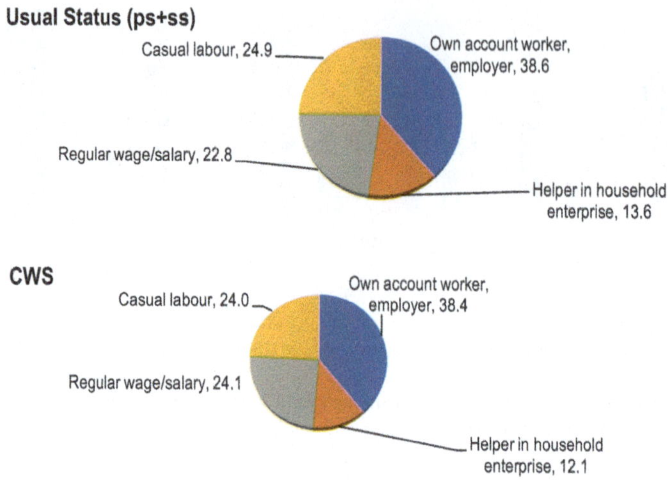

Fig. 10 Percentage distribution of persons working by broad status in employment. *Source* Based on PLFS Annual Report, 2017–18

As per the NSSO estimates of 2011–12, count of informal labour was a whopping 453.4 million out of a total of 473.8 million[8] or 93% of the total employed people. This went up to 466.48 million out of a total of 471.3 million or approximately 99% of the working people in 2017–2018.[9]

Workers in informal employment are generally represented by a high presence of self-employed and casual workers. This is also reflected in the 2017–18, which shows that 52.2% of the All India workforce (UPSS) is self-employed; 25% are casual, and 22.8% are regular salaried workers. In rural India (Table 6 and Fig. 10), the share of self-employed workers is as high as 57.8% of which 41% are own-account workers. Only 29.1 are casual workers, whereas only 13.1% are working as regular salaried workers (Table 6 and Fig. 10). The same pattern also can be seen with respect enumeration of types of workers by the CWS approach as shown in Table 7 and Fig. 10.

Further evidence of informality, among regular/salaried employees, is captured in the PLFS, 2017–18, which shows that 71.1% of the workers in non-agricultural regular wage/salaried (PS+SS) do not have any written job contract. About 54.2% of them are not eligible for paid leave and 49.6% are without any social security

[8]The calculation of the workforce is done on the basis of the projected population calculated on the basis of Census 2011 and growth rates provided in NSSO EUS report 2012. The formula is seen as: A = A1 (census population) *(1 + R (rate of growth of specific segments/100)^82/100 for 2017–18. The projected population for 2012 was provided in the EUS report. The population of rural male and female; urban male and female were calculated separately to project the total population. Multiplier was used from respective NSSO reports to work out the LFPR and WPR (NSSO 2012).

[9]The calculation of workers in informal employment = self-employed workers + casual workers + regular workers without a written contract.

benefit. One of the major indicators of such rising informality is that people in regular employment are willing to work for longer hours. Under the Factory Act, 1948 the length of a normal working day was 8 hours a day, with one hour of overtime, for 6 days a week. By these standards, a worker should be working between 48 and 54 hours a week. However, the PLFS shows that, on an average, a regular worker is working 58.1 hours a week, largely because of the flexibility that has been introduced within the system under the banner of labour reforms. What is even more worrisome, as per the same report, between 7 and 9% of regular workers are available for additional work for 12–14 hours a week. At the same time, 9–12% of the employers of own-account enterprises are also available for additional work for an average of 12–15 h a week. Approximately 10% of the casual workers are willing to do additional work for 14–15 h a week. Thus, at the current juncture, workers are both overworked and underpaid. Despite relatively high economic growth rates of GDP in the reforms era, withdrawal of the Indian state from several key areas in the social sector has only aggravated the vulnerability of the masses. In fact, many of these workers do not have adequate recognition as a 'worker' and are outside the scope of any labour legislation which sets out the parameters of workers' rights.

4 Concluding Remarks

Apart from long-term structural changes, organically connected with the so-called economic reforms since the early 1990s, it would appear that the last quinquennium has been particularly stressful on the employment front, as is evident from all the major data sources. Much of it is on account of the two major disruptions by the Union Government, namely, demonetisation in November 2015 and the rolling out of the ill-conceived Goods and Services Tax (GST), within 7 months of the demonetisation. As pointed out by the last Economic Survey (by the Government of India), there are serious negative fallouts of these measures including on employment generation. As per the CMIE-CPHS data, about 1.5 million jobs were lost during the first 4 months of 2017, which was attributed to demonetisation. The same data source pointed out that in 2018, the Indian economy lost a whooping 11 million jobs. There were reports of large-scale retrenchment of workers, substantial instances of return migration (from urban to rural areas) and an increase in the employment demand under MGNREGA, etc.

In passing, we may note that a major basis for rosy claims on the employment front, advanced by the current government spokespersons, is on account of the presumed success of the so-called the Pradhan Mantri Mudra Yojana (PMMY). However, as a recent study notes, under this programme, the share of substantial loans (above Rs. 5 lakhs), which have the potential to create jobs, was as little as 1.3% of total disbursement in 2017–18. The average loan size of Rs. 52,700 appears to be far too small to have any employment generation potential. But if one goes by the total disbursement under the Mudra Yojana, which was worth Rs. 2,53,677.10 crores and distributed to 4.81 crores beneficiaries in 2017–18 (without examining the issues of viable business model, employability, etc.) and simply counting each beneficiary a net addition to employment, clearly one can arrive at fantabulous figures of employment increases!

Finally, with respect to schemes and programmes, we would like to stress here that the performance of any government with respect to relevant indicators must include how it deals with the vulnerable sections of the population. In this context, the performance of the government in recent years with respect to MGNREGA ought to be considered an appropriate benchmark. By now, there are quite a few studies (e.g. Rajendran Narayanan et al. 2018), which show that this job guarantee scheme—which is a kind of lifeline to those at the bottom of India's economic and social hierarchy—has been continuously hammered by the current government. For instance, the budget allocation during the current union government regime has not only been insufficient but going down in real terms. In fact, adjusting for inflation, the allocation for 2018–19 is substantially lower than what it was in 2010–11. Two, the functioning of the scheme has been persistently plagued during the last few years by a problem of "pending wages"; for the year 2016–17, the total amount of pending wages (i.e. the amount the to be paid by the union government to the state governments for works already performed) for the country as a whole was around Rs. 11,000 crores. This obviously becomes a major disincentive for the state government to run the scheme in a demand-driven sense. Third, by delinking the MGNREGA wage rates from the Minimum Wages Act, 1948 and choosing not to increase the former in real terms has dealt yet another blow to the functioning of the scheme and consequently large segments of the most vulnerable segments of India's workers. In our judgment, the way MGNREGA has been dealt with is possibly the most damning indictment of the current NDA government at the Centre.

To conclude: to make sense of the multiple dimensions of the world of work in India, including the quantity and quality of jobs, both in the organised and unorganised sector, it is obvious that there are serious structural and persistent employment problems that the country is confronted with. The basic question, with respect to labour and employment, has to do with the strategies of appropriate economic transformation that is inclusive and can generate decent work. The period since the early 1990s has been anything but what can be considered a move towards an appropriate strategy. Based on whatever evidence we have, the policies adopted by the NDA government since 2014 have made it even worse.

Appendix

See Tables 1, 2, 3, 4, 5, 6 and 7.

Table 1 Unemployment rates (in %) according to usual status (ps+ss) and current weekly status (CWS) from 1972–73 to 2017–18 (PLFS)

Round (year)	Rural				Urban			
	Male		Female		Male		Female	
	Usual status (ps+ss)	CWS	Usual status (ps+ss)	CWS	Usual status (ps+ss)	CWS	Usual status (ps+ss)	CWS
(1)	(2)	(3)	(4)	(5)	(6)	(7)	(8)	(9)
PLFS (2017–18)	5.8	8.8	3.8	7.7	7.1	8.8	10.8	12.8
68th (2011–12)	1.7	3.3	1.7	3.5	3.0	3.8	5.2	6.7
66th (2009–10)	1.6	3.2	1.6	3.7	2.8	3.6	5.7	7.2
61st (2004–05)	1.6	3.8	1.8	4.2	3.8	5.2	6.9	9.0
55th (1999–2000)	1.7	3.9	1.0	3.7	4.5	5.6	5.7	7.3
50th (1993–94)	1.4	3.1	0.9	2.9	4.1	5.2	6.1	7.9
43rd (1987–88)	1.8	4.2	2.4	4.4	5.2	6.6	6.2	9.2
38th (1983)	1.4	3.7	0.7	4.3	5.1	6.7	4.9	7.5
32nd (1977–78)	1.3	3.6	2.0	4.1	5.4	7.1	12.4	10.9
27th (1972–73)	1.2	3.0	0.5	5.5	4.8	6.0	6.0	9.2

Source PLFS Annual Report 2017–18, Statement 31, Page 83
Note The figures are to be read along with the explanatory note given in the PLFS Annual Report 2017–18 for comparability

Table 2 LFPR (in %)

LFPR (in %)		Rural		Urban	
		Usual (ps+ss)	CWS	Usual (ps+ss)	CWS
Male	1993–1994	56.1	54.7	54.3	53.8
	1999–2000	54	53.1	54.2	53.9
	2004–05	55.5	54.5	57	56.6
	2009–10	55.6	54.8	55.9	55.6
	2011–12	55.3	54.5	56.3	56.1
	2017–18	54.9	54.4	57	56.7

(continued)

Table 2 (continued)

LFPR (in %)		Rural		Urban	
		Usual (ps+ss)	CWS	Usual (ps+ss)	CWS
Female	1993–1994	33	27.6	16.5	15.2
	1999–2000	30.2	26.3	14.7	13.8
	2004–05	33.3	28.7	17.8	16.8
	2009–10	26.5	23.1	14.6	14.1
	2011–12	25.3	21.5	15.5	14.8
	2017–18	18.2	16.1	15.9	15.3

Source PLFS Annual Report 2017–18, Statement 7, Page 51
Note The figures are to be read along with the explanatory note given in the PLFS Annual Report 2017–18 for comparability

Table 3 GDP share and percentage distribution of usually working persons (ps+ss) by industry of work, 1977–78 to 2017–18

Broad industry division	NSS round	Rural		Urban		GDP Share
		Male	Female	Male	Female	
Agriculture	PLFS (2017–18)	54.95	73.19	5.38	9.07	14.8
	68th (2011–12)	59.2	74.5	5.6	8.7	14.3
	66th (2009–10)	62.5	78.9	5.9	11.8	15.0
	61st (2004–05)	66.2	81.4	6	14.7	19.2
	55th (1999–2000)	71.2	84.1	6.5	14.6	23.3
	50th (1993–94)	73.7	84.7	8.7	19.3	28.3
	43rd (1987–88)	73.9	82.5	8.5	21.8	30.9
	38th (1983)	77.2	86.2	9.7	25.5	34.5
	32nd (1977–78)	80.4	86.8	10.2	25.1	37.3
Mining & quarrying	PLFS (2017–18)	0.46	0.17	0.56	0.15	3.0
	68th (2011–12)	0.6	0.4	0.9	0.3	2.1
	66th (2009–10)	0.8	0.3	0.7	0.3	2.3
	61st (2004–05)	0.6	0.4	0.9	0.2	2.8
	55th (1999–2000)	0.6	0.4	0.9	0.4	3.0
	50th (1993–94)	0.7	0.5	1.3	0.7	3.3
	43rd (1987–88)	0.7	0.5	1.3	0.9	3.2
	38th (1983)	0.6	0.4	1.2	0.8	2.9
	32nd (1977–78)	0.5	0.3	0.9	0.6	2.4

(continued)

Table 3 (continued)

Broad industry division	NSS round	Rural		Urban		GDP Share
		Male	Female	Male	Female	
Manufacturing	PLFS (2017–18)	7.66	8.14	22.39	25.22	18.1
	68th (2011–12)	8.2	9.6	22.4	26.6	16.1
	66th (2009–10)	7.1	7.6	21.9	25.8	16.0
	61st (2004–05)	8	8.7	23.6	25.4	15.3
	55th (1999–2000)	7.3	7.7	22.5	23.2	15.3
	50th (1993–94)	7	7.5	23.6	23.6	14.7
	43rd (1987–88)	7.6	7.5	26	26.9	14.8
	38th (1983)	7.1	6.5	27	26	14.6
	32nd (1977–78)	6.5	6.1	27.6	29.4	14.1
Electricity, water, etc	PLFS (2017–18)	0.47	0.03	1.3	0.63	2.2
	68th (2011–12)	0.3	0.1	1.4	1.1	1.9
	66th (2009–10)	0.2	0	0.7	0.4	1.9
	61st (2004–05)	0.2	0	0.8	0.2	2.1
	55th (1999–2000)	0.2	–	0.8	0.2	2.3
	50th (1993–94)	0.3	–	1.2	0.3	2.2
	43rd (1987–88)	0.3	–	1.2	0.3	1.9
	38th (1983)	0.2	–	1.1	0.2	1.6
	32nd (1977–78)	0.2	–	1.1	0.1	1.4
Construction	PLFS (2017–18)	14.5	5.34	11.73	4.12	8.1
	68th (2011–12)	13.1	5.1	10.7	4.3	7.7
	66th (2009–10)	11.4	4.2	11.5	5.1	7.8
	61st (2004–05)	6.9	1.7	9.3	4.5	7.6
	55th (1999–00)	4.5	1.2	8.8	5.5	6.5
	50th (1993–94)	3.3	1.1	7	4.9	6.7
	43rd (1987–88)	2.7	3.2	5.8	4.3	6.7
	38th (1983)	2.3	0.9	5.1	3.7	6.7
	32nd (1977–78)	1.7	0.7	4.2	2.6	7.5
Trade, hotel & restaurant	PLFS (2017–18)	7.85	3.05	20.8	10.12	
	68th (2011–12)	8	3.6	26	13.1	16.4

(continued)

Table 3 (continued)

Broad industry division	NSS round	Rural		Urban		GDP Share
		Male	Female	Male	Female	
	66th (2009–10)	8.2	3.1	27	12.4	16.7
	61st (2004–05)	8.3	2.8	28.1	13.1	16.2
	55th (1999–2000)	6.8	2.3	29.3	16.4	14.6
	50th (1993–94)	5.5	2.2	21.9	10.7	12.7
	43rd (1987–88)	5.2	2.4	21.5	10.9	12.5
	38th (1983)	4.4	2.2	20.2	9.9	12.0
	32nd (1977–78)	4	2.3	21.6	9.8	11.5
Transport, storage & communications	PLFS (2017–18)	4.9	0.17	9.71	0.8	
	68th (2011–12)	4.3	0.2	11.8	3.2	10.6
	66th (2009–10)	4.2	0.3	10.5	1.5	9.9
	61st (2004–05)	3.9	0.2	10.7	1.6	8.3
	55th (1999–00)	3.2	0.1	10.4	2	6.5
	50th (1993–94)	2.2	0.1	9.8	1.5	5.5
	43rd (1987–88)	2.1	0.1	9.8	1.2	5.3
	38th (1983)	1.7	0.1	10.1	1.7	5.0
	32nd (1977–78)	1.3	0.1	9.8	1.2	4.5
Other services	PLFS (2017–18)	9.21	9.91	28.12	49.88	34.8
	68th (2011–12)	6.4	6.7	21.4	42.7	30.9
	66th (2009–10)	5.6	5.7	21.8	42.7	30.2
	61st (2004–05)	5.9	4.6	20.7	40.2	28.6
	55th (1999–00)	6.1	4.3	20.9	37.8	28.5
	50th (1993–94)	7.1	4	26.4	38.8	26.3
	43rd (1987–88)	6.4	3.7	25.3	33.6	24.2
	38th (1983)	6.2	3.4	24.8	31.4	21.8
	32nd (1977–78)	5.4	3.7	24.5	31.1	19.8
All	x	100	100	100	100	

Note GDP shares are 3 years moving average and figures from 1976–77 to 2012–13 are in 2004–05 constant prices, whereas figures for 2016–17 to 2018–19 are in 2011–12 constant prices and the share of GVA

Source LFPR are based on NSS Report No. 554: Employment and Unemployment Situation in India, 2011–12, Statement 5.11 and Annual Report PLFS, 2017–18, Appendix Table 26 and GDP shares are calculated from data available at sectoral from CSO

Table 4 Sector-wise growth rate of employment, 1980–2016 (as percentage of total employment)

KLEMS industry description	1981–82	1989–90	1999–00	2009–10	2010–11	2011–12	2012–13	2013–14	2014–15	2015–16	2016–17
Agriculture, hunting, forestry and fishing	1.80	2.17	0.04	−1.99	−1.96	−1.92	−3.47	−0.21	−3.50	−3.62	−3.62
Mining and quarrying	6.54	1.88	0.12	−0.26	−0.22	−0.17	−1.69	1.58	−1.69	−1.80	−1.76
Food products,beverages and tobacco	3.10	3.80	2.01	1.48	1.51	1.53	−0.02	3.23	−0.07	−0.20	−0.13
Textiles, Textile Products, Leather and Footwear	3.04	−1.90	0.53	−3.18	1.17	−1.76	−2.79	0.82	−2.54	−2.31	−3.11
Wood and products of wood	3.32	1.52	5.42	−4.37	−4.34	−4.30	−5.92	−2.66	−5.94	−6.06	−6.19
Pulp, paper,paperproducts,printing and publishing	2.81	0.20	4.72	−0.89	−0.83	−0.77	−2.27	1.02	−2.23	−2.31	−2.29
Coke, refined petroleum products and nuclear fuel	3.15	2.01	−2.12	7.59	−7.09	−4.12	−1.51	1.72	−1.60	−1.76	−1.70
Chemicals and chemical products	2.92	4.66	1.08	−0.04	0.32	0.66	−0.60	2.91	−0.15	−0.08	−0.12
Rubber and plastic products	2.95	8.98	2.13	5.33	5.41	5.49	3.85	7.16	3.92	3.85	3.81
Other non-metallic mineral products	3.26	1.02	1.11	1.63	1.73	1.82	0.32	3.63	0.38	0.29	0.33
Basic metals and fabricated metal products	3.11	0.87	4.06	2.84	2.93	3.03	1.52	4.87	1.69	1.69	1.67
Machinery, nec	3.24	6.26	7.77	4.61	4.73	4.85	3.29	6.64	3.46	3.46	3.40
Electrical and optical equipment	3.05	4.29	2.23	24.61	−7.01	15.83	10.27	12.23	10.06	9.14	9.90
Transport equipment	0.39	−7.26	−0.47	14.90	14.68	9.66	−3.73	2.88	−0.45	−0.61	−0.53
Manufacturing, nec; recycling	3.15	2.26	0.56	3.89	3.92	3.94	2.33	5.58	2.28	2.15	2.19
Electricity, gas and water supply	4.28	1.98	0.70	5.90	0.11	0.00	1.69	4.97	1.72	1.63	1.66

(continued)

Table 4 (continued)

KLEMS industry description	1981–82	1989–90	1999–00	2009–10	2010–11	2011–12	2012–13	2013–14	2014–15	2015–16	2016–17
Construction	6.96	2.16	3.65	9.42	9.59	9.76	7.91	11.31	8.15	8.17	7.85
Trade	5.04	3.72	4.09	1.32	1.34	1.35	−0.21	3.04	−0.27	−0.41	−0.34
Hotels and restaurants	4.99	1.44	5.36	4.02	4.06	4.09	2.47	5.73	2.43	2.30	2.34
Transport and storage	9.30	3.21	4.89	2.44	2.44	2.44	0.85	4.08	0.76	0.60	0.68
Post and telecommunication	9.91	6.04	8.35	−1.62	−1.52	−1.43	−2.92	0.39	−2.86	−2.95	−2.95
Financial services	9.29	6.95	0.19	5.40	5.41	5.42	3.72	6.95	3.64	3.49	3.50
Business service	9.13	6.72	10.80	9.05	9.08	9.11	7.19	10.45	7.16	7.03	6.85
Public administration and defense; compulsory social security	0.07	2.03	0.70	0.06	1.39	2.27	−2.54	0.69	−2.63	−2.79	−2.75
Education	1.14	4.79	4.11	3.13	3.13	3.13	1.52	4.74	1.42	1.27	1.33
Health and social work	0.64	2.32	5.10	3.40	3.45	3.49	1.91	5.18	1.90	1.79	1.83
Other services	1.16	7.18	1.99	3.15	3.32	3.49	2.03	5.43	2.28	2.30	2.26
Total economy	2.42	2.40	1.28	0.61	0.81	1.02	−0.51	2.94	−0.16	−0.08	0.06

Source RBI-ILO Key Labour and Employment Market Indicators, 2018

Table 5 Average wage/salary earnings (in Rs.)

survey period 2017-18	Rural			Urban		
	Male	Female	Person	Male	Female	Person
(1)	(2)	(3)	(4)	(5)	(6)	(7)
	Per month					
	Regular wage/ salaried employees in current weekly status					
July-September 2017	12659	8777	11878	17314	13895	16538
October-December 2017	13005	8534	12133	18014	15078	17359
January–March 2018	14445	8549	13351	18277	14779	17483
April-June 2018	14024	9895	13207	18353	14487	17473
Average	13533	8939	12642	17990	14560	17213
	Self-employment work in current weekly status					
July-September 2017	8493	4342	8111	15935	7488	14824
October-December 2017	8807	4104	8304	16110	7478	14873
January–March 2018	8864	4121	8340	15958	6453	14591
April-June 2018	9657	3921	8963	16265	6556	14878
Average	8955	4122	8430	16067	6994	14792
	Per day					
	Casual labour engaged in works other than public works					
July-September 2017	253	166	232	314	192	294
October-December 2017	265	172	243	318	186	297
January–March 2018	270	175	249	328	189	307
April-June 2018	282	179	262	335	201	316
Average	268	173	247	324	192	304
	In MGNREG public works					
July-September 2017	141	135	136			
October-December 2017	161	138	147			
January–March 2018	171	165	168			
April-June 2018	142	131	136			
Average	154	142	147			
	In public works other than MGNREG public works					
July-September 2017	158	142	154			
October-December 2017	157	144	153			
January–March 2018	152	134	143			
April-June 2018	138	119	129			
Average	151	135	145			

Source Compiled from PLFS Annual Report 2017–18, Statement 22, 23, 24 and 25

Table 6 Percentage distribution of workers in usual status (ps+ss) by broad status in employment

All India	Self-employed			Regular wage/salary	Casual labour	All
	Own-account worker, employer	Helper in household enterprise	All self-employed			
(1)	(2)	(3)	(4)	(5)	(6)	(7)
Male (Rural)	48.0	9.8	57.8	14.0	28.2	100.0
Female (Rural)	19.0	38.7	57.7	10.5	31.8	100.0
Person (Rural)	41.0	16.9	57.8	13.1	29.1	100.0
Male (Urban)	34.9	4.3	39.2	45.7	15.1	100.0
Female (Urban)	23.7	11.0	34.7	52.1	13.1	100.0
Person (Urban)	32.6	5.7	38.3	47.0	14.7	100.0
Male (Rural+Urban)	44.1	8.2	52.3	23.4	24.3	100.0
Female (Rural+Urban)	20.2	31.7	51.9	21.0	27.0	100.0
Person (Rural+Urban)	38.6	13.6	52.2	22.8	24.9	100.0

Source Annual Report PLFS, 2017, Appendix Table 19

Table 7 Percentage distribution of persons working according to CWS by broad status in employment

All India	Self-employed			Regular wage/salary	Casual labour	All
	Own-account worker, employer	Helper in household enterprise	All self-employed			
(1)	(2)	(3)	(4)	(5)	(6)	(7)
Male (Rural)	**47.3**	**9.2**	**57.9**	**14.5**	**27.6**	100
Female (Rural)	**20.0**	**34.7**	**56.3**	**12.3**	**31.4**	100
Person (Rural)	**41.3**	**14.9**	**57.6**	**14.0**	**28.4**	100
Male (Urban)	34.0	4.2	39.6	46.5	14.0	100
Female (Urban)	22.1	10.0	34.0	54.9	11.1	100
Person (Urban)	31.7	5.3	38.5	48.1	13.4	100
Male (Rural+Urban)	43.3	7.7	52.4	24.1	23.5	100
Female (Rural+Urban)	20.6	28.0	50.2	23.9	25.8	100
Person (Rural+Urban)	38.4	12.1	51.9	24.1	24.0	100

Source Annual Report PLFS, 2017, Appendix Table 38

References

Amin, S. (2019, July 01). The new imperialist structure. *Monthly Review*.

Babic, M., Fichtner, J., & Heemskerk, E. M. (2017). States versus corporations: Rethinking the power of business in international politics. *The International Spectator, 52*(4), 20–43.

Baran, P. A., & Sweezy, P. M. (1966). *Monopoly capital: An essay on the American economic and social order*. New York: Monthly Review Press.

Basu, K. (2016). *Globalization of labor markets and the growth prospects of nations*. World Bank Policy Research Working Paper 7590.

Galbraith, J. K. (1967). *New Industrial State*. Princeton and Oxford: Princeton University Press.

GoI. (2019, July). Economic survey 2018–19 (Vols. I and II). Ministry of Finance, Government of India.

Harvey, D. (2005). *A brief history of neoliberalism*. Oxford: Oxford University Press.

Hymer, S. (1969). Multinational Corporation and International Oligopoly: The Non-American Challenge, Center Discussion Paper, No. 76. New Haven, CT: Yale University, Economic Growth Center.

ILO. (2019). *World social and economic outlook: Trends to 2019*. Geneva: International Labour Office.

Jha, P. (2009). *The well-being of labour in contemporary Indian Economy: what's active labour market policy got to do with it?* Employment working paper, no.39, International Labour Office, Employment Analysis and Research Unit, Economic and Labour Market Analysis Department. Geneva: ILO.

Jha, P. (2017). Labour conditions in contemporary India. [book auth.]. In P. Patnaik (Eds.), *ICSSR explorations and surveys: Economics Volume 3, Macroeconomics*. Delhi: Oxford University Press.

Narayanan, R., & Madhubala, P. (20016) A triple blow to job guarantee scheme. The Hindu, 16 May 2018.

NSSO. (2012). Employment and unemployment situation in India (July 2011 to June 2012). National Sample Survey Organisation, Delhi.

Papola, T. S., & Kannan, K. P. (2017). *Towards an India wage report*. New Delhi: ILO.

Patnaik, P. (2005). *The economics of the new phase of imperialism*. New Delhi.

Reuters. (2019, August 08). Worst downturn ever for Indian auto industry, 350,000 Lay-Offs: Report, NDTV Profit. https://www.ndtv.com/business/tens-of-thousands-losing-jobs-as-auto-sector-crisis-deepens-report-2081478.

Stiglitz, J. (2018, November 1). The american economy is rigged and what we can do about it. Scientific American. https://www.scientificamerican.com/article/the-american-economy-is-rigged/.

Sweezy, P. (1994). *The triumph of financial capital*. Monthly Review Press.

Varma, S. (2019). Govt. Report Reveals Shocking Condition of Workers in India. NEWSCLICK. Retrieved June 12, 2019, from https://www.newsclick.in/govt-report-reveals-shocking-condition-workers-india.

World Bank. (2018). *South Asia Economic Focus, Spring 2018: Jobless Growth?* Washington, DC: World Bank.

Structural Change and Rural Households in India: An Analysis of the Nature of Transformation in Their Economic Activities

Vinoj Abraham

Abstract The rural economy in India has been witnessing a transformation in terms of a shift in the economic activities undertaken by members of the household. This paper looks into this transformation during the period 1993–94 to 2011–12. In order to look at the transformation within households, we take households as the unit of analysis and analyse the changes that occur within households. We use the NSS unit-level data of Employment–Unemployment rounds for the analysis. There is a shift from agriculture sector to non-agriculture sector employment in case of males. For females too, the share in agricultural employment declined but the corresponding rise was in two activities, education and domestic activities. The near stagnancy of employment in manufacturing, transport, storage and communication and financial and other services, both for males and females, point to the lack of diversification of output growth in the rural areas, which in turn signals the lack of interlinkage with the urban sector. It can be seen that the rural households, from being agricultural households with a rudimentary division of labour and limited specialization within the households, there is increasing division of labour both within the household and in the production site. Within the household, the functions of caregiving and social reproduction is increasingly becoming a specialized activity of the women in the household, while male members engage in economic activity. The typical male HoH is now moving away from agriculture to non-agricultural sources of livelihood, and the sons in these households are moving towards acquiring better levels of education, which probably by the next generation would accentuate the process of shift to non-agricultural employment among males. Meanwhile, the concentration of women in the domestic sector may get further enhanced.

V. Abraham (✉)
Centre for Development Studies, Prasanth Nagar, Thiruvananthapuram, Kerala, India
e-mail: vinoj@cds.edu

N. K. Mishra (ed.), *Development Challenges of India After Twenty Five Years of Economic Reforms*, India Studies in Business and Economics,
https://doi.org/10.1007/978-981-15-8265-3_10

1 Introduction

The agricultural sector in India after a decade of productivity stagnation during the mid-1990s to mid-2000s has improved its growth to reach about 3.75% per annum since mid-2000s (Chand and Parappurathu 2012). The rural economy has been undergoing gradual changes, with rural markets, both for output and inputs deepening, rural infrastructure becoming thicker, with increasing electrification, deeper penetration of mobile telephony and enhanced road networks (Fan, Gulati, and Thorat 2008). A key outcome of the ongoing changes in the rural sector had been the shift in the population dependent on agriculture. Studies have noted that the employment structure in rural India has started showing signs of diversification towards non-agricultural sector (Binswanger 2013). Studies have also looked into the factors that trigger a shift from the agriculture sector. From a household perspective, the shift from agriculture is a very crucial break away from the past. Agriculture is not only a livelihood source but a way of life. Most rural households had agriculture as their livelihood source for many generations. The rural agrarian society is structured around agricultural production, distribution and consumption. The shift from agriculture sector entails manifold changes to the economic activities of the household. The conventional division of labour in terms of gender, skill and age would be replaced by new arrangements. However, this aspect of the household in the context of shift to the non-agriculture sector in India is not explored much.

Indian economy is undergoing a structural transformation with the contribution of agriculture sector in Gross Domestic Product (GDP) consistently declining for the last three decades, while that of service sector, rising (Papola 2012). The shift from agriculture as the primary source of livelihood to other sources can occur under different conditions. An economy undergoing structural transformation experiences a rise in agricultural productivity, a fall in agricultural employment and a shift of surplus labour from agriculture to other sectors (Lewis, 1954). This kind of a transformation also entails that within rural households the activities that are undertaken by their members would change. Inter-generational occupational mobility may take the form of the older males who are less educated but more experienced remain attached to agriculture while the younger ones who are more educated but less experienced shift to the non-agricultural sector. With shift in male employment to the more productive non-agricultural sector and rising incomes the gendered division of labour may become sharply defined. Females may either remain attached to agriculture or withdraw from paid labour market for care services. With rising incomes from non-agricultural sector, the younger ones may now spend more years in school to enhance future expectations in the labour market. If the shift to non-agricultural sector is not the outcome of a structural transformation, but that of worsening agricultural conditions then the rural household may change differently. If the absolute production and living conditions in the agriculture sector is worsening relative to that of the non-agricultural sector, then the entire households may shift from agriculture to non-agriculture sector. Inter-generational occupational mobility may be limited, though spatial mobility may take place. Women's work may accentuate with double burden of both care work and paid work.

This paper looks into such changes that rural households have undergone during the period 1993–94 to 2011–12. The analysis would be done keeping the above context of structural transformation versus distress induced shift to non-agricultural sector. The key questions that I seek answers are; Who moves from agriculture? And to what activity? Who stays put? These questions are analysed keeping the household as the unit of analysis. In analysing the questions posed above, it is hoped that some of the key dimensions of changes that are occurring within rural households may come to the fore.

We use the NSS unit-level data of Employment–Unemployment rounds for the analysis. The choice of period broadly fits into the period that saw a rise in non-agricultural employment in rural areas. The choice of the latter year is constrained by the availability of data. We keep relationship status as a primary variable in understanding economic activity diversification. We consider the following relationship statuses, Head of Household (HoH), spouse of Head of Household, Son of Head of Household and spouse of the son of Head, all co-residing. Given the structure of the data, it is not possible to analyse such relations who are not co-residing. We are not able to analyse the data for daughters as most daughters move to the male spouses' household or establish new household units along with the male spouses. In either case, women in their status as daughters may be difficult to capture. This may not pose a problem as the data does capture spouses, and this is the familial role entrusted on women by society. Similarly, though there are women-headed households, we are not able to discuss this as the samples would be too thin from the surveys to have a meaningful discussion.

The paper is divided into six sections. Following the introduction, the major shifts in economic activities in rural areas are explored in Sect. 2. The shift in economic activities is subjected to further scrutiny on the basis of household relationship status in Sect. 3. Section 4 provides broad directions to the causes of the structural transformation. Section 5 looks into the patterns in inter-generational mobility in activity and Sect. 6 gives the conclusions.

2 Shift in Economic Activities

The rural household in India has been witnessing a transformation. The transformation is in terms of a shift in the economic activities undertaken by members of the rural household. Tracing the change between 1993–94 and 2011–12 the key economic transformation we note is the gradual shift in focus of employment from agriculture sector to other sectors. The share of the total population working in agriculture sector in rural areas was 30% in 1993–94 (Table 1). While about 22% was in other activities, about 19% were undergoing education and another 19% were engaged in domestic activities. The share of population engaged in agriculture declined to 23% by 2011–12, a drop of nearly 7% points, while the share of population engaged in

Table 1 Activity status by gender

Period	Sex	Activity						
		Agriculture	Non-Agriculture	Unemployed	Education	Domestic activities	Others	Total
1993–94	Male	39.64	14.15	1.07	23.24	0.49	21.42	100
	Female	19.79	3.55	0.33	15.05	38.17	23.11	100
	Total	29.99	9	0.71	19.26	18.8	22.24	100
2011–12	Male	31.94	21.56	1.15	30.44	0.42	14.49	100
	Female	13.16	4.42	0.53	25.11	42.17	14.61	100
	Total	22.76	13.18	0.85	27.83	20.83	14.55	100

Source NSSO unit level records of the Employment–Unemployment Surveys for the years 1993–94 and 2011–12

non-agriculture sector employment increased from 9 to 13%. The population engaged in education increased to 28% and that in domestic activities increased from 19 to 21%.

The share of total working population (agriculture + non-agriculture) remained more or less constant for males at about 54% during the period 1993–94 to 2011–12. However, there was a shift to non-agriculture sector employment for males, which increased from 14 to 22%, correspondingly, the share of agricultural employment declined from 40 to 32%. While for females, though the agricultural employment declined from 20 to 13%, the corresponding rise was in two activities, education and domestic activities.

It can be noted that though there is a shift away from agricultural sector both for males and females, the entry to non-agricultural employment in the rural areas is gender-specific, with the employment in non-agricultural sector limited to males and females moving away from the labour market and entering to either education or domestic activities.

Table 2 shows the distribution of the working population according to industrial classification. Among the male working population, there was a decline in employment in the agricultural sector from 74% in 1993–94 to 59% in 2011–12 (Table 2). This decline in agricultural employment was associated with a dramatic increase in employment in the construction sector, which increased from 3.2 to 13%. In trade, hotels and restaurant, there was a marginal increase from 6 to 8% during the period. In all other sectors, the share of employment remained more or less stagnant. Among females, the share of working population declined from 23 to 18%. Within the reduced women labour force now, there was a decline in agricultural employment from 85 to 74%. Among females also there was a rise in construction employment from 1 to 5%, and a marginal rise in both manufacturing and community and personal services, by about 2% point each.

Table 2 Employment of persons categorized by Gender and industries

	1993–94		2011–12	
Industry	Male	Female	Male	Female
Agriculture, hunting, forestry and fishing	73.7	84.78	59.16	74.48
Mining and Quarrying	0.75	0.48	0.55	0.38
Manufacturing	7.06	7.47	8.2	9.55
Electricity, gas and water	0.3	0.04	0.31	0.09
Construction	3.22	0.96	13.07	5.07
Wholesale and retail trade & restaurants and hotels	5.56	2.18	8.03	3.59
Transport, storage and communication services	2.24	0.07	4.1	0.11
Financial, insurance, real estate and business services	0.43	0.09	1.21	0.32
Community, social and personal services	6.75	3.91	5.38	6.42
Total	100	100	100	100

Source Same as Table 1

It can be seen from above that the share of employment in agriculture had declined in the rural areas, both for males and females and the main sector for non-agricultural employment was construction. Almost 70% of the shift in employment for males and nearly 50% of the non-agricultural employment was in the construction sector. In short, the shift to non-agricultural employment in rural areas, is a replacement to construction, without much diversification to other non-agricultural employment in rural areas.

The near stagnancy of employment in manufacturing, transport, storage and communication and financial and other services, both for males and females, point to the lack of diversification of output growth in the rural areas, which in turn signals the lack of inter-linkage with the urban sector. Binswanger-Mkhize (2013) also argues that the growth of rural non-agricultural employment is partly due to poor inter-linkage between the rural and urban sectors. Given the high rate of output growth of the economy during the period, especially in the services sector, the poor penetration of growth to the rural areas point to the fault lines that are developing between the rural economy and the urban.

3 Shift in Economic Activities by Household Relation Status

From the household's perspective what kind of a shift has been taking place in employment? Is it that some members of the households are leaving agriculture while some remain within agriculture? Looking at the data, in 1993–94 about 68% of the households were agricultural households, where all working members of the household were in agriculture sector (Table 3). More than 21% of the households were such households where all working members worked in non-agricultural activities. And nearly 11% of the households had mixed households, where working members were engaged in both agriculture and non-agriculture activities. Looking at the shift, between 1993–94 and 2011–12 the pure agricultural households declined from 68 to 54%, a decline of 14% points, and the pure non-agricultural households share increased from 21 to 35%. While that of the mixed households remained at 11% throughout the period. From the above, it can be inferred that households are converting themselves from agriculture to non-agriculture households fully, while

Table 3 Distribution of households according to Agriculture, Non-agriculture and Mixed Activities

Share of Households	1993–94	2011–12
Share of HH with all working members in agriculture	67.92	53.97
Share of HH with all working members in non-agriculture	21.45	35.22
Share of mixed households	10.63	10.81
Total	100	100

Source Same as Table 1

there is no intermediate transition of having mixed households. Why is this so? Why does households shift completely to non-agricultural activities rather than a more risk-averse strategy of having mixed activities? There are two possible arguments that can be made. One plausible answer is this. The contours of the labour market are getting more stringently defined. As a household shift from agriculture to non-agriculture sector the number of members in the labour market from each household is declining. For instance, a household with many members working in agriculture now shifts to non-agriculture sector. A few members may migrate to newer locations for short periods. The remaining members may withdraw from agriculture and may engage in care work, or undergo education. Another plausible explanation may be that the households who find agriculture unviable anymore, move to new sectors. But since such mobility is due to poor agricultural outcomes the household and market work may remain similar.

Who moves within household and to what activity? For this, we look into the relationship status of the members of the household and associated changes in economic activities. The most prominent economic activity in 2011–12 continues to be agriculture, but this is limited to the male head of the household. Nearly 57% of all heads of households (HoH) in rural areas were engaged in agricultural activities (Table 4). Only 21% of the Spouses of HoH were engaged in agriculture, among sons only 18% were engaged in agricultural activities, and among spouses of sons, only 15%

Table 4 Share of Population in Economic Activity and Relationship Status: Rural India (in percent)

Activities						
Relation status	50th Round (1993–94)					
	Agriculture	Non-Agriculture	Unemployed	Education	Domestic activities	Others
Male HoH	68.91	25.18	0.14	0.6	0.27	4.9
Spouse of HoH	32.36	5	0.13	0.08	60.96	1.47
Son	24.37	8.48	1.72	37.91	0.46	27.06
Spouse of Son	25.45	2.79	0.56	0.36	70.34	0.51
68th Round (2011–12)						
Male HoH	56.8	36	0.11	0.81	0.27	6.01
Spouse of HoH	21.92	6.09	0.26	0.04	70.13	1.57
Son	17.56	13.76	2.04	51.34	0.44	14.86
Spouse of Son	14.54	4.14	0.93	1.25	78.96	0.18

Source Same as Table 1

were in agriculture. Among Male HoH about 25% were engaged in non-agricultural activities in the rural areas, but among spouses of both head of the household and sons, the largest share of activities was in domestic activities, 70 and 79%, respectively. Among sons, the participation in non-agricultural activities was also low at 13.7%, while the largest share was participation in education, about 51%. So it can be noticed that for the male HoH agriculture is the primary economic activity, while for spouses it is domestic activities and for the sons, it is undergoing education.

Between 1993–94 and 2011–12, there is a substantial shift towards non-agricultural employment for HoH, from 25 to 36% of the HoH population and correspondingly a decline in agricultural employment. Similar fall in agriculture is noted among all relation status. But the decline in agriculture employment is not compensated to non-agricultural employment, as noticed in the male HoH population. Though there is a marginal rise in non-agricultural employment among all other relations considered, the substantial rise in case of women is towards domestic activities, for the spouse of HoH increasing from 60 to 70% and for the spouse of sons increasing from 70 to 79% share. For sons themselves, the substantial shift was from agricultural employment to education, which increased from 39 to 51%.

Thus the emerging long-term picture from the rural households is that head of households are moving away from agriculture to non-agriculture employment and sons are increasingly going to schools, and women, be it spouses of HoH or of sons, are withdrawing from the labour market.

However, among the working women in rural areas, a much larger share of women are engaged in agriculture. Even when the total share of HoHs in agriculture is 61%, nearly 78% of spouses of HoH are engaged in agriculture (Table 5). And for nearly 56% of the sons engaged in agriculture, 78% of their spouses were engaged in agriculture. In other words, an overwhelmingly large share of women were engaged in agriculture work, compared to males, be it spouses to HoH or sons. Comparing between the two periods, there is a marginal shift for women towards non-agricultural activities. But the consistent and largest increase for women is in domestic activity.

In short, the rural households from being agrarian in nature, where all members of the households were engaged in agriculture, be it heads of households, children or spouses a gradual but definite transition is underway. The channel of transition is in the following manner. The typical heads of households are moving away from agricultural activities to non-agricultural sources of employment, the typical sons

Table 5 Share of Workers by Industry and Relationship Status: Rural India (in percent)

	Industry	Male head of Household	Spouse of Head	Son	Spouse of Son
1993–94	Agriculture	73.23	86.61	74.18	90.13
	Non-Agriculture	26.77	13.39	25.82	9.87
2011–12	Agriculture	61.21	78.26	56.06	77.84
	Non-Agriculture	38.79	21.74	43.94	22.16

Source Same as Table 1

are moving away from agriculture to education mostly, with some non-agricultural employment. The spouses of both the HoHs and sons are moving away from agriculture to domestic activity, with some very marginal presence in non-agricultural employment.

From the above analysis, it can be argued that within the rural households there is increasing division of labour both within the household and in the production site. Within the household, the functions of caregiving and social reproduction are increasingly becoming a specialized activity of the women in the household, while male members engage in economic activity. The typical male HoH is now moving away from agriculture to non-agricultural sources of livelihood, and the sons are moving towards acquiring better levels of education, which probably by the next generation would accentuate the process of shift to non-agricultural employment among males. Meanwhile, the concentration of women in the domestic sector may get further enhanced.

4 Male HoH: Does Age Matter? Or Period Matters?

We had noted that the share of male HoHs in agriculture had declined from 69% to 57%, correspondingly the share in non-agricultural employment increased from 25 to 36% during the period 1993–94 to 2011–12. This distribution is for the population of all age groups.

A shift in employment from agriculture to non-agricultural activities during the period may occur due to two accounting factors. One possibility is that the share of HoHs in agriculture sector belonging to different age groups may have different propensities to be in the agriculture sector. For instance, with better education and skills than their previous generation, the younger HoH population may prefer to be out of agriculture, while the older HoH population remain put in agriculture. Another possibility is that, the propensities to be in agriculture do not differ across age groups, but across all age groups, there is a shift from agriculture to other activities. In other words, it is the period that this population lived in, that encouraged a shift from agriculture to non-agriculture rather than the changes in preferences across age groups.

From Table 6 below it can be seen that there is a much stronger period effect. There is a decline in agricultural employment during the period 1993–94 to 2011–12. But this decline is not much different across age groups. All age groups experienced a decline in agricultural employment share by about 10% points. The change in agricultural employment across different age groups compared across years show that the difference between age groups for the same occupations are not very large, except for the III–II between 1993–94 and 2011–12. In this group, we see that the older group(60–70) in 2011–12 had seen a larger fall in non-agricultural employment as well compared to their younger cohort (50–60), but this is because of a shift in economic activity from being employed to 'others' probably being pensioners or rent dependent.

Table 6 Share of Economic Activities of Male HoH by Age Cohort and Year

Survey year	Birth Year Cohort	Age	Agriculture	Non-Agriculture	Unemployed	Education	Domestic activities	Others
1993–94	1963–73	40–50(I)	71.74	26.56	0.08	0.01	0.15	1.46
	1953–63	50–60 (II)	74.26	19.33	0.04	0.02	0.47	5.88
	1943–53	60–70 (III)	64.87	11.78	0.02	0.07	0.75	22.51
2011–12	1981–91	40–50 (I)	61.14	37.75	0.09	0	0.15	0.88
	1971–81	50–60 (II)	62.49	30.89	0.1	0	0.41	6.11
	1961–71	60–70 (III)	56.09	15.62	0.04	0.03	0.79	27.43
Period effect								
	2011 minus 1993	40–50	−10.6	11.19	0.01	−0.01	0	−0.58
		50–60	−11.77	11.56	0.06	−0.02	−0.06	0.23
		60–70	−8.78	3.84	0.02	−0.04	0.04	4.92
Age Effect								
	II–I (1993–94)		2.52	−7.23	−0.04	0.01	0.32	4.42
	II–I (2011–12)		1.35	−6.86	0.01	0	0.26	5.23
	III–II (1993–94)		−9.39	−7.55	−0.02	0.05	0.28	16.63
	III–II (2011–12)		−6.4	−15.27	−0.06	0.03	0.38	21.32

Thus, from the Table given below, what comes out is that a key feature of the transformation in the rural areas is that it is not dependent on individual features such as age or factors that are associated with age, such as education, health or age composition of population. Rather, what seems to be important in the shift are the social and economic conditions that encourage the rural population towards non-agricultural activities.

Comparing the key changes across the age cohorts of the Head of the Households, the following observations may be made from Table 7 with regard to the structure of economic activity among Indian rural households.

For the Male HoH of age 40–50: There is a compensated shift for the male HoH from agricultural employment to non-agricultural employment during 1993–94 to 2011–12(a fall of-10.6% in agriculture and a gain of 11.2% in non-agriculture sector). But for the spouse of HoH, a similar reduction in agricultural employment by −11.1%, there is no compensated employment in the non-agricultural sector. The compensated rise is in domestic activities. For the son of HoH for a decline in agricultural employment and 'others' (probably young children who did not attend

Table 7 Net Change in Activity Status between 1993–94 and 2011–12 by age cohorts of Male HoH

	Agriculture	Non-Agriculture	Unemployed	Education	Domestic activities	Others
Member	Male HoH age group 40–50					
Male HoH	−10.6	11.2	0.0	0.0	0.0	−0.6
Spouse of HoH	−11.1	1.5	0.1	0.0	9.6	−0.1
Son	−9.9	2.2	0.7	18.5	−0.2	−11.4
Spouse of Son	−9.8	−0.2	0.1	1.9	8.7	−0.6
	Male HoH age group 50–60					
Male HoH	−11.8	11.6	0.1	0.0	−0.1	0.2
Spouse of HoH	−9.4	1.6	0.1	0.0	8.0	−0.3
Son	−11.6	12.0	0.5	2.1	0.4	−3.3
Spouse of Son	−12.9	1.2	0.3	1.0	10.8	−0.4
	Male HoH age group 60–70					
Male HoH	−8.8	3.8	0.0	0.0	0.0	4.9
Spouse of HoH	−7.2	1.7	0.1	0.0	4.9	0.5
Son	−10.3	14.1	−1.3	−0.5	0.0	−2.1
Spouse of Son	−11.4	0.6	0.3	0.4	10.1	0.0

Source Same as Table 1

schools in the 1990s), the compensated rise is in education. And for the spouse of the son for a decline in agriculture employment the compensated rise is, as in the case of her mother-in-law, to domestic activities.

For the Male HoH of age 50–60: As the Male HoH is in this age group, the shift in employment from agriculture continues across all members of the household, but a key change from the younger HoH is that now along with the HoH, the sons are also fully compensating to non-agricultural sector, while women move completely into domestic activities.

For the Male HoH of age 60–70: All the trends mentioned above continues, except that the male HoH now, instead of moving from agriculture to non-agriculture, moves into the 'others' category, probably as not working and retired, while the largest increase in non-agriculture employment is noted for the son now. Women, continue to move out of agriculture to domestic activities.

5 Intergenerational Changes in Activity Status

Though we had noted that there was a change in the activity status across relation status, this does not imply that this happens within the same household. Ideally, the question of who moves within the household, the analysis should look into the households that saw a shift in employment to newer sectors. But such an analysis cannot be taken up for want of panel data on household mobility for the same period of analysis.[1] The next best proxy is to look into what happens to the rest of the members when the HoH remains in agriculture, and contrast with his mobility to another sector. This would help us to see if the mobility from one sector occurs within households, or do the entire households move to newer sectors.

Table 8 shows the share of sons engaged in an activity corresponding to their father's activity. In 1993–94, among the fathers who were engaged in agriculture only, 29% of their sons were in agriculture (Table 8). Their sons were mostly out of labour force, 66% of them were in 'others', undergoing education. In 2011–12, the share of such sons who followed their father in agriculture declined to 24%. But this decline saw a small increase in non-agriculture employment, along with a similar increase in others as well. Sons following father's occupation in the non-agricultural sector were much smaller, only 15%, but this increased to 18% in 2011–12. The most important component of increase is in case of fathers not in labour force, probably as pensioners, rent dependent or indisposed. About 49% of sons whose fathers in 'others', were in agriculture in 1993–94. But in 2011–12, this declined to 36% and in turn, their share increased in non-agriculture activity from 25 to 41%. This implies that when fathers were not in the labour market, the mobility of sons is highest, towards non-agricultural employment.

[1] India Human Development Surveys (IHDS) does provide a panel data, but the period available for meaningful inter-generational comparison is too short.

Table 8 Son's Activity Status matched to father's Activity Status (in percent)

	1993–94				2011–12			
Activity of HoH	Activity of_Son				Activity of_Son			
	Agri	Non-Agri	Other	Total	Agri	Non-Agri	Other	Total
Agriculture	29.34	4.65	66.01	100	24.3	7.22	68.47	100
non agriculture	6.14	15.16	78.7	100	2.98	18.4	78.62	100
Others	49.06	24.55	26.4	100	36.26	41.53	22.21	100
Total	24.37	8.23	67.4	100	17	13.08	69.92	100
age of HoH = 40n50								
Activity of HoH	Activity of_Son				Activity of_Son			
	Agri	Non-Agri	other	Total	Agri	Non-Agri	other	Total
Agriculture	34.66	4.59	60.75	100	25.09	5.95	68.96	100
non agriculture	8.38	19.31	72.31	100	3.59	20.56	75.85	100
Others	30.22	21.18	48.6	100	17.01	25.05	57.94	100
Total	27.69	8.73	63.58	100	16.61	11.86	71.53	100
age of HoH = 50n60								
Activity of_Son	Activity of_Son				Activity of_Son			
	Agri	Non-Agri	other	Total	Agri	Non-Agri	other	Total
Agriculture	56.56	9.8	33.64	100	49.49	16.23	34.29	100
non agriculture	15.08	38.34	46.58	100	8.32	50.68	41.01	100
Others	40.79	29.66	29.55	100	32.79	44.58	22.63	100
Total	47.44	16.59	35.96	100	35.44	28.77	35.79	100
age of HoH = 60n70								
Activity of_Son	Activity of_Son				Activity of_Son			
	Agri	Non-Agri	other	Total	Agri	Non-Agri	other	Total
Agriculture	64.59	14.54	20.87	100	62.29	21.4	16.31	100
non agriculture	16.96	57.85	25.19	100	9.31	71.41	19.28	100
Others	56.26	26.01	17.73	100	36.47	46.5	17.03	100
Total	56.79	22.58	20.63	100	46.06	36.94	17	100

Source Same as Table 1

When we classify the father–son pairs according to the age of fathers, for the young father (40–50 age group) the father's presence in non-agriculture occupation led to about three-fourth of all such father's sons (72.31%) to participation in others, mainly into education in 1993–94. The same trend is seen in 2011–12 as well. For the fathers in the age group 50–60 who are engaged in agriculture, about 56% of their sons were in the same industry. While in 2011–12, the share of sons declined to less than 50%. On the other hand, while 38% of their sons follow their father's industry in non-agriculture sector, during 93–94, this share increased to more than 50% by 2011. For the fathers' age group 50–60, about 65% of sons followed their father's industry in agriculture and about 57% of sons followed their father in non-agriculture sector. However, in 2011–12, the father–son pair in agriculture declined in 62% such pairs in non-agriculture sector increase to 71.41%.

In summary, among the older parents, those who were engaged in non-agricultural sector, a large share of such sons are in the non-agricultural sector and over time such preferences seem to be accentuating. While among older parents, those who were engaged in agricultural sector, though a large share of their sons were also engaged in agriculture, over time such preferences were declining. Among younger parents, there is a shift away from agriculture for their sons, but the shift is towards 'others' mostly into education.

Drawing from Appendix Tables 11 and 12, Table 9 above summarizes the change in father and son's industry during the period 1993–94 to 2011–12. The highest presence of sons in father's industry is within agriculture. In 1993–94, 86% of sons followed their father in agriculture. In Manufacturing and Trade sector (wholesale and retail trade), also about 60% of the sons followed their father's industry in 1993–94. In mining and quarrying and construction sector, about half the sons followed their father's industry. In the rest of the sectors, only 40% (or less) of the sons worked in the same industry as their father.

Between 1993–94 and 2011–12, there have not been large changes in the son's presence in the father's employment sector. The sectors namely agriculture, electricity, gas, water, trade restaurant and hotels show a marginal decline in the share of sons joining the father's industry. In all the other sectors, there is a marginal increase. Correlation coefficient between 2 years is at 0.79 which supports the argument that there has been very little change in the way inter-generational industrial shifts in employment occurred between the two periods.

The primary capital for agricultural sector is land. The nature of shift from agriculture to non-agriculture sector may be governed by the access to land. We now look

Table 9 Comparing Father and Son in the same industry

Occupation of HoH	1993–94	2011–12	Difference
Agriculture, hunting, forestry and fishing	86.32	77.08	−9.24
Mining and Quarrying	52.87	87.61	34.74
Manufacturing	61.93	65.16	3.23
Electricity, gas and water	26.66	17.76	−8.9
Construction	55.82	73.88	18.06
Wholesale and retail trade & restaurants and hotels	58.05	53.06	−4.99
Transport, storage and communication services	22.63	30.65	8.02
Financial, insurance, real estate and business services	39.12	39.48	0.36
Community, social and personal services	37.36	44.3	6.94
R			0.7983

Source Same as Table 1

Table 10 Son's employment share according to land size, and fathers' employment (per cent)

	1. HoH in Agriculture				2. HoH in Non-Agriculture			
	1993–94		2011–12		1993–94		2011–12	
	Agri	Non-agri	Agri	Non-agri	Agri	Non-agri	Agri	Non-agri
Landless	90.0	10.0	100.0	0.0	39.5	60.5	12.4	87.6
<1 hectare	83.3	16.7	74.1	25.9	12.6	87.4	25.3	74.7
1 to 2 hectare	86.2	13.8	80.9	19.1	29.3	70.7	50.8	49.2
2 to 5 hectare	89.3	10.7	83.8	16.2	40.6	59.4	52.4	47.6
>5 hectare	90.0	10.0	87.1	12.9	32.1	67.9	58.3	41.7

Source Same as Table 1

at the role of land in the inter-generational mobility in economic activity from agriculture to non-agriculture sector. Table 10 shows two panels, one with HoH engaged in agriculture and the other with HoH in non-agriculture sector. The table shows the share of sons of HoHs in agriculture and non-agriculture sector classified according to the land size owned by the household. As can be seen from panel 1, in 1993–94 if the household was landless and the father worked in the agriculture sector, then 90% of the sons also worked in the sector as agricultural worker. In 2011–12, 100% of such sons were agricultural workers. If the household was landless and father worked in a non-agricultural sector, then about 65% of sons followed their father in 1993–94, which increased to 88% by 2011–12. In other words, if the households did not own this crucial asset, land, then sons typically followed what fathers did. There was no possible option for any inter-sectoral mobility.

However, if the households owned land, then as the land size increased, then there is a greater probability of sons of fathers in agricultural sector joining the agricultural sector. For instance, in 1993–94 when the land owned was less than a hectare, 83% of the sons joined father in agriculture, while the land size was above 5 hectares, 90% of the sons joined father in agriculture.

Yet, between 1993–94 and 2011–12, more of such sons whose fathers were in agriculture and owned land of some size, left agriculture. Moreover, smaller the land size larger was the propensity for sons to leave agriculture, despite fathers being in agriculture. This is in contrast with the landless agricultural workers. When one was landless, there was greater propensity to be in agriculture, but when one holds land, then land size matters inversely for sons to remain in agriculture.

Looking at the panel 2, it is interesting to note that if the households owned land and even if the fathers worked in non-agriculture sector as the size of the land increased, there was an increasing tendency for sons to shift to agricultural activity. For instance, only 13% of the sons whose fathers were in non-agricultural sector and owned land less than one hectare were in agriculture. But for such fathers, who owned more than 5 hectares of land 32% of their sons engaged in agricultural activities. Surprisingly, we find that this propensity of sons of non-agricultural fathers to join agricultural increased across size classes by some measure between 1993–94 and 2011–12. This implies that the shift from agriculture to non-agriculture sector for sons whose fathers were in non-agricultural employment was governed largely by land ownership. In short, it can be seen that landless households had to depend on the father's occupational choice to decide on son's occupation, while landed households seem to choose between agriculture and non-agricultural employment depending on land size, and father's occupation had a less prominent role to play in such cases.

6 Conclusion

After a long period of stagnancy, the period 1993–94 to 2011–12 had witnessed a marked reduction in the population dependent on agriculture and a rise in non-agricultural employment. This paper looked into the changes taking place in the economic activities of rural households in the above context of structural transformation. The change, though in its initial stages, reorganizes the division of labour within the household. Moreover, the skill demands of the non-agricultural sector and the prospects of higher earnings in the non-agricultural sector revamps the nature of social reproduction envisaged by the agrarian societies. Such emerging prospects in the non-agricultural sector change the conventional role played by the members of rural households.

The analysis in this paper shows that there is a marked shift of households from agriculture to non-agricultural employment. However, this shift is gender-specific, with the males moving to non-agricultural employment and the females moving mostly from agricultural activities to unpaid domestic activities, reducing their participation in the active labour market. However, the inter-sectoral mobility of males was limited to a narrow set of rural non-farm sectors such as construction. Though the female labour participation is declining, among those who are in the labour market there is a movement towards non-agricultural sectors, mostly to construction activities. The lack of diversification of employment to other rural non-farm activities point to the weak inter-linkages with the urban productive sector.

The shift to non-agricultural sector is marked by the conversion of entire households from agriculture to non-agriculture sector. Very few households explored a more risk-averse strategy of diversification instead of conversion. Apparently, this sort of inter-sectoral mobility may appear to be distress driven. But what seems to be at work is that as males move to non-farm sector, females in the household withdraw from the labour market. Thus, such households, whose labour participation has dwindled get accounted as non-agricultural households.

Looking at members within the households, for the head of the household the most prominent activity was agricultural employment, but this had declined during the study period. In its place, rural non-agriculture employment was gradually becoming prominent. For the spouses of the male HoH, along with the shift of males to non-agricultural sector, they withdrew from agricultural activities to unpaid domestic activities, probably now engaged in care services for the household. The children, both males and females, had shifted their primary economic activity from agricultural employment to attending educational institutions, probably responding to the demand for higher skills in the non-agricultural sector. It seems to show that the activities within the rural household are getting increasingly specialized with a clearly demarcated division of labour in terms of who participated in the market, and who did care services. The shift of male head of households to non-agriculture sector also seems to invigorate aspirations about their young ones, now attending schools instead of being part of the agricultural workforce.

Though the change in rural employment pattern during this period had implications on the members of the household, the transformation was not triggered by individual- or household-level factors. As Persons seem to shift out of agricultural activities, whatever be their age or gender. But joining the non-agriculture sector was age- and gender-specific. The change was probably caused by the socio-economic conditions that encouraged rural families to shift to non-agricultural activities.

In terms of inter-generational mobility, firstly, there was very limited inter-generational mobility across industries. The highest presence of sons in father's industry is within agriculture throughout the period. In terms of change, when fathers were engaged in non-agricultural sector their adult sons also joined the same sector, but if fathers were in agriculture sector there is an increasing preference for their adult sons to shift to non-agriculture sector. The shift from agriculture to non-agriculture sector for sons whose fathers were in non-agricultural employment, was governed largely by land ownership. Landless households had to depend on the father's occupational choice to decide on son's occupation, while landed households seem to provide greater choices to sons while father's occupation lost prominence.

Acknowledgements I acknowledge the excellent research assistance provided by Mr. Chacko Babu for this work. I also thank discussants and participants of the international seminar on "Developmental Challenges of India after Twenty Five Years of Economic Reforms" 16–18 March, 2018, by the Department of Economics, Banaras Hindu University, Varanasi, Uttar Pradesh for comments on the paper. All errors are mine.

Appendix Tables

Inter-generational mobility in Industry 1993–94 (Tables 11, 12)

Table 11 Distribution of sons' occupation by father's occupation in 1993–94

1993–94										
Occupation of HoH	Occupation of Male Child									
	1	2	3	4	5	6	7	8	9	Total
1	86.32	0.31	3.57	0.11	2.11	2.53	1.45	0.35	3.25	100
2	27.51	52.87	6.14	0	6.56	1.94	3.85	0	1.13	100
3	20.33	0.16	61.93	0.19	4.39	3.97	2.11	0.58	6.35	100
4	48.99	0	8.82	26.66	1.42	1.47	4.87	1.9	5.87	100
5	26.45	1.09	7.13	0.25	55.82	1.51	1.74	0	6.01	100
6	23.47	0.34	7.23	0.24	1.42	58.05	2.1	0.73	6.41	100
7	38.2	0.38	9.75	0	6.34	11.4	22.63	0.41	10.88	100
8	25.77	0	5.66	0.69	1.38	12.34	12.16	39.12	2.88	100
9	42.75	0.15	4.73	0.22	2.65	7.86	2.98	1.3	37.36	100
Total	75.7	0.56	7.1	0.18	3.32	5.52	1.86	0.53	5.23	100

Source NSSO unit level records of the Employment–Unemployment Surveys for the years 1993–94 and 2011–12

Table 12 Distribution of sons' occupation by father's occupation in 2011–12

2011–12										
Occupation of HoH	Occupation of Male Child									
	1	2	3	4	5	6	7	8	9	Total
1	77.08	0.25	3.8	0.12	7.73	4.64	2.87	0.87	2.64	100
2	5.93	87.61	1.22	0	2.51	2.24	0.5	0	0	100
3	10.5	0.7	65.16	0.63	9.67	6.3	4.16	0.64	2.23	100
4	14.2	0	6.21	17.76	15.96	10.17	4.32	16.03	15.34	100
5	10.6	0.1	5.14	0.03	73.88	4.68	3.02	0.4	2.16	100
6	15.33	0.18	9.76	0.03	10.56	53.06	5.89	1.91	3.28	100
7	20.03	0.34	10.64	0	18.54	14.04	30.65	1.24	4.53	100
8	14.27	0	4.78	1.09	4.21	13.33	8.58	39.48	14.25	100
9	22.49	0.14	6.37	0.72	7.16	9.93	6.37	2.51	44.3	100
Total	57.99	0.62	8.6	0.22	14.5	8.41	4.02	1.29	4.35	100

Source NSSO unit level records of the Employment–Unemployment Surveys for the years 1993–94 and 2011–12

References

Binswanger, H. P. M. (2013). The stunted structural transformation of the Indian economy: agriculture, manufacturing and the rural non-farm sector. *Economic and Political weekly, 48*(26–27), 5–13.

Chand, R., & Parappurathu, S. (2012). Temporal and spatial variations in agricultural growth and its determinants. *Economic & Political Weekly, 47*, 26–27.

Fan, S., Gulati, A., & Thorat, S. (2008). Investment, Subsidies, and pro-Poor Growth in Rural India. *Agricultural Economics, 39*(2), 163–170.

Lewis, W. A. (1954). Economic development with unlimited supplies of labour. *The Manchester School, 22*(2), 139–191.

Papola, T. S. (2012), Structural changes in the Indian economy: emerging patterns and implications. Working Paper No. 2012/02, Institute for Studies in Industrial Development, New Delhi, June.

Wage Employment, Informality, and Social Networks in Indian Labor Market

Rajendra P. Mamgain

Abstract This chapter shows how a majority of available regular employment—generally considered better over other forms of employment, is devoid of any social security and largely contributed by informal enterprises. Among regular salaried workers, the situation of contractual workers on social security entitlements is worrisome. The degree of such informality of employment is comparatively high in low-end occupations. More so, access to regular salaried employment is significantly influenced by the social background of workers. SCs, STs, and Muslims are largely concentrated in informal sector wage employment. The chapter argues how informational asymmetries in urban labor market create unequal labor outcomes in terms of access to employment and income and demonstrates that despite a notable progress in the penetration of information technology in India, social networks still remain critical in providing job information to regular wage employment. Even a large proportion of employers in formal private sector frequently use social networks for job postings. The new forms of job search such as web job portals are largely being used by educated job seekers looking for jobs in the private formal sector. The likelihood of using social networks in job search is comparatively high among low-educated and male job seekers. The chapter concludes that apart from the lack of employment opportunities in general, the quality of employment is a major casualty in the current dispensation of liberal economic policies of last two-and-half decades or so. The share of precarious employment is widespread and tended to increase over the years. This dismal situation on the front of employment though attracted attention of political class in recent times but yet to be translated into reality with a comprehensive time-bound agenda of creation of employment that ensures tenurial security, social security, dignity, and decent earnings to workers.

R. P. Mamgain (✉)
S. R. Sankaran Chair (Rural Labour), National Institute of Rural Development and Panchayati Raj, Hyderabad, India
e-mail: mamgain.rp@gmail.com

N. K. Mishra (ed.), *Development Challenges of India After Twenty Five Years of Economic Reforms*, India Studies in Business and Economics,
https://doi.org/10.1007/978-981-15-8265-3_11

1 Introduction

Decent employment is instrumental in achieving economic and social development all over the world (ILO 2014; World Bank 2012). However, access to such employment opportunities to a growing labor force remains a big challenge across the globe, more so in developing countries like India. The experience of a consistently high economic growth rate of over 5% in India since the onset of 1980s and its accelerated pace after the economic reforms of 1990s has had limited impact on creating employment opportunities for its growing labor force outside the farm sector (Papola and Sahu 2012). So dismal was the pace of employment creation during the decade of 1990s that it was dubbed as a period of 'jobless growth.' But for a brief period of reasonable growth in employment between 2004–05 and 2011–12, the scenario has been grim and in the recent years, there are apprehensions of declining job opportunities, particularly amid the persistence of economic recession and increasing automation across the world (OECD 2017; ILO 2014; IHD 2016; Abraham 2017).

About 6.18 million jobs, mainly that of women, were lost in India during the period between 2011–12 and 2017–18, as per the estimates based on the latest data of the Periodic Labor Force Survey (PLFS) of National Statistical Office (NSO) of Government of India by Kannan and Raveendran (2019). The survey also reported a fast decline in the female labor force participation rates particularly in the rural areas of the country, mainly driven by 'discouraged withdrawal' from the labor market.

Unlike the faster structural changes in gross domestic product (GDP), the structure of employment in the post-liberalization period, has changed at an abysmally slow pace in India. About half of the country's workforce is tasked in occupations related to agriculture and allied activities at abysmally low-income levels, contributing a mere 14% to the national GDP (IHD-ISLE 2014, p. 26). The decline in the proportion of such occupations has been rather slow. Wage employment constitutes about 46% of total employment comprising almost equal shares of regular salaried jobs and casual wage jobs.

The job market in the post-liberalization era has witnessed a sea change in virtually every aspect of employment be it job information, hiring practices, or the nature of employment itself, which is getting increasingly casual and contractual, with little or no social and tenurial security at all. Although the share of regular salaried employment in total employment has witnessed a sizeable improvement, most of it has been led by contractual jobs without any social security, both in public and private enterprises. Moreover, access to regular salaried employment is significantly influenced by the social background of workers with notable underrepresentation of scheduled castes (SCs), scheduled tribes (STs), other backward classes (OBCs), and Muslims in private corporate sector employment where most jobs are on the offer (Mamgain and Tiwari 2017). Thus, informal mode of employment, with low earnings and limited or no social protection still accounts for about 84% of total employment in India (ISLE-IHD 2014; Srivastava and Naik 2017).

Associated with the increasing informality in wage employment is the role of job information in labor market (Stigler 1961, 1962; Spence 1973). It is argued that equal access to job information improves labor market outcomes from the perspective of job seekers and employers alike. However, such free flow of information is hampered for job seekers in segmented labor markets, resulting in inequality in productivity, wage earnings, and upward mobility (Kannapan 1977; Papola 1981). Information asymmetries in the labor market were expected to disappear with the rapid penetration of Information Technology (IT) in recent years. However, contrary to such expectations, a fairly high proportion of job seekers still depend on their social networks for job information, thereby dwarfing the potential of IT in the labor market. The use of social networks is comparatively more important for those searching contractual/casual jobs in the middle and low-rung occupational hierarchies in both formal and informal sector enterprises.

In brief, the faster economic growth witnessed during the late 1990s till recently has hardly been able to ameliorate the persistent deficit of quality employment; thus, resulting in the rise in under-employment and educated unemployment in India. Against this backdrop, the author seeks to analyze the nature and magnitude of informal employment both in formal and informal sector enterprises based on empirical data and examines the changing nature of job information and hiring practices in the ICT (Information–communications technology) age that is bypassing the socially marginalized sections rather than integrating them in the mainstream. Primary data from four metropolitan cities has been gathered for this purpose.

The paper comprises five sections. The following Sect. 2 dwells on the nature and magnitude of informal employment based on NSSO (National Sample Survey Organization) data on employment and unemployment, particularly for the years 2004–05 and 2011–12. Since NSSO data do not provide information on contractual workers (who are generally counted under the category of regular employment) and sources of job search information, we have used primary data collected from the cities of Lucknow, Delhi NCR, Pune, and Coimbatore (Mamgain 2019) to understand informality and related importance of social networks in access to paid wage employment in the urban labor market in Sects. 3 and 4, respectively. The purpose is to examine how sources of job information help in getting jobs in the labor market. Section 4 also examines how the source of information determines the access to quality of job in terms of its nature and income. Equally important would be to analyze the nature and access of job information to the job seekers belonging to various socio-economic groups. It is generally believed that information about job opportunities is relatively weak in case of migrants to cities, women, marginalized communities, and those with low educational attainments. The concluding section summarizes the main features of informality and the role of social networks in the urban labor market.

2 Wage Employment and Informality

A little less than half of the Indian workforce is absorbed in wage employment, which includes regular salaried jobs and casual wage works (Table 1). Regular wage employment has long been associated with jobs in the formal or organized sector of the economy, whereas casual wage employment is largely, if not only, associated with work in the informal or unorganized sector. Moreover, opportunities for regular salaried jobs are largely concentrated in urban areas, while casual wage works are mainly located in rural areas thus, indicating unequal access to employment opportunities. Although wage employment witnessed a sizeable annual growth since 2004–05 mainly led by a growth of regular employment, yet most of the jobs created in the period, particularly in private sector, do not 'fit' into ILO's broad framework of 'decent' work ensuring tenurial and social security to workers. The quality of regular employment has seriously eroded after the economic reforms of early 1990s as regular workers even in the formal sector are increasingly facing informal work conditions indicated in several reports and studies (NCEUS 2007, 2009; Kannan 2014).

The author first looks at the composition of regular employment—the most sought after form of employment, i.e., which type of enterprises are major employers of regular salaried workers. For understanding this, he has categorized the enterprises/employers into three types: (a) public sector enterprises consisting of all kinds of government departments, autonomous/subordinate organizations supported by

Table 1 Nature of employment in India (in percent)

	1993–94	2004–05	2011–12	2017–18
Rural				
Self-employed	58.2	60.2	55.9	57.8
Regular	6.4	7.6	8.7	13.1
Casual	35.4	32.8	35.4	29.1
Total	100	100	100	100
Urban				
Self-employed	42.7	45.4	41.9	38.3
Regular	38.9	39.5	43.3	47.0
Casual	18.4	15.1	14.8	14.7
Total	100	100	100	100
All India				
Self-employed	55.01	56.9	52.2	52.2
Regular	13.05	14.3	17.9	22.8
Casual	31.95	28.9	29.9	24.9
Total	100	100	100	100

Source NSSO data on employment and unemployment, various rounds; and PLFS data for 2017–18

government finances, etc.; (b) private sector enterprises consisting of public and private limited companies/organizations, voluntary and other firms/organizations (broadly matching the features of private organized sector; and (c) informal sector enterprises including proprietary/partnership firms, and individual employers households employing domestic help, security guards, etc. The data thus grouped are comparable for the years 2004–05 and 2011–12, whereas the same is not strictly comparable for the earlier period 1999–2000.

Based on the above criteria, around 30% of regular salaried workers were employed in public sector, another 22.6% in private sector, and the remaining 47.5% in informal sector, including about 1.4% with employer households in 2011–12 (Fig. 1). There is a significant change in the share of regular employment over the years across different types of enterprises—a sizeable decline in the share of public enterprises with a corresponding increase in the share of private corporate sector. However, the share of informal enterprises in creating regular employment was high, hovering around 48% (Mamgain and Tiwari 2017).

Indian workforce suffers from huge informality in employment—about 93% of workers are characterized as informal workers without any social security benefits. By using the criteria of social security and tenurial security to wage workers, Srivastava and Naik (2017) have estimated the magnitude of informality in wage employment in India. According to their estimates, over 61.4% of wage employment in the formal sector was of informal nature in 2011–12. Further, about half of employees among regular workers were in informal jobs. The share of informal workers significantly increased by over ten percentage points between 2004–05 and 2011–12, including that in case of regular employment (Table 2). The intensity of informal employment in formal sector wage employment varied significantly across different industry divisions. Manufacturing, construction, trade, and hotels suffer

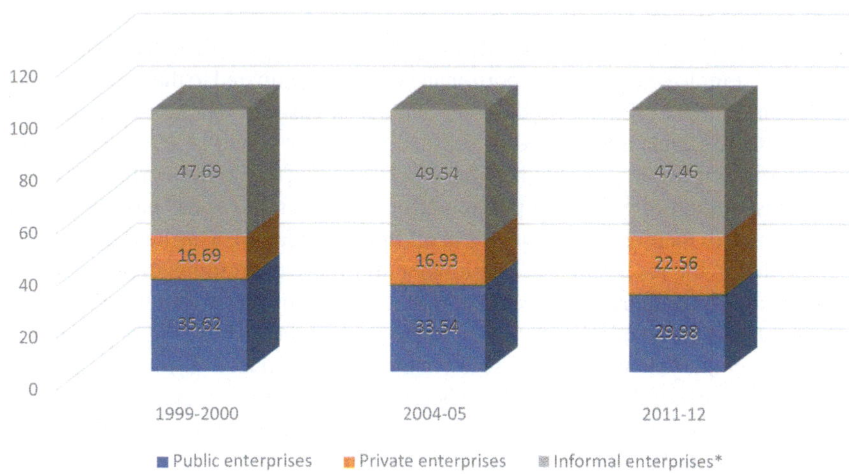

Fig. 1 Regular salaried employment by type of enterprises. *Source* Calculated from NSSO data

Table 2 Percentage of informal employment among wage workers in the formal sector

	Regular wage workers			All wage workers		
Formal sector	2004–05	2009–10	2011–12	2004–05	2009–10	2011–12
Public sector	23.3	31.7	28.2	27.1	39.3	41.5
Private sector	61.4	66.4	68.8	73.4	75.2	76.9
Public and private sector	40.3	48.7	50.2	51.6	58.1	61.4

Source Srivastava and Naik's (2017) calculations based on NSSO unit-level data on employment and unemployment, various rounds

with high degree of informality as around three-fourths of regular workers working therein are categorized as informal workers. More importantly, the rise in the share of informal employment in wage employment was widespread across different industry segments in the formal sector during 2004–05 and 2011–12 (Ibid). Even in the public sector, the proportion of informal employment among regular employees increased by five percentage points from over 23% in 2004–05 to over 28% in 2011–12. By including casual wage workers, the share of informal employment in total wage employment in public sector jumped sharply from 27% to over 41% during the period. Industry divisions such as hotels, education, and administration witnessed a significant rise in the share of informal workers among regular workers in public sector (Ibid).

2.1 Representation of Various Social Groups in Regular Salaried Jobs

As is well known, the share of socially marginalized groups such as STs and SCs in casual wage employment is disproportionately high as compared to their share in total population. In 2011–12, among the total number of casual wage labor the share of STs, SCs, OBCs, and Others stood at 12.8%, 30.9%, 42.0%, and 14.4%, respectively. The opposite is true particularly in regular employment in the private corporate sector. The representation of SC/ST in public sector regular employment has been fairly proportionate to their respective shares in all India population. This has been largely possible due to the reservation of employment for these two groups in public sector employment. It has improved since the 1990s after the active involvement of judiciary in the implementation of job reservation in the public sector. However, opportunities for regular employment in public sector significantly reduced in the aftermath of economic reforms of the early 1990s, wherein the share of contractual and informal employment increased but without any provisions of reservation for the deprived sections in such jobs. Muslims too are grossly under-represented in public sector employment and their relative share in such jobs has not improved much over the years. The reasons for their under-representation in such jobs and need for affirmative measures to promote their share have been well outlined in the recommendations of the Sachar Commission (2006), and recently by Kundu Committee (2014).

In case of regular employment in the private sector, the share of SCs, STs, and Muslims is still low in proportion to their share in population, but more so in case of STs and Muslims. OBCs also remain under-represented in private sector employment but their representation tended to improve due to faster growth in their employment during 2004–05 to 2011–12. In the informal sector regular wage employment, however, SCs and Muslims are fairly represented (Table 3).

The case of OBCs is worth mentioning in the context of their representation in regular employment opportunities in the country. They experienced a rapid improvement in their share in regular wage employment in public sector as well as private sector, but yet remain underrepresented in proportion to their share in total population. The rise in the share of OBCs in public sector could be directly due to reservation.

Table 3 Representation of different socio-religious groups in regular salaried employment by type of enterprise (in percent)

Socio-religious group	Public enterprises	Private enterprises	Informal enterprises	Total	% workers
	1999–2000				
ST	7.06	3.33	3.92	4.95	11.1
SC	16.15	11.46	13.56	14.16	20.3
Muslim	5.82	7.27	13.26	9.66	9.9
OBCs	23.26	24.83	29.5	26.53	33.1
OCs	47.71	53.12	39.77	44.7	25.8
All	100	100	100	100	100
	2004–05				
ST	6.47	2.29	3.16	4.12	9.8
SC	18.22	12.38	17.73	16.99	19.9
Muslim	6.48	5.31	12.45	9.24	10.3
OBCs	28.08	30.62	34.84	31.86	37.5
OCs	40.75	49.4	31.82	37.79	22.5
All	100	100	100	100	100
	2011–12				
ST	8.52	2.55	3.53	4.8	10.2
SC	17.75	12.08	17.45	16.33	19.1
Muslim	5.91	7.53	15.01	10.59	11.7
OBCs	30.63	31.2	35.44	33.04	37.6
OCs	37.19	46.64	28.56	35.23	21.4
All	100	100	100	100	100

Source Mamgain and Tiwari's (2017) calculation based on NSS unit record data on employment and unemployment

But the rise in their share in private and informal sector is worthwhile to mention (Table 3). This has been associated with significant improvement in their educational levels in recent years and faster withdrawals from farm-related jobs. Other Classes (upper caste) are represented in proportionately larger share than their population share in regular employment in public as well as private sector. The higher growth in employment for SCs, STs, and OBCs has been gradually bridging the gap with their relative share in such employment (Table 3). This is definitely a positive trend which can be associated with higher economic growth that created regular employment opportunities in private as well as informal sector particularly after 1999–2000, benefitting the marginalized groups.

2.2 *Informality in Regular Salaried Jobs by Type of Enterprises*

Given the relatively higher growth rate in private sector regular jobs between 2004–05 and 2011–12, it is necessary to know the quality of regular employment generated. By following the framework of formal/informal employment on the basis of written job contracts (as a measure of tenurial security) and social security benefits to workers (see NCEUS 2007; Srivastava and Naik 2017), it is expected that all regular employees working in public as well as private organized sector should have at least written job contracts and social security. Surprisingly, a significant 38% of regular workers working in public sector do not have any written job contract and social security indicating the precarious nature of employment. This has been true for all regular employees in public sector belonging to various social groups but more so for Muslims, SCs, and STs (Table 4).

In case of the private sector, the proportion of regular workers having some form of job contract along with social security is expectedly very less (30.5%) as compared to public sector (61.73%), thereby indicating the vulnerability of almost 70% of regular employees in private sector. Similar to public sector, the extent of such vulnerability is more so in the case of Muslims, STs, and SC regular workers as compared to OBCs and OCs in private sector. As obvious, almost all regular workers in the informal sector are most vulnerable from the perspective of their job contract and social security (Table 4). In brief, an overwhelming majority of regular salaried employees in India do not have any form of written job contract and social security, implying the magnitude of precariousness or uncertainty of such employment opportunities. Muslim and SC regular workers suffer maximum with such vulnerability.

Has such vulnerability of workers has reduced over the years? In fact, it has significantly increased during the period 2004–05/2011–12, as the proportion of workers without job contract and social security increased by almost ten percentage points both in public and private sectors. In the most recent period (2011–12 to 2017–18), the proportion of regular workers without any written job contract increased from 64.7% to over 71%, and that of those without any social security benefits (such as

Table 4 Share of regular salaried employees having written job contract and social security (in %)

Socio-religious group	Public Enterprises	Private Enterprises	Informal Enterprises	Total
	2004–05			
ST	64.66	24.49	4.50	38.05
SC	66.27	29.42	2.94	28.98
Muslims	63.95	30.81	3.61	20.45
OBC	68.61	37.52	5.74	29.49
OCs	72.50	48.88	8.88	40.73
Total	69.21	41.47	5.94	33.17
	2011–12			
ST	59.98	20.25	5.71	36.30
SC	58.63	24.04	3.20	24.74
Muslims	52.55	17.91	1.57	12.71
OBC	57.19	30.44	4.34	24.59
OCs	68.81	34.85	7.83	35.20
Total	61.73	30.52	4.77	27.66

Source Mamgain and Tiwari's (2017) estimates based on NSS unit record data on employment and unemployment

public provident fund, pension, gratuity, health and maternity benefits) declined from 55.4 per to 49.6% (PLFS-NSO 2019). This general deterioration in the quality of regular employment has been witnessed by workers from all social groups but more so by Muslims (Table 4).

3 City-Level Features of Employment and Informality

Having examined the macrofeatures of wage employment and extent of informality therein at the macrolevel, this section analyzes wage employment and informality in urban areas based on a sample survey of 3000 households in four cities during 2014–15 (Mamgain 2019). However, before the analysis, it would be useful to understand the broad features of the sample urban households. Over 60% of the population among sample households belongs to the 18–45 years age group—the focus age group of the study. Since the focus population groups are SC and ST, a substantive proportion of the sample constituted SC and ST households. About 12% of the sample population was Muslim. Migrants constituted around 8% of the sample population, though the ratio was very high (14.8%) in Pune, and between 5 and 7% in other cities. On considering a much broader aspect of migrant population, i.e., those not born in the city of enumeration, the proportion of such population jumps to over 40% in Delhi and least 10.5% in Coimbatore (Table 5). Over 70% of the sample population had high school and above education including one-third with graduate

Table 5 Broad features of sample population

Characteristics	Lucknow	Delhi/NCR	Pune	Coimbatore	All
Sample HHs	700	1100	700	500	3000
Sample population	3338	4755	2656	1798	12,547
Population in age group 18–45 yrs (in %)	60.90	62.20	63.80	62.20	62.20
Social background (%)					
SC and ST	50.80	38.20	32.40	41.80	40.80
OBC	28.60	22.10	30.10	53.10	30.00
Others	20.60	39.80	37.50	5.10	29.20
Place of birth (%)					
City of enumeration	78.22	59.45	61.67	89.49	69.22
Other city/town	7.88	13.94	14.78	5.01	11.22
Village	13.90	26.60	23.56	5.51	19.56
Migrant@ (%)	6.60	6.00	14.80	5.20	7.90
Not born in the city (%)	21.78	40.55	38.33	10.51	30.78
Literacy rate (%)	89.32	91.2	92.21	93.55	91.24
Educated persons (high school and above) (%)	69.18	74.74	69.12	63.30	70.45

Note Following the Census definition, we have treated migrant population to the city as those persons whose last place of residence was different than the current one in the city and residing there for less than 10 years
Source Mamgain (2019)

and above educational levels. It merits mention here that such demographic features of the sample households should not be generalized as these are necessarily not representative of the city's population universe due to its different purpose. However, it adds important information on the nature of employment and job search in the urban labor market in recent years.

3.1 *Characteristics of Employment*

Since the survey aimed at understanding the job search practices among salaried workers in the age group 18–45 years, most of the workers in the sample households were working in regular salaried jobs in all cities, ranging from nearly 44% in Lucknow to over 59% in Pune (Table 6). Contractual employment has emerged as a new form of employment where workers are not directly employed by a principal employer but employed through a contractor for specific jobs (third party hires). In Delhi and Lucknow, the proportion of contractual workers was high—32.0% and 26.7%, respectively, whereas the proportion of such workers was least at 14.97% in Pune. This form of recruitment is being increasingly used by employers to not

Table 6 Distribution of workers (18–45 yrs) by their job/work status (in percent)

Job/work status	Lucknow	Delhi/NCR	Pune	Coimbatore	Total
Self-employed	22.90	12.30	20.20	10.90	17.00
Regular salaried	43.60	51.70	59.20	58.37	53.32
Contractual	26.70	32.00	14.90	21.97	24.14
Casual	5.90	3.20	5.20	8.80	5.20
Apprenticeship trainee	0.80	0.90	0.40		0.50
Total	606	1047	1339	478	3470

Source Mamgain (2019)

only reduce labor costs but to also control labor. The share of such workers both in public and private sectors has increased substantially over the years, particularly after the economic reforms of the early 1990s. For example, the share of contractual workers in the organized manufacturing sector in India increased sharply from 13.9% in 1995–96 to 34.0% in 2011–12 (Goldar and Suresh 2017). Nearly one-fifth workers were self-employed in Lucknow and Pune sample and over one-tenth in Delhi and Coimbatore, respectively. Apprenticeship trainees strictly are not workers but their services are growingly being used by the employers for the production of goods and services. The proportion of such apprenticeship trainees, however, is less than 1% among the sample workers.

Gender-wise there is not much difference in the work status of men and women. But it differs significantly among workers belonging to various social groups. The proportion of contractual and casual workers was higher among ST and SC workers as compared to those belonging to OBCs and OC social groups (Fig. 2). On the other hand, the proportion of regular salaried workers was higher by about six percentage points for OBCs and OCs than ST/SCs. In other words, workers belonging

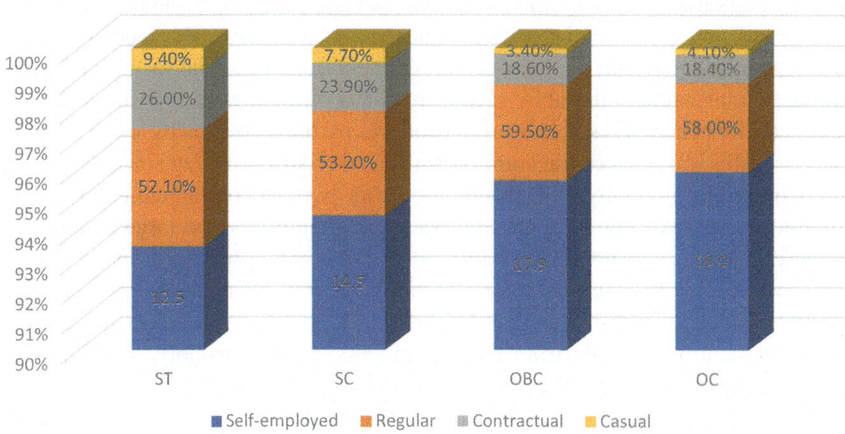

Fig. 2 Job/Work Status of Workers by Their Social Group. *Source* Mamgain (2019)

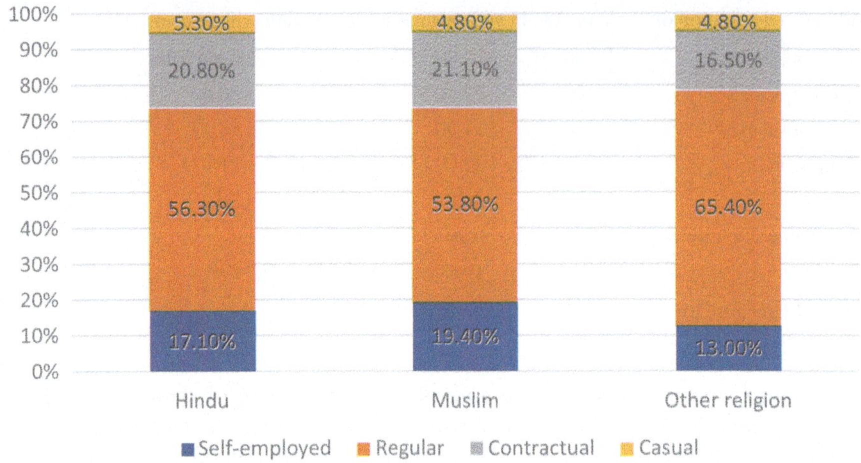

Fig. 3 Job/Work Status of Workers by Their Religious Group. *Source* Mamgain (2019)

to SC/ST communities have relatively poor quality employment. This pattern has been observed at the national level as well (ISLE-IHD 2014; Mamgain and Tiwari 2017). Religion-wise, work status of workers belonging to Hindu and Muslim religions is almost similar to a marginally higher proportion of self-employed workers among Muslims. However, workers belonging to other religions were proportionately more in regular salaried jobs (Fig. 3).

3.2 *Coverage of Social Security Benefits*

Wage workers have been classified into three categories based on the nature of their contract and coverage of social security benefits, viz. fully covered by social security benefits, partially covered by social security benefits, and no social security benefits. Among regular workers in public sector, over half of them were fully protected by social security benefits. A sizeable proportion was partially covered by social security benefits. In this way, the general notion of full social security coverage in public sector employment has gradually diluted with the faster pace of contractual employment in public sector in recent decades. In private sector enterprises, a large majority of regular employees was not covered fully by social security benefits. Nearly half of regular workers in private sector were partially covered by social security benefits (Table 7). About one-third of regular workers in private sector were not getting any social security benefits from their employers. Understandably, a majority of those working in private unincorporated enterprises or informal enterprises were not receiving any social security benefits. These patterns at city level broadly follow the macro patterns as observed earlier (Tables 2, 3 and 4).

Table 7 Percentage share of employed persons covered by social security benefits@

Type of work/Enterprise	Without social security	Partially covered	Fully covered
Regular			
Public	20.4	27.4	52.2
Private/MNCs	32.5	47.1	20.4
Others	60.9	34.8	4.3
Total	30.7	43.7	25.6
Observations	662	940	551
Contractual			
Public	39.6	47.8	12.6
Private/MNCs	47.6	42.6	9.8
Others	51.9	40.7	7.4
Total	46.0	43.7	10.3
Observations	325	309	73

Note @If an employed person gets earned leave, medical leave in case of sickness and contributory provident fund from her/his employer, she/he is termed as 'fully covered' by social security benefits. In case she/he gets any of the above mentioned social security benefits, she/he is categorized as 'partially' covered. Those who do not get any of the above mentioned social security benefits are categorized as 'without social security'
Source Mamgain (2019)

The situation of contractual workers on social security entitlements is worrisome as an overwhelming majority among them is not fully covered by social security benefits. As high as 40% of contractual workers in public sector and nearly half in private sector were not receiving any social security benefits (Table 8).

How the degree of such informality of employment varies for persons working in different occupations in our sample cities? Let us first look at regular workers. Lack of informality is widespread across various occupational groups of workers. However, the degree of informality is very high in the occupational groups such as sales and service works, crafts and related works, and plant and machinery operators. At the top ladder of occupational hierarchies, comparatively a higher proportion of workers are protected by social security benefits, indicating the criticality of such workers to employers. Contractual workers, though few in top-end occupations, also enjoy relatively better social security benefits than those working in bottom end occupations. Almost 80% of contractual workers working in machine operating and elementary occupations were not getting any social security benefits (Table 8).

In brief, apart from the lack of employment opportunities in general, the quality of employment is a major casualty in the current dispensation of liberal economic policies of the last two decades or so. The share of precarious employment is widespread tended to increase over the years. Socially marginalized groups and those working in lower end occupational hierarchies do suffer more with such informality in the labor market and thus has serious implications for their income earnings and well-being.

Table 8 Percentage share of employed persons covered by social security benefits$

NCO	Without social security	At least one	Fully covered	Obs
Regular				
Legislators, Senior Officials, and Managers	9.6	44.9	45.5	198
Professionals	13.9	48.5	37.6	431
Technicians and Associate Professionals	29.7	43.6	26.7	610
Clerks	37.6	38.6	23.8	189
Service and Sales Workers	44.0	43.8	12.3	350
Skilled Agri. and Fishery Works	25.0	25	50.0	4
Craft and Related Works	49.6	38.9	11.6	224
Plant and Machine Operators and Assemblers	47.7	44.9	7.5	107
Elementary occupations	35.0	35	30.0	40
Total	30.7	43.7	25.6	2153
Contractual				
Legislators, Senior Officials, and Managers	32.2	52.6	15.3	59
Professionals	41.5	40.6	17.9	123
Technicians and Associate Professionals	41.1	50.3	8.6	209
Clerks	53.8	35.9	10.4	106
Service and Sales Workers	49.2	45.9	5.0	120
Skilled Agri. and Fishery Works	82.6	15.2	2.2	46
Craft and Related Works	62.0	31.7	6.3	79
Plant and Machine Operators and Assemblers	76.0	20.2	3.8	104
Elementary occupations	81.0	17.5	1.6	189
Total	46.0	43.6	10.4	711

Note $ Same as @ in Table 7
Source Mamgain (2019)

4 Social Networks and Access to Employment

How informality in employment is inked with access to job information in labor market is examined in this section. Economic theories have clearly recognized the role of information in labor markets by bringing together employers and job seekers in a competitive economy to maximize their earnings/productivity (Stigler 1961, 62; Spence 1973). However, the lack of access to such free and timely information, both to employers and job seekers creates rigidities and imperfect competition in the labor market. It is argued that free flow of information is hampered in segmented labor markets, resulting in inequality in productivity, wage earnings and upward mobility (Kannapan 1977; Papola 1981). More recent literature shows how the success rate of getting job and negotiation for wages depends on access to information, its source, and quality (O'Connor 2013). In this section, an attempt is made to understand the sources of job information used by the employed persons for finding their current employment in select cities. It also examines how the source of information determines the access to better quality jobs. Equally important is analyzing the nature and access of job information to job seekers belonging to various socio-economic groups. It is generally believed that information on job opportunities is relatively weak in the case of migrant workers, women, socially marginalized communities, and those with low educational attainments.

The most prominent source of job information is informal social networks, which include friends, relatives, family members, caste networks, etc. The importance of social networks in providing access to labor market information is well documented in earlier studies as well (Papola 1981; Harriss et al. 1990). Newspaper advertisements along with web portals were the source of information for nearly 22% persons. For about 4.63% of workers, employee referral was the source of job information. About 5% said they had directly approached the employers. Unlike in the past, employment exchanges are no longer a major source of job information. Interestingly, social contacts/networks emerged as the most important source of job information for a majority of employed persons (Table 9). These included family members, friends, relatives, caste/community networks, co-villagers, migrants, employee referrals, etc.

This pattern in the use of different sources of job information is similar among different cities. For instance, family connection as a source of job information was relatively stronger in Lucknow and Coimbatore as compared to Delhi and Pune. In Coimbatore, caste/community network seems to be more effective in getting a job as compared to the other three cities in the survey. Newspaper advertisements have been cited by a sizeable number of persons in all cities except Coimbatore. Web portals have emerged an important source of job information with the highest proportion (13.3%) of employed persons in the Delhi sample using this source for finding their current job.

Do sources of job information vary for men and women workers in the labor market? Broadly speaking, social networks are the main source of job information for both men and women. However, friends/acquaintances as the main source of job information were of lesser importance for women workers as compared to

Table 9 Source of information for current employment, city-wise (in percent)

Source of Job Information	Lucknow	Delhi/NCR	Pune	Coimbatore	Total
Family connections	22.92	13.61	20.50	24.45	19.36
Friends/acquaintances	44.31	43.05	41.61	60.92	45.12
Employee referral	4.92	5.15	5.54	0.44	4.63
Newspaper advertisements	13.92	14.38	19.06	8.52	15.33
Electronic web portals	3.40	13.31	5.77	0.87	6.98
Placement agencies/Staffing companies	0.51	0.78	0.46	0.22	0.53
School/college	0.51	0.78	0.08	0.66	0.44
Campus placement	0.17	1.85	0.91	0.22	0.97
Directly approaching employers	8.32	6.12	4.40	2.84	5.39
Contractor/middleman	0.68	0.19	1.59	0.44	0.85
Employment exchanges	0.00	0.10	0.08	0.22	0.09
Others	0.34	0.68	0.00	0.22	0.29
Total	100	100	100	100	100
No. of persons	589	1029	1317	458	3393

Source Mamgain (2019)

their male counterparts. For over 18% women newspapers were the main source of their job information, whereas about 14% men used this source of information. The proportion of women (8.1%) directly approaching the employer for job was almost double than men (4.2%) (Table 10). Such behavior of job search information has also been reported in earlier studies. City-wise, there is a significant difference in the sources of job information both for employed men and women (see Mamgain 2019). For example, only one-third of women respondents got job information from their friends/acquaintances social network in Lucknow and Delhi as compared to 57.4% in Coimbatore, and 43% in Pune. Also, the proportion of women directly approaching employers for job information was higher in Lucknow and Delhi as compared to Pune and Coimbatore.

The predominance of social networks as sources of job information is true for workers belonging to various social groups albeit with relatively lesser dependence on such sources among OCs. There is a significant variation in friend/acquaintance as a source of job information among workers belonging to various social groups. Proportionately more OC workers used newspaper advertisements and web portals as compared to SC and OBC. Campus placement cells were the main source of job information for about 2% of OC workers as compared to about 0.6% for SCs and OBCs. It merits mention here that although job information through college placement cells may be accessible to all, the cut-off marks for such placements are generally high wherein SCs and OBCs often remain at a disadvantageous position due to their (non-English) educational background (Chakravarty and Somanathan 2008).

Table 10 Source of information for current employment by gender and social groups

Source of job information	Gender		Social group			
	Male	Female	STs	SCs	OBCs	OCs
Family connections	19.34	19.41	8.42	20.91	19.82	18.33
Friends/acquaintances	46.83	41.17	30.53	46.40	47.57	42.92
Employee referral	4.90	4.00	16.84	3.87	5.35	3.74
Newspaper advertisement	14.02	18.34	34.74	14.59	12.88	16.59
Electronic web portal	7.73	5.27	5.26	5.10	6.64	9.30
Placement agencies/Staffing companies	0.55	0.49	0.00	0.26	0.59	0.78
School/college	0.34	0.68	0.00	0.53	0.50	0.35
Campus placement	1.06	0.78	1.05	0.62	0.59	1.65
Directly approaching employers	4.22	8.10	1.05	6.15	5.15	5.21
Contractor/middleman	0.72	1.17	2.11	0.97	0.59	0.87
Employment exchanges	0.13	0.00	0.00	0.18	0.10	0.00
Others	0.17	0.59	0.00	0.44	0.20	0.26
Total	100	100	100	100	100	100
No. of persons	2368	1025	95	1138	1009	1151

Source Mamgain (2019)

Thus, it is seen that dependence on social networks for job information is comparatively more among SCs and OBCs as compared to OCs. This is in contrast to earlier studies which showed how due to weak social networks SC job seekers in the urban labor market suffer higher unemployment incidence (Banerjee 1983; Harriss et al. 1990). However, this has been observed here in case of STs who are largely dependent on other sources of job information rather than social networks.

The popularity of social networks in providing job information to job seekers across different types of enterprises is more than evident although in varying degrees. Understandably, they are most important media for dissemination of information on job opportunities in informal private enterprises, followed by private enterprises and least important in case of public enterprises (Table 11). Electronic job portals and newspaper advertisements are important sources of job information for public sector employment as about 40% of respondents employed in such enterprises received job information from these two sources. This holds true for those working as regular as well as contractual workers in public sector enterprises. In case of those working in private sector enterprises, over one-fourth among them received job information from electronic job portals and newspaper advertisements. For those working in informal enterprises on contractual basis, much less than one-fifth received job information through electronic job portals and newspaper advertisements. For a sizeable number of employees, employee referrals were the main source of job information particularly for contractual jobs and that too in private sector and informal sector enterprises.

Table 11 Job search information by type of enterprise (in percent)

Job search information	Public	Private/MNCs	Others@	Total
Regular				
Social networks	54.4	63.5	96.0	62.4
Employee referrals	1.3	5.5	0.0	4.8
Electronic job portals	28.8	14.6	4.0	16.8
Newspapers	12.7	13.2	0.0	13.0
Placement agencies/HR firms	1.1	0.6	0.0	0.7
Campus placement	0.0	1.3	0.0	1.1
Others	1.8	1.2	0.0	1.3
Total	100.0	100.0	100.0	100.0
Contractual				
Social networks	46.9	52.2	72.4	51.8
Employee referrals	6.2	8.7	10.3	8.2
Electronic job portals	21.0	22.0	10.3	21.3
Newspapers	19.1	13.6	6.9	14.5
Placement agencies/HR firms	1.2	0.9	0.0	0.9
Campus placement	0.6	1.6	0.0	1.3
Others	4.9	1.0	0.0	1.8
Total	100.0	100.0	100.0	100.0

Note Others include private-sector small enterprises which are not categorized as limited companies
Source Mamgain (2019)

Thus, social networks were dominant source of job information in private as well as informal enterprises in the urban labor market (Table 11).

4.1 Determinants of Using Social Network for Job Search

While recognizing the importance of social networks, it is important to understand the factors influencing the use of such networks for job search in the urban labor market. There are various factors, viz. age, gender, social group, migration, education, occupation, income, and location that may affect a job seeker's decision to use social network to look for jobs in the urban labor market. For this logistic regression was applied to estimate the effect of these variables on the decision of a job seeker to use social network as job search method.

Table 12 depicts the results of logistic regression. It has captured the effect of age, gender, social groups, education, income, migration, and occupation on the chances of using social network as job search method. Some interesting features that emerged are as follows. The probability of using social networks for job search

Table 12 Decision to use social network as job search method by workers

Social network	Coefficient	Odds ratio	Standard error	Z	P > |Z|
Constant	1.310162	3.706772	0.4155845	3.15	0.002
Education	−0.1084206	0.8972501	0.014536	−7.46	0.000
Income	−0.000024	0.999976	0.000004	−6.2	0.000
Age	0.0051559	1.005169	0.0064026	0.81	0.421
Gender	0.2327063	1.262011	0.0893738	2.6	0.009
Migrant	−0.1867969	0.8296122	0.0846618	−2.21	0.027
SC	0.9419804	2.565056	0.2419145	3.89	0.000
OBC	1.014645	2.758384	0.2434637	4.17	0.000
General	1.134315	3.109042	0.240744	4.71	0.000
Occupation I	−0.5597004	0.5713802	0.2096146	−2.67	0.008
Occupation II	0.1057418	1.111535	0.2096475	0.5	0.614
Occupation III	0.2147643	1.23957	0.2197797	0.98	0.328
Delhi	−0.0115424	0.988524	0.1194289	−0.1	0.923
Pune	−0.1327892	0.8756496	0.1235746	−1.07	0.283
Coimbatore	1.065867	2.903354	0.1684976	6.33	0.000
Total Observations	3232				
LR $chi^2(14)$	517.05				
Pseudo R^2	0.1222				

Note Education is measured as number of years of education; income reflects per capita monthly income of workers; age in number of years. Except for these three variables, other variables are categorical. For gender, social group and occupation dummies are used as females, STs, and Occupation IV (elementary occupations), respectively. Lucknow is used for city dummy. For details, see Mamgain (2019)

tends to reduce with every increase in the numbers of years of education. This is statistically significant as its odds ratio shows that one year increase in education reduces the odds in favor of using social network as job search method by around 11%. In other words, job seekers with the high level of education do not employ social network as job search method as intensively as compared to those with the low level of education. Similarly, as the income levels of workers increase, the odds in favor of using social networks decline significantly. The level variable 'age,' however, does not have any significant impact upon the likelihood of using social network for job search in the urban labor market, and thus is in conformity with the earlier studies (Banerjee 1983).

It is seen that the coefficient of sex dummy is significantly different from zero at 1% level of significance and the odd ratio for male dummy indicates that male job seekers shift the odds in favor of using social network by about 26.2% as compared to their female counterparts. Next, the dummy variable capturing migration shows that if the job seeker is a migrant it reduces the odds in favor of using social network as job search method. This implies that migrants have less social fabric to explore jobs in the urban labor market.

The social belonging of job seekers has a significant bearing on using social networks for job search. The three-social group dummies are statistically significant from zero and they increase the odds which favor the choice of employing social network as job search method by job seekers compared to the omitted category, ST. To note that the job seekers from higher caste groups employ social network as a job search method to a greater extent compared to the lower caste group (say, ST and SC).

The chances of using social network for job search significantly differ with the type of occupational group of workers. The declining values of odds ratios with rising occupational hierarchies reconfirms that the chances of workers using social networks in top-end occupations for jobs are significantly lower than those in lower occupational hierarchies in the urban labor market in India.

Finally, the effect of location or city on the decision to use social network as job search method is measured through the usage of location dummies. The coefficients on dummies—Delhi and Pune—are not found to be different from zero. However, Coimbatore is significantly different from zero which indicates that compared to Lucknow, social network is used to a greater degree to search for a job in Coimbatore. In other words, the use of social networks in Delhi, Pune, and Lucknow is almost identical, whereas the same is significantly different and higher in Coimbatore.

In brief, social networks are significant in providing job information and access to jobs in the urban labor market, particularly for low-end informal employment/occupations fetching low income to job seekers.

5 Conclusion

The 1990s economic reforms induced high growth development trajectory in India has been rather sluggish in bringing the desired rate of growth in employment opportunities and related structural changes therein. An overwhelmingly large majority of employment is informal in nature without any social security to workers. Due to a variety of reasons, there has been an increasing pace of informalization in employment in the organized segment of the Indian economy, which was once considered a major source of stable job with reasonable social security. Such kind of informalization is widely spread across different industry segments in the formal sector including both public and private enterprises. More recent evidences emerging from various studies have also indicated a high pace of contractualization and casualization of employment opportunities both in public and private formal sectors. Moreover, the access to 'decent jobs,' particularly in private formal sector, is a proportionately unequal among populations belonging to different socio-religious groups. Socially backward groups like SCs, STs, and OBCs have proportionately lower share in private sector jobs as compared to other or upper caste groups in proportion to their shares in the overall population. OBCs albeit remain under-represented in private formal sector jobs, but their representation has improved in the recent years due to faster growth in their employment. However, SCs, STs, and Muslims remain largely concentrated in informal sector wage employment.

Associated with the high prevalence of informal wage employment, sources of job information have become highly informal in nature for a large majority of wage workers despite great strides in the penetration of information technology in India. Social networks comprising close family members, friends, relatives, co-villagers, etc., are still critical in providing job information to wage workers, especially in informal enterprises and private formal sector enterprises for jobs pertaining to low-end occupational hierarchies. The new forms of job search such as web job portals are largely being used by educated job seekers looking for jobs in formal sector. This pattern in sources of job information in the urban labor market among job seekers only reiterates the limited access to job information in labor markets remains segmented, thus hampering the free flow of job information to job seekers, and resultant efficiency and productivity of enterprises.

Apart from the lack of employment opportunities in general, the quality of employment has been a major casualty in the current dispensation of liberal economic policies during the last two-and-half decades. The share of precarious employment is widespread and has tended to increase over the years. This dismal situation on the employment front has attracted the attention of political class in recent times but it has yet to be translated into effective policy measures with a time-bound agenda for the creation of employment that ensures tenurial stability and social security as also dignity and decent earnings to workers. This indeed is a daunting challenge, which if left entirely to the market forces would create another set of economic and social upheavals that could become very difficult to contain.

Acknowledgments The earlier version of this paper was presented in the 59th Annual Conference of the Indian Society of Labor Economics at Indira Gandhi Institute of Development Research, Mumbai. I am thankful to Professors S. Mahendra Dev, Alakh N. Sharma, Amitabh Kundu, Arup Mitra, and S. Madheswaran and participants of the Conference for providing their valuable comments.

This paper is based on a larger study on *Job Search, Hiring Practices and Discrimination in Urban Labor Market*, undertaken by the author for the Indian Council of Social Science Research, New Delhi. However, the views expressed are the author's own.

References

Abraham, V. (2017). Stagnant employment growth: Last three years may have been the worst. *Economic and Political Weekly, 52*(38), 13–17.

Banerjee, B. (1983). Social networks in the migration process: Empirical evidence on chain migration in India. *The Journal of Developing Areas, 17,* 185–196.

Chakravartry, S., & Somanathan, E. (2008). Discrimination in an elite labor market? Job placements at IIM-Ahmedabad. *Economic and Political Weekly, 43*(44), 45–50.

Goldar, B. N., & Suresh, R. (2017). Contract labor in organized manufacturing in India. In K.P. Kannan, R.P. Mamgain, & P. Rustagi (Eds.), *Labor and development-essays in honour of T.S.Papola.* New Delhi: Academic Foundation.
Harriss, J., Kannan K. P., & Rodgers, G. (1990). *Urban labor market structure and job access in India: a study of Coimbatore*, Research Series 92, Centre for Development Studies, Trivandrum, and International Institute for Labor Studies, Geneva.
ILO. (2014). *World of work report 2014-developing with jobs.* Geneva: International Labor Organisation.
Institute for Human Development (IHD) and Indian Society of Labor Economics (ISLE). (2014). *India: Labor and employment report 2014- workers in the era of globalization.* New Delhi: Academic Foundation.
Institute for Human Development (IHD). (2016). *India: Labor and employment report 2016*. New Delhi: Oxford University Press.
ISLE-IHD. (2014). *India labour and employment report 2014- workers in globalised world, New Delhi: Indian society of labour economics and institute for human development.*
Kannan, K. P. (2014). *Interrogating inclusive growth: Poverty and inequality in India.* New Delhi: Routledge.
Kannan, K. P., & Raveendran, G. (2019). From jobless to job losses growth: Gainers and losers during 2012–18. *Economic and Political Weekly, 54*(44).
Kannapan, S. (1977). *Studies of urban labor market behavior in developing areas.* Geneva: International Institute of Labor Studies.
Kundu Committee. (2014). Report of the Post Sachar Evaluation Committee (PSEC), (Chairman: Amitabh Kundu), Government of India, Ministry of Minority Affairs, New Delhi.
Mamgain, R. P., & Tiwari, S. (2017). Regular salaried employment opportunities in India: Nature, access and inclusiveness. *The Indian Journal of Labor Economics, 60*(3), 415–436.
Mamgain, R. P. (2019). *Formal labor market in urban India: Job search, hiring practices and discrimination.* New Delhi: Sage Publications.
NCEUS–GoI, . (2007). *Report on conditions of work and promotion of livelihoods in the unorganised sector*. Government of India, New Delhi: National Commission for Enterprises in the Unorganised Sector.
NCEUS–GoI, . (2009). *The challenge of employment: An informal economy perspective.* Government of India, New Delhi: National Commission for Enterprises in the Unorganised Sector.
O'Connor, L. T. (2013). Ask and you shall receive: Social network contacts' provision of help during the job search. *Social Networks, 35,* 593–603.
OECD. (2017). *OECD Employment Outlook 2017*, Paris.
Papola, T.S. (1981). *Urban informal sector in a developing economy.* New Delhi: Vikas Publishing House.
Papola, T. S., & Sahu, P. P. (2012). *Growth and structure of employment: long-term and post-reform performance and emerging challenges.* ISID Occasional Paper Series, 2012/1, New Delhi: Institute for Studies in Industrial Development.
Sachar Commission. (2006). *Social, economic and educational status of the Muslim community in India*, Prime Minister's High Level Committee, Cabinet Secretariat, Government of India, New Delhi, November. (Chairman: Rajinder Sachar).
Spence, M. (1973). Job market signaling. *The Quarterly Journal of Economics, 87*(3), 355–374.
Srivastava, R.S., & Naik, A. (2017). Growth and informality in the Indian economy. In K.P. Kannan, R.P. Mamgain, & P. Rustagi (Eds.), *Labor and Development-Essays in honour of T.S.Papola.* New Delhi: Academic Foundation.
Stigler, G. J. (1961). The economics of information. *Journal of Political Economy, 69*(3), 213–225.
Stigler, G. J. (1962). Information in the labor market. *Journal of Political Economy, 70*(5), 94–105.
World Bank. (2012). *World development report 2013: jobs.* Washington D.C.: World Bank.

Entrepreneurial Avenues for Scheduled Tribe Communities in Nonfarm Enterprise Sector: Prospects and Challenges

Partha Pratim Sahu and Manik Kumar

Abstract This paper explores the role of social group identity on private enterprise ownership in India. Drawing data from NSSO-Unincorporated Non-Agricultural Enterprises Survey: 2010–11 and 2015–16, the paper seeks to analyse how caste discrimination continues to exist and hinder economic participation for specific groups. The disadvantageous castes, especially Scheduled Tribes (STs) not only own a disproportionately low share in the private business economy but also operate at low-end activities with low levels of productivity and earnings and there is hardly any improvement in their participation during the period under study 2011–16. However, there are significant variations in enterprise ownership among marginalized groups across type and location of enterprise, scale of operation and a host of other characteristics. This paper obtains some interesting results which have important policy implications. The analysis also opens up a rich research agenda, including further investigation of various issues regarding tribal entrepreneurship in India.

1 Introduction

With shrinking livelihood opportunities especially in rural areas, agricultural workers being pushed out of agriculture and severe distress-driven out-migration, there is an urgent need to generate employment and/or entrepreneurial avenues in the place of residence, which will ensure higher productivity, secured and sustainable livelihood. In the recent past, we have noticed that there has been an unprecedented employment

This paper liberally draws from first author's earlier works on this theme, Sahu 2017. The usual disclaimer applies for any errors, inaccuracy or omission.

P. P. Sahu (✉) · M. Kumar
Centre for Entrepreneurship Development (CED), NIRDPR, Hyderabad, India
e-mail: ppsahu@gmail.com

M. Kumar
e-mail: maniktiwary@gmail.com

N. K. Mishra (ed.), *Development Challenges of India After Twenty Five Years of Economic Reforms*, India Studies in Business and Economics,
https://doi.org/10.1007/978-981-15-8265-3_12

setback across the broad sectors of the economy. Although various segments of non-farm sector have shown some positive employment growth, its size, type and quality of employment generated raise doubt. The employment generated in this sector is inadequate not only to accommodate workers moving out of agriculture but also to the new entrants to the labour market. During the last two decades or so, we have also observed a sharp decline in the rural female labour force participation rate and rise in the share of youth population. In view of these changes, entrepreneurship development alone can ensure sustainable livelihoods and create employment opportunities at the local level.

Of late enterprises in the manufacturing and services sector have shown encouraging potential to generate employment. However, these sectors are suffering from a low level of technology, limited access to inputs and credits and an unfavourable market environment. To ensure local employment generation at rising levels of productivity, skill development of both aspiring and existing entrepreneurs and workers engaged therein will be crucial. Linking these enterprises with the market, formal institutions and large enterprises will also enhance their capability to scale up their production and expand employment. But in spite of numerous skill and entrepreneurship development programmes, we have not witnessed any significant change in the entrepreneurship scenario. Not only new and aspiring entrepreneurs are struggling but also the existing entrepreneurs are finding it difficult to run and scale-up. Most of the policies to promote entrepreneurship are not based on systematic and scientific thinking. Therefore, we have seen that a vast bulk of entrepreneurs are neither innovative nor significant job creators.

We argue that there exists a strong caste dimension to the issues of discrimination and exclusion in ownership of non-farm enterprises and livelihood avenues. Prior works have attempted to understand the processes and factors that block or resist business participation by specific communities such as Scheduled Tribes (STs) and Scheduled Castes (SCs). These groups are often constrained to start any new livelihood avenue in non-farm segment business due to limited access of resources, inadequate entrepreneurial abilities and lack of social networks and most of them end up in activities similar to their family/parental business. Marketing obstacles further restrict the possibility to start up a new venture and/or scale up the existing ones. Lack of access to formal institutions relating to credit, market, skill and training also obstructs the possibilities of upward mobility. There are a plethora of schemes and policies under various government ministries but there is no evidence of any visible improvement and no systematic evaluation of these policies and provisions has also been undertaken. During last 5–6 years, a series of policy initiatives such as Goods and Service Tax (GST), demonetization, reforms in banking transactions, the ease of doing business, direct benefit transfers (DBT) and ICT/digitization have been rolled out in an attempt to transcend small and informal enterprises to a formal set-up and improve their accessibility to formal institutions and improve their livelihood status. But these initiatives have not only created opportunities but also thrown up challenges, threat and distrust.

The SCs and STs together account for a quarter of India's population. While between 1991 and 2001, there was no change in their share, the latest available census estimate, however, indicates a marginal rise. The share of SCs and STs population, taken together, marginally increased from 24.6 in 1991 to 25.2 (STs = 8.60 and SCs = 16.60) in 2011. Although there are several strands of protective and affirmative policies in place to alleviate and moderate discrimination against specific groups, negative discrimination against disadvantageous caste continues to exist and some of them even have aggravated. There is a voluminous literature on social and economic discrimination and/or social exclusion contributing to the understanding of these facets. But the role of caste-based differences in ownership of non-farm enterprises has remained as one of the most under-studied areas in the context of contemporary policy changes.

Drawing unit-level data from NSSO-Unincorporated Non-Agricultural Enterprises Survey: 2010–11 and 2015–16,[1] the present paper seeks to analyse how social group identity[2] continues to play a crucial role in the participation of for specific groups, i.e. STs in non-farm livelihood avenues. These groups not only own a disproportionately low share (with respect to their population weight) but also operate in low-end activities with low levels of productivity and earnings. However, there are considerable variations among these groups across type and location of enterprise, scale of operation and a host of other characteristics of a non-farm enterprise and its owner. To mainstream, these disadvantaged groups into the growth process and thus making it more inclusive has been the key challenge for policymakers. Given the increasingly shrinking livelihood space for the STs, this paper attempts to unfold the possibility of expanding livelihood opportunities for ST communities in the non-farm enterprise sector. The paper also discusses how to mainstream livelihood strategies for these groups in the existing rural institutions, tools and instruments through a convergence approach.

The paper has been organized into six sections. While Sect. 1 introduces the broad issues of discussion, Sect. 2 takes a broad look at the existing studies and discusses the issues and policies related to the participation of SCs and STs in the private business economy. Section 3 describes the ownership pattern by social groups across broad activity categories such as manufacturing, trading and other services activities. Section 4 analyses the industry-wise pattern of participation of STs in non-farm enterprise sector, based on two rounds of NSS data sets. Section 5 briefly ponders over the performance difference among enterprises owned by various social groups. Section 6 concludes the paper while presenting its key findings along with a series of issues which need further probe. It also highlights how rural entrepreneurship for STs Communities can be mainstreamed in the existing rural development institutions.

[1]Non-agricultural enterprises which are not incorporated (i.e. registered under Companies Act, 1956) were covered in the survey. Further, the domain of 'unincorporated enterprises' excluded (a) enterprises registered under Sections 2m(i) and 2 m(ii) of the Factories Act, 1948 or bidi and cigar manufacturing enterprises registered under bidi and cigar workers (condition of employment) Act, 1966, (b) government/public sector enterprises and (c) cooperatives. Thus, the coverage was restricted primarily to all household proprietary and partnership enterprises. In addition, Self Help groups (SHGs), Private Non-Profit Institutions (NPIs) including Non-Profit Institutions Serving Households (NPISH) and Trusts were also covered (NSSO 2012).

[2]This paper focusses only on Scheduled Tribe (ST) communities.

2 Review of Issues, Policies and Prior Works

In addition to constitutional provisions, there are policies, initiatives, preferential treatments to overcome institutionalized caste-based deprivations. These policies include reservation in jobs and access to higher education, exclusive or subsidized allocation of resources and benefits. One may argue that over the years, some sections of the tribal population might have been benefited from various policies and witnessed some improvements in their situation, but various forms of discrimination and relative deprivation continue to remain in our society. Moreover, we could have new disadvantageous castes emerging as dominant in several pockets of rural India. Recent studies extensively document various dimensions of discrimination and exclusion in access to land, job, credit, health, education, housing, basic amenities and other public services (World Bank 2011; Harriss-White and Prakash 2010; Thorat 2002; Desai and Dubey 2011; Papola 2012; Pal 2016; Kumar 2013).

Several researchers have attempted to understand the process and factors that promote and block business participation by specific communities (Harriss-White, Vidyarthee and Dixit 2014; Deshpande and Sharma 2013, 2015; Vidyarthee 2011, 2015; Iyer et al. 2013; Kapur et al. 2014; Thorat and Sadana 2009). Urbanization, education, assets (landholdings), social networks, access to information, etc., have been used as explanatory variables to explain Dalit participation in private business economy (Murphy, 2006[3] as cited in Harriss-White and Vidyarthee 2010). The SCs and STs are often constrained to start any new business due to limited resources, inadequate entrepreneurial abilities and lack of social networks and most of them end up in activities similar to their family/parental business (Jodhka 2010).[4] Marketing obstacles further restrict the possibility to start up a new venture and/or scale up the existing ones. Limited participation in business activities also obstructs the possibilities of skill formation and upward mobility. All these factors offer a substantive basis for policy recommendations.

India has an elaborate and systematic institutional framework to support enterprise development. These policies include fiscal and tax incentives, credit and financial incentives such as the priority sector lending, grants and subsidies and infrastructure assistance in the form of industrial estates and promotion of industrial clusters. The Government of India also has schemes for entrepreneurial and managerial development, marketing support, export promotion, skill development and technology up-gradation programme.[5] Specifically, to promote entrepreneurship there

[3]Murphy, C. (2006) The Power of Caste Identity in Private Enterprise Ownership, M. Sc. thesis in Economics and Development, Oxford University.

[4]The study further pointed out that 41% of the surveyed respondents started their business with the initial investment of less than Rs. 25,000/-, raising funds mainly from own savings; these enterprises were also found to be operating at a very low scale; a significant proportion of them reported annual turnover below Rs. 1 lakh.

[5]For detailed discussion see various issues of SIDBI Report on Micro, Small and Medium Enterprises Sector; Annual Reports of the Ministry of Micro, Small and Medium Enterprises, Government of India.

is an elaborate institutional set up with various programmes towards skill development, vocational education and training. For instance, an entrepreneurship development scheme is currently being developed by the Ministry of Skill Development and Entrepreneurship to educate and equip potential and early stage entrepreneurs across India, to connect entrepreneurs to peers, mentors, incubators, to support entrepreneurs through Entrepreneurship Hubs, to catalyse a culture shift to encourage entrepreneurship, to encourage entrepreneurship among under-represented groups, to promote Entrepreneurship amongst women and to foster social entrepreneurship and grassroots innovations (Govt. of India 2015). Wide networks of Indian Institutes of Entrepreneurships (IIEs), Entrepreneurship Development Institutes (EDIs), MSMEs Development Institutes; MSME Tool Rooms have been in place, but we have not yet witnessed any significant improvement in entrepreneurship nor there has been any marked improvement in the participation of backward social groups, particularly SCs and STs. There are other interventions such as Start-up Village Entrepreneurship Program (SVEP) under National Rural Livelihood Mission (NRLM), Rural Self Employment Training Institute (RSETI), MUDRA loan to promote entrepreneurship and livelihood opportunities, with special focus on youth, women and backward region. Few of these entrepreneurship development and training programmes are exclusively targeted to SCs and STs. These programmes are also specially conducted in rural/less developed areas and no fees are charged from SCs and STs. There are multiple agencies, including banks, training institutes and industry associations, playing a crucial role in providing continuous and long-term hand-holding, mentoring and advisory services to both potential and existing entrepreneurs.

In addition, there are several employment generations and anti-poverty programmes initiated by the State and Central Government to promote self-employment and entrepreneurship through provisioning of assets, skills and other support to the unemployed and the poor. In many of these programmes, a specific share of the total target (number of beneficiaries) is exclusively earmarked for SCs and STs. At the state level as well, many initiatives are undertaken, such as providing free plots, loans at subsidized interest rates, relaxations in lending norms for term loans, providing training programmes, etc., to empower the entrepreneurs of the SCs and STs communities. The large private corporate sector, as a part of Corporate Social Responsibility (CSR), has envisaged steps for the creation of entrepreneurs from SCs and STs (FICCI 2006; CII-ASSOCHAM 2007).[6] These include maintaining a database of entrepreneurs belonging to SCs and STs, providing mentoring in quality control, productivity and cost standards, ensuring greater access to capital, facilitating a business partnership with enterprises owned and promoted by SCs and STs, collaborating with SIDBI, NABARD[7] for creation of entrepreneurs from SCs and STs and so on. Thus, various government ministries and industry associations have been endeavouring to improve their participation in business, but there is no

[6]The Federation of Indian Chambers of Commerce and Industry (FICCI); The Confederation of Indian Industry (CII); The Associated Chambers of Commerce of India (ASSOCHAM).

[7]Small Industry Development Bank of India (SIDBI) and National Bank for Agriculture and Rural Development (NABARD).

evidence of any visible improvement. However, no systematic evaluation of these policies and provisions has been undertaken.

3 Ownership Pattern by Type of Enterprise: Aggregate Analysis

This paper is based on the two rounds of enterprise survey on un-incorporated non-agricultural enterprises, i.e. 2010–11 and 2015–16,[8] which provides information on manufacturing, trading activities and service sector enterprises. The paper covers only proprietary and partnership enterprises[9] operating in 25 branches of manufacturing activities, 5 under trading activities and 15 under the services sector[10] (For a detailed description of activity category, see Appendix 1). During the period under study, the absolute number of enterprises increased significantly in all the activity categories. The total number of enterprises grew from 559.6 lakhs in 2010–11 to 616.1 lakhs in 2015–16. Within the non-farm enterprises sector, manufacturing witnessed a growth of 2.7%; trading 2.1% and services enterprises 1.1% during 2011–16. This period also saw a significant shift of enterprises from rural to urban locations and growth in urban enterprises was significantly faster than that in rural located enterprises. This holds true for all the three broad sectors, manufacturing, trading and services activities.

In rural manufacturing-OAEs segment, STs and SCs owned 6.9 and 16.8%, respectively, of total enterprises during 2015–16. So far, as the rural establishments are concerned, STs and SCs owned 4.5 and 9.2% of enterprises, respectively. As we move to urban areas, the share of enterprises owned by SCs and STs are lower as compared to rural areas (Table 1).

The proportion of enterprises owned by STs remained more or less stable while those owned by SCs declined during 2011–16. In rural OAEs segment, the STs-owned enterprises declined in manufacturing, while their share increased in case of trading and service sector activities. In rural areas, we could see a shift from manufacturing to trading and service sector enterprises both in OAEs and establishment. In urban areas,

---

[8]OAEs and establishments are two types of enterprises covered in this survey. **Own-account Enterprise**: An enterprise, which is run without any hired worker employed on a fairly regular basis1, is termed as an own account enterprise. **Establishment**: An enterprise which is employing at least one hired worker on a fairly regular basis is termed as establishment. Paid or unpaid apprentices, paid household member/servant/resident worker in an enterprise are considered as hired workers (NSSO 2012).

[9]Classification of enterprises based on ownership includes proprietary, partnership, Govt./public sector, private limited company, public limited company, co-operative society, trust, non-profit institutions. More than 95% of enterprises are in the category of proprietary (i.e. enterprises wholly owned by a single individual).

[10]While the mapping exercise (Sect. 4) is based on all segments of un-incorporated non-agricultural enterprises, the performance analysis (Sect. 5) is based only on manufacturing segment.

Table 1 Proportion of enterprises owned by various social groups (%)

Location/Type of Enterprises	2010–11					2015–16				
	No. of Units (in Lakhs)	% of enterprises owned by				No. of Units (in Lakhs)	% of enterprises owned by			
		STs	SCs	OBCs	Others		STs	SCs	OBCs	Others
1	2	3	4	5	6	7	8	9	10	11
Rural_OAEs										
Manufacturing	90.9 (33.7)	7.4	17.2	47.7	27.7	104.2 (36.6)	6.9	16.8	52.6	23.7
Trading activities	98.8 (36.6)	7.3	15.0	46.6	31.1	101.1 (35.5)	8.4	14.0	51.0	26.6
Other services	80.4 (29.7)	4.8	17.6	47.3	30.3	79.4 (27.9)	5.0	17.8	53.0	24.1
All	270.1 (100)	6.5	16.5	47.2	29.8	284.7 (100)	7.0	16.1	52.1	24.8
Rural_Ests.										
Manufacturing	9.7 (37.5)	3.9	8.6	47.5	40.0	9.1 (33.4)	4.5	9.2	52.0	34.3
Trading activities	6.1 (23.5)	3.3	7.0	42.7	46.9	6.7 (24.7)	3.3	5.3	47.6	43.8
Other services	10.0 (39.0)	4.9	8.5	46.6	40.0	11.4 (41.9)	5.9	10.7	50.7	32.7
All	25.7 (100)	4.2	8.2	46.0	41.6	27.3 (100)	4.8	8.8	50.4	36.0
Urban_OAEs										
Manufacturing	52.6 (25.9)	1.6	11.0	52.0	35.5	62.7 (26.9)	1.4	10.7	57.4	30.5
Trading activities	78.2 (38.6)	1.6	10.9	40.8	46.7	92.0 (39.4)	1.6	9.9	45.2	43.3
Other services	72.1 (35.5)	1.6	15.8	42.3	40.2	78.6 (33.7)	1.7	13.0	49.2	36.1
All	203.0 (100)	1.6	12.7	44.2	41.5	233.3 (100)	1.6	11.1	49.8	37.5
Urban_Ests.										
Manufacturing	17.8 (29.3)	0.9	5.5	43.8	49.8	19.2 (27.0)	0.9	5.5	47.6	45.9
Trading activities	22.9 (37.7)	0.5	3.2	31.2	65.1	28.4 (40.2)	0.6	2.8	37.6	59.0
Other services	20.1 (33.0)	0.9	5.7	37.1	56.4	23.2 (32.8)	1.3	5.0	45.5	48.2

(continued)

Table 1 (continued)

Location/Type of Enterprises	2010–11					2015–16				
	No. of Units (in Lakhs)	% of enterprises owned by				No. of Units (in Lakhs)	% of enterprises owned by			
		STs	SCs	OBCs	Others		STs	SCs	OBCs	Others
All	60.8 (100)	0.8	4.7	36.8	57.7	70.8 (100)	0.9	4.3	42.9	51.9

Note (i) OAEs = Own account enterprises; Ests. = Establishments; (ii) The ‘**not recorded cases**’ have been excluded from the analysis
(iii) Figures in the parentheses are percentage distribution of enterprises across the type of enterprise
Source Authors’ own estimates based on unit-level data on un-incorporated non-agricultural enterprises, 2010–11 and 2015–16

the share STs-owned enterprises are lower as compared to their rural counterparts even in the same activity.

4 Disaggregated Scenario

In this section, we have identified six branches of activity, where the share of STs-owned enterprises is high. The share of ST-owned enterprises varies significantly across industry groups. An analysis at disaggregated level of industrial classification suggests that in Rural_OAEs segment in beverages, transport equipment, wood products, pharmaceutical, water transport and accommodation, the share of SCs-owned enterprises was high during 2010–11. But during 2015–16, among these industry groups only three continue to appear in the top six categories. In a few new activities, such as basic metal, warehousing, machinery and financial services, etc., the share of ST-owned was high (Table 2). Thus, during this 5-year period, ST entrepreneurs lost their share in few activities but managed to start a business in new manufacturing activity as well as in services sector. Similarly, for rural_establishments, urban OAEs and establishments segment we saw significant reshuffling. But it is interesting to note that the share of ST-owned enterprises declined during 2011–16, operating in the same industry groups. So it may be corroborated that their existing enterprises were becoming less remunerative and they were pushed to explore in other sectors. A more disaggregated analysis is called for whether the entry of ST entrepreneurs to new activities is productivity-driven or distress-driven. During 2015–16, we observed a large number service sector enterprises were started by ST, as it is understood that the capital/investment needed to start a new enterprise in services sector is less as compared to that in manufacturing and trading activities. We also noticed that even in same industry group as we move on a scale ladder, i.e. from OAEs to establishment (and move from rural to urban locations), the share of ST-owned enterprises declined. Thus, both locational and scale factors are at work and affect the participation of ST in business activities.

The ST-owned enterprises were limited to very few select activities in the un-incorporated manufacturing sector. Moreover, those enterprises were largely in traditional industry groups with the highly labour-intensive production process. In other words, their presence in capital-intensive/non-agro-based industry groups is very negligible. To start or run enterprises in these sectors seems to require a high degree of skill and training and also a large amount of investment. There are also significant rural–urban variations. Even within the same product line, the ST-owned enterprises were higher in rural areas as compared to urban areas. Over the years, the urban areas seem to pose greater degree of entry barriers for the ST entrepreneurs. Both scale and locational attributes thus operate adversely for these groups to participate in the private business economy.

We also analysed the sector-wise distribution of enterprises within ST-owned enterprises. We found that in the un-incorporated enterprise sector the industry-wise distribution of STs-owned enterprises were highly skewed and unevenly distributed

Table 2 Top Six Industry Groups in terms of Share of ST-Owned Enterprises

Location/Type of enterprises	2010–11			2015–16		
	Code	Description	% age	Code	Description	% age
1	2	3	4	5	6	7
R_OAEs	M3	Mfg. of beverages	72.7	M3	Mfg. of beverages	73.8
	M22	Mfg. of other transport equipment	36.4	M16	Mfg. of basic metals*	51.9
	M13	Mfg. of pharmaceuticals, medicinal chemical and botanical	32.8	S1	Accommodation	30.7
	M8	Mfg. of wood and products of wood and cork, except furniture	18.2	S5	Warehousing and storage*	24.7
	S4	Water transport	17.3	M20	Mfg. of machinery and equipment*	18.5
	S1	Accommodation	16.3	S8	Financial service activities except insurance and pension funding*	16.9
R_Ests.	M3	Mfg. of beverages	35.8	S5	Warehousing and storage*	20.9
	M16	Mfg. of basic metals	31.8	M3	Mfg. of beverages	12.3
	S3	Land transport	8.2	S3	Land transport	10.2
	S4	Water transport	7.8	S1	Accommodation*	9.4
	M23	Mfg. of furniture	6.5	M23	Mfg. of furniture	8.7
	M22	Mfg. of other transport equipment	5.7	M15	Mfg. of other non-metallic mineral products*	8.4
U_OAEs	M16	Mfg. of basic metals	42.2	M3	Mfg. of beverages	22.7
	M3	Mfg. of beverages	24.2	M8	Mfg. of wood and products of wood and cork, except furniture	8.4
	M8	Mfg. of wood and products of wood and cork, except furniture	7.4	M19	Mfg. of electrical equipment*	3.2
	T3	Other wholesale trade	4.3	S2	Food service activities*	3.1

(continued)

Table 2 (continued)

Location/Type of enterprises	2010–11			2015–16		
	Code	Description	% age	Code	Description	% age
	M10	Printing and reproduction of recorded media	3.6	S3	Land transport*	2.6
	M14	Mfg. of rubber and plastics products	2.9	M16	Mfg. basic metals*	2.2
U_Ests.	S4	Water transport	67.0	M7	Mfg. of leather and related products	2.5
	M9	Mfg. of paper and paper products	7.3	S1	Accommodation*	2.4
	S10	Printing and reproduction of recorded media	3.5	S3	Land transport	2.2
	M7	Mfg. of leather and related products	3.1	S2	Food services activities*	2.0
	S3	Land transport	2.5	S5	Warehousing and storage*	1.8
	M12	Mfg. of chemicals and chemical products	2.5	M21	Mfg. of motor vehicles, trailers and semi-trailers*	1.6

Note (i) OAEs = Own account enterprises; Ests. = Establishments; R = Rural; U = Urban; (ii) The '**not recorded cases**' have been excluded from the analysis. (iii) * denotes new industry groups appearing in top six category during 2015–16. (iv) M = Manufacturing activities; T = Trading activities; S = Other services

Source Authors' own estimates based on unit-level data on un-incorporated non-agricultural enterprises, 2010–11 and 2015–16

across industry groups (Table 3). Six industry groups such as retail trade, land transport, wearing apparels, wood and wood products, beverages, tobacco products, etc., accounted for more than 75% total enterprises in rural_OAEs segment in 2015–16. This pattern holds true not only in OAEs and establishments segments but also both in rural and urban locations. But the concentration of ST-owned enterprises was more skewed in OAEs than that in establishment, and in rural than that in urban areas. Of the top six industry groups (in terms of incidence as well as the weight of tribal entrepreneurship), about four or five continued to appear in 2015–16. To explain such pattern, besides castes there are other factors at work such as education, household net income, access to formal institutions, parental entrepreneurship and inter-generational business links. These are issues which require more detailed analysis.

Table 3 Industry-wise distribution of STs-Owned enterprises (%): Top Six

Location/Type of enterprises	2010–11			2015–16		
	Code	Description	% age	Code	Description	% age
1	2	3	4	5	6	7
R_OAEs	T4	Other retail trade	39.0	T5	Other retail trade	41.7
	M8	Mfg. of wood and products of wood and cork, except furniture	12.0	S3	Land transport	9.6
	S3	Land transport	8.3	M6	Mfg. of wearing apparel	6.6
	M3	Mfg. of beverages	7.0	M8	Mfg. of wood and products of wood and cork, except furniture	6.3
	S15	Other community, social and personal service activities	5.0	M4	Mfg. of tobacco products*	5.4
	M6	Mfg. of wearing apparel	4.7	M3	Mfg. of beverages	5.3
	Total of top six		**76.0**	**Total of top six**		**74.8**
	All Total		100.0	All Total		100.0
R_Ests.	S3	Land transport	27.8	S3	Land transport	27.4
	T4	Other retail trade	12.9	T5	Other retail trade	11.4
	S2	Food service activities	9.1	S2	Food service activities	7.6
	M2	Mfg. of food products	8.5	M2	Mfg. of food products	7.4
	M3	Mfg. of beverages	5.0	M23	Mfg. of furniture	7.3
	M23	Mfg. of furniture	4.4	M15	Mfg. of other non-metallic mineral products*	6.1
	Total of top six		**67.7**	**Total of top six**		**67.2**
	All Total		100.0	All Total		100.0
U_OAEs	T4	Other retail trade	31.8	T5	Other retail trade	34.7
	S3	Land transport	13.5	S3	Land transport	14.8
	S15	Other community, social and personal service activities	10.3	M6	Mfg. of wearing apparel*	11.4
	S2	Food service activities	7.3	S2	Food service activities	8.9

(continued)

Table 3 (continued)

Location/Type of enterprises	2010–11			2015–16		
	Code	Description	% age	Code	Description	% age
	T3	Other wholesale trade	6.1	S15	Other community, social and personal service activities	6.2
	M8	Mfg. of wood and products of wood and cork, except furniture	5.9	M8	Mfg. of wood and products of wood and cork, except furniture	2.9
	Total of top six		**74.9**	**Total of top six**		**78.9**
	All Total		100.0	All Total		100.0
U_Ests.	T4	Other retail trade	18.4	T5	Other retail trade	20.6
	S2	Food service activities	12.2	S2	Food service activities	15.8
	S3	Land transport	7.7	S15	Other community, social and personal service activities*	8.5
	M17	Mfg. of fabricated metal products, except machinery	6.6	S3	Land transport	5.4
	T1	Trade and repair of motor vehicles and motorcycles	6.0	M17	Mfg. of fabricated metal products, except machinery	5.3
	M9	Mfg. of paper and paper products	5.1	M6	Mfg. of wearing apparel*	5.1
	Total of top six		**56.0**	**Total of top six**		**60.6**
	All Total		100.0	All Total		100.0

Note (i) OAEs = Own account enterprises; Ests. = Establishments; R = Rural; U = Urban; (ii) The '**not recorded cases**' have been excluded from the analysis. (iii) * denotes new industry groups appearing in top six category during 2015–16. (iv) M = Manufacturing activities; T = Trading activities; S = Other services

Source Authors' own estimates based on unit-level data on un-incorporated non-agricultural enterprises, 2010–11 and 2015–16

5 Performance Differences

The social group identity not only plays a crucial role in participation but also in the economic performance of these enterprises. Several key structural ratios must be considered to explain the performance differences between the ST-owned enterprises and those by other social groups. Standard structural coefficients such as per worker productivity, capital–labour ratio provide considerable insights about the relative efficiency of enterprises. The share of ST-owned enterprises is not only low but also the economic returns to their enterprises are lower as compared to those owned by

Table 4 Share of Principal Characteristics by Social Group/Caste of the Owner: 2015–16 **(Manufacturing Sector)**

Location	Type of Enterprises	% share of enterprises					% share of Workers				
		STs	SCs	OBCs	Other	All	STs	SCs	OBCs	Other	All
1	2	3	4	5	6	7	8	9	10	11	12
Rural	OAE	6.9	16.8	52.6	23.7	100	8.1	17.0	53.0	21.9	100
	Establishment	4.6	9.1	52.0	34.3	100	3.0	7.7	47.7	41.7	100
	All	6.7	16.2	52.5	24.5	100	6.9	14.7	51.7	26.7	100
Urban	OAE	1.4	10.6	57.4	30.5	100	1.4	11.1	58.7	28.8	100
	Establishment	0.9	5.5	47.6	45.9	100	0.7	4.6	43.4	51.3	100
	All	1.3	9.4	55.1	34.1	100	1.1	7.8	50.9	40.3	100
		% share of Gross Value added					% share of Fixed Asset (Owned)				
		STs	SCs	OBCs	Other	All	STs	SCs	OBCs	Other	All
Rural	OAE	5.6	13.9	59.3	21.2	100	4.7	14.1	59.1	22.1	100
	Establishment	2.1	6.5	49.3	42.1	100	1.5	4.9	48.5	45.2	100
	All	4.1	10.7	55.0	30.2	100	3.6	10.9	55.5	30.0	100
Urban	OAE	1.1	8.5	57.8	32.6	100	1.2	9.3	53.0	36.6	100
	Establishment	0.6	3.6	39.8	56.0	100	0.4	1.9	30.0	67.7	100
	All	0.7	5.1	45.2	49.0	100	0.6	4.3	37.3	57.8	100

Source Authors' own estimates based on unit-level data on un-incorporated non-agricultural enterprises, 2015–16

other social groups. In this section, we used the unit-level data on un-incorporated enterprise sector, 2010–11 and 2015–16,[11] and estimated the share of enterprises, workers, gross value added (GVA) and fixed assets across social groups and also estimated the productivity gaps between these groups, **focussing only on manufacturing activities**. Manufacturing sector has often been recognized as the engine of growth, but its contribution to total Gross Domestic Product has remained stagnant during the last four decades. To boost manufacturing growth, a series of policies such as National Manufacturing Policy, SEZs, FDI, industrial corridors and so on has been initiated. As discussed in Sect. 4, the participation of ST communities in manufacturing activities seems to be more difficult due to the requirement of relatively higher investment and relevant skill. In addition, most of the state's schemes and policies are focussed more towards manufacturing activities, rather than on trading and other services activities. In view of these, it is pertinent to analyse not only the participation but also their economic performance of SC communities vis-à-vis other social groups, focusing on the manufacturing sector.

In rural OAEs segment, STs owned and managed 6.9% enterprises which accounted for 8.1% of employment, 4.7% of fixed capital and 5.6% of share in GVA (Table 4). There has been a marginal decline in the share of fixed assets, GVA,

[11]Due to space limitation, we have presented estimates for the period 2015–16 only.

Table 5 Select Performance Differences across Social Group/Caste of the Owner: 2015–16 **(Manufacturing Sector)**

Benchmark-OTHERs	Type of Enterprises	Per Enterprises GVA			Per Worker GVA		
		STs	SCs	OBCs	STs	SCs	OBCs
1	2	3	4	5	6	7	8
Rural	OAE	0.91	0.93	1.26	0.84	0.89	1.20
	Establishment	0.37	0.58	0.77	0.78	0.87	1.03
	All	0.49	0.54	0.85	0.77	0.81	1.12
Urban	OAE	0.72	0.75	0.94	0.77	0.70	0.89
	Establishment	0.51	0.53	0.68	0.80	0.74	0.87
	All	0.39	0.37	0.57	0.69	0.62	0.81

Source Authors' own estimates based on unit-level data on un-incorporated non-agricultural enterprises, 2015–16

number of employment and number of enterprises in ST-owned enterprises during the past 5 years. In terms of all variables, even within ST-owned enterprises, the share significantly varies as we move from OAEs to establishments and also from rural to urban areas. In establishments segments, the share ST-owned enterprises are lower as compared to OAEs. Similarly, STs owned and managed a higher share of enterprises in rural areas as compared to their urban counterparts. This pattern also holds true for fixed capital and GVA as well. In both OAEs and establishments segments, a huge gap between the share in enterprises and that in other principal characteristics was observed and within each segment also there are significant gaps among different social groups. It follows from the above discussion that the ownership of enterprises by different social groups (along with the host of other factors) is associated with the performance indicators of an enterprise.

Tables 5 and 6 provide estimates of the ratio of per worker and per enterprise GVA across social groups both for OAEs and establishments operating in rural and urban areas. It shows that per enterprise (and per worker) gross value added for the ST-owned enterprises are lower as compared to those owned by higher castes (other social groups). This pattern holds true both in OAEs and establishments and also in rural and urban areas (Table 5). The ratio of labour productivity in rural OAEs between higher caste (others)-owned enterprises and the ST-owned was 1:0.91, while it is 1:0.37 in establishment. Similarly, the ratio of per enterprise gross value added between high caste-owned and that of ST-owned enterprises was 1: 0.84 and 1: 0.78 in rural OAEs and establishment segments, respectively.

The STs-owned enterprises also fared worse, in terms of per worker and per enterprise productivity, as compared to those owned by other backward social groups such as SCs and OBCs (Table 6). Thus, in terms of relative efficiency, ST-owned does not perform better than those owned and managed by SCs, OBCs and other castes. A more detailed industry-wise analysis is essential to arrive at a better understanding of the implications of social group identity on the economic performance of these enterprises. It would also be interesting to identify situations under which the conditions

Table 6 Select Performance Differences across Social Group/Caste of the Owner: 2015–16 **(Manufacturing Sector)**

Benchmark-STs	Type of enterprises	Per Enterprises GVA			Per Worker GVA		
		SCs	OBCs	Others	SCs	OBCs	Others
1	2	3	4	5	6	7	8
Rural	OAE	1.02	1.39	1.10	1.06	1.43	1.19
	Establishment	1.54	2.06	2.67	1.13	1.33	1.29
	All	1.09	1.72	2.02	1.06	1.46	1.30
Urban	OAE	1.03	1.30	1.38	0.91	1.16	1.30
	Establishment	1.04	1.33	1.95	0.93	1.09	1.25
	All	0.96	1.46	2.56	0.89	1.17	1.45

Source Authors' own estimates based on unit-level data on un-incorporated non-agricultural enterprises, 2015–16

of these enterprises will improve. Success in reducing the performance gap between the ST-owned and higher caste-owned enterprises will depend to a large extent on providing an enabling environment that nurtures businesses run by ST community.

6 Conclusion

In recent years, Government has embraced the promotion of entrepreneurship and small businesses with ever greater enthusiasm, but the overall outcome has been far from satisfactory and bulk of entrepreneurial ventures are solo and microentrepreneur, which are neither innovative nor significant job creators. We have also observed that most of these enterprises continue to operate at a low scale without any scale-up planning and vision. The concept of entrepreneurial abilities, role of institutions, financial and non-financial incentives, overall development strategies are all important while designing a sustainable entrepreneurship development strategy. It is even more challenging in a country like India when there are a strong gender and social group dimensions to this strategy.

Notwithstanding, the lack of systematic, comprehensive data and limited prior works, it is apparent that the proportion of enterprises owned and managed by STs is low as compared to other social groups and disproportionally low as compared to their share in total population. It is also disheartening to see that, over time, their shares declined, even if the absolute number of total enterprises has grown. From our analysis, we found that participation of STs in private business economy is of low order and is limited to very few product lines, such as leather, beverages, textile and wearing apparels, wood and wood products and so on. The phenomenon of under-representation is amply visible from our data set. Further, we did not find any significant improvement in their participation, although there are a series of government policies and schemes, especially during the period under study, i.e. 2011–16. Further, in terms of select performance indicators (based on partial productivity ratios), the enterprises owned by STs operate less efficiently than that owned by other social groups. Besides, social group identity, there must be a host of constraints such as institutional, technological and marketing that hold back these enterprises to operate at the very bottom of the productivity hierarchy and to grow faster at rising levels of productivity. Undoubtedly, a more systematic and detailed probe is called for.

Our findings call into question any perception that ST entrepreneurs are innately less entrepreneurial than that of other social groups. There are a number of empirical studies that have tested whether expanding access to capital would help microentrepreneurs grow their businesses. But these have consistently found that SCs and STs find it difficult to access finance from formal financial institutions. Common explanations are that ST-owned enterprises have low returns to capital, or that STs are less able to make sound or timely enterprise investments. The existing data sets, however, cannot address these and several other aspects that need to be probed for a well-informed and fact-based policy for promotion of enterprises among SCs and STs communities. Therefore, it is imperative to include new variables in the existing surveys and/or exclusive surveys need to be undertaken both for aspiring and existing ST entrepreneurs.

To conclude, caste has been a systemic barrier for certain disadvantageous groups to participate in private business activities. To overcome these barriers, one important step would be to develop a comprehensive and policy-sensitive database focusing on disadvantageous and discriminated groups, which could be placed in the public domain, making identification and intervention more effective. Moreover, in order to supplement secondary data sources, field survey, case studies are also needed to be undertaken. Subject to these limitations, the results of this paper calls for more relevant data and detailed study for better understanding of the continued incidence of under-representation, exclusion and discrimination of STs in India, who remain in the marginal spaces of the formal and informal business economy. In addition, the differences between the processes and relationship among enterprises owned by various social groups as well as between rural and urban need further probe.

For setting up new enterprises and/or scaling up of the existing ones owned by ST communities, especially in rural areas, it is essential to assess the magnitude of the constraints and challenges faced by them and mainstream it in the overall rural development strategy. The Gram Panchayat Development Plan (GPDP) can play a direct role in identifying sectors, sub-sectors and activities by their respective business potential and devise a mechanism to prioritise resource allocation and help in the overall direction of policy towards the achievement of holistic rural development, entrepreneurship and livelihood avenues could be one of them. While undertaking monitoring and evaluation of various livelihood and entrepreneurship development programmes under rural development ministry and its departments, a checklist of questions could be addressed to different authorities, agencies and ministries in respect of the intervention area. To illustrate a few: whether entrepreneurship promotion for ST community a central objective of the programme; what is the nature and extent of entrepreneurship and livelihood generation envisaged in the programme; what are the major constraints in creating the envisaged entrepreneurship development; is it sustainable; and so on. Thus, Gram Panchayat Development Plan (GPDP) could be truly an effective tool to mainstream entrepreneurship and livelihood challenges for STs in the rural development strategies and overall economic policies.

At least from a policy perspective, it is important to tailor entrepreneurship policies, keeping in mind, the need, abilities and market outreach of aspiring and existing ST entrepreneurs. It is also important, while designing entrepreneurship support programs, to include initiatives to help entrepreneurs cope with the psychosocial aspects, stresses and conflicts inherent in risk-taking. The overall enabling environment relating to policy, incentive structures and improvements in vital physical and institutional infrastructure (power, transport and information network), access to better credit, training and skill and effective regulatory mechanism will be crucial to improve the participation by marginalized social groups in private business economy and also scale up their existing business.

Appendix 1

Coverage of the survey in terms of National Industrial Classification—2008 codes

Description of activity category	Notations used in tables/report
Cotton ginning, cleaning and bailing	M1
Manufacture of food products	M2
Manufacture of beverages	M3
Manufacture of tobacco products	M4
Manufacture of textiles	M5
Manufacture of wearing apparel	M6
Manufacture of leather and related products	M7
Manufacture of wood and products of wood and cork, except furniture; mfg of articles of straw and plaiting materials	M8
Manufacture of paper and paper products	M9
Printing and reproduction of recorded media	M10
Manufacture of coke and refined petroleum products	M11
Manufacture of chemicals and chemical products	M12
Manufacture of pharmaceuticals, medicinal chemical and botanical products	M13

(continued)

(continued)

Description of activity category	Notations used in tables/report
Manufacture of rubber and plastics products	M14
Manufacture of other non-metallic mineral products	M15
Manufacture of basic metals	M16
Manufacture of fabricated metal products, except machinery and equipment	M17
Manufacture of computer, electronic and optical products	M18
Manufacture of electrical equipment	M19
Manufacture of machinery and equipment n.e.c	M20
Manufacture of motor vehicles, trailers and semi-trailers	M21
Manufacture of other transport equipment	M22
Manufacture of furniture	M23
Other manufacturing	M24
Repair and installation of machinery and equipment	M25
Manufacturing activities	**M**
Non-Captive Electricity Generation and Transmission	E*
Wholesale and Retail Trade of motor vehicles and motorcycles	T1
Repair and maintenance of motor vehicles and motorcycles	T2*
Activities of commission agents	T3
Other wholesale trade	T4
Other retail trade	T5
Trading activities	**T**
Accommodation	S1
Food service activities	S2
Land transport	S3
Water transport	S4
Warehousing and storage	S5
Support activities for transportation, postal and courier activities	S6
Information and Communication	S7
Financial service activities except insurance and pension funding	S8
Other financial activities	S9
Real estate activities	S10
Professional, Scientific and Technical activities	S11
Administrative and support service activities	S12

(continued)

(continued)

Description of activity category	Notations used in tables/report
Education	S13
Human Health and Social work	S14
Other community, social and personal service activities	S15
Other services	**S**
All	**M + E+T + S**

*Note**New activities covered in 2015–16
*Source*NSSO 2018

References

CII–ASSOCHAM. (2007). Proposed concrete steps by indian industry on affirmative action for scheduled caste and scheduled tribes (*mimeo*), New Delhi.

Desai, S., & Dubey, A. (2011). Caste in 21st century India: Competing narratives. *Economic and Political Weekly, 46*(11), 40–49.

Deshpande, A., & Sharma, S. (2013). Entrepreneurship or survival?: Caste and gender of small business in India. *Economic and Political Weekly, 48*(28), 38–49.

Deshpande, A., & Sharma, S. (2015). Disadvantage and discrimination in self-employment: Caste gaps in earnings in indian small businesses, Working Paper No. 236, Centre for Development Economics, Department of Economics, Delhi School of Economics.

FICCI. (2006). *FICCI's agenda for affirmative action.* New Delhi: Federation of Indian Chambers of Commerce and Industry.

Government of India. (2015). National policy for skill development and entrepreneurship-2015, Ministry of Skill Development and Entrepreneurship.

Harriss-White, B., & Vidyarthee, K. (2010). Stigma and regions of accumulation: Mapping Dalit and Adivasi Capital in the 1990s. In B. Harriss-White & J. Heyer (Eds.), *The comparative political economy of development: Africa and South Asia* (pp. 317–349). Routledge Studies in Development Economics.

Harriss-White, B., & Prakash, A. (2010). Social discrimination in India: A case for economic citizenship. Oxfam India Working Papers Series, September 2010.

Harriss-White, B., Vidyarthee, K., & Dixit, A. (2014). Dalit and Adivasi participation in India's business economy. *Journal of Social Inclusion Studies, 1*(1), 76–105.

Iyer, L., Khanna, T., & Varshney, A. (2013). Caste and entrepreneurship in India. *Economic and Political Weekly, 48*(6), 52–60.

Jodhka, S. S. (2010). Dalits in business: Self-employed scheduled castes in Northwest India. *Economic and Political Weekly, 45*(11), 41–48.

Kapur, D., Shyam Babu, D., & Bhan Prasad, C. (2014). *Defying the odds: The rise of the dalit entrepreneurs.* Random House India Publication.

Kumar, S. M. (2013, March). Does access to formal agricultural credit depend on caste? *World Development, 43*, 315–328.

NSSO. (2012). *Operational Characteristics of Unincorporated Non-agricultural Enterprises (Excluding Construction) in India, NSS 67th Round, (July 2010 – June 2011).* Government of India: National Sample Survey Office.

NSSO. (2018). Operational characteristics of unincorporated non-agricultural enterprises (Excluding Construction) in India, NSS 73rd Round, (July 2015 – June 2016), National Sample Survey Office, Government of India.

Pal, G. C. (2016). Caste and access to public services: 'Intensified' disadvantages. *Economic and Political Weekly, 51*(31), 102–107.

Papola, T. S. (2012) *Social exclusion and discrimination in the labor market*, ISID Working Paper No. 2012/04.

Sahu, P. P. (2017). Expanding livelihood strategies for marginalized communities in India: Opportunities and challenges. In D. N. Reddy & K. Sarap (Eds.), *Rural labour mobility in times of structural transformation* (pp. 151–180). Palgrave Macmillan.

Thorat, Sukhadeo. (2002). Oppression and Denial: Dalit discrimination in the 1990s. *Economic & Political Weekly, 37*(6), 572–578.

Thorat, S., & Sadana, N. (2009). Caste and ownership of private enterprises. *Economic and Political Weekly, 44*(23), 13–16.

Vidyarthee, K. K. (2011). Dalit and Adivasi Participation in the Indian Business Economy, Paper presented in a conference titled "Rethinking Development in an Age of Scarcity and Uncertainty: New Values, Voices and Alliances for Increased Resilience, September 19–22, 2011, York.

Vidyarthee, K. K. (2015). Regional patterns in Dalit and Adivasi Participation in India's Business Economy, Chapter 6, India Rural Development Report 2013–14, IDFC Rural Development Network, Orient Blackswan Private Limited (pp. 107–143).

World Bank. (2011). *Poverty and social exclusion in India.* Oxford University Press-World Bank.

MGNREGS and Rural Labour Market in India

Ashok Pankaj and Mondira Bhattacharya

Abstract With a minimum guarantee of 100 days of employment to every rural household whose adult members volunteer to do unskilled manual work at a prescribed minimum wage rate, and about one-fourth of the total rural households actually availing of this guaranteed employment every year since 2008, the MGNREGS has created unmistakable impacts on India's labour market, especially rural, through employment creation in public works programme, provision of minimum wage, and multiplier effects. For example, there has been a rise in wages in nominal and real terms. Male–female and rural–urban wage disparities have come down. There has been a dent in the largely monopsonic rural labour market and empowerment of the casual labour through their increased bargaining position. This paper examines some of the labour market impacts of the MGNREGS.

1 I

The Mahatma Gandhi National Rural Employment Guarantee Scheme (MGNREGS), originated from the Mahatma Gandhi National Rural Employment Guarantee Act (2005), (MGNREGA) is a massive public works programme to provide guaranteed employment to rural households. The scheme is universal within rural areas. Any adult members of a rural household can avail up to 100 days of demand-based wage employment in public works programme at a guaranteed minimum wage rate. The legal guarantee includes unemployment allowance equal to the total wages to be earned in case of inability of the state to provide employment on demand, minimum wages, compensation for delay in wage payment and worksite facilities.

A. Pankaj (✉) · M. Bhattacharya
Council for Social Development, New Delhi, India
e-mail: ashokkpankaj@gmail.com

M. Bhattacharya
e-mail: mbhatta234@gmail.com

N. K. Mishra (ed.), *Development Challenges of India After Twenty Five Years of Economic Reforms*, India Studies in Business and Economics,
https://doi.org/10.1007/978-981-15-8265-3_13

Since the extension of the programme to all the rural Districts in 2008, the programme was implemented initially in 200 Districts, extended to another 130 Districts in 2007, about one-fourth of the total rural households have been availing about 50 days of employment per household every year. About 50% of the employment days have been earned by women, about one-fifth by the Scheduled Castes (SCs) and slightly less than one-fifth by the Scheduled Tribes (STs).[1] A significant proportion of the employment days have been provided in the lean season, with a view to preventing distress migration of casual labour. In some of the dry regions, with limited agricultural and non-agricultural activities, the programme has been of great help to casual labour in general but to others as well.

As on 14 February 2020, a total of 3019.67 crore person days have been generated with a total expenditure of 573,073.73 crores. More than 60% of the above expenditure has been spent on wages that have been earned by rural households. A large number of assets pertaining to water conservation and harvesting, land development, flood control and drought proofing, rural connectivity and agriculture and allied activities have been created since the commencement of the programme. Most of these assets are community-owned, but a large number of them since 2014–15 have been created on individual land for the uplift of individual beneficiaries, which have created significant impacts on their income and livelihood conditions (Pankaj and Bhattacharya 2018). These assets, apart from serving the purpose of direct job creation, have triggered economic activities in the local area with income, employment and multiplier effects (Pankaj 2012).

Apart from distinct features, the sheer size of implementation of the programme in terms of job and assets creation across rural India has been mammoth. It has created unmistakable impacts, especially on the rural labour market that has been largely monopsonic. Other characteristics of India's rural labour market are seasonal unemployment, massive under-employment and male–female employment and wage disparities. Evidences suggest that the implementation of the programme for more than a decade has created various kinds of impacts on rural labour market. Some of them pertain to the rise in rural wages in nominal and real terms, decrease in male–female wage disparity, reduction in seasonal migration and empowerment of rural labour. This paper examines impacts of the MGNREGS on India's rural labour market, with reference to (a) rise in wages, including male–female and rural–urban wage disparities and (b) empowerment of labour through their increased bargaining position.

[1] Authors calculation from MGNREGA website www.nrega.nic.in.

2 II

2.1 Impacts on Wages

There have been two major aspects of the impacts of MGNREGS on wages. One is awareness of the provision of minimum wages and another is upward push to wages, especially of rural casual labour.

2.1.1 Minimum Wages in Social Imagination

Section 6 of the MGNREGA, 2005, made a provision for applying the minimum wage of agricultural labourer, as per the minimum wages act, 1948, for MGNREGS work until the Central Government has decided to notify a separate wage rate. Section 6 (1) of the Act says: "Notwithstanding anything contained in the Minimum Wages Act, 1948, the Central Government may, by notification, specify the wage rate for the purposes of this Act… Provided further that the wage rate specified from time to time under any such notification shall not be at a rate less than sixty rupees per day". Clause (2) of Section 6, however, states: "Until such time as a wage rate is fixed by the Central Government in respect of any area in a State, the minimum wage fixed by the State Government under Section 3 of the Minimum Wages Act, 1948, for agricultural labourers, shall be considered as the wage rate applicable to that area" (p. 11).

The Minimum Wages Act has been in existence in India since 1948. However, this Act has been flagrantly violated. Also, there has been an abysmally low level of awareness about it, especially in rural areas. In urban areas and industrial sectors, there has been some adherence to the provisions of the Minimum Wages Act, partly because of greater monitoring and enforcement mechanisms and partly because of a greater level of awareness. An important contribution of the MGNREGA lies in making the concept of minimum wages popular in rural areas, so much so that the minimum wages under MGNREGA became the reference wage rate for negotiating other rural wages. Studies have shown a high level of awareness about the minimum wages under MGNREGA (Pankaj 2008, 2012). Prior to the MGNREGS, in rural areas, the provision of minimum wages act was largely unheard of.

Until MGNREGS, the wage rate in agriculture was determined apparently by demand and supply factors, but there were various kinds of distortions in the labour market, which were also an influence on rural wages. The free play of demand and supply factors in the determination of wages has been obstructed by the excess supply of unskilled labour, seasonality of demand largely because of the seasonal character of agriculture, male–female disparity in employment and wages and erstwhile socio-economic practices like payment of wages in kind, bonded and attached labour and *begar* and *jajmani* system. The limited mobility of rural labour was also a factor that was the reason for suppressed wages in agriculture and rural areas. Because of a variety of such factors, the wage rate was often suppressed at a low rate. It was determined by a pluarality of economic and non-economic, including social factors.

An important contribution of the MGNREGS lies in making the notion of minimum wages a part of the social conscience of casual rural labour. While the Act has made a provision for the payment of minimum wages, as a part of guarantee, very soon the notion of minimum wages caught the imagination of rural labour, so much so that the MGNREGS wage rate became a reference point for negotiation between workers and their employers. Although even under the MGNREGS, the payment of minimum wages remained unfulfilled, workers were aware of the provision of the legal guarantee of minimum wages and used to raise this issue in their discussion with the implementing agencies. Studies on MGNREGS show that a large number of workers were aware of the provision of minimum wages and asserted their rights for the same. Often, workers clash with the officials over the issue. There is such a high level of awareness about the provision of minimum wages that if officials insist for productivity linked wage payment, as per the provision of the guidelines of MGNREGS, they retort back asking whether you get your wages based on productivity of your work.

Another important consequence of the awareness of the minimum wages under MGNREGS is the frequent use of the MGNREGS wage rate for negotiating other rural wage rates. It has been observed that while negotiating wage rates for other casual work including various agriculture works, rural workers often cite MGNREGS wages as a benchmark and refuse to accept lower than the MGNREGS wage rate. This has implications for the rural labour market as a whole. Under the provision of the minimum wages act, states notify wage rate under agriculture. But this has never been enforced. People do not know about the notified wage rate. Also, because of the entrenched unequal power relations between landlord and labourers, minimum wages are not enforced in agriculture. Moreover, the state is weak in enforcing wage rate because of the local political economy and existing power relations between landlords and agricultural workers. Since in the case of MGNERGS, the employer is state, it is feasible to enforce minimum wages.

In the initial years of implementation of the MGNREGS, there was a high level of activism around the programme. A large number of civil society organizations, media and other socially conscientious individuals were not only helping in generating awareness about the programme but they also became a watchdog of workers' rights. There was unprecedented enthusiasm about the prospects of the programme, as this was the first rights-based employment guarantee scheme at all India level. Prior to MGNREGS, there was a state-level employment guarantee programme in Maharashtra. Moreover, it was an assertion of rights-based approach to development. The protagonists of the programme took it as a cause of rights-based development and demonstrated extra vigilance for the protection of the rights of workers. As a result of the above, there was a high level of awareness about workers' rights under the programme. This included awareness about the minimum wages. For the first time in rural India, people started talking of minimum wages.

2.1.2 Impacts of MGNREGS on Wages

Gulati et al. (2013) have contested the impacts of MGNREGS on the growth of wages of casual labour. They have argued that a significant rise in the wages of rural labour between 2004–05 and 2011–12 has been due to heavy demand for labour in construction activities, which generated a huge amount of wage employment for casual labour. While construction and other activities might have played a role in this regard, it is argued in this paper that the impacts of MGNREGS cannot be missed out, although one can contest the share of contribution of MGNREGS to the rise in casual labour wages. There has been an upward push of wages due to MGNREGS for a number of reasons, which can be explained as (a) additional employment effects, (b) increased bargaining position and (c) reduced vulnerability through assured employment.

2.1.3 Additional Employment Effects

Firstly, MGNREGS has created a huge amount of additional employment in the economy which has benefitted about one-fourth of the total rural households since 2008. The numbers of households who have benefitted out of the programme are more than the total numbers of landless rural households. These are the households who are dependent on casual labour for their livelihood. To illustrate the point, as per the socio-economic caste census 2011 data, 537,013,83 landless manual labour rural households earn their livelihood through wage employment. In 2010–11, 549,542,25 rural households (about 102.33% of the landless manual labour households) were provided employment under MGNREGS on an average of 47 days per household at the average wage rate of 101.93 rupees per day. In the same year, a total of 257.15 crore person days of additional employment were generated in the rural economy. A sum of rupees 25,686.53 crores was earned by these households as wages. The number of households provided employment varied from year to year that has stabilized around 5 crore every year since 2009–10, except 2014–15 in which it fell down to less than four crore.

This additional employment created some kind of supply-side pressure on casual labour, particularly in the rural economy. In other words, it contracted the supply of that many number of person days in the rural economy. Had MGNREGS not been there, these many labourers would have remained available in the local economy. Since it is a vulnerable group and given the condition of supply exceeding demand of such workers, with limited buyers, these factors have a tendency to suppress the wage rate.

One can argue that MGNREGS merged two programmes, viz. Sampporna Gramin Rozgar Yojana (SGRY) and National Food for Work Programme (NFFWP). So in a sense, it substituted the existing employment programmes, with no additional employment benefits. However, the total person days generated under these two programmes were much lower than the total person days generated in MGNREGS. Also, SGRY and NFFWP were implemented in a limited number of Districts. They were not universal. The number of households who actually benefitted out of these two programmes was much lower than the number of households who get benefitted under MGNREGS. Even when we account for employment days generated under SGRY and NFFWP, the additional employment generated under MGNREGS exceeds by a huge number. One can, further, argue that in rural India, there are surplus labour and huge numbers of underemployed workers. So MGNREGS, even though created huge amount of employment days, might not have been able to negate the effects of surplus labour and underemployed rural workforce. Also, most of these additional days of employment were created during the lean season when there was hardly any competitive demand for wage labour from other sectors of the rural economy. Moreover, about 50% of these employment days were earned by women who in any case did not have alternative employment avenues and hence were unutilized labour. Their joining of workforce could hardly create any pressure. Therefore, additional employment days generated under MGNREGS might not have created supply-side scarcity. Therefore, there could not be a significant impact on the upward push of wages due to MGNREGS.

It is argued here that MGNREGS has contributed to the upward push of rural wages precisely by pulling women out from low-wage employment under agriculture, providing employment to the vulnerable poor households during the lean period and by providing them cushion to bargain better wages and look for better employment opportunities.

2.2 *Increased Bargaining Position*

Even though it is assumed that there have been no substitution effects of MGNREGS employment days, these additional days of employment provided them cushion not to sell their labour at an absolutely cheap rate. In monopsonic rural labour market of casual labour with abundant supply and limited demand, the wage rate is also determined by other than demand and supply factors. These factors include their economic vulnerabilities, seasonal character of employment and lean season drought of employment.

On an average a household earns about 50 days of employment that varies from state to state. In some states, they have generally been earning an average of 60–70 days. With 60–70 days of assured employment on a guaranteed minimum wage, there is an increase in their bargaining position. Moreover, a large number of women, who were generally offered abysmally low wages, joined the programme and refused to accept any employment at a much lower wage rate. Huge numbers of unskilled women workers with limited paid employment opportunities have resulted in suppressed wages. Also, since many of the agricultural activities like paddy plantation, weeding, plucking, etc., are performed majorly by women, the withdrawal of women even temporarily from these activities, as they get alternative employment opportunities created a shortage of supply for those agricultural activities.

In conditions of workers earning only limited days of employment in agriculture, which continues to be largely seasonal in rainfed areas, and their migration for job, the pressure of MGNREGS on rural wages could be limited. For example, during our field survey in Dungarpur District of southern Rajasthan, it was observed that there was a demand for not more than 25–30 days of employment in agriculture. In non-agriculture, the main source of employment was public works including MGNREGS. After exhausting the above, casual rural labour used to migrate to Udaipur, Ahmedabad in search of wage employment. Now, in such a condition, it is unlikely that MGNREGS was able to create much upward pressure on the wages of casual labour. But these are extreme conditions, prevalent in only limited number of Districts.

But in the conditions of relatively greater agricultural and other allied activities and availability of a good number of employment in non-agricultural sectors, the MGNREGS employment competed with agriculture and other activities, thereby creating supply shortage and generating upward push to casual rural labour wages. An indication of the pressure of MGNREGS on agriculture and other wages is a clamour for stopping MGNREGS work during agriculture season. In many states, farmers demanded to stop MGNREGS work during agriculture season, as they were facing a shortage of labour due to competition with MGNREGS work. The clamour was so vociferous that many a state formulated a calendar, of course unofficially, for MGNREGS work to avoid competition between MGNREGS and agriculture work, especially during the peak season. Also, there were lobbying by the farmers' groups to restrict MGNREGS work to the lean season.

MGNREGS wage rate has also served as a benchmark wage rate for rural labour. The MGNREGS wage rate has been continuously revised upward. In nominal terms, MGNREGS wage rate has risen almost three times since its inception. Initially, the state agriculture wage rate was MGNREGS wage rate, except that it was not to be less than 60 rupees from 2006–07 to 2008–09 that was revised to a minimum of rupees 100 for 2009–10 and 2010–11. Since 2011–12, it has been linked to the consumer price index. A look at the MGNREGS wage rate since 2006–07 shows significant rise across all states. Table 1 shows the state-wise compound annual growth rates (CAGR) of MGNREGS wages.

It shows that between 2005–06 and 2013–14, there was an increase of 12.15% per annum in MGNREGS wage rate. This was the period of relatively high employment growth and also higher growth in casual labour wages. The high employment growth during this period increased demand for workers and MGNREGS work competed with other work. In other words, there was a competitive demand for casual labour that created upward pressure on casual labour wages. In contrast to that, during the period between 2014–15 and 2018–19, the MGNREGS wage rate grew by merely 4.68%. During this period there was a net loss of job and there was also a slow growth in the wage rate of casual labour. Again this can be interpreted as less competitive demand for casual labour that slumped their wages.

Table 1 Increase in MGNREGS wage rate in nominal terms (2005–06 to 2018–19)

States	CAGR (2005–2013)	CAGR (2014–2018)
Assam	13.67	3.14
Andhra Pradesh	9.29	4.95
Bihar	10.64	1.55
Gujarat	16.66	3.82
Haryana	12.30	4.46
Himachal Pradesh	11.97	1.48
Jammu & Kashmir	18.19	4.33
Karnataka	15.62	6.85
Kerala	5.35	6.33
Madhya Pradesh	13.82	2.60
Maharashtra	19.34	4.84
Manipur	12.76	4.54
Meghalaya	10.96	4.29
Orissa	14.63	2.64
Punjab	8.95	4.66
Rajasthan	10.73	4.18
Tamil Nadu	9.19	7.62
Tripura	12.28	3.37
Uttar Pradesh	13.65	2.91
West Bengal	12.31	3.11
India	**12.15**	**4.68**

Source Calculated by the authors using MGNREGS notified wage rates obtained from www.nrega.nic.in

2.2.1 Reduced Vulnerability Through Assured Employment

Most of the casual labourers in rural India are extremely vulnerable because of their low income and assets base, compounded by the seasonal character of employment in agriculture. In lean season, a large number of them either migrate to urban areas in search of wage employment or borrow money from landlords or moneylenders. This is to survive them, as they do not have savings to last for long and in the absence of employment during the lean season, they can not afford to sit for long. If they migrate, they are able to escape the clutches of landlords/moneylenders, but if they stay there, they often borrow from them and get indebted. In many of the cases, they repay the loan by working on their fields (of landlords). In such a condition, their wage rate is not determined at the market wage rate. They often agree to work at a wage rate lower than even the prevailing market wage rate.

Now, because of the assured employment under MGNREGS, many of such workers stay at their places instead of migrating. There are evidences to suggest that there has been a reduction in distress migration of casual rural labour. More importantly, they do not borrow money from the moneylenders, as they get employment under MGNREGS during the lean season. In fact, a large proportion of MGNREGS employment is created during the lean season. This has also helped in their increased bargaining position.

Women have taken great advantage of the provision of assured employment. Unskilled rural women prior to MGNREGS had limited opportunities for paid employment. They would agree to any wage rate, which was offered to them. Because of poverty, all adult members of the poor households work to ensure a minimum income. Women often join workforce to supplement family abysmally low income. The MGNREGS gave them an opportunity to paid employment at a guaranteed wage rate, which was at least in the initial years of the programme was higher than the market wage rate of a female labour. As a consequence of this alternative opportunity of higher earnings with limited number of employment days, many of them withdrew from the extremely low-paid agriculture work. Consequently, farmers have to offer higher wages to employ women in agriculture.

2.2.2 Increase in Wages

An examination of the trend in agriculture male–female labour and MGNREGS wage rate shows a zigzag path. In the initial year of implementation, the rural male wage rate was slightly higher than that of the MGNREGS wage rate, but that of rural female was slightly lower. While rural male labour wage rate remained above the MGNREGS wage rate throughout the period, the female wage rate exceeded that of MGNREGS in 2009–10 and has been higher than that since 2009–10. It is to be noted that the proportion of female workforce in agriculture has increased and that of male worker has reduced which has been described as "feminization of agriculture". Now, because of MGNREGS, in which women have earned about 50% of employment days, many of them have pulled out of agriculture labour in which they were working at a suppressed wage rate. The withdrawal of women labour from agriculture, as they got alternative employment, created a shortage of female labour for agriculture. It is worthwhile noting that certain activities of agriculture like plantation of paddy, weeding, cotton plucking, etc. are mainly performed by women. In a sense, women have a monopoly position over the supply of labour for certain agricultural activities. Now with MGNREGS, they got alternative employment with a more conducive working environment. They withdrew from low wage rate employment. Since a number of agricultural activities are performed only or majorly by women, their withdrawal led to a push of agricultural wages to attract them for such activities. Thus, MGNREGS worked as alternative employment provider to women thereby created supply-side shortage which pushed women wage rate, as it can be seen in Fig. 1. It shows, in the initial years of implementation of MGNREGS, the wage rate of agricultural female labour was lower than that of MGNREGS. In the initial years, women had started joining MGNREGS and their share kept increasing. With their increased participation in MGNREGS, there was a pressure of their withdrawal from

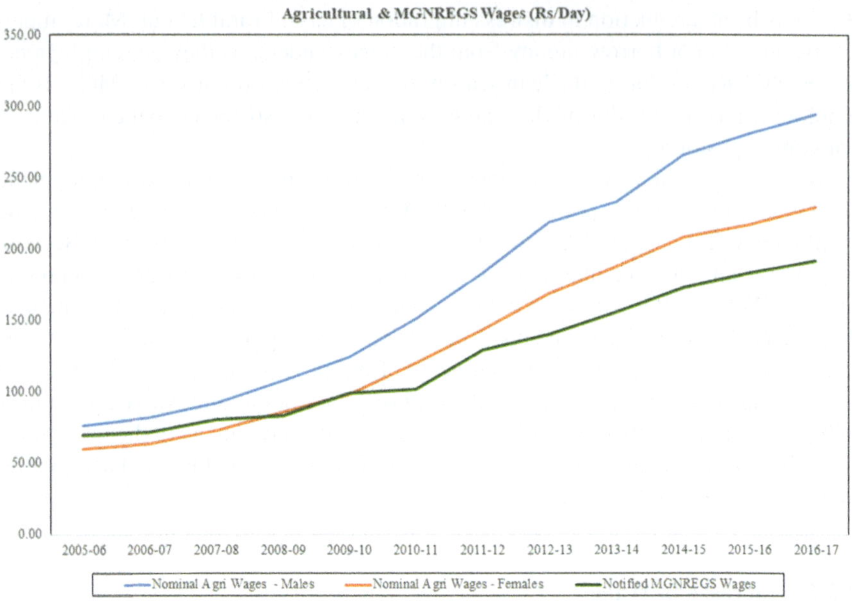

Fig. 1 Male and female agricultural labour and MGNREGS wage rates: a comparison. *Sources* Prepared by the authors. MGNREGS wages obtained from www.nrega.nic.in, and agricultural male and female wage rates obtained from the Agricultural Wages in India, Ministry of Agriculture and Farmers Welfare, Government of India

agricultural activities. That to a certain extent created supply shortage for agriculture, thereby pushing upward female agricultural labour wage rate.

Table 2 shows compound annual growth rates in agricultural wages and it is seen that during the initial years of MGNREGS (2005–2013) the growth rates in agricultural wages for both males and females were approximately 15% which declined to nearly 5% in the recent years (2014–2016).

An examination of the trend in the growth of real wages since 2004–05 shows that the wage rate of casual labour (all India) has grown by 7.75%, between 2004–05 and 2011–12 much higher than 3.91% of regular worker (Kannan and Raveendran 2019) The growth was significant across most of the states, but remarkably higher in some of the states which were leading in terms of employment generation under MGNREGS. For example, during the same period, the growth of in real wages of Tamil Nadu, Andhra Pradesh, Kerala, Jharkhand, M.P. was higher than some other states with relatively low employment generation. The growth in real wages during 2011–12 to 2017–18 declined compared to 2004–05 to 2011–12 (Srivastava and Padhi 2020) but this was also because of slackening of implementation of the MGNREGS and various other changes. The additional employment generation under MGNREGS was weak as there was a decline in other employment opportunities that weakened the additional employment effects of MGNREGS.

Table 2 Trends in growth rates of male and female agricultural casual labour wage rates

States	2005–05 to 2013–14		2014–15 to 2016–17	
	Males	Females	Males	Females
Andhra Pradesh	18.74	19.17	7.65	7.18
Assam	15.50	16.78	6.60	9.30
Bihar	15.57	17.52	7.07	5.52
Gujarat	9.84	11.11	4.02	7.77
Haryana	14.98	15.75	2.39	1.93
Himachal Pradesh	11.90	10.76	6.09	8.01
Karnataka	16.07	16.39	8.10	9.16
Kerala	14.63	16.84	4.30	5.88
Madhya Pradesh	15.57	16.11	10.90	10.83
Maharashtra	10.50	11.27	−6.81	−5.13
Orissa	17.21	13.23	10.15	12.84
Punjab	15.05	15.78	8.10	8.76
Rajasthan	15.69	16.67	6.86	9.67
Tamil Nadu	16.22	15.44	3.88	8.49
Uttar Pradesh	14.24	14.72	1.54	5.35
West Bengal	16.75	16.87	7.51	9.99
India	**14.93**	**15.38**	**5.25**	**5.09**

Source Calculated by the authors using data on male and female agricultural wage rates from Agricultural Wages in India, Ministry of Agriculture and Farmers Welfare, Government of India

2.2.3 Reduced Male–female and Rural–Urban Wage Disparity

There has been male–female and rural–urban wage disparities in India's labour market. There are multiple reasons for that. However, post MGNREGS, there has been some reduction in both male–female and rural–urban wage disparity. This could be partly attributed to MGNREGS.

In 2004–05, the all-India average daily wage of a casual rural male and female worker was 55.03 and 34.94 rupees respectively. There was a difference of about 20 rupees (Karan and Selviraj 2008: 43). At all India level, the average daily wage of a female casual worker was 63% of that of a male worker. The difference was much higher in some states. For example, there was a difference of 69.11 rupees in Kerala, the highest among all the states. The practice of discriminatory wages in case of casual workers is found both in rural and urban areas. Realization of equal wages for male and female workers under MGNREGS has significant implications for the rural labour market. If women are able to earn higher wages under MGNREGS, there is a likelihood that in most cases, they would not be willing/available to work for less than what they are getting under MGNREGS. The reduction in the supply of women workforce, because of their joining of MGNREGS, create supply-side pressure on the labour market, so much so that there is an upward revision of female wages.

3 III

3.1 Conclusion

The MGNREGS is the largest public works programme with a view to creating employment for providing minimum income guarantee to rural households. In fact, the programme has created a huge amount of additional employment in rural areas that has been largely availed by the most vulnerable households like landless, and marginalized workers like SC, STs and women. Over more than 10 years of its implementation, it has created various kinds of impacts. An important impact of the programme has been on India's labour market, particularly rural that has been characterized by various kinds of distortions for a number of economic and non-economic factors. The depressed wages of rural casual labour is one such distortion. Some of them are related to entrenched social practices.

An important impact of MGNREGS has been a rise in wages of casual labour in agriculture and non-agriculture as well, although for some, the rise in wages of casual labour in this phase has been due to high demand of labour in construction activities. This, however, does not rule out the impacts of MGNREGS. Firstly, the huge amount of additional employment generated under MGNREGS competed with other such demand for casual labour. The net result was a contraction in the supply of labour amidst the expansion of demand for labour. Consequently, there was an upward push to casual labour wages. Apart from creating effects of additional employment, MGNREGS also pushed casual labour wages because of the processes of job creation that provided guaranteed employment at minimum wages and that through self-selection targeted the most vulnerable and deserving households. The landless households, SC, ST and women workers have been its greatest beneficiaries. By reducing their vulnerability and increasing their bargaining position, MGNREGS has empowered them to negotiate higher wages. In a sense, apart from direct push to rural wages, it has also made an indirect push. A major contribution of MGNREGS lies in correcting some of the distortions in India's labour market.

References

Gulati, A., Jain, S., & Satija, N. (2013). *Rising farm wages in India: The 'pull' and 'push' factors*, commission for agricultural costs and prices. Department of Agriculture & Cooperation, Ministry of Agriculture, Government of India/New Delhi, April.

Government of India. *Agricultural Wages in India*, Directorate of Economics and Statistics, Department of Agriculture, Cooperation and Farmers Welfare, Ministry of Agriculture and Farmers Welfare.

Karan, A. K., & Selviraj, S. (2008). *Trends in wages and earnings in India: Increasing wage differentials in a segmented labour market*. ILO Asia-Pacific Working Paper Series. New Delhi: ILO sub-regional office for South Asia.

Kannan, K. P., & Raveendran, G. (2019). From jobless to job-loss growth: gainers and losers during 2012–18. *Economic and Political Weekly, 54*(44), 38–44.

Pankaj, A. (2008). *Processes, institutions and mechanisms of implementation of NREGA: Impact Assessment of Bihar and Jharkhand*. Delhi: Institute for Human Development.

Pankaj, A. (2012). *Right to work and rural India: Working of the Mahatma Gandhi National Rural Employment Guarantee Scheme (MGNREGS)*. Delhi: Sage Publication.

Pankaj, A., & Bhattacharya, M. (2018). *Socio-economic Impacts of 'Category-B' Assets under MGNREGS*, Council for Social Development, New Delhi. ISBN Number 978-93-5321-440-1.

Srivastava, R., & Padhi, B. (2020). *Collapse in Wages/Salary Income Growth in India, 2011–12 to 2017–18*, WP-01/2020, IHD-CES Working Paper Series, Institute for Human Development, New Delhi.

The Mahatma Gandhi National Rural Employment Guarantee Act, 2005, No 42 of 2005 with Schedulesas amended in 2014, Universal Law Publishing Co: New Delhi.

References

Subcontracting Linkages in the Informal Manufacturing Sector in Uttar Pradesh

Udai Bhan Singh

Abstract The study examines the subcontracting dynamics of informal manufacturing enterprises in Uttar Pradesh using nationally representative NSSO data of non-agricultural enterprises between 2010 and 2016. The results show that the incidence of subcontracting has decreased in rural areas among own-account enterprises and establishment (2–5 worker) category but it has increased in urban areas among these enterprises during the study period. There is negligible evidence to show that workers are much more efficient and productive in firms involved in subcontracting as compared to non-subcontracted enterprises. Rather, the study found that subcontracted enterprises created more jobs than non-subcontracting ones. It also found that the gross value addition (GVA) per worker in more than three-fourth subcontracted enterprises is below notional income, which indicates that a majority of labour-intensive enterprises come into the subcontracting system only as means for survival.

1 Introduction

The Indian economy has witnessed high economic growth in the post-reform period in which the role of the informal sector has been commendable. The informal sector in India is large and persistent, accounting for about 90% of employment and 40% of value addition in the manufacturing sector in 2005–06 (Moreno-Monroy et al. 2012). It is often argued that if the informal firms can become more dynamic and productive, it would not only lead to further accumulation and expansion of the informal firms but also generate higher incomes for the majority of the workforce in the sector. Given the centrality of the informal sector in developing countries to employment, enhancing poverty-level incomes prevalent in this sector is a major policy concern. In this regard, the linkages of modern sectors with informal enterprises are believed to be achieving the goal (Meagher 2013). One kind of linkage that has been of long-standing concern

U. B. Singh (✉)
Yunus Social Business Centre, Amity Business School, Amity University Rajasthan, Jaipur, India
e-mail: udaieco@gmail.com

N. K. Mishra (ed.), *Development Challenges of India After Twenty Five Years of Economic Reforms*, India Studies in Business and Economics,
https://doi.org/10.1007/978-981-15-8265-3_14

for both policymakers and scholars in India is subcontracting or the outsourcing of a part of the production process by a larger firm to a smaller or tiny enterprise (Nagraj 1984; Basole et al. 2015). Subcontracting is generally defined as a situation where the firm offering the subcontract requests another independent enterprise to undertake production or carry out the processing of a material, component, part or subassembly for it according to specifications or plans provided by (Holmes 1986; Taymaz 2005).

Due to the paucity of resources and limited market access of informal enterprises, subcontracting can play an important role in employment generation and inclusive growth. There exist two distinct views regarding the subcontracting relationship between formal and informal enterprises and their impact on the informal sector. First, the '*dualistic view*' contends that large firms take to subcontracting labour-intensive production activities to traditional informal enterprises to minimize labour costs. Due to intense pressure of cost competition exerted on informal enterprises, the linkages between formal and informal enterprises results in a downward spiral of wage, worsening labour conditions, as also the creation of survivalist characteristics of informal enterprises (Portes 1994; Tokman 1978). Nonetheless, subcontracting arrangements keep the activities of informal enterprises going; eventually contributing to the stagnation of the informal sector (Moreno-Monroy et al. 2012).

The second is the '*development view*' which harbours a positive perspective of subcontracting between large and small enterprises. It argues that the linkages between tiny and micro-enterprises and large enterprises lead to employment generation to a greater extent and it makes small firms more efficient, productive and specialized. Formal enterprises encourage technological up-gradation, productivity, growth and accumulation of capital in subcontracted firms, and also ease demand and credit constraints for small units (House 1984; Ranis and Stewart 1999; Arimah 2001). The adherents of this approach believe that the subcontracting arrangement not only reduces the labour costs of formal firms, but it even increases the productivity of informal enterprises. According to them, firms in subcontracting relationships should be more productive than their non-subcontracted counterparts. Several more studies have highlighted the importance of networking and clustering for the growth of informal firms (Pyke 1992; UNCTAD 1994). Although a majority of informal firms have a few common problems, these firms are in the best position to help each other build a good network in the horizontal integration and can also achieve specialization enabling vertical integration. Networking is beneficial, especially for small enterprises. Moreover, patterns of subcontracting as a specific form of networking are associated with specific types of industrial clusters (Rama et al. 2003; Berger and Piore 1984; Holmes 1986; Ceglie and Dini 1999).

In India, subcontracting literature is consistent with both views. Marjit (2003) argues that formal sector enterprises subcontract to the capital-intensive segment of the informal sector, purchasing intermediate inputs from the latter. It observed that expansion of the export-oriented formal sector due to trade liberalization significantly contributed to the growth of a particular segment of the informal sector which supplies intermediate inputs to the export sector. Similar evidence has been found by Kar and Marjit (2009) in the case of Indian firms during 1984–85 to 2000–01. Contrary to this, based on NSS data, Sahu (2010) and Bhattacharya et al. (2013) have found that productivity per worker and asset base is higher for non-subcontracted enterprises as compared to subcontracted firms. This finding is consistent with the stagnation view that describes subcontracting as a medium of exploitation of informal enterprises. According to this view, a formal firm subcontracts the labour-intensive segment of its production process to informal firms to cut down its cost. Intense competition among informal sector enterprises for securing linkages with the formal sector units leads to further cost-cutting among the informal units, thus strengthening survivalism over accumulation (Basole et al. 2015).

It has been observed that subcontracting in India is predominantly of the traditional putting out type wherein the subcontracting firm is often being a home-based enterprise. Almost 50% of the nine million women in the informal manufacturing workforce are home-based workers. They continue to work for the same enterprise mainly due to their weak bargaining power, debt bondage, deferred payments, competition with other suppliers and so on (NCEUS 2007). A similar result has been reported by Chen et al. (1999) and Mehrotra and Biggeri (2007), which indicate that subcontracting, lead to an expansion of the traditional component of the informal sector, even when it is linked to the dynamic formal sector. However, in case of capital-intensive industries such as machinery, transport equipment and vehicles, evidence shows that subcontracting between multinational enterprises and local suppliers involves several layers of subcontracting and the informal sector firms can only associate themselves among the lowest tiers due to their huge technological deficiency even though such contractual relations carry the possibility of technological spillovers (Uchikawa 2011).

The states of India are varied in terms of socio-economic development, expansion of industries in rural and urban areas and their impact on local economy, climate conditions, etc. Thus, an aggregate level study of India cannot capture the dynamics of subcontracting arrangements among informal manufacturing enterprises. Uttar Pradesh (U.P.) is a classic case wherein the regions of the state are highly heterogeneous. For instance, the western and eastern regions are at two extremes of the spectrum in terms of per capita income, which at Rs. 20,846 is almost double in the western region than Rs. 11,392 in the eastern region. Almost 70% of the Net State Domestic Product (NSDP) comes from non-farm sector (GoUP 2012–13). Trade, transport, communications and public and private services together contribute more than one-third of NSDP. Although the regions have largely retained their share of NSDP since 1980, yet, in per capita NSDP, there is a large difference between the western and eastern regions, while the central and southern regions appear at par (Srivastva and Ranjan 2016). According to the sixth Economic Census (2012–13) of U.P., Amroha, Bulandshahar, Meerut, Aligarh, Bareli, Badaun, Kanshiram Nagar, Etawah and Moradabad districts (western U.P.) reported the maximum number of enterprises per thousand population; however, Gonda, Sonbhadra, Shravasti, Balrampur districts (eastern U.P.), Chitrakoot and Hamirpur (southern U.P. or Bundelkhan) and Unnao and Kheri (central U.P.) recorded the lowest growth in enterprises. This shows the level of disparity in industrialization and the spread of enterprises across various regions of U.P.

Rural non-farm sector is the key to employment and output growth in rural U.P. as the employment share of this sector rose from 17.8% in 1987–88 to 27.2% in 2004–05 (Ranjan 2009). The percentage of households engaged as self-employed in the non-farm sector is highest in the western and eastern regions as compared to the other regions. Besides, only 10.79% of workers in the state have regular jobs as against 18.45% in the country. The informal sector is quite large in U.P. as about 91.5% of workers are employed in the informal sector. Srivastva and Ranjan (2016) show that the state economy is not generating enough good jobs, which is reflected in a high level of unemployment among the youth with a tertiary level of education. This is also a big reason for a large number of seasonal and temporary migrations, especially in eastern and southern regions of the state. Singh and Mishra (2016) presenting findings from the survey of 889 households and 145 household enterprises of four economic regions (Akbarpur from eastern region, Saharanpur from western region, Hamirpur from southern region and Kannauj from central region), point that remittances are the main source of the start-up of small enterprises in eastern and southern regions. Thus, linkages of tiny and micro-enterprises with modern formal manufacturing enterprises can be created possibilities of employment generation, market access, and technological advancement for the informal sector in U.P. Although several studies have been done so far on subcontracting in India, there is hardly any state-specific study available on subcontracting issues. The present study attempts to bridge this gap in the literature.

The rest of the paper is categorized into the following sections: Section two discusses data and analytical framework. Section three examines the pattern and magnitude of subcontracting by the scale of enterprises, regions and broad industry categories. The fourth section describes the nature of operations in subcontracting and non-subcontracting enterprises. Section five describes the relationship between subcontracting and productivity. It also discusses the employment generating potential of different manufacturing groups. The sixth section tries to understand the potential of subcontracting enterprises by comparing the GVA per worker with notional income. Section seven discusses the major problems faced by the subcontracted enterprises, while the last section sums up the discussion with respect to U.P.

2 Data and Analytical Framework

The study has used the NSS 67th round (2010–11) and 73rd round (2015–16) unit record data. Some necessary adjustments have been made to make both rounds comparable. This study aims to comprehend the dynamics of subcontracting arrangements in informal manufacturing enterprises across the scale of enterprises and industries. Only those non-agricultural enterprises which have less than ten workers have been taken up in the study. They have been referred to as informal enterprises in this study. While NSS 67th round and 73rd round use National Industrial Classification (NIC) 2008, some new industries have been added in the 73rd round. Therefore, the author has constructed a concordance table to make sub-industries comparable.

Following Singh and Mishra (2016), the sub-industry categories of manufacturing are as follows:

M1: Food products, beverages and tobacco products.

M2: Cotton ginning, cleaning and baling, textiles, wearing apparel, leather and leather products.

M3: Wood and wood products, paper and paper products, printing, etc.

M4: Petroleum products, chemicals, pharmaceuticals, rubber, plastics, metals, metal products, machinery and equipment, etc.

M5: Remaining manufacturing activities.

To understand the dynamics of informal enterprises, the same are generally categorized as own-account enterprises (OAEs) and establishments. But this is too broad a category. However, the constraints faced by enterprises are often co-related with their size. The present study considers the following categories among informal manufacturing enterprises: OAEs, the establishments with 2–5 workers, establishments with 6–9 workers and total establishment.

3 Subcontracting Intensity in Informal Manufacturing Enterprises

Traditionally, the linkages between the informal and formal manufacturing sector have generally been weak and subtle (Sahu 2010). A very large number of informal manufacturing activities have been operating independently from formal manufacturing sector; the informal manufacturing sector has been producing a final product for the consumer market rather than intermediate products for formal sector (Papola 1991). But globalization and liberalization have opened up opportunities for tiny and micro-informal enterprises to associate themselves with formal enterprises and increase their profit. Of late, a substantial number of informal manufacturing enterprises have been expanding their scale of operations in the global production chain through technological linkages, market linkages, financial and raw material support by formal manufacturing enterprises. Notwithstanding the disparities in the incidence of subcontracting across, the scale of enterprises and sub-industries groups in various regions of the state.

Considering Uttar Pradesh as a case for the study, in 2015–16 almost 34.92% of urban enterprises and 15.69% of rural enterprises are working under the subcontracting arrangement. The incidence of subcontracting is higher in urban enterprises compared to those in rural areas across all enterprise categories. In urban areas, a much larger proportion of subcontracted enterprises belong to the establishment 2–5 worker category followed by OAEs in 2015–16. However, the incidence of subcontracting is almost same in establishment 2–5 worker category and OAEs in rural areas. Overall, the incidence of subcontracting has been declining significantly

Table 1 Intensity of subcontracting in informal manufacturing enterprises

Scale of Enterprise	2010–11			2015–16		
	Rural	Urban	Total	Rural	Urban	Total
OAEs	29.86	30.35	30.03	16.25	37.47	23.86
Est. 2–5 workers	6.04	10.74	8.90	8.99	23.21	17.79
Est. 6–9 workers	20.42	25.42	23.71	16.79	41.89	37.43
Total Est.	7.88	12.98	11.03	9.48	26.24	20.29
Total	28.06	26.63	27.52	15.69	34.92	23.36
Region						
Western	38.41	25.77	32.75	30.47	41.74	36.32
Central	29.57	11.81	22.21	12.02	17.05	14.29
Eastern	20.96	39.68	26.46	8.39	43.21	17.00
Southern	0.00	0.76	0.26	2.55	0.92	2.00
Total	28.06	26.63	27.52	15.69	34.92	23.36
Broad NIC Group						
M1	23.67	27.83	24.91	19.92	12.37	17.95
M2	36.69	36.40	36.57	17.01	38.25	26.03
M3	26.97	14.65	22.62	5.86	41.36	20.54
M4	8.27	11.86	9.98	14.15	36.52	24.79
M5	0	0	0	0.00	12.81	12.69
Total	28.06	26.63	27.52	15.69	34.92	23.36

Source NSS 67th and 73rd rounds unit record data

between 2010–11 and 2015–16. Table 1 depicts an interesting trend; that the incidence of subcontracting has decreased among OAEs and establishment 2–5 worker categories in rural areas between 2010–11 and 2015–16, however it has increased among OAES and establishment 2–5 worker enterprise categories in urban areas during the same period. The decrease in subcontracting incidence in rural areas can be attributed to less expansion of rural markets due to poor outreach of government policies and industrial growth.

Region-wise also the incidence of subcontracting in manufacturing enterprises across the state is quite diverse. In the urban areas, nearly 41.74% of enterprises in the western regions and 43.21% of enterprises in the eastern region are working under the subcontracting arrangement in 2015–16. However, in southern region enterprises, the incidence of subcontracting is minimal (0.92%). It is surprising to see that the proportion of subcontracting declined rapidly in rural areas between 2010–11 and 2015–16 for all three regions, i.e. western, central and eastern wherein it was higher than the urban areas of these regions. There is no evidence of subcontracting arrangement in the southern region in 2010–11 probably due to lack of appropriate amenities, market linkages and technological transfers by formal enterprises. However, in 2015–16, the share of subcontracting in case of urban areas of all these regions reveals a significant increase.

There is a visible difference in intensities of subcontracting in different manufacturing sub-industries over the period of 5–6 years in both rural and urban areas. The data (Table 1) show the overall growth of subcontracting in the informal manufacturing industries categorized into five major groups. In rural areas, subcontracting incidence has declined drastically between 2010–11 and 2015–16 in informal manufacturing enterprises along with all the major sub-industry groups, viz. food products, beverages and tobacco products, cotton ginning, cleaning and baling, textiles, wearing apparel, leather and leather products and wood and wood products, paper and paper products, printing, etc. However, in the urban areas, subcontracting has declined only in the M1 category that is food products, beverages and tobacco products. In contrast, cotton ginning, cleaning and baling, textiles, wearing apparel, leather and leather products and wood and wood products, paper and paper products, printing, etc., in urban U.P. have witnessed a significant increase in subcontracting over the 5–6 years study period. While subcontracting has declined in M1, M2 and M3 categories in rural areas, M4 presents quite a different picture in which subcontracting incidence has increased by almost six%. Further, there was no evidence of subcontracting in M5 category in 2010–11 but a bit of it is seen in urban areas in 2015–16. The overall growth of subcontracting intensities in manufacturing industries, especially in the case of urban areas may be attributed to technological up-gradation, better access to market and other uplifting factors.

Table 2 represents the proportion of subcontracting intensities by scale of enterprises and broad NIC groups. The pattern of subcontracting is seen differently in all the five manufacturing groups concerning the scale of enterprises. It is clear that M2

Table 2 Proportion of subcontracting by scale of enterprises and broad NIC group

Broad NIC Group	OAEs	Est. 2–5 workers	Est. 6–9 workers	Total Est.	Total
2010–11					
M1	27.22	1.80	0.00	1.60	24.91
M2	39.57	13.22	34.60	17.20	36.57
M3	25.13	6.03	8.13	6.22	22.62
M4	9.63	9.95	19.24	11.27	9.98
M5	0	0	0	0	0
Total	30.03	8.90	23.71	11.03	27.52
2015–16					
M1	20.15	1.54	10.94	2.19	17.95
M2	25.98	25.04	38.49	26.52	26.03
M3	20.83	17.42	34.99	19.35	20.54
M4	24.67	20.70	43.45	25.15	24.79
M5	6.55	10.52	44.61	16.95	12.69
Total	23.86	17.79	37.43	20.29	23.36

Source NSS 67th and 73rd rounds unit record data

and M4 categories have witnessed higher incidence of subcontracting in 2015–16. However, a drastic decline has been observed in M3 category over the 5–6 years' study span. In 2010–11, the major share of subcontracting (39.57%) in OAEs is in manufacturing of Cotton ginning, cleaning and baling, textiles, wearing apparel, leather and leather products followed by food products, beverages and tobacco products which are 27%. Both these categories have witnessed a decline in 2015–16 among OAEs. The subcontracting in establishments where 2–5 workers are engaged in different manufacturing industries was low in 2010–11 compared to 2015–16. Only in M2 category of manufacturing, subcontracting in the establishment 2–5 workers category was 13.22% which almost doubled to 25.04% in 2015–16 which is a case of growth of subcontracting in establishments. Also, the establishment 6–9 worker category has shown a significant rise in subcontracting, especially in the M3 (wood and wood products, paper and paper products, printing, etc.); and M4 (petroleum products, chemicals, pharmaceuticals, rubber, plastics, metals, metal products, machinery and equipment, etc.), and remaining manufacturing activities between 2010–11 and 2015–16. In all the four manufacturing groups, the proportion of subcontracting has declined overall for different scale of enterprises except the M4 category in which the share of subcontracting has increased in 2015–16.

4 The Nature of Operations

The nature of operations of subcontracted and non-subcontracted enterprises may be perennial, seasonal or casual. Enterprises which are perennial in nature run more or less throughout the year. The second type is seasonal which runs occasionally, that is, for a particular season or during fixed months of a year, and casual enterprises are the ones which run for a total of at least 30 days in the preceding (of the NSS survey) 365 days. One can expect that the return of perennial enterprises is always better than the other two. But it depends on other factors also such as the scale of operations, demand for products, availability of working capital, etc. Table 3 depicts whether the nature of operations is the same in different types of enterprises and sub-industry categories in subcontracting arrangement or they are significantly different. In general, subcontracted enterprises are more perennial in nature as compared to non-subcontracted enterprises. About 98% of OAEs in the subcontracting system are perennial compared to 93.74% in non-subcontracted enterprises. A significant number of non-subcontracted enterprises are seasonal, which is minimal among subcontracted enterprises. A minuscule number of enterprises operations are casual in both subcontracted and non-subcontracted systems.

Considering the broad NIC categories, manufacturing enterprises that are 100% perennial in nature in subcontracting are M4 and M5. The manufacturing industry of Cotton ginning, cleaning and baling, textiles, wearing apparel, leather and leather products (M2 category) also operates throughout the year for about 98% of subcontracting units and 94% of non-subcontracting units.

Table 3 Nature of Operations in Subcontracting Arrangement, 2015–16

	SC			NSC		
	Perennial	Seasonal	Casual	Perennial	Seasonal	Casual
Scale of Enterprise						
OAEs	97.98	0.81	1.20	93.74	3.18	3.08
Est. 2–5 workers	98.61	0.24	1.14	97.51	1.98	0.51
Est. 6–9 workers	100.00	0.00	0.00	95.25	4.72	0.03
Total Est.	98.94	0.19	0.88	97.29	2.25	0.46
Total	98.10	0.74	1.16	94.26	3.04	2.70
Broad NIC Group						
M1	95.75	0.37	3.88	93.57	5.94	0.49
M2	98.68	0.28	1.04	94.34	0.74	4.92
M3	95.98	4.02	0	96.5	2.79	0.71
M4	100	0	0	92.72	6.11	1.17
M5	100	0	0	100	0	0
Total	98.1	0.74	1.16	94.26	3.04	2.7

Note SC shows subcontracted and NSC shows non-subcontracted
Source NSS 73rd round unit record data

5 Subcontracting and Productivity

There is a general belief that enterprises working under a subcontracting system are more productive than those that are not. In order to check its veracity, we use structural coefficients such as gross value addition (GVA) per worker (labour productivity), capital–labour ratio[1] and worker per enterprise. There is negligible evidence to show that workers are much more efficient and productive in subcontracted firms than non-subcontracted firms. At the aggregate level, labour productivity was less in subcontracted enterprises as compared to non-subcontracted enterprises, but the difference of estimated labour productivity between subcontracted and non-subcontracted enterprises has decreased significantly during 2010–11 to 2015–16. It is indicative of a substantial improvement in labour productivity in subcontracted enterprises. The trend is similar for all types of subcontracted enterprises. Within the subcontracting system, labour productivity is higher in establishment than OAEs both in 2010–11 and 2015–16. OAEs reported a significant growth in labour productivity compared to all categories of establishment over the 5-year study period.

[1]Gross value added per worker and fixed capital per worker was estimated at constant 2004–05 prices.

Table 4 Labour productivity, capital–labour ratio and employment potential by scale of enterprises

Enterprise Type	2010–11		2015–16	
	SC	NSC	SC	NSC
GVA per worker (Rs.)				
OAE	11785.9	25663.36	23383.11	30934.56
Est. 2–5 workers	32837.85	46546.92	49556.23	51134.27
Est. 6–9 workers	37407.76	47249.27	50087.49	63401.9
Total Est.	34245.64	46633.11	49962.75	52360.32
Total	12976.97	29077.68	26643.89	34073.13
Capital–labour ratio (Rs.)				
OAE	23940.84	69037.06	41816.56	55611.12
Est. 2–5 workers	63910.7	126352.6	83051.21	78247.9
Est. 6–9 workers	52516.07	129422.8	78172.43	74136.29
Total Est.	60400.52	126729.7	81907.02	77837.85
Total	25870.62	78412.59	46715.69	58862.85
Worker per enterprise				
OAE	1.7	1.5	1.9	1.5
Est. 2–5 workers	3.5	2.9	3.6	2.9
Est. 6–9 workers	7.1	6.9	7.2	6.8
Total Est.	4.6	3.4	4.5	3.3
Total	1.9	1.8	2.3	1.8

Source NSS 67th and 73rd rounds unit record data

Also, it is important to understand which sub-industry categories have had higher labour productivity in the subcontracting system. From Table 4, it is clear that GVA per worker is low in all sub-industry categories involved in subcontracting as compared to those that are not. There are some manufacturing industries such as wood and wood products, paper and paper products, printing, etc., in which, a small difference appeared in labour productivity between subcontracted and non-subcontracted units in 2015–16. However, M1 enterprises such as food products, beverages and tobacco products show quite the opposite picture with high difference in labour productivity between subcontracted and non-subcontracted units. Within subcontracted enterprises, wood and wood products, paper and paper products, printing, etc., have witnessed highest labour productivity followed by M4 category sub-industries involved in petroleum products, chemicals, pharmaceuticals, rubber, plastics, metals, metal products, machinery and equipment, etc., while labour productivity in M1 has been less than one-third of M3. The relatively low productivity in subcontracted enterprises compared to non-subcontracted enterprises may be attributed to labour-intensive nature of work, utilization of outdated technologies, inadequate access to both input and output markets and proliferation of middleman (Sahu 2010). Besides these factors, the exploitative nature of large enterprises is also because of low productivity in subcontracted tiny enterprises as very often they pay less than the market prices to small enterprises (Papola and Mathur 1983).

Capital–labour Ratio, however, is observed to be lower in subcontracted enterprises compared to non-subcontracted ones in both years, viz. 2010–11 and 2015–16. A similar pattern was observed for OAEs and both categories of establishments (with 2–5 workers and 6–9 workers), and across the sub-industry categories (Table 4). The subcontracted units have the potential to generate employment with the lower capital requirement if there is a growing demand for their products. Overall, it is visible that the subcontracting system has a positive impact on job creation as enterprises working under linkages with larger units have created more jobs compared to those who are not. This difference has widened between subcontracted and non-subcontracted firms during 2010–11 to 2015–16, especially in establishment 6–9 workers units involved in petroleum products, chemicals, pharmaceuticals, rubber, plastics, metals, metal products, machinery and equipment (M4 category) which have created more jobs compared to other sub-industry categories (Table 5).

6 Choice or Survival

It is not clear from the discussion thus far whether GVA per worker generated by enterprises under the subcontracting system is adequate to protect the livelihood needs of workers or not. This requires obtaining some indicator of adequacy. Following National Commission for Enterprises in the Unorganised Sector NCEUS (2007), we have computed notional income[2] (minimum floor income) of a worker from Employment and Unemployment Survey of NSS and used it as a benchmark to judge the adequacy of GVA per worker of enterprises. While NCEUS (2007) used this for OAEs only, this study has extended it to establishments also, even though it is not as accurate in case of establishments as is in case of OAEs.

Table 6 confirms that in almost 88.56% of subcontracted enterprises GVA per worker is below the notional income, while it is much less in case of non-subcontracted enterprises (78.21%) in 2015–16. This pattern is almost common in across all scales of enterprises and broad NIC groups. However, the proportion of enterprises having linkages with master units, and GVA per worker below notional income has declined significantly between 2010–11 and 2015–16. Nonetheless, OAEs are still in a worse situation as compared to the establishment as in about 92.72% OAEs GVA per worker is below than notional income under the subcontracting arrangement which is quite higher than 50.22% in the establishment 6–9 workers category in 2015–16. On the other hand manufacturing enterprises in wood

[2]Notional minimum income = minimum floor level wage x working days per year x earning units per family.

Two notional income for the years 2010–11 and 2015–16 were computed to compare GVA per worker during two rounds of NSS. The notional income was Rs. 36702 and Rs. 50260 in 2010–11 and 2015–16, respectively.

Table 5 Labour productivity, capital–labour ratio and employment potential by broad NIC groups

NIC	2010–11		2015–16	
	SC	NSC	SC	NSC
GVA per worker (Rs.)				
M1	9730.607	28812.57	13379.96	35802.72
M2	13849.07	24052.13	23936.43	28357.1
M3	11340.29	33639.38	42138.6	43274.85
M4	25797.73	34673.36	34886.15	39128.42
M5	0	50180.65	96457.86	91252.93
Total	12976.97	29077.68	26643.89	34073.13
Capital–labour ratio (Rs.)				
M1	14570.58	80225.3	25891.41	66689.33
M2	26815.59	70995.9	42830.83	59545.46
M3	30687.46	80209.54	61089.16	49328.03
M4	52340.84	90325.89	66504.73	55124.27
M5	***	174107.6	61058.34	129027.7
Total	25870.62	78412.59	46715.69	58862.85
Worker per enterprise				
M1	1.6	1.8	2.1	1.9
M2	2.1	1.8	2.1	1.6
M3	1.3	1.9	2.4	1.8
M4	2.9	2.0	2.7	2.2
M5	***	2.6	4.6	2.8
Total	1.9	1.8	2.2	1.8

Source NSS 67th and 73rd rounds unit record data

and wood products, paper and paper products, printing, etc., petroleum products, chemicals, pharmaceuticals, rubber, plastics, metals, metal products, machinery and equipment, etc., activities have reported more growth in GVA per worker between 2010–11 and 2015–16. In almost one-fourth of these enterprises GVA per worker is more than notional income. It is clear that enterprises involved in making food products, beverages and tobacco products; cotton ginning, cleaning and baling, textiles, wearing apparel, leather and leather products came into the subcontracting system for survival rather than choice as in more than 90% of these enterprises GVA per worker is below the notional income. Significantly, the proportion of similar non-subcontracted enterprises with GVA per worker less than the notional income is fairly less as compared to subcontracted enterprises (Table 7).

Table 6 Percentage of enterprises having GVA per worker below notional income

Enterprise type	2010–11		2015–16	
	SC	NSC	SC	NSC
Scale of enterprise				
OAE	97.16	77.24	92.72	81.83
Est. 2–5 workers	64.69	44.01	61.34	58.42
Est. 6–9 workers	50.94	48.26	50.22	45.90
Total Est.	60.46	44.54	58.73	57.17
Total	95.22	71.94	88.56	78.21
Broad NIC Group				
M1	99.38	70.80	97.99	75.65
M2	95.74	80.87	92.71	82.73
M3	92.27	61.84	79.68	71.59
M4	79.13	68.35	74.15	75.37
M5	0.00	26.98	36.66	9.55
Total	95.22	71.94	88.56	78.21

Source NSS 67th and 73rd rounds unit record data

Table 7 Severe problems faced by subcontracted enterprises (in %)

	2010–11			2015–16		
	SC	NSC	Total	SC	NSC	Total
Erratic power supply	16.59	20.94	19.9	18.85	17.34	17.73
Shortage of raw materials	11.08	10.66	10.76	9.29	4.97	6.1
Shrinkage of demand	24.29	30.84	29.27	37.11	42.35	40.99
High cost of credit	11.94	12.77	12.57	11.27	15.3	14.25
Non-recovery of financial dues	12.36	12.13	12.18	10.14	12.99	12.25
Non-availability of labour	1.11	1.56	1.45	0.29	0.64	0.55
Non-availability of skilled labour	***	***	***	0.28	1.08	0.88
Labour dispute	0.51	0.38	0.42	0.04	0.01	0.02
Others	22.12	10.72	13.45	12.73	5.31	7.24
Total	100	100	100	100	100	100

Note *** shows this option was not available in the 67th round
Source NSS 67th and 73rd rounds unit record data

7 Major Problems in Subcontracting Linkage

Do subcontracted and non-subcontracted informal enterprises face similar problems in their operations or, linkages with larger units help subcontracted enterprises to minimise their problems? The study finds that shrinkage of demand for products is a major problem faced by both subcontracted and non-subcontracted enterprises, although its magnitude is relatively less in subcontracted enterprises. Almost 37.11% of enterprises acknowledge shrinkage of demand as their major problem. Thus, tiny and small enterprises come into subcontracting practices to avail better opportunities for market access even though the nature of exploitation by master units is well known. So, subcontracted enterprises face the challenge of being exploited at two levels: less payment at the hands of subcontracting master units, and inadequate recognition in the local market. Besides, erratic power supply and high-cost credit are other major problems for both subcontracted and non-subcontracted enterprises. It appears that subcontracted enterprises have no hardly any advantages while coping with operational problems. Most subcontracting arrangements are skewed in favour of the contractors thereby enabling the master units to dictate their terms. They often engage in arm twisting practices such as delayed payments, undue price-cutting, strict quality control, sudden slash in orders and lack of continuity in placing orders. Further, their own low resource base and inadequate managerial capacity of subcontractors put the subcontracted units in a more disadvantageous position (Sahu 2010).

8 Conclusion

Subcontracting arrangements between formal and informal firms can be used to modernize small and tiny informal enterprises in several ways such as technological up-gradation, employment and income generation, market access, capital accumulation and so on. But there is evidence that these linkages have led the informal enterprises towards stagnation as larger firms have exploited this linkage as a cost-cutting measure. In recent years, however, there has been decentralized production through subcontracting and 'putting-out' arrangements in India. The present study has used enterprise-level data from the informal manufacturing sector in the country to understand the dynamics of linkages of formal sector enterprises with informal enterprises. Based on evidence from 67th round (2010–11) and 73rd round (2015–16) of NSS unit-level data, it has been found that informal enterprises in urban areas are more into subcontracting arrangements compared to their rural counterparts, and the intensity of subcontracting is greater among relatively large enterprises. The extent of subcontracting significantly varies among the sub-industry categories. The study shows that subcontracted works are prevalent in both labour-intensive and capital-intensive enterprise. In 2015–16, almost one-fourth enterprises in M2 and M4 NIC categories, viz. cotton ginning, cleaning and bailing, textiles, wearing apparel, leather and leather products; petroleum products, chemicals, pharmaceuticals, rubber, plastics, metals, metal products, machinery and equipment, etc., were working on subcontracting arrangements. There has been a reshuffling in the pattern of subcontracting by sub-industry categories during 2010–11 to 2015–16. The extent of subcontracting has increased more than two times among relatively capital-intensive enterprises (M4); however, it has declined significantly among labour-intensive enterprises (M2).

Also, the manufacturing sector in Uttar Pradesh appears to be supporting both views stagnation and development with respect to subcontracting. Furthermore, subcontracting linkages between formal and informal enterprises have developed mainly in the western region which is also the most industrialized part of the state, lending credence to the development view.

The study shows that enterprises that are working in subcontracting arrangements have created more employment in comparison to non-subcontracted enterprises in U.P., which is in line with the view that subcontracting linkages create more employment. A similar pattern is found across the scale of enterprises and sub-industry categories. But productivity is lower among subcontracted enterprises than in non-subcontracted enterprises, which means that the terms of trade are worse for subcontracted enterprises. While trying to understand whether GVA per worker generated by subcontracted enterprises is adequate to protect the livelihood needs of workers or it's just a survival strategy of informal enterprises. The study found that in almost 89% of subcontracted enterprises GVA per worker is below the notional income in 2015–16. This percentage is relatively higher in labour-intensive enterprises, i.e. mostly OAEs, and in M1 and M2 sub-industry categories (food products, beverages and tobacco products, cotton ginning, cleaning and baling textiles, wearing apparel, and leather products, etc.), which implies that large firms exploit informal manufacturing firms and use them for cost-cutting. Shrinkage of demand for products is the main problem reported by subcontracted enterprises. Ideally, the purpose of informal enterprises, who work on subcontracting linkage, is to use the network of formal firms for market access. Erratic power cuts and shortage of raw materials are other problems, which affect the productivity of informal subcontracted enterprises. Similarly, Sahu (2010) observes that the nature of the extent of assistance received by subcontracted firms from the master or contracting units in the form of technical assistance, financial support, supply of raw material and provision of training is relatively less prevalent in rural areas, which supports the stagnation view of the subcontracting linkage.

There is a huge opportunity for informal enterprises in subcontracting. Master units or subcontracting firms will have to show greater involvement with informal enterprises in the form of technological guidance, timely supply of raw material, timely payments, transport and market access, etc., rather than use subcontracted firms as cost-cutting measures. On the other hand, informal firms those which are large and employ workers should be provided credit support and market independent. These would make relatively large informal enterprises more efficient and stable to lead the growth path of informal sector independent of subcontracting linkages with formal firms.

References

Arimah, B. C. (2001). Nature and determinants of linkages between informal and formal sector enterprises in Nigeria. *African Development Review, 13*(1), 114–144.

Basole, A., Basu, D., & Bhattacharya, R. (2015). Determinants and impacts of subcontracting: Evidence from India's unorganised manufacturing sector. *International Review of Applied Economics, 29*(3), 374–402.

Berger, S., & Piore, M. J. (1984). *Dualism and discontinuity in industrial societies.* Cambridge: Cambridge University Press.

Bhattacharya, R., Bhattacharya, S., & Sanyal, K. K. (2013). Dualism in the informal economy: Exploring the Indian informal manufacturing sector. In: S. Banerjee & A. Chakrabarti (Eds.), Development and sustainability: India in a global perspective. Springer.

Ceglie, G., & Dini M. (1999). *SME cluster and networking development in developing countries: The experience of UNIDO*, Working Paper, No. 2. Private Sector Development Branch, UNIDO, Vienna.

Chen, M. A., Sebstad, J., & O'Connell, L. (1999). Counting the invisible workforce: The case of homebased workers. *World Development, 27*(3).

GoUP. (2012–13). Economics and statistics review. Economics and Statistics Division, Government of Uttar Pradesh.

Homes, J. (1986) The organisation and locational structure of production subcontracting. In: A. J. Scott, M. Storper (Eds.), Production, work and territory: The geographical anatomy of industrial capitalism. Allen & Unwin, Boston, MA.

House, W. J. (1984). Nairobi's informal sector: Dynamic entrepreneurs or surplus labour. *Economic Development and Cultural Change, 32*(2), 277–302.

Kar, S., & Marjit, S. (2009). Urban informal sector and poverty. *International Review of Economics and finance, 18,* 631–642.

Marjit, S. (2003). Economic reform and informal wage a general equilibrium analysis. *Journal of Development Economics, 72*(1), 371–378.

Meagher, K. (2013). Unlocking the unformal economy: A literature review on linkages between formal and informal economies in developing countries, WIEGO working paper no. 27 April.

Mehrotra, S., & Biggeri, M. (2007). Child labour and subcontracted home-based manufacturing in low and middle-income Asia. Retrieved from https://mafiadoc.com/child-labour-and-subcontracted-home-based-manufacturing-in-low-_5add3a287f8b9a6b8f8b4651.html.

Moreno-Monroy, A. I., Pieters, J., & Erumban, A. A. (2012). Subcontracting and the size and composition of the informal sector: Evidence from Indian Manufacturing, IZA discussion paper August.

Nagraj, R. (1984). Sub-contracting in Indian manufacturing industries: Analysis, evidence and issues. *Economic and Political Weekly, 19,* 1435–1453.

NCEUS. (2007). Conditions of work and promotion of livelihoods in the unorganized sector, National Commission for Enterprises in the Unorganized Sector (NCEUS), New Delhi: Government of India.

Papola, T. S., & Mathur, R. S. (1983). Inter-sector linkages in the metal engineering industry in Kanpur, India. In S. Watanabe (Ed.), *Technology, marketing and industrialization: linkages between large and small enterprises.* Macmillan India: New Delhi.

Papola, T.S. (1991). Industry and employment recent Indian experience, ISID Foundation Day Lecture (Mimeo).

Portes, A. (1994). When more labor can be less: Labor standards, development and the informal Economy. In C. Rakowski (Ed.), *Contrapunto. The informal sector debate in Latin America.* Albany: State University of New York Press.

Pyke, F. (1992). *Industrial development through small-firm co-operation.* Geneva: ILO.

Rama, R., Ferguson, D., & Melero, A. (2003). Subcontracting networks in industrial districts: The electronics industries of Madrid. *Regional Studies, 37*(1), 71–88.

Ranjan, S. (2009). Growth of rural nonfarm employment in Uttar Pradesh: Reflections from recent data. *Economic and Political Weekly, 44*(4), 63–70.
Ranis, G., & Stewart, F. (1999). V-goods and the role of the urban informal sector in development. *Economic Development and Cultural Change, 47*(2), 259–288.
Sahu, P. P. (2010). Subcontracting in India's unorganized manufacturing sector a mode of adoption or exploitation. *Journal of South Asian Development, 5*(1), 53–83.
Singh, U. B., & Mishra, N. K. (2016). Dynamics of non-farm informal enterprises in rural Uttar Pradesh: A disaggregated analysis. *Journal of Regional Development and Planning, 5*(1).
Srivastva, R., & Ranjan, R. (2016). Deciphering growth and development: Past and present. *Economic and Political Weekly, 51*(53), 32–43.
Taymaz, E. (2005). Are small firms really less productive? *Small Business Economics, 25*, 429–445.
Tokman, V. E. (1978). An exploration into the nature of informal-formal sector relationships. *World Development, 6*(9–10), 1065–1075.
Uchikawa, S. (2011). Linkage between organised and unorganised sectors in Indian machinery industry. *Economic and Political Weekly, 46*(1), 45–54.
UNCTAD. (1994). *Technological dynamism in industrial districts: An alternative approach to industrialization in developing countries*. New York: United Nations.

Skill Inequality Among Social Groups in India: Regional Analysis in Uttar Pradesh

Ishwar Chandra Awasthi and Puneet Kumar Shrivastav

Abstract Even though the overall social group inequality in general education has reduced, yet inequality in technical education and vocational training has increased over the last decade in all regions in the state of Uttar Pradesh. There is evidence of increasing inequalities in skill attainment across various regions and among social groups in the state. This paper attempts to explore the regional imbalances of growth in formal and non-formal skill formation through technical and vocational education and training (TVET) along with general education and its distribution across social groups in India's most populous state. Secondary data from the National Sample Survey Organization's (NSSO) quinquennial surveys for 2004–05 and 2011–12 have been used to explore skill formation as a whole in the state and among various social groups across different regions to investigate the disparities in skill attainment. Thereafter, the authors have conducted a primary survey in four districts in two economic regions of the state that validates their findings. Atkinson and Thiel indices have been used to decompose the inequality in skill attainment, showing the share of within-group and between-group inequalities for all the four economic regions of the state using NSSO data.

1 Introduction

Social inequalities among various groups have been deeply ingrained in India's age-old caste system that has exacerbated various forms of discrimination in both the society and the labor market (Deshpande and Newman 2007; Jodhka and Newman 2007; Jodhka and Shah 2010; Thorat and Newman 2007). Discrimination has resulted in inequality in accessing resources like education, skill, health, jobs, and so on. Labor

I. C. Awasthi (✉)
Institute for Human Development, Delhi, India
e-mail: icawasthi@gmail.com

P. K. Shrivastav
Giri Institute of Development Studies (GIDS), Lucknow, India
e-mail: puneetshrivastav1@gmail.com

N. K. Mishra (ed.), *Development Challenges of India After Twenty Five Years of Economic Reforms*, India Studies in Business and Economics,
https://doi.org/10.1007/978-981-15-8265-3_15

market disparities are evident in securing jobs even with the same level of education and skill sets primarily because of social discrimination and prejudices (Awasthi and Shrivastav 2017). There are evidences of growing inequalities and disparities across regions, sectors, gender, and social groups (Saxena and Kumar 2017). The studies also suggest that inequalities among social groups have increased in the post-reform period (Pal and Ghosh 2007; Prasad 2013). Further, some have reported that inequalities among the social groups have declined in terms of social indicators (Desai and Kulkarni 2008) but increased in respect of economic indicators (Basole 2014; Kapoor2013).

The available research clearly demonstrates that poverty is directly correlated with the level of human capabilities and entitlements. Knowledge, skills, and competencies have become the basic premise for employability, enterprise competitiveness, and economic and social sustainability (ILO 1997). The role of skill and education has had an encouraging impact on raising productivity, employability, and human capital formation and has a profound positive influence in reducing the level of poverty and destitution. Skill development is central to improving productivity and is one of the important sources of growth and improved living standards (Christoph and Berg 2009; DFID 2008; ILO 2008; OECD 2013; Sanghi and Srija 2015). The role of skills in improving productivity, incomes, and equitable access to employment opportunities seems particularly clear and robust (Bennell 1999).

India is in transition to a knowledge-based economy and its competitive edge will be largely determined by the abilities of its people to create, share, and use knowledge more effectively (Dahlman and Utz 2005; Goel 2009). This transition requires India to transform its workers into knowledge workers who would be flexible, analytical, adaptable, and multi-skilled. Therefore, a better education and skill formation facility is a need of the hour. A greater amount of educational ability is a sign of more skilled and productive workers who in turn are responsible for the increase in the economy's output of goods and services. This huge requirement of skilled and educated persons cannot be met unless the large chunk of deprived and marginalized sections of the society is transformed into knowledge and skilled workers. The composition of economically disadvantaged social groups, popularly referred to as lower castes, accounts for about 72% of Indian population of which 18.9% are scheduled castes (SCs), 8.7% are scheduled tribes (STs) and 44% are other backward castes (OBCs) (GoI 2015). The corresponding percentage share of disadvantaged social groups in Uttar Pradesh (U.P.) is 78% of which SCs comprise 23.8%, STs 1.1%, and 53.8% are OBCs (ibid).

Uttar Pradesh, the country's most populous state, ranks 13 out of the country's 15 major states ahead of only Assam and Bihar in terms of human development index (Government of Uttar Pradesh 2008). The proportion of population below poverty line (BPL) in U.P. was estimated to be 29.4% (30.45% in rural and 26.0% in urban areas) in 2011–2012 as against 21.9% BPL at the all India level. Uttar Pradesh ranked tenth among states having the highest proportion of people living in poverty (Awasthi and Shrivastav 2017).

Huge inequalities in terms of critical socio-economic indicators such as landholdings, higher education, wealth distribution, and multidimensional poverty are persisting in Uttar Pradesh (Awasthi and Shrivastav 2017; Goli et al. 2015). Using Theil and Atkinson indices for decomposition analysis, it was found that 'between' group or inter-group inequalities contribute more to the total inequality in land-holding, whereas 'within' or intra-group inequalities contribute maximum to total inequality in education and wealth status of different castes in rural Uttar Pradesh (Awasthi and Shrivastav 2017). The Theil and Atkinson indices of education inequality show that more than 90% of the contribution is made by within-group inequalities in the state. However, inequalities within group are much lower among general castes compared to SCs/OBCs (Goli et al. 2015). The probability of getting into services (jobs) or well-paid jobs is higher among the general or upper castes than the lower castes (Awasthi and Shrivastav 2017).

Spanning a large part of the Indo-Gangetic plains in northern India, Uttar Pradesh is divided into four regions having huge social, economic, cultural, and geographical diversity. Based on the regional dynamics of the state, it is expected that skill development status would have variations across social groups among different regions. Thus, this paper focuses on the regional imbalance of growth in formal and non-formal skill formation through technical and vocational education and training (TVET) across social groups in U.P. The main objective of the paper is to decompose inequality within groups and between groups in educational and skill attainment in all the four regions in the state. In addition, it also cross-validates the status of disparity through a primary survey carried out in two economic regions in U.P.

The paper comprises six sections including a brief background in this introductory section. The second section deals with the data and methodology, followed by the status of skills in U.P. across regions and social groups utilizing NSSO data presented in the third section. The fourth section discusses the inequality and decomposition across the social groups and regions in educational and skill attainment in U.P. The fifth section focuses on evidence from the primary survey about the skill differentials among individuals across four districts in two regions namely Western U.P. and Bundelkhand. The last section summarizes the findings and suggests policy imperatives.

2 Data and Methodology

The paper is based on the NSSO employment and unemployment survey unit-level data for two rounds, i.e., 61st and 68th for the years 2004–05 and 2011–12. General education, technical education, and vocational training are used as indicators representing the skills. The levels of general education have been grouped in eight established categories. Similarly, technical education and vocational training have been grouped into five and three categories, respectively. To show the variation in the status of skill development, the aforementioned indicators at national level (India), state level (U.P.), and regional level (Eastern, Western, Central, and Bundelkhand) have been considered. The authors have included all age groups in their analysis in general and also made some projections for the young (15–29 years) age group population.

Bivariate tables have been used to show different indicators such as general education, technical education, vocational training, region, source of training, social group, etc. Also, Thiel and Atkinson models have been used to measure inequalities while different indices have been utilized to decompose the inequality into education and other indicators of skill in the selected regions (Goli et al. 2015; Awasthi and Shrivastav 2017).

The primary data have also been used in order to supplement the current scenario information on variations in skill attainment. Based on the analysis of stock of skill (educational and skill attainment level) from unit-level NSSO data, evidences from the primary survey data have been collected from 500 individuals in four districts from two economic regions: Western Uttar Pradesh, a relatively developed region, and the not so developed Bundelkhand region or Southern Uttar Pradesh. Further, two districts have been selected from each region—one relatively developed district and another not so developed on the basis of the score of a district-wise composite index computed for each district. To compute the district-wise composite index, seven indicators have been taken into consideration as per the availability of data. Three indicators of demand side of skills, viz. number of small-scale industries per hundred thousand population, number of registered working factories per hundred thousand population and average number of workers per registered working factory, and three indicators of the supply side, viz. literacy rate, number of ITIs (industrial training institutes) per hundred thousand population, and number of polytechnics per hundred thousand population have been taken along with the per capita income. The methodology of calculating the index is similar to that of the Human Development Index (HDI).On the basis of the composite index, Jhansi district (relatively developed district) and the Banda district (relatively not so developed district) in Bundelkhand region and Gautam Buddha Nagar district (relatively developed district) and Etah district (not so developed district) in the western region have been selected for primary investigation. The primary survey has been conducted in 2017. The data have been collected from a total of 500 individuals—125 from each of the four selected districts.

3 Status and Growth of Education and Skill in Uttar Pradesh

3.1 Educational Attainments in Uttar Pradesh

The data analysis shows that overall literacy has improved perceptibly over the years both at the all India level as well as in U.P. state. But illiteracy is still a huge problem in the state. In 2005–05, nearly half of the state's population (49.1%) was illiterate, which declined to about 40.4% in 2011–12 (Table 1). The corresponding figures for All India were 40.3 and 31.75%, in 2004–05 and 2011–12, respectively.

Table 1 Level of educational attainment in 2004–05 and 2011–12 for all age groups (in %)

General education	2004–05		2011–12	
	U.P.	India	U.P.	India
Not literate	49.13	40.28	40.37	31.7
Below primary	18.06	18.18	18.61	18.03
Primary	11.18	13.81	12.27	13.9
Middle	9.68	12.46	11.43	13.74
Secondary	4.96	6.8	7.04	9.85
Higher secondary	3.64	3.87	5.18	6.2
Diploma/Certificate course	0.23	0.83	0.25	0.88
Graduate	2.27	2.92	3.36	4.32
Postgraduate and above	0.85	0.84	1.48	1.39

Source NSS unit-level data for 61st and 68th rounds

In spite of the large number of illiterates, there has been significant progress in the literacy rates in the state over the years due to expansion of educational institutions and increasing awareness about the value of education in improving the human life.

Below primary-stage education comprises about 18% at both state and national level which is a major chunk at the lowest pyramid of the education system. There is a minuscule variation in this category at All India and the state level; however, as we move up the ladder, the variations appear to be sharper between the state and national levels.

The percentage of population educated up to primary level is nearly 14% in both the periods at the national level, while in U.P., the share is low at 12.3% in 2011–12—slight improvement (one percentage point) over 2004–05. U.P. has made substantial improvement in the middle level, and secondary and higher secondary levels of education yet when compared to All India level its percentage share is lower for all the levels of education. The percentage share of technical education (diploma and certificate courses) is abysmally low in U.P. with the share during 2004–05 to 2011–12 improving marginally (0.23–0.25%). While efforts at the promotion of technical education bore some fruit in other states as reflected by the All India share (nearly 1%), U.P. has failed miserably in improving its technical education base during this period resulting in a woefully low level of human capital base. There has been a massive expansion of higher education (graduate and postgraduate levels), but the pace of expansion for postgraduate education, in particular, has been higher in U.P. as compared to All India. Educational expansion (both general and technical) has grown at a sluggish pace in U.P. in comparison to that of All India.

3.2 Educational Attainments Across Social Groups

There has been a consistent improvement in educational attainment across all social groups in U.P. The weaker section has shown improvement in terms of achieving literacy as compared to the upper section in 2011–12 over 2004–05. The highest achievement in literacy is among ST category (16%) followed by SCs (11.7%), OBCs (8.9%), and 'general' (7.3%) in 2011–12 over 2004–05 (Table 2).

STs appear to have gained in terms of percentage share at all educational levels with about 7.5% increase in tertiary education followed by about 5.5% gain in secondary education and rest in primary education in 2011–12 over 2004–05, primarily because their share in the total population is minuscule (Table 2). Among the SC, the major growth is seen in up to middle-level education wherein there is an increase of around 8% (from 2.5% in 2004–05 to 12% in 2011–12) followed by secondary education (about 3.5% gain) and tertiary education (only 0.5% gain during the period under study). In OBCs, the major gain in literacy is concentrated at the secondary education level as out of 9% more than 6% concentration is found

Table 2 Educational attainment by social groups in U.P. for all age groups (in %)

	ST	SC	OBC	General	U.P.
2004–05					
Not literate	59.1	58.0	52.0	34.0	49.1
Below primary	16.4	18.1	18.7	16.6	18.1
Primary	10.8	10.1	11.1	12.5	11.2
Middle	8.1	8.6	9.2	11.8	9.7
Secondary	1.8	2.5	4.4	8.8	5.0
Higher secondary	1.6	1.7	2.8	7.5	3.6
Diploma/Certificate course	0.0	0.1	0.2	0.5	0.2
Graduate	1.9	0.8	1.3	6.1	2.3
Postgraduate and above	0.4	0.3	0.4	2.4	0.9
2011–12					
Not literate	43.1	46.3	43.1	26.7	40.4
Below primary	18.2	19.6	18.8	16.9	18.6
Primary	9.4	12.4	12.3	12.2	12.3
Middle	9.6	11.7	11.3	11.7	11.4
Secondary	5.2	5.2	6.9	9.6	7.0
Higher secondary	3.6	3.1	4.4	9.5	5.2
Diploma/Certificate course	1.2	0.2	0.2	0.5	0.3
Graduate	8.6	1.2	2.3	8.3	3.4
Postgraduate and above	1.1	0.3	0.8	4.5	1.5

Source Computed by authors using NSS Unit-level data for 61st and 68th rounds

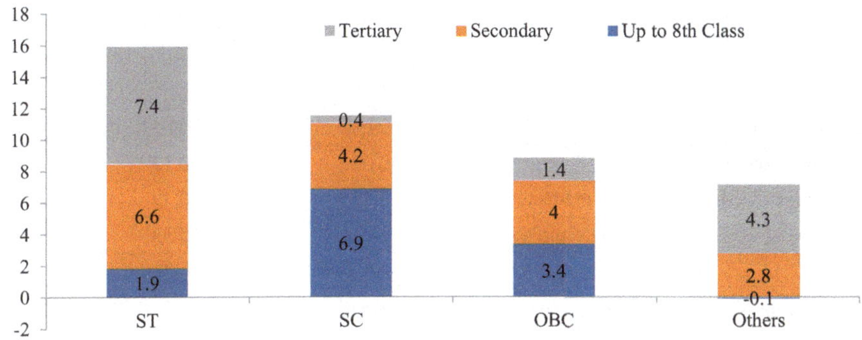

Fig. 1 Distribution of total achievement in literacy in 2012 over 2004–05 across the social groups (in %). *Source* Table 2

between 8 and 12th standards. In the 'general' category, clustering is noted at the tertiary level of education, as out of a total gain of 7% during the period 2004–05 to 2011–12, the major achievement (more than 4%) is seen in tertiary education (Table 2, Fig. 1).

The above data show that the pyramid of educational achievement still corresponds with that of the social hierarchy with both the upper caste and tertiary and higher education being at the tip of the pyramids. Major improvement in tertiary education is mostly concentrated among upper caste, followed by OBCs toward secondary education, while the SCs are still moving toward primary education from illiteracy despite the fact that there has been a huge upsurge in efforts toward literacy programs for the lower sections of the society (Fig. 1).

However, notwithstanding the noteworthy improvement in the educational levels in the state, there are still variations across regions and across social groups. For instance, in the Western region, the overall illiteracy has declined by more than 7% and the highest gain in terms of percentage share of increment in literacy has been noted among the STs (19%), followed by the SCs (10.63%), 'general' (7.71%), and OBCs (7.29%) in 2011–12 over 2004–05.

3.3 Status of Technical Education

Although India is one of the fastest growing economies in the world, yet its share of technical manpower in the labor force is abysmally low. This has been one of the major reasons for huge unemployment and low wage premiums associated with jobs. An overwhelmingly large majority of population (98%) does not have any technical education in India; this proportion is even higher in U.P. (99%) (Table 3). Thus, less than two percent of the country's labor force is trained in technical education. A minuscule proportion of the labor force received technical education during the periods 2004–05 and 2011–12 and their pace of growth has been tardy and slow.

Table 3 Status of technical education in U.P. and India for all age groups (in %)

	2004–05		2011–12	
	U.P.	India	U.P.	India
No technical education	99.38	98.47	99.17	98.3
Technical degree	0.08	0.19	0.12	0.28
Diploma or Certificate (below graduate level)	0.33	0.93	0.39	1.0
Diploma or Certificate (graduate and above level)	0.21	0.41	0.33	0.43
Total	100	100	100	100

Source From NSSO unit-level data for 61st and 68th rounds

The percentage of its young-age population (15–29 years) having received skill and training is just about 3.3% in 2011–12 (GoI 2011–12).

An overwhelmingly large majority of population (as high as 98%) are without technical education at all India level and this proportion is even higher in the State of U.P. (99%). Undergraduate diplomas or certificate-level education have a relatively larger share in technical education as compared to postgraduate technical degrees or diplomas. The share of undergraduate diplomas is around one percent at the all India level and in U.P. it is even lower at 0.3%. At the postgraduate level, diplomas are scarce at less than half a percent of the total sample population in 2004–05, and it is almost status quo in 2011–12 at the all India level. In U.P. the situation is still worse—this proportion being miserably low at 0.21% in 2004–05 with a minuscule improvement to 0.33% in 2011–12—making it unlikely that there would be any dramatic change in the situation in the near future in view of its population size.

Technical degree-level education is still lesser among people—not even a quarter of 1%, which is disturbing and indicative of the sorry state of affairs. Virtually, all the efforts at providing skills through technical education appear to be made practically no impact on the ground. One of the significant reasons for the low level of technical education is due to a lack of quality and low value attached to such education, which has little or no connection with the labor market demand.

3.4 Status of Vocational Training

The level of skill training also is dismally low in the country as compared to other developed and industrialized countries. This has seriously hampered the realization of demographic dividend among the young-age population. Although skilling efforts have been continuing as a part of skill development initiatives taken at the national and state levels, yet the pace of skill development is a slow-moving exercise. At the all India level, the proportion of skill training, both formal and non-formal put together, is 11.3% in 2004–05 with a marginal increase (11.6%) in 2011–12. This speaks of the tardy pace of skill training initiatives despite the fact that there are numerous skill-imparting programs initiated by various ministries and line departments. The

Table 4 Levels of skills training in India and U.P. for all age groups (in %)

	2004–05		2011–12	
	U.P.	India	U.P.	India
Formal training	1.62	3.68	1.1	3.02
Non-formal training	6.65	7.75	6.8	8.6
Did not receive any vocational training	91.73	88.57	92.1	88.38

Source From NSSO unit-level data for 61st and 68th rounds

proportion of formal training has been appallingly low at 3.7% in 2004–05, and it further declined to 3.0% in 2011–12 (Table 4).

It speaks of the very low institutional and training capacity available for the burgeoning new entrants in the labor force. About 80% of the new entrants in the workforce have had no opportunity for skill training. The proportion of non-formal training has been double than that of formal training in 2004–05 and it increased almost three times in 2011–12. In U.P., the level of skill training, both formal and non-formal, has been much lower than the all India level. Formal training in the state also has been alarmingly low at 1.6percent in 2004–05 and it further shrunk to 1.0% in 2011–12 showing the lackadaisical approach of the state government toward skill initiatives (Table 4). Even non-formal training has remained stagnant (6.7–6.8%) during 2004–05 to 2011–12. A vast majority of the population (90%) in the most populous state lacks skill training that eventually results in an army of the low productive population with serious ramifications on productivity and severe socio-economic implications. Such a low share in skill training of population is a matter of serious concern for the polity of the state. Although the Government of U.P. has created U.P. Skill Development Mission in 2011 to promote skill development initiatives in the state, yet the progress has remained awfully unsatisfactory due to limited institutional capacity of skilling in the face of required skill training needs. This is clearly a policy challenge for the state (Government of Uttar Pradesh 2013).

3.5 Status of Vocational Training and Technical Education in the Young Age Group

In the area of vocational training among the young-age group (15–29 years) the state fares poorly with respect to the national average. The status of vocational training in the state is very low with only 8.2% of the youth in this age group having received vocational training as against the national average of 11.3% in 2004–05 (Table 5). Formal training accounts for just about 1.28%, while non-formal training for about six percent in 2011–12 and surprisingly the proportion of both types of vocational training declined in 2011–12 over 2004–05. Region-wise, the performance of the eastern region and Bundelkhand is much poor as compared to the western and central regions, which show a relatively better performance in the non-formal training sphere.

Table 5 Status of vocational training for the age group (15–29 years)

Vocational training	Western	Central	Eastern	Bundelkhand	U.P.	India
2004–05						
Formal	2.24	2.27	0.76	0.73	1.62	3.68
Non-Formal	7.9	14.98	2.02	0.94	6.65	7.75
DNR	89.86	82.75	97.22	98.33	91.73	88.57
Total	100	100	100	100	100	100
2011–12						
Formal	1.39	1.74	0.92	1.52	1.28	3.79
Non-Formal	7.88	10.66	2.05	0.44	5.87	7.34
DNR	90.73	87.6	97.03	98.04	92.85	88.87
Total	100	100	100	100	100	100

Note DNR—Did not receive
Source From NSSO unit-level data for 61st and 68th rounds

Bundelkhand and eastern regions present a typical case of severe underdevelopment as compared to other economic regions in the state. Majority of districts in the eastern region and Bundelkhand are most backward and least developed, while the situation is distinct in the districts in the central and western region. While the central region is ahead of other regions in terms of vocational training, the western region follows at the second position with respect to the provision of vocational training through non-formal sources.

Similarly, the status of technical education for the young age group in the state has been horribly low at just about 1.5% in 2011–12. This is lower by 1.69 percentage points as compared to the all India figure of 3.2% (Table 6). The pace of progress in the status of technical education in the state during the period has been very slow. At the regional level, the relative position of eastern and Bundelkhand regions are worse than the other two regions under study, although Bundelkhand region has shown improvement in the latter period i.e. 2011–12. The status and progress of vocational and technical education clearly show that the progress in the state has been very low in the young age population and it has serious policy implications on the labor market if the trend is not arrested by scaling up the vocational and technical education under the skill mission policy of the state.

4 Decomposition of Educational and Skill Inequality in U.P.

The Theil and Atkinson decomposition analyses are performed to estimate within- and between-group inequalities among the social groups in general education, technical education, and vocational training attainment. The results of the study using the two indices reveal that overall caste group inequality in general education has reduced, but in the case of technical education and vocational training, it has increased

Table 6 Status of technical education for the age group (15–29 years)

	Year	No technical education	Technical degree	Diploma or certificate (below graduate level)	Diploma or certificate (graduate and above level)
India	2004–05	97.41	0.28	1.62	0.69
	2011–12	96.79	0.48	2.03	0.71
U.P.	2004–05	99.07	0.12	0.46	0.36
	2011–12	98.46	0.20	0.80	0.53
Western	2004–05	99.07	0.1	0.45	0.38
	2011–12	98.42	0.11	0.93	0.54
Central	2004–05	98.44	0.34	0.64	0.58
	2011–12	97.37	0.17	1.27	1.20
Eastern	2004–05	99.3	0.04	0.4	0.26
	2011–12	99.08	0.26	0.40	0.26
Bundelkhand	2004–05	99.72	0	0.26	0.02
	2011–12	97.85	0.71	1.07	0.37

Source From NSSO unit-level data for 61st and 68th rounds

in 2011–12 over 2004–05 in all the four regions of the state (Table 7). Both the indices have produced almost similar results.

There is clear evidence of regional imbalance of inequality in the state. The analysis shows that, in terms of general education attainment, the eastern region of U.P. has the highest score of inequality (0.416) followed by central (0.402) and western (0.392) regions, while Bundelkhand region has the lowest score (0.386) in 2004–05. The analysis also shows that over the period of time total inequalities have declined in the case of general education for all the regions in the state in 2011–12. The rate of reducing inequalities is slow in western (5%) and eastern (10%) regions, while it is highest for Bundelkhand (24%) followed by central (11%) region during the period. This is because the rate of growth of literacy rate among the weaker sections is highest in Bundelkhand region as compared to the total literacy rate between the last two censuses (Government of Uttar Pradesh 2015). The Bundelkhand economic package also has had a significant impact in reducing the inequalities in the region at a faster rate. Various government policies such as Universal Elementary Education (UEE) and the Right of Children to Free and Compulsory Education Act 2009 at the national level and, in 2011, at the state level have made a major contribution in bridging the inequality gap in the state.

The results also reveal that out of the total caste inequalities more than 90% is due to within-group inequalities, while the remaining are due to between-group inequalities in all the four regions of the state. Bundelkhand region has the highest share (96%) of within-group inequality followed by western (94%), eastern (93%), and central (90%) regions for the year 2004–05. In the case of general education

Table 7 Region-wise skill inequality decomposition and its transformation during 2004–05 and 2011–12

Skill indicators	Region	Measures of inequality	2004–2005			2011–12			Change
		Name of indices	Within Group	Between Group	**Total**	Within Group	Between Group	**Total**	
General education	Western	Thiel	0.370	0.022	**0.392**	0.351	0.020	**0.371**	Declined
		Atkinson	0.335	0.018	**0.353**	0.323	0.026	**0.349**	Declined
	Central	Thiel	0.364	0.037	**0.402**	0.336	0.023	**0.359**	Declined
		Atkinson	0.332	0.031	**0.363**	0.327	0.023	**0.350**	Declined
	Eastern	Thiel	0.388	0.027	**0.416**	0.358	0.017	**0.375**	Declined
		Atkinson	0.333	0.023	**0.356**	0.338	0.017	**0.355**	Declined
	Bundelkhand	Thiel	0.373	0.012	**0.386**	0.275	0.017	**0.292**	Declined
		Atkinson	0.331	0.012	**0.343**	0.293	0.022	**0.315**	Declined
Technical education	Western	Thiel	0.027	0.000	**0.028**	0.037	0.001	**0.038**	Increased
		Atkinson	0.015	0.000	**0.015**	0.021	0.000	**0.021**	Increased
	Central	Thiel	0.025	0.000	**0.026**	0.062	0.001	**0.063**	Increased
		Atkinson	0.014	0.000	**0.014**	0.034	0.000	**0.034**	Increased
	Eastern	Thiel	0.021	0.000	**0.021**	0.021	0.000	**0.021**	Constant
		Atkinson	0.012	0.000	**0.012**	0.012	0.000	**0.012**	Constant
	Bundelkhand	Thiel	0.007	0.000	**0.007**	0.032	0.000	**0.032**	Increased
		Atkinson	0.004	0.000	**0.004**	0.017	0.000	**0.017**	Increased
Vocational training	Western	Thiel	0.017	0.000	**0.018**	0.026	0.000	**0.027**	Increased
		Atkinson	0.025	0.000	**0.025**	0.037	0.000	**0.037**	Increased
	Central	Thiel	0.023	0.000	**0.024**	0.032	0.000	**0.032**	Increased
		Atkinson	0.031	0.000	**0.031**	0.043	0.000	**0.043**	Increased

(continued)

Table 7 (continued)

Skill indicators	Region	Measures of inequality	2004–2005			2011–12			Change
		Name of indices	Within Group	Between Group	**Total**	Within Group	Between Group	**Total**	
	Eastern	Thiel	0.006	0.000	**0.006**	0.010	0.000	**0.010**	Increased
		Atkinson	0.008	0.000	**0.008**	0.015	0.000	**0.015**	Increased
	Bundelkhand	Thiel	0.004	0.000	**0.004**	0.006	0.000	**0.006**	Increased
		Atkinson	0.007	0.000	**0.007**	0.011	0.000	**0.011**	Increased

Source Computed by authors using NSSO unit-level data for 61st and 68th rounds

attainment, the share of within-group inequality in total caste inequality has increased in all the regions except Bundelkhand region in 2011–12 over 2004–05.

The score of indices shows that the total caste group inequalities in technical education attainment have increased in 2011–12 over 2004–05 for western, central, and Bundelkhand regions, while the score of the eastern region has remained constant. Across the regions, western region (0.028) has the highest score of total inequality followed by central (0.026), eastern (0.021), and Bundelkhand regions (0.007) in 2004–05. The results show that the total inequalities have increased in the case of technical education in the three regions: Bundelkhand, western, and central, respectively, in 2011–12 over 2004–05. The ratio of inequalities has gone up by more than 3.5 times in Bundelkhand region, followed by central region (1.5 times) and western region (0.3 times), while the eastern region has shown status quo on the total caste inequality score. These results sufficiently validate inter-regional disparity in the access and distribution of technical education in the state.

The analysis further reveals that in the case of technical education, out of the total caste inequalities, more than 95% contribution is due to within-group inequalities and remaining due to between-group inequalities in all the four regions of the state for both the time periods. In eastern and Bundelkhand regions, it is about 100% for both the time periods. The share of within-group inequality has increased in the central region to 98.4% in 2011–12 from 96.2% in 2004–05.

In the case of vocational training attainment, the total inequality has gone up in 2011–12 over 2004–05 for all the economic regions of U.P. Maximum inequality has been found in the central region, followed by western, eastern and Bundelkhand regions for the year 2004–05. In 2011–12, the inequality has increased in the western region taking it to number one position from number two position in 2004–05, followed by central, eastern, and Bundelkhand regions. The results of within-group and between-group inequalities show that social group inequalities not only persist in all the four regions but have increased over the period under study.

The overall inter-regional disparity is due to differences in the required level of infrastructure in terms of availability of Technical Education and Vocational Training (TEVT) institutions per hundred thousand population. It was highest in Bundelkhand region, followed by central, eastern, and western regions in 2000–01. Again in 2014, Bundelkhand region has the highest level of infrastructure followed by western, central, and eastern regions in terms of availability of TVET institutions per hundred thousand population (Government of Uttar Pradesh 2014). Still, there is a lack of the number of institutions and infrastructure facilities and availability of seats per hundred thousand population in Industrial Training Institutes (ITIs) and Industrial Training Centers (ITCs). Availability of these institutions for per hundred thousand population is only 74 in the state, as compared to the national average of 110. A similar scenario exists in the case of diploma institutions (Government of Uttar Pradesh 2013).

There may be two possible reasons for increasing inequality at a faster rate in western and central regions. First, these regions are relatively developed, urbanized, and have a better economic status. People in these regions have access to information, and the economic and social infrastructure is in a position to take advantage of opportunities as compared to other regions. This is eventually leading to an increasing total caste inequality in these regions.

The other reason for rising social inequality is inaccessibility of vocational training which requires a certain level of pre-educational qualification. Among the lower (SC, ST) sections and OBCs, the dropout rate being high at the primary and middle levels, they are unable to acquire vocational training.

4.1 Region-Wise Intra-Social Group Skill Inequality Decomposition and Its Transformation

The results of Theil and Atkinson index have also revealed caste-specific within-group inequalities in education (Table 8). It is found that inequality in general education within the disadvantaged group is higher as compared to the 'general' category or higher castes for all the regions in both the time periods. While in the case of TEVT, the situation is just reverse—lower inequality prevailed within the weaker sections (SC, ST, and OBCs) and higher inequality was found within the upper caste group (general) in all the regions.

Table 8 Transformation in caste-specific inequalities in general education, technical education and vocational training in different regions of U.P.

Region	Measures	Social group	2004–05	2011–12	Change
General education					
Western	Thiel Index	General	0.336	0.306	Declined
		OBC	0.391	0.377	Declined
		SC	0.386	0.362	Declined
		ST	0.439	0.343	Declined
	Atkinson Index	General	0.344	0.332	Declined
		OBC	0.335	0.341	Increased
		SC	0.317	0.329	Increased
		ST	0.359	0.358	Declined
Central	Thiel Index	General	0.327	0.277	Declined
		OBC	0.387	0.358	Declined
		SC	0.397	0.377	Declined
		ST	0.413	0.424	Increased
	Atkinson Index	General	0.342	0.309	Declined
		OBC	0.333	0.341	Increased
		SC	0.308	0.324	Increased
		ST	0.294	0.322	Increased

(continued)

Table 8 (continued)

Region	Measures	Social group	2004–05	2011–12	Change
Eastern	Thiel Index	General	0.332	0.302	Declined
		OBC	0.411	0.373	Declined
		SC	0.411	0.387	Declined
		ST	0.408	0.464	Increased
	Atkinson Index	General	0.341	0.328	Declined
		OBC	0.336	0.343	Increased
		SC	0.319	0.336	Increased
		ST	0.323	0.338	Increased
Bundelkhand	Thiel Index	General	0.324	0.206	Decline
		OBC	0.390	0.318	Decline
		SC	0.399	0.285	Decline
		ST	0.000	0.355	Increased
	Atkinson Index	General	0.328	0.256	Declined
		OBC	0.332	0.320	Declined
		SC	0.333	0.294	Declined
		ST	0.000	0.292	Increased
Technical education					
Western	Thiel Index	General	0.070	0.113	Increased
		OBC	0.010	0.006	Declined
		SC	0.013	0.013	Increased
		ST	0.050	0.210	Increased
	Atkinson Index	General	0.038	0.062	Increased
		OBC	0.006	0.004	Declined
		SC	0.007	0.007	No change
		ST	0.027	0.119	Increased
Central	Thiel Index	General	0.062	0.120	Increased
		OBC	0.012	0.064	Increased
		SC	0.006	0.003	Declined
		ST	0.000	0.038	Increased
	Atkinson Index	General	0.035	0.066	Increased
		OBC	0.006	0.034	Increased
		SC	0.004	0.002	Declined
		ST	0.000	0.028	Increased
Eastern	Thiel Index	General	0.045	0.055	Increased
		OBC	0.018	0.017	Increased

(continued)

Table 8 (continued)

Region	Measures	Social group	2004–05	2011–12	Change
		SC	0.012	0.003	Declined
		ST	0.000	0.000	No change
	Atkinson Index	General	0.025	0.031	Increased
		OBC	0.010	0.009	Increased
		SC	0.006	0.002	Declined
		ST	0.000	0.000	Increased
Bundelkhand	Thiel Index	General	0.014	0.065	Increased
		OBC	0.006	0.037	Increased
		SC	0.002	0.001	Increased
		ST	0.000	0.000	Increased
	Atkinson Index	General	0.008	0.036	Increased
		OBC	0.004	0.020	Increased
		SC	0.001	0.001	No change
		ST	0.000	0.000	No change
Vocational training					
Western	Thiel Index	General	0.026	0.034	Increased
		OBC	0.015	0.026	Increased
		SC	0.012	0.018	Increased
		ST	0.000	0.053	Increased
	Atkinson Index	General	0.038	0.050	Increased
		OBC	0.021	0.034	Increased
		SC	0.016	0.025	Increased
		ST	0.000	0.079	Increased
Central	Thiel Index	General	0.035	0.032	Declined
		OBC	0.018	0.037	Increased
		SC	0.019	0.023	Increased
		ST	0.031	0.000	Declined
	Atkinson Index	General	0.050	0.047	Declined
		OBC	0.022	0.048	Increased
		SC	0.023	0.031	Increased
		ST	0.029	0.000	Declined
Eastern	Thiel Index	General	0.006	0.010	Increased
		OBC	0.006	0.011	Increased
		SC	0.004	0.007	Increased
		ST	0.000	0.006	Increased
	Atkinson Index	General	0.010	0.017	Increased

(continued)

Table 8 (continued)

Region	Measures	Social group	2004–05	2011–12	Change
		OBC	0.009	0.017	Increased
		SC	0.005	0.009	Increased
		ST	0.000	0.012	Increased
Bundelkhand	Thiel Index	General	0.007	0.007	Increased
		OBC	0.001	0.009	Increased
		SC	0.007	0.004	Declined
		ST	0.000	0.000	No change
	Atkinson Index	General	0.011	0.012	Increased
		OBC	0.002	0.015	Increased
		SC	0.011	0.005	Declined
		ST	0.000	0.000	No change

Source Computed by authors using NSSO unit-level data for 61st and 68th rounds

In the case of general education, western U.P. has the highest inequalities within upper caste (0.336), followed by eastern (0.332), central (0.327), and Bundelkhand regions (0.324) for the year 2004–05. A similar trend has been found in 2011–12.

Again, western U.P. has the highest inequalities within the upper caste in technical education attainment (0.070), followed by central (0.062), eastern (0.045), and Bundelkhand regions (0.014), respectively, for the year 2004–05. In 2011–12, the trend has changed with the central region being at the top (0.120), followed by western (0.113), Bundelkhand (0.065), and eastern (0.055) regions with respect to within-upper caste inequalities.

In the case of vocational training, central U.P. has the highest within-upper caste inequalities (0.035), followed by western (0.026), Bundelkhand (0.007), and eastern (0.006) regions for the year 2004–05. In 2011–12, the trend has changed with the western region being at the top (0.034), followed by central (0.032), eastern (0.010), and Bundelkhand (0.007) regions with respect to within-upper caste inequalities.

In the case of general education attainment, within-caste group inequalities have declined for all the castes in all the regions in 2011–12 over 2004–05. A singular exception according to results from Theil's index is the ST group wherein the intra-group inequality has increased in all regions except in the western region in 2011–12 over 2004–05.

In case of technical education attainment, within-caste group inequalities have declined for OBCs in all the regions (except Bundelkhand), while for SCs it declined in central and eastern regions in 2011–12 over 2004–05. Rest of the caste groups have shown an incremental change in within-group inequality for all regions in 2011–12 over 2004–05 (as per results of Thiel Index). In case of vocational training attainment, within-caste group inequalities have increased for all the social groups in all the regions in 2011–12 over 2004–05. However, it has declined for 'general' and ST categories in the central region and for SCs in Bundelkhand region.

5 Evidences from the Primary Survey

5.1 Educational and Skill Attainments Across Regions

Nearly one-third (32%) of the surveyed population possesses general education while nearly half of them (49%) have received vocational training, and the remaining about one-fifth (19%) have received technical education. Thus, two-thirds of the sample population has received some kind of skill training in different trades for varying durations. The higher proportion of skill training in the sample population is also due to higher reflection of sample from the vocational and technical education providers. Across regions, Bundelkhand region has a higher sample in general education (36%) as compared to the western region (29%). The proportion of skilled (vocational and technical taken together) sample is higher in the western region (71%) than in Bundelkhand region (65%). However, the share of technical education is higher in Bundelkhand region and a fraction of vocational education is higher in the western region (Table 9).

It is found from the field that the share of 'others' social group in vocational education is highest across the social group in Bundelkhand region.

The reason for a higher share in technical and vocational education in the western region is primarily being a relatively developed region with higher industrial entrepreneurship that has generated better demand for such education and training. Bundelkhand, being a relatively less developed region, has relatively more programs focusing on general education and training that has spurred such activities.

Looking at the skill spectrum within districts, it is noted that Gautam Budh Nagar which is a relatively developed district in the western region has a huge proportion of skilled persons in the sample (89%), while Etah district which is relatively less developed has about 65% of those who have received a vocational and technical education, and rightly so. However, the trend appears to be opposite in the case of the districts in Bundelkhand region. The relatively developed Jhansi district in the region has a lower share of sample having vocational and technical education (50%) while the less developed Banda district has a larger proportion of people with skill education.

Vocational education has a larger share than that of technical education in the surveyed sample. It is palpably clear that skilling has a positive impact on accessing

Table 9 Region-wise distribution of individuals surveyed by types of education

Type of education/Region	Bundelkhand	Western	Total
General	89 (35.6)	72 (28.8)	161 (32.2)
Vocational	107 (42.8)	138 (55.2)	245 (49.0)
Technical	54 (21.6)	40 (16.0)	94 (18.8)
Total	250 (100)	250 (100)	500 (100)

Source Field Survey, 2016–17

employment than general education. The analysis clearly shows that regional differentiation is pronounced with larger share and preference for vocational and technical education in the western region as compared to Bundelkhand region and there is a fairly good share of such education among all the categories of the labor force (Table 10).

The data presented in Table 11 reveals that out of total 500 respondents, OBCs have performed well in terms of overall education in both the regions. However, comparing across regions, OBCs in the western region have performed better in terms of overall education compared to Bundelkhand region.

It is clearly evident from the secondary data analysis that disparities have reduced during 2004–05 to 2011–12 across each social category in general education across the regions of the state but have increased in technical and vocational education and training (TVET) which are closer indicators of skill development. However, the primary survey has revealed that the participation of disadvantaged social groups has increased in general, vocational and technical education. Evidently, this suggests that government policy initiative has had a positive impact on enhancing human capital base in the state.

6 Conclusion

The paper shows that despite significant improvements in the literacy levels and educational achievements, illiteracy is still a huge challenge in Uttar Pradesh, particularly among the disadvantaged sections. The level of technical skill attainment is dismally low in the state. Although there has been an improvement during the two quinquennial periods, yet its extent is minuscule. Surprisingly, OBCs have witnessed a decline in this respect. SCs have the highest proportion in 'not literate' category and they are concentrated in the lowest rung of educational structure, while 'Others' or upper castes are highly represented in the higher education stratum.

The proportion of technical education that includes technical degree, diploma and certificate (below degree and degree and above) in the state is appallingly low, less than 1% in 2011–12. The level of skill training, both formal and non-formal, has been much lower in U.P. than the all India level. Formal training in the state was alarmingly low at 1.6% in 2004–05 and it further shrunk to 1.0% in 2011–12. One of the main reasons for low level of vocational and technical education is the lack of quality and low value attached to such education which has little or no connection to the labor market demand.

The overall social group inequality in general education has reduced but in the case of technical education and vocational training, it has increased in 2011–12 over 2004–05 in all the four regions of Uttar Pradesh. Out of the total social (caste) inequalities, more than 90% contribution is due to within-group inequalities and remaining due to between-group inequalities in all the four regions of the state.

The central region has the highest percentage share in technical and higher educational levels of education in 2004–05, but in 2011–12, the western region picked up

Table 10 District-wise distribution of individuals surveyed by types of education

Type of education	Bundelkhand region				Western region				Total
	Banda		Jhansi		Etah		Gautam Budh Nagar		
	Male	Female	Male	Female	Male	Female	Male	Female	
General	12	15	35	27	33	25	13	1	161
Vocational	43	29	18	17	54	5	72	7	245
Technical	24	2	23	5	8	0	32	0	94
Total	79	46	76	49	95	30	117	8	500

Source Field Survey, 2016–17

Table 11 Region-wise distribution of individuals by type of education across social groups (in %)

Type of education	Bundelkhand				Western			
	SC	ST	OBC	Other	SC	ST	OBC	Other
General	6.0	0.2	8.2	3.4	3.2	0.0	7.8	3.4
Vocational	6.0	0.2	9.2	6.0	6.0	0.6	13.2	7.8
Technical	3.2	0.0	5.8	1.8	1.4	0.0	5.2	1.4
Total	15.2	0.4	23.2	11.2	10.6	0.6	26.2	12.6

Source Field Survey, 2016–17

and reported the highest proportion in TVET. The maximum inequality has been found in central region, followed by western, eastern and Bundelkhand regions for the year 2004–05. In 2011–12, the inequality has vastly increased in the western region and it has shifted to number one position in the latter period followed by central, eastern, and Bundelkhand regions.

In the case of vocational training attainment, the total inequality has gone up in 2011–12 over 2004–05 for all the economic regions of Uttar Pradesh. The inequality scores of vocational training present more or less similar trend as in the case of technical education.

One of the main factors responsible for the central region to be advance in technical and higher educational attainment could be its proximity to state capital that has numerous developmental activities and provides better opportunities. Similarly, the western region being agriculturally prosperous helps in establishing stronger linkages to industrial activities that fuel the demand for higher education as well as technical vocational training. Another reason is the fact that some part of it falls under the National Capital Region (NCR), which too spurs growth in the education and skilling spheres.

Though inequalities still persist in terms of access across regions and among social groups yet recent evidence, based on primary investigation, clearly indicates that disparities have reduced across social groups and their participation has increased in vocational and technical education.

From a policy point of view, there is a need for more focused interventions for the disadvantaged social groups in order to improve their education and skill attainment and ensure better access to the labor market for a genuinely inclusive growth process.

References

Awasthi, I. C., & Shrivastav, P. K. (2017). Inequalities in economic and educational status among social groups in India: Evidences from a village-based study in Uttar Pradesh. *International Journal of Social Economics, 44*(6), 774–796.

Basole, A. (2014). Dynamics of income inequality in India: Insights from world top incomes database. *Economic and Political Weekly, 49*(40), 14–16.

Bennell, P. (1999). Learning to change: Skills development among the economically vulnerable and socially excluded in developing countries. *Employment and Training Paper*, Employment and Training Department, International Labour Organization (ILO), Geneva.

Christoph, E., & Berg, J. (2009).The role of employment and labour markets in the fight against poverty. In *The Role of Employment and Labour Markets*, International Labour Organization (ILO), Geneva.

Dahlman,C., &Utz, A. (2005). *India and the knowledge economy.* World Bank Institute Resources, The World Bank.

Desai, S., & Kulkarni, V. (2008). Changing educational inequalities in India in the context of affirmative action. *Demography, 45*(2), 245–270.

Deshpande, A., & Newman, K. (2007). Where the path leads: The role of caste in post-university employment expectations. *Economic and Political Weekly, 42*(41), 4133–4140.

DFID. (2008).*Growth-building jobs and prosperity in developing countries.* Department for International Development, UK.

Goel, V. P. (2009). Technical and Vocational Education and Training (TVET) System in India for Sustainable Development. India Country Paper, International Centre for Technical and Vocational Education and Training, UNESCO-UNEVOC.

Goli, S., Maurya, N., & Sharma, M. (2015). Continuing caste inequalities in rural Uttar Pradesh. *International Journal of Sociology and Social Policy, 35*(3/4), 252–272.

Government of India. (2015). Employment and Unemployment Situation among Social Groups In India 2011–12., NSS 68th Round NSSO Ministry of Statistics & Programme Implementation.

Government of India. (2015). National Policy for Skill Development and Entrepreneurship. New Delhi. Retrieved from https://www.skilldevelopment.gov.in/assets/images/SkillIndia/policybooklet-Final.pdf

Government of Uttar Pradesh. (2008). *Human Development Report of Uttar Pradesh.* Lucknow: UNDP.

Government of Uttar Pradesh. (2013). *Uttar Pradesh Skill Development Policy.* Lucknow: Department of Vocational Education Government of Uttar Pradesh.

Government of Uttar Pradesh. (2014). *District-wise Development Indicators.* Lucknow: Department of Planning.

Government of Uttar Pradesh. (2015). *Annual Action Plan 2015.* Lucknow: Department of Planning.

International Labour Organization. (1997). *Vocational training and lifelong learning of women.* Geneva: United Nations Division for the Advancement of Women, International Labour Organization (ILO).

International Labour Organization. (2008). *Skills for improved productivity, employment growth and development*, Report V, International Labour Organization (ILO), Geneva.

Jodhka, S. S., & Newman, K. (2007). In the name of globalization, meritocracy, productivity, and the hidden language of caste. *Economic and Political Weekly, 42*(41), 4125–4132.

Jodhka, S. S., & Shah, G. (2010).Comparative contexts of discrimination: caste and untouchability in South Asia, *Working Paper Series No. 4,* Indian Institute of Dalit Studies, New Delhi.

Kapoor, R. (2013). Inequality matters. *Economic and Political Weekly, 48*(2), 58–65.

OECD. (2013). *Indicators of skills for employment and productivity: a conceptual framework and approach for low-income countries.* A Report for the Human Resource Development Pillar of the G20 Multi-Year Action Plan on Development, OECD, and the World Bank in collaboration with ETF, ILO, and UNESCO.

Pal, P., & Ghosh, J. (2007). Inequality in India: a survey of recent trends. *DESA Working Paper No. 45 ST/ESA/2007/DWP/45*, United Nations Department of Economic and Social Affairs, New York, NY, July.

Prasad, S. (2013). Polarization, inequality and inclusive growth: Kerala's experience in the reform period. *Journal of South Asian Studies, 1*(2), 91–103.

Sanghi S., & Srija, A. (2015). Skill development and productivity of the workforce, *Economy Matters*, Confederation of Indian Industry (CII), New Delhi.

Saxena, P. K., & Kumar, A. (2017). Skill differentials in India. *Working Paper No, 6/2017*, Chetanya Kasyap Foundation (pp. 1–52).

Thorat, S., & Newman, K. S. (2007). Caste and economic discrimination: Causes, consequences and remedies. *Economic and Political Weekly, 42*(41), 4121–4124.

Agrarian Question

Structural Transformation and the Agrarian Question in the Indian Economy

Some Disturbing Concerns from a Labourist Perspective

K. P. Kannan

Abstract Structural transformation is profoundly linked to several political, socio-economic and technological factors. From a labourist perspective the transfer of surplus labour from agriculture to industry, for example, is a function of higher wages and productivity in industry. This paper is essentially attempting to interrogate the structural transformation in the Indian economy from the point of shifts in employment away from agriculture in terms of its content. While this transition would be of great interest and consequence to both capital and labour, there is the third actor, i.e. the state. The renewed debate has brought in the role of the state and rightly so. The state in a country like India promised national economic development through a political process of universal franchise in a multi-party electoral system. This factor is important to note to understand the role of the state in addressing the question of agrarian transition. By deploying a measure of 'Rurality of Employment' to include non-agricultural rural employment activities that push the agrarian transition in the wider context of rural transition, this paper finds that this structural transformation away from agriculture is not accompanied by a structural transformation away from rural employment and the rural nature of urban employment. Second, we look at the regional spread and find a four-fold pattern where only a few states qualify for a meaningful structural transformation even in the limited sense of moving away from the agricultural sector for majority employment. Third, we look at the social dimension of this structural transformation and find its partial character because it is limited to three out of five broad social groups. From our analysis of the partial nature of India's structural transformation with weak foundations, an important lesson from a developmental point of view is the need for a concerted strategy of employment-led development of the rural economy.

K. P. Kannan (✉)
Honorary Fellow, Centre for Development Studies, Trivandrum 695011, India
e-mail: kannankp123@gmail.com

Laurie Baker Centre for Habitat Studies, COSTFORD, Trivandrum, Thrissur 695573, Kerala, India

N. K. Mishra (ed.), *Development Challenges of India After Twenty Five Years of Economic Reforms*, India Studies in Business and Economics,
https://doi.org/10.1007/978-981-15-8265-3_16

1 Introduction

Ever since economic development literature accepted the three divisions of the economy into (a) primary sector consisting of agricultural and related activities, (b) secondary sector consisting of industry and construction and (c) tertiary sector consisting of all service-oriented activities, scholars were looking at the pace and timing of the process of structural transformation that is understood as a movement away from a dependence on the primary sector—often referred to as agricultural sector—in terms of both income and employment. If a major share of income as well as employment in an economy is generated from secondary and tertiary sectors, then the economy is characterized by a structural transformation. Since Lewis (1954) and (1955) conceived of the possibility of economic development for poor labour surplus economies by transferring the surplus labour from agriculture with zero marginal productivity to the higher productivity sectors in non-agriculture, especially industry, the process of structural transformation became a task of the newly independent states in poorer countries. India's national economic development vision and plan, no doubt, fits into this idea of sectoral shift away from agriculture. However, it took more than six decades since independence for the Indian economy to mark its structural transformation in 2011–2012 defined in the above sense.

Although this question of structural transformation might look like a technical issue, it is well known that it is profoundly linked to several political, socio-economic and technological factors. From a labourist perspective the transfer of surplus labour from agriculture to industry, for example, is a function of higher wages and productivity in industry. As the process goes on it raises wages in agriculture to an inflexion point where wages in agriculture equals that of the high productivity sector, i.e. industry. This implies a point where the zero marginal productivity of labour ceases to exist. This could also be accelerated by a process where the productivity in agriculture is also raised through technological and/or organizational changes. Scholars who adopt a Marxian methodology to understand this question has posed it as a process of development of capitalism in poor economies. Their focus on developing countries such as India has posed the issue as one of understanding the agrarian question (see Thorner 1982; Patnaik 1990; Byres 1991; Akram-Lodhi 2010). The renewed debate on the agrarian question in developing countries has indeed provided greater clarity on the role of agriculture in economic and social transformation with particular focus on the role of peasantry. Terry Byres provided clarity by formulating specific questions in the debate on agrarian question as one of agrarian transition. These may be summarized in terms of three issues: (1) the internal dynamic in agriculture and the possibility of the development of capitalism within it; (2) the possibility of accumulation of surplus in agriculture that could finance industrialization and (3) the nature and type of exploitative agrarian relations (as between peasants and landlords) and the possibility of political alliance between peasants and industrial workers. The net result of a successful agrarian transition would be the development of capitalism not only in agriculture but also in all sectors of the economy.

In the context of these issues, there has been a renewed interest in debating the agrarian question with specific reference to India. The outcome of one such attempt has been documented in the volume on *Critical Perspectives on Agrarian Transition: India in the Global Debate* edited by Mohanty (2016). The contributions in the volume explicitly recognize that the agrarian transition question goes beyond agriculture,[1] that colonialism and its historical impact has a bearing on the current context, that the independent national state has made several interventions in agriculture and that the current phase is also marked by the emergence of a neoliberal economic order characterized by globalization. It is in this background that Mohanty contextualizes the Indian situation with the following questions: (1) What are the significant changes emerging in India's agrarian economy and society under the impact of neoliberal reforms and global capitalism? (2) Are these changes indicating the transition from rural/semi-feudal economy to urban-industrial capitalist economy? (3) Is this transition conforming to, or deviating from, the classical model of transition from feudalism to capitalism? (4) How have different regions and states in India, being at different stages of development, experienced and responded to this agrarian transition? (5) How are various agrarian classes and interest groups responding to this transition'? (Mohanty 2016: 2).

It would be a tall order to claim that all these important questions are sought to be answered in this paper. What we are essentially attempting is to interrogate the structural transformation in the Indian economy from the point of shifts in employment away from agriculture in terms of its content, by keeping these questions in mind.

While this transition would be of great interest and consequence to both capital and labour, there is the third actor, i.e. the state. Here the state in a developing country like India has been attempting a structural transformation in a context where there is a large segment of peasantry often referred to as small and marginal farmers located in between a small segment of rich/large farmers and a sizeable segment of landless agricultural labourers. In that sense, the process of structural transformation of the economy marked by a shift away from agriculture for a majority of the people for income and employment in India since 2011–2012 assumes importance.

For labour, the situation is more complex than one would expect. Wage labour is not the majority in the universe of working people even for the whole economy. Even in 2011–2012 when the Indian economy marked its structural transformation, the share of wage labour was only 48% while the remaining 52% were classified as self-employed (see Table 1). Within wage labour, a majority of them are called casual workers underlining their insecure work status. The main category of self-employed includes peasants in agriculture who are categorized as marginal and small farmers but who are also compelled, more often than not, to send members of their families for wage labour to supplement the family income. The self-employed or peasant-like category in non-agriculture is also significant. Given the high incidence of poverty and vulnerability, the quality of employment and the corresponding income earning capacity has emerged as a major issue of concern. For capital, especially

[1] See Foreword by T. J. Byres.

Table 1 The compositional picture of labour shifting away from agriculture

Category	Employment (million)				Real Wages (Rs./day at 2004–2005 prices)	
	1993–1994	%	2011–2012	%	1993–1994	2011–2012
Total workers in agriculture	236.23	100.0	225.39	100.0		
(1) Regular workers	3.28	1.4	1.89	0.8	46.04	107.81
(2) Casual workers	90.07	38.1	75.49	33.5	39.01	79.77
(3) Self-employed	142.88	60.5	148.01	65.7		
Total workers in Non-agriculture	132.60	100.0	245.95	100.0		
(1) Regular workers	47.13	35.5	85.08	34.6	135.50	227.16
(2) Casual workers	26.23	19.8	62.60	25.5	54.10	93.84
(3) Self-employed	59.24	44.7	98.27	39.9		

Source Computed from unit level data from the 50 and 68th Rounds of NSS

non-agricultural capital, there is the concern on supply of wage goods to workers in non-agriculture. Although the question of extracting a surplus from agriculture (through taxation and/or other means) for financing industrialization has been flagged as an important question, it has not been an effective one so far. However, capital may be said to be concerned about agriculture and the rural economy especially in large developing economies like India as a potential market for its goods.

The renewed debate has brought in the role of the state and rightly so. The state in a country like India promised national economic development through a political process of universal franchise in a multi-party electoral system. This factor is important to note to understand the role of the state in addressing the question of agrarian transition. The state can be said to be concerned with the third issue mentioned earlier, i.e. the nature and type of exploitative agrarian relations in so far as it wants to discourage pre-capitalist agrarian relations to increase agricultural output. It is concerned about supply of wage goods for industrialisation (especially food and raw materials) and hence started a process of public investment in agricultural infrastructure. It also knows that agriculture is the largest sector of employment and as such there is an employment concern although it consciously tries, limited by overall political economy, to increase employment outside agriculture. The state is also concerned to develop the agricultural rural economy as a market for non-agricultural goods and services.

The larger context in which national economic development was conceived and executed by the state in India has undergone profound changes in 1991 when it formally adopted neoliberal economic reforms within a global context of liberalization, privatization and globalization that was summed up as Washington Consensus. An earlier debate in India on the 'mode of production in Indian agriculture' could not arrive at a consensus on the development of capitalism in Indian agriculture (see, e.g. Thorner 1982). But it is quite evident that Indian agriculture is a complex mix of the influence of pre-capitalist institutions as well as increasing market-related transactions in land, labour, credit and product with significant state interventions.

Beginning with the initiation of neoliberal economic reforms the Indian economy has been witnessing a higher growth trajectory with increasing sectoral inequality, among other inequalities, as between agriculture and non-agriculture. Right from the mid-1950s, the contribution of agriculture to the national income has been less than half and it steadily declined to around 15% by 2013. However, a majority of the population was dependent on the primary sector of agriculture and allied activities, from 64% in 1993–1994 to 48% in 2011–2012, thus marking a formal threshold of achieving structural transformation. But the question we ask is to what extent this structural transformation a substantive one. First, we look at the nature of dependence on employment. By deploying a measure of 'Rurality of Employment' to include non-agricultural rural employment activities that push the agrarian transition in the wider context of rural transition, we find that this structural transformation away from agriculture is not accompanied by a structural transformation away from rural employment and the rural nature of urban employment (i.e. agricultural activities in urban areas). Second, we look at the regional spread and find a four-fold pattern where only a few states qualify for a meaningful structural transformation even in the limited sense of moving away from the agricultural sector for majority employment. Third, we look at the social dimension of this structural transformation and find its partial character because it is limited to three out of five broad social groups. Of the three groups, one is a socially and economically advantaged group (called Others) with a higher incidence of non-poor, better quality of employment and higher education. The second group is a socially and economically less advantaged group (Muslims) with a tradition of higher incidence of non-agricultural occupations. The third group is a socially disadvantaged group (SC) whose move away from agriculture seems to be driven more by distress and indignity than a case of vertical labour mobility. In that sense, the structural transformation is a partial one from a social point of view as well. These results are then discussed in the light of the studies that have flagged the preponderance of informal—i.e. insecure—employment in the Indian economy.

2 Overall Structural Transformation in the Indian Economy

There is no doubt that since the launching of neoliberal economic reform policies there has occurred a slow but steady structural transformation of the Indian economy away from agriculture both in terms of income and employment. However, such structural transformation has not been accompanied by a significant increase in agricultural productivity and consequent surplus generation for industrialization. It would appear that it is the result of the expansion of the non-agricultural sector through greater investment especially infrastructure, easier access to capital by the private sector, liberalization of bank credit for consumption including housing and a flexible approach to implementing labour legislation in favour of capital. The result has been a boom in construction that attracted a significant share of labour away from agriculture to work as casual workers mostly, if not only, in urban areas. Industrial expansion in the formal sector witnessed very little of new job creation but allowed for more employment and output expansion in the informal sector. Service sector grew at a faster rate than industry and agriculture, although its ability to absorb new labour has been limited. The net result is an increase in intersectoral inequality in product per worker (a broad measure of labour productivity). The inequality ratio of 4.25 in 1993–1994 increased to 5.16 in 2011–2012, i.e. the value of output per worker in non-agriculture is 5.16 times higher than that in agriculture. This is contrary to the expectations of the Lewisian process of the transfer of surplus labour from agriculture to non-agriculture.

During this phase (1993–2012) agricultural sector has also witnessed significant changes. Agricultural activity came to be dominated by market transactions whether it is in land, labour, credit and output. That does not mean pre-capitalist agrarian institutions have undergone significant changes. Earlier forms of unfree labour may have been morphed into new forms of unfree labour (see, e.g. Breman et al. 2009) with continuing low wages as well as job and wage discrimination based on social identity and gender (see Papola and Kannan 2017 for an analysis of the wages across sectors, rural-urban, gender and social identity). Development of capitalistic labour relations and exploitative framework has not erased the category of peasants but in fact increased their presence in absolute and relative terms (see the category of self-employed in agriculture in Table 1). In fact, there is a significant category of peasantry both small and marginal although close to half the land is under large landholders.[2] Regionally varied growth in productivity, the large presence of peasantry of small and marginal farmers as well as landless agricultural labourers along with a small segment of rich capitalist agriculturists characterize the current scenario in Indian agriculture.

These seemingly contradictory processes of change in agriculture have been such that the agricultural sector continues to experience the highest incidence of poverty, low wages, insecure employment and poor conditions of work. As we shall see later, there is a social dimension to this scenario where the dependence of the socially disadvantaged sections on agriculture for their employment and income is considerably higher (for a detailed documentation and analysis of the situation see, e.g. NCEUS 2008). Although the political alliance between the peasantry and wage workers is much talked about, very little of sustained organizational and/or mobilizational action has taken place despite such objective conditions as the persistence of a large mass of labouring poor in both agriculture and non-agriculture as peasants (self-employed) and insecure wage workers, i.e. casual status workers.

Yet, without a full resolution of the agrarian question or questions, agriculture has ceased to be the largest provider of employment in India. At the same time,

---

[2]84% of cultivators are marginal and small farmers with one and two hectares of land, respectively.

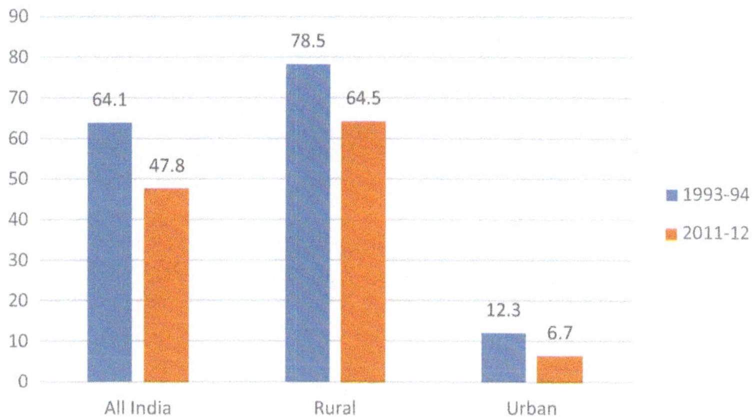

Fig. 1 Percentage share of workers in agriculture. *Source* Computed from unit level data from the 50 and 68th Rounds of the National Sample Survey

industry has not been able to absorb a higher share; instead employment is equally divided between the secondary and services sectors. In effect, the non-agricultural sector has emerged as the biggest employment and income-generating sector. In 1993–94 agriculture accounted for 64% of employment and 30% of national income that got reduced to 48 and 15%, respectively, by 2011–2012 (see Fig. 1 for the shift in share of employment in agriculture, including rural and urban areas, during this period). Such a drastic reduction in the share of income has also increased the intersectoral income inequality enormously as between agriculture and non-agriculture as mentioned earlier.

Not only the share of workers in agriculture reached less than half by 2011–2012, the absolute number of workers in agriculture also came down as compared to 1993–1994, from 236.24 to 225.39 million. It meant that the incremental workforce of 91.6 million during this period has wholly been absorbed by the non-agricultural sector along with 10.9 million of those already engaged in agriculture. This has meant a 4.6% decline in employment in agriculture. This overall absorption of additional labour is no doubt massive although not adequate to match the increase in labour force.

However, a close examination of the shift in employment in terms of the composition of the workers by labour status (i.e. regular, casual or self-employed) suggests that those who left agriculture seem to be mostly casual wage labour. The peasants as a group officially classified as self-employed in agriculture have in fact registered an increase both in absolute terms as well as in their share in the total agricultural workforce (see Table 1). This is not a sign of increasing proletarianization but increasing peasantization of Indian agriculture that is not in tune with the spread of capitalist market relations and transactions in Indian rural economy. The share of the self-employed in Indian agriculture increased from 61% to 66% during 1993–2012.

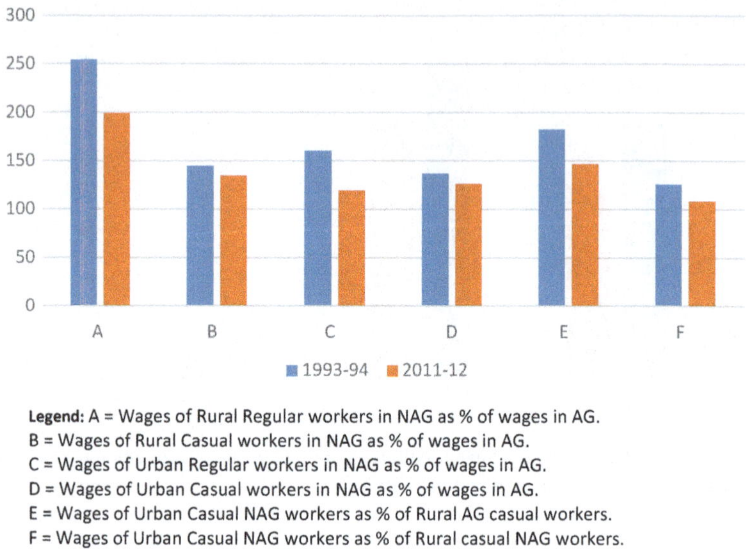

Fig. 2 Wage relativity for segments of workers. *Source* Computed from unit level data from the 50 and 68th Rounds of the National Sample Survey

The situation in the non-agricultural sector points to an increasing, albeit slow, trend in proletarianization going by the increase in the share of wage labour from 55 to 60% during this period (see Table 1). Wages in the non-agricultural sector are expectedly higher than in agriculture for both casual and regular workers but the smaller margins (see Fig. 2) camouflage the interstate differences that have accelerated the migration of casual labour to the southern and western states from the rest of the country (Fig. 3).

Does this mean that the rural economy in India has ceased to be the main provider of employment and income to the majority of the people? For this, we need to go beyond the agricultural sector and examine employment in the rural economy, or what we call, rurality of employment.

3 The Continuing Predominance of Rurality of Employment

From this aggregate picture, it is tempting to conclude that a structural transformation has finally come about despite continuing issues of low wages, inadequacy of employment and consequent persistence of poverty. A closer examination reveals that the direct dependence of the workers on agriculture may have declined but not their overwhelming dependence on the rural economy for employment and, consequently, on income. This is because while much of the movement of labour was away from

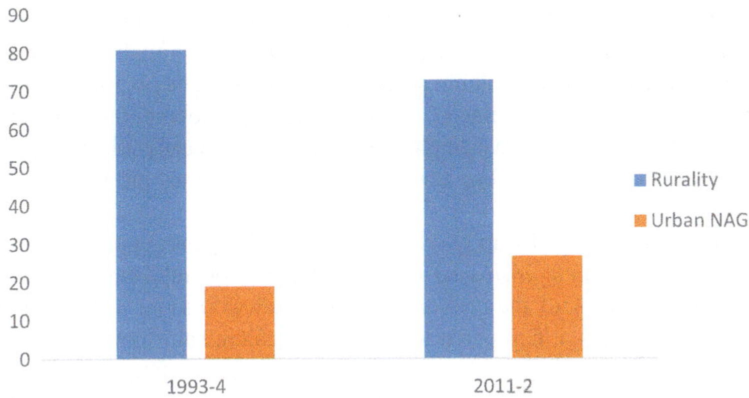

Fig. 3 Rurality of Employment in India (Rural AG + Urban AG + Rural NAG). *Source* Computed from unit level data from the 50 and 68th Rounds of the National Sample Survey

agriculture to non-agriculture, it was less so from rural to the urban economy. Therefore, we measure employment that is based on rurality. This 'rurality of employment' consists of workers in agriculture in rural and urban areas as well as those working in non-agriculture in the rural areas.

The rurality of employment declined from close to 81% of total workforce in 1993–1994 to 73% in 2011–2012. Therefore, the labour transition away from agriculture has been divided between rural and urban non-agricultural sectors. While the agricultural sector witnessed a decline of 10.85 million workers the rurality of employment increased by about 46.6 million. The urban non-agricultural sector absorbed another 56.56 million (see Table 2).

Table 2 Rurality of Employment in India (Percentage distribution of employment Rural AG + Urban AG + Rural NAG)

Category	1993–1994		2011–2012	
	Million workers	%	Million workers	%
Rurality of employment	298.28	80.9	344.22	73.0
Urban NAG	70.56	19.1	127.12	27.0
Total	368.84	100.00	471.34	100.00
Wage workers and Self-employed in Rurality of Employment				
1. Regular workers	18.87	6.3	28.76	8.3
2. Casual workers	105.45	35.4	120.38	35.0
3. Wage workers (1 + 2)	124.32	41.7	149.14	43.3
4. Self-employed	173.95	58.3	195.08	56.7
5. Rurality	298.28	100.0	344.22	100.0

Note AG means agriculture and NAG means Non-agriculture
Source Computed from unit level data from the 50 and 68th Rounds of NSS

But this movement away from agriculture has not significantly benefitted the labouring poor to lead a life of dignity and security. Although wages in non-agriculture is higher than agriculture, a majority continues to be poor and vulnerable. Such a phenomenon was examined from the point of employment and social security. Those who continue to have employment and social security arising out of their employment are classified as 'formal workers' and the others as 'informal workers'.[3] Given the pro-capital orientation and policies of the state, employment with security has been given the go-by and in its place labour-cheapening policies have been encouraged resulting in an increased share of 'insecure' or 'informal workers' even in the organized sector of the economy. Of the total workforce in India 92% are such informal workers, a figure that has refused to change during the entire period of economic reforms.

Despite a continuing but slow decline in poverty and vulnerability notwithstanding since the early 1990s, a majority of India's population continues to be poor and vulnerable. By taking the international poverty line of 2 Purchasing Power Parity Dollars per capita per day in 1993–1994, our calculations show that 85% of Indian population was poor and vulnerable that has now declined to 64% as of 2011–2012.[4] Therefore the movement away from agriculture to non-agricultural has not addressed the larger question of employment security, its quality and income arising out of wages. However, we need to ask here as to the significance of the movement away from agricultural employment.

While the share of agricultural employment declined from 64 to 48%, the share of rural employment declined from 81% to only 73%. What this signifies is that the share of rural non-agricultural employment increased from 17 to 25%. There is no estimation of national income by rural and urban economies but we reckon that rural GDP is around 50%.[5] This points to the sharp increase in rural-urban income inequality although it is considerably less than the intersectoral inequality as between agriculture and non-agriculture.

While agriculture has ceased to be the major provider of employment to the workers, the rural economy has not and that shows the limitations of the structural transformation in the Indian economy. The agrarian transition question may be said to be replaced by a rural transition question in so far as employment and livelihood of an overwhelming share of Indian workers and their families are concerned. The

[3]For a detailed analysis of the link between informality of employment and poverty and vulnerability see, NCEUS (2008).

[4]The 2 PPP$ in the 1990 s was revised to 3.2PPP$ in 2010 to reflect the depreciation in the value of the dollar.

[5]We indirectly estimate the GDP originating from the rural economy by multiplying the number of agricultural workers with product per worker in agriculture and adding it to the number of non-agricultural workers in rural areas with the economy-wide product per worker in non-agriculture. This gives us a 55% of GDP originating from the rural economy. Since the product per worker in non-agricultural sector in rural areas is likely to be less than that in urban non-agricultural sector, it is quite possible that this gives a higher GDP in rural non-agricultural sector than what we presume to be. Hence, it is safe to reckon the share of GDP originating from the rural economy at around 50%.

need to focus on the rural economy from a developmental perspective that provides employment to more than 70% of Indian workforce becomes an imperative. The steady neglect of the rural economy, more so since the economic reforms than earlier, will not only manifest in terms of a highly unequal India but also a source of social and economic crisis from time to time as already manifested in farmers' suicides (see Reddy and Mishra 2009) and the largely distress induced migration of rural labour to urban as well as more prosperous rural areas.

From the perspective of labour, what such a scenario raises is a developmental question anchored in decent employment. This transformation of the agrarian question into a rural question warrants urgent social and political attention.

Given the continental size of the country and the unequal pace of socio-economic transformation and the consequent developmental outcomes, there are two employment dimensions that we need to examine from an agrarian transition point of view. These are (a) regional, and (b) social.

4 Regional Dimension of Structural Transformation and Rurality of Employment

Given the sub-continental nature of India's geography and economy, the regional dimension of any economic characteristic assumes importance while interpreting the national aggregate economy. Since structural transformation is understood as an important marker of a turning point in any given economy, this assumes all the more important from a regional perspective. Our regional analysis of these issues has revealed a limited or partial nature of this transformation. Broadly speaking it consists of four groups of states, i.e. (i) states attaining structural transformation with a high per capita income, (ii) states attaining structural transformation with a low per capita income, (iii) states with no structural transformation so far but registering high per capita income and (iv) states with no structural transformation so far and continuing to be in the group of low per capita income. High and low per capita income here is used in relation to the national average.

What do we make of this differentiated scenario presented in Table 3? States in Group 1 no doubt present a desirable outcome because, on the face of it, it is accompanied by relatively higher per capita income. There are nine states in this group accounting for one third of the country's population in 2011. Most of them also report higher ranks in agricultural product per worker except Maharashtra and Tamil Nadu although these two states have front-run status in industrialisation and urbanization. However, our test of Rurality of Employment suggests that except the small state of Goa there is no state in this group (or any other) which has reported a structural transformation in the sense of a movement away from rural employment for majority of the workers. The State of Kerala comes closest with 56% of employment in terms of 'rurality' followed by Tamil Nadu with 61%.

Table 3 States ranked according to characteristics of structural transformation, 2011–2012

State	AG-GDP (%)	AG-E (%)	Rurality of Emp (%)	Rank in			
				Per cap Income	Agr product per worker	Non-Agr product per worker	HDI
1	2	3	4	5	6	7	8
1. Structural transformation with high per capita income							
Goa	3.7	3.7	41.4	1	1	1	3
Haryana	16.8	40.9	68.8	3	4	4	8
Maharashtra	8.3	49.1	63.0	4	24	3	6
Gujarat	13.1	46.9	62.2	5	9	7	10
Tamil Nadu	8.5	33.5	61.1	6	17	11	7
Uttarakhand	10.8	46.7	75.0	7	13	5	13
Punjab	22.8	35.8	66.7	10	3	16	4
Kerala	9.9	20.4	56.0	9	5	12	1
Karnataka	15.3	48.5	67.9	13	16	13	11
2. Structural transformation with low per capita income							
Tripura	23.8	24.4	77.7	14	2	24	5
West Bengal	17.6	36.8	68.5	18	10	23	12
J&K	21.7	40.2	77.6	19	8	25	9
Rajasthan	21.3	49.9	81.1	20	15	20	16
Jharkhand	16.9	49.5	81.1	23	22	19	18
Manipur	19.8	38.0	77.0	25	11	28	5
3. No structural transformation but high income							
Sikkim	10.4	55.7	77.0	2	19	2	5
Himachal	16.9	58.4	92.6	8	18	8	2
Nagaland	26.6	63.2	81.5	11	6	6	5
AP(Undivided)	18.9	52.5	75.1	12	14	14	14
4. No structural transformation and low income							
Mizoram	20.9	53.8	67.1	15	12	15	5
Arunachal	30.7	65.9	83.7	16	7	9	5
Meghalaya	15.6	56.3	84.6	17	25	17	5
Chhattisgarh	19.2	71.8	83.9	21	28	10	22
Odisha	17.2	54.8	86.9	22	26	18	21
MP	23.5	57.7	79.0	24	21	22	19
Assam	21.8	54.3	86.9	26	20	21	15
Uttar Pradesh	23.0	51.9	80.6	27	23	27	17
Bihar	23.5	61.6	90.7	28	27	26	20

(continued)

Table 3 (continued)

State	AG-GDP (%)	AG-E (%)	Rurality of Emp (%)	Rank in			
				Per cap Income	Agr product per worker	Non-Agr product per worker	HDI
1	2	3	4	5	6	7	8
All India	15.1	47.8	73.0				

Note AG-GDP (%) means share of agriculture in total GDP; AG-E(%) means share of agriculture in total employment. HDI values are for 2007-08 and taken from *India Human Development Report* prepared by the Institute for Applied Manpower Research (renamed as National Institute for Labour and Employment), New Delhi. Source: GDP data from Economic Survey 2013 and HDI ranking based on HDI values from IAMR (2011). All other calculations are based on unit level data from the 68th Round of NSS

Group 2 states are those attaining structural transformation but continue to be in the league of poorer states, if not the poorest, by per capita income. They account for 18% of the total population. At the same time, their product per worker in non-agriculture is also considerably below the national average. What kind of a structural transformation is this? This could be a case of movement of workers away from agriculture because of very low capacity for labour absorption in a gainful sense but ending up in low wage employment outside agriculture whether in rural or urban areas. This is reflected in a much higher dependence on rural non-agricultural employment. Therefore, the rurality of employment is much higher than in Group 1 states. There are six states in this group with West Bengal reporting the lowest rurality at 68.5% of total employment and the highest in Rajasthan and Jharkhand with 81%.

Group 3 states belong to a set where one cannot mark a full structural transformation because the share of employment in agriculture continues to be well above 50% despite a much lower share of income. But these are not poorer states with low per capita income; in fact, they are to be counted as those with high per capita income with a relatively higher product per worker in non-agriculture. There are four states here accounting for a mere eight percent of the country's population. In terms of rurality of employment, these states report a high share ranging from 75% in Andhra Pradesh (undivided) to as high as 93% in Himachal Pradesh. It would appear that their high per capita income arises largely from a high product per worker in non-agriculture except for the State of Nagaland.

Group 4 perhaps represents the most difficult part of the structural transformation story because it is a combination of no structural transformation, low per capita income accompanied by low product per worker (indicating low labour productivity) in both agricultural and non-agricultural sectors. The only exception is the State of Arunachal Pradesh where the per capita income and product per worker are relatively higher than the others in the group. There are nine states in this group including the most populous states of Uttar Pradesh and Bihar. This group accounts for close to 38% of the total population, the highest share among the four groups.

The rurality of employment is quite high in all but Mizoram. Except for the smaller states of Mizoram, Arunachal Pradesh and Meghalaya, all the remaining six states also belong to a category where the achievement in basic development indicators—as for example represented by the Human Development Index—is the least among other Indian states. The broad association between relatively high human development and structural transformation is something that also needs to be noted in this regional picture. Investment in human development creates favourable conditions in the form of increasing labour productivity as well as ability to seek out employment opportunities outside agriculture.

The overall picture, therefore, is one of partial structural transformation covering 15 states accounting for half the total population. Even here the six states in Group 2 continue to be low per capita income states that dim their transformative performance. However, the nine states reporting structural transformation with better economic performance give a partial picture of the nature of economic transformation under way in India. Three out of the four states in Group 3 without structural transformation but with relatively better economic performance are likely to join the Group 1 given their relatively lower dependence on agricultural sector for employment ranging from 52% for Andhra Pradesh (undivided), 56% for Sikkim and 58 for Himachal Pradesh. All these states also belong to a group of better performance in human development compared to the Group 4 states. However, it will take a much longer period of time to talk about a rural transformation as indicated by the rurality of employment.

There is nothing inherently wrong in depending on rural non-agricultural employment but the challenge here is one of generating adequate decent employment with higher labour productivity that will assure a decent standard of living to a majority of the people. That calls for a greater focus on the rural economy with a transformative developmental agenda.

5 The Social Dimension of Structural Transformation

In the discussion on the agrarian question in the Indian context, largely held within the Marxian framework, there is hardly any serious incorporation or factoring of the social dimension in terms of the entrenched ideology of social hierarchy. While this is often referred to as the 'caste factor', it transcends all religions in India and needs to be viewed as an ideology of 'social hierarchy' which is closely, if not perfectly, linked to economic inequality. In our earlier work, we have followed a five-fold classification to reflect the broad social hierarchy in the Indian society. The social groups are ST, SC, Muslim, Hindu-OBC and Others. In an overwhelming number of economic and development indicators, the last group is found to be on the top, followed by OBC, Muslim, SC and ST in a descending order (see Kannan 2019).

First the question of dependence on agriculture. In 1993–1994, only one social group, i.e. Muslim, had a major share of their workforce in non-agriculture. This could be due to the historical and traditional factors wherein Muslim communities were found to be in the artisanal and crafts and trading occupations with a significant

Table 4 Percentage share of workers in Agriculture and Non-Agriculture Sectors

	1993–1994		2011–2012	
	AG	NAG	AG	NAG
Rural + Urban				
ST	82.4	17.6	70.0	30.0
SC	71.1	28.9	48.0	52.0
Muslim	45.0	55.0	30.3	69.7
OBC			52.9	47.1
Others			38.1	61.9
OBC + Others	61.5	38.5	47.5	52.5
Rural				
ST	86.8	13.2	76.3	23.7
SC	80.4	19.6	59.6	40.4
Muslim	64.7	35.3	47.2	52.8
OBC			67.7	32.3
Others			64.7	35.3
OBC + Others	77.8	22.2	66.9	33.1
Urban				
ST	21.4	78.6	12.8	87.2
SC	18.4	81.6	7.3	96.7
Muslim	8.3	91.7	4.0	96.0
OBC			10.0	90.0
Others			3.9	96.1
OBC + Others	11.7	92.3	6.5	93.5

Source Computed from unit level data from 50th and 68th Rounds of NSS

presence in urban areas. By 2011–2012, we find that three social groups—Muslims, Others and SC—are no longer dependent on agriculture for majority employment. Therefore, there is a clear social dimension to the structural transformation (or lack of it in many states). It would, therefore, be interesting to examine the distribution of the incremental workforce during 1993–1994 and 2011–2012. The relevant findings are presented in Tables 4 and 5. The largest movement away from agriculture has been reported by SC, followed by Muslim and then by the combined group of Others and OBC.[6]

The movement of SC or Dalits away from agriculture is significant. Historically, they were the landless or land-poor and hence had to work mostly as attached labour in agriculture and related activities. The lack of gainful and regular employment opportunities in a fast-changing labour relations regime in agriculture could be one

[6]This combining is due to the non-availability of separate data for Hindu-OBC group in 1993–1994. Going by the separate data for these groups in 2011–2012, it would appear that it is the group of Others that has moved away from agriculture in a decisive sense.

Table 5 Distribution of additional workforce between 199–1934 and 2011–2012

Social group	AG	%	NAG	%	Total	%
OBC + Others	−7.68	−15.1	58.57	+115.1	50.89	100
Muslim	+2.13	+9.2	21.00	+90.8	23.11	100
SC	−6.82	−34.8	26.43	+134.8	19.61	100
ST	+1.52	+17.1	7.37	+82.9	8.89	100
Total	−10.85	−10.6	113.37	+110.6	102.52	100

Source Computed from unit level data from the 50 and 68th Rounds of NSS

reason for this faster movement. Another reason could be the new consciousness about their dignity coupled with the fact that agricultural work often begets very low wages as well as conditions of work that bear a mark of earlier subordinate status. The higher aspirations of the better educated younger generation could have also added to this movement.

The next group is that of the Muslim who have traditionally been largely, if not wholly, engaged in non-agricultural activities. They now have the lowest share of workers in agriculture at 30%.

The third is the combined group of Others and OBC with 48% of employment in agriculture. Separate data available for 2011–2012 show that the share of the socially advantaged group of Others is now only 38, mostly as the landed class, in agriculture, whereas a majority of 53% of OBC continue to be in agriculture. For the Others, the movement away from agriculture could be induced by better opportunities for employment with higher wages and security although it is by now politically recognized that there is a layer of economically poor among the socially advantaged grouped here as Others. To a lesser extent, this could also be the case for those belonging to OBC although it has a higher share of land-poor and hence labouring poor than the social group of Others.

Majority of OBCs continues to be in agriculture although that share is only marginally higher than 50%. It is the group of ST that is still largely dependent on agriculture with 70% of employment.

Therefore, the structural transformation in terms of the overall economy's major share of employment and income has a social dimension is mainly applicable to three social groups, i.e. the socially advantaged group of Others, Muslims and SCs. Of these, the first group has the lowest incidence of poverty while the other two have the second and third highest incidence of poverty (see Kannan 2019).

But this agrarian transition is only technical if we shift the focus from agriculture to the Rurality of Employment (see Table 6). While the three social groups of SC, Muslims and Others have moved out of agriculture their dependence on the rural economy is considerable. What it means is that their employment is mostly dependent on agriculture (located in rural or urban areas) and in rural non-agricultural employment. While there is a reduction in Rurality of Employment since 1993–94, its importance cannot be ignored. Here again the social group with the lowest dependence is that of Others (consisting of Upper caste Hindus, Jains, Sikhs, Christians

Table 6 Distribution of workers (%) in terms of rurality of employment

Soc group	Year	All AG	Rural NAG	Rurality
Others+OBC	1993–1994	61.55	16.73	78.27
	2011–2012	47.54	22.48	70.01
	Difference	−14.01	5.75	−8.26
Muslim	1993–1994	45.03	22.93	67.95
	2011–2012	30.26	32.15	62.41
	Difference	−14.76	9.22	−5.54
SC	1993–1994	71.11	16.70	87.81
	2011–2012	48.00	31.38	79.37
	Difference	−23.11	14.67	−8.44
ST	1993–1994	82.41	12.29	94.70
	2011–2012	70.09	21.35	91.44
	Difference	−12.33	9.06	−3.27
Total	1993–1994	64.05	16.82	80.87
	2011–2012	47.82	25.21	73.03
	Difference	−16.23	8.39	−7.84
OBC	2011–2012	52.91	23.99	76.89
Others	2011–2012	38.10	19.82	57.92

Source Computed from unit level data from the 50th and 68th Rounds of NSS

and all others except Muslim) with 58% of their employment. They are followed by Muslims (62%), OBC (77%), SC (79%) and ST (91%).

A mere shift of labour from agriculture to non-agriculture need not necessarily be a transition from low quality (including low wage) employment to good quality employment. At the higher level of the social hierarchy, the transition is backed by better initial conditions including assets, higher education and stronger social network. At the lower end, it could be a horizontal movement from one type of low quality work to another type. Table 7 is illustrative of this broad transition. There is a clear hierarchy in terms of educational attainment, employment status and wage earnings. The socially advantaged have the highest incidence of higher education resulting in a higher employment status (as Regular workers) and the highest wage income. The next is the OBC group followed by Muslim, SC and then the ST.

6 Structural Transformation and Agrarian Transition

These findings of the spatial and socio-economic characteristics of the structural transformation in the Indian economy need to be placed and understood in the larger

Table 7 Educational attainment, labour status and wage income by social group

Soc Group	Secondary level of education or above (% to total wage workers)		Labour Status among all wage workers				Wage income per household (in Rs)	
			% of Regular Workers		% of Casual Workers			
	1993–1994	2011–2012	1993–1994	2011–2012	1993–1994	2011–2012	1993–1994	2011–2012
Others + OBC	24.7	39.4	40.0	47.2	60.0	52.8	22079	139261
SAG	NA	57.3	NA	69.0	NA	31.0		199440
OBC	NA	29.9	NA	35.6	NA	64.4		103148
Muslim	11.2	19.6	30.3	36.4	69.7	63.6	15363	87622
SC	6.2	18.8	14.5	24.2	85.5	75.8	13634	86759
ST	5.4	15.1	12.3	18.4	87.7	81.6	13620	83106
All Popn	16.4	29.6	29.2	37.4	70.8	62.6	18707	96113

Source Computed from unit level data from the 50th and68th Rounds of NSS

context of the process of economic change in general and the discussions on the agrarian question in particular.

Indian agriculture during the colonial period faced intense stagnation as a result of the colonial policy of rack-renting and absence of any land reforms in favour of poor peasants and agricultural labourers. Therefore, agriculture at the dawn of independence warranted special attention by way of land reforms and public investment to create the necessary infrastructure such as irrigation and related collective goods.

Independence came with the launching of a national economic development plan and a process of state-directed development path. While agriculture received some attention in terms of public investment, price support, subsidies, greater access to institutional credit and so on, land reforms were mainly confined to the ending of big landlordism with very little redistribution of land. Agricultural labourers, by and large landless, received very little attention except in the form of fixation of minimum wages that was observed more in its breach than implementation.

At the sub-national level, agriculture received some attention from the state governments given the fact that it was a state (provincial) subject under the Constitution. Here again the focus was on farmers—small and big cultivators—and not much on agricultural labourers with some rare exceptions like Kerala. Incidence of absolute poverty was highest among agricultural labourers followed by small peasants often referred to as marginal and small farmers.

While land distribution continued to be skewed, the proportion of medium and large farmers was small. But they stood to benefit from the Green Revolution that was launched in the mid-1960s in several parts of the country, if not all. Farmers' movements also received political attention and this resulted in minimum support prices for food grains as well as several input subsidies as in fertilizers and electricity. Farm mechanization took place but was uneven.

The third phase is the emergence of a neoliberal economic policy regime and the concomitant emergence of a neoliberal state. However, the compulsions of electoral politics demanded concessions and compromises from the state to continue to pay some attention to basic developmental challenges such as education and health and selected forms of poverty alleviation measures. At the regional level some state governments, dictated by regional political factors, paid relatively more attention to welfarist policies that eased the poverty situation. Later, this was also followed by the national governments dictated by electoral political compulsions and hence remained inadequate and often lagging in implementation.

The emergence of the neoliberal policy regime witnessed a steady erosion of the importance given to the agricultural sector in general and rural economy in particular. The long term developmental objectives suffered a setback. Public investment in agriculture declined and rural development was mostly welfarist (limited provisioning for manual employment known as MG-NREGS, extremely limited, almost miniscule, financial subsidies for housing for the poor, etc.). Despite some form of minimum support prices, many agricultural raw materials and commodities were allowed to be imported under the guise of trade liberalization, and access to bank credit was diluted in the name of agriculture. More and more dependence on the market created a situation whereby land under food grains was diverted to more remunerative cash crops and industrial raw material crops such as cotton. The entry of big corporations, both national and multinational, in the market for seed, pesticides and other agricultural inputs increased the risks of farmers. Farmers distress got manifested in the extreme measure of suicides that took place in several states (see, e.g. Reddy and Mishra 2009). For a while, farmers' movements of the earlier kind got weakened but of late new movements started emerging demanding more positive state intervention.

All these and more in an emerging and essentially neoliberal state was of course taking place in the larger global context of the failure of the socialist experiment and the steady push for neoliberal economic regimes on a global scale. Neoliberal policies were consciously promoted and pushed into the developing countries by the IMF, World Bank and the WTO controlled largely and decisively by the rich Western capitalist democracies.

From the point of the agrarian question of development of capitalism in the Indian economy, there was very little differentiation within the peasantry although regional variations are significant. If we take a long-run period of more than six decades, what we observe is the continuing inequality in land distribution, an increase in the share of small and marginal farmers as a result of further fragmentation of land and a decline in the share of agricultural labourers. Given the slow pace of transformation of agriculture, employment opportunities declined leading to a shift of wage labour from agriculture to non-agriculture and the absorption of additional labour into the non-agricultural economies in rural and urban areas, more rural than urban.[7]

The shift of wage labour from agriculture to non-agriculture is largely a horizontal shift from low-paid insecure work (informal employment) in agriculture to low-paid (but higher than agriculture) insecure work in non-agriculture. Given the increasing educational levels and some expansion in urban services, there has been some increase in regular work—some employment security—but they also tended to be of informal kind with no guarantee of employment.

From the point of the agrarian question, the emergence of a strong capitalist global framework with neoliberal economic policies is a significant development. The ascendancy of finance capital was a new development in such a scenario. In developing countries like India, it benefitted a small segment consisting of big capitalists, the middle class with educational capabilities and the political and bureaucratic class that saw the emergence of new opportunities for rent seeking on an unprecedented scale. This also led to a system of crony capitalism.

Therefore, it is not the internal development of capitalism within agriculture that was unfolding. It is the power of the new emergent capitalism globally and its national variation that all those dependent on agriculture as well as the rural economy faced. The balance of forces tilted in favour of the urban in general and big capitalists, educated middle class, those engaged in speculative activities as in land and stock market and those in the financial sector in particular.

[7]Between 1993–94 and 2011–2012 rural employment in non-agriculture increased from 62 to 113 million (82%) and the urban non-agriculture from 71 to 127 million (79%).

Small scale producers and small traders including those who are nothing but disguised wage workers as in the case of at least one-third of those classified as self-employed in India also suffered in varying degrees along with farmers and rural and urban labourers. It is this phenomenon that has led to the stubborn figure of 92% of India's workers as informal, in the sense of insecure and largely casually employed, workers.

Therefore, the agrarian question in India from the point of its working people—farmers and labourers—is a subset of a larger employment question in a fast-growing large economy manifested as jobless growth and informalization of even existing employment resulting in the persistence of poverty and vulnerability despite a measure of progress due to welfarist programmes. The question of informality of employment, its social correlates, and high incidence of poverty and vulnerability have been documented and discussed in detail in NCEUS (2008). Strategies, policies and measures to transform such a scenario have been discussed in NCEUS (2009). However, the adoption of such a strategy of levelling up was highly constrained by the political economy of power that dominated the neoliberal economic reforms in India. Surveying the persistence and dynamic of this vast mass of small producers referred to as petty commodity production (PCP), Harriss-White (2012) concludes that PCP in India survives by multiplication and does not lead to more advanced forms of accumulation. It is worth quoting her diagnosis here.

> "Relations of exchange, of reproduction, the behaviour of social institutions in which PCP is embedded and contradictory relations with the state all contrive to prevent accumulation trajectories from PCP from being anything but a rare event. PCP may sometimes be the unintended outcome of development projects, but it is more commonly the outcome of capitalist development, here to stay, as modern a kind of capitalism as the corporation, but with an incoherent set of economic projects imposed on it and developed from it, and with a plurality of political expressions which serve to disenfranchise it. One next step for scholars would be to make a detailed mapping of the economic sectors, ecological-political regions, technologies, exchange relations and trajectories of multiplication associated with PCP.
>
> Agriculture is leaking labour as never before, while capital-biased plans are laid for the hitherto most labour-absorptive sectors of the non-farm economy. What is to be done, what can be done, for the common man and woman who are petty producers in India today are most important development questions with different kinds of politics: whether and how to release constraints through a new wave of politically engineered collective activity, through the destruction of obstacles to accumulation, through the destruction of PCP itself, through ignoring work but expanding social protection to lower the risks of reproduction or by other means that are at present uncelebrated in the literature that has been reviewed here. It would seem that the stakes are high" (2012: 144–5).

7 Conclusions

After a long drawn-out process of economic change the Indian economy is technically on a trajectory of structural transformation. However, it is far from the expected process of transformation through an expansion of income and employment in manufacturing but from a combination of activities under the rubric of non-agricultural activities. Increasing domination of market transactions has not led to any clear cut trajectory of development of capitalism in agriculture per se but there is agreement in the overall process of capitalist economic relations in the economy as a whole. The increasing migration of labour from agriculture to non-agriculture and the rural-urban continuum associated with it (Reddy 2017) that was earlier subsumed under 'footloose labour' (Breman 1996) makes any analysis of changes within agriculture quite challenging. Given the dependence of labour on the rurality of employment, the force of structural transformation looks quite weak. From a development point of view such a process has been noted for countries in South Asia in sharp contrast to countries in East and Southeast Asia (Islam 2017). From a policy perspective, this ought to form the basis for a more focused approach to rural economic development to lift it from its lower level equilibrium to a higher level equilibrium.

The second agrarian question of accumulation in agriculture, though not part of our enquiry, has also not been supported by empirical studies in the sense of the availability of a surplus for industrialization. The source of accumulation for rich farmers seems to have diversified with both agricultural and non-agricultural production as well as combining with trading and money lending (see, e.g. Harriss-White 2012; Lerche 2013). But the neoliberal globalization has also laid out the ground for accumulation in agriculture by corporate capital through dispossession of land of the peasantry (in the name of Special Economic Zones, mining and so on), increasing commercialisation of inputs like seeds and fertilizer and often engaging in marketing of agricultural produce through corporate-owned retail stores. On the other hand, the low level of income of marginal and small farmers and the low level of wages for agricultural labourers drive them also to diversify their sources of income. This has raised some to conclude whether the agrarian transition has bypassed the Indian farmers (Lerche 2013) as formulated by its classical question. This was in response to an investigation of the thesis of Henry Bernstein, an early participant in the debate on agrarian transition, who took the position that the agrarian question in the Global South is no longer relevant given the neoliberal globalization and its ability to find non-agricultural sources for accumulation/industrialization (Bernstein 1996 and 2006).[8] But broadly agreeing with Bernstein, Lerche has in fact argued for a 'formulation that allows for a continued investigation into the actual processes of agrarian change that clearly are taking place in India' (2013: 400). However, contributors to the volume edited by Mohanty (2016) are more cautious and have

[8]In his 'Revisiting Agrarian Transition', Bernstein elaborates his thesis by recognizing the complexities in the current process of globalization and its impact on agrarian countries and concludes as follows: 'The challenges to analysis that the diversity and complexity of current agrarian change present cannot be grasped adequately by regarding inherited notions of transition as simply false 'predictions', hence discarding what they offer to inform investigation of current realities, above all concerning class formation, class struggle and how, and how much, accumulation (and what kinds of accumulation) proceeds. In short, much of their approach to framing the central questions of agrarian political economy remains valid, even if some of the answers provided might be found wanting as historical interpretation or applications to contemporary realities or both. Indeed, this is simply to recognize the demand of grasping how capitalism changes across all its spaces from global divisions of labour and flows of capital and commodities, through vastly different national economies to similarly diverse countrysides and agrarian structures' (2016: 85).

argued that the terms of reference of the agrarian question are still relevant although they recognize the change in the larger external and the internal situation. Surveying some of the recent studies relating to the agrarian question in India, Reddy (2016) concludes that the process of capitalist development in Indian agriculture as part of a larger process of capitalist development has great relevance for the understanding of agrarian transition although the question of agriculture as a source of capital for industrialization may have lost its significance.

Given the interlinking of agriculture and non-agriculture for employment and the persistence of small producers on the one hand and the overall strategy of neoliberal globalization for cheapening the cost of labour on the other, the importance of an alliance between peasantry (including the agricultural labourers) and the wage labour and self-employed in the vast informalized segment in non-agriculture (what Harriss-White refers to as PCP) has become all the more crucial. This perhaps is a powerful question among the three agrarian questions (referred to in the beginning) that continues to have a great relevance. It will have to address the basic questions of right to work, education, health and housing, and social security along with work-based rights of minimum wages and decent conditions of work. However, such a process of sustained alliance building is also not quite evident in the Indian political landscape.

From our analysis of the partial nature of India's structural transformation with weak foundations, an important lesson from a developmental point of view is the need for a concerted strategy of employment-led development of the rural economy. This in our view calls for a structural transformation agenda in both agriculture and non-agriculture in the rural economy with decent employment and higher productivity and income. Under what conditions such a transformation becomes feasible would be an interesting question to ask from the standpoint of the debate on agrarian transition.

Appendix

See Table 8.

Table 8 The compositional picture of labour shifting away from agriculture in rural and urban areas in India

Category	Employment (million)				Real wages (Rs./day at 2004-2005 prices)	
Rural						
	1993–1994	%	2011–2012	%	1993–1994	2011–2012
A. Agriculture	**226.31**	**100.0**	**216.21**	**100.0**		
1. Regular workers	2.96	1.3	1.53	0.7	41.14	84.86
2. Casual workers	86.37	38.2	72.74	33.6	33.64	67.80
3. Wage labour (1 + 2)	89.33	39.5	74.27	34.3		
4. Self-employed	136.98	60.5	141.94	65.7		
B. Non-agriculture	**62.04**	**100.0**	**118.83**	**100.0**		
1. Regular workers	15.59	25.1	26.87	22.6	104.84	170.04
2. Casual workers	15.38	24.8	44.89	37.8	48.90	91.59
3. Wage labour (1 + 2)	30.97	49.9	71.76	60.4		
4. Self-employed	31.07	50.1	47.07	39.6		
Urban						
A. Agriculture	**9.92**	**100.0**	**9.18**	100.0		
1. Regular workers	0.32	3.2	0.36	3.9	93.92	213.92
2. Casual workers	3.70	37.3	2.75	30.0	45.00	78.88
3. Wage labour (1 + 2)	4.02	40.5	3.11	33.9		
4. Self-employed	5.90	59.5	6.07	66.1		
B. Non-agriculture	**70.56**	**100.0**	**127.12**	**100.0**		
1. Regular workers	31.54	44.7	58.21	45.8	151.50	257.19
2. Casual workers	10.85	15.4	17.71	13.9	61.55	99.80
3. Wage labour (1 + 2)	42.39	60.1	75.92	59.7		
4. Self-employed	28.17	39.9	51.20	40.3		

Source Computed from the 50th and 68th Rounds of NSS

References

Bernstein, H. (1996). Agrarian questions then and now. *The Journal of Peasant Studies, 24*(1–2), 22–59.

Bernstein, H. (2006). Is there an agrarian question in the 21st century? *Canadian Journal of Development Studies, 27*(4), 449–460.

Breman, J. (1996). *Footloose labour: Working in India's informal economy*. Cambridge, New York and Melbourn: Cambridge University Press.

Breman, J., Guerin, I., & Prakash, A. (2009). *India's unfree workforce: Of bondage old and new*. New Delhi: Oxford University Press.

Harriss-White, B. (2012). Capitalism and the common man: Peasants and petty production in Africa and South Asia. *Agrarian South: Journal of Political Economy, 1*(2), 109–160.

Islam, R. (2017). 'Structural transformation and alternative pathways to the lewis turning point'. In Reddy and Sarap (Eds.).

Kannan, K. P. (2014). *interrogating inclusive growth: Poverty and inequality in India.* New Delhi and Oxon: Routledge.

Kannan, K. P. (2019). *India's socvial inequality as durable Inequality,* Centre for Development Studies, Working Paper No. 489, June, Thiruvananthapuram.

Lewis, A. W. (1954). 'Economic development with unlimited supplies of labour', Manchester School, Vol. 22.

Lewis, A. W. (1955). *The theory of economic growth.* London: Allen and Unwin.

Lerche, J. (2013). The agrarian question in neoliberal India': Agrarian transition bypassed. *Journal of Agrarian Change, 13*(3), 382–404.

Mohanty, B. B. (Ed.). (2016). *Critical perspectives on agrarian transition: India in the global debate.* Oxon and New York: Routledge.

NCEUS (National Commission for Enterprises kin the Unorganised Sector). (2008), *Report on conditions of work and promotion of livelihoods in the unorganised sector.* New Delhi: Academic Foundation.

NCEUS. (2009). *The challenge of employment in India: An informal economy perspective.* New Delhi: Academic Foundation.

Papola, T. S. & Kannan, K. P. (2017), *Towards an India wage report.* ILO Asia-Pacific Working Paper Series, ILO DWT for South Asia and Country Office for India, New Delhi.

Reddy, D. N., & Mishra, S. (Eds.). (2009). *Agrarian crisis in India.* New Delhi: Oxford University Press.

Reddy, D. N. (2016). Contours of the agrarian question: Towards political question of 'the peasantry' in contemporary India in Mohanty (Ed.).

Reddy, D. N., & Sarap, K. (Eds.). (2017). *Rural labour mobility in times of structural transformation.* Singapore: Palgrave Macmillan.

Failing Agriculture and Frazzled Farmers: The Inside Story of India's Most Populous States—UP and Maharashtra

Rakesh Raman and Khursheed Ahmad Khan

Abstract Distress of agriculture and disquietude of farmers remain a matter of grave concern for the Indian economy. The deceleration in growth of production and productivity, increase in unviability of agriculture, decimal rate of growth of farmers' income, steep rise in their indebtedness, surge in risk and uncertainty caused by frequent crop failures, etc. have acquired all India character and brought the sector to the brink and made life tough for those dependent on it. The popular debate whether it is crisis of the sector or that of the peasantry seems futile and infructuous as the present crisis engulfs both and its conceptualization and interventions required to negotiate it warrants integrating them. The present write up captures crisis of agriculture by developing an index incorporating indicators that reflect situation of agriculture and the agriculturists in an effort to establish that condition is really alarming, and the crisis of agriculture is slowly engulfing the whole nation. The paper uses secondary data collected from Directorate of Economics and Statistics, Department of Agriculture and Cooperation, Ministry of Agriculture, Government of India and different States and chooses and normalizes indicators using UNDP methodology, to first compute state-level crisis of agriculture for fourteen major states of India and then at the regional and district level for two most populous states of India Uttar Pradesh and Maharashtra. It ranks the geographical units in terms of the index to establish that though crisis is more acute in states like Tamil Nadu, Kerala, Karnataka, Maharashtra, etc. but low-intensity crisis exists also in states like UP, Bihar, MP where things are normally stated to be in order. Further, based on primary survey conducted of over one thousand farming households of different farm size and social categories in three worst affected districts each for UP and Maharashtra, the crisis of agriculture is captured at the farmers level for more comprehensive set of indicators using principal component analysis. A simple linear regression has been used to determine the respective weights of individual indicators

R. Raman (✉)
Department of Economics, Banaras Hindu University, Varanasi 221005, India
e-mail: rraman88@gmail.com

K. A. Khan
Department of Economics, Samastipur College, Samastipur, Bihar, India
e-mail: khursheedak86@gmail.com

N. K. Mishra (ed.), *Development Challenges of India After Twenty Five Years of Economic Reforms*, India Studies in Business and Economics,
https://doi.org/10.1007/978-981-15-8265-3_17

in construction of the composite index. The work concludes that agriculture and farmers face high- and low-intensity crisis, respectively, in states of Maharashtra and Uttar Pradesh, however, the intensity within a particular state varies across regions with acute problem in some regions and relatively relaxed status in some other. It explores the inter-connectedness between level of development of a region and position of farmers and agriculture there and finds no perceptible flow. A deeper investigation of the problem at the farmers' level helps the authors to conclude that the problem of crisis has social orientation, i.e. it varies across farmer caste groups (with high intensity of crisis among farmers belonging to the lower caste) and landholding size (with graver problem for small and marginal farmers). The paper calls for decentralised policy interventions to tackle region-specific issues and adoption of farmer centric policy to resurrect the sagging spirit of frazzled farmers and rekindle a hope in them that agriculture is not failing and has a distinct future as a profession.

1 Introduction

Among a vast majority of factors that are threatening to derail the onward march of the Indian economy and draw red in its report card of inclusiveness, precarious position of agriculture and deep affliction of farming community are significant. The deceleration in growth of production and productivity in agriculture, increase in its unviability, decimal rate of growth of farmers' income and steep rise in their indebtedness, surge in risk and uncertainty caused by frequent crop failures, troubles for the peasantry, etc. are no longer characteristic features of a handful of states like Maharashtra, Kerala, etc. but are engulfing even the northern Indian states of Punjab, Haryana and Uttar Pradesh—traditionally viewed as epitomes of prosperous agriculture. The failing agriculture and frazzled farmers facing a deluge of problems have together created an environment of gloom and desolation in rural India raising serious doubts over the sustainability of the growth momentum.

The troubles of the agricultural sector and tribulations of farmers, have, of late, attracted the attention of academia as well as government, and agriculture that had lost charm in the neo-liberal wave has suddenly become the cynosure of public debate. There are, however, three very crucial aspects that are either missing or have been overlooked by those actively engaged in the field: First, the debate relating to 'sector' versus 'farmers' as the focal point of policymaking still remains unsettled. This has resulted in great theoretical confusion as to the nature of present crisis being 'agrarian' or 'agricultural' and has prevented us from understanding whether the solution lies in measures to increase production and productivity in agriculture, or in efforts to raise farmers' income and improve their well-being. This confusion has reduced the efficacy of policy interventions immensely. Second, there has been a tendency to pay attention only to the troubled regions where the problem has reached alarming proportions and neglect regions where on the surface things look 'okay.' Hence, while there exists a plethora of work pertaining to problems of farmers and agriculture for states such as Maharashtra (Vidharbha), Kerala and Andhra Pradesh, the issues of typically agricultural states like Uttar Pradesh (U.P.), Bihar, etc. have barely drawn attention of both policymakers and researchers. This has led to the popular perception that agriculture and farmers in these states are better off and prima facie face no threat. Thirdly, there has been a tendency to go in for sweeping generalizations based on macro data as well as fascination for meta-analysis without seeking access to the inside story of farmers. Conclusions have been drawn on the basis of statistics that are not so appropriate and indicators that capture only limited dimensions. This has tended to seriously undermine the validity of findings as also the success of policies based on such studies.

Such serious omissions and commission make it imperative to have a comprehensive study on the problems of both farmers and the agricultural sector, based on primary first-hand interactions with the farmers, for states in which the problem is reaching a crescendo as well as those where it is at a nascent stage. It is precisely this that the present paper attempts to do. The paper is structured into four sections: Section-I introduces the conceptual 'farmer' versus 'agriculture' question and based on extant literature attempts to establish whether the problem should be branded as 'agrarian' or an 'agricultural' crisis. The section also briefly mentions the methodology adopted in the present study. Section-II provides a macro perspective of the crisis scenario by capturing the scenario at the state level for fourteen major states of India and at the regional and district levels for two chosen states viz. Uttar Pradesh and Maharashtra. Section-III is based on a primary survey conducted in over one thousand farming households in the two states in an attempt to capture, measure and analyze the extent of problems faced by agriculture as well as farmers. The final section sums up the discussion and stresses the need to have a farmer centric and region-based approach to alleviate the problem.

2 Concept and Methods

Contemporary literature is though aghast mourning the failure of agriculture and grieving the plight of farmers in India (Gulati et al. 2003; Rao 2009; Siddiqui 2015; Ghosh 2016; Raman and Khan 2018), yet is divided on the nature of the crisis and causes of its origin. Assadi (2006) has made an excellent job of classifying the debate. He finds four distinct strands of thought of which two appear dominant and appealing. The first of these treats the present problem as a problem of the agricultural sector and calls it 'agricultural crisis.' It puts emphasis on the problems of the 'sector' and not so much on farmers, and supports sector-specific strategy. The second view treats the present crisis as an 'agrarian crisis,' i.e. as a problem of the farming community/peasantry (which might as a supplementary effect affect the agricultural sector). This is the Marxist critique, spearheaded by Patnaik (2003) and others, which locates the crisis in the larger context of ambiguous path of capitalist development in India manifested in the neo-liberal policy or imperialist globalization that has linked the poor unprotected peasantry with the global market. This approach calls for steps to handle the problem of marginal and small farmers. We briefly discuss the debate as under.

Agricultural Crisis—The first approach puts emphasis on the 'sector' and the faulty way in which it has evolved. It traces the root of crisis to the 1980s when the terms of trade started going against agriculture (Bose 1981; Rudra 1982; Balagopal 1988) and policies with urban bias began to dominate the state policies with farming gradually appearing as a losing proposition; a phenomenon that intensified after the launch of the economic reforms. It highlights factors ailing the agricultural sector picking up four for exclusive emphasis viz. deceleration in growth of production and productivity in agriculture, decline in the capacity of agriculture to absorb labour, fall in profitability of cultivation and increase in the indebtedness and vulnerability of farmers that have discouraged investment in agriculture. These, the view claims, are sector-specific issues and affect all farming groups simultaneously.

Deceleration in the growth of agriculture started from mid-1990s and increase in input use efficiency have been highlighted as the chief worry for agriculture by many such as Sidhu (2002), Chand et al. (2007), Chand and Parappurathu (2011), etc. Pillai (2007), Bhalla and Singh (2009), Reddy and Mishra (2009), Barah and Sirohi (2011), etc. support this view. Deshpande (2002), Galab et al. (2006) examined how the growth rate of production of important food crops drastically slowed down over the years, particularly after the 2000s calling it a crisis situation. The deceleration of agricultural growth in the 1990s complicated the employment issue in rural India resulting in livelihood crisis. Agriculture that provided a safe refuge to people in rural areas, has failed miserably in this endeavour in recent times. Bhalla and Hazell (2003), Sharma (2005), Pillai (2007) and others have seen falling employment elasticity of agricultural output as a symbol of crisis.

Falling profitability of agriculture has been highlighted as a major crisis factor that is leading to the deceleration of agricultural growth. Sen and Bhatia (2004) argue that there have been significant changes in the structure of costs of production for more than two decades, reflecting the changes in the technology, and relative prices of inputs that have made it difficult for the farmers to recover the cost from sale of produce. Mishra (2007) and Ramasamy and Kumar (2007) have highlighted low or negative profitability of cotton growers in different Indian states. There are a number of other studies that have attempted a detailed analysis of profitability of different crops in relation to the cost of cultivation over a period of time (Kamlakar and Narayanamoorthy 2003; Deshpande and Arora 2010; Sainath 2010). Falling profitability and unviability of agriculture coupled with increasing uncertainty has increased the indebtedness of farmers and reduced their capacity to invest and bring about improvement in agriculture (Deshpande 2002; Reddy and Mishra 2009; Deshpande and Arora 2010). The combined effect of the two has resulted in reduced private investment in agriculture, promoted reverse tenancy and made agricultural technology inaccessible to the bulk of farmers thereby reinforcing deceleration of agriculture.

The 'agricultural crisis' argument thus calls for specific policies to resurrect the sector such as raising production and productivity, developing the non-farm sector to provide subsidiary livelihood opportunity to farmers, price support and marketing system to give to the farmers their due and, of late, waiving loans of farmers. Specific issues concerning specific groups of farmers are not given much credence and it is hoped that through macro-economic intervention at the top, things could be made to improve for the sector and everybody associated with it.

Agrarian Crisis—The second view associates crisis with the agrarian structure of the economy and calls it 'agrarian crisis.' It looks at the crisis as a crisis of certain agrarian classes, arising out of the relationship of these classes to other classes. The view claims that neo-liberal policies have surreptitiously but consciously promoted monopoly capitalism making the state withdraw and focus on protecting the interest of capitalists leaving the deprived sections including peasantry at the mercy of capitalists who have exploited them. It has forced the government to follow a policy of deliberate price deflation in agriculture causing terms of trade to move against the peasantry and giving undue advantages to the capitalists (Patnaik 2006). Theoretically speaking, as monopoly capitalism develops peasantry gradually withdraws acreage from the subsistence requirement and shifts to production for the metropolitan market. As they move to commercial/cash/hybrid crops they incur heavy losses due to uncertainty and the high costs involved.

The Green Revolution initiated the evolution of capitalist mode of production in India, a trend that was reinforced by neo-liberal policy (Assadi 1998; Ramachandran 2010; Basole and Basu 2011). The agrarian structure created by the capitalist mode of production has affected agriculture in many ways. It has opposed institutional reforms (Sharma 2005) and resulted in intermediaries monopolizing land ownership and extracting rent from both recorded and unrecorded tenants. It has also resulted in increasing the pace of marginalization. As marginalization has taken place, it has complicated the fortune of agriculture and agriculturists in more ways than one. Just to point a few—First, resource-constrained small and marginal farmers have become unable to invest in modern inputs resulting in lower productivity and income. Second, the non-viability of the size of holdings has compelled peasants to undertake commercial crops characterized by market-led instability and uncertainty. Third, the land market has gone in favour of large owners. The socially deprived and marginal farmers are being forced to sell their uneconomical size of land at throwaway prices to landlords. Fourth, the small farmer group has faced some constraints in the access to institutional credit, subsidies, and because of illiteracy, ignorance and poverty it is not able to reap the benefit of government schemes that are actually meant for them.

The 'agrarian crisis' view thus highlights the problem from the side of the majority small and marginal farmers brandishing the capitalist mode of production and monopoly capitalism as the chief factor making the farmers frazzled and pushing them to the brink. It calls for reversal of neo-liberalism, a more active and pro-peasant role of the government rather than steps to boost the agricultural sector per se.

Summing up—A cursory look at the *agriculture versus agriculturist debate* tells us that the *real debate is related to the primacy of class relations and peasant concern in the leftist approach and critical importance being attached to the agriculture sector* *in the first approach.* While the leftist approach claims that so long as agriculture is unviable, increasing output won't be possible and if possible, won't solve the problem of farmers. Therefore, it won't be sustainable. The other approach advocates a comprehensive long-term growth strategy for agriculture which, it hopes, would ultimately trickle down to benefit the farmers. Though there is no denial of the fact that the agricultural policies in the nation over the years have created a conflict between agriculture and farmers, especially the small and marginal ones, and made agriculture an unviable occupation for the bulk of them, yet it would be wrong to say that just by addressing the concern of small and marginal farmers the present crisis can be effectively handled and that the agricultural sector can be put back on track and vice versa. Economic reforms are irreversible in nature and there is no question of completely going back on neo-liberalism. International experience shows that agriculture has witnessed a robust growth and the farming community has prospered even when nations have adopted 'neo-liberal' policies. Working blindly in favour of peasantry would compel us to adopt steps that might go against the interest of poor and the vulnerable urban population. *The present crisis is not just a crisis of peasantry or agrarian crisis*; it is part of a broader crisis that engulfs the entire agricultural sector. We prefer to call it the **Crisis of Agriculture**. We end this section by concluding that the present crisis is the crisis of the agriculture that has two facets—crisis of the agricultural sector, and crisis of the peasants who are dependent on it; it is neither the first nor the second but a combination of the two.

3 Methodology and Tools

The study measures the crisis of agriculture at the macro level for fourteen major states of India and regions and districts of two chosen states UP and Maharashtra. Based on the primary survey of 1080 farmers of these states, it also explores the ground reality. Availability of suitable indicators and their comparability across states worked as a major hindrance in the choice of appropriate indicators for capturing the crisis of agriculture at the macro level. It forced the study to take only four indicators (shown in Table 1). The indicators though do not give very reliable quantitative estimate of the crisis, yet are able to supply the general trend and ranking of states, regions and districts. The primary data analysis, however, does not cause such problem and comprehensive and suitable indicators have been easily generated and used.

The state-level data for the indicators have been taken from the Directorate of Economics and Statistics, Department of Agriculture and Cooperation, Ministry of Agriculture, Government of India, while district-level data have been taken from the Ministry of Agriculture of the respective states. In order to neutralize the effect of year to year fluctuations in agriculture the study has taken data for the triennium. For the state-level index data for the triennium ending TE 2011 has been taken, while for district-level crisis index of two triennium years—triennium ending in the year 2004 (TE04) and triennium ending in the year 2015 TE2015 have been included. Figures

Table 1 List of indicators used to capture the crisis of agriculture

S.N.	Used at both macro and micro-level	S.N.	Used only at micro-level
1	Land condition of farmers-cropping intensity	5	Access and quality of modern technology used
2	Yield of major crops	6	Dwindling livelihood opportunities
3	Indebtedness of farmers	7	Unviability of agriculture
3.1	Per hectare outstanding loan	7.1	Profitability of Cultivation
3.2	Debt asset ratio	7.2	Percentage of Expenditure Covered by Income from Agricultural Activities
3.3	Debt income ratio		
4	Net per capita availability of food grains		

Source Primary survey

for the new millennium only have been included as the situation of agriculture has worsened at a fast pace during about this time only. For the computation of crisis index at macro level, HDI methodology has been used.

For primary survey, data for the chosen indicators have been generated through the survey of farming households. Multi-stage stratified random sampling method has been used. Resource constraint forced the study to omit some regions and choose three regions each from the two states. The omission, however, does not cause much worry as the omitted 'Central Region' of U.P. does not have distinguishing agricultural feature, and 'Greater Mumbai' and 'Konkan' in Maharashtra are hardly agricultural. The first stage was choice of districts. For this all the districts of U.P. and Maharashtra were ranked separately in terms of crisis index for the two trienniums 2004 and 2015 and from each region the district with maximum deterioration (in terms of crisis indicated by its rank) was chosen. In the second stage, from each district three blocks were chosen by ranking blocks on the basis of block level agricultural development index (developed for the purpose). This has been done to capture the impact of agricultural development on crisis of agriculture. Hence, from each district agriculturally the most advanced block, the most backward block and the one in the middle were chosen. In the third stage, from each block on random basis one village was chosen. Thus, from each state three districts, nine blocks and nine villages were chosen. Table 2 shows the list of districts, blocks and villages chosen for the study. The final stage was selection of farming households. This was based on proportional stratified random sampling: farming households belonging to each class of farmers—marginal, small, medium, etc. were chosen so as to have an idea about the relationship between size of land holding and crisis of agriculture. Sample size was a major worry and resources forced the researchers to make a compromise here so it was decided to take 60 samples from every village. Thus, altogether 1080 samples (three villages from each district x sixty samples x three districts = 540 samples each from the two states).

Table 2 List of chosen regions, districts, blocks and villages

Uttar Pradesh				Maharashtra			
Region	**District**	**Block**	**Village**	**Region**	**District**	**Block**	**Village**
Western	**Meerut**	Mawana Kalan	Mawana Khurd	**Western**	**Kolhapur**	Karvir	Wadange
		Rajpura	Masuri			Kagal	Bidri
		Sarurpur Khurd	Dabathuwa			Bhudargarh	Gargoti
Bundelkhand	**Jalaun**	Jalaun	Bhitara	**Marathwada**	**Parbhani**	Parbhani	Shingnapur
		Dakore	Act			Gangakhed	SuppaTunda
		Kadaura	Atta			Jintur	Bori
Eastern	**Kushi**	Hata	Tharuadih	**Vidharbha**	**Yavatmal**	Arni	Jawala
		Tamkuhi	Gauri Abrahim			Wani	Dahegaoan
		Dudahi	Rakwa Dulma Patti			Zari Zamni	Wadange

Source Field study

4 Failing Agriculture and Frazzled Farmers: A Macro Perspective

The growth process of Indian economy has seen progressive worsening of the agricultural sector with time. The crisis of agriculture that started from southern states has taken a pan India character with only the intensity varying. Based on the indicators mentioned in Table 1 and the method mentioned above, crisis of agriculture index has been computed for major states. Table 3 mentions the result. Different states have been ranked in terms of crisis and have been divided into different categories viz. very high, high, moderate, low and very low based on the index score. Higher index value in the table reflects higher level of crisis.

Table 3 clearly reflects that perilous form of the crisis exists in Tamil Nadu, Kerala, Karnataka, Andhra Pradesh and Maharashtra where the intensity is very high (0.650 and above). However, preliminary signs of lingering crisis of low intensity are noticeable in the northern states, i.e. Punjab, Haryana and Uttar Pradesh. We can

Table 3 Crisis index across fourteen major Indian states

Category	State	Crisis index	Rank	Category	State	Crisis index	Rank
Group-'A' Very High > 0.650	Tamil Nadu	0.746	1	Group 'C' Moderate 0.448–0.548	Bihar	0.475	10
	Kerala	0.717	2				
	Karnataka	0.673	3				
	Andhra Pradesh	0.672	4		West Bengal	0.468	11
	Maharashtra	0.668	5	Group 'D' Low 0.347–0.447	Uttar Pradesh	0.439	12
Group 'B' High 0.549–0.649	Rajasthan	0.575	6				
	Orissa	0.556	7	Group 'E' Very Low 0.346 & Below	Haryana	0.341	13
	Madhya Pradesh	0.556	8		Punjab	0.232	14
	Gujarat	0.549	9				

Source Authors' computation from secondary data

broadly draw three very important conclusions here—First, crisis of agriculture is an all India phenomenon, only its intensity varies across states. Second, the crisis is more intense in southern India than the northern states which have low index scores on this count. Third, though the factors initiating and intensifying the crisis might vary among states, most of them suffer from some common ailments like high cost, problem in realizing remunerative prices and indebtedness.

The study has chosen India's two most populous states Maharashtra and Uttar Pradesh for a detailed analysis. While Maharashtra represents in some loose manner western and southern India where the intensity of the crisis is high and farmer suicide common, Uttar Pradesh showcases the broader image of eastern and northern India. The two states are very big in size and by no means homogeneous entities. Maharashtra is divided into five regions: Greater Mumbai, Western, Marathwada, Konkan and Vidharbha, which are widely different from each other in terms of natural endowments, level of infrastructure development, and are undergoing differential long-term structural changes. Since Greater Mumbai is not typically agricultural and Konkan is completely different in terms of topography, crops grown and ownership patterns these have been left out in the study (Khan and Raman, 2016). Uttar Pradesh has four economic regions Western, Eastern, Central and Bundelkhand. The Western and Central regions of the state are comparatively in better position in terms of access to agricultural resources, whereas the Eastern and Bundelkhand region are suffering from marginalization and poor utilization of resources. Since, basic features of Central region are covered by inclusion of Western region, for cost and time consideration, we have left out this region in our analysis. Table 4 shows crisis of agriculture index for the chosen regions of the two states.

Table 4 Region-wise crisis index in Uttar Pradesh and Maharashtra

Regions	Crisis index			% Growth rate of crisis Index		
	TE04	TE11	TE15	TE04 to TE11	TE11 to TE15	TE04 to TE15
Uttar Pradesh						
Western	0.296	0.301	0.335	1.69	11.3	13.18
Bundelkhand	0.428	0.432	0.474	0.93	9.72	10.75
Eastern	0.378	0.400	0.428	5.82	7.00	13.23
All	0.352	0.363	0.395	3.21	8.68	12.17
Maharashtra						
Western	0.594	0.533	0.55	−10.27	3.189	−7.407
Marathwada	0.514	0.493	0.543	−4.086	10.141	5.642
Vidharbha	0.578	0.575	0.59	−0.519	2.608	2.0761
All	0.565	0.537	0.563	−5.060	4.80	−0.501

Source Computed by authors based on secondary data

Table 5 (Maharashtra) and Table 6 (Uttar Pradesh) present the results of crisis of agriculture at the district level using the indicators and methodology already discussed. As district-wise absolute figure of crisis would not have revealed much, we have classified districts into five categories very high, high, moderate, low and very low (as done earlier with respect to states) for two time periods: the triennium ending 2004 (TE04) and 2015 (TE15). Clearly, as the classification is based on the spread of score within a particular state the values are not comparable between states. In other words, since Maharashtra has high crisis index value in very high crisis index we have put those districts which have an index score of > 0.723, the corresponding category district for U.P. has score of > 0.391.

Tables 5 and 6 show movement of districts in the intervening time period and give some very interesting results—First, there exists crisis of agriculture in the two states. Since Maharashtra has overall higher intensity of crisis so naturally, the crisis across regions here is higher than in U.P. Secondly, within a particular state the intensity of crisis varies significantly across regions. Hence, while Vidharbha and Western regions suffer the most in Maharashtra, Marathwada is relatively better off. Table-5 shows that of the eight districts of Marathwada, none fell in the very high or high category in 2004 and only one was so in 2015, while for Western and Vidharbha more districts lay in the very high or high category. In U.P., Bundelkhand is the worst performer (all seven districts of the region lie in very high and high category in both time periods) while the situation is far better in the Western and Eastern regions (Table 6).

Poor performance of Bundelkhand is often attributed to poor infrastructure, a contention that is not supported by facts. Prakash and Raman (2015) through infrastructural utilization index have shown that in the stressed region of Bundelkhand there is no dearth of infrastructure. In fact, poor return on agriculture, uncertainty

Table 5 Categorisation of districts in terms of crisis index (Maharashtra)

Category and index Score	Crisis index (TE04)		Crisis index (TE15)	
	Region	Districts	Region	Districts
Very high > 0.723	W = 1, T = 1	Solapur	T = 0	–
High 0.722–0.645	W = 4, M = 0 V = 3, T = 7	Nagpur, Gadchiroli, Sangli, Wardha, Ahmednagar, Nasik, Pune	W = 1, M = 1 V = 3, T = 5	Solapur, Wardha, Yavatmal, Nanded, Nagpur
Moderate 0.645–0.566	W = 2, M = 3 V = 2, T = 7	Beed, Chandrapur, Satara, Yavatmal, Nanded, Osmanabad, Nandurbar	W = 5, M = 3 V = 3, T = 11	Chandrapur, Pune, Gadchiroli, Satara, Jalna, Latur, Beed, Nasik, Sangli, Amravati, Ahmednagar
Low 0.565–0.487	W = 1, M = 3 V = 4, T = 8	Dhule, Latur, Amravati, Akola, Buldhana, Bhandara, Aurangabad, Jalna	W = 1, M = 2 V = 3, T = 6	Washim, Buldhana, Nandurbar, Osmanabad, Akola, Parbhani
Very low < 0.486	W = 2, M = 2 V = 1, T = 5	Washim, Hingoli, Jalgaon, Kolhapur, Parbhani	W = 3, M = 2 V = 1, T = 6	Aurangabad, Kolhapur, Dhule, Hingoli, Jalgaon, Bhandara

Note W = Western, M = Marathwada, V = Vidharbha, T = Total
Source Computed by authors

and poverty among farmers have resulted in poor utilization of available infrastructure. Eastern region is also going along the same path of development. Contrary to this, the Western region not only has good infrastructure but also has higher utilization of infrastructure as well leading to better performance.

Third, a very interesting point here is the relatively low difference in crisis intensity across the regions in the worst crisis state Maharashtra. For the low crisis state U.P., however, if we compare the high performing Western region with the worst affected Bundelkhand region, the average score of latter was found to be 1.45 times higher in TE04 and 1.41 times in TE15. It also shows that within U.P. we have the troubled Bundelkhand region which is worse than Western Maharashtra. This justifies the contention that **within crisis infested states/regions there could be some comfortable zones while within the so-called less troubled states/regions there could be some difficult zones**. Fourth, within a particular state the relative position of different regions is changing. Thus, for Maharashtra the Western and Vidharbha regions have swapped their ranks in terms of crisis intensity between TE04 and TE15. Vidharbha which was lying at second spot in TE04 has moved to number one in TE 15. Table 6 shows that while index score of Western Maharashtra has declined by 7.41% that of Vidharbha has increased by 2.08%. Table 6 also

Table 6 Categorisation of districts in terms of crisis index (Uttar Pradesh)

Category and index Score	Crisis index (TE04)		Crisis index (TE15)	
	Region	Districts	Region	Districts
Very high > 0.391	W = 1, C = 3 B = 6, E = 10 T = 20	Lucknow, Lalitpur, Sonebhadra, Chitrakoot, Allahabad, Mirzapur, Pratapgarh, Kaushambi, Mahoba, Varanasi, S. R. Nagar, Jhansi, Banda, Kanpur, Balrampur, G. B. Nagar, Hamirpur, Raebareli, Gorakhpur, Ballia	W = 6, C = 5 B = 7, E = 17 T = 35	Sonebhadra, Mirzapur, G. B. Nagar, Lucknow, Lalitpur, Chitrakoot, Allahabad, Mahoba, Kanpur, Varanasi, Pratapgarh, Kaushambi, Ballia, Bahraich, Jalaun, Hamirpur, S. R. Nagar, Balrampur, Jhansi, Deoria, Kushinagar, Faizabad, Shravasti, Ghaziabad, Raebareli, Ghazipur, Bijnor, Fatehpur, Saharanpur, Banda, Muzaffar Nagar, Gonda, J. P. Nagar, Ambedkar Nagar, Hardoi
High 0.390–0.353	W = 3, C = 3 B = 1, E = 10 T = 17	Faizabad, Sultanpur, Jaunpur, Fatehpur, Unnao, Bijnor, Agra, Farrukhabad, Basti, Azamgarh, Sitapur, Mau, Gonda, Siddharth Nagar, Jalaun, Deoria, Ghazipur	W = 6, C = 2 E = 7 T = 15	Farrukhabad, Jaunpur, Basti, Gorakhpur, Mau, S. K. Nagar, Sitapur, Sultanpur, Kannauj, Meerut, Moradabad, Agra, Unnao, Bareily, Azamgarh
Moderate 0.352–0.316	W = 7, C = 2 E = 4 T = 13	Firozabad, Shravasti, Kannauj, Kushinagar, JP Nagar, Hardoi, Bahraich, Lakhimpur Kheri, Etah, S. K. Nagar, Ghaziabad, Saharanpur, Muzaffarnagar	W = 2, C = 2 E = 1 T = 5	Lakhimpur Kheri, Chandauli, Mathura, Barabanki, Etawah
Low 0.315–0.275	W = 8, C = 1 E = 2 T = 11	Meerut, Barabanki, Ambedkar Nagar, Bareily, Chandauli, Auraiya, Etawah, Mainpuri, Budaun, Baghpat, Mahamaya Nagar	W = 4, E = 1 T = 05	Firozabad, Siddharth Nagar, Baghpat, Rampur, Badaun

(continued)

Table 6 (continued)

Category and index Score	Crisis index (TE04)		Crisis index (TE15)	
	Region	Districts	Region	Districts
Very low < 0.274	W = 7 E = 1 T = 8	Moradabad, Mathura, Aligarh, Maharajganj, Buland Shahar, Shahjahanpur, Rampur, Pilibhit	W = 8, E = 1 T = 9	Etah, Maharajganj, Pilibhit, Mahamaya Nagar, Shahjahanpur, Aligarh, Buland Shahar, Auraiya, Mainpuri

Note W = Western, C = Central, B = Bundelkhand, E = Eastern, T = Total
Source Computed by authors

shows that Solapur district of Western Maharashtra that was lying in very high crisis category in TE04 has improved its position and moved to high category in TE15. Similarly, two districts of the region that were in high category in TE04 have moved to moderate category in TE15. This shows that within the same region while some districts witness improvement, some other undergo deterioration over a period of time. Further, the underlying factors vary across regions. It calls for a more disaggregated study and initiative. In U.P., the relative position of regions has not changed over a period of time. A heartening finding is that for Maharashtra the crisis index as a whole has declined by 0.501% (though it has worsened between TE11 and TE15). The index score for different regions has by and large not increased much. In fact, it has gone down in Western Maharashtra but marginally increased in Marathwada (5.65%) and Vidharbha (2.07%). During the last decade, irrigation facilities and market conditions have improved in Western Maharashtra, which as a result has seen a change in the cropping pattern in favour of farmers. A large number of farmers have minimized their risk by shifting to horticulture and floriculture which are highly profitable. The farming community of Marathwada and Vidharbha, on the other hand, are still producing cotton and soyabean which have relatively high cost of are costly for cultivation (Mishra 2006). The high cost of production and poor return due to market imperfections have resulted in fall in profitability, thereby intensifying the crisis in this region (Deshmukh 2010).

A point of concern for U.P. is that although it is a low crisis state yet over the period of time under study deterioration has taken place there (Raman and Khan 2017). Table 4 shows that for all the regions of U.P., the crisis score has increased between TE04 and TE15. The index for U.P. as a whole has witnessed an increase of 12.17% between TE04 and TE15. What is worse is that the deterioration is more pronounced in case of Eastern region (13.28%) and Western region (13.18%). Seven districts from the Eastern region (Faizabad, Ambedkar Nagar, Shravasti, Bahraich, Deoria, Kushinagar, Ghazipur) and five from Western region (Bijnor, Saharanpur, Muzaffarnagar, J. P. Nagar (Amroha), Ghaziabad) which were earlier lying in the high and moderate crisis categories, respectively, have moved to the very high category in TE15. This has two very important implications for the state economy—first, deterioration has taken place in Western and Eastern regions that have been traditional agriculture strongholds of the state. This has serious long-term implications for the state. Second, crumbing agriculture in the face of no manufacturing and almost non-existent rural non-farm sector in Eastern region is going to be catastrophic for this region.

5 The Agricultural Fiasco: Inside Story

The macro level analysis though gives a general trend of the crisis situation, yet it has its own limitations appearing primarily from the use of limited number of indicators for which data is available, and absence of direct interaction with the ultimate sufferers, i.e. farmers. We present findings of primary survey of over 1080 farmers collected in the sample districts of U.P. and Maharashtra using all the indicators mentioned in Table 1, and assigning weights based on principal component analysis. For keeping things short, the paper does not mention factor loading and provides only the final crisis index. Table 7 presents some important results pertaining to crisis of agriculture—first, it shows that agriculture is not in a comfortable position in the two states; there exists crisis of low intensity in almost all parts of these states. It also shows that crisis score is considerably high for blocks of Maharashtra as compared to the same in Uttar Pradesh. Secondly, it reflects that there exists wide inter-region variation in crisis even within these states. It is evident that there is relatively high crisis in Jalaun (Bundelkhand) and low crisis in Meerut (Western) in U.P. Similarly, Yavatmal (Vidharbha) has very high crisis as compared to Kolhapur (Western) in Maharashtra.

Table 7 Crisis Index at the block/village/farmer level

Category of blocks	Uttar Pradesh			Maharashtra		
Advanced block	Meerut 0.379	Mawana Kalan[a]	0.375	Kolhapur 0.536	Karvir	0.517
		Rajpura	0.395		Kagal	0.556
		Sarurpur Khurd	0.367		Bhudargad	0.535
Block lying in middle	Kushinagar 0.424	Hata	0.434	Parbhani 0.546	Parbhani	0.537
		Tamkuhi	0.432		Gangakhed	0.593
		Dudahi	0.407		Jintur	0.509
Backward block	Jalaun 0.497	Jalaun	0.468	Yavatmal 0.563	Arni	0.555
		Dakore	0.499		Wani	0.546
		Kadaura	0.525		Zari Jamni	0.59

[a]For every district the blocks have been arranged in order of the level of their agricultural development

Source Computed by authors based on primary survey

The secondary data-based study has shown that Bundelkhand region of Uttar Pradesh and Vidharbha of Maharashtra are the worst affected regions. Vidharbha is one of the most vulnerable regions of Maharashtra. It has low 'adaptive capacity' to climate change, including adjustments in resources and technologies. The region faces a number of problems such as low rainfall, lack of irrigation, low micro-nutrients in soil, poor government support and procurement mechanism. The region grows two main crops soyabean and Bt cotton. The adoption of Bt cotton, which is more sensitive to shortage of water in the region without assured irrigation and irregular rainfall, has made cotton cultivation a high risk–high cost cultivation system. Failure of monsoon has resulted in farmers' sufferings and loosing all that they had, at times forcing them to commit suicide. Similarly, Bundelkhand is the most backward region of U.P. The quality of land here is not very suitable for agriculture; rainfall is erratic, and irrigation facilities sparse. The region hardly has any industry so there is excessive dependence on agriculture. Farmers in the region are very poor and most of them do not have sufficient resources to carry out cultivation using even modest technology. They face high cost of cultivation and frequent crop failure and most of them for want of resources are forced to sow the land only once in a year or even leave a significant portion of the land fallow.

The crisis index scores prima facie show that there is a negative relationship between the level of development of a region and crisis of agriculture as advanced districts (Meerut and Kolhapur) have low crisis and backward districts (Jalaun and Yavatmal) have high crisis. In order to get a deeper picture of this relationship and examine it at the block level, the blocks were classified into three categories on the basis of crisis index and we did a cross tab with their rank in agricultural development.

Table 8 Cross tab of crisis index and level of agricultural development of blocks

	Uttar Pradesh			Maharashtra		
	Advanced Block	**Medium Block**	**Backward Block**	**Advanced Block**	**Medium Block**	**Backward Block**
High Crisis	Hata, Jalaun	Dakore	Kadaura	Arni	Gangakhed, Kagal	ZariJamni
Medium Crisis	Mawana Kalan	Rajpura, Tamkuhi	Dudahi	Parbhani	Wani	Bhudargarh
Low Crisis	---	---	Sarurpur Khurd	Karvir	-	Jintur

Source Computed by authors based on primary survey

The results are tabulated in Table 8. The table shows that the relationship between level of agricultural development and intensity of crisis is completely hazy at the block level. For U.P., of the nine blocks taken up four blocks that fall in high crisis zone are of three types (advanced-2, medium-1 and backward-1) in terms of agricultural development. Further, Sarurpur Khurd block that is backward in agricultural development is a low crisis block. In the medium crisis level also all three kinds of blocks fall. In U.P., moderate crisis district Kushinagar has one block (surprisingly its agriculturally advanced block Hata) in high crisis zone and other blocks in medium zone. The picture is more or less the same for Maharashtra. Here also backward blocks Bhudargarh and Jintur fall in low crisis category while advanced blocks Parbhani and Arni lie in the middle crisis category. Hence, just creating infrastructure at the block level does not improve the position of farmers.

Third, block-wise comparison of the two states reveals that while in UP all the blocks of less crisis infested district (Meerut) have lower crisis index as compared to blocks of high crisis infected district (Jalaun), the relationship is not so obvious in Maharashtra. In Maharashtra, some block (Kagal) of less crisis infested district Kolhapur have higher crisis score as compared to some blocks (Arni and Wani) of crisis-ridden district Yavatmal. Thus, even in the better performing districts, there are acute problems related to agriculture. This clearly shows two things—one, that crisis is deep rooted in Maharashtra and even in those districts where things look not as bad at the macro level, at the ground level deterioration is severe. Two, as the crisis intensifies in a region its impact spreads in less troubled areas as well.

Fourth, crisis of agriculture is a result of multiple issues: development, economic condition of farmers and social condition, each interlinked with the other. Agricultural development covers only one aspect of crisis and does not make any rigid statement about the crisis situation of different farmers and social groups. An attempt to relate crisis of agriculture with farm size and farmers' caste yielded very interesting results (Table 9). The Table clearly shows that for both the states crisis intensity is related to the type of farmers. **Marginal and small farmers have higher crisis index as compared to the semi-medium and medium farmers**. For measuring the extent to which crisis depends on the size of land, we clubbed the farmer group into two groups: marginal and small, and semi-medium, medium and large) and did the '*t*' test to find whether means of these land groups differ or not, the difference was found statistically significant at 5%.

A clear and emphatic relationship was found between crisis of agriculture and caste of farmers. Table 9 shows that in both the states crisis index was low for upper caste farmers and high for OBC and SC farmers (ST farmers were not found in the survey area). An attempt to see whether difference is statistically significant revealed that while the difference between upper caste and OBC farmers was not significant, a clear difference (five per cent level) was noticeable if we compare the SC farmers with upper caste and OBC farmers clubbed together. **This means that the crisis of agriculture has caste orientation and crisis is high in lower caste farmers.**

A deeper investigation of the issue reveals that in UP land ownership has caste orientation as bulk of SC farmers (89.8%) is marginal and small. Only 10.1% SC farmers fell in semi-medium or above category. On the contrary, only 52.8% of the

Table 9 Crisis of agriculture and farm size and farmers' caste group

Crisis of agriculture based on farmer categories			Crisis of agriculture based on caste of farmers		
Farmer Categories	**Uttar Pradesh**	**Maharashtra**	**Caste Group**	**Uttar Pradesh**	**Maharashtra**
Marginal	0.46	0.562	**Upper Caste**	0.406	0.526
Small	0.419	0.569	**OBC**	0.416	0.563
Semi-medium	0.411	0.536	**SC**	0.503	0.571
Medium	0.382	0.505			
Large	0.395	0.491			

Source Computed by authors based on primary survey

upper caste farmers surveyed were in small and marginal farmer category. Hence, saying that marginal and small farmers have high crisis intensity automatically means that SC farmers have high crisis intensity. The situation is, however, different in Maharashtra where out of the 540 farmers surveyed, 75% belonged to the upper caste category while small and marginal for OBC and SC was 51.3 and 42.38%, respectively. Thus, even after falling in relatively higher land size category SC farmers in Maharashtra have higher crisis of agriculture intensity. Hence, for Maharashtra, crisis definitely is severe among SC caste group.

The relationship between size class and productivity and profitability of agriculture has been explored by Chandra (2001), Sidhu (2002), Sukhpal et al. (2008), Gaurav and Mishra (2011) and a host of others. The literature identifies few factors that go against marginal and small farmers such as inability to use latest technology resulting in low productivity, high cost of production, higher level of indebtedness and reliance on non-institutional finance. The present study investigated these issues and endorsed some of these and rejected others. It was found that the cropping intensity and productivity per hectare in rupees for marginal and small farmers in both the states were higher than that of medium and large farmers. For example, per hectare productivity was Rs 72635.66 and 45084.25, respectively, for U.P. and Maharashtra, respectively, for marginal farmers while for medium farmers the figure stood at Rs. 65475.06 and 27573.81 in U.P. and Maharashtra, respectively. High productivity was on account of better and more intensive utilization of available land. However, very high cost of production, adherence to old technology, high dependency of population (large family size dependent on land), greater reliance on non-institutional credit, inability to get remunerative price for their product all combined together to turn the tide against marginal and small farmers. High dependence of population results in very low per capita food grain availability among marginal farmers and severely reduces the capacity of these farmers to face crop failure. High cost of production significantly depresses the profitability per hectare. Hence, despite having high productivity in Rs/per hectare the marginal farmers have very low profitability per hectare. The marginal and small farmers in the survey area could meet a relatively small percentage of their total expenditure through income from agriculture; for the rest, they have to depend on casual income from other sources. Very often when casual employment is not available they borrow money to meet the expenses. They thus fall into a debt trap. The primary survey revealed that on an average a marginal farmer in U.P. had an outstanding loan of Rs. 76446.52 (Rs. 71429.43 in Maharashtra). They had very high debt to gross value added (GVO). A significant portion of the loan was taken to meet current consumption expenditure in the event of insufficient income from agriculture. Not surprisingly, it came from non-institutional sources.

6 Determinants of Crisis of Agriculture at Micro-Level

Identifying determinants of the crisis is a very tricky and difficult issue. This is because there is an overlap between the indicators of crisis and causes of crisis. For example, farmers' indebtedness is a very important indicator of crisis, which at the same time is an important cause of crisis. Hence, if we run a regression farmers' indebtedness would appear both on the left- and right-hand side of regression equation thereby creating the problem of identity. To establish any cause–effect relation between crisis index and its variable, a normal regression has been run. In this process, we have insured that those variables that appear in the computation of crisis index do not appear as a predictor or explanatory variable on the right-hand side. But, if we drop the variables that have been used in the computation of crisis from the list of regressors, the explanatory power of the model nose-dives. The condition of running a predictor regression, however, forces us to do this. Thus, as the regression result shows the value of R^2 obtained is very low. Table 10 gives the list of regressors, their units of measurement and the expected sign of the coefficient (theoretically conceivable).

We used ANOVA model that reflected a statistically significant overall regression model with a p-value of (0.000) which is less than 0.05 (95% confidence interval). This implies that the model is a good fit. Therefore, we can go ahead and examine the coefficient of indicators to determine which economic indicators contribute more weight in the economic distress (Table 11).

Table 10 List of variables for regression analysis

SN	Variables	Explanation	Unit	Expected sign
1	Farmer groups/land size	Crisis is expected to be related to size of holding	Binary (0 = Marginal and Small, 1 = Others)	Negative
2	Social groups/caste	Crisis has a social context	Binary (0 = SC, 1 = Others)	Negative
3	Irrigation	Can be used as proxy for resources of farmers	Binary (1 = Adequate., 0 = Not- Adequate)	Negative
4	Sources of loan	Has direct bearing on cost of production	Binary (0 = Institutional 1 = Non-Institutional)	Positive
5	Problem of availability of labour	Affects wage component of cost	Binary (0 = No, 1 = Yes)	Positive
6	TFP (Total Factor Productivity)	Proxy for technology used	Normalized	Negative
7	Availability of alternative livelihood	Supplementary income source	Normalized	Negative

Source Computed by authors based on primary survey

Table 11 Model summary

Model	A	β_1	β_2	β_3	β_4	β_5	β_6	β_7*
Value of unstandardized coefficients	0.455	−0.027	−0.059	−0.034	0.021	0.022	−0.029	−0.013
Standardized coefficients		−0.091	−0.212	−0.145	0.044	0.092	−0.2	−0.109
t Value	42.696	−2.555	−4.988	−3.657	2.133	2.135	−6.222	−2.403
R Square (0.479)								

Source Computed by authors

$$\begin{aligned}\text{Crisis Index} = {} & \alpha + \beta_1\text{Farmer Groups} + \beta_2\text{Social Group} + \beta_3\text{Irrigation} \\ & + \beta_4\text{Sources of loan} + \beta_5\text{Problems of Labour} + \beta_6\text{TFP} \\ & + \beta_7\text{livelihood opportunity} + u_t\end{aligned}$$

The table clearly indicates that status of social group (0.212) is the main determining factor of crisis followed by total factor productivity (0.200), irrigation facilities (0.145), alternative livelihood opportunity (0.109) and land holdings (0.091), whereas the source of loan and labour problem has low explanatory power. Those variables that have high explanatory and influencing power are highly influenced by long-term growth process which has been prevailing since the 1970s (Era of Green Revolution). Over time, institutional changes, market processes and demographic pressure have brought two remarkable changes in the rural structure. First, the proportion of small and marginal holdings has increased and second, the capitalist mode of production has prospered. In the capitalist mode of production, a three-tiered pyramid of the farming communities exists in the rural economy. At the wide base are located the poverty-stricken and socially marginalized farmers who fly around the poverty line and live in distress condition. The middle tier is formed by the upwardly mobile farmers who come from the creamy layer of OBC engaged in a prolonged and, often, frustrating battle to rise above the poverty line and join the mainstream. Small but politically powerful farm lobbies occupy the peak of the pyramid. *It is important to note that this pyramid is an outcome of policy regimes that have prevailed so far in the agrarian economy.*

7 Conclusion

From the afore-mentioned explanation it is sufficient to establish three very pertinent points—First, the sector vs farmer debate relating to agriculture is futile as there has been overall deterioration in agriculture. There are issues both at the sector and farmers' level, thus adoption of a balanced perspective is required. Second, the crisis of agriculture is now an all-India phenomenon and different states and regions vary only in terms of intensity of the same. So, we cannot talk about crisis infested region(s) and crisis-free region(s). Different states and regions differ in terms of nature and intensity of crisis. Although there can be some common problems, yet the underlying causes of crisis, and chief factors responsible for its initiation and perpetuation might differ across states/regions/districts demanding the adoption of region-specific policies. Third, formulation of macro-level policies to resurrect the agricultural sector and troubled farmers would have limited success. The primary survey has clearly established that the left perspective is correct and that the crisis definitely has a social orientation. It is more severe for the small and marginal farmers and the weaker or lower caste groups. Since these sections or castes face specific kinds of problems, a specific set of policies is required to handle their issues. Policies adopted to give a boost to the agricultural sector in general would, in all likelihood, have only temporary and superficial effect on the severely affected farmer categories. It is imperative to take specific measures for these social sections.

Thus, in order to resurrect the agricultural sector and rejuvenate farmers, the government should adopt region-specific and farmer centric policies. Region-specific policies should be based on a detailed district and block-level study that could identify the main problem areas and specific issues faced by agriculture and farmers of the particular region. Farmer centric policies should address the specific issues faced by the troubled farmers. Brief suggestions on region-centric and farmer centric policies are discussed as under.

Adoption of Farmer centric policies—The principal component of farmer centric policies should be to ensure sufficient return to farmers from farming activity. Two important interventions are required from this angle: (i) Provision of remunerative prices and checking price deflation: This calls for developing an efficient agro-marketing network with very effective involvement of government agencies and fixation of prices that are farmer friendly. The state should intervene to resolve the problem of sale of agricultural products. Minimum support prices (MSPs) for key crops are not regularly revised and upward revisions are generally not adequate enough. A system of determination of MSP at district level may be developed and revision of MSP be based on rate of inflation in the economy and cost of production with inputs from farmer groups. The poor farmers should be protected from vagaries of the international market. Hence, during years of shortages of agricultural commodities farmers should be allowed to reap reasonable benefits and prices should not be deliberately depressed by pushing up imports. The decision is definitely going to be tough as it results into a clash of interest of farmers and consumers (who prefer cheap imports) but government should attempt to strike a balance.

(ii) Reducing the cost of production: it in turn depends on provision of extension of services, increasing public investment in rural development and mitigating risks associated with farming by offering dependable crop insurance. For minimizing input costs, high-quality agricultural inputs should be made available at the appropriate time and at affordable prices. This can be done through member-based farmers' cooperatives free from bureaucratic intervention and controls. The government should provide subsidies especially for marginal farmers by the cash transfer scheme.

Region-specific policies Though there are some common issues and measures that are to be adopted in an effective manner everywhere, yet special issues of different regions must be dealt with by adopting region centric approach. The analysis of regional dimension of crisis of agriculture clearly shows that because of their peculiarities the policies that are relevant for Jalaun (Bundelkhand region) and Yavatmal (Vidharbha region) are not going to be appropriate for Meerut and Kolhapur (Western regions of U.P. and Maharashtra). For example, irrigation is the major cause of concern in Bundelkhand and Vidarbha. To handle this issue the government should enhance irrigation facilities and improve irrigation systems. There is a need to replenish groundwater through water harvesting. Measures like arrangement of underground pipelines for water could be promoted so as to reduce water loss in transportation. The government should also lay emphasis on micro-irrigation systems and precision farming. Another important intervention required is in the area of crop insurance in the district. This is more crucial in these districts as frequent monsoon failure results in pauperization of farmers. The problem is more severe in Yavatmal (Vidharbha) where farmers have shifted to Bt Cotton farming and crop failure is very frequent. Similarly, the specific issues of Meerut and Kolhapur need to be studied and appropriate steps need to be undertaken. The objective of this paper is not to come up with specific suggestions rather to emphasize emphasize the need for farmer centric and region centric policies based on findings of the primary survey.

We can conclude by saying that agricultural sector is failing and farmers are frazzled and under severe duress. The problem has acquired an all India proportion and on the economic front is taking its toll on the sector that still supports more than half of the nation's workforce and supplies food to the population. On the social front, the distress has hit the small and marginal farmers the hardest widening the gulf in the society. To add to it, severe livelihood crisis in the rural areas is further complicating the crisis in agriculture. If the government moves in a planned manner and gives proper emphasis on non-farm sector especially rural manufacturing, it would, on the one hand, reduce dependence on agriculture and reverse the trend of sub-division of land holdings and on the other provide surplus income that can be pooled back and invested in agriculture. The need of the hour is comprehensive district and region level planning as piecemeal efforts are not going to achieve the desired results. It's high time that serious consideration is given to the problem of farmers else the crisis of agriculture would intensify in states and would have very serious repercussions for not just the agriculture sector and farmers but the bulk of population.

References

Assadi, M. (1998). Farmers' suicide: Signs of distress in rural economy. *Economic and Political Weekly*, *33*(14), 747–748.

Assadi, M. (2006). Agrarian crisis and farmers' suicide in India: Dimension, nature and response of the state in Karnataka. *The Indian Journal of Labour Economics*, *49*(4).

Balagopal, K. (1988). Rich peasant, poor peasants. *Seminar*, *352*, 19–23.

Barah, B. C., & Smita, S. (Eds.). (2011). *Agrarian distress in India: Problem and remedies*. New Delhi: Concept Publishing Company Pvt. Ltd.

Basole, A., & Basu, D. (2011). Relations of production and modes of surplus extraction in India: Part II-'informal' industry. *Economic and Political Weekly*, *46*(15).

Bhalla, G. S., & Hazell, P. (2003). Rural employment and poverty: Strategies to eliminate rural poverty within a generation. *Economic and Political Weekly*, *38*(33).

Bhalla, G. S., & Singh, G. (2009). Economic liberalization and Indian agriculture: A state-wise analysis. *Economic and Political Weekly*, *44*(52), 34–44.

Bose, P. (1981). Farmer's agitation. *Seminar*, *257*, 58–62.

Chand, R., Raju, S. S., & Pandey, L. M. (2007). Growth crisis in agriculture: Severity and options at national and state levels. *Economic and Political Weekly*, *30*(24).

Chand, R., & Parappurathu, S. (2011). Historical and spatial trends in agriculture: growth analysis at national and state level in India. In *Workshop on policy options and investment priorities for accelerating agricultural productivity and development in India*. New Delhi.

Chandra, D. (2001). Crucial agriculture problems facing small farmers. *Political Economy Journal of India*, vol.*10*, I–4.

Deshmukh, N. (2010). Cotton growers: Experience from Vidharbha. In R. S. Deshpande & S. Arora (Eds.), *Agrarian crisis and farmers suicide*. New Delhi: Sage Publication.

Deshpande, R. S. (2002). Suicide by farmers in Karnataka: Agrarian distress and possible alleviatory step. *Economic and Political Weekly*, *37*(25), 2601–2610.

Deshpande, R. S., & Arora, S. (Eds.). (2010). *Agrarian crisis and farmers' suicide*. New Delhi: Sage Publication.

Galab, S., & Reddy, D. N. (2006). Agrarian crisis: looking beyond the debt trap, *Economic and Political Weekly*, *41*(19).

Gaurav, S. & Mishra, S. (2011). *Size-class and returns to cultivation in India: A cold case reopened*. Mumbai: Indira Gandhi Institute of Development Research. cited on August 20, 2017

Ghosh, J. (2016). 25 years of economic reforms: Agriculture. Available at http://www.macroscan.org/fet/jul16/pdf/Economic_Reforms.pdf cited on May 20, 2019

Gulati, A., & Mullen, K. (2003). Responding to policy reform: Indian agriculture in the 1990s and after. Working Paper No. 189, Stanford Center for International Development, Stanford.

Khan, K. A., & Raman, R. (2016). Indian agriculture in dire straits: Evidences from primary survey of Maharashtra. *Journal of Economic Development*. Patna University.

Kamlakar, S. S., & Narayanamoorthy, A. (2003). Impact of liberalization on domestic agricultural prices and farm income. *Indian Journal of Agricultural Economics, 58*(3), 353–364.

Mishra, S. (2006). Farmers' suicides in Maharashtra. *Economic and Political Weekly, 41*(16), 1538–1545.

Mishra, S. (2007). *Risks, farmers' suicides and agrarian crisis in India: Is there a way out?*. Mumbai: Indira Gandhi Institute of Development Research.

Patnaik, U. (2003). *Global capitalism, deflation and agrarian crisis in developing countries*, Social Policy and Development Programme Paper Number 15, October 2003, United Nations Research Institute for Social Development.

Patnaik, U. (2006). Unleashing the market: Global capitalism, deflation, and agrarian crisis in developing countries. In M. John et al. (Eds.), *Contested transformations: Changing economies and identities in contemporary India* (pp 53–83). New Delhi: Tulika Press.

Prakash, A., & Raman, R. (2015). Regional dimension of performance of agriculture: An analytical study of Uttar Pradesh, *Research Fronts: A Peer Reviewed Journal of Multiple Science, Arts and Commerce, V*, 34–44. ISSN 2250–2653.

Pillai, S. (2007). Agrarian crisis and the way out. *The Marxist, 23*(3).

Ramachandran, V. K., et al. (2010). *Socio-economic survey of three villages in Andhra Pradesh: A study of agrarian relations*. New Delhi: Tulika Books.

Raman, R., & Khan, K. A. (2017). Crisis of agriculture in Uttar Pradesh: Investigating acuteness and antecedents. *Amity Journal of Agribusiness, 2*(1), 13–27.

Raman, R., & Khan, K. A. (2018). Regional dimensions of crisis of agriculture: experiences from farmer level survey in Uttar Pradesh. *Journal of Regional Development and Planning, 7*(1).

Ramasamy, C., & Kumar, D. S. (2007). Regional difference in farm profitability in Indian agriculture. In *National seminar on agrarian distress: causes and remedies national centre for agricultural economics and policy research*. New Delhi.

Rao V. M., (2009) 'Farmer's distress in a modernizing agriculture- the tragedy of the upwardly mobile: An overview. In D. Narasimha Reddy & S. Mishra (Eds.), *Agrarian crisis in India* (pp. 164–98). New Delhi: Oxford University Press.

Reddy, N., & Mishra, S. (2009). *Agrarian crisis in India*. New Delhi: Oxford University Press.

Rudra, A. (1982). *Indian agricultural economics: Myths and reality*. New Delhi: Allied.

Sainath, P. (2010). Farm suicides: A 12-year saga. *India Together*. Open Access also available at https://www.thehindu.com/opinion/columns/sainath/Farm-suicides-a-12-year-saga/article16811575.ece. Cited on January 20, 2020

Sen, A., & Bhatia, M. S. (2004). *State of the Indian Farmer: A millennium study- cost of cultivation and farm income* (Vol. 14). New Delhi: Academic Foundation.

Sharma, A. N. (2005), Agrarian relations and socio-economic change in Bihar. *Economic and Political Weekly, 40*(10).

Siddiqui, K. (2015). Agrarian crisis and transformation in India. *Journal of Economics and Political Economy, 2*(10) 1453/jepe.v2i1.122.

Sidhu, H. S. (2002). Crisis in Agrarian economy in Punjab: Some urgent steps. *Economic and Political Weekly, 37*(30), 3132–3138.

Sukhpal, S., Kumar, M., & Kingra, H. S. (2008). Indebtedness among farmers in Punjab. *Economic and Political Weekly, 43*(26), 130–136.

Labor Mobility

Labour Mobility in Historical Perspective from East U.P, South U.P and North Bihar: Contours of Changes and Continuity

Tulika Tripathi

Abstract Mobility is a fundamental trait of human beings, from the memory immemorial. However, its duration and location and the characteristics of mover keeps on changing. In this paper, we have tried to understand the present nature of mobility over two decades, i.e. 1996–2016 for two regions of Bihar and Uttar Pradesh, which remained to be a poverty concentrated zone in India. In this paper, we have contextualised current pattern of mobility in context to the past patterns of mobility, since mobility is very closely related with the resources and social capital of an individual to which she/he belongs and the source and destination locations. The short run mobility and circular migration has increased among men and new and richer locations to move have been opened during this time period. People from this region have started to migrate to Gulf countries which was earlier only limited to migrating to domestic destinations, that too particularly to Mumbai, Delhi, Gujarat, etc. While long run circular migration has seen new destinations, short run local migration to the same district have increased many folds. Survey observation suggests that the expansion of real estate and service sector have created low skills job catering to flexible job requirements of low skill agriculture workers and small farmers of the same district. However, having stated the change in the pattern of mobility, not everything has changed. The mobility pattern across the socio-economic group remains the same. To be more clear, poor, less educated moving to nearer destinations and better off moving to far off destinations is evident. And returns of those moving to far off places are higher than those moving to nearer destinations. Similarly, those moving to far off place do so for longer durations and those moving to nearer destinations are moving for shorter durations. Further, this paper has looked at the change in road and transportation and banking and financial services as an enabler of frequent mobility and mobility to far off places. Survey results suggest large improvement in terms of road quality and reach of road to the villages. Due to better road networks mostly private transportation like taxi and auto have reached to these villages taking many workers every day/week or month to their respective work locations. These villages now have taxi and auto stand, banking facilities such as ATM, internet and

T. Tripathi (✉)
CSEP, SSS Central University of Gujarat, Gandhinagar, India
e-mail: hello.tulika@gmail.com

N. K. Mishra (ed.), *Development Challenges of India After Twenty Five Years of Economic Reforms*, India Studies in Business and Economics,
https://doi.org/10.1007/978-981-15-8265-3_18

post offices, enabling frequent mobility at one end, and enabling mobility to far off places for longer duration at the other. Since it has eased to reach homes quickly in case of any emergency or to send money as and when needed. So in nutshell, far off destination to move is opened, short run circular migration has increased. However, the characteristics of those migrating to various places for different locations remains the same. Road, transportation, ICT and financial services have played a very important role in changing the nature of mobility from this region of India.

1 Introduction

Mobility has always been an intrinsic part of human civilization. People need a certain minimum of social and economic resources in order to be able to mobile. It is, therefore, no coincidence that wealthy people and societies tend to be generally more mobile than relatively poor people and societies (Haas 2009). A fundamental paradox is that while constraints are likely to motivate people to move, but at the same time they need resources to do so. Thus, mobility is both a cause (among many) and a consequence (among many) of processes of social transformation, which underpin living standard and livelihood expansion. Mobility begets access to resources and better access to resources facilitates mobility. Therefore, historically, people from wealthy regions have been more mobile than poor regions and/or mobility have made those regions richer. People from south and west regions of India, especially from the coastal belt, i.e. Kerala, Gujarat and Tamil Nadu, have been migrating for trade and services and not just as labourers. Therefore, we find a very strong Gujarati and Tamil/Telegu domestic and international diaspora (Tumbe 2018). Further, the migration literature suggest the crucial role played by social networks in helping people at both the places; origin and destination (Mani and Riley 2019; Bertoli and Ruyssen 2018; Bashi 2007). These social networks in form of linguistic and regional diaspora help people from their background to enter the new destination. Helps include information, job offers, accommodation, economic support, social relations, etc. Of all these access to information is so important that it restricts mobility within the same group of people and/or area flowing through these diaspora. Conversely, relatively lower long term spatial mobility and smaller information sets have reduced the chances of acquiring capital among many social groups, including the Dalits and Adivasis, and also stunted the development of their diasporas (Tumbe 2018). The links established by the Punjabis, Gujaratis, Malayalis and Tamilians during the colonial period were critical in extension of their internal and international diasporas. They were followed globally by the Telegus and Kannadigas, while erstwhile dominant UP and Bihari lagged behind in relative terms. Because, migration from UP and Bihar was in form of indentured labourers and recruiters in British Army had no agency to create a strong social network. Therefore, we still find the historical streams and pattern of migration and more mobile regions are wealthiest ones and vice versa. Here, two things are important; pattern and type of activity of migration/migrants. In light of historical facts, one can observe the following pattern of continuity in the mobility of people.

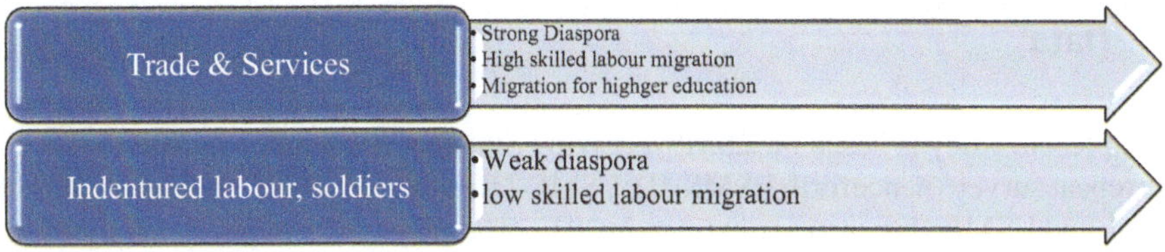

A case of East and South UP and North Bihar: If we believe in eastward migration hypothesis into Indo-Gangetic valley it received inward migration between 2000 BCE and 300 BCE and even after that (Tumbe 2018). Bihar and Uttar Pradesh are located on the great filed of Ganga Yamuna doab of Indo-Gangetic valley. These two states have most fertile lands, excellent environment for cattle rearing, full of natural resources and traditionally well-fed people. Therefore, it naturally led to a dense settlement of population in this region and less mobility of the people from this area. Measures like passport, taxes on using roads and crossing border during the Mauryan period might have further prevented in/outmigration. Also, this region in the north is blocked by great Himalayan range where the passes are snow blocked, therefore, no going towards East Asia and no trade, social and culture exchange was possible. On the other side, Ganga Yamuna doab had rivers, dividing it from Delhi and northern India. That is why we find limited domestic circular migration from this belt to other parts of country for religion and trade, etc.; Ashoka and Mahavira are two great religious migrants of Bihar. However, in modern times, i.e. pre-independence period, the majority of migration remains limited to indentured labour for plantation and recruitment of soldiers in British Army during World War II from this region. These two groups; one working as slave and other as soldiers would have little agency and capacity to establish a strong network with the people of the place of origin and destination. That is why there is no singular diaspora emerged from this side. Bhojpuri diaspora is identified very late which might loosely cover this area. This diaspora particularly emerged in Africa and East Asia (Trinidad, Fiji, etc.), with no connection whatsoever with the people of Uttar Pradesh and Bihar. Nationally, during Independence movement and after that there was migration from this region to northern India and especially Delhi. Many political leaders like Rajendra Prasad, Pandit Nehru, Shastri, Lohiya and so on so forth migrated from UP and Bihar to Delhi. Thus from this region in near history, we see mostly domestic and circular migration towards northern India particularly Delhi. This migration then was not remained limited to political leaders, and since then the spur of migration ever increasing for services and labour. Uttar Pradesh harbours nearly one-fifth of India's population and it experienced net outflow of 2.7 million people during 1991–2001. Similarly, Bihar also registered the same phenomenon where the net outmigration is around 1.7 million people during the same time period. Rural to urban migration, which from

18 to 38% of intra-state and inter-state migrants, respectively, is predominantly a phenomenon among males (Bhagat and Mohanty 2009).

2 Data

The present study is based on LSMS-I (Living Standard Measurement Survey-I) and its repeat survey (henceforth LSMS-II). LSMS-I was carried out in 1997 by the World Bank and LSMS-II is carried out by us in 2017. The survey was focused on migration and poverty belt of India, which is Eastern and Southern Uttar Pradesh and Northern Bihar. LSMS-2 selected 21 villages out of the original 124 villages of LSMS-1 and revisited same households to construct a panel of households and members. Thus, we have cross section data of around 900 households for two points of time, which is 1997 and 2017. Remarkably, 1990s are the time when road, transportation and communication started expanding in India. Globalisation and capitalist expansion ensured that infrastructure and market expansion took over which have led to increase in labour mobility. The present work uses this household data from two time periods by forming a panel of households to look at labour mobility characterised by the endowment and social characteristics of household. Against this backdrop the present paper is focussed on these two backward states of India, Uttar Pradesh (U.P) and Bihar which have very low level of urbanisation and are considered to be poverty and outmigration belt of India. The migrants from these regions are often more disdainfully referred as ‘Bhaiyas’.

The paper is an attempt to understand the mobility and its pattern in this belt. The key to understanding migration in India is by looking at the two Ds, i.e. duration and destination of migration. The paper is organised as following: Sect. 3 examines changes in two decades in duration of mobility using LSMS data of Uttar Pradesh and Bihar. Section 4 analyses the change in destination of migration. This entire analyse is done in the three districts of Uttar Pradesh and four districts of Bihar, which is part of East U.P, South U.P and West Bihar. Section 5 shows the availability of road and transport and its role played in migration. Further, Sect. 6 looks at the availability of banking and communication, and its role played in recent change in migration. Further, Sect. 7 uses the household endowment of vehicle and its impact on pattern of migration.

3 Duration; Short Run and Long Run Mobility

In case of UP and Bihar, the structural transformation led to decline in agriculture profitability but didn’t lead to the growth of secondary sector. The growth of tertiary sector and real state have mostly created low level work (ILO 2017, Jha, undated, FICCI 2015). Due to which employment elasticity and agricultural wages fell in both the states (Chavan and Bedamatta 2006, Jha undated). As a result, we see lots of labour force moving out of agriculture and joining the casual labour force in construction and services.

Continues: There could be various forms of mobility, often distinguished on the basis of duration and destination. It is true that there has been faster mobility of labour in recent times. Its quantum has increased significantly, be it to nearby or far off places. Mobility of labour to adjacent town or city accompanied by better connectivity has changed the earlier form of mobility which was of longer duration. The shortest duration migrations of less than a day or week are called commuting and affect over 10 million people around the major urban centres. Slightly longer duration migrations, in spells of a few months each, with no spell lasting more than six months is known as seasonal migrations/short run migration. Short run migration has increased from 1996–1997 to 2016–2017. A larger part of labour is resorting to short run migration in our survey data as compared to earlier round. By default, short run migration is mostly possible in case of places nearer to residence. It is shown that short run migration is mainly observed in the same district and long term mobility is to far off places. We distinguish these two forms of mobility based on duration. Short run migration are those who report to be at home for nine or more months and long term mobility means who are reported to be at home for less than nine months. Means short run migrants are circular migrants they go for shorter duration often for 2–3 months or lesser, while the long run migrants visit home annually or biannually and therefore remains absent for entire year. Increasing urbanisation, expansion of city boundaries, higher demand for labour in nearby towns, expansion of construction and transport industry, better rail and road connectivity, lowering down of transportation cost and declining family size have promoted short run migration. Construction sector is the most favourable destination for short run migrants as it provides necessary flexibility to match up with seasonality of agriculture. Moreover, labour absorption in agriculture is also going down. Transport sector has also contributed in short run migration. Works like rickshaw pulling, taxi/auto/bus/truck driving provide flexible working period and thus could be combined with farming activities. Therefore, it is most convenient for rural labour to seek job in these sectors and, therefore, we observe an expansion in activity status of individuals as daily wage labours. When we compare short run mobility (Tables 1 and 2) and long term mobility in LSMS-1 and LSMS-2, we find that people moving to far off places have increased. Interstate mobility was quite low in LSMS-1, but it has registered substantial presence in LSMS-2. International mobility is also observed in LSMS-2, particularly to middle east. In the past decade, the locus of emigration to the Gulf shifted from south India to north India, and the Bhojpuri speaking tracts of eastern Uttar Pradesh and western Bihar dominate the unskilled labour flow outside India, much like a century and a half ago. The billions of dollars of remittances from the Gulf that once touched the west coast of India have finally made its way to Ganga.

Further, males are larger in numbers in mobility as compared to women (Table 3), another historically established pattern, remains the same. For instance, between 1838 and 1917 over 2,00,000 Indian labourers migrated to British Guiana and less than a third returned to India. Almost all the migrants traced their roots to the

Table 1 Short run mobility for economic activity: 9 months or more at home

District	LSMS-1			LSMS-2			Total
	Same district	Other districts-same state	Other districts-different states	Same district	Other districts-same state	Other districts-different states	
Jehanabad	67.24	23.84	8.92	88.17	12	0	100
Saharsa	1.45	29.5	69.05	73.5	3.03	23.47	100
Vaishali	37.93	37.93	24.15	90.52	9	0	100
Banda[a]	69.09	22.14	8.77	96.13	4	0	100
Allahabad	73.05	5.25	21.7	95.59	4.41	0	100
Gorakhpur	83.94	8.03	8.03	96.31	2.88	0.82	100
Total	56.74	17.59	25.67	90.45	5.63	3.92	100

[a]Now known as Chitrakoot
Source LSMS-1 and Field Survey

Table 2 Long term mobility: less than 9 months at home

District	LSMS-1				LSMS-2				Total
	Same district	Other districts-same state	Other districts-different states	Outside India	Same district	Other districts	Other states	Outside India	
Jehanabad	76.45	10.08	13.47	0	0	13.68	86.32	0	100
Saharsa	0	12.41	87.59	0	1.03	4.09	94.87	0	100
Vaishali	31.99	36.02	31.99	0	0	8.02	90.69	1.3	100
Banda[a]	47.22	5.56	47.22	0	3.98	6.68	89.34	0	100
Allahabad	0	50	50	0	4.32	11.45	80.19	4.04	100
Gorakhpur	0	24.15	51.7	24.15	0	1.09	76.23	22.68	100
Total	21.94	21.35	52.14	4.56	1.57	5.95	85.3	7.19	100

[a]Now known as Chitrakoot
Source LSMS-1 and Field Survey

Table 3 Economic activity by sex- LSMS-2

	Short run mobility			Long run mobility				
Sex	Same District	Other districts-same state	Other districts-different states	Same District	Other districts-same state	Other districts-different states	Outside India	Total
Male	89.69	5.26	5.05	1.39	5.48	85.82	7.31	100
Female	91.27	6.03	2.7	3.07	4.21	87	5.73	100
Total	90.45	5.63	3.92	1.5	5.4	85.89	7.22	100

Source Field Survey

Bhojpuri-speaking tracts of the Gangetic plains, a core area of the Great Indian Migration wave. Only a sixth were upper castes, rest of all were from low caste or outcaste and middling artisan and agricultural castes and mostly men (Tumbe 2018). Further, if we solely look at the change in duration of migration, pattern almost continues for the long run migration over the two-decade time period. There is almost no change in individuals migrating for 9 or more months in one spell. And the short duration of migration 4–6 months and 7–9 months shows slight increase followed by almost similar decrease in migration for shorter duration, i.e. 1–3 months (Fig. 1).

Our analysis of over two decades time period suggests that not much has changed in the duration of migration besides a small increase in migration for 6–9 and 4–6 months in one spell (Tables 3 and 4).

Changes: Further, our survey from the two rounds over two decades time suggest the change occurred between SES communities in duration of migration. In fact, individuals from the well-off communities, i.e. upper caste, higher MPCE class and land class are migrating for longer duration; they are absent for the entire year. The gendered pattern of migration remains the same; a one of flow for men and fixity

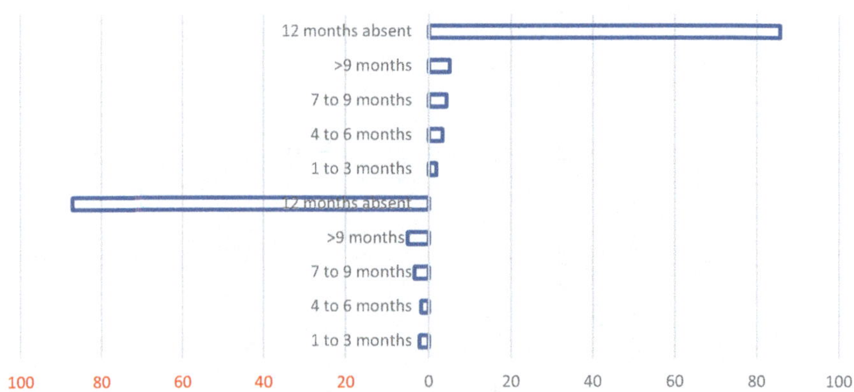

Fig. 1 Change in duration of migration from 1997 to 2016 *Source* LSMS-1 and Field Survey

Table 4 Duration of migration (East UP & West Bihar)

	1997					2016				
	1–3 months	4–6 months	7–9 months	>9 months	12 months absent	1–3 months	4–6 months	7–9 months	>9 months	12 months absent
Male	2.56	2.73	5.8	6.66	82.25	2.85	6.2	7.39	8.84	74.71
Female	1.95	0.88	0.78	3.41	92.98	0.82	0.29	1.35	1.31	96.22
Upper caste	2.92	0.97	2.19	13.63	80.29	0.47	1.17	2.1	8.41	87.85
OBC	1.99	2.19	2.98	2.78	90.06	1.52	3.79	3.46	5.1	86.13
SC/ST	2.22	2.05	2.73	1.54	91.47	2.64	3.44	5.91	2.64	85.37
Muslim	2.58	1.55	10.82	10.31	74.74	0.9	1.49	4.48	12.54	80.6
Poorest	1.76	3.27	5.29	1.51	88.16	4.23	5.71	6.98	5.71	77.35
Poorer	1.94	1.94	3.87	2.66	89.59	0.8	2.59	3.69	5.78	87.14
Poor	1.19	1.9	2.14	2.38	92.38	1.07	1.95	3.31	2.63	91.03
Rich	2.99	2.35	3.84	6.18	84.65	2.03	3.55	3.95	5.17	85.31
Richest	3.21	0.2	2.41	11.45	82.73	0.87	2.73	3.6	6	86.8
0–0.5	2.74	1.92	4.25	5.62	85.46	2.26	3.72	4.17	3.92	85.94
0.5–1	1.31	3.49	4.37	1.75	89.08	0.28	2.92	4.18	5.71	86.91
1–3	1.57	1.39	2.61	6.96	87.48	1.26	2.09	5.13	7.54	83.98
3–5	0.49	2.43	3.4	1.94	91.75	4.6	5.17	4.6	5.75	79.89
5+	3.71	1.31	2.84	5.24	86.9	0	1.99	1.32	5.96	90.73

Source LSMS-1 and Field Survey

for women. Men leave their wife at home to take care of the surviving parents and entire family mostly moves if the parents have passed away (Tumbe 2018). The long duration migration for men has reduced by 10% while it has increased by 8% for the women. If we analyse these numbers with the change in duration of mobility across land class and MPCE quintiles, we find that there is rise in the long run migration for well-off individuals, individuals from large landholding and higher MPCE quintiles. The result also suggests that in cases of long term migration men travel frequently to the native place, to run farming on inherited land, while women doesn't need to do the same. Long term migration has increased for upper caste individuals from 80 to 87% over two decades while other categories of short run migration have declined. Short duration migration increased for OBC and SC/ST and long duration migration declined. Interestingly there is a rise in Muslims migrating for longer duration. It is backed by the historical waves of migration of weavers, especially *Momin* Muslim communities migrated towards the textile towns of Bombay in the nineteenth century. It has contributed to the emergence of a new corridor being established towards Maharashtra (Tumbe 2018) followed by Surat in the twentieth century (Field survey of weavers of Varanasi 2012). Within the MPCE quintile poorer individuals are doing short duration migration. Short duration migration of 1–2 months and seasonal migration of 4–9 months have increased over two decades time period. While the richest individuals are moving for longer duration, the biggest contributor to this group is women relatively to men (Figs. 1 and 2). If we look at the land class category it reinstates the same argument of increasing absentee landlords, where the long run migration have increased while individuals from the smaller landholding groups are either short run or are seasonal migrants. This also shows the reduced profitability and lucrativeness of agriculture as an employment opportunity.

Therefore, while the pattern of migration between male and female and SES category remains the same, i.e. better off moving out first either permanently or for longer duration, poorer communities are short run and seasonal migrants, mostly migrating for shorter duration. But the pattern of duration of migration has changed in two decades time period, frequent commuting and seasonal migration are replaced by long duration migration by better off individuals. It also shows that Lewisian turning point never occurred in this part of India, as individuals still rely on income from agriculture back at home. This result also indicates the lack of well-paid and secure, permanent jobs for individuals in the cities, along with higher cost of living.

Thus today, male migration from East UP and West Bihar extends in all directions within the Indian subcontinent, especially westwards and southwards, with a new line opening to the Gulf countries particularly for semiskilled and unskilled workers. While Gujaratis and Punjabis dominated the earlier waves of migration, the later phase was dominated by South Indians, especially Telegus and Tamilians, current wave of migration is dominated by UP and Bihar. However, the migration from UP and Bihar in comparison to South Indians, Gujarati and Punjabis restricts to domestic migration and of low skilled labours.

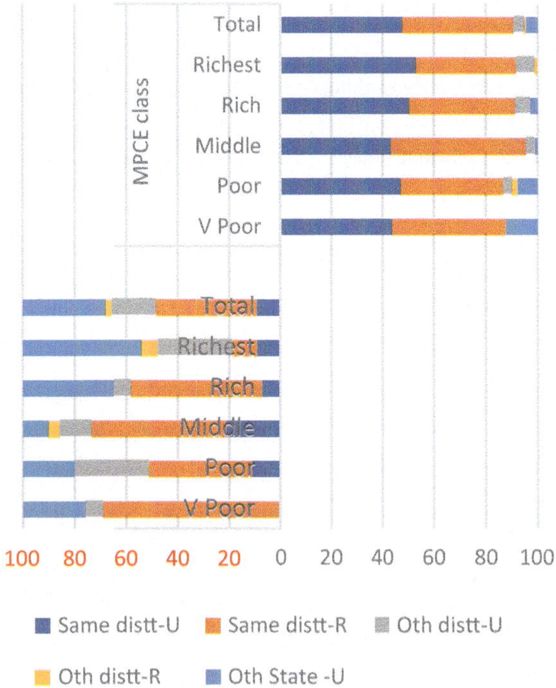

Fig. 2 Change in destination of migration in East UP and West Bihar—Income class *Source* LSMS-1 and Field Survey

4 Destination of Short Run and Long Run Mobility: Changes

Urban centres are always preferred destination, be it now or two decades ago, as Lewis theorise in his dual sector model. The migration destination to same district and other districts in the same state was mostly used by poor MPCE quintiles and land class, however, the rich and upper caste also migrated to urban centres of other states (Table 5 and Figs. 2, 3, 4). Over two decades the class-caste pattern of migration remains the same, the change, however, occurred in terms of tremendous increase in migration within the same district and sharp decline in migration to other states. Further, the decline in migration to other states happened among upper caste, higher MPCE quintile and higher land class. From our field survey, we understand that the rising service and construction sector in the small towns and cities have generated some job opportunities there, which not only made the cities like Allahabad, Gorakhpur, Patna more employable but increased the short run migration and, therefore, frequent commuting by the poorer communities. It has also increased the migration to the nearby urban centres. Thereby also increasing frequent commuting and seasonal migration.

Table 5 In 1997, only about 4% of the population was working outside, which rose to 10% by 2017

There is a bare increase in women working outside the village in comparison to men						
	LSMS-1 1997			LSMS-2 2017		
Sex	Same village	Outside village	Total	Same village	Outside village	Total
Male	94.3	5.7	66.7	79.7	20.3	45.5
Female	99.3	0.7	33.3	98.7	1.3	54.5
Total	96.0	4.0	100.0	90.1	9.9	100.0

Source LSMS-1 and Field Survey

Fig. 3 Change in destination of migration in East UP and West Bihar—Land class. *Source* LSMS-1 and Field Survey

5 Availability of Transport and Communication

Apart from sustained labour demand in an increasingly multi-polar world of multiple migration destinations, mobility seems to have been further spurred by reduction of travel costs and the revolution of communication technology, connecting people over increasingly distant places (cf. Castells 1996). Expansion of transport and communication has also contributed in labour mobility. Therefore, it makes sense to examine

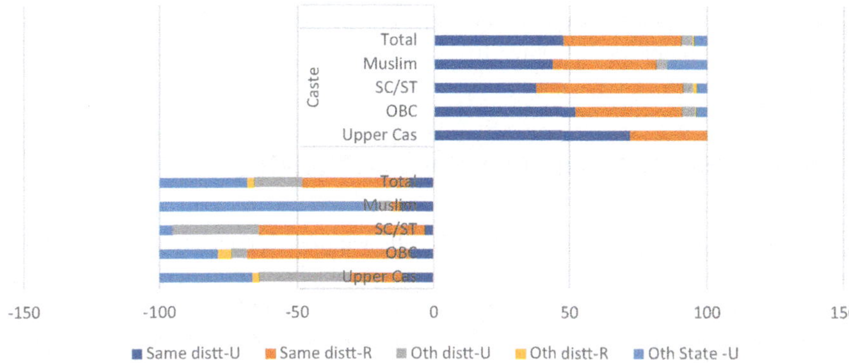

Fig. 4 Change in destination of migration in East UP and West Bihar—Caste. *Source* LSMS-1 and Field Survey

this. In this section, we have analysed village level availability of road, mode of transport and communication. We also include financial facilities as it might have a role in reducing frequent commuting and promoting long term mobility. Our field data shows that almost all villages have road connectivity, mostly metalled road (*pacca* road). Out of 21 villages of our sample, 6 villages have paved roads and only 1 village has trail road. Retail trade has witnessed phenomenal expansion in India and there has been diversification of consumption basket of rural population, away from food to non-food consumption. Consumer goods have entered into consumption basket. A barter-based village economy has been converted into cash transaction. Selling of surplus to market and filling deficit by buying from market is a growing practice in rural India. Thus, market has reached rural India in a big way in post globalisation era. This has been facilitated by better transport, communication and banking system. Thus, private means of transport like taxi/auto have emerged as the main mode of transport to cities from these villages. Public transport like availability of bus stops is still limited. These privately run shared vehicles though cater to the need of the most villagers but their frequency could depend upon the availability of number of passengers and sometimes could be very infrequent. It has surely improved the connectivity of the villages to the cities. Yet it is still a constraint for women, women with children, older and disabled. Particularly the running time of these taxi/auto matches to the mobility requirement of labourers, i.e. early morning and evening and, therefore, limiting the mobility for rest of population. Therefore, our results of migration pattern between male and female shows still relatively migration from this belt is male dominated. The increase in volume of migration is also because of improvement in road and connectivity. However, transport facilities and their stops are generally at the prime location of villages, which also require substantial distance to cover particularly for the labourer class as they often live in the farthest corner of village. This distance has to be covered by foot, further limiting the mobility of most needy with already burdens/sufferings, women and young mothers. This is one of the reasons for women staying in the villages and demanding work near their homes and limiting the mobility of women for economic activities (Table 6).

6 Availability of Communication and Banking

Apart from road transport, better communication and banking system has also influenced labour mobility. It has also impacted on type of labour mobility. Faster communication has removed the compulsion of staying near to family and, therefore, might have worked as incentive for long term mobility. But, this also means more frequent visit to the village, thereby reducing duration of migration and converting erstwhile long term mobility into short run mobility and frequent commuting. Moreover, changes in banking system have ensured that workers do not need to visit village to hand over earnings. Rather, this is done through banking system or through various apps. Nevertheless, it cannot be said with certainty in what direction this impact has been. But it is sure that labour mobility has been impacted by these changes. Mobile phone has reached every household. In our focus group discussion, villagers reported that in 1996–1997 only 'big people' (*Bdaka ghare*) have telephones, but now every individual in household has mobile as reported in the asset section of our survey. Once upon a time what was done by money order facilities in post offices, with further improving to the money order delivered at doors, making it easier for homebound women to receive money. And easier for males to go far off places (Table 7).

We have further looked at the availability of banking system and internet in the villages. Various researches have suggested that banking system has eased the fund transfer and thereby reduced the limitation to work closer to home (IFAD 2009; Madianou and Miller 2011; Mashayekhi and Branch 2015; Orozco 2016; UNCTAD 2015). Similarly, the internet has played a huge role in terms of sending and receiving information through mobile phones, internet, and many apps (Horst 2006). Our FGD in these villages suggest that people remain connected with their employers through phones and WhatsApp. The young and educated also use it to search and fill online job vacancies. Many researchers have found similar results. None of our study villages have these facilities, though they are available in the nearby towns and it takes on average 15 min to an hour to reach these facilities. Cheaper mobile data have also eased the access to internet through mobile phones. After foot, bicycle and followed by motorcycle is the most frequent used transport to reach to these facilities. We looked at ownership of these vehicles by the distance covered by the villagers. The bicycle is the most common mode of transport and ownership of motorised vehicle remains very low. Therefore, no wonder we see most people covering these distances on foot. This indicates communication has favoured the rich, youth and male and, therefore, higher mobility of this group.

Table 6 Road and transport 2016–2017

District	Village	Road type	Bus stop (no)	Distance to facility (in Km)	Transport to reach to facility	Time taken to reach in mnt.	Taxi/Auto stand (no.)	Distance to facility in Km	Transport to reach to facility	Time taken to reach in mnt
Jahanabad	Ismailupr	Pakka road	2	3	Foot	0.45	2	1	Foot	15.00
	Dahuha	Pakka road	2	2	Foot	0.30	yes	0	Foot	0.05
	Sakrauhrah	Pakka road	2	3	Foot	0.30	2	3	Foot	0.30
Saharsa	Modhara	Pakka road	2	7	Foot/vehicle	0.40	2	2	Foot/vehicle	0.10
	Gamraho	Kutcha road	yes	0.5	Foot	0.05	yes	0.5	Foot	0.05
	Manikpur	Paved road	yes	0.5	Foot	0.05	yes	0.5	Foot	0.05
Vaishali	Jamalpur	Paved road	2	2	Foot	0.20	2	1	Foot	0.15
	Kutubpur	Pakka road	2	0.5	Foot	0.10	yes	0	Foot	0.05
	Mohanpur	Paved road	2	4	Foot/vehicle	0.30	2	4	Foot/vehicle	0.30
Banda	Madain	Pakka road	2	20	Foot/vehicle	0.50	2	3	Foot	0.50
	Karaundh	Pakka road	2	15	Motor vehicle	0.30	yes	0	Foot	0.05
	Pathara	Pakka road	2	6	Motor vehicle	0.20	yes	0	0	0.05
	Audha	Paved road	2	13	Motor vehicle	0.35	yes	0	Foot	0.10
Allahabad	Tarav	Pakka road	yes	0.5	Foot	0.10	yes	0.5	Foot	0.10
	Hathigan	Pakka road	2	6	Motor vehicle	0.20	yes	0.3	Foot	0.05
	Beeker	Pakka road	2	2	Cycle	0.15	2	2	Cycle	0.15

(continued)

Table 6 (continued)

District	Village	Road type	Bus stop (no)	Distance to facility (in Km)	Transport to reach to facility	Time taken to reach in mnt.	Taxi/Auto stand (no.)	Distance to facility in Km	Transport to reach to facility	Time taken to reach in mnt
	Sandwa Khurd	Trail only	2		Foot	0.25	2		Foot	0.25
Gorakhpur	Parsawna	Paved road	2	3	Motorcycle	0.20	yes	0	Foot	0.05
	Ghoradeor	Paved road	2	7	Cycle	0.35	2	7	Cycle	0.35
	Dihwa Bujurg	Pakka road	2	6	Cycle	0.30	2	6	Cycle	0.30
	Kurwa	Pakka road	2	12	Foot/vehicle	0.40	2	2	Foot	0.35

Source Field Survey

Table 7 Financial system and internet 2016–2017

District	Village	Bank	Distance to facility	Transport to reach to facility	Time taken to reach	ATM	Distance to facility	Transport to reach to facility	Time taken to reach	Cyber café	Distance to facility	Transport to Reach to facility	Time taken to reach
Jahanabad	Ismailupr	2	2.5	Cycle	0.20	2	1	1	0.20	2	1	Foot	0.20
	Dahuha	2	2	Cycle	0.20	2	2	3	0.20	2	7	Foot/vehicle	1.30
	Sakrauhrah	2	4	Cycle	0.25	2	4	3	0.25	2	4	Cycle	0.25
Saharsa	Modhara	2	4	Foot/vehicle	0.20	2	7	7	0.20	2	2	Foot/vehicle	0.10
	Gamraho	2	3.5	Motorcycle	0.20	2	3.5	4	0.20	yes	0.5	Foot	0.50
	Manikpur	2	4	Motorcycle	0.15	2	3	4	0.15	2	3	Motorcycle	0.15
Vaishali	Jamalpur	2	2	Foot/vehicle	0.20	2	6	4	0.25	2	6	Motorcycle	0.25
	Kutubpur	2	0.5	Foot	0.10	2	0.5	1	0.10	2	0.5	Foot	0.10
	Mohanpur	2	4	Foot/vehicle	0.30	2	1.5	6	0.15	2	1.5	Foot/vehicle	0.15
Banda	Madain	2	29	Cycle	2.30	2	20	6	0.40	2	20	Foot/vehicle	0.35
	Karaundh	2	2	Motorcycle	0.15	2	15	4	0.30	2	15	Motorcycle	0.30
	Pathara	2	6	Cycle	0.46	2	6	4	0.20	2	6	Cycle	0.40
	Audha	yes	1	Foot	0.70	2	28	4	1.00	2	13	Motorcycle	0.35
Allahabad	Tarav	2	2	Cycle	0.15	2	2	3	0.15	2	2	Cycle	0.15
	Hathigan	2	3	Cycle	0.20	2	3	3	0.20	2	3	Cycle	0.20
	Beeker	2	2.5	Cycle	0.15	2	2	3	0.15	2	2	Cycle	0.15
	Sandwa Khurd	2		Motorcycle	0.35	2		4	0.00	2		Foot/vehicle	1.00
Gorakhpur	Parsawna	2	3	Motorcycle	0.20	2	3	3	0.20	2	3	Cycle	0.20

(continued)

Table 7 (continued)

District	Village	Bank	Distance to facility	Transport to reach to facility	Time taken to reach	ATM	Distance to facility	Transport to reach to facility	Time taken to reach	Cyber café	Distance to facility	Transport to Reach to facility	Time taken to reach
	Ghoradeor	2	3	Cycle	0.15	2	7	3	0.35	2	3	Foot	0.30
	Dihwa Bujurg	2	6	Cycle	0.30	2	6	4	0.00	2	6	Cycle	0.30
	Kurwa	2	3	Cycle	0.30	2	3	3	0.30	2	3	Cycle	0.30

Source: Field Survey

Table 8 Worked outside village and had vehicle

	Cycle	Bike	Car	Total
yes	84.0	15.7	0.4	89.8
Location of work and availability of vehicle				
	cycle	bike	car	Total
Same District	84.3	15.0	0.8	94.1
Other Districts	60.0	40.0	0.0	3.7
Other states	100.0	0.0	0.0	2.2
Total	83.7	15.6	0.7	100.0

Source Field Survey

7 Household Endowments of Transportation and Level of Mobility

What post offices have done to the remittances, that is done by motorised two wheelers vehicles for mobility. From the analysis of household asset ownership, it is clear that there is a sharp rise in ownership of mobiles and motorcycles. While mobile has increased the connectivity, motorcycle has increased the short D-D (duration and destination) migration easy and frequent as suggested in Sects. 3 and 4. Whether working in village or outside, around 89% have any vehicle. Around 15% of the household have motorcycle/scooter. Those who are working in other districts owns more motorcycle/scooter than those working in the same district. The construction of roads under MGNREGA and Pradhan Mantri Gram Vikas Yojana has played a significant role in improving connectivity of village and road quality. It, in turn, increases the ownership of motorcycle, because still most of the village either doesn't have bus/taxi stand or if has the frequency of bus and taxi is low or inconvenient. Therefore, motorcycles in the villages and on the roads of UP and Bihar are the most obviously found and seen vehicle. And a fun fact, it became an important demand in dowry for a graduate with job from poor SES community or without job from higher SES community, shows a social premium in must having a object, i.e. motorcycle for boys (Table 8).

8 Conclusion

Therefore, as discussed in the introduction, while other parts of India benefited from their wealthy and educated diaspora in and outside the country, migration from UP and Bihar mostly remains inter-state or intra-state, of low skilled and less educated labours. Primarily because this area was agriculture belt. As much as 68% of workers was working in agriculture and contributing 39% to state GDP in 1993 in UP and 65% was working in agriculture and contributing 50% to state GDP of Bihar in

1993. As a result when agriculture gradually became unprofitable, its contribution to GSDP in UP & Bihar declined to 20 and 18%, respectively, in 2018–10 (EPWRF, accessed on 12 Feb 2020). Only a very small percentage of population of upper caste who were traditionally educated actually moved out at higher positions and became absentee landlords. But the majority being agricultural labour found job in construction sector as unskilled labour as suggested by our analysis. Further, the coastal belts of India also received immigrants from outside such as Parses, Muslims, Portuguese which not only encouraged trade but also improved the social relations from other continents. But this belt only faced extortion in agriculture through various land and agricultural tax regime, no social or trade exchange which kept this region mostly orthodox, backward and illiterate. So a regional pattern in temporary labour migration is evident in the low income central and north Indian states mostly circular and seasonal migration dominated by young male (Keshri and Bagat 2013), whose remittances are sustaining the loss-making agriculture. Historically, economy of the states based on trade and business flourish, because whenever the regime became difficult for traders and business people, they moved to other countries or regions and thereby creating a strong network between the places of their migration (Sindhis, Baniya). Since UP and Bihar are dependent on agriculture with a fixity of land, this movement is not possible whatever is the regime. As a result, neither they benefited from agriculture activities nor could develop strong network of exchanges through migration.

In our analysis, we have looked at differential in short run and long run labour mobility across household income levels and land endowments. Our result suggests that long term migration to far off places by rich and upper caste and higher land-holding group and short term migration is to the nearer places by poorer communities. The big story about work-related migration in this belt lies between two poles of short and long run migrations which were earlier seasonal and permanent migration. This is the world of semi-permanent migration, where migrants seem to have discovered 'secret of perpetual migration' (Tumbe 2018). However, as hypothesised that household endowment affects one's capability to mobility, we find that the better off workers are migrating to far off places and generally for longer duration. Workers in lowest income quintile are confined to same district with short run migration; only some of them are going to other state and doing long run migration. International migration is reported only in household from the highest income group (LSMS 2016).

Road transportation and banking and connectivity have played a major role in change of duration and volume of migration. Data shows an improvement in reach of roads particularly metaled road. However, there is substantial variation in terms of quality of roads; they are better at the entrance but gets poorer as one enters to the corners of the villages which are generally occupied by the poor and low caste people. Further, taxi and auto have reached to the villages but again the access to them is very selective, and, therefore, one has to travel long to reach them. We don't have data on the frequency of taxi/auto availability, which can be another constraint. Only one village has a bus stop, which also requires travel of 5 Kms. Therefore, household ownership of motorized vehicle seems to have revolutionised frequent commuting. However, still large number of frequent commuters seems to use cycle, of course, from mostly poorer income groups. Car remains a much luxury. We don't have data on the difficulty faced by this group of people in frequent commuting while mostly doing short run migration, but these are the people who are investors to the village economy; travelling in acute lack of personal/public transport can hint at their struggle and constraint. Further, the migration of young and male and better educated to far off places and better work shows the constraint played by unavailability of transportation in villages particular for women, which is a great constraint for employment opportunity for women. At the end, we can't deny the improvement in basic infrastructure road and transport, banking and information communication and its role played in increasing migration: circular or short run, however, its quantity and quality remains a concern.

References

Bashi, V. F. (2007). *Survival of the knitted: Immigrant social networks in a stratified world*. Stanford: Stanford University Press.

Bhagat, R. B., & Mohanty, S. (2009). Emerging pattern of urbanization and the contribution of migration in urban growth in India. *Asian Population Studies, 5*(1), 5–20. https://doi.org/10.1080/17441730902790024.

Bertoli, S., & Ruyssen, I. (2018). Networks and migrants' intended destination. *Journal of Economic Geography, 18*(4), 705–728.

Castells, M. (1996). *The network society: The information age: economy, society and culture, Vol. I: The rise of the network society*. Cambridge, MA, Oxford, UK: Blackwell Publishers.

Chavan, P., & Bedamatta, R. (2006). Trends in agricultural wages in India 1964–65 to 1999–2000. *Economic and Political Weekly*, 4041–4051.

De Hein, H. (2009): Mobility and human development. In *Working paper*. International Migration Institute, University of Oxford.

Horst, H. A. (2006). The Blessings and burdens of communication: Cell phones in Jamaican transnational social fields. *Global Networks, 6*(2), 143–159.

International Fund for Agricultural Development (IFAD). (2009). Sending Money Home to Africa, Remittance markets, enabling environment and prospects. Available from: http://www.ifad.org/remittances/pub/money_africa.pdfINTERNATIONAL.

Keshri, K., & Bhagat, R. B. (2013). Socioeconomic determinants of temporary labour migration in India. *Asian Population Studies, 9*(2), 175–195. https://doi.org/10.1080/17441730.2013.797294.

Living Standard Measurement Study. (2016). *Funded by ICSSR*. New Delhi.

Mani, A., & Riley, E. (2019). *Social networks, role models, peer effects, and aspirations*. WIDER Working Paper 2019/120. Helsinki: UNU-WIDER.

Madianou, M., & Miller, D. (2011). Mobile phone parenting: Reconfiguring relationships between filipina migrant mothers and their left-behind children. *New Media & Society, 13*(3), 457–470.

Mashayekhi, M., & Branch, C. D. (2015). Remittances and financial inclusion. In *13th coordination meeting on international migration* (pp. 12–13). New York.

Orozco, M. (2016). *Understanding income, remittances and financial access in Latin America and the Caribbean: The case of El salvador*. Washington, DC. Available from: http://www.thedialogue.org/wp-content/uploads/2016/11/Orozco_Understanding-Income-2.pdf.

Taylor, J. E. (1999). The new economics of labour migration and the role of remittances in the migration process. *International Migration, 37*, 63–88.

Tumbe C. (2018). *India moving*. Penguin.

UNCTAD. (2015). Access to Financial Services As a Driver for the Post-2015 Development Agenda. Policy Brief No.35 (September 2015) Available from: http://unctad.org/en/PublicationsLibrary/presspb2015d7_en.pdf.

Migrating to the Roads in the Cities in Uttar Pradesh: Some Reflections

Bhaskar Majumder and V. Narayan

Abstract The members, mostly male, from the distressed households in the rural regions migrate to the cities in India in search of jobs and stand on the public roads each morning. These street labourers are hired by employers for engagement at the bottom of the labour market understood by the work profile. These labourers are supposedly free to offer their labour power to any buyer at perceived labour-equivalent wage rate and refrain from questioning the working conditions that often remain adverse as much as the adverse initial conditions at their outmigration zone; these adverse conditions incapacitate them to bargain. This paper examines if migration of the street labourers in all the six million-plus populated cities of Uttar Pradesh reflects migration under distress and if labour is forced in nature. The paper also addresses the institutional questions by legal provisions and suggests at the end what are to be done.

1 Introduction

In any million-plus populated city in India, one observes an assembly of mostly male persons standing on the crossing of roads ready to offer their labour power. Most of them migrate from near and far, intra-state and inter-state. These migrated labourers do not have any idea where they will be absorbed and for what tenure. These labourers are free hand and ready to work manually. Supply of labour finds its market in the urban economy through a brief negotiation between the labourers and the employers. While some are absorbed, others stay behind as residue. The next morning some more labourers may join the residue assembly that hides the temporary exit of cross-sections of reserve labourers from the crossings of roads. The short-term production relation between the employer and the labourers often does not go beyond the working hours of a day. The labourers are not tied to any particular employer. Each one is free to untie the work relation. The engagement is oral; there

B. Majumder (✉) · V. Narayan
G B Pant Social Science Institute, Allahabad 211019, India
e-mail: majumderb@rediffmail.com

N. K. Mishra (ed.), *Development Challenges of India After Twenty Five Years of Economic Reforms*, India Studies in Business and Economics,
https://doi.org/10.1007/978-981-15-8265-3_19

is no legal/written contract. The works done by the labourers include earthworks, head-load works, construction works or any manual work that the employers offer and the worker agrees to execute. The tenure of job depends on the quantum of work and the ability-cum-willingness of the labourer to work in exchange of wages. The tenure of job, thus, varies from very short-term like for a day, to medium-term like a few months. The location of the worksite is limited to the city itself or to the urban fringes.

The crossing of roads where the labourers wait for job is called labour *chauraha* in Uttar Pradesh. Labour *chaurahas* are not worksites; they are crossings of roads of different directions, which are assembly points for the job-seeking migrant labourers. These labour *chaurahas* generally get formed adjacent to bus depots, railway stations and markets as the labourers come by train/bus to the city depending on distance and travel cost, which they bear on their own. All of them move out from their native villages in search of jobs. The assembled labourers on the street crossings can also be called street labourers, not in the sense that they have no residential address, but in the sense that public roads become their living spaces by compulsion in absence of better alternatives to live and to search jobs in the cities. The local administration does not obstruct them from occupying space on the public road since it is for short periods per day, generally from 6:00 a.m. to 10:00 a.m. There is no display board to show geographic existence of labour *chaurahas*. These *chaurahas* have evolved from its embryonic stage since unrecorded past. These labourers generally are not accompanied by their family members. The labourers are not paid any advance wage when they are offered employment. This implies apparent freedom of the street labourers to offer labour power to any buyer. They do not have any long-term employment guarantee or attachment with any particular employer and they remain in circulation over several employers and cities.

The city where the labourers assemble has to be large by size of population, infrastructure, trade and business, and industries. The workers usually migrate from poverty-zone to search for jobs. Most of the labourers come from landless households generally during off-agricultural seasons each year in the absence of scope to work as agricultural labourers or as tenants in their native villages. Cultivation remaining seasonal in most parts of India, the landless wage-labourers and marginal farmers migrate to other places during off-agriculture seasons (Oberai and Singh 1983: 30; Sahu and Das 2010: 103; Korra 2011: 68). Inter-state migration shows mostly migration from poorer region to less poor region (Nceus 2008: 96). Most of the migrant labourers belong to castes at the bottom of the Hindu social hierarchy (SCs and OBCs) but labourers from high castes may also migrate to cities to get engaged in manual jobs since the sociocultural scenario in India's rural areas do not allow people from high caste households to get engaged in manual-menial works. These migrant households earn income below subsistence level at the root and so they are forced to migrate elsewhere for survival. Being mostly illiterate and poor, they remain as manual labourers at the bottom of the labour market in the unorganized segment of the economy. The rural to urban migration is not determined by the actual or expected wage-differential because there is no wage rate in rural areas in absence of any job opportunities during off-agricultural season. The non-farm rural activities and restricted access to shrinking common resources cannot retain them for long in the rural areas; hence, they migrate to cities for any job at any wage rate for survival.

The population of cities accelerates due to rural-urban migration and natural increase of population (UN-HABITAT 2003). Urbanization shows increasing carrying capacity of the city to attract population from outside through expanding economic opportunities. The material standard of living has distanced gradually from dependence on land-cum-agriculture to urban living for an increasing number and percentage of the population. The literature on urbanization focused on unnumbered indicators that included rural territorial annexation and its transformation into a city (Ramachandran 1992; Kundu 1994; Bhagat 2011; Bhagat and Mohanty 2009; Saxena 2014). It took half a century for UP to register urban population as a percentage of rising total population from 12.9 in 1961 to 22.3 in 2011 parallel to 31.2% for all-India in 2011. In 2001 as well as in 2011 there were six million-plus populated cities in UP, namely, Lucknow, Allahabad, Agra, Kanpur, Varanasi and Meerut.

The paper addresses the following questions: Does migration of the street labourers reflect migration under distress? Does the unity of street labourers and local labourers by similar initial conditions lead to rising bargaining power of these labourers? Do the street labourers know the legal provisions for them? The final question is, what is to be done?

In order to address the first question we take three basic indicators at the household level: (i) land owned, (ii) income earned, (iii) indebtedness; all at the root rural areas from where the labourers migrate. We call it migration under distress if the livelihood security of these people remains endangered in the rural areas in the absence of regular job-cum-income opportunities in combination with debt bondage. The juxtaposition is, if distress remains at the destination also by the adopted indicators of (iv) processes of labour engagement and consequences by wage payment and (v) work environment at the city destination. The Bonded Labour System (Abolition) Act 1976, enacted by the Government of India, declared the practice of bonded labour as illegal. If the same or similar initial conditions exist, then we call it forced labour, one degree less than being bonded labour, since they are not physically confined to the creditor as is the case with bonded labourers. The ILO Forced Labour Convention, 1930 (No. 29) considered forced labour as 'all work or service extracted from any person under the menace of any penalty and for which that person has not offered himself (or herself) voluntarily' (ILO 2007: 19; UNDP 2015: 41). Forced labour is 'not defined by the nature of the work being performed (which can be either legal or illegal under national law) but rather by the nature of the relationship between the person performing the work and the person exacting the work' (ILO 2012: 19). We expand the connotation of forced labour to include labour that is offered by the labourers in adverse environments over which they have no control. In order to address the second question, we examine the tenure of jobs of the migrant labourers, their working hours and work environment, and wage rate in the city labour market. While it is difficult to examine wage-differential, if any, between the migrant and non-migrant labourers intra-city and inter-city because of the differences in work profile, the point of time and job tenure, we may examine if any conflict arose because of the migrant street labourers waiting on the crossing of public roads for jobs. In order to address the third question, we examine the Acts formulated by the state that pledged to protect these street labourers and if the migrant labourers are aware of these Acts.

The rest of the paper is structured as follows. Section 2 presents the methodology, sample and study zone. Section 3 examines the causes and consequences of migration of labourers to wait on public roads in the cities. The nature of state intervention by the Acts is discussed in Sect. 4. Finally, Sect. 5 offers conclusions and recommendations.

2 Methodology, Sample, and Study Zone

All six million-plus populated cities in UP from Census, 2011 are selected. Pilot visits were made in each city to find out the locations/road crossings where labourers wait early in the morning. There were a total of 80 identified labour *chaurahas* in these six cities in UP in 2012. A total of 24 were selected, four from each city based on geographic dispersal and the number of visible labourers early in the morning prior to their getting jobs (Box 1).

Box 1 Study zone

Selected zone and labour *Chaurahas*	Number	Names
State	1	UP
City*	6	Allahabad, Kanpur, Lucknow, Agra, Meerut, Varanasi
Name of selected labour *chaurahas*	24	Rambag, Rajapur, Allahpur, Jhusi (Allahabad); Lalbangla, Mulganj, KDA, Govindpur (Kanpur); Engineering College, Udayganj, Nishant, Goyel Chauraha (Lucknow); Kamal Nagar, Loha Mandi, Shadra, Sikandra (Agra); Begum Bridge, Jail Chungi, Bagpat Adda, Sagasa (Meerut); Chetganj, Gurudham, Maidagini, Durgakund (Varanasi)

Note *Each one is the Head Quarter of the respective district

We took the help of catalysts who constitute the sub-sample in selecting labour *chaurahas*. These included 24 contractors, one each from the selected labour *chaurahas*, as well as 24 labour mates who facilitated in the supply of labourers. We had informal conversations with 12 representatives of labour unions and 10 representatives of NGOs (Box 2).

Box 2 Core sample and sub-sample

Core sample	Number
Labourers	240
Sub-sample	–
Contractors	24
Labour Mates	24
Representatives of labour unions	12
Representatives of NGOs	10

Note Core Sample and Sub-Sample are non-additive

We did not find any register maintained by the city administration to find the total number of street labourers, and we could not enumerate the total number of these labourers on the *chaurahas*. Based on pilot visits we selected 40 migrant labourers from each of the six cities that varied intra-state and inter-state. We selected a total of ten (10) male labourers from each labour *chauraha*. The intra-state migrant labourers constituted 80.8% and the rest were inter-state (Table 1).

Of all the migrant labourers, 90.0% were males. Of the male labourers, 80.8% were intra-state. Of the female migrant labourers, 54.2% were intra-state. Of all the labourers, 29.6% were SCs, 45.0% OBCs, 7.9% Minority (Muslims), 2.5% STs and 15.0% from General Castes. Further, 93.3% of the labourers were in the working age group of 18–60 years. Illiterate constituted 41.7% of the labourers. Of the literate labourers, 41.2% had education up to primary level (Field Survey 2012). The labourers migrated intra-state (UP) and inter-state, the latter from the adjoining states of Bihar, Jharkhand, Madhya Pradesh and Chhattisgarh (Box 3).

Table 1 Distribution of migrant labourers in selected cities of UP

Destination cities	Migrant labourers				Total
	Intra-state		Inter-state		
	Number	%	Number	%	Number
Agra	29	14.9	11	23.9	40
Allahabad	33	17.0	7	15.2	40
Kanpur	40	20.6	0	0.0	40
Lucknow	26	13.4	14	30.4	40
Meerut	35	18.0	5	10.9	40
Varanasi	31	16.0	9	19.5	40
Total Labourers	194 (80.8)		46 (19.2)		240 (100.0)

Source Field Survey, 2012

Box 3 Inter-state and intra-state migrant labourers to the selected cities in UP

Destination cities	Intra-state migrants (By Districts in UP)	Inter-state migrants
Allahabad	Mirzapur, Azamgarh, Pratapgarh, Allahabad, Ballia, Bhadohi, Bahraich, Jaunpur	Madhya Pradesh, Chhattisgarh
Kanpur	Sultanpur, Faizabad, Allahabad, Unnao, Fatehpur, Raebareli, Basti, Lucknow, Kanpur, Kanpur Dehat, Mahoba, Ballia, Kaushambi	–
Lucknow	Raebareli, Unnao, Sultanpur, Hardoi, Barabanki, Gonda, Bahraich, Lakhimpur Kheri	Bihar, Chhattisgarh
Agra	Agra, Jhansi, Mathura, Farrukhabad, Aligarh, Auraiya, Mahoba	Madhya Pradesh
Meerut	Meerut, Agra, Moradabad, Muzaffarnagar, Hapur, Baghpat, Shahjahanpur, Bareilly, Sitapur	Bihar, Madhya Pradesh, Jharkhand
Varanasi	Varanasi, Sonebhadra, Mirzapur, Ghazipur, Mau, Chandauli, Sultanpur, Azamgarh, Pratapgrah, Bhadohi	Madhya Pradesh, Bihar

Source Field Survey, 2012

3 Causes and Consequences of Migration of Labourers to the City Roads

The major reason for migration to the city roads was landlessness or inadequate landholding that failed to fulfil the subsistence needs of the households at the migration zone. 54.6% of the migrant labourers were landless. Of those having land, 67.8% had land less than 2.0 acres. Thus, the landholders had marginal landholding (Table 2).

Purchase-cum-investment on land was beyond the capacity of the landless households; marginal landholding was inadequate to sustain the households by subsistence

Table 2 Size of landholding of migrant labourers at root

Landholding (Acres)	Intra-state		Inter-state		Total	
	Number	%	Number	%	Number	%
Landless	112	57.3	19	41.3	131	54.6
Up to 1.0	26	13.4	12	26.1	38	15.8
1.0–2.0	28	14.4	8	17.4	36	15.0
2 .0–4.0	19	9.79	4	8.7	23	9.6
4.0–6.0	3	1.5	1	2.2	4	1.7
Above 6.0	6	3.1	2	4.3	8	3.3
Total	194 (80.8)		46 (19.2)		240	100.0

Source Field Survey, 2012

Table 3 Employment and wage rtes in MGNREGA by gender in rural areas, 2011

Labourers migrated	Job card owners (As % of Total)	Man days created		Wage rate (Rs.) per day	
		Male	Female	Male	Female
Intra-state (UP)	33.8	25	11	93.00	100.00
Inter-State	7.9	19	17	92.00	87.00
Total Labourers	41.6	24	14	93.00	93.00

Source Field Survey, 2012

guarantee. Non-farm rural activities like animal husbandry and forestry could not be relied upon due to shrinking common resources. Rural public works like MGNREGA also could not absorb the labourers (Table 3).

41.3% of the migrant labourers were employed for a period of less than three months per year, and 79.7% were employed for a period less than six months in the rural economy implying compulsion for the most to migrate (Table 4).

The derivative reason got reflected in income below subsistence requirements. Almost 95% of the migrant households earned income less than Rs. 2,500.00 per month including households earning no income (Table 5).

Landlessness, short-duration employment and low income led to indebtedness. 24.2% of the migrant labourers were indebted, which was 24.7% of all intra-state labourers, and 21.7% of all inter-state labourers. 89.7% of the households borrowed from non-institutional sources, namely, *mahajans*, relatives and friends. 75.9% of all the households borrowed from *mahajans* (informal money lenders). The institutional sources were banks. Indebtedness was because of expenditure on health, rituals and food (Table 6).

Informal information, and not formal advertisement through print or electronic media, helped the labourers to migrate to stand on the roads of cities. The local administration was indifferent about the assembly on the road crossings. Physical visibility of these street labourers helped them get jobs. 78.8% of the migrant labourers got works for a tenure of more than six months per year at the destination. This was

Table 4 Employment tenure of the migrant labourers per year at root

Employment tenure (Months)	Intra-state		Inter-state		Total	
	Number	%	Number	%	Number	%
Less than 3	79	40.7	20	43.5	99	41.3
3–6	72	37.1	18	39.1	90	37.5
6–9	42	21.6	5	10.9	47	19.6
Above 9	1	0.5	3	6.5	4	1.7
Total labourers	194 (80.8)		46 (19.2)		240	100.0

Source Field Survey, 2012

Table 5 Income of the households of migrant labourers per month at root

Income per month (Rs.)	Intra-state		Inter-state		Total	
	Number	% of total	Number	% of total	Number	% of total
No income	25	12.9	7	15.2	32	13.3
Below 500	49	25.2	11	23.9	60	25.0
501–1,000	55	28.3	16	34.8	71	29.6
1,001–1,500	28	14.4	6	13.0	34	14.2
1,501–2,500	28	14.4	5	10.9	33	13.7
Above 2,500	9	0.5	1	2.2	10	4.2
Total Labourers	194 (80.8)		46 (19.2)		240	100.0

Note The unemployed section in the working age and unpaid home workers reported no income
Source Field Survey, 2012

Table 6 Borrowing by migrant labourers by sources at root

Borrowing (Rs.)	Workers	Sources of borrowing				Total
		Institutional	Non-institutional			
		Banks	Mahajans	Relatives	Friends	
Less than 10,000	No.	1	23	5	1	30
	% of Total	1.7	39.7	8.6	1.7	51.7
10,001–25,000	No.	2	12	1	1	16
	% of Total	3.4	20.7	1.7	1.7	27.6
25,001–50,000	No.	2	7	0	0	9
	% of Total	3.4	12.1	0.0	0.0	15.5
Above 50,000	No.	1	2	0	0	3
	% of Total	1.7	3.4	0.0	0.0	5.2
Total labourers	No.	6	44	6	2	58
	% of Total	10.3	75.9	10.3	3.4	100.0

Source Field Survey, 2012

similar for both intra-state and inter-state migrants. 65.9% of the labourers earned between Rs. 2,001 and Rs. 5,000 per month in the cities (Tables 7 and 8).

The street labourers negotiated with the employers and the contractors to fix the wage rate. 59.6% of the labourers got wages at time rate. The major labour absorption sector was construction works. The average wage rate per day for migrant labourers was Rs. 177.00; with Rs. 176.00 for intra-state and Rs. 180.00 for inter-state. The average working days per month were 18 and the average working hours per day was 9.0. Both varied between cities. 72.1% of the migrant labourers used to carry cash savings to their rural root, while 12.1% used to remit through co-workers, friends and relatives. 7.9% of the labourers could not save anything. The inter-state migrant labourers used to visit their native places once in six months while the intra-state

Table 7 Job tenure for the migrant labourers per year at destination

Job tenure (Months)	Intra-state		Inter-state		Total	
	Number	%	Number	%	Number	%
Less than 3	1	0.5	3	6.5	4	1.7
3–6	42	21.6	5	10.9	47	19.6
6–9	72	37.1	18	39.1	90	37.5
Above 9	79	40.7	20	43.5	99	41.3
Total Labourers	194 (80.8)		46 (19.2)		240	100.0

Source Field Survey, 2012

Table 8 Income of migrant labourers per month at destination

Income brackets (Rs.)	Intra-state		Inter-state		Total	
	Number	%	Number	%	Number	%
Up to 1,500	7	3.6	2	4.3	9	3.8
1,501 to 2,000	20	10.3	8	17.4	28	11.7
2,001 to 3,000	38	19.6	7	15.2	45	18.8
3,001 to 4,000	55	28.3	11	23.9	66	27.5
4,001 to 5,000	41	21.1	6	13.0	47	19.6
Above 5,000	33	17.0	12	26.1	45	18.7
Total Labourers	194 (80.8)		46 (19.2)		240	100.0

Source Field Survey, 2012

migrant labourers once in three months, implying non-confinement of labourers de jure and confinement de facto (Field Survey 2012).

80.8% of the migrant labourers reported non-availability of first aid and safety kit on the worksite; 80.4% reported absence of toilet; 79.2% reported absence of restroom/shed; 97.5% reported availability of drinking water at worksites (Field Survey 2012). Thus, the work environment was adverse for the migrant labourers (Box 4).

Box 4 Work environment for migrant labourers

Work environment
Insecurity, drudgery, abusive behaviour of employer, wage-cut, pressurized to work more hours for same wage, no protection against injury, no leave, no night shelter and no provision of food.

Source Field Survey, 2012

In terms of living conditions, 50.8% of the migrant labourers were homeless in the city; 15.0% lived in *Jhopris*, while 10.8% were commuters on daily basis (Field Survey 2012). Living homeless at the destination is a major reflection of migration to the road—for temporary jobs as well as for spending nights.

Table 9 Average wages per month of migrant labourers at root and destination

Locations	Migrant labourers	Average wages (Rs.)	Number of workers	% of labourers
Root	Intra-state	877.5	194	80.8
	Inter-state	724.3	46	19.2
	Grand average	848.2	240	100.0
Destination	Intra-state	3253.2	194	80.8
	Inter-state	3366.3	46	19.2
	Grand average	3274.9	240	100.0

Note Income data in the rural outmigration zone was based on income per month reported by 54.6 per cent of the labourers who were landless and worked as wage-labourers in agriculture and related rural activities
Source Field Survey, 2012

The rural average wage per month (of root) was an estimation based on approximately 15 days work per month that the migrant labourers might have worked there mostly as agricultural labourers. For intra-state labourers, it was Rs. 877.5 per month and for inter-state labourers it was Rs. 724.3. The city workday per month on average was 18 for both intra-state and inter-state migrant labourers. The average wages per month at the destination for the migrant labourers was around four times what they used to earn at the root for both intra-state and inter-state. This higher urban wage rate was because of the nature of urban works catering to urban market by commoditization of resources many of which had often been shared cost-free in rural areas. The agricultural wage rate had no impact on the urban wage rate (Table 9).

4 Did Street Labourers Reflect Forced Labour?

Force is physical-psychological-institutional—all or a combination of these may go together. Even in absence of physical coercion one may feel forced to leave the root because of inter-generational poverty and indebtedness. 'Labour may be forced not only owing to physical force….but also owing to hunger and poverty which compels (a worker) him to accept employment for remuneration which is less than the statutory minimum wage' (ILO 2001:9). 'Migration to cities may not necessarily emancipate them for they move from one disadvantaged condition to another adverse inclusion' (Roy 2013: 41).

In a situation of work at piece rate and in a non-comparable frame of labour-hours, the condition of paying less than the minimum wage rate does not reflect much, apart from the fact that the minimum wage rate as announced by the State Government remains far from being implemented for the workers in circulation in the unorganized segment in India. The migrant labourers waiting on the crossings of public roads in the cities in India as a gateway to enter into the labour market did not come within the scrutiny of the ILO so far (ILO 2001: 2).

'The ultimate purpose of forced labor—into which workers enter through failed systems of recruitment—is almost always economic exploitation through payments to workers below the level that appeared to have been mutually agreed upon and negotiated' (Andrees and Belser 2009: 4). We observed violation of wage negotiations by wage-cut and imposition of long working hours since the negotiation was oral and unequal. The excess supply of labourers on the labour *chaurahas* in the cities in UP on a daily basis lessened their bargaining power. Extremely unequal relations between the city-based employers and migrant labourers posed doubt on the possibility of a wage rate 'mutually agreed upon and negotiated'. The labourers negotiated the wage but any bargaining for fixation of wage rate by the street labourers made such negotiation fractured, mainly because of the adverse conditions of the labourers which forced them to enter into the city labour market. Since these labourers were mostly migrants from rural areas, who were illiterate and poor and indebted, their voices were suppressed. They had no exchangeable assets and no elastic time for job search, since not getting job in one day would mean starving for most of them. Being migrants, they could not expect to hire productive assets from any asset owner for providing services in the city. In the absence of secure space, they could not shoulder the risk of buying any productive assets in the city, even if they acquired the economic capacity, as they would not be able to protect those. The *chauraha*-specific labour contractors did not have much role to play in wage negotiations. The labour unions were apathetic towards these workers, which reinforced the disempowerment of the labourers.

The positive rural-urban wage-differential was not the determinant of migration for these labourers. The very fact that most of them had no job for tenure more than six months in the rural areas parallel to their landlessness forced them to migrate to the cities. Historically, the urban nature of work for wages at piece rate or time rate offers a wage rate higher than the rural one. But since jobs were not available at the outmigration zone for most of the year, any comparison of wage rates between rural and urban to explain migration is meaningless. That the labourers used to get jobs on an average of 18 days per month and over six to nine months per year at the destination implied the positive probability of getting jobs in the selected cities in UP. This also implied that these cities had the capacity to carry these labourers who waited for jobs. These jobs were manual, low-quality and delinked from education and skill.

The job contract was oral, delinked from any commitment on job security. The job itself was not regular. The employers went on changing within a short time-span. Once the employer-specific work was over, the labourers would come back to their *chaurahas* to search for another job and another employer, or move to another city. They had no effective power to influence the wage rate. It was determined from the demand side because of the unlimited supply of labourers on the crossing of roads. Employment of one fraction of the labourers did not create any vacuum in the *chaurahas*. These labourers reflected free entry into, and free exit from, the city labour market. This is not to be seen as 'free wage-labour' for it was not webbed in the macro market mechanism and it operates locally in fragments in a rudimentary form. The rural economy in parallel reflected the inertia of landlords to invest on land to retain labourers. The practice of money lending made the dependent landless labourers indebted to the money lenders. This indebtedness forced the labourers to migrate in a condition of never-ending outstanding debt repayment.

More than half of the migrant labourers were homeless in their destinations. City-housing was a remotely attainable good for them as they were not permanent migrants and were unable to maintain two residential houses. The work environment showed their adverse inclusion at the bottom of the labour market in the city. The migrant labourers had no preference for any particular city and were ready to move to any city in India. The poverty of the adjoining states, namely, Bihar, Jharkhand, Madhya Pradesh and Chhattisgarh, was the cause of outmigration from these states. The intra-state migrants came from many districts of Uttar Pradesh (Box 3). The implication is that the survival instinct of the labourers forced them to migrate from their native places to reach the occupation space even if that meant being homeless at the destination. They migrated on their own delinked from any networking. There was no *thekedar* (contractor) to take them to a specific employer for work. There was no system of advance wages for them. They waited on the crossing of roads in the expectation of getting engaged as wage-labourer through an employer/contractor. They had no ex-ante information about the worksites or the nature of work and they often did not come in contact with the employer when he operated through his agents. The labour *chaurahas* were the assembly points of available labourers who were ready to work on demand. The demand side was revealed when the contractors reached the *chaurahas*, generally on a motorcycle with a pillion rider, to select the required number of labourers based on the fulfilment of the skill required and the wage rate agreed upon. The labourers encircled the man on the motorcycle to negotiate and offer themselves for work. The negotiation would be usually settled, the contractor would go back after telling the labourers to join the job. The labourers would decide their mode of transport and reach the worksite by the specified time. The labourer was free not to accept the offered wage rate in which case he would search for another employer or starve or go back to the village; the last option would be unwelcome except for daily commuters. Hence, the labourer preferred any wage rate to the absence of job or to a prolonged wait on the road since early morning. The migrant labourers went back to their native places once they completed their works at the city destination. There were a number of reasons for going back like rural living preferred to urban living by kinship-rituals-culture-tradition, work in agriculture sector and repayment of outstanding debt. As most of them opined, had they got assured job opportunities at their native places on a regular basis even at a wage rate much lower than that of the urban wage rate they would have been less inclined to migrate to urban areas. We call it forced labour since the labourers had to migrate in an initial condition of landlessness, indebtedness and absence of subsistence guarantee at the root. The labourers migrated to large cities to wait on public road being unaware of the nature of works they will be asked to perform in an unknown location. This is irrespective of the length of time the labourers spent at the destination (ILO 2012). The adverse inclusion of the street labourers in terms of absence of any security card, job card, registration, insurance and derivative indicators at the city destination was the result of the adverse conditions at the migration zone.

It is often argued that migrant labourers changes matrix of local labour market, often inviting intra-labour conflict and thus two sections of workers are confronted with each other. Based on the wage rates by types of works the migrant labourers were engaged in and juxtaposing those vis-a-vis the wage rates that the local labourers used to earn in the same city, it was difficult to compare if the migrant labourers subsidized the local labour market or occupied a space not totally engaged by the local labourers. There are multiple sub-segments within the unorganized city-based labour market reflected in different work profiles and different wage rates at piece and time. The work profile like street hawking, vegetable vending, rickshaw pulling, auto-rickshaw pulling, card-load working were observed for the local labourers while the migrant labourers were on-wait to get engaged mostly in construction works without any ownership over work tools and head-load workers at night linked with loading and unloading of goods in the surface transport system linked with trade and commerce.

We observed normal co-existence between labourers engaged in different sub-segments of the city-based labour market. The street labourers were from the same or similar states; this was conducive to their harmonious co-existence at the bottom of the labour market. The migrant street labourers did not crowd out the local labourers. The street labourers, most of whom were intra-state migrants, lived in the same culture zone as the local labourers. Most of the labourers were in multiple distress-driven occupations, so that a '*bhai chaara*' (fraternity) developed among the migrant and local labourers. One conjecture is that the labourers, both local and migrants, were brought up under similar sociocultural conditions that bond them in a low-level equilibrium. Occupying public road by the migrant labourers was not a concern for the local labourers, not because that public road was non-excludable by use but for the simple reason that all accepted public road as their own. Nor it was a matter of concern for the city administration because of the blurred distinction between private space and public space, apart from annexation of public space for private use in the selected cities in UP. Economic distress united the labourers—local and migrants. This was, however, delinked from any labour union and so the unity could not get crystallized as a powerful platform for the labourers to effectively bargain for wage rate, working hours and job security. The street labourers were incapacitated to enter into the organized labour market because of their irrelevance for urban industrial jobs, obstructing them from being organized as an industrial working class. Supply of labour by the street labourers created demand for labour in the city economy that made the urban wage rate flexible downward but still remaining much above the wage rate in the rural agricultural job. The wage-differential, however, was not the determinant of rural-urban migration.

Since the street labourers migrated on their own, it was their responsibility to find living space, which most of them failed to do. The work-cum-living of the street labourers in the cities did not confer them a city identity. They used to go back to their native places each year not because they were mostly homeless in the destination cities but because of the initial conditions that centred on land-agriculture, house, environment, social relations, family attraction and debt repayment.

5 State Intervention: Acts

India is a signatory to the Forced Labour Convention, 1930 and to the Abolition of Forced Labour Convention, 1957, with ratifications dated 30 November 1954 and 18 May 2000, respectively (ILO 2007: 128–129; Mishra 2001: 8). The ILO Declaration on Fundamental Principles and Rights at Work adopted in 1998 pledged to eliminate all forms of forced or compulsory labour (ILO 2007: 1). It remains indecisive which Acts enacted by the Government of India encompass the migrant street labourers in the cities (GoI 2011:4-6).

The Inter-State Migrant Workmen (Regulation of Employment and Conditions of Service) Act, 1979, of the Government of India applies to every 'establishment' employing 'five or more inter-State migrant workmen' recruited through a 'contractor' that includes a sub-contractor by whatever name called, 'with or without the knowledge of the principal employer in relation to such establishment'. The Act provides that 'No principal employer of an establishment to which this Act applies shall employ inter-state migrant workmen in the establishment unless a certificate of registration in respect of such establishment issued under this Act is in force'. The contractor must have a license to recruit workmen with prior information provided on 'the terms and conditions of the agreement or other arrangement under which the workmen will be recruited, the remuneration payable, hours of work, fixation of wages….' (GoI 1979).

The migrants to the cities in UP were from 'similar states' by language-culture so that assimilation at the bottom of the labour market was natural from the supply side. From the demand side, the employers in the cities in UP were neutral between intra-state or inter-state migrant labourers so long as their skill requirement was fulfilled. We did not find any gap between the inter-state and intra-state migrant labourers geo-culturally because of the geographic vastness of UP that virtually internalized labourers at the bottom from the Hindi-speaking adjoining states. The 1979 Act pledged 'to ensure suitable conditions of work to such workmen having regard to the fact that they are required to work in a State different from their own State' (GoI 1979: 8). Neither the contractors nor the labourers had any idea about the provisions of the 1979 Act. The obscure employer–employee relation made fixing the responsibility of security of the labourers on the employer difficult. The local administration was conspicuous by its absence from shouldering any protective role for the labourers waiting on labour *chaurahas* in the selected cities in UP.

The Minimum Wages Act, 1948 of the Government of India, had provisions to 'fix the number of hours of work which shall constitute a normal working day' and 'minimum time rate wages for piece work' in tune with the provisions of the Payment of Wages Act, 1936 (GoI 1948: 8). The rural wage rate (Rs. 848.2 per month or Rs. 56.5 per day if the labourer worked for 15 days per month) was far below the minimum wage rate declared by the Government of UP. The urban wage rate for labourers on labour *chaurahas* per day was Rs. 181.94 that was also far below the minimum wage rate announced by the Government of UP. The minimum wage rate per day as declared by the Government of UP through Order dated 26 January 2014 was Rs. 284.63 for unskilled, Rs. 313.10 for semi-skilled and Rs. 350.72 for skilled labourers (GoUP, Order No. 194/36-3-2014-07/04 dated 26.01.2014).

The 1948 Act made it mandatory for every employer to maintain 'registers and records giving such particulars of employees employed by him, the work performed by them, the wages paid to them, the receipts given by them....' (GoI 1948:10). We did not find any such registers maintained by the employers/contractors since the jobs were based on hire and fire often outside public scrutiny. The labourers had no idea about the existence of any such Act. The Labour Union representatives in the organized sector were indifferent about the street labourers. The modus operandi of labour employment through labour *chaurahas* in the cities of UP reflected its own dynamics that was outside the orbit of the state. The migrant labourers had no information about any such Acts. It remains a hypothetical question what they could have done had they had the information.

6 Conclusions and Recommendations

The street labourers waiting on road crossings of the selected cities reflected a case of forced labour. The labourers migrated unobstructed; first destination was city roads to stand for physical visibility and probable second destination was workspace in and around the city. The outmigration was from 'similar states' by language and culture to nip in the bud any possibility of conflict between the in-migrant labourers and the local labourers. Also the big cities provided economic opportunities that retained the labourers for the major period of the year. To sum up,

- The major reason for migration to cities was distress at the root characterized by landlessness or inadequate landholding that failed to fulfil the subsistence needs of the households.
- Physical visibility of the migrant street labourers on city roads helped them get jobs for tenure of more than six months per year at the destination.
- The average wages per month at the destination for the migrant labourers, both intra-state and inter-state, was around four times what they used to earn at the root. The agricultural wage rate had no impact on the urban wage rate.
- The positive rural–urban wage-differential was not the determinant of migration for these labourers. The joblessness of most of them for more than six months in the rural areas parallel to their landlessness forced them to migrate to the cities.
- The assembly of street labourers did not show any sign of solidarity or conflict.
- The migrant street labourers did not crowd out the local labourers, the work profile remaining different.
- Economic distress of the households of the labourers as the initial condition was the plank of unity among the labourers in the city. This was delinked from any labour union. Hence, the local unity did not get crystallized as a platform for the labourers to bargain.

The supply of labour by migrant labourers waiting on public roads was their adverse inclusion at the bottom of the city-based labour market and an example of forced labour for the following reasons:

1. The labourers had to migrate from the rural region to the cities in adverse economic conditions characterized by landlessness and indebtedness (initial condition).
2. The labourers had to wait unauthorized on the public roads in the cities (processes).
3. The labourers had no control over their work relations in the city economy (consequences).
4. The labourers were confined de facto for they had no right to leave while on job (consequences).

We recommend a dual strategy to stop forced labour. The long-term strategy is to ensure regular wage-employment at the root rural areas through rural public works, and the short-term strategy is to ensure social security of the labourers at the destination.

We propose introducing an Act by the Government of India to address the minimum needs of street labourers. Pending this, we propose that the city administration

- recognizes the existence of the street labourers and provide roofed labour colonies with sanitation facility for accommodating the assembled migrant labourers;
- provides the labourers identity cards;
- identifies the private contractors/employers and makes them accountable by registering the labourers encompassing both inter-state and intra-state migrant labourers engaged by them, and ensuring their security at the worksite;
- provides night shelter for the in-migrant labourers with basic utilities like drinking water, first aid kit, toilet and blanket for the migrant labourers;
- makes sure that the employer provides safe drinking water, sanitation, cost-free medical care for all the labourers encompassing both inter-state and intra-state migrant labourers;
- assists the street labourers in distress with a toll-free Help Line number.

References

Andrees, B., & Belser, P. (2009). *Forced labour*. Lynne Rienner, London: Coercion and Exploitation in the Private Economy'.

Bhagat, R. B. (2011). Emerging pattern of urbanization in India. *Economic and Political Weekly, 46*(34), 10–12.

Bhagat, R. B., & Mohanty, S. (2009). Emerging Pattern of urbanization and the contribution of migration in urban growth in India. *Asian Population Studies, 5*(1), 5–20.

Government of India. (1948). The Minimum Wages Act.

Government of India. (1979). The Inter-State Migrant Workmen (Regulation of Employment and Conditions of Service) Act.

Government of India, Ministry of Labour and Employment. (2011). Report of the Working Group on Labour Laws and Other Regulations for the Twelfth Five Year Plan (2012–2017).

International Labour Organisation (ILO). (2001). A perspective plan to eliminate forced labour in India. Declaration/WP/2/2001, Geneva.

International Labour Organisation (ILO). (2007). *Eradication of forced labour*. Geneva: Report III.

International Labour Organisation (ILO). (2012). *Global estimate of forced labour*. Geneva.

Korra, V. (2011). Nature and characteristics of seasonal labour migration: A case study in Mahabubnaga district of Andhra Pradesh. *Indian Journal of Labour Economics, 54*(3), 527–544.

Kundu, A. (1994). Pattern of urbanization with special reference to small and medium towns in India. In G. K. Chandra (Ed.), *Sectoral issues in Indian economy*. New Delhi: Har Anand Publications.

Mishra, L. (2001). A perspective plan to eliminate forced labour in India. In *Working Paper*. Geneva: ILO.

Nceus, G. (2008). *Report of the conditions of work and promotion of livelihood in the unorganized sector*. New Delhi.

Oberai, A. S., & Singh, H. K. M. (1983). *Causes and consequences of internal migration: A study in the Indian Punjab*. New Delhi: Oxford University Press.

Ramachandran, R. (1992). *Urbanization and urban system in India*. New Delhi: Oxford University Press.

Roy, T. (2013). Bringing economics back in labour history: A study of the historical patterns of labour supply in India. *Indian Journal of Labour Economics, 56*(1), 37–56.

Sahu, G. B. & Das, B. (2010). Urban labour market and the return of migration, *Review of Development and Change, XV*(2): 129–152.

Saxena, K. B. (2014). Urban growth and exclusion of the poor. *Social Change, 44*(4), 493–504.

UNDP. (2015). *Human development report*. New York: Oxford University Press.

UN-Habitat. (2003). *United Nations human settlement programme*. London: The Challenge of Slums. Earthscan Publications Ltd.

Government of India. (1979). The Inter-State Migrant Workmen (Regulation of Employment and Conditions of Service) Act.

Government of India, Ministry of Labour and Employment. [illegible] Report of the Working Group [illegible]

[illegible]

Mobility and Threshold Social Security

Pushpendra and Dipak Kumar Singh

Abstract Migrants predominantly work in the unorganised sector which employs over 90% of the workforce and is characterised by low earnings, informal contracts, insecure jobs, fluctuations in employment, poor working conditions and low level of social security, resulting in extremely poor living standards and precarity for its workers. The social policy in India too has followed the dichotomy of organised and unorganised sector by developing a dual system of social security—a comprehensive, portable social security for organised sector employees who usually have regular salaried jobs and a minimalist social security for unorganised sector workers who are the most vulnerable groups—socially as well as economically. Building upon the ILO Social Protection Floor recommendation, the paper argues for reimagining social security as an intervention to make drastic improvements in the living standard of the entire workforce of India. It highlights three weaknesses in the existing social security system—one, they are based on a reductionist package of social insurance and social assistance; two, they lack a threshold push to make a real change in the lives of beneficiaries and three, the prevailing policy environment seeks to keep workers in abominable conditions in the name of expanding employment opportunities. However, both high as well as some low-income countries have shown that social security can be successfully used to uplift the living standard of vast majority of masses. Rather than treating growth and social security as binaries, a developing country like India, the paper argues, needs to make departure from the growth objectives it has hitherto followed and invest massively into people's lives. To overcome the historic weaknesses of social security programmes in India, the gap between formal and informal sector must be minimised. The paper strongly argues for making Employees Provident Fund (EPF) and Employees State Insurance (ESI)—the two flagship programmes designed for the organised sector—universal social security programmes in India. This would require work at several levels—right

---

Pushpendra (✉)
Tata Institute of Social Sciences (TISS), Patna, India
e-mail: pushpendra1962@gmail.com

D. K. Singh
Department of Environment, Forest and Climate Change, Government of Bihar, Patna, India
e-mail: dksingh1992@yahoo.in

N. K. Mishra (ed.), *Development Challenges of India After Twenty Five Years of Economic Reforms*, India Studies in Business and Economics,
https://doi.org/10.1007/978-981-15-8265-3_20

from working out technical details, registration of a very unstable workforce, finding resources and bringing similar initiatives by a host of public actors under a common 'threshold' framework. The paper also recognises the need for other securities that can be derived from schemes and programmes related to food and nutrition security; work security in rural and urban areas; cash support; and improvement in housing, surrounding settlement and workplace; and call for combining these with universal EPF and ESI, is termed by the authors as 'threshold security'. For migrants, all social security programmes and schemes must have an inbuilt portability clause. This would require investing into technology platforms, overcoming exclusions created by the requirements of domicile, adhering to the principle of non-discrimination and equal citizenship, recognising the contributions made by migrants in the growth and development of the country, and amending the basic design of some crucial funds for inter-state portability of resources so that they finally reach the workers.

1 Introduction

This chapter is being written in a particular background. The novel coronavirus pandemic, known as COVID-19, has caused the severest global health crisis since the Spanish Flu of 1918–1920. Till the time of writing this paper, globally it has infected more than ten million persons and has claimed over half a million lives. India though like other Asian and African countries has witnessed less virulence of the disease, has lost more than 15,000 lives while more than half a million persons have got infected. Taking cue from experiences of some countries in containing the spread of the virus by breaking the human to human contact chain, India imposed a curfew-like lockdown from 25 March 2020 which was in phases extended up to 31 May 2020. However, the lockdown triggered a massive exodus of intra-state and inter-state migrants from towns and cities, particularly industrial growth centres. For more than eight weeks, the optics of desperate attempts by the migrants to return to their native places unfolded a spectre of human misery in India, unprecedented since the Partition.

Amidst all these, optics apart, what was perplexing to know through newspaper reports and some quick surveys by universities and civil society groups[1] that more than the fear factor of corona virus, the main reasons behind the exodus of migrants were the loss of sources of income, low savings, lack of access to food, loss of accommodation at worksites or inability to pay rent, unbearable conditions of living in the context of forced indoor life in the slums and labour colonies, inability to

[1](Survey reports, all accessed on 2 June 2020. Azim Premji University: https://cse.azimpremjiuniversity.edu.in/covid19-analysis-of-impact-and-relief-measures/, Stranded Workers Action Network (SWAN): https://covid19socialsecurity.wordpress.com/, Ideas for India: https://www.ideasforindia.in/topics/poverty-inequality/how-has-covid-19-crisis-affected-the-urban-poor-findings-from-a-phone-survey.html, National Council of Applied Economic Research: http://www.ncaer.org/data_details.php?dID=28, Jan Sahas: https://9f10ca96-9d6f-4573-8373-ed4c52ef9c6a.filesusr.com/ugd/d70f23_f18accd3b4404f789889b53fa27d99c8.pdf.

maintain social distancing, hygiene and so on. As the lockdown kept extending, the migrants were further gripped with the fear that they would exhaust savings which were precious for their families back home. In several cases, they were forced to seek reverse remittance from their families to meet their daily expenses and to meet the cost of their return. According to the Centre for Monitoring Indian Economy, COVID's immediate impact on employment was the loss of over 100 million jobs.[2] These reports and visuals helped bring the plight of migrants at the centre-stage of the pandemic as well as development discourse. The vulnerabilities of migrants were too exposed to be ignored. The fact that India's workers, particularly the migrants, are impoverished and have minimal capacity to withstand joblessness and income shock has been proved beyond doubt in this crisis.

In this backdrop, the paper attempts to build a strong case for revisiting India's social security architecture. As various studies (Jhabvala and Subrahmanya 2000; Dev 2002; Agrawal and Anupama 2013; Majumdar and Borboa 2013) have highlighted, the existing social security provisions are grossly inadequate to meet the requirements of the migrants when in need, particularly in the condition of en mass loss of jobs and livelihoods. In this chapter, we briefly assess the policy and legal framework of social security in India and argue for reconceptualising social security as a redistribution strategy that creates comprehensive entitlements for migrants and other workers. Drawing from some successful experiences from India and abroad, we suggest ways to make social security system relevant for unorganised workers and portable for migrants.

The paper is divided into three sections. The introduction sets the context of COVID-19 pandemic which has prompted us to search for new ways of strengthening social security of migrants and other workers. In the second section, we discuss how precarity is embedded in the nature of informal sector employment and how that makes migrants and other workers extremely vulnerable and severely deprived. The third section examines the weaknesses of existing social security edifice for adequacy and threshold through which we try to answer: why social security programmes have not succeeded in transforming the quality of life of migrants and workers? We propose a transformative framework of social security for unorganised workers including migrants that put particular emphasis on narrowing the gap between social security available for organised sector and that for unorganised sector workers. We also discuss the issue of portability of migrant rights.

2 Poverty, Vulnerability and Precarity

Intercensal data establish that migration has accelerated between 2001 and 2011 (Economic Survey 2016–2017). However, owing to several complexities and problems with both Census and NSSO in the estimation of migrants (Srivastava 2011;

[2]https://www.cmie.com/kommon/bin/sr.php?kall=warticle&dt=2020-06-02%2011:43:41&msec=800. Retrieved on 05 June 2020.

Dandekar and Ghai 2020), it is not possible to arrive at a precise estimate of the number of migrants and its disaggregation in terms of intra-state, inter-state, long-term, and short-term circular and seasonal migrants. Moreover, both the sources are quite old. Definitional problems have particularly led to under-estimation of circular and seasonal migration as well as female migration. However, it can be assumed that the number of migrants would be over 100 million (Economic Survey 2016–2017) of which 55 million might be inter-state migrants. Both long-term and short-term circular and seasonal migrants are by and large constituted by those employed in the informal sector as casual or low-paid regular wage workers, and also those who work as self-employed in low-earning occupations.

While writing on migration, one faces two-fold difficulties—first, methodological and definitional issues that do not allow estimating precise number or proportion of circular and seasonal migrants. And second, the paucity of data regarding the characteristics of migration and migrants which does not allow assessing the nature of their employment, the magnitude of unemployment and under-employment, earnings and access to social security benefits. Hence, we will be using data related to the unorganised sector to get a sense of the economic vulnerabilities faced by migrants since they overwhelmingly work in the unorganised sector.

The overall percentage of workers in informal employment has been hanging around 92% of total employed workers (see Table 1). The chief characteristics of this massive informal sector are unregulated terms and conditions of employment,

Table 1 Distribution of workers by category of sector

Sector of employment	Organised		Unorganised		Total	
	(%)	(No.)	(%)	(No.)	(%)	(No.)
2004–2005						
Formal	53.44	33.4	0.35	1.4	7.61	34.8
Informal	46.56	29.1	99.65	393.5	92.39	422.6
Total	14	62.5	86.34	394.9	100.00	457.4
2011–2012						
Formal	45.35	37.1	0.41	1.6	8.18	38.7
Informal	54.65	44.7	99.59	389.5	91.82	434.2
Total	17.30	81.8	82.70	391.1	100.00	472.9
2017–2018						
Formal	48.95	44.3	0.74	2.8	10.00	47.1
Informal	51.05	46.2	99.26	377.9	90.00	424.1
Total	19.21	90.5	80.79	380.7	100.00	471.2

Source NSSO 61st Round, 68th Round and Periodic Labour Force Survey (PLFS)[a] 2017–2018 (Numbers are in millions)

[a]The figures of PLFS are not strictly comparable with NSSO Rounds due to the difference in the sampling method. The proportion of organised sector/formal employment is likely to be slightly higher in PLFS because of sampling bias in favour of households with better educational attainments.

unwritten contract, small scale operations, ease of entry but also hire and fire of workers at will, labour-intensive work, low productivity of labour and lack of social security for workers (Agrawal and Anupama 2013). 64.9% of regular wage/salaried workers, 67.8% of contract workers and 95.3% of casual workers do not have a written job contract (Bureau 2015–2016). The number of workers without written contract went up from 74% in 2004–2005 to 79% (85% in rural areas and 73% in urban areas) in 2011–2012 (NSSO, 68th Round 2011–2012). Only 20.6% of workers (other than self-employed) had availed paid leave. Only 21.6% of them had availed at least one or more of the three social security benefits in the form of pension, gratuity or health care and maternity. In fact, 71.2% of workers were not eligible for these social security benefits. Another 7% had no idea about such provisions. Self-employed workers (primarily own account workers), contract workers and casual labour, who are likely to be devoid of any social security, constituted 83% of all workers (see Table 2).

Unemployment has steadily risen in the recent decade (see Fig. 1). The Periodic Labour Force Survey (PLFS 2017–2018) shows an actual decline in the number of employed people. The projection of unemployment varies as experts differ on the projection of labour force, new entry and exit from the labour market. For example, while the Bureau (2015–2016) projected the unemployment rate at 5%, the Centre for Monitoring Indian Economy projected it at 8.2%. Moreover, under-employment

Table 2 Structure of employment in India (percentages)

Year	Self-employed	Regular/Salaried	Casual	All
1993–1994	54.8	13.2	32.0	100.0
1999–2000	52.9	13.9	33.2	100.0
2004–2005	55.9	14.8	29.3	100.0
2011–2012	51.9	18.7	29.4	100.0
2015–2016	50.0	17.0	33.0	100.0

Source Various rounds of NSSO and Labour Bureau

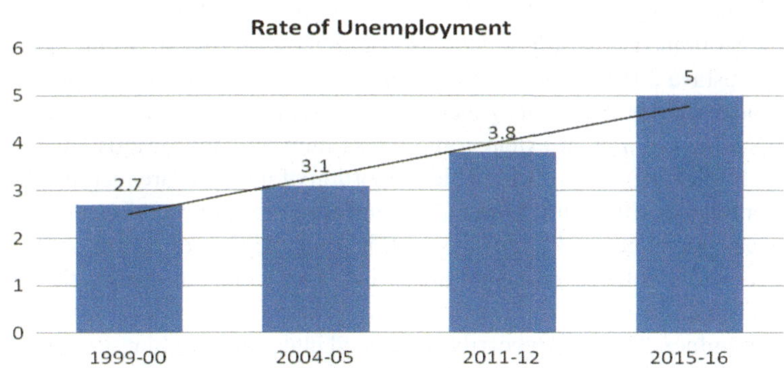

Fig. 1 Unemployment *Source* NSS, EUS and Labour Bureau

Table 3 Average monthly earnings by employment status, 2015–2016

Income categories	Self employed (%)	Regular wage/Salaried (%)	Contract workers (%)	Casual labour (%)	Total workers (%)
Up to ₹5000	19.2 (41.3)	3.2 (18.7)	1.4 (38.5)	19.5 (59.3)	43.3
₹5001–₹7500	12.2 (26.2)	3.3 (19.5)	1.0 (27.9)	8.2 (25.0)	24.7
₹7501–₹10,000	8.1 (17.4)	3.2 (19.0)	0.8 (20.3)	3.9 (12.0)	16.0
₹10,001–₹20,000	5.2 (11.1)	4.0 (23.6)	0.4 (11.0)	1.1 (3.5)	10.7
₹20,001–₹50,000	1.6 (3.5)	3.0 (17.7)	0.1 (2.1)	0.1 (0.3)	4.8
₹50,001–₹1,00,000	0.2 (0.4)	0.2 (1.4)	0.0 (0.1)	0.0 (0.0)	0.4
Above ₹1,00,000	0.0 (0.1)	0.0 (0.2)	0.0 (0.0)	0.0 (0.0)	0.1
All income groups	46.6 (100.0)	17.0 (100.0)	3.7 (100.0)	32.8 (100.0)	100.0

Source Labour Bureau, Employment and Unemployment Survey, 2015–2016

is rampant. Bureau (2015–2016) data show that of all workers, up to 35.5% worked for less than 12 months in a year.

As Table 3 clearly shows, low wages is the foremost challenge of the workforce in India. Two-thirds of self-employed as well as contract workers and more than 84% of casual workers earn just up to 7500 per month. These classes of workers constitute 83% of the workforce. Even among regular wage or salaried workers, close to 40% earn up to 7,500 per month and 57% earn up to 10,000 per month only. Similarly of all workers, 84% earn up to 10,000 per month only and less than 5.5% earn Rs. 20,000 a month or more.

We are well aware of the serious implications of such low wages such as persistence of poverty, the inability of the workers to deal with even minor economic shocks, predominantly single male or female migration, and compromises made on living conditions and meeting food and health needs in order to send remittances. We will desist from further getting into it and, instead, discuss several non-wage issues that too make migrants vulnerable. The short-duration and seasonal out-migrants are much more likely to be from SC/ST, from land-poor households and bottom quintiles. More than two-fifth of the seasonal migrants belong to SC or ST communities (Srivastava 2019). Lower social profile exposes them to social discrimination in the labour market. Migrants generally come with low educational background and skills which to a great extent compromise their attempt towards upward class mobility (NSSO 2010). A considerable proportion of migrants are recruited through labour contractors who control their terms and conditions of recruitment. They also have a weak social network at the destination, thus they are often left on their own when faced with violence, monetary needs and other situations such as the need for a caregiver in case of illness.

It is this vulnerability and precarity that forced inter-state migrants to flee the cities during the lockdown. An analysis of occupation-related data of those migrants who registered with the Government of Bihar for their return to the state from different inter-state destinations by Shramik Special trains not only confirm that they were employed in the unorganised sector but also throw further light on their social composition (for the occupational profile of return migrants in Bihar, see Table 4). 95% of them were males and the same percentage was in the working age group of 15–59 years. Over 80% belonged to Scheduled Castes, Scheduled Tribes, Other Backward Classes and Extremely Backward Classes. They engaged in a wide range of activities at the destination, with a whopping 65% of them engaged in construction work.

In a nutshell, informal nature of employment, lack of social security, growing unemployment and under-employment and low wages make the condition of informal sectors workers precarious. Within them, migrants find themselves in a more precarious situation due to additional constraints imposed by lack of portability of entitlements, lower social profile, lack of opportunity of upward mobility, weak social network, etc. All these make it imperative to adopt a social policy that emphasises on addressing these issues through appropriate and adequate social security measures and designing a strong implementation apparatus so that the vicious cycle of poverty and precarity of workers and migrants can be ruptured.

Table 4 Occupational profile of migrants who returned to Bihar by Shramik special

Broad occupational profile of return migrants	Number	Percentage
Agriculture[a]	14,557	1.2
Banking and Financial services	3,607	0.3
Computer and IT	13,964	1.1
Construction	809,753	65.6
Electronic and Electricals	20,572	1.7
Food processing	5,823	0.5
General services	219,499	17.8
Health services	14,696	1.2
Automobile and Generator mechanic	49,836	4.0
Textiles and Handloom	21,556	1.7
Others	79,563	6.4
All occupations	12,35,262	100.0

[a]Low figure for agriculture-related activities may be due to lean agricultural season when the lockdown was imposed

Source https://covidportal.bihar.gov.in, Government of Bihar

3 Reimagining Social Security

3.1 *Current Edifice of Social Security*

Social security of migrants, mainly circular and seasonal migrants, should be approached from three perspectives—from the perspective of their mobility which involves a change of place (migration); their poor economic, social and educational background (poverty and deprivation); and they are being part of the unorganised workforce (value of labour). These are not mutually exclusive; instead they bring out different dimensions of social security requirements of both, migrants and non-migrants. They have a great degree of overlap, except that migrants face restrictions on accessing schemes because of issues related to portability and also face more problems concerning housing than local workers.

None of the above is addressed by the Interstate Migrant Workmen Act, 1970. The Act does not apply on informal ways of recruitment which is, in practice, the rule rather than the exception. Moreover, the benefits accruing to the worker under the Act, if all norms are followed, are actually minimal limited to wages, leaves, suitable accommodation, etc. The maximum liability of a registered contractor for a registered Migrant worker during any crisis, such as the present one, would have been to provide return fare to his/her place of residence. Similarly, The Unorganised Workers' Social Security Act, 2008 is a classic example of a highly reductionist approach to social security. It limits its ambit to life and disability, health and maternity, and old age protection and leaves other social security needs up to the state governments. It excludes a large number of informal workers like agricultural workers, construction workers and informal workers in the formal sector, and ignores the working conditions of the informal workers and the particular problems of the women workers (Majumdar and Borbora 2013). It did not give any new benefit to workers instead notified pre-existing 10 schemes in its schedule[3] some of which are rather defunct. The Government of India in 2019 introduced a new bill, called The Code on Social Security, 2019 in the parliament which is under the pre-legislative consultation process.[4] The Bill is almost a reproduction of the 2008 Act and is limited to life and disability cover; health and maternity benefits; and old age protection.[5]

---

[3]The Act was promulgated following the Report of the National Commission for Enterprises in the Unorganised Sector (NCEUS 2006). The NCEUS had recommended a National Social Security Scheme with additional components of health insurance not only for self but for spouse and children, sickness allowance and maternity benefits for women workers or spouse of men workers; Provident Fund-cum-unemployment relief for workers below the age of 60 years and a National Social Security Fund for unorganised workers. These recommendations did not find a place in the final Act.

[4]Bill No. 374 of 2019. https://labour.gov.in/sites/default/files/375_2019_LS_Eng_0.pdf. Retrieved on 28 May 2020.

[5]For a brief commentary on the Code, see https://scroll.in/article/964108/how-india-can-strengthen-its-social-security-code-to-include-the-422-million-workers-left-behind. Retrieved on 12 June 2020.

The social security edifice of India chiefly consists of schemes that can be divided into two categories. The first category includes contributory schemes of old age pension; contributory schemes of life, accidental and disability insurance; and schemes related to medical assurance/insurance. These three types of schemes are either contingency oriented or for future security. However, except the scheme related to medical insurance, provisions under pension or insurance schemes are quite less, their coverage is low and they are meant to support the beneficiaries only in case of contingencies and old age. The second category of schemes is related to food and nutrition; rural employment and cash support. While under the National Food Security Act 2013, public distribution system, mid-day meal and supplementary feeding through *anganwadi* centres provide crucial survival food and nutrition security to a large majority of the country, rural employment programme under Mahatma Gandhi National Rural Employment Guarantee Act is a source of cash during unemployment period. It has the potential of providing a rural household up to approximately 20,000 per annum provided the household gets 100 days of employment. In reality, during 2019–2020, the scheme provided an average of just 48.39 days of employment to a household at the average wage rate of Rs.182.09, thus providing a beneficiary household Rs. 734 a month. *[For details of social security schemes in India, see the note provided at the end of the chapter].*

The exiguous entitlements under these schemes have provided some relief in times of exigencies such as death, accidents, disability, medical emergencies requiring hospitalisation or during old age and also given crucial survival support to unorganised sector workers. However, they have been proved grossly inadequate in making a visible impact on the living standards of workers which we have discussed in Sect. 2.

3.2 Minimalist Versus Threshold Social Security

For a very long time, the ILO Social Security (Minimum Standards) Convention, 1952 (No. 102) has influenced the understanding of social security in terms of preventive measures which emphasised on measures that help workers in contingent times.[6] Further, the ILO Social Protection Floors Recommendation 2012 (No. 202)[7] elevated the right to social security as a human right, moving beyond treating social security as a protection against certain life risks and social needs, and called for reconceptualising social security as an essential tool to prevent and reduce poverty, inequality, social exclusion and social insecurity; to reduce differences within and among the region, to promote equal opportunity and gender and racial equality, and to support the transition from informal to formal employment. Social security, it argued, would

[6]The ILO Convention identified nine branches of social security which are (i) medical care; (ii) sickness benefit; (iii) unemployment benefit; (iv) old-age benefit; (v) employment injury benefit; (vi) family benefit; (vii) maternity benefit; (viii) invalidity benefit and (ix) survivors' benefit. The Convention also defined minimum standards for each of them. In India, social security in the organised sector more or less follows these components.

[7]It was adopted in the 101st Session of the International Labour Conference in 2012.

help stimulate aggregate demand in times of crisis and beyond, and help support a transition to a more sustainable economy.

The principles laid down in the Social Protection Floor open possibilities of income support, regulation of wages and other measures to narrow the gap between formal and informal employment and ensure decent work conditions. It also conceptualises inclusive urbanisation that ensures a basic level of decent living including housing, water supply, sanitation and environmental hygiene and capability enhancing measures such as quality education and acquisition/upgradation of skills.

Does such conceptualisation of social security encroach upon the general economic functions, particularly market-based economic functions? We argue that social security and general economic functions should not be seen in binary. The purpose of economic growth should be the same—end deprivations among masses and achieve everyone's well-being. Experiences of several countries have also shown the success of economic growth in improving living standards but those have been the direct result of social intervention rather than of simple economic growth (Dreze and Sen 1991). We, therefore, argue that a multi-dimensional, inclusive and equity-oriented conceptualisation of social security sets a social policy agenda for the state, markets, industry associations, trade unions, civil society organisations and other actors and would require them to re-orient their goals accordingly.[8]

From this perspective, existing migration and social security related legislations and schemes in India suffer from three major problems: a) reductionism; b) inadequacy to cross the threshold and c) incoherence. Reductionism limits the choices to a minimalist package in the name of effectiveness, constraints of resources and manageability. A threshold is the level at which something starts to happen or have an effect. When a scheme is designed to be minimalist in terms of scale, it fails to effect a change. If a minimum level of decent living in old age requires x amount, a support which is one-fourth of x amount will not help attain decency instead will only allow living a wretched life in old age. Incoherence arises because of adverse policy climate where the State considers labour protection antithetical to labour market flexibility, perceived as one of the essential conditions for attracting investments. Coherence would require the market, government and all others to commit to comprehensive social security to address deprivations and other issues mentioned earlier.

The threshold approach to social security contrasts with the minimalist approach hitherto pursued in India. If social security has to perform a greater transformative role, then the emphasis has to be on promotional aspects of social security. Dreze and Sen (1991) differentiate between two aspects of social security—protection and promotion. While the former is concerned with preventing a decline in living standard in general and in the basic conditions of living in particular; the latter is concerned with achieving higher incomes and living standards. In developed countries where living standard is high and the size of poor is relatively small,

[8]On the debate why governments should involve themselves in social security, see Burgess and Stern (1991), Dreze and Sen (1991).

contingency-based social security system works reasonably well, whereas in India a social security system will have to adopt promotion strategies that can raise living standards. In the following pages, we have tried to present an outline of a social security system for India which is based on four guiding principles: i) narrowing the gap between organised and unorganised sector social security; ii) reducing social insecurities in everyday life in the *present* by ensuring a minimum decent living standard; iii) creating mechanisms to take care of old age and contingency needs and iv) ensuring delivery of social security in a way that it does not disincentivise spatial mobility. Setting threshold-level security as the goal, these principles combine aspects of protection and promotion with a strong emphasis on the latter. Regarding migration, the approach is not to prevent it but remove any disadvantages associated with spatial mobility.

3.3 Narrowing the Gap Between Organised and Unorganised Sector

At present, there is a clear distinction between the nature of social security cover available to the organised sector workers in the form of Employees Provident Fund (EPF) and Employees State Insurance (ESI), as compared to the benefits available for the unorganised workers provided under the 2008 Act or otherwise. The EPF, managed by Employees Provident Fund Organisation (EPFO), has three components—a) a provident fund created for every employee based on equal contributions by the employee and employer which is fully availed by the employee after retirement or even earlier, and fully or partly, in case of unemployment; b) a pension fund in the form of superannuation pension, retiring pension or permanent total disablement pension to the employees with the benefit of widow or widower's pension, children pension or orphan pension payable to the beneficiaries of such employees and c) employee deposit-linked life insurance where the employee is insured for up to Rs. 6 lakh.

The ESI, managed by Employees State Insurance Corporation (ESIC), offers extensive benefits to its subscribers[9] that take care of various conditions from sickness; maternity; disablement and death due to employment injury or occupational

[9]Benefits under ESI include (a) medical benefit for the insured person and his/her family that include in-patient treatment, domiciliary treatment, specialist consultation, imaging services, artificial limbs and aids, etc. through a vast network of ESI hospitals as well as its empanelled hospitals; (b) sickness benefit with full or part payment of wages extendable up to 2 years; (c) maternity benefit usually for 26 weeks with full wage; (d) disablement benefit in the form of 90% of wages; (e) dependants' benefits in the form of 90% of wage every month if death occurs due to employment injury or occupational hazards; (f) other benefits in the form of funeral expenses, vocational rehabilitation, physical rehabilitation, old age medical care, unemployment allowance at 50% wage up to 2 years due to closure of factory/establishment, retrenchment or permanent invalidity, and medical care for self and family during the period of unemployment allowance, and also provision for skill upgradation at the expenses of the ESIC.

hazard; to unemployment allowances and skill upgradation. An interesting feature of the ESI Scheme is that the contributions are related to the paying capacity as a fixed percentage of the workers' wages, whereas they are provided social security benefits according to individual needs without distinction.

For organised sector, therefore, the social security creates an appreciable level of capacity to take care of short-term exigencies and periodical needs, like sickness, injury, education and marriage of children, short-term unemployment, etc. From the perspective of migrants, both EPFO and ESI benefits are portable. EPFO has launched a unified portal and (portable) Universal Account Number (UAN). In most of the schemes of the unorganised sector, benefits accrue at a future date—in the event of old age, death or disablement. This explains the reluctance of workers to subscribe to them. This can be understood as the effect of 'time inconsistency' (Banerjee and Duflo 2011).[10] This psychological factor combined with the core financial sense of the Net Present Value (NPV) of the future benefits vis-à-vis the current investments makes most of these schemes at least appear to be unattractive for the intended beneficiaries.

Hence, we argue that membership of the EPF and ESI should be made compulsory for the entire workforce—organised as well as unorganised sector workers in India.[11] EPFO and ESIC can be entrusted to manage the services for unorganised workers also. The government should create a separate welfare fund under them to meet the cost of employer's contribution if the worker is a self-employed or casual worker or wherever the employer or employee or both are not in the position to pay their contribution.

Undeniably, such a proposition is not easily implementable. On the contrary, it is far more complicated than it might appear. For example, what wage floor will be used to calculate the contribution of employees and employer/government, given the diversity of occupation, income, payment system, job fluctuations and period of unemployment of unorganised workers? How to ensure that the contribution is not too low to make the threshold impact? Universalising EPF and ESI would also require registration of all workers in the country and providing them with a unique identification number as envisaged in the Unorganised Workers Social Security Act, 2008 and a system of regular updating of their data. Both EPF and ESI would require dismantling restrictions on their subscription such as the size of the enterprise and cap on salary up to Rs. 15,000 per month to include all workers since due to these restrictions the schemes cover less than half of organised sector workers. Though Massive expansion of ESI hospital and domiciliary facilities may be required, the state and central governments will have to agree to gradually bring ESIC facilities

[10]According to Banerjee and Duflo, 'Research in psychology has now been applied to a range of economic phenomena to show that we think about the present very differently from the way we think about the future (a notion referred to as "time inconsistency")'.

[11]Report of the Working Group on Migration (2017: 34), in the context of health security, recommends 'covering contract and even unorganised workers under ESI'. However, there is no further discussion on this in the Report. Duggal (2006) argues for restructuring ESI to accommodate the entire workforce by removing all restrictions for coverage under the Act like wage limits, numbers employed, etc.

and general health services under a common governance mechanism so that access to universal primary health care is not compromised. On top of it, bringing social security of organised and unorganised sector workers on the par would require re-orienting the economic and social policies towards formalisation of economy. This will clearly be an epoch-making departure from the economic dispensation that has become the hallmark of developing countries' economy. The government should form a Commission to suggest a roadmap to roll out the new social security programme which aims at ensuring up to par benefits for unorganised workers.

We have successful examples of functioning of some welfare funds at the state level, for example in Kerala, that demonstrate the feasibility of delivering provident fund, gratuity, unemployment relief, social assistance and insurance cover to life, disability and accidents, and several other benefits, similar to those offered by the EPF and ESI, to a range of unorganised workers with diverse occupations and differential earnings and risks associated with each of them (NCEUS 2006). The functioning of the Mathadi Workers' Welfare Board in Maharashtra is another example which has been successfully working since 1969 and has gradually expanded workers' welfare by starting its own hospitals on the line of ESI and providing provident fund, insurance and other assistance.

The sceptics would raise the issue of feasibility of such massive social security through public provisioning in a developing country like India where resources are limited, the economy has taken a hit in recent years, the unemployment rate is high, and seasonal and low quality employment are rampant. Our estimates put the cost of ESI at slightly less than 1% of the GDP.[12] Regarding the EPF, the entire cost of employer and employee contributions come to 5.6% of the GDP, whereas the actual cost is likely to be around 4.5% of the GDP if employees share a portion of the cost.[13] As Dreze and Sen (1991) have shown from the example of China, Sri Lanka, Cuba, Costa Rica, Chile and Jamaica, countries with low per capita GNP, such scepticism is often exaggerated and, to some extent, misleading. Moreover, taking a giant leap towards formalisation would have extraordinary spin-off effects on the economy in the form of massive investments in water, sanitation, housing, and other urban and rural infrastructure, correcting demand-side weaknesses by infusing purchasing power in half a billion workforce, and constant skill upgradation to deal with the problem of redundancy and unemployment. This would also save resources that are spent on treating preventable diseases, and avoid frequent disruptions in work. This will, in the medium to the longer run, substantially reduce the need for state subsidy in social security programmes by improving market wages, work and living conditions and purchasing power of workers.

[12]The calculation is based on the assumption that the average earning of 84% of 47 crore workforce is Rs. 10,000 per month, and in their case, the employer contribution will be met by the government. The total premium to be borne by the government will be 183,300 crores.

[13]Considering 24% contribution of employer and employees for 84% of 47 crore workforce whose average monthly income is Rs. 10,000 per month, the total contribution will be 11.37 lakh crore. However, if the employees can pay Rs. 6,000 per annum, then the cost will come down to 9 lakh crore.

Meeting the cost of EPF and ESI for unorganised sector workers does not require all *new* resources. Five important existing sources can be tapped. First, existing sectoral schemes targeted at different segments of the unorganised workforce, for example, construction workers, beedi workers, handloom weavers, handicraft artisans, mines workers, etc. These schemes are supported by specific welfare funds. Second, various state governments have also established welfare funds for unorganised workers including those who are either self-employed or casual labourers. Some of these have been working efficiently. Hence, all targeted funds at central and state levels can be brought under the broad umbrella of the EPFO and ESIC through negotiation with states. Third, the universalisation of the EPF and ESI will result in redundancy of several existing schemes that are, a la Kabeer (2010), piecemeal and fragmented, resulting in savings from them. Fourth, the central and state governments should consider levying a new cess in sectors wherever possible on the line of Building and Other Construction Workers Welfare Cess Act (1996). And fifth, the employer of regularly employed informal workers in organised and unorganised sectors should be directed to pay employers' contribution. There can be creative ways of bringing in accountability of the employer, for example, asking their contribution for the total number of workers employed in a year. This will also require making written contracts mandatory which will be a step towards formalisation of labour markets.

The measures as mentioned above will still leave some gaps in the financing of a universal EPF and ESI which the central and state governments should jointly finance. Additionally, we have some successful social security programmes and micro initiatives managed and/or promoted by NGOs, trade unions, workers' collectives and employers. Ways can be found to bring such initiatives under a common broad framework while maintaining their autonomy. For example, these agencies as well as state governments should have the autonomy to add provisions over and above the threshold level decided under the EPF and ESI.

More than the financial feasibility of implementing comprehensive schemes like ESI and EPF, the bigger challenge is government's push to greater participation of private sector in the health insurance market and investment of pension funds in the capital market, thereby weakening low cost and low-risk social insurance schemes. In the case of the EPF, employees are given the choice of opting for the EPF or the New Pension Scheme (NPS) which is given tax incentives. However, investing the pension fund in the capital market exposes it to the volatility of capital market while the employee is lured by the attraction of higher return (Kannan 2015). Similar is the case of ESI where members have been given an option to exit by choosing a health insurance product from the market, and giving substantial tax rebates on payment of medical insurance premium (Duggal 2015). Both 'reforms' are accompanied by the recent relaxation of labour laws, including the abolition of inspections of enterprises employing up to 40 persons.

3.4 Other Essential Social Security Measures

The Public Distribution System (PDS) as envisaged in the National Food Security Act, 2013 should be converted into a universal programme. This will eliminate wilful or inadvertent errors in beneficiary selection and costs incurred on targeting, and promote self-selection process, besides other benefits such as plugging leakages in the system, reducing wastage due to under-utilisation of grains and cost incurred on storage. The cost of expansion of the programme is likely to be marginal. Similarly, other schemes under the Act—ICDS, MDM and Matritva Sahyog—should not only continue but entitlements under the programmes must be progressively reviewed as the working-class households overwhelmingly stand to benefit from these schemes. Food grain distribution and cooked meal programmes must not be converted into cash transfer as a cash transfer will cause fluctuations in entitlements depending on fluctuations in the market prices. It may also allow diversion of money to meet other requirements at the cost of food security, for example, in a patriarchal society an alcohol-addicted male may get away with money to spend on his addiction.

The demand-based rural public works programme, MGNREGA, should not only continue but family entitlements should be expanded from 100 days to 200 days in a year, with fair wages. An urban public works programme should also be launched which can be utilised to massively improve the urban infrastructure particularly in housing, water supply, sanitation, hygiene, drainage, solid waste management and condition of work units, particularly in dominated by the working class. The urban works programme may be used as a wage subsidy programme in case of micro and small enterprises, if required.

For migrants, the central and state governments should pay particular attention to improving urban settlements and housing. This is a multi-dimensional complicated issue and requires a separate detailed discussion. The basic elements of a good housing security for circular and seasonal migrants would depend on how they are provided affordable rental accommodations, how standards of accommodation at worksites are codified to make them livable; and, for long-term migrants and other low-income organised and unorganised sector workers, how slums are strategically put under redevelopment for affordable, safe, livable, one and two-bedroom (with kitchen and toilet) accommodations with hygienic surroundings. These require going beyond individual owner-based approach to planning for housing security to city, locality and group-based planning. In rural areas, apart from the individual owner-based subsidy, access to homestead land must be part of housing security, particularly for the landless labourers.

Pradhan Mantri Kisan Samman Yojana (PM-KISAN) provides income support to even those who own a few decimals of land. Several small landowners-cum-wage labourers-cum tenants are its beneficiaries who also migrate to work. This cash support through direct benefit transfer is particularly useful for purchasing agricultural inputs and paying wages for agricultural operations before harvesting. Similarly, public provisioning of education and skill development has helped make the workforce, including migrants, educated and appropriately skilled, and it remains a crucial social security measure. Any emergency causing massive disruptions such as the COVID-19 pandemic, drought and floods require special social assistance not only in the form of relief but rehabilitation, income support, enterprise revival support, etc. Mitigation of such contingency should be incorporated in the social security architecture.

3.5 Portability of Entitlements for Migrants

The next important issue is ensuring the intra- and inter-state portability of schemes. Under this category, five schemes/programmes are important from the perspective of migrants. They are (i) PDS scheme; (ii) Integrated Child Development Scheme (ICDS); (iii) Mid-day Meal and other non-teaching incentives; (iv) school education and (v) benefits under Building and Other Construction Workers Welfare Board (BOCWWB). Portability of PDS entitlements is possible by delinking individuals from the household. In this regard, the 'One Nation One Card' will be a big move though it may take some time to make PDS universally portable. Portability of ICDS, schooling of children and mid-day meal are complicated and require more than technological fix. Right from the admission of new children on a seasonal basis in anganwadi centres/schools to getting an additional quota of ration for them, portability of school enrolment and attendance certificate on a seasonal basis, getting any non-teaching incentives for seasonal migrant children and removing other barriers in learning such as language, caste/community and cultural barriers are all difficult questions. They require flexibility in the administrative procedures, quick responsiveness, studying the usual pattern of migration and making planning in advance, cooperation at source and destination between state and civil society organisations, administrative divisions in case of intra-state migration and state governments in case of inter-state migration. There are some successful examples of inter-state coordination such as cooperation between Odisha and Andhra governments for the education of children of seasonal migrant families working in brick kilns.

Portability of benefits under BOCWWB has been facing technical and bureaucratic hurdles. Under the Act, the worker is registered with the district authority in his home state. If the worker has worked in a different state where cess is deducted from the employer, the cess remains with the state government at the destination. However, the worker is denied any welfare under the Board for not having worked in the home state and not contributing to the cess pool of the home state. At present, there is no portability of cess pool based on the domicile of the worker making worker the ultimate sufferer. This is likely to be the case with some other welfare funds too.

4 Conclusion

In India, COVID-19 pandemic has exposed all dimensions of the fragility of unorganised sector workers in general and migrants in particular. How to deal with that fragility has been the binding thread throughout this chapter. We began with the current socio-economic context in which migration takes place in India. While the high regional disparity in terms of agricultural, industrial and urban growth creates the condition for intra- and inter-state migration, the outcome of migration (and labour in general) is determined by the most crucial characteristics of economic growth in India, that is, overwhelming predominance of unorganised sector. It is this sector that continuously churns out abysmal living standards and precarity for its workers.

The social policy in India too has followed the dichotomy of the organised and unorganised sector by developing a dual system of social security—a comprehensive, portable social security for the organised sector employees who usually have regular salaried jobs and minimalist social security for unorganised sector workers who are the most vulnerable groups—socially as well as economically and constitute over 90% of the workforce. We briefly analysed the weaknesses and limitations of the existing legislative framework and schemes that are meant for the unorganised sector workers including migrants and concluded that they are inherently incapable of lifting the living standard of workers to a dignified human existence. At best, they can support them to survive barely and deal with contingencies in a minimalist sense and at worst fail to support at all when caught up in bureaucratic technicalities of selection errors and lack of portability.

Building upon the ILO Social Protection Floor recommendation, we then argued for reimagining social security as an intervention to make drastic improvements in the lives of the entire workforce of India. We analysed three weaknesses in the existing social security system—first they are based on a reductionist package of social insurance and social assistance; second, they lack a *threshold* push to make a real change in the lives of beneficiaries and third, the prevailing policy environment seeks to keep workers in abominable conditions in the name of expanding employment opportunities. However, both high as well as some low-income countries have shown that social security can be successfully used to uplift the living standard of the vast majority of masses. Rather than treating growth and social security as binaries, a developing country like India needs to invest massively into people's lives.

The gap between the formal and informal sector must be minimised to overcome the historical weaknesses of social security programmes in India. In this regard, we proposed making Employees Provident Fund (EPF) and Employees State Insurance (ESI)—the two flagship programmes designed for the organised sector—universal social security programmes in India. This would require work at several levels—right from working out technical details, registration of a very unstable workforce, finding resources and bringing similar initiatives by a host of public actors under a common 'threshold' framework.

A combination of universal EPF and ESI and some other useful securities derived from existing schemes and programmes related to food and nutrition security; work security in rural and urban areas; cash support; and improvement in housing, surrounding settlement and workplace will prove, what we call ‘threshold security’ removing the ‘time inconsistencies’ where the present is compromised in lieu of a promise of somewhat better (distant) future.

For migrants, all social security should have an inbuilt portability clause. This would require investing into technology platforms, overcoming exclusions created by the requirements of domicile, at least for social security purposes, adhering to the principle of non-discrimination and equal citizenship, recognising the contributions made by migrants in the growth and development of the country, and amending the basic design of some crucial funds for inter-state transfer of resources so that they finally reach the workers.

The COVID-19 crisis has shaken up lives and livelihoods of tens of millions but is also knocking us to re-imagine our collective future where migrants and other workers can live with a sense of dignity and security.

Note

A brief note on prominent social security schemes in India.

1. *Pension*: Pradhan Mantri Shram Yogi Maan-dhan (PMSYM) is for workers in the unorganised sector with a maximum income of Rs. 15,000 per month. The worker will get Rs. 3000 per month with the benefit of family pension in case of her/his death. Atal Pension Yojana (APY) is open to all, without any income criteria. The subscriber can opt for monthly pension ranging from Rs. 1000 to Rs. 5000 by payment of the stipulated contribution regularly. In case of both the schemes, the age limit at entry level is 18–40 years and the pension starts after attaining the age of 60 years.
2. *Insurance*: Pradhan Mantri Jeevan Jyoti Bima Yojana (PMJJBY) is available to people between 18 and 50 years of age with an annual premium of Rs. 330. It provides coverage of Rs. 0.2 million in case of death of the subscriber. Pradhan Mantri Suraksha Bima Yojana (PMSBY) is an accident insurance scheme available to people between 18 and 70 years of age with an annual premium of Rs. 12 only. In case of accidental death or full disability, the payment is Rs. 0.2 million while in case of partial permanent disability, the payment is Rs. 0.1 million. Both the schemes are open to all.
3. *Medical*: Ayushman Bharat Pradhan Mantri Jan Arogya Yojana (AB PM-JAY) provides for cashless treatment up to Rs. 500,000 a year in case of secondary and tertiary care hospitalisation with inbuilt portability through an e-card to any empanelled public or private hospital in India. The selection of beneficiaries is made on the basis of deprivation and occupational criteria of the Socio-Economic Caste Census (SECC) 2011. Given the selection criteria, in all likelihood the overwhelming majority of the beneficiaries are labouring classes including migrants and its easy portability is highly suitable to migrants. The scheme is far below the level of benefits of ESIC. It neither covers wage loss nor out-patient expenses

if hospitalisation is not required. Moreover, those households not enlisted in the SECC 2011, either by omission or commission, are excluded from the scheme.

4. *Food and Nutrition*: All schemes related to food security come under integrated umbrella of the National Food Security Act, 2013. Under the Targeted Public Distribution System (TPDS), Antyodaya Anna Yojana (AAY) beneficiary households get 35 kg of highly subsidised foodgrains. New beneficiaries, called Priority Households (PHH), get five kg of foodgrains per person per month at the same subsidised price. Besides, every pregnant woman and lactating mother is entitled to free of charge meal during pregnancy and six months after the childbirth, through local *anganwadi* (under Integrated Child Development Services Scheme), and maternity benefit (under Indira Gandhi Matritva Sahyog) of no less than Rs. 6000. As regards food security of children, the Act provides for free of charge meal to children in the age group of six months to six years through local *anganwadi*, and in the case of children in the age group of six years to fourteen years (or up to class VIII), free of charge one mid-day meal every day except on school holidays to be provided through government and government-aided schools and schools run by local bodies (under Mid-day Meal Scheme). The majority of beneficiaries of ICDS and MDM schemes come from the poor and labouring classes including migrants. However, selection errors and issues related to linking with Aadhaar and biometric identification have left a considerable section of deserving poor out of its purview. Portability of food security-related schemes has been a long-pending demand. So far, there are pilot programmes regarding portability of PDS rations in some states. During the COVID-19 lockdown, the Central government announced its decision to implement 'One Nation One Ration Card' from 1 July 2021. However, all states have still not joined the scheme. A major destination state Delhi is yet to join the scheme, thus limiting its usefulness. Further, portability of ICDS benefits and MDM is also an issue that is yet to be resolved.
5. *Housing*: Pradhan Mantri Awas Yojana (Urban) and Pradhan Mantri Gramin Awas Yojana are two housing-related schemes where the beneficiary gets either interest subsidy or central assistance. In rural areas, SCs, STs, Economically Weaker Sections (EWS) and women can take advantage of interest subsidy up to 3% or up to 2 lakh. In urban areas, central assistance of 1–1.5 lakh is available for in situ slum redevelopment with private participation, or construction of a house by those belonging to EWS or for affordable housing by private or public sector builders where they reserve at least 35% houses for EWS. Interest subsidy of different slabs amounting not more than up to 2.67 lakh for different socio-economic groups is available under a credit-linked subsidy scheme. These schemes are primarily meant for EWS which includes unorganised sector workers and migrants. However, urban housing is highly complicated and it is doubtful to what extent the scheme can improve access to minimum decent housing for migrants and other unorganised workers.
6. *Employment*: Mahatma Gandhi National Rural Employment Guarantee Act (MGNREGA) is a demand-based rural employment programme under which the

government is obliged to provide up to 100 days of employment to a rural household. All MGNREGA workers are unorganised workers and an overwhelming number of them are likely to be circular and seasonal migrants too.

7. *Cash Support*: Family Benefit Scheme provides onetime cash support to a family who has lost its bread earner. The Pradhan Mantri Kisan Samman Nidhi Yojana provides cash support of Rs. 6,000 in four instalments to all farmers (with certain exclusion criteria). Since a considerable number of unorganised workers and migrants come from very small farmers, they too benefit from the scheme. However, the landless wage earners as well as tenants are outside the purview of the scheme. At present, there is no regular cash support scheme for unorganised workers and migrants. Workers' welfare boards in some sectors have the mandate to provide cash support to its members in specific conditions.
8. *Social Security during Disasters*: The current disaster management act and relief code provide for state action in case of a disaster in the form of various types of relief and rehabilitation measures to be announced by the government. Such relief includes food support, treatment, compensation in case of death, etc.

References

Agrawal, S. K. & Anupama. (2013). Social protection policies for the urban informal sector: The Indian perspective. In N. Chandhoke & S. K. Agrawal (Eds.), *Social protection policies in South Asia* (pp. 35–77). New Delhi: Routledge.

Banerjee, A. V., & Duflo, E. (2011). *Poor economics: A radical rethinking of the way to fight global poverty*. Noida: Random House India.

Burgess, R., & Stern, N. (1991). Social security in developing countries: What, why, who, and how? In E. Ahmad, et al. (Eds.), *Social security in developing countries* (pp. 41–80). New Delhi: Oxford University Press.

Bureau, L. (2015–2016). *Report on fifth annual employment and unemployment survey*. Government of India: Ministry of Labour and Employment.

Dandekar, A., & Ghai, R. (2020). Migration and reverse migration in the age of COVID-19. *Economic and Political Weekly, 55*(19), 28–31.

Dev, S. M. (2002). Growth mediated and support-led social security in the unorganised sector in India. *Indian Journal of Labour Economics, 45*(2), 219–242.

Dreze, J., & Sen, A. (1991). Public action for social security: Foundations and strategy. In E. Ahmad, et al. (Eds.), *Social security in developing countries* (pp. 3–40). New Delhi: Oxford University Press.

Duggal, R. (2006). Need to Uuniversalise social security. *Economic and Political Weekly, 41*(32), 3495–3497.

Duggal, R. (2015). Saving the employees' state insurance scheme. *Economic and Political Weekly, 50*(17), 17–20.

Government of India. (2017). *Economic survey 2016–2017*. New Delhi: Oxford University Press.

Jhabvala, R., & Subrahmanya, R. K. A. (2000). Meeting the basic needs: The unorganised sector and social security. In R. Jhabvala & R. K. A. Subrahmanya (Eds.), *The unorganised sector: Work security and social protection* (pp. 17–29). New Delhi: Sage Publications.

Kabeer, N. (2010). *Gender and social protection strategies in the informal economy*. New Delhi: Routledge.

Kannan, K. P. (2015). Corporate capitalism in the name of social security. *Economic and Political Weekly*, *50*(12), 30–32.
Majumdar, A., & Borbora, S. (2013). Social security system and the informal sector in India: A review. *Economic and Political Weekly*, *48*(42), 69–72.
Ministry of Housing and Urban Poverty Alleviation. (2017). *Report of the working group on migration*. Retrieved from http://mohua.gov.in/upload/uploadfiles/files/1566.pdf.
National Commission for Enterprises in the Unorganised Sector. (2006). *Social security for unorganised workers: Report*.
National Sample Survey Office. (2010). Migration in India. Report No. 533. NSSO 64th Round. Government of India: Ministry of Programme Implementation.
National Sample Survey Office. (2011–2012). NSSO 68th Round, Government of India: Ministry of Programme Implementation.
National Sample Survey Office. Periodic Labour Force Survey 2017–2018. Government of India: Ministry of Programme Implementation
Srivastava, R. (2011). Labour migration in India: Recent trends, patterns and policy issues. *The Indian Journal of Labour Economics*, *54*(3), 411–440.
Srivastava, R. (2019). Emerging dynamics of labour market inequality in India: Migration, informality, segmentation and social discrimination. *Indian Journal of Labour Economics*, *62*(2), 147–171. https://doi.org/10.1007/s41027-019-00178-5.

Mapping of Migrants Based on Caste, Origin, and Destination: An Insight into the Sugarcane Cutter Migrants in Maharashtra

Anurag Asawa

Abstract Temporary migration is often used interchangeably with circular, seasonal, short-term, and spontaneous migration. The data (NSSO and Census) reveals that there is an upward trend in migration because of employment opportunities. Seasonal migration is a routine phenomenon for people in the five districts of the arid Marathwada region of the Maharashtra—Beed, Jalgaon, Ahmednagar, Nasik, and Jalna. Analysis of more than 95000 respondents reveals that more than 75% of migrants belong to five castes—Vanjari (28.49%), Maratha (20.34%), Banjara (13.0%), Bhill (8.55%), and Dhangar (6.92%). This paper attempts to map the migration process in the state and seeks to throw light on the preferred destination of the migrants originating from a particular district belonging to a specific caste.

1 Introduction

Humans have been on the move since time immemorial. While early human beings moved in search of food, shelter, and mates, not much has changed down the ages as people continue to relocate out of choice or necessity in search of better work opportunities and living conditions. Nowadays people are found to be moving away from the place of their origin not only in search of work, or to study but also to escape conflicts, terrorism, and in response to the adverse impact of climate change, or natural disasters and even large-scale development projects. The UN Migration Agency (IOM) defines a migrant 'as any person who is moving or has moved across an international border or within a country away from his/her habitual place of residence, regardless of (1) the person's legal status; (2) whether the movement is voluntary or involuntary; (3) what the causes for the movement are; or (4) what the length of the stay is'. This paper is confined to internal migration, or movement within a country, in India, and more specifically within the western state of Maharashtra. More people in India leave their homes for greener pastures within the country in a

A. Asawa (✉)
Gokhale Institute of Politics and Economics, Pune, India
e-mail: anurag@gipe.ac.in

N. K. Mishra (ed.), *Development Challenges of India After Twenty Five Years of Economic Reforms*, India Studies in Business and Economics,
https://doi.org/10.1007/978-981-15-8265-3_21

year than those crossing international borders globally. According to the 2001 Census of India, the total number of migrants in the country was 315 million, which is more than the United Nations' global estimate of 272 million international migrants in 2019 (UN 2019). Migration takes place because households diversify their economic activities outside the traditional agricultural sphere by sending out members to work in urban areas in the lean period (Keshri and Bhagat 2012). Migration may acquire many forms, and there is significant diversity in migratory patterns (Smita 2008). Depending upon their duration, migration cycles range from a few weeks to some months (7–9 months) and may occur once or several times in a year. Migration for agricultural work, for example, is often of short duration and may take place several times each year, with families making trips of four to eight weeks for sowing, harvest, or transplantation activities. This type of migration commonly features small family groups traveling over short distances and working in highly scattered areas, making them difficult to trace. Migration can result in the permanent relocation of an individual or household, which may be termed as a permanent migration. But if individuals migrate, leaving their families and land and property in the area of origin or residence, they may do so with the intention of coming back. This short-term migration is more likely to happen if the individuals have precarious jobs in the destination areas, or if the cost of permanent relocation is high as compared to its benefits. In such a case, although individuals or groups may find a toehold in the destination areas, such migration may be termed as semi-permanent or long-term circular. Many studies have found that migration is not a choice instead it is a part of the normal livelihood strategy of the poor, (Mc Dowell and Haan 1997) and it occurs all the time and is triggered not just by emergency, or distress.

Migration within India is predominantly short-distance with around 60% of migrants changing their residences within their district of birth and 20% within their state (province), while the rest move across state boundaries. Estimates of short-term migrants vary from 15 million (NSSO 2007–2008) to 100 million (Deshingkar and Akter 2009). Migration in India is primarily of two types: (a) Long-term migration, resulting in the relocation of an individual or household and (b) Short-term or seasonal/circular migration, involving back and forth movement between a source and destination. If the duration of stay away from home is between thirty days to six months, it is termed temporary or short-term migration. Temporary migration is often used interchangeably with circular, seasonal, short-term, and spontaneous migration. If individuals, or groups of individuals, migrate for temporary periods, either moving from place to place or to a fixed destination, such migrants are seasonal, temporary, or circular migrants (Srivastava 2011). These migrants belong to the poorest and deprived sections of society typically comprising the Scheduled Castes (SCs), Scheduled Tribes (STs), and Other Backward Castes (OBCs) (Srivastava and Desgupta 2010).

As per the Census 2001, Maharashtra witnessed the largest in-migration of the population over ten years (1991–2001) from different states. The total number of in-migrants into the state was 3.2 million. The number of out-migrants from the state during the decade was 0.89 million. Thus, the total net migrants, including those who came from abroad, were 2.3 million. In comparison, the number of net migrants in 1991 was only 0.87 million showing significant growth of net migrants into Maharashtra during these ten years. Out of 3.2 million in-migrants from other states during the said decade, 2.6 million (or 79.6%) moved into urban areas. The source states of in-migration into Maharashtra were Uttar Pradesh (0.9 million), Karnataka (0.4 million), Madhya Pradesh (0.27 million), Gujarat (0.24 million), Bihar (0.22 million), and Andhra Pradesh (0.19 million). Among distant inter-state male migrants, work/employment has been cited as the primary reason for migration (Uttar Pradesh—73.0%; Bihar—79.1%). From the adjoining states, 'marriage' and 'moved with households' were cited as important reasons for migration (Census of India 2011). Marriage is the most prominent reason for migration among females. Table 1 presents data on the percentage distribution of migrants according to reasons for migration in Maharashtra as per the 2001 census and the National Sample Survey Organization's (NSSO) 64th round of survey conducted in 2007–08. The major reasons for migration are considered to be 'employment', 'business', 'education', 'marriage', and 'others'. Reasons such as natural disasters, social/political problems, housing problems, migration of parents are clubbed in 'others'. The data shows an upward trend in migration because of employment. Almost half the number of male migrants have stated employment as the reason for relocation in 2007–08 as against 37.18% in 2001. Thus, one of the main reasons for migration can be attributed to employment seeking behavior. However, for females, the single most important reason for migration can be traced to marriage.

Table 2 shows that 92.2% of rural and 94.4% of urban temporary migrants were not employed. Table 3 shows that besides agriculture (61.8%), construction activity (15.9%) in rural areas is seen to be generating sizeable employment for temporary migrants. However, in urban areas, it is other services (34.0%) followed by construction (19.3%) that emerged as job generators.

Table 1 Percentage distribution of migrants by reason for migration: comparison of Census data and NSS 64th round data, Maharashtra

Reason for Migration	Census 1991			Census 2001			NSS 64th round		
	Male	Female	Person	Male	Female	Person	Male	Female	Person
Employment	24.16	1.61	10.05	37.18	2.70	16.55	50.28	1.31	14.22
Business	11.43	1.43	5.17	1.00	0.10	0.46	4.91	0.05	1.33
Education	5.34	1.28	2.80	2.63	0.65	1.45	5.72	1.46	2.58
Marriage	1.24	62.43	39.50	0.68	59.13	35.64	2.70	78.87	58.79
Others	57.84	33.26	42.47	58.52	37.42	45.90	36.39	18.31	23.08

Source A report on Migration Particulars' based on data collected in state sample of 64th round of National Sample Survey (July, 2007–June, 2008), Vol. I, Table no.1, page no 4, Directorate of Economics and Statistics, Planning Department, Government of Maharashtra

Table 2 Broad activity status

Broad activity status	Rural			Urban		
	Male	Female	Person	Male	Female	Person
Agriculture	50.9	71.2	57.4	14.7	15.9	15
Non-agriculture	1.9	0	1.3	2.7	0	2
Mining and quarrying	12.3	7	10.7	11.8	4.3	9.9
Manufacturing	0	0	0	0	0	0
Construction	17.1	9.9	14.8	17.6	17	17.5
Trade, hotel and restaurant	5	2.1	4.1	11.9	16.8	13.1
Other services	2.1	0.8	1.7	3	0	2.2
All Employed (a)	2.8	3.2	3	26.1	44.7	30.7
Not Employed (a)	92.2	94.4	92.9	87.7	98.8	90.5
Total	100.0	100.0	100.0	100.0	100.0	100.0

Source A report on Migration Particulars' based on data collected in state sample of 64th round of National Sample Survey (July, 2007–June, 2008), Vol. I, Table no. 10, page no 10, Directorate of Economics and Statistics, Planning Department, Government of Maharashtra

Table 3 Percentage distribution of temporary migrants by employment activity

Broad activity status	Rural			Urban		
	Male	Female	Person	Male	Female	Person
Agriculture	55.3	75.5	61.8	16.7	16.1	16.6
Non-agriculture	44.7	24.5	38.2	83.3	83.9	83.4
Mining and quarrying	2.1	0	1.4	3.1	0	2.2
Manufacturing	13.4	7.5	11.5	13.4	4.4	10.9
Construction	18.5	10.5	15.9	20.1	17.2	19.3
Trade, hotel, and restaurant	5.4	2.2	4.4	13.6	17	14.5
Transport	2.3	0.9	1.8	3.4	0	2.4
Other services	3.1	3.4	3.2	29.7	45.3	34.0
Total	100.0	100.0	100.0	100.0	100.0	100.0

Source A report on Migration Particulars' based on data collected in state sample of 64th round of National Sample Survey (July, 2007–June, 2008), Vol. I, Table no. 11, page no 10, Directorate of Economics and Statistics, Planning Department, Government of Maharashtra

2 Present Study

For the first time, the NSSO 55th round had separately estimated the number of short duration out-migrants. The NSSO 64th round has taken the extra effort to cover seasonal/temporary migration. The census, which is the other important source of migration data, is mainly concerned with current and permanent migration and does not attempt to capture seasonal or short-term flows of labor (Keshri and Bhagat

Table 4 Total Coverage of field survey

Years	No. of migrants	No of migrants from outside state	No. of castes covered	No. of factories where migrants worked	No. of districts from where laborers migrated
2004–05	7483	39	46	25	25
2005–06	16670	203	55	36	23
2006–07	13916	218	43	30	25
2007–08	17452	177	53	33	29
2008–09	16874	289	55	38	30
2009–10	9740	266	66	24	24
2010–11	7784	35	50	18	26
2011–12	3649	3	42	34	22
2012–13	1742	0	33	20	15

Source Field survey

2012). The two main secondary sources of data on population mobility in India do not adequately capture seasonal and circular migration due to differences over the definitions of migrants, reasons for migration, and stock versus flow concept of migration. These limitations necessitate collecting primary data exclusively on seasonal migration, especially for sugarcane cutter migrants. This has been done over a period of nine years from 2004–05 to 2012–13 through a structured questionnaire with the help of purposive sample methods.[1] Sugarcane cutter migrants of Maharashtra are essentially temporary or seasonal migrants where movement is from a rural origin to a rural destination. Workers from rural areas of Beed, Jalgaon, Ahmednagar, Nashik, and Jalna districts migrate to the sugar belt of Maharashtra, comprising seven districts—Nashik, Ahmednagar, Pune, Satara, Sangli, Kolhapur, and Sholapur, every year during the sugarcane harvest period which generally starts in the month of October and lasts up till March.

This paper is confined to tracing the flow of sugarcane cutter migrants based on their caste, origin, and destination so as to understand patterns of migration by social groups.

The head of the household was contacted at the workplace. Information about the number of male and female members in the family, caste, age, and education level, and current as well as last three years working destination, the number of children accompanying the migrant family, their education level and age group, etc. have been gathered. The total number of respondents is 95310. Table 4 shows that respondents belong to on an average 49 different castes and every year almost 30 factories were visited by enumerators which spread over almost 28 districts of the state.

[1]This daunting exercise was performed by workers of an NGO 'Janarth' located in Aurangabad. Janarth ran schools for the sugar cutter migrant children at the site itself until the Right to Education Act came into force in the year 2013.

Table 5 Distribution of male and female migrant laborers by age group

Age Group	Male	Female	Total
Up to 35	59347 (62.28)	73768 (77.88)	133115 (70.1)
36 to 59	33431 (35.1)	20385 (21.53)	53816 (28.3)
60 & above	2485 (2.6)	574 (0.6)	3059 (1.6)
Total			189990 (100)

Note Figures in parentheses shows percentage
Source Field Survey

3 Profile of Migrants

3.1 Age

The ability to earn income mostly depends on the capability and/or productivity of the person which is mainly affected by the age of laborers. The same is true for the migrants who work as sugarcane cutters. As per Table 5, the highest percentage (70.1) of migrant male and female laborers belongs to the age group of 'up to 35 years' that is the most appropriate age group to do strenuous physical work. Surprisingly, the number of females is relatively more than that of males in this age group. The reverse can be seen in the 36–59 years age group wherein almost 35% are males and only 22% are female migrant workers.

3.2 Education

The overall education level of migrant labor is very poor (Table 6), although that of males is slightly better than females. Of the total, almost 85% female migrants are illiterate, as compared to their male counterparts (64.6%). Middle-level education (between 5th and 8th standards) is the most common level among both males (13.15%) and female (7.36%) migrants. Less than 2% of the migrant has studied after matriculation.

3.3 Social Groups

Respondents in the study belong to 85 different castes (see Table 7). Every second migrant belongs to the Other Backward Caste (OBC) category and out of them almost every third migrant belongs to Vanjari caste. The general category, which is primarily of Marathas, contributes around 21% of the migrants. Five castes from Schedule Caste (SC), namely Matang, Mahar, Buddha, Chambhar, and Harijan constitute the third highest group among the respondent migrants. Though the share of Schedule Tribe

Table 6 Distribution of male and female by the general educational level

Education Level	Male	Female	Total
Illiterate	61536 (64.6)	80589 (85.08)	142125 (74.8)
Up to primary	10102 (10.6)	5193 (5.48)	15295 (8.1)
5th to 8th standards	12524 (13.15)	6966 (7.36)	19490 (10.3)
9th to 10th standards	8024 (8.42)	1686 (1.78)	9710 (5.1)
Above 10th standards	3077 (3.23)	293 (0.31)	3370 (1.8)
Total			189990 (100)

Note Figures in parenthesis shows percentage
Source Field Survey

Table 7 Distribution of migrants by social group/sub-caste

Sr No	Caste	Migrant	Sr No	Caste	Migrant
1	Vanjari	27157 (28.49)	44	Kandali	34 (0.04)
2	Maratha	19387 (20.34)	45	Tirmali	33 (0.03)
3	Banjara	12389 (13.)	46	Gavali	31 (0.03)
4	Bhill	8145 (8.55)	47	Dhobi/parit	29 (0.03)
5	Dhangar	6597 (6.92)	48	Vakar	29 (0.03)
6	Mahar	3950 (4.14)	49	Holar	28 (0.03)
7	Matang/Mang	2742 (2.88)	50	Pujari	27 (0.03)
8	Buddha	2257 (2.37)	51	Joshi	26 (0.03)
9	Muslim	1639 (1.72)	52	Ghisadi	25 (0.03)
10	Lamani	1129 (1.18)	53	Gurav	20 (0.02)
11	Matang	916 (0.96)	54	Sonar	18 (0.02)
12	Lonar	895 (0.94)	55	Jogi	17 (0.02)
13	Naik	747 (0.78)	56	Nandiwale/jondhali	17 (0.02)
14	Harijan	641 (0.67)	57	Pathan	17 (0.02)
15	Chambhar	634 (0.67)	58	Christian	16 (0.02)
16	Koli	616 (0.65)	59	Nandiwale/jondh	14 (0.01)
17	Kokani	524 (0.55)	60	Dhakar	13 (0.01)
18	Ramoshi	507 (0.53)	61	Pardeshi	13 (0.01)
19	Mali	483 (0.51)	62	Pawara	11 (0.01)
20	Hatgar	378 (0.4)	63	Kadhodi	9 (0.01)
21	Gosawi	315 (0.33)	64	Patil	9 (0.01)
22	Wadari	276 (0.29)	65	Kunbi	8 (0.01)
23	Gujar	273 (0.29)	66	Panchal	8 (0.01)
24	Mang	236 (0.25)	67	Dhobi	7 (0.01)

(continued)

Table 7 (continued)

Sr No	Caste	Migrant	Sr No	Caste	Migrant
25	Thakar	202 (0.21)	68	Garudi	7 (0.01)
26	Lohar	165 (0.17)	69	Nandiwale/gondhali	7 (0.01)
27	Kumbhar	151 (0.16)	70	Vasava	7 (0.01)
28	Sutar	143 (0.15)	71	Brahmin	5 (0.01)
29	Nhavi	134 (0.14)	72	Shimpi	5 (0.01)
30	Gopal	125 (0.13)	73	Katkari	4 (0)
31	Kaikadi	105 (0.11)	74	Tambat	4 (0)
32	Pardhi	102 (0.11)	75	Wari	4 (0)
33	Valhar	93 (0.1)	76	Khatik	3 (0)
34	Rajput	76 (0.08)	77	Padavi	3 (0)
35	Teli	61 (0.06)	78	Lakhan	2 (0)
36	Mavachi	59 (0.06)	79	Bhai	1 (0)
37	Kolhar	53 (0.06)	80	Birad	1 (0)
38	Adivasi	51 (0.05)	81	Dhor	1 (0)
39	Wani	45 (0.05)	82	Gamit	1 (0)
40	Lingayat	42 (0.04)	83	Kahar	1 (0)
41	Bhoi	41 (0.04)	84	Parit	1 (0)
42	Gola	40 (0.04)	85	Vaidya	1 (0)
43	Beldar	39 (0.04)	86	Caste not given	206 (0.25)
	Grand Total				95313 (100)

Note Figures in parenthesis shows percentage
Source: Field Survey

(ST) in the sample is only 9.75%, Bhill alone comprises 8.5% of migrants under study. Although, the respondents belong to more than eighty castes, yet more than 75% of migrants belong to only five castes—Vanjari (28.49%), Maratha (20.34%), Banjara (13%), Bhill (8.55%), and Dhangar (6.92%). Every fifth migrant belongs to Maratha caste and almost every third migrant is Vanjari by caste. Therefore, further analysis is done only for the migrants belonging to these top five castes.

Beed, Ahmednagar, Jalgaon, Aurangabad, and Nashik are districts of origin for almost 80% migrants. Ahmednagar, Pune, Nashik, Kolhapur, and Satara are the top five districts of destination for almost 77% of migrants. The highest percentage (41.44) of migrants belongs to Beed district. The number of migrants from Nashik and Aurangabad districts is almost equal. Ahmednagar district is the most preferred destination district one out of every fourth migrant headed there during 2004–05 to 2012–13. Pune district is the next favorite destination for migrant labor with 22.6% of them working in the factories located there. A good number (7.45%) of migrants also went to Belgaon district, which is part of adjoining state Karnataka.

Table 8 Districts of origin, destination, and corresponding caste of the migrant's Respondents migrated from (origin) top five districts

		Respondents working (destination) in the top 5 districts		Respondents belongs to top 5 Caste	
Beed	39493 (41.44)	Ahmednagar	23132 (24.27)	Vanjari	27157 (28.49)
Ahmednagar	14424 (15.13)	Pune	21541 (22.6)	Maratha	19387 (20.34)
Jalgaon	9001 (9.44)	Nashik	13368 (14.03)	Banjara	12389 (13.0)
Aurangabad	6379 (6.69)	Kolhapur	8702 (9.13)	Bhill	8145 (8.55)
Nashik	6350 (6.66)	Belgaon	7105 (7.45)	Dhangar	6597 (6.92)
Total of 5 districts (Origin)	75647 (79.37)	Total of 5 districts (Destination)	73848 (77.48)	Total of 5 caste	73675 (77.3)
Total Respondents	95313 (100)				

Note Values shown in the parentheses of the second last row are the percentage of the top five districts of the origin, destination and caste to the total number of the respondents in the respective categories
Source Field Survey

4 Mapping of Migration

It is observed that there is a definite pattern in the migration of sugarcane cutter laborers in terms of caste and choice of migration destination. There is a need to study the combination of the district of origin and destinations of the migrants belonging to different castes. Table 9 traces the flow of migration from origin to destination. Top five districts from which migrants moved outside in decreasing order are Beed, Ahmednagar, Jalgaon, Aurangabad, and Nashik. Out of the top five districts of origin, only two districts viz. Ahmednagar and Nashik could find a place in the list of top five preferred destinations also.

Ahmednagar is the most preferred workplace followed by Pune, Nashik, Belgaon, and Kolhapur. Of the total migrants who moved to Ahmednagar in search of work, 88% belong to five districts, namely Beed, Ahmednagar, Jalgaon, Aurangabad, and Nashik. Among them, almost 30% belong to Ahmednagar itself and every fourth migrant comes from Beed. Although very few migrants from Nashik work in the Ahmednagar, Belgaon, Kolhapur, and Pune district, yet the highest percentage (38.36%) of workers from Nashik work in Nashik only. Sugarcane cutter migrant hailing from the Beed and Ahmednagar go out of the state and work in Belgaon. Kolhapur is preferred by the migrants who belong to Beed. Out of almost 91% workers of Pune, the majority of them have migrated from Beed (71.25%) followed

Table 9 Flow of migration from origin to destination

Districts Destination/Workplace	Districts Origin					Total of 5 districts*
	Beed	Ahm'gar	Jalgaon	Aur'bad	Nashik	
Ahmednagar	5922 (25.6)	6736 (29.12)	2874 (12.42)	3960 (17.12)	843 (3.64)	20335 (87.9)
Belgaon	5502 (77.44)	797 (11.22)	1 (0.01)	2 (0.03)	NA	6302 (88.7)
Kolhapur	3501 (40.23)	171 (1.97)	69 (0.79)	29 (0.33)	2 (0.02)	3772 (43.34)
Nashik	298 (2.23)	1806 (13.51)	4267 (31.92)	669 (5.0)	5128 (38.36)	12168 (91.02)
Pune	15349 (71.25)	3380 (15.69)	479 (2.22)	291 (1.35)	111 (0.52)	19610 (91.03)

*In the last column, for example, 20335 is the number of migrants belonging to the top five districts from where they have migrated, which constitutes 88% of the total migrants who migrated to Ahmednagar. Please read other values in the same column accordingly
Source Field Survey

by Ahmednagar (15.69%), Jalgaon (2.22%), Aurangabad (1.35%), and Nashik (0.52%).[2]

4.1 Caste and District of Origin

After understanding the flow of migration between and among the districts, the flow of migration based on caste and district of origin is discussed in this section. The first row and first column of Table 10 show the name of the district of origin and caste of migrants, respectively.

The highest number of migrants belongs to Beed. Interestingly, the total number of migrants from Beed (39493) is more than the total number of migrants belonging to the other four districts (36154). It is discernable from Table 10 that almost 80% of the migrants from the top five districts belong to five castes except for migrants hailing from Aurangabad district where only 68% of migrants belong to the aforementioned five castes (see the first column under the heading—Total of 5 castes).

Of the migrants from Beed, 42.15% of migrant belongs to Vanjari caste followed by Maratha (33.63%), Dhangar (6.54%), and Banjara (2.42%) caste. The same is true for migrants from Ahmednagar except for Bhill caste as in Beed they are at the bottom (0.5%) but here they are in second last (1.34%). Bhill (39.29%) tops the ladder for migrants from Nashik district. In Jalgaon, the highest position is occupied

[2]Note that row total is addable but not the column as it quite possible that migrants who belong to one district let's say, Nashik may not be working in any one of the districts listed in the table (in column). That's why total of five districts opposite of Kolhapur is summing up to 43.34% only.

Table 10 Distribution of migrants migrated from top five districts-(origin) caste-wise

Caste\District	Beed	Ahmednagar	Jalgaon	Aurangabad	Nashik
Banjara	956 (2.42)	263 (1.82)	4604 (51.15)	2438 (38.22)	1871 (29.46)
Bhill	198 (0.5)	193 (1.34)	1338 (14.87)	610 (9.56)	2495 (39.29)
Dhangar	2582 (6.54)	1309 (9.08)	80 (0.89)	84 (1.32)	28 (0.44)
Maratha	13283 (33.63)	3364 (23.32)	152 (1.69)	507 (7.95)	136 (2.14)
Vanjari	16646 (42.15)	6797 (47.12)	1395 (15.5)	692 (10.85)	528 (8.31)
Total of 5 castes	33665 (85.24)	11926 (82.68)	7569 (84.09)	4331 (67.89)	5058 (79.65)
Total number of migrants	39493 (100)	14424 (100)	9001 (100)	6379 (100)	6350 (100)

Source Field survey
Note Figures in parentheses are percentage values

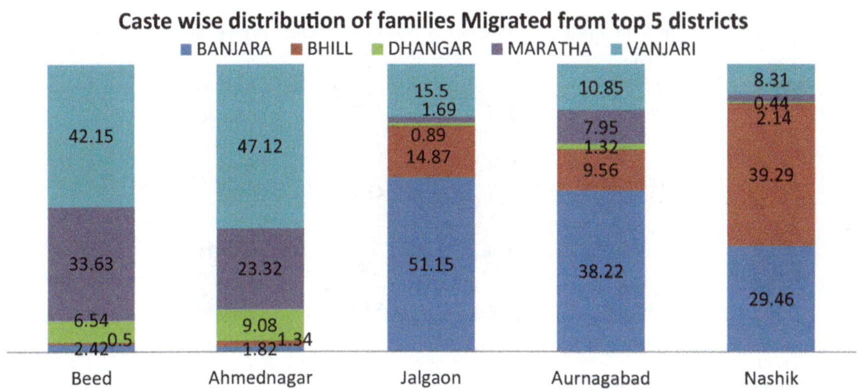

Fig. 1 Distribution of migrants migrated from top five districts—caste-wise. *Source* Field survey

by migrants of Banjara caste (51.15%). Banjaras are also at the top (38.22%) in Aurangabad district but with a lower percentage in comparison to Jalgaon (Fig. 1).

4.2 Caste and District of Destination

One also needs to understand the relation between caste and most preferred destination or workplace. Table 11 and Fig. 2 show the preferred workplace of the migrants belonging to different castes. Ahmednagar and Pune stand at first and second place, respectively, in consideration of the preferred workplace or destination. Belgaon is the least preferred.

Out of total migrants working in the five mentioned districts, more than 75% belong to the top five castes except for Kolhapur where only half of the migrants are

Table 11 Caste-wise distribution of families working in the top five (destination) districts

Caste	Ahmednagar	Kolhapur	Nashik	Pune	Belgaon
Banjara	4852 (20.98)	305 (3.5)	3764 (28.16)	654 (3.04)	70 (0.99)
Bhill	1120 (4.84)	87 (1.0)	3482 (26.05)	320 (1.49)	6 (0.08)
Dhangar	823 (3.56)	1739 (19.98)	354 (2.65)	1560 (7.24)	1006 (14.16)
Maratha	3463 (14.97)	1192 (13.7)	450 (3.37)	9424 (43.75)	1994 (28.06)
Vanjari	7434 (32.14)	1212 (13.93)	2385 (17.84)	5720 (26.55)	3372 (47.46)
Total of 5 caste	17692 (76.48)	4535 (52.11)	10435 (78.06)	17678 (82.07)	6448 (90.75)
Total families (working districts)	23132 (100)	8702 (100)	13368 (100)	21541 (100)	7105 (100)

Source Field Survey

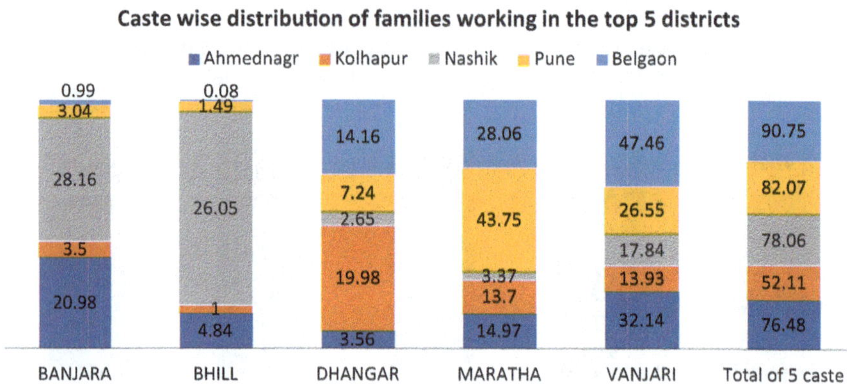

Fig. 2 Caste-wise distribution of families working in top five districts (destination). *Source* Field survey

from these five caste groups. Among those migrants who had migrated to Ahmednagar, percentage of Vanjari is the highest (32.17). Migrants belonging to the Dhangar caste top the list of migrants who worked in Kolhapur. Around every second and fourth migrants belonging to Vanjari and Maratha castes, respectively, prefer to work at Belgaon. Migrants belonging to Maratha caste are the largest in Pune (43.75%).

4.3 Caste and District of Origin: Microanalysis of the Movement of the Migrants

In this section, an attempt has been made to trace the movement of migrants from the origin by distributing them as per the working place vis-à-vis their caste. This exercise throws light about the preferred destination choice of a migrant of specific caste, originating from a particular district.

The related data is presented in Table 12, which is disaggregated into five parts; each pertaining to a specific caste. The names of the districts in the first row correspond to the district of origin, while the destination districts are represented column-wise. To understand the caste-wise movement of migrants an example has been presented as follows—In the top five districts of origin and destination, there are 21135 migrants belonging to Vanjari caste, which is almost 78% of the total 27157 Vanjari migrants in the sample (refer Table 7). Out of them, i.e., 21135, 6250 (29.57%) hail from Ahmednagar district. However, 3768 of them, or, 51.2% of 6250 migrate

Table 12 Distribution of destination, origin, and caste of the migrants

Vanjari[1]

Working place	Origin of migration					Grand total*
	Ahm'gar	Auran'ad	Beed	Jalgaon	Nashik	
Ahm'gar	3768 (51.2)	167 (2.27)	3024 (41.09)	363 (4.93)	37 (0.5)	7359 (34.82)
Pune	944 (16.91)	34 (0.61)	4511 (80.8)	85 (1.52)	9 (0.16)	5583 (26.42)
Belgaon	37 (1.16)	NA	3156 (98.81)	1 (0.03)	NA	3194 (15.11)
Satara	410 (15.26)	8 (0.3)	2259 (84.1)	8 (0.3)	1 (0.04)	2686 (12.71)
Nashik	1091 (47.17)	44 (1.9)	143 (6.18)	574 (24.82)	461 (19.93)	2313 (10.94)
Total	6250 (29.57)	253 (1.2)	13093 (61.95)	1031 (4.88)	508 (2.4)	21135 (100)
	Maratha[2]					
Pune	1443 (16.25)	25 (0.28)	7393 (83.26)	13 (0.15)	5 (0.06)	8879 (55.68)
Ahm'gar	1084 (34.12)	374 (11.77)	1666 (52.44)	44 (1.38)	9 (0.28)	3177 (19.92)
Belgaon	374 (20.55)	1 (0.05)	1445 (79.4)	NA	NA	1820 (11.42)
Satara	182 (14.63)	2 (0.16)	1059 (85.13)	1 (0.08)	NA	1244 (7.8)
Kolhapur	71 (8.6)	1 (0.12)	743 (89.95)	11 (1.33)	NA	826 (5.18)
Total	3154 (19.78)	403 (2.53)	12306 (77.17)	69 (0.43)	14 (0.09)	15946 (100)
	Banjara[3]					

(continued)

Table 12 (continued)

Vanjari[1]						
Working place	Origin of migration					Grand total*
	Ahm'gar	Auran'ad	Beed	Jalgaon	Nashik	
Ahm'gar	131 (3.14)	1674 (40.08)	238 (5.7)	1822 (43.62)	312 (7.47)	4177 (45.32)
Nashik	70 (2.05)	138 (4.04)	17 (0.5)	1761 (51.49)	1434 (41.93)	3420 (37.11)
Auran'ad	2 (0.26)	334 (43.89)	26 (3.42)	357 (46.91)	42 (5.52)	76 (8.26))
Pune	19 (3.36)	108 (19.08)	97 (17.14)	265 (46.82)	77 (13.6)	566 (6.14)
Gujrat	NA	122 (41.78)	1 (0.34)	168 (57.53)	1 (0.34)	292 (3.17)
Total	222 (2.41)	2376 (25.78)	379 (4.11)	4373 (47.45)	1866 (20.25)	9216 (100)
	Bhill[4]					
Nashik	37 (1.18)	171 (5.45)	10 (0.32)	815 (25.99)	2103 (67.06)	3136 (66.89)
Ahm'gar	96 (10.14)	274 (28.93)	40 (4.22)	277 (29.25)	260 (27.46)	947 (20.2)
Gujrat	NA	33 (13.81)	NA	121 (50.63)	85 (35.56)	239 (5.1)
Pune	45 (21.03)	46 (21.5)	83 (38.79)	34 (15.89)	6 (2.8)	214 (4.56)
Auran'ad	6 (3.95)	77 (50.66)	NA	33 (21.71)	36 (23.68)	152 (3.24)
Total	184 (3.92)	601 (12.82)	133 (2.84)	1280 (27.3)	2490 (53.11)	4688 (100)
	Dhangar[5]					
Pune	290 (22.82)	10 (0.79)	965 (75.92)	5 (0.39)	1 (0.08)	1271 (35.61)
Ahm'gar	368 (48.94)	49 (6.52)	320 (42.55)	3 (0.4)	12 (1.6)	752 (21.07)
Belgaon	291 (40.3)	(0.0)	431 (59.7)	NA	NA	722 (20.23)
Kolhapur	40 (9.52)	2 (0.48)	377 (89.76)	1 (0.24)	NA	420 (11.77)
Satara	69 (17.08)	3 (0.74)	332 (82.18)	NA	NA	404 (11.32)
Total	1058 (29.64)	64 (1.79)	2425 (67.95)	9 (0.25)	13 (0.36)	3569 (100)

Percentage of migrants belonging to (1) Vanjari (2) Maratha (3) Banjara (4) Bhill, and (5) Dhangar caste working in and migrated from the discussed top five districts are 77.83, 82.25, 74.39, 57.56, 54.1 of their castes in the entire sample

Source Field study

within the district itself. But they constitute only around one-third (34.82%) of the migrant labor working in Ahmednagar district.

The last column of the table gives the caste-wise grand total of migrants working in each district. Hence out of 21135 Vanjari migrants working in the top five destination districts, 7359 (34.82%) are working in Ahmednagar, followed by 5583 (26.42%) in Pune, then 3194 (15.11%) in Belgaon, 2686 or 12.71% in Satara, and 2313 (10.94%) are working in Nashik district. Thus, the entire table can be interpreted in the same manner. It may be noted that the grand total in each column is total of values in the respective column, but the same is not the case for percentage which is given in parentheses; but for the row values, grand total in the last column is the outcome of the addition of each cell of that particular row and value in the parentheses is the percentage of the migrant of the particular cell to the grand total of the respective row. The migration patterns of the top five castes are thus discussed in the following paragraphs.

4.3.1 Vanjari Migrants

Of the total Vanjari migrants, almost 78% have migrated from the given top five districts and out of them, maximum have migrated from Beed (61.95%) district, followed by Ahmednagar (29.57%). The two most preferred destinations for this caste are Ahmednagar (34.82%) and Pune (26.42%). In Belagaon, almost 98.1% of Vanjari migrants and 80% of Vanjari migrants in Pune hailed from Beed district. In Nashik, almost every second Vanjari migrant came from Ahmednagar while one-fifth of them had moved within Nashik district itself.

4.3.2 Maratha Migrants

As per the survey, every fifth (20.34%) respondent belongs to the Maratha Caste (Table 7) and almost 97% of them belong to only two districts: Beed (77.17%) and Ahmednagar (19.78%). Pune is the most preferred migration destination of Marathas as they constitute more than half (55.68%) of its working migrant population. Around 20% prefer to work in Ahmednagar, and 34% of the Maratha migrant labor in Ahmednagar has migrated within Ahmednagar itself. Belgaon comes in third place as a preferred working place for Maratha migrants comprising 11.42% of its migrant population.

4.3.3 Banjara Migrants

Out of the total 9216 (74.39% of total Banjara respondents in the study), almost every second, fourth, and fifth migrant belonged to Jalgaon (47.45%), Aurangabad (25.78%), and Nashik (20.25%) districts, respectively. Around 45 and 37% of the Banjara migrants headed for Ahmednagar and Nashik, respectively, as their chosen destinations. Out of the 4177 Banjara migrants working in Ahmednagar, 43% belong to Jalgaon while 40% to Aurangabad. However, a good 42% of Banjara migrant population in Nashik district has moved for work within the district only. Comparatively, less number of Banjara migrants prefer to work in Aurangabad (8.26%) and out of them, the maximum (44%) are from within the district itself.

4.3.4 Bhill Migrants

Taking into account migration from the top five districts to top five destinations, Bhills constitute 57.56% of the total Bhills migrants in the sample (Table 12). However, if two more districts of origin–Nashik and Jalgaon–are added then the percentage for the community leaps to 93.71% (Table 13). It means these two districts contribute almost 39% of Bhills migrants in the study. The highest number of Bhill migrants hails from Nashik (32.62%), followed by Dhule district with 28.52 migrants and Beed occupies the last position (1.74%). Among all the Bhill migrants, the maximum preferred to work in Nashik (45.2%) and Gujarat (35.82%), and among 60% of the Bhills working in Nashik had moved within the district itself. Almost the same is the case of Bhill migrants working in Aurangabad where out of 159 migrants, every second migrant belonged to Aurangabad.

4.3.5 Dhangar Migrants

Of all the major castes in the study, the Dhangars have been found to have migrated in the most scattered way. On considering the top five districts of origin, it would cover only 54.15% of the total Dhangar migrants in the sample. More interestingly, after the inclusion of two more districts like Sangali (12.46%) and Osmanabad (8.96%), it would cover only about 68.85% of the total Dhangar migrant respondents (Refer Table 13). Almost every second migrant belongs to Beed district while every fourth is from Ahmednagar district. It seems that their working districts are more or less the same, which means they do not relocate great distances. Almost every second migrant who worked in Kolhapur belonged to Sangli.

5 Conclusion

Migration within India is predominantly short-distance with around 60% of migrants changing their residences within their district of birth and 20% within their state (province), while the rest move across state boundaries. Estimates of short-term migrants vary from 15 million (NSSO 2007–2008) to 100 million. These migrants belong to the poorest and deprived sections of society typically comprising the Scheduled Castes, Scheduled Tribes (STs), and Other Backward Castes (OBCs).

Table 13 Distribution of destination, origin, and caste of the migrants (after adding two more districts)

	Bhill							
Working place	Districts of origin							Grand Total
	Ahm'nagar	Aur'bad	Beed	Jalgaon	Nashik	Dhule	Nandurbar	
Nashik	37 (1.07)	171 (4.96)	10 (0.29)	815 (23.62)	2103 (60.96)	310 (8.99)	4 (0.12)	3450 (45.2)
Gujrat	NA	33 (1.21)	NA	121 (4.43)	85 (3.11)	1743 (63.75)	752 (27.51)	2734 (35.82)
Ahmednagar	96 (9.09)	274 (25.95)	40 (3.79)	277 (26.23)	260 (24.62)	98 (9.28)	11 (1.04)	1056 (13.83)
Pune	45 (19.23)	46 (19.66)	83 (35.47)	34 (14.53)	6 (2.56)	19 (8.12)	1 (0.43)	234 (3.07)
Aurangabad	6 (3.77)	77 (48.43)	NA	33 (20.75)	36 (22.64)	7 (4.4)	NA	159 (2.08)
Grand Total	184 (2.41)	601 (7.87)	133 (1.74)	1280 (16.77)	2490 (32.62)	2177 (28.52)	768 (10.06)	7633
Working place	**Dhangar**							
	Ahm'dnagar	Aur'bad	Beed	Jalgaon	Nashik	Osmanabad	Sangli	Grand Total
Pune	290 (20.71)	10 (0.71)	965 (68.93)	5 (0.36)	1 (0.07)	129 (9.21)	NA	1400 (30.82)
Belgaon	291 (29.82)	NA	431 (44.16)	NA	NA	254 (26.02)	NA	976 (21.49)
Kolhapur	40 (4.46)	2 (0.22)	377 (42.03)	1 (0.11)	NA	1 (0.11)	476 (53.07)	897 (19.75)
Ahmednagar	368 (48.94)	49 (6.52)	320 (42.55)	3 (0.4)	12 (1.6)	NA	NA	752 (16.56)
Satara	69 (13.35)	3 (0.58)	332 (64.22)	NA	NA	23 (4.45)	90 (17.41)	517 (11.38)
Grand Total	1058 (23.29)	64 (1.41)	2425 (53.39)	9 (0.2)	13 (0.29)	407 (8.96)	566 (12.46)	4542

Source Field Study

As per the Census 2001, Maharashtra witnessed the largest in-migration of the population during ten years (1991–2001) from different states. The total number of in-migrants into the state was 3.2 million. Major contributing states toward this movement were Uttar Pradesh (0.9 million), Karnataka (0.4 million), Madhya Pradesh (0.27 million), Gujarat (0.24 million), Bihar (0.22 million), and Andhra Pradesh (0.19 million). Among distant inter-state male migrants, work/employment has been cited as the primary reason for migration (Uttar Pradesh—73.0%; Bihar—79.1%). From the adjoining states, 'marriage' and 'moved with households' were cited as important reasons for migration (Census of India 2011).

For the first time, the NSSO 55th round separately estimated the number of short duration out-migrants. Thereafter, NSSO 64th round took the extra effort to cover seasonal/temporary migration. The census, which is the other important source of migration data, is mainly concerned with current and permanent migration and does not attempt to capture seasonal or short-term flows of labor. However, these two main secondary sources of data on population do not adequately capture seasonal and circular migration due to differences over the definitions of migrants, reasons of migration, and stock versus flow concept of migration. These limitations necessitate collecting primary data exclusively on seasonal migration.

This paper is confined to tracing the flow of sugarcane cutter migrants in Maharashtra based on their caste, origin, and destination so as to understand patterns of migration by social groups. They are essentially temporary or seasonal migrants wherein movement is from a rural origin to a rural destination. Workers from the rural areas of Beed, Jalgaon, Ahmednagar, Nashik, and Jalna districts in the arid Marathawada region migrate to the sugar belt of Maharashtra, comprising seven districts—Nashik, Ahmednagar, Pune, Satara, Sangli, Kolhapur, and Sholapur, every year during the sugarcane harvest period which generally starts in the month of October and lasts up till March. The information has been collected over a period of nine years with the help of an NGO working among the migrant workers. The field survey covering 95310 respondents, who belonged to more than 85 different caste groups, in 30 sugar factories across 28 districts in Maharashtra.

The study found the highest percentage (70.1) of migrant male and female laborers belonging to the age group of 'up to 35 years' that is the most appropriate age group to do physical work. Surprisingly, the number of females is relatively more than that of males in this age group. The overall education level of migrant labor is very poor, although that of males is slightly better than females. Almost 85% female migrants are illiterate, as compared to their male counterparts (64.6%). Middle-level education is the most common level among both male (13.15%) and female (7.36%) migrants and less than 2% of them have studied beyond class ten.

Respondents in the study belong to 85 different castes. Every second migrant hails from the Other Backward Caste (OBC) category. General category, which is primarily of Marathas, contributes around 21% of the respondent migrants. Five castes from Schedule Caste (SC), namely Matang, Mahar, Buddha, Chambhar, and Harijan constitute the third highest group among the respondents. Though the share of Schedule Tribe (ST) in the sample is only 9.75%, Bhill alone comprises 8.5% of migrants under study. Although, the respondents belong to more than eighty castes, yet more than 75% migrants belong to only five castes—Vanjari (28.49%), Maratha (20.34%), Banjara (13%), Bhill (8.55%), and Dhangar (6.92%). Therefore, further analysis is done only for the migrants belonging to these top five castes.

It is observed that there is a definite pattern in the migration of the migrant labor in terms of caste and choice of migration destination. Beed, Ahmednagar, Jalgaon, Aurangabad, and Nashik are districts of origin for almost 8% of migrants. Almost 80% of the migrants from the top five districts belong to the five aforementioned castes except for migrants hailing from Aurangabad district where only 68% of migrants belong to these caste groups. Ahmednagar, Pune, Nashik, Kolhapur, and Satara are the top five districts of destination for almost 77% of migrants. Out of the top five districts of origin, only two districts viz. Ahmednagar and Nashik also made it to the list of top five preferred destinations. Ahmednagar is the most preferred workplace followed by Pune, Nashik, Belgaon, and Kolhapur.

The highest number of migrants (41.44%) belongs to Beed. Interestingly, the total number of migrants from Beed (39493) is more than the total number of migrants belonging to the other four districts (36154). Among them, the highest numbers are from Vanjari and Maratha castes, and they prefer Ahmedabad and Pune districts as their work destinations. Jalgaon, Nashik, and Beed are the districts where the maximum percentage of the migrants belongs to Banjara, Bhill, Dhangar caste migrants and their preferred workplaces are Ahmednagar, Nashik, and Pune, respectively. Of all the major castes in the study, the Dhangars have been found to have migrated in the most scattered way.

The flow of migrants is from less developed areas to more developed areas, and the caste of migrants also indicates that they belong to the poor strata of the population. Marathas, from the general or upper-caste category, are a 'surprise' inclusion as they are seen as a very influential community in some parts of the state. The majority of families belonging to this community live in the rural area which is why their numbers seem to be high in seasonal migration.

Acknowledgements This paper is part of a study supported by Janarth (an Aurangabad-based NGO). I am thankful to Janarth for their support in collecting primary data.

Appendix 1: Total Coverage: Distribution of Working Place

Sr No	District	No. of factories	No. of talukas	No. of Migrants	Crushing capacity *
1	Ahmednagar	15	11	22113	40954
2	Aurangabad	5	3	1738	11458
3	Belgaon	4		6387	11416
4	Gujrat	4		3297	11416
5	Hingoli	2	2	565	5000
6	Jalgaon	1	1	1	2500
7	Jalna	1	1	20	2500
8	Kolhapur	10	6	7221	37700
9	Nanded	2	1	2254	5000
10	Nashik	5	4	12968	9750
11	Pune	11	4	27392	36104
12	Sangli	5	3	2748	11750
13	Satara	4	3	6431	10800
14	Solapur	3	1	2063	9500

(continued)

(continued)

Sr No	District	No. of factories	No. of talukas	No. of Migrants	Crushing capacity *
15	Yavatmal	1	1	112	2500
	Total	73	41	95310	204348 (Average-13890)

Source Field Survey

Appendix 2: Details of All Factories, Location, Number of Migrants Working and Crushing Capacities

Sr No	Name of the factory	District	Tehsil	No of Migrants	Crushing Capacity (Mt/year)
1	Ashok S S K	Ahmednagar	Shrirampur	58	2600
2	Agasti SS K	Ahmednagar	Akole	1794	2500
3	Annasaheb mane gurale S S K	Aurangabad	Gangapur	41	2854
4	Bhima S S K	Pune	Daund	2312	2500
5	Bhima shankarS S K	Pune	Ambegaon	7	2500
6	BardoliS S K	Gujrat		505	2854
7	Barashiv hanuman S S K	Hingoli	Aundh	122	2500
8	Dr. Baburaobapujitanpure S S K	Ahmednagar	Rahuri	241	4250
9	Baramati agro Ltd. Sugar division	Pune	Baramati	687	3500
10	Bhauraochavan—unit I S S K	Nanded	Ardhapur	1694	2500
11	Bhauraochavan—unit II S S K	Nanded	Ardhapur	560	2500
12	Chhatrapati S S K	Pune	Indapur	4684	3500
13	Chatrapati Rajaram S S K	Kolhapur	Karvir	1600	2200
14	ChhatrapatiShahu S S K	Kolhapur	Kagal	460	2500
15	Dnyaneshwar S S K	Ahmednagar	Newasa	5897	5000
16	Dattashetkari S S K	Kolhapur	Shirol	1465	7000
17	Daulatshetkari S S K	Kolhapur	Chandgad	260	3500
18	Dudhgandha-vedganga S S K	Kolhapur	Kagal	54	3500
19	Dudhgangakrishna S S K	Belgaon	Chikodi	2717	2854
20	Daund sugar S S K	Pune	Daund	66	3500
21	DeshbhaktaRatnappannaKumbhar S S K	Kolhapur	Hatkangale	147	5000
22	Gangamai sugar industries S S K	Aurangabad	Sillod	21	2500

(continued)

(continued)

Sr No	Name of the factory	District	Tehsil	No of Migrants	Crushing Capacity (Mt/year)
23	Gurudatta sugars, takalwadi S S K	Kolhapur	Shirol	560	3500
24	Gangapur S S K	Aurangabad	Gangapur	1344	2000
25	Ganesh S S K	Ahmednagar	Kopargaon	2732	1750
26	Halasidhanath S S K	Belgaon	Chikkodi	1203	2854
27	Hiranyakeshi S S K	Belgaon	Hukeri	2344	2854
28	HutatmaKisanvirAhir S S K	Sangli	Walwa	13	1250
29	Indapur S S K	Pune	Indapur	2733	5000
30	Jarandeshwer S S K	Satara	Koregoan	514	2500
31	Kadwa S S K	Nasik	Dindori	2388	1250
32	K.k.wagh S S K	Nashik	Niphad	338	1250
33	KarmayogiShankarraoPatil S S K	Pune	Indapur	2291	5000
34	Kranti S S K	Sangli	Palus	857	2500
35	Krishna S S K	Satara	Karad	4979	5000
36	Kopargaon S S K	Ahemednagar	Kopargoan	131	2500
37	Kumbhikasari S S K	Kolhapur	Karvir	169	3000
38	Madhuka S S K	Jalgaon	Yawal	1	2500
39	MulaSS K	Ahemednagar	Newasa	6651	2500
40	Mahua S S K	Gujrat		377	2854
41	Madhi S S K	Gujrat		2279	2854
42	Malegaon S S K	Pune	Baramati	29	4000
43	Mukteshwar sugar mills ltd	Aurangabad	Gangapur	136	2854
44	NiphadSS K	Nashik	Niphad	6553	3500
45	Nasik S S K	Nashik	Nasik	1548	1250
46	New Phaltan Sugar Works Ltd. S S K	Satara	Phaltan	542	1300
47	Nirabhima S S K	Pune	Indapur	8543	1250
48	Padmashri Dr. VitthalraoVikhePatil S S K	Ahmednagar	Rahata	366	4000
49	Parner taluka S S K	Ahmednagar	Parner	411	1250
50	Purna S S K	Hingoli	Vasmatnagar	443	2500
51	Prasad Sugars & Allied Products Ltd.	Ahmednagar	Rahuri	62	2854
52	Pandurang S S K	Solapur	Malshiras	121	2500
53	Rameshwar S S K	Jalna	Bhokardan	20	2500
54	Rajaram BapuPatilS S K	Sangli	Walwa	56	1250
55	Renuka S S K	Belgaon		123	2854

(continued)

(continued)

Sr No	Name of the factory	District	Tehsil	No of Migrants	Crushing Capacity (Mt/year)
56	Sangamnerbhag S S K	Ahmednagar	Sangamner	1768	3500
57	Someshwar S S K	Pune	Baramati	5099	2500
58	Shriram S S K	Satara	Phaltan	396	2000
59	Shrinathmhaskoba S S K	Pune	Daund	941	2854
60	Sanjivani (takli) S S K	Ahmednagar	Kopargaon	1701	2500
61	SaswadMali Sugar Factory Ltd. S S K	Solapur	Malshiras	1898	2500
62	Sharad S S K	Kolhapur	Hatkanangale	1185	2500
63	Sant eknath S S K	Aurangabad	Paithan	196	1250
64	Shankar S S K	Yavatmal	Yavatmal	112	2500
65	Saikripa S S K	Ahmednagar	Shrigonda	21	1250
66	Shrigonda S S K	Ahmednagar	Shrigonda	45	2000
67	Sahakar Maharshi Shankarao Mohite Patil S S K.	Solapur	Malshiras	44	4500
68	Tasgaon S S K	Sangli	Palus	1421	1750
69	Tatyasaheb Kore Warana S S K	Kolhapur	Panhala	1321	5000
70	VasantraoDadaPatil S S K	Nashik	Deola	2141	2500
71	VasantdadaShetkari S S K	Sangli	Miraj	401	5000
72	Virudeshwar S S K	Ahmednagar	Pathardi	235	2500
73	Vyara S S K	Gujrat		136	2854

Source Field Survey

References

Census. (2011). Office of the registrar general & census commissioner, ministry of home affairs. Government of India. Available at https://censusindia.gov.in/.

Deshingkar, P. & Akter, S. (2009). Migration and human development in India. Human Development Research Papers (2009 to present) HDRP-2009-13, Human Development Report Office (HDRO), United Nations Development Programme (UNDP), revised April 2009.

Keshri, K., & Bhagat, R. (2012). Temporary and seasonal migration: Regional pattern, characteristics and associated factors. *Economic and Political Weekly, 47*(4), 81–88.

McDowell, C., & de Haan, A. (1997) Migration and sustainable livelihoods: A critical review of the literature, IDS Working Paper 65, Brighton: IDS.

Smita, S. (2008). Distress seasonal migration and its impact on children's education, Project Report, Consortium for Research on Educational Access, Transitions and Equity (CREATE), Falmer, UK. Retrieved from http://www.create-rpc.org/pdf_documents/PTA28.pdf.

Srivastava, R., & Desgupta, R. (2010). *Small steps lead the way.* America India Foundation.

Srivastava, R. (2011). Internal migration in India: An overview of its features, trends and policy challenges. In: *Internal Migration in India Initiative National Workshop on Internal Migration and*

Human Development in India. Workshop Compendium, vol. 2, Workshop Papers, 6–7 December 2011
United Nations. (2019). *Global issues – Migration.* Retrieved from, January 5, 2020, https://www.un.org/en/sections/issues-depth/migration/index.html.

Internal Migration and Inclusive Development: Insights from the Field

Jhilam Ray, Farhat Naaz, Poulomi Khasnobis, and Rajarshi Majumder

Abstract Migration is a universal phenomenon. From time immemorial, women and men have travelled in search of better living. There are two separate streams of migration. The first one is at the upper end of human capital hierarchy, to fill in existing surplus demand in the labour market of destination regions. Consequently, this process is highly selective in nature—in terms of skills and training, age and gender. The second stream emerges due to 'Push factors' or distress conditions in the source regions (relative to the destination)—economic hardships in the form of low wages, high unemployment, heavy population pressure, etc. in the native places and the lure of better earning opportunities in the economically vibrant destination region. This process is a coping mechanism of poor families and helps them come out of poverty. Thus, migration can be both discriminatory and egalitarian. Another issue is the emerging pattern of identity and conflict between natives and migrants in several parts of the country. Social inclusion of migrants is sometimes at jeopardy and goes against the ethos and economics of one nation–one labour market principle. Using field data from three districts of Bengal in India, this paper seeks to understand issues like who migrates—what are the social, economic and institutional factors that determine migration decisions; what are the socio-economic disparities between migrants/natives and various socio-religious groups regarding education, employment and earnings; whether migration is a successful route out of poverty; perception of natives in receiving regions about migrant workers and how migrants assimilate. It also explores the humanitarian issues related to migration through case studies to help us understand vulnerability of migrants.

J. Ray · F. Naaz · P. Khasnobis · R. Majumder (✉)
Department of Economics, University of Burdwan, Burdwan 713104, West Bengal, India
e-mail: rmajumder@eco.buruniv.ac.in

J. Ray
e-mail: jhilam@rediffmail.com

N. K. Mishra (ed.), *Development Challenges of India After Twenty Five Years of Economic Reforms*, India Studies in Business and Economics,
https://doi.org/10.1007/978-981-15-8265-3_22

1 Background

Oscillating between considering people as a favourable factor for economic growth and viewing them as a drag to the growth process, the debate on looking at people and population growth from the human capital context or the human development context has caught the imagination of many economists for ages. While the former treats people as active economic agents and inputs to the production process, the latter looks at human beings as the benefactor of the process of growth. The mercantilist view, which dominated economic thought during the sixteenth and eighteenth centuries, considered increase in population as a blessing. Higher population meant higher number of soldiers and increase in the number of productive workers. On the other hand, the physiocrats were suspicious about the advantages of population growth and some of them insisted that shortage of food was a possibility that ought to be taken into account by a nation if population increased continuously. Now, population of any region can change through the natural processes of birth and death, and through movements of population or migration. Over the last three hundred years or so, the natural process has stabilised across the globe. With advances in science and technology, preventive and curative medical facilities have improved tremendously leading to convergence of death rates. Socio-economic progress at the macro level and changes in micro decision-making at the household level have led to a fall in birth rates as well. As a result, migration has emerged as an important factor behind population changes—both temporary and permanent. Migration has also become a part of worldwide process of urbanisation and industrialisation. It signals social and economic change, and can be regarded as a human adjustment to economic, environmental and social situation.

What is the size of migrant population in the globe and in India? Today every seventh individual on earth is a migrant, that is, away from their place of origin or usual residence. According to a conservative estimate of the United Nations Department of Economic and Social Affairs (UNDESA), more than a billion people in the world are migrants (2013). Of these, more than three fourths are internal migrants: footloose people within their own country. The same institution estimates that close to 46 million people in India are migrants—staying at places outside their home state.

However, these estimates depend on how we define migration in the first place. Defining migration (especially internal migration) is a controversial issue. At one end of the spectrum, migration is defined as movement of people over some distance (or at least from one 'migration-defining area' to another) and from one 'usual place of residence' to another. At the other end of the spectrum, the definition of migration discards the requirements that migration must involve a change of residence and a move across some distance (Kok 1999). Standing (1984) suggested that one should rather use a change in 'activity space' as a criterion to define migration. However, it is virtually impossible to determine whether there has been a change in 'activity space' or not unless research or census questionnaire specifically makes provision for the appropriate information to be obtained. Shryock et al. (1976) defined migrants as those persons who are moving relative to labour market areas. The most accepted and widely used approach to define migration is—*a change in usual place of residence and a move from one migration-defining area to another*. The UN estimate earlier mentioned is based on the administrative unit of provinces/regions/states as a migration-defining area in the large countries like China and India. Some of these areas are larger in area and population than some mid-European countries. If smaller administrative units like districts are used, then the number would jump significantly. Also, people are constantly on the move—migrating and then also coming back to their place of origin—and getting estimate of that stock is quite a difficult task. Considering these issues, India is said to have close to 450 million migrants—taking both intrastate and interstate migrants together—implying that one third of Indians stay outside their place of birth/usual residence [Census of India 2011; NSSO 2007–08]. This is more than the population of USA, and close to the population of USA, UK and Germany combined. A large part of them move due to marriage, birth and with family, but more than a fifth or about 90 million are temporary economic migrants or footloose workers—a size higher than the entire population of Germany, and three times that of Canada. Thus, the issue of migration in India is humongous and necessitates considerable attention from researchers and policy makers. That the issue has not been analysed with due importance so far came to focus when the global pandemic of early 2020 uprooted the migrants overnight and threw them to the road - many dying in an effort to reach home - and the adminstrators were clueless about what to do!

2 Review of Literature

Ravenstein (1885) was the foremost proponent who claimed that migration is an economic decision. Neoclassical theorists took this forward, and the basic models (Lewis 1954; Ranis and Fei 1961) portray how modern sector grows through capital accumulation and movement of labour from traditional to modern sector in lure of higher wages. Todaro (1969) [also Harris and Todaro (1970)] evolved this further to note that migration occurs in response to *expected* income differentials to account for rural–urban migration even in presence of urban unemployment in less developed countries. However, contrary to the neoclassical view, historical experience suggests that migration does not lead to equalisation of wages across space and sector as several factors not only perpetuate the old socio-economic differences between source and destination regions, but new differences are also created by the migration process itself leading to systematic and recurring migration between regions. This is especially true when people with low skills, without economic opportunities at home, travel each year to regions where some work is available in particular seasons (for example, agricultural workers during harvesting season, brick kiln workers in dry season, etc.).[1] Thus, the process of migration, especially within a particular developing country, seems to follow the trail suggested first by Lee (1966) who fragmented the force behind migration into push and pull factors. Push factors like poverty, political instability, unemployment, etc. pushes potential migrants to move out of a region, whereas pull factors like vibrant economy, better job opportunities, etc. attract migrants to move in. Migration decision is influenced by factors that are determined at an individual level, household level, community level and regional level, and in turn affects those factors. Net migration in a region is thus determined by the relative strength of both pushes and pulls there. Thus, as long as such *pull*-s and *push*-es exist, migration would continue. Piore (1979) contradicted this theory and held that migration is not caused by push factors like low wages and high unemployment in the sending countries but by the pull factors in the receiving country. These and other issues that link migration with development and poverty and the existing literature have been comprehensively discussed by de Haan (2006). Empirical studies, in general, echo the Todaro–Lee–Piore concept that migration is in response to the gap between actual economic position in source region and expected situation in destination region. These include Deshingkar and Grimm (2005) and Banga and Pritish (2010) who discuss internal migration and role of remittances in global perspective across countries and continents. At the national level, studies by Rele (1969), Srivastava and Sasikumar (2003), Srivastava (2005), Rafique et al. (2006), Mitra and Murayama (2008), Wouters (2008), Kundu (2007), Roy and Debnath (2011), Taralekar et al. (2012), Naaz and Majumder (2016), Mahapatro (2012), Coffey et al. (2015), Abbas (2014) refer to uneven regional development, search for better jobs and diversification of livelihood as main reasons for (male) migration in India. Area- or sector-specific studies on migration in India such as Mukherjee (2004), Sundari (2005), Deshingkar and Akhter (2009), Rodgers and Rodgers (2011), Majumder and Mukherjee (2012), Bora (2014) also confirm this notion. Naaz and Majumder (2016) takes a more nuanced approach and differentiates between two different streams of migrants—one which includes people with high levels of human capital moving mostly from urban to urban centres, and two, those with low human capital moving in search of low-end jobs mainly from rural to urban areas. This supports the views of Kundu and Sarangi (2007) who pointed out that though both poor and rich households migrate, poor households send few members out to create a diversified and external support system for livelihood, while the better off households mostly migrate en masse, relocating the entire family for enjoying better amenities and status at urban metropole.

A large part of such migrants are females, moving after marriage, or family members moving with rest of the household. The individuals in these cases have no say in the decision to move, but they bear the consequent impacts—both positive and negative. At the same time, the condition of the household and its members across dimensions of assets, physical and human capital, gender and age composition, etc. do exert an influence on the household's decision on whether to migrate, when to migrate and who would migrate. Similarly, the duration of migration also varies from a few months in a year to long-term migrants who migrated two generations back and have settled down in a new place. The reasons, impetus and also the socio-economic import of long-run migration would differ substantially from short-term migration. Surprisingly, while the literature on migration is voluminous, there is not much work that looks at both these type of migrants at the micro level—focussing on the processes and results of short-term and long-term migration on households.

This paper is an attempt to address this research gap by using case studies from three districts of Bengal state in the eastern part of India.

3 Database and Methodology

Since independence, India has maintained a clear agenda towards potent fiscal federalism aimed at balanced statewise economic progress. Despite this effort, the issue of disparities in regional economic output has persisted over many years (Mathur 1983, 1987, 1992; Majumder 2005; Stewart and Moslares 2014). States, and districts within states, vary in terms of infrastructure, economic conditions, employment opportunities and aggregate development. Thus, there is considerable out-migration from relatively backward districts and in-migration into relatively advanced districts. Two backward districts of the state of Bengal—Malda and Purulia—which have a long history of repetitive or temporary migration have been selected to study the condition of such out-migrants at micro level. Also, as a contrast, a developed district of the same state—Bardhaman—which too has a long history of attracting migrants from not only surrounding districts but neighbouring states as well into its myriad mines and factories has been selected for the study. Those in Asansol are mostly long-term migrants from the backward districts of not only Bengal but also of Bihar and Jharkhand, and have settled down with their families in urban areas of west Bardhaman. Here, the urban centre of Asansol which is home to a large proportion of long-term migrants was especially selected. Municipal wards from Asansol city and villages from Malda and Purulia districts were selected through purposive sampling to represent locations that had a mix of both migrants and natives/non-migrants. Thereafter, random sampling was used to select households from the two groups—migrants and non-migrants, in proportion to their share in population. In total, the survey covered 245 households in Malda, 281 in Purulia, and 210 in Bardhaman district. Of these, 498 were migrant households.

4 Temporary Migration: Driving Factors

People migrate from the place where push factors outweigh the pull factors and move to a place where pull factors outweigh the push factors. These factors may be of two kinds—economic and non-economic. Movement in search of employment or better income may be termed economic factors, whereas marriage, education, family movement and so on may be designated as non-economic factors. At the macroeconomic level, it has been observed that male migration in India is mostly economic, whereas female migration is predominantly for non-economic reasons (Naaz and Majumder 2015). While rural male migrants are observed to be better educated compared to non-migrants, female migrants in both rural and urban areas have less education compared to the non-migrant females (Naaz and Majumder 2016). It is also argued that rural–urban temporary migration is age and gender selective, and peaks for the young adult males whose physical productivity is relatively higher than the rest (Esipova et al. 2013; IOM 2015). There is also a recurring argument that it is the poor asset-less rural people who migrate in search of job (though this has been questioned in recent times by researchers; see Kundu and Sarangi 2007; Kundu 2007). Another observation is that people from large families migrate more as there are surplus hands and not enough food at home (Kothari 2002; Gurung 2012). It is also argued that temporary seasonal migrants from rural areas are more likely to be single males rather than married males (Singh 1986). This has been now challenged by recent data which supports the view that men migrate more after marriage when the family responsibility rests upon them and that migration is a family strategy (Gordon 1981; de Haan 1997).

This paper therefore tries to examine if field data could throw some light on the aforementioned issues and bring out the correlates of the process of temporary migration from rural areas. For the purpose, a Binary Logistic Regression Function is used where the dependent variable is whether an individual is temporary migrant or not (=1 if migrant, =0 otherwise). The causal variables identified for the study are age, gender, education represented by completed years of formal schooling, marital status, social class, family size and land owned (in *Kathas*[2]) as a proxy of asset. Also included in the regression are age squared and land owned squared to account for non-linearity of the impact of these two variables.

Given the above discussion, status (Y_{ij}) of the i-th member of the j-th household may be either of the two—temporary migrant ($Y_{ij} = 1$) or non-migrant ($Y_{ij} = 0$). This status would depend on the household-specific characteristics (X) and individual-specific characteristics (Z). Thus,

$$P\left[Y_{ij} = 1 | X_j, Z_i\right] = \frac{e^{\alpha + \beta X_j + \pi Z_i}}{1 + e^{\alpha_j + \beta X_j + \pi Z_i}}, \quad (1)$$

or the Log Odds Ratio would be given by

$$LOR_{ij} = \alpha + \beta X_j + \pi Z_i, \quad (2)$$

where X and Z are vectors of variables as mentioned earlier. Estimated coefficients β and π provide the impact of explanatory variables on the Log Odds Ratio of being a temporary migrant vis-a-vis being a non-migrant. The impacts of changes in the explanatory variables on the probability are obtained as marginal effects or e^{β} and e^{π}. To exclude child migration who move mostly with their family and are not decision makers, the analysis includes only those who are 14+years of age in the sample. Descriptives of the sample data are reproduced in Table 1. The regression results are discussed as follows.

Table 1 Determinants of migration—sample descriptives

Characteristics/Variables	Pooled			Malda			Purulia		
	Mean	Low	High	Mean	Low	High	Mean	Low	High
% Migrant	20.1			23.0			17.2		
Age (years)	35	15	90	30	15	85	36	15	90
Years of Schooling	4	0	21	6	0	21	4	0	15
Family Size	5	1	10	5	2	9	5	1	10
Land Possessed (in *kathas*)	35	0	200	21	0	200	45	0	180
% Males	52.8			54.4			51.5		
% Married	72.0			68.9			74.7		
% Hindu ST	43.9			17.7			66.7		
% Hindu SC	24.0			34.3			15.0		
% Muslims	12.4			26.7			–		
Number of Observations	1779			827			952		

Source Authors' calculation based on Field Survey (2017–18)

4.1 Pooled Regression—All

From the results shown in Table 2, we observe that seasonal/temporary out-migration from the two selected districts of Bengal (Purulia and Malda) is indeed age and gender specific. Probability of migration increases with age initially but comes down eventually as shown by positive coefficient of age and negative coefficient of age squared. Males are twenty times more likely to migrate than females. Marital status is also significant and there is evidence that married males are three times more likely to migrate than unmarried males. Family size is an important determinant too, but contrary to popular perception, members of large families are less likely to migrate as shown by the significantly negative coefficient. Migration is also driven by asset poverty as probability of migration decreases as quantity of land possessed increases. Probability of migration is significantly higher for Hindu Scheduled Tribes (STs) and Muslims compared to Hindu Others (or Hindu upper castes). Education as indicated by completed years of formal education seems to increase probability of migration, though the impact is statistically insignificant.

These results are also brought out by Figs. 1 and 2 which show a hump in probability of migration around age 25–45 years, a secular decline in migration probability as land size increases and the higher migration propensity of males.

4.2 Split Regression—All

If we segregate across the two districts, the results provide interesting insights into the heterogeneity of migration process. While the results remain almost identical for

Table 2 Determinants of migration—logit regression (14 + population)

Dependent Variable	Whether Temporary Migrant (or not)					
Causal Variables	Pooled		Malda		Purulia	
	Beta	Marginal Impact	Beta	Marginal Impact	Beta	Marginal Impact
Age (years)	0.053** (0.07)	1.05	0.066 (0.14)	1.07	0.047 (0.25)	1.05
Age Squared	−0.01** (0.02)	1.00	−0.001** (0.04)	1.00	−0.001* (0.13)	1.00
Years of Schooling	0.014 (0.31)	1.01	−0.009 (0.68)	0.99	0.022 (0.35)	1.02
Gender Dummy Males (control group: females)	3.045** (0.01)	21.02	3.814** (0.01)	45.35	2.500** (0.01)	12.18
Marital Status Dummy (Married) (control group: unmarried)	1.124** (0.01)	3.08	1.329** (0.01)	3.78	−0.130** (0.03)	0.88
Family Size	−0.162** (0.01)	0.85	−0.187** (0.01)	0.83	1.023** (0.01)	2.78
Land Possessed (in *kathas*)	-0.008* (0.12)	0.99	−0.002 (0.85)	0.99	−0.010* (0.16)	0.99
Land Possessed squared	–	–	−0.001 (0.21)	0.97	0.001 (0.97)	1.00
Social Group Dummy (Hindu ST) (control group: Hindu Gen)	0.218* (0.20)	1.24	–	–	0.592** (0.04)	1.81
Social Group Dummy (Hindu SC) (control group: Hindu Gen)	−0.013 (0.91)	0.99	−0.185 (0.50)	0.83	0.183 (0.61)	1.20
Social Group Dummy (Muslim) (control group: Hindu Gen)	0.169 (0.49)	1.18	0.154 (0.60)	1.28	–	–
Nagelkerke R-squared	0.339		0.424		0.268	
Log-likelihood Ratio	1346 **		620.2**		707.8**	
Correct Classification (%)	82.9		81.5		83.4	

(continued)

Table 2 (continued)

Dependent Variable	Whether Temporary Migrant (or not)					
Causal Variables	Pooled		Malda		Purulia	
	Beta	Marginal Impact	Beta	Marginal Impact	Beta	Marginal Impact
Number of Observations	1779		827		952	

Source Authors' calculation based on Field Survey (2017–18)
Note: * and ** denote significance at 20% and 10% levels, respectively. Figures in parentheses are p-values

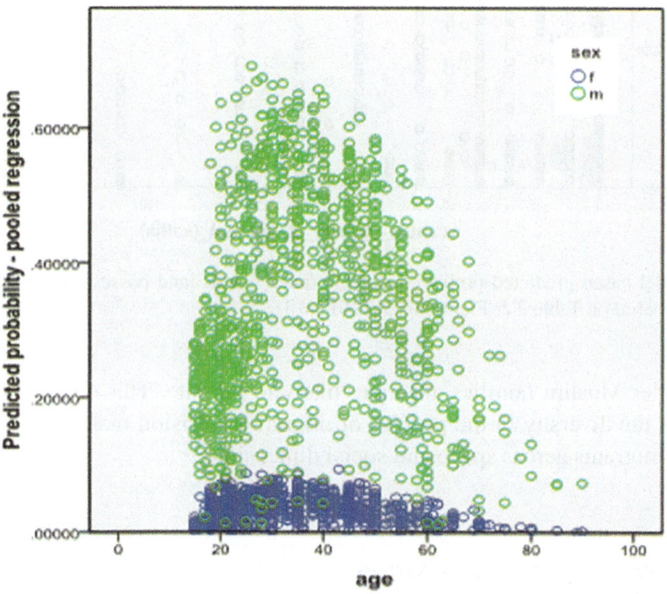

Fig. 1 Model-based predicted probability of migration across age by gender. *Source* Authors' calculation based on Table 2 & Field Survey (2017–18)

age, gender and land possessed, for the rest of the causal factors, the two districts provide a contrasting picture. In Malda, education seems to decrease the probability of migration. In Purulia, being married decreases the probability of migration and larger family size increases such probability. Also, the social class effects are now more pronounced with STs in Purulia and Muslims in Malda showing remarkably higher propensity to migrate compared to the reference category. The gender division is also starker in Malda with males almost fifty times more likely to migrate than females, while in Purulia males are twelve times more likely to migrate than females. Thus, in Purulia, it is the single educated male from larger tribal families who are more prone to migrate compared to Malda where married males with less education

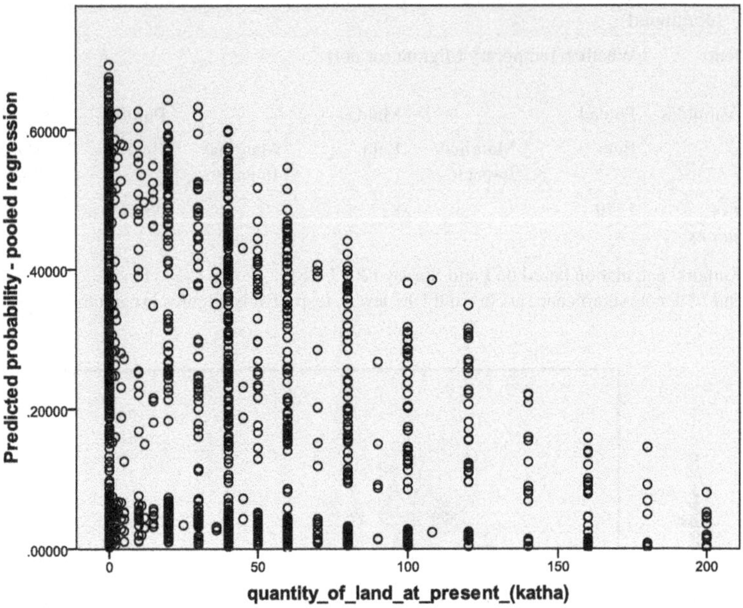

Fig. 2 Model-based predicted probability of migration across land possessed. *Source* Authors' calculation based on Table 2 & Field Survey (2017–18)

from smaller Muslim families are more likely to migrate. This contrasting picture underlines the diversity in the process of migration decision-making as well as the profile of migrants across space and social dimensions.

4.3 Pooled Regression—Males

It is a reality that temporary/seasonal internal migration in India is dominated by males. The survey results discussed above also support this fact as males are significantly more likely to migrate than females. Hence, the researchers further decided to focus more on male population and explore whether results discussed above hold true when only males are considered. It is observed from Table 3 that the impacts are almost similar. Age still has a positive but non-linear impact on probability of migration. Married men are about four times more likely to migrate than unmarried men. Higher amount of land possessed brings down propensity to migrate. STs and Muslims are more likely to migrate than the reference category of Hindu upper caste men. The only difference now is that education has a negative coefficient, indicating that men with relatively less years of formal education are more likely to migrate than the educated ones.

Table 3 Determinants of male migration—logit regression (14 + males)

Dependent Variable	Whether Temporary Migrant (or not)					
Causal Variables	Pooled		Malda		Purulia	
	Beta	Marginal Impact	Beta	Marginal Impact	Beta	Marginal Impact
Age (years)	0.039 (0.23)	1.04	0.065* (0.16)	1.07	0.001 (0.99)	1.00
Age Squared	−0.001** (0.04)	1.00	−0.001** (0.05)	1.00	0.001 (0.48)	1.00
Years of Schooling	−0.003 (0.88)	0.99	−0.008 (0.73)	0.99	−0.013 (0.63)	0.99
Marital Status Dummy (Married) (control group: unmarried)	1.350** (0.01)	3.86	1.401** (0.01)	4.06	1.412** (0.01)	4.11
Family Size	−0.185** (0.01)	0.83	−0.198** (0.01)	0.82	−0.156** (0.02)	0.86
Land Possessed (in *kathas*)	−0.007* (0.17)	0.99	−0.002 (0.80)	0.99	−0.006 (0.45)	0.99
Land Possessed squared	0.001 (0.60)	1.00	0.001 (0.21)	1.00	0.000 (0.80)	1.00
Social Group Dummy (Hindu ST) (control group: Hindu Gen)	0.101 (0.63)	1.11	–	–	0.348 (0.26)	1.42
Social Group Dummy (Hindu SC) (control group: Hindu Gen)	−0.029 (0.90)	0.97	−0.084 (0.77)	0.92	−0.179 (0.65)	0.84
Social Group Dummy (Muslim) (control group: Hindu Gen)	0.024 (0.93)	1.02	0.314 (0.31)	1.35	–	–
Nagelkerke R-squared	*0.166*		*0.200*		*0.142*	
Log-likelihood Ratio	*1091.2**		*534.3**		*541.9**	
Correct Classification (%)	*70.1*		*68.9*		*72.7*	

(continued)

Table 3 (continued)

Dependent Variable	Whether Temporary Migrant (or not)					
Causal Variables	Pooled		Malda		Purulia	
	Beta	Marginal Impact	Beta	Marginal Impact	Beta	Marginal Impact
Number of Observations	*940*		*450*		*490*	

Source Authors' calculation based on Field Survey (2017–18)
Note * and ** denote significance at 20% and 10% levels, respectively. Figures in parenthesis are p-values

4.4 Split Regression—Males

When we segregate across districts, we find that there are some subtle differences. The age selection process is more pronounced in Malda than in Purulia. Also, as before, the selection across social classes follows the demographic pattern of the two districts—STs in Purulia and Muslims in Malda are more prone to migration.

4.5 Summary

The survey results show that temporary seasonal migration is mostly a distress phenomenon. People without adequate (farm) land in rural areas, mostly married males with little formal education and belonging to the socially disadvantaged groups (STs and Muslims) are more likely to migrate. Also calculated is the predicted probability of the average person, as well as several counterfactuals for the pooled data and district-level data (Table 4).

The average unmarried male from Hindu upper caste household is 35 years of age, has just four years of formal schooling and comes from a household of five members with 35 *kathas* of land. For this person, predicted probability of migration is just 19%. As a contrast, if we consider the median person who is married, thirty years old, from an ST or Muslim landless family of four persons, without any formal schooling, the predicted probability multiplies three times to become 62%.

Looking at the district-level data separately, the average person in Malda is younger, with more formal schooling, and less amount of land under possession. For this person, the predicted probability of migration stands at around 30%. Predicted probability of migration for the contrasting person in this district with characteristic variables as mentioned before is more than double at 70%.

For Purulia, the average person is older: 36 years of age, with just four years of formal schooling, comes from a household of five persons with 45 *kathas* of land in possession. The average person has substantially lower predicted probability of migration (than Malda)—just about 12%. The contrasting person in this case is five

Table 4 Expected probability of migration—average and contrasts

Characteristics/Variables	Pooled		Malda		Purulia	
	Sample Average	Contrast	Sample Average	Contrast	Sample Average	Contrast
Age (years)	35	30	30	30	36	30
Years of Schooling	4	0	6	0	4	0
Family Size	5	4	5	4	5	4
Land Possessed (in *kathas*)	35	0	21	0	45	0
Is Male	YES	YES	YES	YES	YES	YES
Is Married	NO	YES	NO	YES	NO	YES
Is Hindu ST/Muslim	NO	YES	NO	YES	NO	YES
Predicted Probability of Migration	0.19	0.62	0.30	0.70	0.12	0.60

Source Authors' calculation based on Tables 1, 2 and Field Survey (2017–18)

times more likely to migrate than the average person, with predicted probability of migration at 60%.

The results, therefore, support the opinion that migration decisions depend on individual as well as household factors, especially in developing countries, where temporary and seasonal migration is a strategy to diversify sources of income and improve total income through remittances (similar to views expressed by Stark and Bloom 1985; Yang 2008; Antman 2012). Whether such a strategy bears fruit at the ground level is a matter of enquiry that has been attempted in the next section.

5 Impact of Migration on Participating Households

It is already inferred that temporary migration is a risk-minimising poverty-mitigating strategy of rural households from disadvantaged social backgrounds. But does migration act as an inclusive process wherein the migrant families improve their economic condition? There are several such questions that beg answer. What is the educational, employment and occupational condition of the migrant households? Do migrant households enjoy better income/consumption levels compared to non-migrants? Are their activities and occupational structures better than the non-migrants? Do they have better housing and household amenities than non-migrants, and enjoy financial inclusion? Such issues have been explored in this section.

As mentioned earlier, the study compared households that send members as temporary/seasonal migrants and those that do not send out migrants. Further, in order to examine whether there is a difference between long-term permanent/semi-permanent migration and seasonal migration in terms of socio-economic outcome of

Table 5 Human Capital position—education of the 18 + sample household members

		Education Distribution					
	Status	Illiterate	Below Primary	Primary Passed	Middle Passed	School Passed	Graduate+
Purulia	Temp Migrants	41.6	20.8	11.6	12.3	12.0	1.6
	Non-migrants	41.8	18.0	13.5	12.0	12.7	1.9
Malda	Temp Migrants	23.7	22.2	19.6	15.6	16.4	2.5
	Non-migrants	27.0	18.3	12.4	16.6	18.7	7.1
Bardhaman	Settled Migrants	7.5	20.7	12.8	33.1	9.9	16.0
	Non-migrants	9.7	15.8	14.7	40.5	7.3	12.0

Source Authors' calculation based on Field Survey (2017–18)

migration, the researchers used a control group of settled migrants from Bardhaman district. The results are discussed as follows (refer Table 5).

5.1 Human Capital Position

The study focused on the human capital position of the 18 + population in the sample. A comparison is drawn between the seasonal migrants (from Purulia and Malda districts), and settled migrants (in Bardhaman district) and non-migrants. It is observed that human capital situation in both Purulia and Malda districts is inadequate with temporary migrant households having relatively poorer human capital situation than the non-migrant households of the same district (Table 5). They have more illiterate and below primary school educated persons, and lesser share of graduates and high school pass outs. The settled migrants in Bardhaman on the other hand have a human capital position that is close to the natives of the district, indicating that after settling down they have been able to improve their educational attainment substantially.

5.2 Participation in Labour Market

Since temporary migration is a strategy to get meaningful employment and raise income level, it is no surprise that Labour Force Participation Rate (LFPR) and Work Participation Rate (WPR) are higher among temporary migrants in both Malda and Purulia as compared to the non-migrant households (Table 6). However, settled migrants in Bardhaman have a lower LFPR and WPR than not only the temporary

Table 6 Labour market statistics

District	Status	Too Young/Too Old	School Going	Domestic Duties	Out of Labour Force	LFPR	Unemployed	WPR
Purulia	Temp Migrants	3.4	21.6	14.1	39.1	60.9	4.2	56.7
	Non-migrants	2.6	23.3	22.1	48.0	52.0	8.2	43.8
Malda	Temp Migrants	3.3	36.0	15.9	55.2	44.8	2.9	41.9
	Non-migrants	13.6	35.8	13.1	62.5	37.5	4.0	33.5
Bardhaman	Settled Migrants	13.6	24.9	18.9	57.4	42.6	3.9	38.7
	Non-migrants	12.4	27.0	22.2	63.6	36.4	3.9	34.5

Source Authors' calculation based on Field Survey (2017–18)

migrants of Purulia and Malda districts but also from the natives of Bardhaman district. Migrant households in Purulia had the highest LFPR and WPR—perhaps reflecting the overall economic stagnancy of the region. Unemployment is highest among non-migrants in Purulia and lowest among migrants in Malda, which is expected as the raison d'être of migration is getting jobs.

5.3 *Work Activity Status*

It is true that the poor can ill-afford to remain unemployed. Hence, LFPR and WPR are generally perverse indicators of economic vibrancy of a region/group, and it is better to look at the type of work/activity to understand the real condition of workers. Workers have been segregated into three broad types. In order of hierarchy and economic benefits, these are regular salaried employment, casual employment and self-employment. It is observed that almost the entire employment among temporary migrants comes from casual work, indicating the precarious nature of the working conditions for them (Table 7). Only a handful of non-migrants in Malda and Purulia are in regular salaried jobs. In contrast, settled migrants in Bardhaman have a more equitable spread over the three types of employment, though there too casual work is marginally dominating. The highest share of regular/salaried job is found among non-migrants in Bardhaman district, indicating that this group is perhaps in the best economic condition.

Table 7 Proportion of workers in different types of employment/activity status

District	Status	Self-Employment	Casual Employment	Regular/Salaried Employment
Purulia	Temp Migrants	0.5	98.8	0.7
	Non-migrants	3.0	85.8	11.2
Malda	Temp Migrants	0.2	99.5	0.2
	Non-migrants	3.0	92.2	4.8
Bardhaman	Settled Migrants	35.4	35.9	28.7
	Non-migrants	22.0	40.0	38.0

Source Authors' calculation based on Field Survey (2017–18)

5.4 Occupational Distribution

Another major indicator of labour market conditions is the occupational distribution of workers. It is observed that seasonal migrants are predominantly into construction work and unspecified manual work in both Purulia and Malda (Table 8). The non-migrants in these two districts, as expected, are mostly in farming occupation as cultivators and agricultural labourers. Presence of migrant workers in clerical and managerial jobs is negligible. This indicates that migrants are mostly engaged in lower rung occupations. The settled migrants in Bardhaman, in contrast, are more in sales, clerical and managerial jobs—occupations that are physically less exerting and more paying.

5.5 Housing and Amenities

The living condition is best reflected in the condition of housing/dwelling and amenities therein. It is observed that in Malda migrant households have relatively poor housing conditions compared to non-migrants (Table 9). In Purulia, migrant households have better houses and electricity but not sanitation or clean cooking fuel. In Bardhaman, however, the settled migrants enjoy better housing conditions, though they have relatively less share of pucca houses.

5.6 Consumption, Poverty and Inequality

In India, economic condition and living standards of people are usually measured by their consumption levels. Though fraught with measurement errors, recall bias and myriad other methodological issues, MPCE (Monthly Per Capita Consumption Expenditure) is still considered as benchmark in determining the economic status

Table 8 Occupational distribution of workers (in %)

Activity	Purulia			Malda			Bardhaman		
	Migrant	Non-migrant	All	Migrant	Non-migrant	All	Migrant	Non-migrant	All
Cultivator	21.5	38.1	26.8	45.6	35.9	41.3	1.0	0.1	1.0
Agricultural Labourer	12.3	13.8	12.8	6.6	10.2	7.4	0.5	0.2	0.3
Industrial Labourer	7.4	7.4	7.4	2.3	1.7	2.2	9.2	6.0	8.0
Construction Labourer	2.0	4.2	2.7	31.4	20.0	31.1	1.3	1.6	1.4
Unspecified Manual Labourer	49.3	11.6	25.0	0.1	0.0	0.0	27.0	45.0	31.6
Handicrafts	2.5	1.1	2.0	2.3	3.4	2.5	16.0	7.0	14.0
Clerical and Managerial	0.3	4.2	1.7	0.0	1.7	0.4	15.0	12.0	15.0
Sales and Others	4.7	19.6	21.6	11.7	27.1	15.1	30.0	28.1	28.7
All	100.0	100.0	100.0	100.0	100.0	100.0	100.0	100.0	100.0

Source Authors' calculation based on Field Survey (2017–18)

Table 9 Conditions of housing and amenities (percentage of households)

District	Status	Pucca Houses	Pucca Toilet	Safe Drinking Water	Clean Cooking Fuel	Electricity
Purulia	Temp Migrants	22.7	6.8	84.6	9.9	73.0
	Non-migrants	12.7	10.2	85.6	21.2	57.6
Malda	Temp Migrants	41.2	20.9	73.3	28.9	73.3
	Non-migrants	62.1	29.3	81.0	29.3	77.6
Bardhaman	Settled Migrants	58.3	77.0	93.1	90.5	100.0
	Non-migrants	65.4	62.1	89.7	90.3	96.6

Source Authors' calculation based on Field Survey (2017–18)

Table 10 Household consumption expenditure (Rs per capita per month at current prices 2016–17)

District	Status	Mean MPCE	Median MPCE	% Below State Poverty Line
Purulia	Temp Migrants	791	570	44.5
	Non-migrants	813	825	74.5
Malda	Temp Migrants	1527	1218	35.2
	Non-migrants	1559	1272	35.5
Bardhaman	Settled Migrants	2580	2030	23.2
	Non-migrants	2521	1742	26.0

Source Authors' calculation based on Field Survey (2017–18)

of a household. The survey also attempted to collect information on consumption expenses and constructed the MPCE figures. It is observed that average MPCE of surveyed households is lowest in Purulia and highest in Bardhaman—in line with the general economic condition of the three districts as exhibited by secondary data too (Table 10).[3] On comparing migrants and non-migrants, it is found that seasonal migrant households in Malda and Purulia have marginally lower average MPCE than the non-migrant families. Since in the earlier section it is noted that migrants mostly come from asset-less poor families, the results here indicate that migration does help them to come up to an economic level closer to that of non-migrants. In Bardhaman, however, the settled migrants have average MPCE that is marginally higher than the natives, indicating that permanent migration is more effective as a coping strategy than temporary migration.

Incidence of Head Count Poverty across districts and family types on the basis of computed MPCE levels was also measured. For it, the state-specific poverty line provided by NITI Aayog/Planning Commission for West Bengal (GoI 2014) has been used. For the year 2011–12, this was Rs 783 for rural areas and Rs 981 for urban areas. It was updated to 2016–17 figures using the Consumer Price Index for Agricultural Labourers (CPIAL) for rural areas and Consumer Price Index for Industrial Workers (CPI-IW) for urban areas. It is observed that, as expected, HCR or

Head Count Ratio is highest among the surveyed households in Purulia, followed by Malda and least in Bardhaman (Table 10). What is more interesting is that while the incidence of consumption poverty is almost similar across migrant and non-migrant families in Malda, in Purulia households with migrant members have remarkably lower incidence of consumption poverty as compared to non-migrant families. In Bardhaman too, settled migrants show lower HCR compared to the natives. Thus, in Purulia, migration as poverty alleviation strategy of the households is remarkably successful. This is also true, but with a lesser degree, for the migrant families settling in Bardhaman.

The study also tried to examine the relative inequality in consumption levels across households. For this, the sample households are pooled together and divided into five quintiles based on their MPCE levels, separately for each of the three districts. Q5 is the highest MPCE bracket and Q1 is the lowest one. Thereafter, the proportion of each household type in each district is examined in the five quintile groups. It is observed that migrant households are more equally spread across the five quintile groups, while the non-migrant households are more polarised near the two ends (Table 11). Thus, inequality seems to be lower within migrant households compared to those within non-migrant households in all the three districts. This becomes clear in Fig. 3 which

Table 11 Distribution of persons across MPCE quintiles for migrants and non-migrants

	Status	Q1	Q2	Q3	Q4	Q5
Purulia	Migrants	14.1	28.9	22.5	17.5	16.9
	Non-migrants	28.7	9.9	19.9	23.3	18.2
Malda	Migrants	22.3	19.4	23.3	18.9	16.1
	Non-migrants	21.6	23.6	13.2	22.8	18.8
Bardhaman	Migrants	20.0	19.0	21.0	21.0	18.0
	Non-migrants	16.0	20.0	12.0	15.0	37.0

Source Authors' calculation based on Field Survey (2017–18)

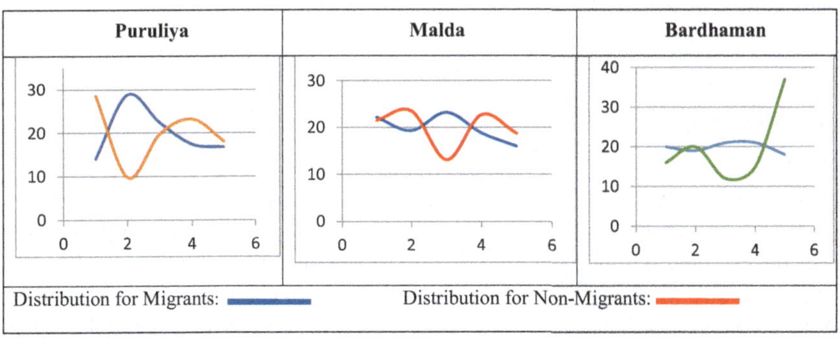

Fig. 3 MPCE distribution across quintiles for migrants and non-migrants. *Source* Author's calculation based on Field Survey (2017–18)

shows that the distribution across MPCE classes is unipolar for migrant households and bipolar for the non-migrant households.

It therefore appears that migration indeed acts as a way out of poverty for rural households. They have improved consumption levels, lower incidence of head count poverty and lower 'within group' inequality. In this, migration seems to be working as an inclusive process, with permanent migration reaping better dividends than seasonal migration.

5.7 Financial Inclusion

Another way to look at the impact of migration is to examine the aspect of financial inclusion. In recent years, there has been an emphasis in policy as well as implementation level towards financial inclusion—making banking and institutional credit services accessible to all. The situation among the surveyed households in this dimension was explored. It appears that making people come to the bank and have bank account has been successful in Bardhaman and Purulia where most households have bank accounts (Table 12). However, this has not been that much successful in Malda. Also, bank accounts are more frequent among migrant households than non-migrants in the two districts mentioned—perhaps because of the remittance factor as sending and receiving money is facilitated when the family has a bank account. In Malda, fewer migrant households have bank accounts compared to non-migrants—perhaps because the monetary transactions there are more through personal channel rather than institutional.

Indebtedness is also higher in Malda compared to Purulia and Bardhaman. Indebtedness is higher among non-migrants in these two districts, while in Malda, indebtedness is more frequent among migrant households. What is alarming is the fact that only a fraction of such loans are from institutional sources, especially in Purulia where it is almost negligible. However, the brighter side is that institutional credit is marginally more frequent among migrant households than non-migrants in all the three districts.

5.8 Summary

The study finds that the success of migration as a coping and poverty alleviation strategy is somewhat mixed. While they do seem to enjoy higher consumption levels, lower poverty and within-group inequality, the nature of employment and earning is questionable. Most of them are in unskilled manual jobs outside the state and the jobs are casual in nature. Housing and amenities are not remarkably better and indebtedness is high, especially in Malda. Also, the situation of the settled migrants is somewhat better than the seasonal/temporary migrants.

Table 12 Penetration of financial instruments among sample households

Activity	Purulia			Malda			Bardhaman		
	Migrant	Non-migrant	All	Migrant	Non-migrant	All	Migrant	Non-migrant	All
% with Bank Account	82.2	78.0	80.4	9.6	13.8	10.6	94.6	91.7	93.7
% Indebted	45.4	34.7	40.9	41.2	48.3	42.9	22.5	25.0	23.3
% Loan from Institutions	4.3	2.5	3.6	10.7	10.3	10.6	19.4	13.3	17.6

Source Authors' calculation based on Field Survey (2017–18)

6 Migration Process and the Human Angle

The analysis thus far has revealed the macroeconomic processes underlying temporary or seasonal migration. It appears that migration does indeed act as a risk mitigating and income augmenting decision for the impoverished. It, however, misses out, an important aspect—the story of the human beings—migrants as we know them—some hard facts of their lives so as to better understand the nuances of migration and the associated pitfalls.

Forced to move in search of livelihoods and better income, migrants often end up paying high costs for doing so. There are increasing instances of sociopolitical identities being aroused across the country as migrant workers often face contempt in destination cities, as they compete for space and civic amenities. Confined to shanties and ghettos in subhuman conditions, their shanties are looked upon as an 'eyesore' on cityscapes. They also become soft targets of local and organised crime and very often fall victim to human trafficking.[4]

Lacking proper documentation and faced with political exclusion (not registered voters in the destination region, and absentees in source areas during elections), migrants are a non-existent constituency lacking a 'lobbying' voice to ensure their basic rights.[5] In addition, the process of migration itself gives rise to further risks and heartbreaks.

Most migration is based on social networks—through family, relatives, friends or the 'neighbourhood uncle', who also doubles as labour contractor or agent. The survey results also come up with the same pattern—seasonal or temporary migration is facilitated mostly by labour contractors (especially in Malda) followed by family/relatives, while long-term settled migration is facilitated more by family members or relatives (Table 13). The dominating pattern of out-migration through labour contractors is through the age-old process known as *Dadon*. In the colonial era, it involved taking loan from the local money lender (who most often was also the local *zamindar* or landlord) as advance payment for agricultural activities before the agricultural season. The repayment was through unpaid labour at the landlord's farm. That precolonial practice seems to have returned in a modified form: nowadays, the local labour contractor provides loan to poor rural households at the start of the agricultural season. The debtors repay the amount by joining the contractor's labour force at construction sites across the country during the lean agricultural season. The wages of migrant labour, thus formed, partly constitute the repayment and partly

Table 13 Channels of migration—percentage shares

Channel	Purulia	Malda	Bardhaman
Family/Relatives	23.8	41.9	60.9
Friends	36.2	–	18.2
Middlemen/Labour Contractors	40.0	58.1	20.9
	100	100	100

Source Field Survey (2017–18)

remittances sent back home. They are mostly asset-less, poorly educated and with no vocational or skill training. The plight of *Qurban*, a migrant from Halna village of Malda district, epitomises the life of most domestic migrants in the region.[6]

In *Qurban*'s Halna village, *Rintu* is the main contractor. Out of 700 households in Halna, at least 300 are on his payroll, working outside the state. *Qurban* had taken a loan of Rs 60,000 for his ailing father from a local labour contractor. It was to be repaid by working 300 days at a construction site near Hyderabad. On a cold January Sunday, when the temperature in the district was plunging, the contractor's men collected 30 men like *Qurban* and put them on a train. All of them had taken advances from *Rintu*. The running wage receivable by the workers for construction work in Telangana, Karnataka and Kerala is Rs 200 per day for a 10–12 h job. There are no leaves or other allowances. The labour contractor arranges for food and accommodation, and deducts Rs 45 each day for it. All medical expenses are deducted from wages receivable. Incidentally, the actual wages at construction sites in these states are not less than Rs 450 per day, leaving a handsome profit for the contractor. You can call it exploitation if you like but that does not change the ground reality. Men like *Qurban* spend on an average 8–10 months on site, returning home for 2–3 months in a year. Once the work gets over at a given site, the contractor shifts the labourers to a new site in a new state perhaps. They earn about Rs 60,000 or Rs 5000 per month when averaged over the year. This amount is attractive one when compared to Malda's current per capita District Domestic Product or DDP of Rs 4245 per month and average MPCE of Rs 1550 for the sample households in Malda district. Thus, there is no dearth of able-bodied males willing to join *Rintu's* workforce. Little wonder, the contractor always has a queue outside his shanty office in the local *haat-tola* (local market).

The lure of this road out of squalor and poverty is so strong that peculiar transformations are taking place at the countryside. The average years of education among boys is gradually coming down as school drop out rate is going up due to assured income from migratory work. With a stagnant local economy, there is no incentive to continue general education and wait for local earning opportunities to materialise. Interestingly, the frequency and duration of girls going to formal schools is improving as family income is stabilising through such assured incomes. A grim fall out of migration is the rise in alcoholism, substance abuse and spread of infectious diseases like HIV as trans-state movements have increased and more and more unsupervised adolescents are going out to work. Absence of a male member in the household for a major part of the year creates insecurity among the women and infirm who stay back—there have been increasing instances of land grabbing, diversion of rightful benefits and a general rise of the henchmen. But workers like *Qurban,* who was dreaming of his daughter's marriage, have little choice than to remain oblivious of such impending dangers.

Unfortunately, for *Qurban*, one day the building under construction where he was engaged collapsed due to poor material and *Qurban* was one of the two workers who died under the rubble.[7] After much bargaining, the construction company agreed to pay Rs 200000 as compensation. By that time, *Qurban*'s father had expired and his wife did not have a bank account in her name. A facilitator took Rs 20000 for arranging things, and *Qurban*'s body finally arrived in his village after ten days in an ambulance for the last rites. *Qurban*'s is not an isolated case in these hinterlands. One of his friends was even less fortunate. He died in a road mishap in Raipur. Since the death occurred outside working hours and off-site, the company did not give any compensation. The cost of bringing the body home was Rs 70000, which is conventionally borne by the labour contractor. The family agreed to perform the last rites in Raipur and *Rintu* paid for the travel. He handed over the remaining Rs 60000 saved in the process to the family who clutched at it as a last straw to tide over the next few months of hunger staring it. Last heard, *Qurban*'s 15-year-old son dropped school and joined the growing river of migrant workers flowing into the country!

7 Conclusion: Not by Any Chance

The authors have nothing further to add—no grand policy suggestion or cleverly thought out-of-the-box solution to such events of human tragedy. Nonetheless, the magnitude of the problems is too big to be brushed under the carpet, given that every third Indian is a person who has forsaken their place of birth or residence to earn livelihood. The need of the hour is to acknowledge the problems, to pay adequate attention to these issues, to debate and discuss at all levels so that the complexities and human stories behind a country on the move are brought to the fore.

Notes

1. See Majumder and Mukherjee (2012) for case study
2. A traditional unit of land measure; one Katha is equal to 720 sq feet in Bengal
3. Bardhaman ranks fourth among the districts of Bengal in terms of per capita DDP, and Purulia ranks second from bottom, whereas Malda ranks fourth from bottom (GoWB 2015)
4. Lynching and mob fury against migrant workers are common; see The Deccan Chronicle, Jan 17, 2018. In addition, the pandemic that struck the world and India in early 2020 came to fore the sufferings and vulnerabilities of migrants and the sheer size of them like never before.
5. According to a report in *The Times of India* on January 30, 2019, in the 2014 elections, there were 834 million registered voters out of which 280 million people did not vote… a large number of these could be temporary migrants, given that there are 450 million internal migrants in the country. 'If NRIs get a right, why not domestic migrants', https://epaper.timesgroup.com/olive/apa/timesofindia/#panel=document
6. Names have been changed to maintain confidentiality
7. The Hindu, Hyderabad, July 24, 2016

Acknowledgments Parts of this study have been separately funded by ICSSR and UGC-SAP. Comments received during a national seminar organised by the Department of Economics, Banaras Hindu University during March, 2018 have been most helpful.

References

Abbas, R. & Verma D. (2014). Internal labour migration in India raises integration challenges for migrants. Migration Policy Institute. Available from https://www.migrationpolicy.org/article/internal-labor-migration-india-raises-integration-challenges-migrants/. Cited 15-8-19.

Antman, F. (2012). Elderly care and intrafamily resource allocation when children migrate. *Journal of Human Resources, 47*(2), 331–63.

Banga, R. & Pritish, S. (2010). Impact of remittances on poverty in developing countries. Working Papers, eSocialSciences. Available from https://EconPapers.repec.org/RePEc:ess:wpaper:id:3100./. Cited 20-02-2019.

Bora, R. S. (2014). Migrant informal workers: A study of Delhi and Satellite Towns. *Modern Economy, 5*, 562–579. Available from http://dx.doi.org/10.4236/me.2014.55053/. Cited 20-02-2019.

Census of India. (2001). Migration tables, office of the registrar general & census commissioner, India, Ministry of Home Affairs, Government of India.

Census of India. (2011). Migration tables, office of the registrar general & census commissioner, India, Ministry of Home Affairs, Government of India.

Coffey, D., Papp, J., & Spears D. (2015). Short-term labor migration from rural North India: Evidence from New Survey Data". *Population Research and Policy Review, 34*(3), 361–80. Available from www.jstor.org/stable/43672135/. Cited 12-02-2019.

de Haan, A. (1997). Rural-urban migration and poverty: The case of India. *IDS Bulletin, 28*(2), 35–47.

de Haan, A. (2006). Migration in the development studies literature: Has it come out of its marginality?. *UNU-WIDER Research Paper 2006/019*. Helsinki: UNU-WIDER. Available https://www.wider.unu.edu/sites/default/files/rp2006-19.pdf/. Cited 12-02-2009.

Deshingkar, P. & Akter, S. (2009). Migration and human development in India. *Human Development Research Paper 2009/13,* UNDP. Available from http://hdr.undp.org/sites/default/files/hdrp_2009_13.pdf/. Cited 18-02-2009.

Deshingkar, P. & Grimm, S. (2005). Internal migration and development: A global perspective. *Overseas Development Institute, IOM Migration Research Series Paper No. 19*. Available from https://www.odi.org/sites/odi.org.uk/files/odi-assets/publications-opinion-files/68.pdf/. Cited 18-02-2019.

Esipova, N., Pugliese, A., & Ray, J. (2013). The demographics of global internal migration. *Migration Policy Practice, 3*(2), 3–6. Available from http://publications.iom.int/system/files/pdf/migrationpolicypracticejournal10_15may2013.pdf. Cited 20-02-2019.

Gordon, E. (1981). An analysis of the impact of labour migration on the lives of women in Lesotho. *Journal of Development Studies, 17*(3), 59–76.

GoI. (2014). *State specific poverty lines for 2011-12*. Available at https://community.data.gov.in/state-specific-poverty-lines-for-2011-12/. Cited 16-08-2018.

GoWB. (2015). *State domestic product and district domestic product of West Bengal 2014-15*. Bureau of Applied Economics and Statistics, Government of West Bengal

Gurung, Y. B. (2012). Migration from rural Nepal: a social exclusion framework. *Himalaya, the Journal of the Association for Nepal and Himalayan Studies, 31*(1), Article 12. Available at http://digitalcommons.macalester.edu/himalaya/vol31/iss1/12. Cited 24-02-2019.

Harris, J. R. & Todaro M. P. (1970). Migration, unemployment and development: A two-sector analysis. *The American Economic Review, 60*(1), 126–142.

IOM. (2015). *World migration report 2015. Migrants and cities: new partnerships to manage mobility*. International Organisation for Migration. Available from http://publications.iom.int/system/files/wmr2015_en.pdf. Cited 12-02-2019.

Kok, P. (1999). *The definition of migration and it's implication: Making sense of recent South African census and survey data*. Available from https://www.commerce.uct.ac.za/Organisations/Demography/SA_Journal_of_Demography/SAJD/Volume%207/SAJDem_1999_7_1_Kok.pdf. Cited 18.05.17.

Kothari, U. (2002). *Migration and chronic poverty,* Chronic Poverty Research Centre, Working Paper No 16, Institute for Development Policy and Management (Manchester: University of Manchester).

Kundu, A. (2007). *Migration and urbanisation in India in the context of poverty alleviation,* Conference Paper - International Conference and Workshop on Policy Perspectives on Growth, Economic Structures and Poverty Reduction. Available at http://networkideas.org/ideasact/jun07/Beijing_Conference_07/Amitabh_Kundu.pdf. Cited 12-02-2018.

Kundu, A. & Sarangi, N. (2007). Migration, employment status and poverty: An analysis across urban centres, *Economic and Political Weekly, 42*(4), 299–306.

Lee, E. S. (1966). Theory of migration. *Demography, 3*(1), 47–57

Lewis, W. A. (1954). Economic development with unlimited supplies of labour. *The Manchester School, 22,* 139–191. https://doi.org/10.1111/j.1467-9957.1954.tb00021.x.

Mahapatro, S. R. (2012). *The changing pattern of internal migration in India: Issues and challenges,* Paper presented at the Paper presented at European Population Conference, Stockholm University, Sweden. Available from https://epc2012.princeton.edu/papers/121017/. Cited 18-02-2019.

Majumder, R., & Mukherjee, Dipa. (2012). Paternal migration child labour and education: A study in brickfield areas of West Bengal. *Journal of Economic & Social Development, VIII*(1), 2012.

Majumder, R. (2005). India's development experience - a regional analysis. In S. K. Thorat, A. Vinoj, J. P. Pradhan, (Eds.), *Industrialization, economic reforms and regional development: essays in honour of Professor Ashok Mathur.* New Delhi: Shipra Publications.

Mathur, Ashok. (1983). Regional development and income disparities in India: A sectoral analysis. *Economic Development and Cultural Change, 31*(3), 475–505.

Mathur, A. (1987). Why growth rates differ within India-An alternative approach? *Journal of Development Studies, 23*(2).

Mathur, A.. (1992). Regional economic change and development policy in India. *Indian Journal of Applied Economics, 1*(2).

Mitra, A., & Murayama, M. (2008). *Rural to urban migration: A district level analysis for India.* IDE discussion paper no. 137, Institute of Developing Economies, Japan External Trade Organization (JETRO). Available from https://ir.ide.go.jp/?action=repository_uri&item_id=38030&file_id=22&file_no=1/. Cited 20-02-2019.

Mukherjee, N. (2004). Migrant women from West Bengal – Livelihoods, vulnerability, Ill-Being and Well Being: Some Perspectives from the Field. *Development Tracks in Research.* New Delhi: Training & Consultancy.

Naaz, F., & Majumder, R. (2015). Internal migration in India: trends, causes and determinants. *Rabindra Bharati University Journal of Economics, IX,* 30–62.

Naaz, F., & Majumder, R. (2016). Workers on the move: migrated labour in india in early 21st century. *The Indian Journal of Labour Economics, 59*(3), 419–40 (Springer). https://doi.org/10.1007/s41027-017-0065-4.

NSSO. (2008). *National sample survey organisation 2007-08 data.* Government of India: Ministry of Statistics and Programme Implementation.

Piore, M. J. (1979). *Birds of Passage: Migrant Labor and Industrial Societies.* Cambridge University Press

Rafique, A, Massey, D., & Rogaly, B. (2006). Migration for hard work: a reluctant livelihood strategy for poor households in West Bengal. *Development Research Centre on Migration, Globalisation and Poverty Working Paper T17.* Available at http://www.migrationdrc.org/publications/working_papers/WP-T17.pdf/. CITED 20-02-2019.

Ranis, G., & Fei, J. C. H. (1961). A theory of economic development. *The American Economic Review, 51*(4), 533–565.

Ravenstein, E. G. (1885). The laws of migration. *Journal of the Statistical Society of London, 48*(2), 167–235.

Rele. (1969). Trends and significance of internal migration in India. Available at http://www.jstor.org/discover/10.2307/25051701?uid=3737496&uid=2&uid=4&sid=21103505391263. Cited 14.02.2014.

Rodgers, G., and Rodgers, J. (2011). Inclusive development? Migration, governance, and social change in rural Bihar. *Economic & Political Weekly*, *46*(23), pp. 43–50

Roy, N., & Debnath, A. (2011). *Impact of migration on economic development: a study of some selected states*. Paper presented at International Conference on Social Science and Humanity 2011 at Singapore. http://www.ipedr.com/vol5/no1/42-H00092.pdf. Cited 18.08.2018.

Shryock, H. S., Jr., Siegel, J. S., & Stockwell, E. G. (1976). *The methods and materials of demography*. New York: Academic Press.

Singh, J. (1986). Marital status differentials in rural to city migration in India. *Genus*, *42*(3/4), 89–106. Available at http://www.jstor.org/stable/29788869. Cited 12-05-2018.

Srivastava, R. (2005). *Internal migration links with poverty and development*. Paper presented at the Regional Conference on Migration and Development in Asia, Lanzhou, China, 14–15 March 2005.

Srivastava, R., & Sasikumar, S. (2003). *An overview of migration in India, it's impacts and key*. Paper presented at the Regional Conference on Migration, Development and Pro-Poor Policy Choices in Asia, 2003 held in Dhaka, Bangladesh. Available at http://www.eldis.org/vfile/upload/1/document/0903/Dhaka_CP_2.pdf. Cited 27.08.2018.

Standing, G. (1984). Conceptualising territorial mobility. In R. E. Bilsborrow, A. S. Oberai, G. Standing, Dover, N.H. *Migration surveys in low income countries: guidelines for survey and questionnaire design*. 31–59.

Stark, O. & Bloom, D. E. (1985). The new economics of labour migration. *American Economic Review, 75*(2), 173–78. Available at http://www.ppge.ufrgs.br/giacomo/arquivos/eco02268/stark-bloom-1985.pdf/. Cited 24.2.2014.

Stewart, R. & Moslares, C. (2014). Regional disparities across Indian states: are the trends reversing? *Journal of Economics and Development Studies, Vol. 2*(3), 95–111. Available at http://jedsnet.com/journals/jeds/Vol_2_No_3_September_2014/7.pdf. Cited 26.05.17.

Sundari, S. (2005). Migration as a livelihood strategy: a gender perspective. *Economic and Political Weekly*, *40*(22–23), Available at https://www.epw.in/system/files/pdf/2005_40/22-23/Migration_as_a_Livelihood_Strategy.pdf. Cited 12-02-2018.

Taralekar, Radha, Waingankar, Prasad, & Tathkar, Pandurang. (2012). A study to assess pattern of migration across India based on Census data. *International Journal of Recent Trends in Science and Technology, 5*(2), 2012.

Todaro, M. (1969). A model of labour migration and urban unemployment in less developed countries. *The American Economic Review*, *59*(March 1969): 138-148.

UN DESA. (2013). *Cross-national comparisons of internal migration: An update on global patterns and trends,* Technical Paper No. 2013/1, United Nations. Available at http://www.un.org/en/development/desa/population/publications/pdf/technical/TP2013-1.pdf. Cited 12-02-2019.

Wouters, F. S. (2008). *Migration, poverty and inequality (Evidence from Burkino Faso)*. IFPRI Discussion paper 00786.

Yang, D. (2008). International migration, remittances and household investment: Evidence from Philippine migrants, exchange rate shocks. *Economic Journal, 118*(528), 591–630.

The manufacturer's authorised representative in the EU is Springer Nature Customer Service Centre GmbH, Europaplatz 3, 69115 Heidelberg, Germany. If you have any concerns regarding our products, please contact ProductSafety@springernature.com

Printed and bound by CPI Group (UK) Ltd, Croydon, CR0 4YY
30/09/2026
02225289-0015